W9-CEV-529

Main Currents in the
History of Education

McGRAW-HILL CATHOLIC SERIES IN EDUCATION

Bernard J. Kohlbrenner, *Consulting Editor*

McCoy · *American School Administration*

Power · *Education for American Democracy*

Power · *Main Currents in the History of Education*

Main Currents
in the
History of Education

EDWARD J. POWER

Professor of Education
School of Education
Boston College

BRIAR CLIFF COLLEGE
LIBRARY
SIOUX CITY, IOWA

McGRAW-HILL BOOK COMPANY, INC.   1962

New York   San Francisco   Toronto   London

MAIN CURRENTS IN THE HISTORY OF EDUCATION

Copyright © 1962 by the McGraw-Hill Book Company, Inc. Printed in the United States of America. All rights reserved. This book, or parts thereof, may not be reproduced in any form without permission of the publishers. *Library of Congress Catalog Card Number* 61-18051

50580

LA
13
.P6

THE MAPLE PRESS COMPANY, YORK, PA.

To Thomas, Richard, Suzanne and Maryann

MR 18 '63   Elem Educ 758   Kellogg - Grant

38642

Preface

The history of education is a theoretical study. It has the same relationship to contemporary education that general history has to contemporary life. History does not solve our problems for us, although it may illuminate our efforts to find solutions. The history of education offers no guarantee that it will answer the pressing present-day questions concerning goals, curricula, methods, costs, and administration. Offering such answers is not its function. It can, however, provide us with some insights into the way these or similar problems have been handled in the past. We may learn from the past, but we do not look to the past to produce the solutions for today's questions. No teacher or prospective teacher can hope to become a better classroom performer merely because he has studied the history of education; on the other hand, if he has some insight into the educational trends of the past, he will be a more adequate educator and a more thoroughly prepared member of his profession. No one can doubt that the history of education, like any other kind of history, is a relevant study, although it would be inaccurate to make extravagant claims for its direct practical outcomes.

A survey of the history of education takes us all the way back to the beginning, when man first inhabited the earth, and then brings us down to the years that immediately precede our own day. This is an immense expanse of time. To cover all of the developments that have taken place in education during those thousands of years would be impossible in a single volume. This book makes no claim for completeness, and of necessity, many details have been omitted. Despite this curtailment, every effort has been made to keep in perspective the educational movements—plans, theories, and schools—and the schoolmen that have had the greatest influence on later educational developments and thus on our own time. The principal purpose of this book, then, is to trace the main currents of educational thought and practice down through the ages. It is intended chiefly as a textbook for undergraduate classes in the history of education.

In two principal ways this book is different from other history of education textbooks: First, in treating of ancient education, it attempts to put schools and educational theories, teachers and learners, in direct relation with life. The schools in past days were real, not fictional institutions, and the students who went to them learned the values that their society had tested and accepted in formal and informal education. In other words, we have tried to make it easy for the twentieth-century students who uses this book to understand that ancient schools and the students who attended them were real. We have also tried to make the relationship between those schools and the theories of education current in both ancient and modern times clearer and more significant. We are interested to know that Plato and Isocrates had educational theories, but we are even more interested to know the relevance such theories had to the actual practice of ancient education and even to our own education. Second, this book has tried to give early Christian and medieval education its proper role in the history of education. The Christian-medieval period was as important in the evolution of educational theory and practice as were the ancient or modern periods. It was a big link in the chain of educational history, and we have not neglected it. In addition, this book is written from a Christian humanistic point of view. Such a point of view must not change the facts of history, but it will discover them, weigh them, and interpret them in Christian perspective. This history of education is not pro-Christian; on the other hand, and what is more important, it is not anti-Christian.

It would be impossible to write a history of education without leaning heavily on the special and general studies that have appeared in the field over a period of many years. The bibliographical section at the end of the book is not only a guide to the student's future reading; it is also the bibliography for this book. It contains the principal sources upon which the book is based. To the authors and publishers whose books were used in preparing this history, sincere thanks are extended. Whenever quotations are made from published sources, a footnote identifies the source.

Edward J. Power

Contents

1

Education in Early Societies

EDUCATION AMONG THE PRIMITIVES

The history of education began with man's inhabitation of the earth. The soil, the trees, other creatures, and life itself were his first textbooks; with them and from them he learned to adjust to, and in some ways to shape, his environment. The goals he sought to achieve were usually nonintellectual, but they belonged, nevertheless, to education in its broadest meaning.[1]

In historical retrospect one discovers all kinds of educational institutions, practices, and theories. To direct our thoughts backward through the ages to the earliest educational activities of man and to try to describe and evaluate his achievements is not easy. Few of the educational events of the intervening centuries are helpful in this reverse projection, and the actual records of educational accomplishments which may be used for landmarks and guides are meager indeed.[2]

Primitive education was practical; it was concerned almost solely with the useful arts. Among the world's first people there was no literary tradition to be preserved and perpetuated, although oral tradition occupied an important place in the preparation of the individual for the kind of life he was going to lead. Without a literary inheritance, the kind of education that in all modern centuries has been judged most useful was of little value. Elements of reading, writing, and computing were

[1] See Thomas Woody, *Life and Education in Early Societies*, The Macmillan Company, New York, 1949, pp. 15–19.

[2] The major sources for our knowledge of prehistoric man and his educational endeavors are the relics of prehistoric people, from which anthropologists are able to draw important conclusions, and the study of so-called contemporary primitives. The value of the latter source is described by W. J. Sollas, *Ancient Hunters and Their Modern Representatives*, St. Martin's Press, Inc., New York, 1915.

1

underdeveloped and found no place in the training of the young. And among the earliest people there were no formal schools.[3]

Education was preparation for life in the most literal interpretation of the phrase. Primitive man had to feed, clothe, and protect himself and those with whom he was associated or for whom he provided. Youth in primitive societies would one day assume the responsibilities of the older generation, and their education was intended to prepare them for such responsibilities. The principles underlying the "curriculum" of primitive education were so obvious that no theoretical justification was needed.[4]

Besides developing skills for the chase, for war, and for the fashioning of crude creature comforts, there was some need for an understanding of the make-up of the tribe and for an appreciation of man's relationship to the spiritual forces which in mysterious and often occult form influenced his life. Tribal lore, along with tribal rites and ceremonies, was expected to provide what might be called social education; the practices of primitive religion, filled with superstition and fear, and some magical formulas to placate the spirits or the gods, fulfilled the role of religious education.[5]

Without a formal agency for education and without a class of teachers, all of life was the school, and every member of society was a teacher. Education and training were informal and often incidental to the day-to-day living of the people who made up a social unit. Man's inner craving for the artistic and the beautiful was not ignored, but in these areas of human endeavor, as in all others, there was a clear, practical orientation. Tools or weapons were ornamented; utensils sometimes carried the symbols of the peoples' values; and the spirits were appeased with specially prepared works of art. Education for this stage of history was conceived in terms of usefulness and conservativism; the most fundamental arts of life dominated and superintended all of education's activities.[6]

If we examine the educational interests of the primitives more closely, we may find that they were of four kinds: (1) those that prepared man to provide food, clothing, shelter, and protection for himself and those dependent on him; (2) those that enabled man to live with his fellows; (3) those that permitted primitive man to feel at home in the world and

---

[3] Woody, *op. cit.,* p. 15.

[4] W. D. Hambly and Charles Hose, *Origins of Education among Primitive Peoples,* St. Martin's Press, Inc., New York, 1926, p. xi.

[5] *Ibid.,* pp. 128–131.

[6] See Frederick Eby and Charles F. Arrowood, *The History and Philosophy of Education: Ancient and Medieval,* Prentice-Hall, Inc., Englewood Cliffs, N.J., 1940, pp. 10–12; and Hambly and Hose, *op. cit.,* pp. 408–409.

at peace with himself, and from which primitive man formed his religious attitudes, practices, and beliefs and his general outlook on life; and (4) those that gave him some skills for expressing his impulse to create and that sensitized him somewhat to the majesty of the world and its beauty. Such skills, though most elementary, gave him tools of language for communication, simple facility in music and ornamentation, and dexterity in dancing and ceremony.

Education or training in the ways of securing life's most essential needs —obligations from which no one was immune—was unquestionably more important than anything else. Yet seldom, if ever, was a direct or conscious process of such training—what we would call a school—organized by society. The necessary knowledge or skill was obtained by children through imitation. Children of primitive tribes engaged in various forms of play, which not only amused them but served as well to strengthen their muscles, sharpen their intellects, and develop their powers of observation, imagination, and invention. Many of the games were mimetic in character: they were adapted from or followed the serious and necessary occupations of adult life. Boys played with the tools and weapons of their fathers. A boy's amusements and games were usually imitations of the activities of adults. And when toys were used or provided, they were often models of boats, shields, spears, bows and arrows, or other common and useful implements. Girls then played house as they do today and copied the work of their mothers in their own miniature world.[7]

As boys and girls grew older, their training, if not more fully organized, seemed at least to be more consciously directed. Youngsters helped their parents in their work and learned by doing. What we may think of as schooling was for primitive man simply a day's work. Since no one was excused from work, no one avoided training or basic education. Another aspect or phase of primitive life, which took a good deal of an adult's time and which may have possessed some educational value for the young, was ritualistic, consisting in ceremonies, dances, and incantations. All of these performances had a certain religious quality about them. Primitive people appealed to their gods or special spirits before a hunt, a military encounter or expedition, a harvest, or some similar pursuit, and often before any important tribal function.[8]

There were also initiatory rituals, which occupied an important role in tribal affairs and from which youth belonging to various tribal groups may have drawn some educational value. Initiation practices differed

[7] Woody, *op. cit.*, pp. 20–23; Hambly and Hose, *op. cit.*, pp. 332–336.

[8] Hambly and Hose, *op. cit.*, pp. 15–20; R. Karsten, *The Civilization of the South American Indians*, Alfred A. Knopf, Inc., New York, 1926, pp. 17–21; and E. B. Tylor, *Primitive Culture*, John Murray, London, 1913, vol. I, chap. 11.

according to tribes, groups, or orders into which young people were being inducted; there may have been many such groups or orders even within a single tribe and therefore many different initiatory ceremonies. Three types seem to have been fairly common: initiation into secret societies, initiation into the ranks of occupational groups, and puberty rites through which youth could gain full tribal membership. Initiatory ceremonies, it was hoped, bestowed special status on the novices undergoing them. Members of secret tribal fraternities may have enjoyed special attention or they may have had unusual privileges; artisan groups protected the secrets of their trade; and young men who passed through the ordeals of puberty rites were accepted as members of the tribe, and the more closely guarded secrets, taboos, or rules of life were communicated to them.

Accounts of the customs of primitive people provide many examples of the different methods devised for initiations. Some of the practices or rites were extremely painful and dangerous; others were plain torture. But boys—and in many tribes, girls—were expected to demonstrate their maturity or their fitness to belong by exposing themselves to the rigors of such ceremonies. Initiations for girls were usually supervised by older women and those for boys by the wisest men of the tribe. Detailed descriptions of such ceremonies are available, but without going into the matter too carefully here, it is possible to give a few of the fairly distinct steps of initiations, which sometimes extended over a period of several years.[9]

Up to the age of ten or so, the child was subject only to the mild discipline imposed by his immediate family. But after the age of ten he became the object of attention of a number of adults who were designated to supervise his initiation or induction into the tribe. As a first step on the road to full tribal membership, he was painted with totemic symbols, flung in the air, and soundly beaten. This was just the first step! A few years later he was called upon to submit to mutilation. This mutilation may have been a scarification of the back or the breast—marks that would last throughout life, possibly for purposes of identification— or it may have been knocking out the front teeth, piercing the nasal septum or the lips, or loosening the scalp.[10] This stage of the initiation process culminated in the exposure of novices to smoke or fire. While these ceremonies were going on, perhaps for weeks, the boy was given little or nothing to eat. Yet he was expected to hunt and supply animals and other things that were essential to the performance of the rituals.

[9] See especially W. B. Spencer and F. J. Gillen, *The Arunta: A Study of Stone Age People,* St. Martin's Press, Inc., New York, 1927; and Hambly and Hose, *op. cit.,* pp. 193–199 and 281–294.

[10] Hambly and Hose, *op. cit.,* p. 130.

As part of the initiation procedure he was thus trained in the skills of a huntsman, or better, he was required to show, under unusual and often extreme pressure, the skill that he already possessed. The entire period for initiation, which may have taken months or years, included a variety of complex totemic dances and ceremonies. At such ceremonies the novices were under the control of a guardian. Silence was expected of them. No doubt other evidences of strength, stamina, maturity, and character were exacted, but whatever form they may have taken, they were all designed to give the young man or woman a chance to prove his mettle. If the novice was successful in withstanding all of the hazards that initiation imposed, he was admitted to full membership in the tribe.[11]

These ceremonies, whether they were initiatory or of some other kind, were thought to possess moral values. Such practices were part of a broad, indefinite, and unwritten educational syllabus. A boy was taught to endure pain, hardship, and hunger; he learned to be obedient and reverent. His duties and his obligations were impressed on him in a solemn manner. Initiations may also have had the social and political values claimed for them. The totemic symbols with which novices were painted may have depicted some of the history and tradition of the tribe, and the dances and ceremonial performances may have served the same purpose, or they may have been primarily religious in their significance.

It is noteworthy that among primitive people children were not separated from their elders but were in close contact with the personal affairs of the adult members of their families and with the general activities of the larger group to which they belonged. By this intimate view of the group and by full participation in its activities primitive children learned. They learned by daily contact with nature. They learned by observation. Unsheltered from the world around them, they viewed life with great freedom. And they learned by participation; they shared in the work, travels, play, and dangers of their tribe.

To a great extent, of course, they learned by trial and error. They leaned heavily on imitation, whether conscious or unconscious, but when what was to be done could not depend on imitation, then trial and error took over. Under such circumstances a learner meets with some degree of success and develops some skill. But even with trial-and-error learning, the young had to be taught to act in a manner that conformed more or less exactly to the experience and traditions of the tribe. There was a prescriptiveness about life, brought on either by the social or the physical

[11] Woody, *op. cit.*, pp. 16–20; Eby and Arrowood, *op. cit.*, pp. 12–22; and A. J. Todd, *The Primitive Family as an Educational Agency*, G. P. Putnam's Sons, New York, 1913, pp. 64–70.

environment or by the spirits which they thought they would offend if they acted otherwise. In this way—trial and error and supervision—the child of the primitives learned to use his bow and arrow, to dress the animal he killed, to cook, to weave, to make pottery. Constant imitation and trial-and-error methods gave each succeeding generation whatever skill it possessed.

In many ways woman was man's equal. Of course her role and status varied from tribe to tribe, but the environment possibly more than anything else suggested or demanded equality or near-equality of the sexes. In general, the status of women was higher among agriculturally oriented primitives than among herdsmen tribes.[12] Usually it was to women that the easier but also the more monotonous tasks were assigned: the care of children and the gathering and preparing of materials for food and clothing. While the work of women tended to be confining, man was free to roam about for much of his work and to expand the horizons of his experience. Men were hunters and warriors. Thus the same circumstances that made for equality of the sexes often operated to elevate men to a position of dominance. No primitive tribe could afford the divisiveness of sharp, rigid class distinctions, but, on the other hand, the regularly accepted practices of life with respect to division of labor militated against equality. So, though primitive woman was valued mainly as an economic asset, this attitude did not set her very far below man, who was valued in the same way. Differences in the training of men and women, of boys and girls were natural and inevitable.[13]

EDUCATION IN EARLY EGYPT

How long man remained in a simple, uncomplicated, primitive state is difficult to say exactly. For our purposes it is not necessary to trace his evolution meticulously. Man made progress. The societies of which he was a part became more complex, and the activities in which he engaged in order to make a living passed from those of hunter and herdsman to artisan and husbandman and beyond. Along with economic and social advancement came new and more carefully organized political units, and with this progress, too, came the creation of social classes. The aristocracies of nature were supplemented by those of privilege, position, and wealth. Men were placed in categories, or their birth placed them

[12] Hambly and Hose, *op. cit.*, pp. 335–336.

[13] W. T. Corlett, *The Medicine Man of the American Indian and His Cultural Background,* Charles C Thomas, Publisher, Springfield, Ill., 1935, pp. 202–244; H. R. Schoolcraft, *Archives of Aboriginal Knowledge,* J. B. Lippincott Company, Philadelphia, 1868, vol. II, p. 63 and vol. IV, pp. 67–70; and P. A. Means, *Ancient Civilization of the Andes,* Charles Scribner's Sons, New York, 1931, pp. 311 ff.

there, and the opportunities of life were assigned according to rank in society.

Education was intimately associated with life's goals. The orientation of utility, so obvious among the primitives, was honored and protected by social convention and legal sanction.[14] The kind of education a boy might expect to receive depended now not so much on the skill and training necessary for sustaining life but on the place he or his family occupied in society. The principle of division of labor was recognized to the extent that certain classes in the population of a political unit were acknowledged to have rights and duties consistent with their station in life. It may seem that the rights too often belonged to the upper classes, the duties to those less fortunately placed in the social hierarchy.[15]

These developments in social, political, and economic life represented man's progress from a less complex existence. They characterized, in most respects, the type of society common in Egypt as early as about 3000 B.C.[16] It was the major function of education in Egypt, as well as in many Oriental countries, to prepare men for life in this kind of society.[17]

Elementary Education in Egypt

Throughout the history of education, the first level of instruction has, almost without exception, found its objectives in the most fundamental needs of the society responsible for organized elementary education. It is not surprising that this should be so, and there are few good reasons for believing that any other way of determining objectives is possible. But in a society such as that in early Egypt, from about 2000 to 1000 B.C., the organization of elementary levels of instruction was not a simple matter. The various classes in society, each with its own special mission, could not be expected to lend any support to popular and uniform elementary education. Noble people did not live as the military classes lived, nor did they face the same problems; neither of these upper classes needed the kind of elementary training or education that seemed most useful to artisans, merchants, and farmers. Below these classes were the slaves—men, women, and children, captives of war or simply an unranked and underprivileged mass of mankind—for whom any kind of formal instruction seemed entirely unnecessary. In addition to the distinction which could be made in the kind of education appropriate for

[14] Hambly and Hose, *op. cit.*, p. 87.

[15] G. C. C. Maspero, *The Dawn of Civilization: Egypt and Chaldaea*, SPCK, London, 1901, pp. 326–336.

[16] J. H. Breasted, *A History of Egypt*, Charles Scribner's Sons, New York, 1912, pp. 32–45.

[17] G. Rawlinson, *The Story of Ancient Egypt*, G. P. Putnam's Sons, New York, 1888, pp. 40–60; and A. Erman, *Life in Ancient Egypt*, Macmillan & Co., Ltd., London, 1894, pp. 105 ff.

each class, there was in Egypt a thriving economy and a growing political system which, although completely supporting the class system, needed nevertheless the services of clerks, copyists, computers, and inspectors to keep it going.[18]

The richness of the Nile Valley made agriculture the very core of Egyptian economy. A landlord might have his laborers till the soil, sow the crops, and bring in the harvest without concerning himself very much about their skill in computation or their facility in writing. But someone had to do the computing and writing, for landlords often had vast holdings, and sharecropping was an established institution in the agricultural feudalism of the times; someone had to know the best time of the year to irrigate, and this involved computing the seasons when the river would overflow its banks to make irrigation possible. Whether such computation was simple or difficult, and what degree of skill was needed are not the subjects of our inquiry at the moment. Besides these matters, many other practical considerations could not be ignored. Irrigation was a much more complicated procedure than simply letting the waters of the Nile spill over the fields; dikes, ditches, docks, and bridges had to be constructed and maintained. Mechanics and the sciences basic to mechanics were developed to serve man in his attempts to control or modify his environment.

Before or perhaps while they were learning to utilize mathematical and mechanical means in controlling nature, Egyptians developed, through borrowing and their own ingenuity, the art of written communication. As time passed, they perfected this art to such an extent that it was used to record far more than the needs of commerce, agriculture, and government. Learned men in the society used the art of writing to preserve their profound and elusive thoughts; the achievements of the people's ancestors were transferred from an oral tradition to a literary inheritance; and above all, perhaps, the balance sheet of a man's life was prepared by scribes employed for this purpose, and the scrolls with the record of this life were entombed with the body of a deceased for the gods to read.[19]

Discoveries in science, computation, writing, etc., were not made in elementary schools. But once these sciences and these arts were known, it became the chief function of many elementary schools to adapt them for their use and communicate them to the young. The boys who were fortunate enough to have the opportunity for formal education—and the majority of boys were not so fortunate—did not gamble away their

[18] Breasted, *op. cit.*, pp. 88 ff.; S. S. Laurie, *Historical Survey of Pre-Christian Education*, Longmans, Green & Co., Inc., New York, 1895, pp. 33 ff.; and Rawlinson, *op. cit.*, pp. 43 ff.

[19] J. H. Breasted, *Development of Religion and Thought in Ancient Egypt*, Charles Scribner's Sons, New York, 1912, chap. 8.

chances for what would be a fuller, finer, and easier life. Schools were not fun but work, and a boy worked hard to absorb the practical curriculum that was organized for him.[20]

Boys who did not attend elementary schools received whatever education and training was deemed necessary for them from their fathers or masters. Education under these auspices, except the training of apprentice scribes, did not give much attention to the tools of education: reading, writing, counting, computing. Girls in ancient Egypt, as well as in most other countries in these very early years, were not sent to school, nor were they, for that matter, given opportunities for learning anything more than the simple domestic arts. The universal view can be stated succinctly: A woman without ability is normal. No argument was formidable enough to open the doors of schools to girls.[21]

It appears, although authorities on the subject do not always agree, that formal education in Egypt was established very early, sometime between 3000 and 2000 B.C. This formal education usually took the form of schools that were elementary in character. But, as we noted above, such schools were organized to serve a particular class in the population. In spite of the positive assertions of some Egyptologists to the contrary, there is no very convincing evidence that these schools were everywhere committed to teaching reading, writing, and arithmetic. That some schools had such objectives is not open to debate; and strangely enough, such objectives were not out of keeping with a school for poorer boys. The time had not yet arrived when literate men could claim social precedence, or when literary achievements and attainments were the mark of social excellence. The arts of communication in rudimentary form were tools for men who worked and were regarded in the same light as the carpenter's hammer or the mason's chisel. Poor boys could aspire to the occupation of the clerk or the vocation of the scribe without disturbing in any way the rigid social barriers that marked off one class from another. Education, whether for manual or literary skills, was vocational training.[22]

Writing, it is said, was first of all a priestly art. The fact that such a skill came in time to be essential to all or most of the classes, though not to all of the people, in no way alters the clearly practical motives associated with priestly writing. This skill, along with all other literary skills,

[20] Woody, *op. cit.*, pp. 55–57.

[21] Maspero, *op. cit.*, p. 320.

[22] Erman, *op. cit.*, p. 329; Rawlinson, *op. cit.*, p. 45; Maspero, *op. cit.*, pp. 283–298; C. H. Oldfather, *Diodorus of Sicily with an English Translation*, Loeb Classical Library, Harvard University Press, Cambridge, Mass., 1933, vol. I, p. 81; and E. A. W. Budge, *A Short History of the Egyptian People*, J. M. Dent & Sons, Ltd., London, 1914, pp. 208–210.

was employed as an instrument for maintaining the position the priestly class enjoyed in the social hierarchy. With such an obviously instrumental character, the tools of learning were communicated to the youth of this class in temple schools.[23] Noble and military classes also came to see the need for reading and writing, and they, too, introduced these skills to the curriculum of their court and military schools. Their method may be thought of as a generalized apprentice system—one which would prepare a royal or noble child to rule and direct or the son of a military leader to follow his father's career. And in addition to the temple, court, and military schools, the needs of government and economics dictated the establishment of department schools. In these schools the young were prepared for specialized careers in civil government or for business.[24]

In the absence of precise documentation, it is somewhat hazardous to venture beyond what has been said about the kinds of elementary schools that flourished in Egypt. For the most part, however, these schools did not undertake to prepare the scribe. His skill, for which the Egyptians in their business pursuits and in their religious life had a great need, involved preparation in a special kind of writing, but little else. People who built the great pyramids and constructed incomparable obelisks with the afterlife in mind may not have hesitated at organizing schools wherein boys could obtain the skill for writing the history of the dead. One may be fairly certain that master scribes trained apprentices to carry on this work, but it is possible also that schools were founded for this same purpose.

Before leaving the subject of elementary education, we should say a word about the intramural experiences of boys in Egyptian schools. First of all, elementary education, formal or informal, began at an early age; if a boy was going to school, he entered when he was about four. And if the slender accounts that treat of education in Egypt can be trusted, the school day was relatively short; the boys were dismissed at the middle of the day. While they were in school they were taught to write, first by tracing letters and then words; and since Egyptian writing was far more difficult than ours with its hundreds of different hieroglyphics, this was a task somewhat more difficult than one might imagine. The curriculum of elementary education was centered on writing, and the kind of writing that was done in the various schools usually identified the social rank of the students in attendance. Each class in society and often each profession or vocation had symbols and signs which had to be mastered, and the school dealt with the type of writing the students were expected to

---

[23] Breasted, *Development of Religion and Thought in Ancient Egypt*, p. 363; Maspero, *op. cit.*, pp. 301 ff.; and A. Erman, *The Literature of the Ancient Egyptians*, Methuen & Co., Ltd., London, 1927, pp. 185–186.

[24] Woody, *op. cit.*, pp. 57–58.

learn. As we have mentioned above, writing was not a general but a very particular skill; and an elementary school organized its work in writing to comply with the kind of vocational training it was commissioned to give.[25]

It would be difficult to arrive at many general conclusions about the curricula of schools in ancient lands. Although we know more about Egypt than we do about China, Assyria, Babylonia, Sumer, or other countries of the ancient world, we do not stand on very solid ground when we attempt a detailed description of Egyptian schools. Progressively more difficult studies in writing and possibly in elementary science and some mechanics led boys through from six to ten years of elementary education. By the time boys were fourteen they were supposed to be ready for life's work. Some had been taught to write; along with writing they had learned something of arithmetic, geometry, and astronomy. Music, too, because it was thought to have some values for moral formation, was taught, and the boys were given an opportunity to learn and sing songs prescribed by the state. Besides this, they were taught to dance, for dancing, in addition to any recreational value it might have had, was often accepted as a form of religious devotion or exercise.[26]

Where teachers came from for these schools, who they were, and what their preparation was for teaching the elements of Egyptian education, we can only guess. It seems clear that the methods they employed were set or fixed and the discipline they imposed strict and harsh. The purposes of elementary training were obvious, and apparently teachers found little or no difficulty in following approved and tested means to achieve these objectives.

Secondary Education in Egypt

Modern education—an educational period that began with the humanistic revival in the fourteenth century and terminated about the end of the nineteenth century—has regularly devoted more attention to secondary than to elementary schools. The educational historian two centuries from now will probably be able to write a much fuller and more accurate account of secondary education from 1350 to 1950 than of elementary education for the same period. What may be true of modern education, however, was certainly not true of ancient education in Egypt. Although from certain sources of information we find evidences of secondary education in this ancient land, it is impossible to give either a very full or a very accurate account of it. The art of writing—the heart of elementary

[25] Maspero, *op. cit.*, pp. 288 f.; and A. B. Gosse, *The Civilization of the Ancient Egyptians*, J. B. Lippincott Company, Philadelphia, 1922, p. 14.
[26] See Eby and Arrowood, *op. cit.*, pp. 70–82.

education—was, it appears, a staple in all formal secondary education.[27] On this level of education the student could give more attention to the style of his writing and composition; he could follow either the copybooks prepared for this purpose or he could acquaint himself with some of the writings, speeches, or religious pronouncements that had risen to places of respect in Egyptian life and letters. Chief among these were the important writings that made up the wisdom literature of Egypt. It was not the function of secondary education to open any new intellectual worlds or to broaden or illuminate fundamental literary or social issues; this was not the time for inculcating or even defending recognized moral or civic values. Secondary schools were probably little more than continuation schools. Apparently without complaint they assumed the functions of perfecting the work of elementary education and tried to make better craftsmen out of the small proportion of boys who continued their formal education in secondary schools.[28]

A somewhat different picture of secondary education may be drawn from the postelementary activities of the young of the upper classes. But with no notable exceptions, these activities were informal, and their guiding motives were found in the determination of the upper classes to perpetuate their code of manners and morals. Our understanding of secondary education in Egypt would be advanced very little by going into the maze of details on which the culture of the upper classes was built.

In the light of what has been said of secondary education here, and taking into account rather significant but unavoidable omissions, the reader should not be surprised to learn that nothing at all can be said about the teachers of these schools, either their actual work in the schools or their preparation for teaching, or about the organization, administration, support, or popularity of secondary education.[29]

Higher and Professional Education in Egypt

The nations that made up the Orient considered education essentially a practical enterprise. Wherever higher or professional education flourished, it had two distinguishing characteristics: It was under the control of priests or professional men, who communicated its skill and content to relatives or social equals, and it was informal in that neither curricula, faculties, nor degrees were fixed or recognized. In the Orient and in Egypt, during ancient times, there were neither colleges nor universities as we know them or as they were known from the twelfth century on-

[27] Maspero, *op. cit.,* p. 401.
[28] *Ibid.,* pp. 283–298.
[29] See Eby and Arrowood, *op. cit.,* pp. 82–95.

ward, although there were some fairly clear examples of higher and professional education.

The temple school, first of all an elementary and secondary school for the sons of priests and others whose social status qualified them to attend, communicated a variety of scientific and historical lore to its students.[30] It seems important to repeat that though these schools were regularly elementary in their outlook, they were also often higher schools. Where the line was drawn between lower and higher education is not easy to discover, but usually, higher education began when the priest who was the teacher in the temple school started to inculcate in his students those skills and attitudes that were the marks of his calling. Whether along with this professional training, for that is what it was, a scientific and literary education of an advanced kind was also given, must for us, at least, remain a mystery; but if secondary education was really a continuation of fundamentals introduced in elementary schools, one may be justified in assuming that higher education under these auspices was not narrowly vocational or professional. It would be a mistake, however, to think that professional or vocational training was not its primary objective.[31]

Almost without exception the testimony that we have agrees on this point: Professional knowledge was regarded as a kind of trade secret, and this knowledge was guarded carefully so that it seldom passed outside the immediate family circle. Higher education, then, was mainly a family affair. Whether for the priest with his divine mysteries or his knowledge of history and science, or for the physician with his magic potions or secret practices, higher education was entwined with the tradition that in it was knowledge which generated power. A real effort was made, usually successfully, by those who occupied a superior station in life to preserve their position by restricting higher and professional learning to those privileged by birth to know its deepest mysteries. It is reasonable to suppose that these restrictions were modified somewhat with the passing of time, but the generally acknowledged higher professions have maintained, nevertheless, a certain exclusiveness down through ancient, medieval, and modern times.

Military and engineering education was not quite as exclusive as education in priestcraft and medicine.[32] Perhaps this was so because Egyptian society seemed to have greater need for these professional skills or because the qualities of mind and body essential in these professions could not be assumed to exist in sufficient number within a small social

[30] Maspero, *op. cit.,* pp. 301 ff.

[31] Woody, *op. cit.,* p. 57; and Erman, *Life in Ancient Egypt,* pp. 329 ff., 352 ff., and 364 ff.

[32] Erman, *Life in Ancient Egypt,* p. 329.

circle. The architect, for example, enjoyed unusual privileges and was much revered. He, even more than a military leader, might be called by the king to manage the affairs of state. Knowing the high place accorded to architects and engineers, we may find the lack of more precise information on the higher education which prepared them a somewhat surprising omission. Preferences in the military establishment were given only to those who had a good literary and scientific education, and technical training for the art of war was left to the tried and true apprentice system of field training and actual combat. Since qualities of blood and birth did not control admission to the military profession, we may suppose that boys of more humble origins often looked forward to a military career;[33] yet we should not assume that military life offered democratic opportunities either for admission or for advancement.

One more professional pursuit needs brief notice here, that of the scribe. For the historian who tries to give an accurate picture of ancient life without abundant detail, the scribe of Egypt poses a difficult problem. There were, it appears, many grades of scribes. Some were prominent, learned, powerful men, resembling lawyers or judges more than clerks, who sat in on the affairs of state and moved in the privileged circles of society; others were simple secretaries, who knew little more than the art of tracing letters. We have already touched on the education of the latter type; of the former we know almost nothing. We may guess that the superior scribes were educated in some kind of higher school, perhaps in the temple schools, but beyond hazarding this guess, we can only say that many of them were qualified for exalted and exacting positions in government. Possibly some of these superior officials who were called scribes were really not scribes in the occupational sense. Since some positions, we know, bore the title of scribe, the mere fact that an able man filled the position did not mean that he had been or would become a professional scribe. He may have been an engineer, a physician, or a military man, and if he was, his education was of the usual type for any one of these professions. It is entirely possible that when he was appointed to a position of some prominence his title made him a scribe.[34]

Passing from the content of higher learning to some other features, such as faculty, facilities, books, and degrees, we can say only this without going into considerable detail: Teachers were themselves professional men, and they used their homes, their offices, or their places of business, and sometimes the temples as the places where they might communicate their secrets and where youth might be given some opportunity for intellectual formation. They had many manuscripts in literature, history, and science, and these manuscripts formed a kind of base around which

[33] Oldfather, *op. cit.*, vol. I, p. 81; and Maspero, *op. cit.*, pp. 283–298.
[34] Maspero, *op. cit.*, pp. 466 ff.; and Eby and Arrowood, *op. cit.*, pp. 100–103.

professional studies were built. Youth passed from these places of higher education when their learning, skill, and maturity were considered to be sufficient. No formal ceremonies launched the novice into the world of affairs.

ANCIENT EDUCATION IN CHINA

China was the home of a very old civilization, older perhaps than that of any other land except Egypt and Babylonia. Yet Chinese culture seems to have had very little direct influence on the general current of Western thought or Western education. Although one of the oldest nations of the world, China, if judged by Western standards, made relatively slow progress up the ladder of civilization. Because of its traditions and its geography, ancient China remained isolated from the people and the world around her. And in some respects the China of today has changed remarkably little from what she was more than two thousand years ago. In customs, relationships among the various classes of society, methods of business and labor, the administration of justice, and in the framework of thought, the practices of the Chinese have been stereotyped and until recent years have been practically unchangeable.[35]

Notwithstanding what others may regard as imperfections, the Chinese tend to accept their way of life with unusual complacency. In the past they were suspicious of innovation and opposed what they thought were barbarian invasions of their culture; only a few decades ago did they open their cities to foreigners.

Preserving existing institutions and guarding their traditions were commitments not taken lightly. It may be said that the fundamental purpose of Chinese education was to impress upon each succeeding generation traditional ideals and customs and thus to prepare youth to take its place naturally and easily in the established and largely inflexible social order. Chinese educational work did not aim directly at the development of human abilities; in actual practice its principal preoccupation was to cram the memory with the maxims and usages of the past.

As we have indicated, China had a very ancient educational system. Schools, academies, and colleges could have been found there a thousand years or more before the Christian era.[36] Using age alone as the standard, we might accord to China a singular position in the history of education. But how well was this long period used? For two thousand years educa-

[35] See C. P. Fitzgerald, *China: A Short Cultural History*, Frederick A. Praeger, Inc., New York, 1958.

[36] P. W. Kuo, *The Chinese System of Public Education*, Teachers College, Columbia University, New York, 1915, pp. 7 ff.

tional progress in China was slow and painful. The great wall of China, the largest artificial structure on earth, erected in the third century B.C., is some evidence of the early civilization of that land, and it indicates especially the ability of the people to achieve success in the arts of construction. It points also to a characteristic of the people, their willingness to be isolated and their unwillingness to change. It is not easy to understand why the inventors of paper, printing, and gunpowder, and the first users of the mariner's compass chose to remain in nearly complete isolation and in a relatively static condition for so many centuries.[37]

Possibly the religious systems which flourished contributed to this apparent retardation. There were three: Confucianism, Buddhism, and Taoism.[38] The first was chiefly the cult of the upper classes, of scholars and government officials; Buddhism and Taoism were religions of the masses. Buddhism, introduced into China near the beginning of the Christian era, appears to have been more influential and more socially significant than Taoism, but in time, we are told, some of its strength was dissipated in the practices of idol worship. Taoism, originally permeated with mysticism and in some ways related to primitive Buddhism, is said to have degenerated into a religion of spells and incantations. No one doubts that the power of religion in China was great. But it is not easy to attribute to its influence the long record of China's apparent unwillingness to move forward, or to charge it with immobilizing minds in superstition or steeping them in paralyzing traditions. Nor is it easy to assess religion's relationship to education, that is, to the day-to-day work of schools. And at the same time one must remember that China's greatest teacher was also a great religious leader. This was Confucius (ca. 551–478 B.C.). He was neither a prophet nor a revealer, but a provincial prefect and a philosopher, who directed his attention to social reform.[39] Throughout his career he sought to reestablish and preserve the customs and ideals of the past. He emphasized the virtues of obedience to parents and superiors, of reverence for ancestors, and an imitation of their lives. Strength and vigor were added to his teachings when he reinforced them with his own example. Among the many precepts, proverbs, and sayings that he left to posterity was the Chinese golden rule, "What you do not want done to yourself, do not do to others."

Confucius began to teach in a private school at the age of twenty-two. In time he gathered or attracted disciples and imbued them with his ideals. Apparently his influence had an indelible character, for genera-

---

[37] Fitzgerald, *op. cit.*, p. 409; and K. S. Latourette, *The Chinese: Their History and Culture*, The Macmillan Company, New York, 1946.

[38] J. K. Shryock, *The Origin and Development of the State Cult of Confucius*, Appleton-Century-Crofts, Inc., New York, 1932, pp. 117 ff.

[39] Woody, *op. cit.*, pp. 114–116.

tions of disciples honored his creed and his code, and he continued to be China's most important teacher long after his death. In this sense a Confucian School was founded and preserved. In his capacity as a schoolmaster, it is claimed, Confucius rejected no pupil with ability and ambition, and he accepted none without these qualities. He is credited with the maxim, "When I have presented one corner of a subject, and the pupil cannot make out the other three, I do not repeat the lesson." It may be fairly doubted, however, that this principle was honored generally in Chinese education. But without attempting to evaluate the practical application of Confucian thought, we can say that Confucius and his followers recognized knowledge, good behavior, fidelity, and uprightness of character as the proper ends of education.[40] These objectives were to be achieved in many ways, no doubt, but the chief means to their attainment was apparently the grading of instruction. Confucian theory, if not practice, seems to have been to organize four levels of education. The first level trained the mind by stimulating reflection and the heart by encouraging practice in virtue. The second level was concerned with correct and fluent speech; the third, with the science of government. The fourth involved practical and theoretical considerations of morals. Although mental training was not omitted, the general purpose of education in the Confucian view was moral development. This purpose, along with other teachings of Confucius, exerted a profound influence upon the Chinese people and their educational doctrines for nearly twenty-five centuries.

Although Confucius erected and standardized traditions in morals and politics, his school of thought was not the only one to claim the allegiance of men's minds. But the complexities of Chinese philosophical and social thought cannot be unraveled in this book. Other features of ancient Chinese education should receive brief notice here.

The family in China had a position of singular importance. Family life was recognized as the basis of all social and civic order; because of its central position the family was venerated. Within the family circle, absolute power was vested in the father. In all matters which concerned the family or any of its members his word was law. The conception of the state as a family, only larger and more widely scattered, made for a ready transfer of the authority which the father had over the family to the emperor, who was empowered to wield absolute authority over his subjects—in this sense, members of his family.

But to return to domestic affairs. Here the relationship between husbands and wives was unenviable. Wives were really a class of slaves. Their position was, of course, consistent with the disdain that the

[40] Kuo, *op. cit.*, p. 18.

Chinese had for women. Even in infancy the inferiority of a girl to a boy was clear. When a boy was born, there was reason for celebration, and the infant was dressed in the best that the family could provide. With the birth of an infant daughter, there were no very obvious signs of joy, and she was dressed in an indifferent manner. It was conventional for a father, when asked to number the children in his family, to count only the sons.

We have already referred to the educational objective accepted by the Chinese. But it should be understood that this general objective included, or could be made to include, social, political, and literary ends as well. The Chinese made no commitment, however, to anything resembling universal education, and made no effort to provide schools for all the people. Nonetheless, education was encouraged by restricting an enormous civil service system and all positions of power and honor to people who were well educated.[41]

To ensure the promotion of the educated and the advancement of the worthy, the state instituted a system of state examinations. These examinations were administered by a board, which periodically permitted candidates to appear before it.[42] All who chose to present themselves, except the sons of barbers and one or two other classes, were allowed to compete. Depending on the age and ability of the individuals who were successful on the examination, opportunities for further education were offered or appointments to positions in the civil service were made. The ladder to success seems to have been related rather intimately to achievement in learning. Such a system of state examinations was completely organized somewhat late in antiquity, probably not before the Christian era in the Occident; but in a rudimentary form such a system may well have existed from about the time of Confucius.[43]

To attend any school in China was probably a rare privilege. At any rate, going to school for the first time was a great occasion. At about six or seven years of age, the child was ready to enter school. To provide schooling parents sometimes pooled their resources and employed a teacher. This they were entirely free to do, for the government was concerned neither with the standards of the school nor the qualifications of the teacher. If parents were successful in engaging a teacher who was competent, the children were lucky, for good teachers were not easy to find; they were much in demand, and they usually commanded a good salary. In the absence of any kind of financial assistance from the government, these privately organized schools usually had to be content

[41] Chang-tu Hu, *China: Its People, Its Society, Its Culture,* Hraf Press, New Haven, Conn., 1960, p. 410.

[42] *Ibid.,* pp. 411–412.

[43] F. Hirth, *The Ancient History of China,* Columbia University Press, New York, 1911, p. 99; and Shryock, *op. cit.,* p. 52.

with whatever quality of teaching they could get. Under such circumstances, education could not have been compulsory, not, at least, in the sense that attendance in a school was required. Yet the educated boy, that is, one with elementary schooling behind him, was not uncommon. If parents were unwilling or unable to procure the services of a schoolmaster, it was possible for boys in some localities to attend schools which were endowed out of the charity of wealthy people. In all of this the state took no active role: there were no public elementary schools, and no public buildings were maintained as schoolhouses, although classes were sometimes held in temples or other public buildings. More often than not, however, school was kept in the home of the schoolmaster or in the room that was provided by some wealthy patron of the school. In the ordinary classroom the furniture consisted of an altar dedicated to Confucius and to the god of knowledge, a desk and chair for the teacher, and desks or stools for pupils. The latter were there only if the students themselves were able to supply them; if not, they sat on the floor. Such rooms were simply places where the exercises of learning could be carried on; no thought was given to creating an educational environment for the broader and deeper formation of students.[44]

When a boy went to school, he went with much ceremony; his first day, as we have suggested above, was a day to remember, and it was hoped that the memories would be pleasant ones. At this time the school boy was given another name, perhaps to accentuate even more the beginning of a new period of life. The first years of school, however, went to make up an indifferent experience. They contained little to remind the boy of the promise held out on the first day of his educational adventure. He learned to read and write, and he was exposed to some training in computation. For most of the students education did not go beyond these elements. Actual teaching practices took no account of the learner's academic interests, if he had any. Students were expected simply to acquire the basic tools. This was done mainly by rote. Only after the names of the characters of the Chinese alphabet were learned was any effort made to teach the meaning of words. The child's instruction in writing was solely mechanical. The expression of thought was at best a secondary consideration, and ingenuity and resourcefulness, traits which Confucius had praised, seem to have had no place in these schools. Fear, not interest, was the motive which kept the child at his studies. Memory was the chief, perhaps the only, faculty thought to be in need of cultivation.[45]

There was nothing very elevating surrounding the experiences of a school day in this land of custom and iron-bound tradition. Yet the

[44] Latourette, *op. cit.*, pp. 788–794.
[45] *Ibid.*, pp. 791–792.

teachers were given considerable respect. Today's readers must find this deferential attitude somewhat surprising, considering that Chinese teachers belonged to a profession which lacked any very seriously applied requirements for admission. The profession was, in fact, open to anyone who chose to enter it. In his work in the classroom the teacher was aided considerably by a generous grant of authority; he assumed the father's place. Discipline was inflexible and severe; no good teacher spared the rod. Any teacher who earned the reputation for moderation in the administration of discipline was considered to be a poor teacher. Aside from his role as a disciplinarian, the teacher was mainly a hearer of lessons.

Accounts of Chinese education are, of course, subject to some variation. China was a large land that could hold diverse practices. It is not unreasonable, therefore, to suppose that changes either in time or setting might require some alteration in the general and brief description we have given of education in that ancient land. As a final word, we might remark that beyond the elementary levels, education in China was not very well organized. We could even accept the statement that there was no organization at all for education on the higher levels. Boys who were able sometimes aspired to more learning than the elementary teacher could give them. They had to satisfy these aspirations, not in high schools and colleges, but through tutorial arrangements with men or older boys who could lay some claim to a scholar's reputation. It is unlikely that many distinctive details of teaching and learning under such conditions could find their way into history. It is entirely possible that tutors opened schools, and it is likely, also, that the needs of government motivated the state to sponsor some special schools. Neither the features of such schools nor the schools themselves, if and when they existed, made a deep imprint on the history of ancient education. Aside from the rich accounts of what may be described as internal history, we find almost no sources that place China in a position of educational influence in the ancient world.

THE FOUNDATIONS OF EDUCATION AMONG THE HEBREWS

Whether one finds the birthplace of Western civilization in Egypt, in Israel, or elsewhere, he cannot possibly overlook the achievements of the Hebrews, made against considerable obstacles, or the contributions they made to the forming of an educational ideal that gained general acceptance in the West. In the first days of their history, the Jews were little different from other primitive people, and what has been said earlier about education among primitive tribes applies also to them. There appears to be no basis for claiming a precociousness for these people; culture and learning did not come any more naturally or easily for them than for any others. Nor can one avoid the conclusion that the slow interchange of ideas which led to what we may call civilization enabled all early peoples to lay a foundation for culture and learning. Isolation slowed progress; amalgamation speeded the growth of an intellectual life which, in either simple or complex form, permitted men to move slowly out of a primitive stage of existence and prepared them to begin building a better world and a finer life for themselves and their progeny.

As a nomadic people the Jews pursued a pastoral calling. Sometime around 1650 B.C. they wandered into Egypt, where they began to acquire some of the civilization of that country, but where they enjoyed little, if any, freedom.[46] In time they became a subjected people, and, in a state of near slavery, were forced to labor for their Egyptian masters.[47] Moses led them from this bondage in about 1220 B.C., and they settled in the land of Canaan. Here they experimented with various types of social and political organization for nearly a century. This was the period of the judges and kings (1150–586 B.C.), and the time, too, when the kingdom was divided into Judah and Israel. In 721 B.C. the Israelites were swept away by the Assyrians; in 586 B.C. the people of Judah became the captives of the Babylonians. From this time began a series of suppressions, which lasted through 175 B.C. and included domination by the Persians (538–333 B.C.) and by the Greeks, Egyptians, and Syrians (332–175 B.C.). Jewish independence was enjoyed from 175 to 63 B.C., when Rome began to master the Jews. The year A.D. 70 marks the end of a period of continual decline in the fortunes of the Jews; from this date they became a persecuted people without a national home and were forced to wander throughout the world.

With such obstacles constantly confronting them, it is remarkable that the Jews were able to preserve their identity, to say nothing of building a culture which became for centuries a source of religious and moral inspiration and knowledge to many peoples. Among the many symbols that gave meaning to the Jew's life, that which stands out especially is a strong note of monotheism. The Jew gave his undivided allegiance to one God. This belief came in time to be surrounded by a body of law, some of it divinely inspired, which called to the Jew's attention his obligations and duties to God. The law became the central feature of Jewish life and the fundamental motivation for learning.[48]

[46] W. M. F. Petrie, *Egypt and Israel*, SPCK, London, 1912, p. 17.

[47] *Ibid.*, pp. 21 ff.

[48] The law should not be thought of as being tantamount to statutes. This would be a far too narrow conception of law and would miss the whole point of Jewish law. The law was, rather, an oral tradition which contained and illuminated life's basic ideals.

Informal Education among the Jews

With the exception of some private schools in the larger towns, all Jewish education during the postexilic period and before the Babylonian captivity was informal. This means that fathers and mothers were charged with the responsibility of giving their offspring a religious and moral education based on the traditions of the people and the law as it was given to them by Moses and interpreted for them by the prophets.[49] The education of children was not an obligation to be taken lightly, for Jehovah had commanded that the law be "taught diligently unto thy children." Apart from instructing children in religion and morals, parents had to prepare them for life in the world and to give them some skill for meeting the multiple demands that a somewhat primitive society might impose. This preparation included physical training as well as an informal apprenticeship for life. How could life be sustained without men who were hunters, herdsmen, and fighters, and women who were skilled in the household arts? And after all of this practical training was accomplished, there was still time for social education, which, it appears, went little beyond games, contests, and dancing. As time passed a regular apprentice system came into existence. Fathers were to teach their sons a trade, and the secrets of the trade were considered to be family property.[50]

Since life among the Hebrews probably did not require the keeping of records or the rendering of reports, as in Egypt, the art of writing did not command the attention of the Jew.[51] Jewish scribes are usually mentioned in the historical sources relevant to the postexilic period, but such scribes were simple clerks who had neither position nor learning—quite different, as we shall see, from the scribes of a later period. The art they possessed, it is assumed, was borrowed from the Egyptians. Without any great need for writing—the Jewish law was inscribed in the heart—and without ready access to good and inexpensive materials for writing, the art itself was not an important part of education's content during those years when Jewish education was solely in the hands of the family. Without any emphasis on writing—and surely there was little in the way of a written literature—reading was not an essential skill. It seems fairly clear that some members of the society were both learned and literate, although it does not follow necessarily that any attention was given either to reading or to writing in Jewish family education.[52]

[49] Woody, *op. cit.*, p. 86.
[50] *Ibid.*, pp. 97–108.
[51] Eby and Arrowood, *op. cit.*, p. 123.
[52] Petrie, *op. cit.*, pp. 31 ff.

Formal Education among the Jews

Perhaps the claim could be sustained that Jewish education was more effective as a purely family practice than it was when it became more fully institutionalized. There seems to be little question that education's history was longer as a family affair than it was as a school's function. But any attempt to prove such a claim would be so subject to involvements and fine distinctions that the possibility of historical illumination would be remote; and in such an exercise the important point would have to be neglected, namely, that the Jewish family, with schools or without them, never relinquished any of its responsibilities for the education of the young.[53] Jewish schools were established to supplement, not replace, the educational activities of the family.[54]

In the postexilic period, the economic life of the Jew was altered somewhat; in the earlier times he had been a farmer or a shepherd; now he became a craftsman, fisherman, or merchant, and he lived in a town, where the economic environment enabled him to profit from his new endeavor. In a more urban than rural setting a class of scribes, who became the educators of the Hebrews, came into existence. The new Jewish scribe was different from either the Egyptian scribe or the earlier Jewish scribe;[55] in a sense he took the place of the prophets of the old order.

These new scribes became the Jews' first great teachers. They were lawyers, interpreters, and writers, and from them the people of Israel received interpretations of God's law and directions for conforming to it. But they were not ordinary teachers or teachers in an ordinary sense; it is doubtful, for example, that they ever limited their activities to classrooms. Their influence was felt, not in guiding teaching and learning processes, but in setting a pattern and tone for a national intellectual and moral life. Nor were these scribes simple men of common origin. The skill and erudition demanded of one who aspired to the scribal order—and this very likely was the ambition of every Jewish boy—required years of leisure for study and sufficient wealth to ensure the opportunity for leisure. Scribes came from a class and in turn became a class. No other occupation merited the same reverence or prestige as that of the scribe.[56]

To become a scribe a young man had first to secure the necessary leisure; and, if nature's endowment of intelligence was generous, he him-

[53] Eliezer Ebner, *Elementary Education in Ancient Israel*, Block Publishing Co., New York, 1956, pp. 29–37.
[54] Deut. 6: 1–9.
[55] See pp. 10 and 14.
[56] Ecclus. 38: 24–39; 11; and Eby and Arrowood, *op. cit.*, pp. 138–140.

self would have to have the drive to study with men who had already
been inducted into the ranks of an intellectual elite. No schools or universities promised the youth that they would start him on his way to
success. Here, as elsewhere in early societies, the bases of an apprentice
system were in evidence; prospective scribes were taught, guided, and
counseled by men who were already members of the guild. Still, this was
not a craft guild in which a skill or trade could be perfected under the
watchful eyes of a master; rather, it was a kind of association, in which
the young could learn from, and be inspired by, those who were already
in possession of knowledge. Though communication of knowledge of the
law was undoubtedly an important element in such associations, it was
through contact, the friction of mind on mind, that understanding and
sometimes wisdom were achieved. Yet with all of its excellence the
scribal order was unable to broaden its scope or extend its vision much
beyond the law. The scribes became myopic in their concern for the law
and were inclined to be rigorous, casuistic, and narrow in its interpretations. With both strengths and weaknesses, however, the scribes were
the intellectual leaders among the Jews and the teachers of a whole
people.

Schools for the people receive no notice in the history of Jewish education until about 200 B.C. This omission of record, of course, need not mean
that such schools did not exist before; in the absence of information about
them, the historian can only suggest that if there was formal or institutionalized education, it may have been carried on in connection with the
temples, the shrines, or the synagogues. The synagogue was surely a
place of meditation, prayer, and instruction; but the instruction sponsored
there was probably an exposition of the law. Though the instruction of
children in lesser branches of education must have been considered
important, there is no definite evidence that synagogues themselves became what we today would call elementary schools. By about 70 B.C.
schools were conducted in or near synagogues, probably simply because
other facilities were not available and those of the synagogue were
satisfactory. On the other hand, a certain amount and kind of instruction, not necessarily in the formal elements of education, was an essential in the synagogue's general purpose.[57]

Schools for elementary education were common by A.D. 64, when the
decree was issued that all Jewish boys had to attend elementary schools.
This decree is attributed to Rabbi Joshua ben Gamala. With it we have

[57] Nathan Drazin, *History of Jewish Education*, Johns Hopkins Press, Baltimore,
1940, pp. 60 ff.; Fletcher H. Swift, *Education in Ancient Israel*, The Open Court
Publishing Company, La Salle, Ill., 1919, pp. 90–91; and Ebner, *op. cit.*, pp.
60–72.

what is, perhaps, the clearest evidence of formal education among the Jews.[58]

These elementary schools were not in their essentials greatly different from elementary schools in any other place at any other time in educational history: reading, writing, and simple computation were taught, as were the social and religious inheritances. No subject was approached with greater care than the law, and for this the chief textbooks were Leviticus and Deuteronomy.[59] Advanced instruction, in which a boy might be engaged when about fifteen years of age, was mainly a continuation of the study of the law; but schools for such advanced instruction could hardly ever be found except in a good-sized town.[60]

The curriculum of Jewish schools was definitely conservative. There was no thought of change and no mention made of progress; boys and girls were expected to memorize the code of life and keep it. This code was neither flexible nor ephemeral; it was to be engraved on the hearts and the souls of children. The chief engravers were parents and teachers. To achieve the objectives common to all Jewish education and to employ the means which were available to the schools, teachers had to adopt methods or techniques of instruction as permanent and inflexible as the goals themselves. The content of the curriculum was truth, completely and perfectly recorded by the scribes, and this content was to be mastered with thoroughness and accuracy.

In the Jewish conception of child nature especially, and also in the belief that all knowledge was assembled and just waiting to be known, one may find the central justification for the educational process adopted and approved by the Jews. Children were judged to be "wild things" who had to be tamed. If they were left to themselves, their natural willfulness would prevail, and they would never achieve the self-discipline or docility that perfect subjection to the law demanded.[61] This view of child nature does not, of course, set the Jews apart in any way; it was accepted, seemingly without question, by all early peoples. But what was accepted theoretically may not always have been applied practically in Jewish child care and education.[62] Jewish children were handled carefully and sternly, but certainly, a way of life which prefaced a Christian conception of man's nature, the severity so common

[58] I. Epstein, *The Babylonian Talmud,* The Soncino Press, Ltd., Bournemouth, Hampshire, England, 1935, pp. 105–106.

[59] Drazin, *op. cit.,* p. 60; and Ebner, *op. cit.,* pp. 38–50.

[60] Eby and Arrowood, *op. cit.,* p. 148.

[61] Prov. 13: 24; 19: 18; 24: 13; and Ecclus. 30: 1–13. See also, Ebner, *op. cit.,* pp. 88–96.

[62] Woody, *op. cit.,* p. 110.

to the time was tempered by the Jewish parent and teacher with some tenderness. Their love for children mitigated, though in no way altered, their sense of duty; parents could and did demand exact conformity to social and religious discipline, but they could do all this without descending to harshness and cruelty.

In the training and education of Jewish girls we may find the main clue to the breadth and vision of these people. In lands around them the conviction had prevailed for centuries and continued to prevail that girls and women were naturally inferior to men and boys. Though fully aware of this traditional degrading of females, the Jews did not accept the concept. It is true that schools, when they were opened, did not admit girls; and in economic, political, and religious activities women were not accorded anything like modern equality; yet certainly motherhood was honored, and Jewish women were the fortunate recipients of respect and reverence. Girls received a careful and thorough domestic training, and in some homes they learned to read and write. A few Jewish women gained great prominence in religion and letters. In no other ancient land were women so fortunate, for in no other land was there this same conception of man or the same understanding of his relationship to one God.[63]

"Fear of the Lord" stands out as the chief motive underlying Jewish life and work. Not only children but all people were admonished and threatened with divine reprisals. This was the unassailable value in life, which permeated emotion, understanding, and the standards of conduct. Fear of the Lord was accepted as the beginning of wisdom. In education this precept was translated to mean that the child was to accept unquestioningly everything taught to him and preserve and transmit inviolably all that he had learned. No other principle could have supported better or served so well the mnemonic methods of instruction that were universally recognized and accepted.[64]

When the basic guiding force in Jewish life was not sufficient to motivate the child in his work, other means were sometimes employed. Punishment of various kinds was a means to stimulate a boy given to sloth; rewards and praise might be used to encourage even greater effort from children already bent to their tasks of absorbing the content of their curriculum. In extreme cases, where boys were hardened recalcitrants, the penalty of death could have been imposed.[65] Consistently

---

[63] Petrie, *op. cit.*, pp. 21 ff.; and E. Renan, *History of the People of Israel*, Roberts, Boston, 1894–1895, vol. I, chap. 8.

[64] Emil Schurer, *History of the Jewish People in the Time of Jesus Christ*, Charles Scribner's Sons, New York, 1891, vol. I, p. 324; and Eby and Arrowood, *op. cit.*, pp. 151–152.

[65] Deut. 21: 18–21.

with the Jew's view of things, however, extreme measures to encourage learning or to exact discipline were resorted to only after more moderate devices had been tried. Reproof and admonition were universally accepted as better motivators than punishment or chastisement.

In the *Talmud,* a collection and codification of Jewish religious and legal ordinances, and of interpretations and discussions of the works and writings of the prophets, fundamental educational ideals are fairly clearly reflected. Although one would certainly not want to accept uncritically a codification of law and life that was put in written form about the second century A.D. as a faithful and necessarily accurate account of Jewish practices common hundreds of years before, the *Talmud* is, nevertheless, a source of information which must not be overlooked. In it the status of the teacher is clearly enunciated: "The teacher precedes the father; the wise man, the king." In their respect for instruction and for the intermediary whose function it was to teach, the Jews apparently remained constant. For prophets, scribes, and rabbis, as well as for teachers concerned with guiding and directing the most elementary phases of learning, the Jews had nothing but reverence. All of these men were teachers; all of them were doing God's work. And the teachers themselves, whatever their rank on the intellectual or social ladder, were dedicated to their vocation. Teaching was not a function to be performed by just anyone; and if we may judge from the various accounts given of Hebrew teachers, aspiring teachers approached their work with timidity and humility. Their obligation was heavy, and they felt it keenly. One would not venture unhesitatingly upon an occupation dedicated to performing God's work. No little share of the success of Jewish education was due to the high quality of Jewish teaching.[66]

After centuries of near isolation, the Jews' intellectual life was affected by the influx of Greek ideals and language. The new current of thought began to be felt three or four centuries before the birth of Christ. The extent of this influence on Jewish education is not easy to evaluate; scholars voice some question as to the nature of its effect and as to whether the effect was permanent or ephemeral. No one can be certain that the influences moved only in one direction, for the moral ideal in education—undoubtedly the distinctive quality of all education among the Hebrews—came in time to demand some attention from the Greeks, especially from the Athenians.

SUMMARY

Life in early societies demanded constant and unrelenting attention to basic necessities. Education, whether it was informal or formal, was

[66] Ebner, *op. cit.,* pp. 51–62.

centered on the practical arts. In this tradition, the practices of primitive peoples were passed on to the Egyptians, to all Oriental nations, and to the Jews. When man changed his mode of living to settle in more or less permanent homes, to engage in agriculture and trade, to organize political units, and to record his inheritance and his day-to-day activities, education passed from informal and incidental emulation, imitation, and indoctrination to formal exercises in mastering skills essential to life in radically altered political and economic societies. The kind of education important to Egyptian life became the standard education for Egyptian schools. The kind of education important to the Jews was reflected in their home training and in the schools which the Jews created and charged with inculcating in youth a knowledge of God's law and a system of moral values.

Questions and Exercises for Study and Discussion

1. What, if any, distinctions were made between education and training among primitive people? How were these people able to get along without schools?
2. If it is true that education among primitive people was fundamentally practical, how would such an emphasis differ from that of later historical periods?
3. Prepare a special report on social education among primitive tribes. In this report give special attention to the role that initiations played, and describe in some detail the initiatory ceremony that interests you most.
4. The trial-and-error method of learning was a principal one among the earth's first people. Describe the steps that might have been taken in a primitive tribe by a boy or girl who was following this method.
5. In your outside reading look for differences in the education and training of primitive men and women. Did the primitives establish any lasting precedents in the education of the sexes?
6. Compare and contrast elementary and secondary education in early Egypt with your own elementary and secondary school experience. Give special attention to purposes, discipline, opportunities for education, class discrimination, vocational curricula, and character formation.
7. Investigate and report on the development of writing in Egypt. Do you find substantial reasons for the more advanced status of the art of writing in Egypt than in some other ancient lands?
8. There are some differences of opinion as to the place and the role of higher education in ancient Egypt. Prepare a report giving the results of your special study of this problem.
9. Describe the status, the duties, and the professional preparation of the Egyptian teachers.
10. How profound and how permanent was the influence of Confucius on Chinese education? Do you detect any Confucian influence on Western educational thought?

11. It has been claimed that the major contribution that the Jews made to Western education was in the form of a moral commitment. What evidence do you find either in support of or in opposition to this claim?

12. The position of teachers among the Jews was more enviable than anywhere else in ancient lands. Was their honorable estate merely an accident of history, or were there intellectual and moral values among the Jews that guaranteed teachers an established place of honor and respect?

2

Greek Educational Ideals
and Practices

Before the time of Homer, about 850 B.C., the people of Greece followed the customs of their ancestors and practiced the primitive arts as the people who lived before them had done. We know little about them or even about the migration to the peninsula of the men who came to call themselves Greeks; we know nothing of the struggles they faced in conquering or in assimilating the inhabitants who may have preceded them there. Still, in spite of all this historical mystery, it is probably true that we today know more about the earliest beginnings of the Greeks than they themselves knew. But our purpose is not to explore the origins of the people with whom we deal.[1] It is, rather, to understand something of the evolution of their culture and the development and form of their educational activities. This purpose may, to a large extent, be achieved by beginning with the age of Homer. Before Homer, it is safe to say, the Greeks lived very much in the manner of other primitive and very early peoples.

Even beginning with Homer, we cannot approach Greek culture and education with any assumptions about its unity. And because the age of Homer is so filled with legends and tales, we cannot be certain of much of anything before the time of the first Olympiad—the beginning of the Olympian games in 776 B.C. Besides, where one may think of a whole people, for example, the Jews, and write in general about their goals and values, the same thing cannot be done with the Greeks. There were many groups of people in ancient Greece, whose racial origins can be somewhat roughly differentiated, and though these various groups, tribes, or clans may have had some common beliefs and purposes, it is

[1] For the reader who is interested in studying the origins of the Greeks: see A. Jardé, *The Formation of the Greek People,* Alfred A. Knopf, Inc., New York, 1926.

the differences among them rather than the likenesses that must concern us most. A book such as this cannot with profit try to give an account of any but the more prominent and influential of these groups. Certainly, for our purposes, the two most important city states in Greece were Sparta and Athens, which represented respectively the Dorians and the Ionians.

In Sparta and Athens, but especially in Athens, we find the foundation and sometimes the model for present-day cultural ideals and educational practices. More than this—there seems to be little real debate on the point—the history of education in the West really begins with the Greeks, for to them the Western world owes its idea and ideal of culture.[2] Pre-Grecian life surely had an effect on the Greeks and in some cases, perhaps, influenced Western civilization directly, but the model for the life of the mind and the culture that would spring from this model was made for the West by the Greeks. The Greeks seem to have been the first to have been conscious of a cultural ideal, and among ancient peoples the Greeks, especially the Athenians, stand pretty much alone as precursors of the arts of mind and expression.[3]

LIFE AND EDUCATION IN SPARTA

Nowhere was education considered more important than in Sparta.[4] Life in Sparta was directed primarily at preserving the *status quo*. As a result of their military prowess and, to some extent, of the accidents of history, the Spartans were the masters of the majority of the people, most of whom were noncitizens, in the city state. Some of these non-citizens may have been able to trace their lineage to tribes that had lived and worked on the plains of Sparta before the Dorians arrived to suppress them; others were captives of war. All the inhabitants of Sparta, except the citizens and a few privileged visitors, led uninspiring lives. Some of them—the perioeci—were freeborn; others—the helots—were serfs or slaves. These subject people were forced to labor for their Spartan masters. To the citizens, therefore, accrued the advantages of leisure to pursue the one art that was considered important: war. By the Spartans and sometimes by their Athenian neighbors, this art was judged to be a liberal one.[5]

[2] Samuel H. Butcher, *Some Aspects of Greek Genius*, St. Martin's Press, Inc., New York, 1916, p. 40.

[3] On this point, see William Boyd, *The History of Western Education*, 6th ed., Adam & Charles Black Ltd., London, 1952, pp. 2–3.

[4] Kenneth J. Freeman, *Schools of Hellas*, 3d ed., The Macmillan Company, New York, 1922, p. 12.

[5] Thomas Woody, *Life and Education in Early Societies*, The Macmillan Company, New York, 1949, pp. 234–240.

Without taking the time or the space to argue the validity of the claim that the Spartan was engaged in a liberal art when he prepared for and waged war, one may venture a contradictory claim. No activity in which the Spartan could have engaged was more practical than training for military efficiency.[6] His life, together with the safety of the city state and the perpetuation of Spartan standards of living, was challenged constantly by the helots, the largest group of subject people in Sparta, and by Sparta's foreign enemies, with whom war was more or less regularly waged. Military efficiency was not simply a luxury to be afforded by a state whose citizens had leisure to use in this way; it was a necessity to be supported without interruption in order to preserve a way of life which the Spartan refused to alter and which his indoctrination, training, and education would not allow him to speculate about.[7]

Between the Spartan and intellectual autonomy as well as physical freedom stood totalitarianism in its purest form. Boys and girls were born and bred to serve the state. This subservience to the state was called citizenship. Severe penalties—ostracism, or death, or, at the least, disgrace—would be visited upon young people who failed in their patriotic duty to dedicate their energy and their lives to the interests of the state. Individual thought, interests, or hopes were to be subordinated to the good of the state. The state's welfare was guaranteed best by military strength, and Sparta became an armed camp. Neither an enemy nor an innovation could easily penetrate the city's borders.

With almost complete freedom from the cares of money making—Spartan citizens were supported from land allotted to them and tilled by their slaves—and with no trade or profession to occupy either their time or their thought, Spartans were free to imbibe and practice the accepted mode of life.[8] Although patriotism and obedience were virtues expected of both men and women, the means used to inculcate these and subsidiary virtues were different for boys and girls. A Spartan woman was not considered a man's equal, but neither was she doomed to a role of servitude. Her first duty was to bear strong, healthy children; her second was to show, by example of deed and word, her complete devotion to the state. Wives and mothers did not engage in actual combat on the field of battle, but with moral strength and resolute patriotism they supported their soldier husbands and sons and encouraged them to give, if need be, their last full measure of devotion to the state. So drilled were women in this sacrificial attitude and so high was the premium

[6] *Ibid.;* Freeman, *op. cit.,* pp. 12–38; and H. I. Marrou, *A History of Education in Antiquity,* Sheed & Ward, Inc., New York, 1956, pp. 15–16.

[7] Plutarch *Lycurgus.* In *Plutarch's Lives,* Loeb Classical Library, Harvard University Press, Cambridge, Mass., 1914–1926, vol. I, pp. 293–297.

[8] Freeman, *op. cit.,* p. 11.

placed on fortitude that a Spartan mother could tearlessly advise her son, about to leave for the frontier and battle, to come home with his shield or on it.[9]

No school was assigned the role of preparing Spartan girls for their mission in life. Aside from play and exercise which might have been taken with boys in the girl's earlier years, the education of a girl was directed by her mother. But this was not an education in the household arts like that given to the women in every other early society. Spartan women were free from toil; all menial tasks, for that matter, all domestic routine, were the work of slaves. It may be said, then, that the education and training of Spartan girls was carried on informally and somewhat incidentally. There was no doubt, however, as to the objective to be achieved, and mothers and society at large were the Spartan girls' teachers.

The life for which the Spartan boy was to be prepared demanded that he be a thoroughly trained citizen, which was equivalent to a demand that he be militarily efficient. These boys needed the persever- ance which comes from firmly held ideals, but they needed also strength, endurance, cunning, and courage. To these basic qualities was added skill in the use of arms and a thorough knowledge of tactics and strat- egy. Such objectives were too important to be left to chance or treated casually. The Spartans' code of life gave the training of boys precedence over all else save war itself. There are many ways of characterizing the Spartan system, but its most striking feature was rigidity. Nowhere in Sparta was conservativism more apparent than in the carefully arranged steps that would enable a boy to ascend a figurative ladder to citizenship and the life of a soldier.[10]

The Education of Boys in Sparta

There may be some slight inaccuracy in referring to the regimen approved for Spartan boys as education. Although authorities do not always agree as to whether these people were literate or illiterate, whether they knew Homer, or whether, in fact, they had any music, art, or literature, it may be too exacting a judgment to maintain that their training was entirely devoid of intellectual discipline.[11] Still, the years Spartan boys spent in what we might call schools were years devoted to

[9] Woody, *op. cit.*, pp. 244–246; S. S. Laurie, *Historical Survey of Pre-Christian Education*, Longmans, Green & Co., Inc., New York, 1895, pp. 240–246; and Clarence A. Forbes, *Greek Physical Education*, Appleton-Century-Crofts, Inc., New York, 1929, pp. 40–44.

[10] For what may well be the best single treatment of Spartan social and educational values, see Werner W. Jaeger, *Paideia: The Ideals of Greek Culture*, Oxford Uni- versity Press, New York, 1945, vol. I, pp. 77–115.

[11] A. S. Wilkins, *National Education in Greece*, Strahan, London, 1873, pp. 39 ff.

38642 BRIAR CLIFF COLLEGE LIBRARY SIOUX CITY, IOWA

systematic physical and military training, and no definite extant evidence shows that any attention was given to such elements of education as reading and writing, to say nothing at all of mental culture.[12]

Tradition attributes intellectual keenness and laconic speech to the Lacedaemonians; their emissaries and generals are said to have been impressive men, fortified with skill and courage and knowledge. But music, art, and literature that did not serve the state's practical objectives, that is, that did not stimulate emotions believed to be related to patriotism, found few patrons and sometimes, according to many authorities, were actually outlawed. Spartans were suspicious of both the novel and the complex; they could, and did, ostracize a man or a boy who, after being on official business in a foreign land, returned to Sparta with a knowledge of rhetoric which he did not conceal.[13]

Intellectual education was not an objective in the Spartan system. Beyond memorizing the laws of the state, acquiring a sketchy knowledge of Homer, and listening to the tales of heroes, genealogies, and military actions of the past, students were apparently given little training that could be called intellectual. Its place was taken by social and ethical education and, of course, by physical and military training. To posterity the Spartan left few mysteries concerning the hierarchy of objectives that he espoused.

To secure the values held to be most desirable, the Spartans, very early in their history, began to develop a system of training from which they permitted few deviations. Their view of life, as well as of law and education, was given to them, it is said, by Lycurgus and was preserved in *Eunomia*. But this lawgiver may have been either a man or a god—tradition honors both claims—or neither, for there is reason to believe the Spartan system was already in the process of evolution before Lycurgus appeared on the scene, and that the system was adopted to meet problems with which Lycurgus could not have been familiar.[14] Whatever the truth may be on this point, the laws of Lycurgus and the system they ordained prevailed with only minor alterations throughout the city state's history. In connection with the laws of Lycurgus it is

[12] Many authors write on this point. Among them, Isocrates (*Panathenaicus*, Loeb Classical Library, Harvard University Press, Cambridge, Mass., 1927–1929, vol. II, pp. 209, 251) held that the Spartans were practically illiterate; Plutarch (*Lycurgus*, in *op. cit.*, vol. I, p. 257) claimed that the Spartans had just enough literary education to "serve them"; J. F. Dobson (*Ancient Education and Its Meaning to Us*, Longmans, Green & Co., Inc., New York, 1932, p. 17) and Forbes (*op. cit.*, pp. 13 ff.) take the position that nothing was allowed in education that did not serve the practical goals of the state.

[13] Freeman, *op. cit.*, p. 21.

[14] J. A. Bury, *A History of Greece*, St. Martin's Press, Inc., New York, 1922, p. 135.

probably worth mentioning that they were contained neither in constitutional nor in statutory codification but in oral tradition.[15]

The first step in preparing boys for citizenship was taken long before
they had attained either physical or mental maturity. Within a few days
after the birth of a male child—and after he had been bathed in wine to
test his endurance—a council of elders appointed to act in the name of
the state inspected the infant. It rested with this council to determine the
boy's fate. Should it, in its wisdom, decide that the boy was of sturdy
stock, strong and healthy, he was given a chance to live as a member
of a citizen household. Any other verdict placed the boy's life in
jeopardy, for without the council's approval the child could not be
reared for the life of a citizen. He was taken to Mount Taügetos and
exposed. There he might be left to die unless the helots or the perioeci
rescued him.[16] To be snatched from the jaws of death from exposure
was not a reentry to the Spartan citizenship circle; rejection by the
council postponed forever a boy's chances of becoming a citizen-soldier.

But the brighter side of the whole affair, if, indeed, it was the brighter
side, was approval by the council. From this time until the lad was
seven, he was left in the care of his mother and his nurses. But the state
had made its claim on him, and this was a claim never to be relinquished.

When the boy reached seven years of age, his father enrolled him in
the state training school, and with this matriculation systematic preparation for citizenship began. Even before this, however, the boys had been
exposed to military life and to adult ideals. They had accompanied their
fathers to *pheiditia*, or military clubs, and had sat on the floor to listen to
the pithy speech of their elders or to snatch food from the mess table.
In a way, the club was as important to the boys as it was to their fathers.
Any Spartan who was unable to contribute his share of the provisions for
the club lost his membership and also his rights as a citizen; his son,
moreover, lost his opportunity for education in the state system. Maintaining solvency was probably a burden which fell more heavily on the
slaves than on the masters, for no Spartan would sacrifice his place as a
citizen if his slaves could be made to produce more wealth for him.
Wealth for its own sake was not, of course, a motive for the Spartans;
all a master wanted was enough to fulfill his obligations as a citizen.[17]
One of a Spartan father's obligations was the complete support of his
sons through the educational system.[18] There was no such thing as state
support of education, although state control was both obvious and in-

[15] Jaeger, *op. cit.*, vol. I, pp. 82–83.
[16] Plutarch *Lycurgus*. In *op. cit.*, vol. I, p. 255.
[17] Woody, *op. cit.*, p. 239.
[18] Freeman, *op. cit.*, pp. 14–15.

flexible. The obligation to pay for the education of one's sons began when, at seven years of age, they became what we would call "wards of the state."

The little boys who were ushered into what, in many respects, was a new life were not entirely unprepared for the rude regimen that faced them. Their infant years had been, in fact, a kind of preparation for what they were now to meet. And at this point we might inject a word of caution to students who have begun to form an image of the first level of formal training in Sparta: In no way did the Spartan school adumbrate the elite boarding schools of later centuries. The lads were organized into "packs" or classes called either *ilai* or *agelai*. It is usually assumed that each of the *ilai* contained sixty-four boys; the exact composition of the *agelai* is unknown. In these packs the boys were foragers and apprentice fighters. They roamed the countryside to exercise their bodies and to pilfer food for their stomachs. A single garment was allowed each boy; with it and whatever else he could improvise or steal he protected himself from the winter's cold and the summer's heat.

The boy's chief teacher was called a *paidonomos*. He was a citizen of rank and a soldier of repute; under his direction a number of assistants carried on the more immediate supervisory functions in connection with the boys' training. It would not be a distortion of history to associate this principal teacher's office with that of the superintendent of a military academy or a commanding general directing military maneuvers. Or one might think of the position as similar to that of a national minister of education, or, even better, of a director of education and training for all the boys of a country.

The assistants, not the *paidonomos,* came in contact with the boys. They corrected them and flogged them and, it may be supposed, gave them specific instructions as well as general directions. But learning by doing was the principle most often honored. Under the leadership of a boy, by which term we mean someone under twenty, who demonstrated his qualifications for leadership, the pack ventured into the territory surrounding the city state; by being exposed to the basic needs for survival the boys learned what they lived.

Life in the open, dependence on one's self, exercise, fighting, foraging, stealing, killing, these were the constants of the curriculum. Stealing was permitted within certain limits; that is, after reaching a stipulated age, probably ten or eleven, a boy could steal certain things from certain classes of people.[19] Such discriminate pilfering was entirely legal. Because most Spartan property was held in common, one may suspect that what was stolen was taken from noncitizen groups. According to the

[19] Plutarch *Lycurgus*. In *op. cit.,* vol. I, pp. 257–259.

testimony of Xenophon in his *Anabasis,* the Spartans were the most skillful highwaymen of the time.[20] Killing, like stealing, was, within certain limits, an approved military exercise. One may doubt that young boys just being inducted into the packs sought mortal encounters with helots or slaves, but as they became older and bolder they did seek to apply some of the many tactics they had been taught. Bands of young men not yet inducted into the professional ranks of the soldier—therefore young men who were not yet citizens—bivouacked in the country, and when their leaders gave the word, they ambushed a lone helot simply to gain the experience of slaughter.[21] But this was no crime. The elders had seen to it that war was declared on the helots each year, not for this purpose only; but in such a manner these assassinations were legalized.

From the ages of seven to eighteen the boys of Sparta were occupied in preparing themselves for the life of a soldier. These years were really devoted to a kind of basic military training.

At seventeen or eighteen the boys became *ephebi* and entered upon a new phase of preparation for the life of a citizen. They were released from their pack schools, took an oath of allegiance to the state, an oath which included a special clause expressing hatred for the state's enemies, and joined new packs. The packs for these older boys tended to be private organizations; that is, they stood somewhere between the military organization itself and the "boarding school" which the young men had just left. A young Spartan with ambition or position recruited as many young men as were willing to join him in his venture. He became the chief. The father of this young chief acted in the capacity of a superintendent for this private army or military unit; over its actions he exercised almost complete authority, and for its accomplishments he felt a good deal of pride and took a great amount of credit. Such private squadrons were in constant competition with one another. They would seek to display their superiority in the gymnasium, on the hunting expedition, in exterminating "enemies" of the state, and in fighting with other squadrons. On appointed days or at a surprise signal, these squads would assemble, fully armed, for the purpose of doing battle with one another. This was no mock warfare, for all of the implements of war known to the day were used to gain victory. For the Spartans these occasions were eagerly anticipated, and memories of them were savored; participants anxiously awaited such jousts in order to demonstrate their skill in the use of arms, their courage and their endurance, and above all, their great devotion to the state.

[20] Xenophon *Anabasis* iv. 6.14. G. Bell & Sons, Ltd., London, 1915.
[21] Plutarch *Lycurgus.* In *op. cit.,* vol. I, p. 291; Isocrates *Panathenaicus.* In *op. cit.,* vol. II, p. 277.

Apparently no Spartan could conceive of a better way for inducting young men into the ranks of citizens. The system never changed in anything except minor accidentals. All of the virtues held to be most desirable, even necessary, for citizenship could be evaluated in such a system. The young man who could meet all of the ordeals with success was judged to be ready to take his position with the elite. Failure was almost too terrible to contemplate, for it meant that the portals of citizenship were closed; the Spartan who was not a citizen was nothing.

At about the age of twenty the period of preparation came to an end. Now the young man took his place in the regular military organization, and, according to some accounts, became a citizen. When a young Spartan became a citizen in a legal sense is a question that remains unanswered, for it is also claimed that he did not achieve the distinction of citizenship until he had spent ten years successfully in military service. In other words, one could accept the age of thirty as the minimum legal age for citizenship. And to all of the training, discipline, and hardship that had gone before was now added the requirement that the young man take a wife. How serious and how binding was this requirement? The Spartan who had not proved himself on the field of battle could not hope to occupy a position of any influence in the councils that managed the affairs of state, and the whole Spartan philosophy of life seemed to commend the married state to the young soldier.[22] Nevertheless it appears, if the original accounts of Spartan life can be trusted, that not all Spartan men married, and such an oversight did not either deprive them of any opportunity to become citizens or strip them of the rights and duties of citizenship. Whatever the truth may be, we can at least say that the common practice was for Spartans to spend ten years on active army duty and then to return to become husbands and fathers.

Active duty was followed by a lifetime of service in a ready military reserve. Every Spartan male who was a citizen was always a soldier, either active or ready for action, and to this end the whole system of education or training was directed.

A general evaluation of Spartan education seems unnecessary, for the strengths of the system, as well as the weaknesses, are obvious.[23] But one might add here the evaluation of Aristotle: that as long as the Spartans were the only Greeks who practiced the art of war with diligence they maintained superiority, but when other city states, some of them with broader purposes and therefore broader education and training, turned

[22] Plutarch *Lycurgus.* In *op. cit.,* vol. I, pp. 247–249.

[23] For a discussion of the failure of Spartan education, see Woody, *op. cit.,* pp. 269–272; and Marrou, *op. cit.,* pp. 24–25.

to the objective of military excellence, the superiority of the Spartans vanished.[24]

ATHENIAN IDEALS AND PRACTICES

What we, as the beneficiaries of models from ancient life, owe to the Spartans can be indicated mainly by pointing to examples of totalitarianism and police states that have plagued mankind down through history. Possibly the Spartans have been judged too harshly; but the original sources, including Xenophon, who was a constant admirer of the Spartan system, do not lead one to a more lenient interpretation. Our inheritance from Athens, though far richer and more human, is not so easy to identify, for this inheritance can hardly be disassociated from our culture as a whole. However, our indebtedness to Athens should motivate us to trace some of her educational and intellectual history, in order that we may see these influences more clearly. The task is not without real difficulties. Life and institutions are never quite as simple or as neat as histories sometimes represent them. Besides, man's life in society is subject to change; it is not a static society that we are trying to describe and understand.

Athenians were imaginative, artistic, creative; they tried to organize a citizen society wherein individual freedom to cultivate what may have been distinctive Athenian qualities of mind could be ensured.[25] More basic than this, they had a vision or ideal of community life, and it was to this ideal that every Athenian citizen paid allegiance. The ideal was not merely political, nor was it primarily educational, literary, or religious; it was all of these, and for want of a better word it may be referred to as culture. No society before had held such a view of the community which, though it had practical ends, was concerned mainly with the higher life and was organized with the ultimate purpose of making men more human.[26]

There can be little question that Athens bequeathed to later generations an imperishable heritage of art, literature, and philosophy. On a plane higher than all forms of expression or modes of thought was the Athenians' ideal of culture. They left, moreover, a model of government, which permitted a high degree of freedom for citizens and opportunity for personal and political initiative. More dramatic and somewhat outside the boundaries of culture is the Athenian defeat of the military

[24] Aristotle *Politics* vii. 13. In *The Works of Aristotle*, Oxford University Press, New York, 1908–1931.

[25] Butcher, *op. cit.*, pp. 1 ff.

[26] On this point, see Marrou, *op. cit.*, pp. 38–39.

power of Persia, a triumph which preserved the future of Western civilization. But these are items to be pursued in a broader history. Now we should turn to the Athenian educational ideal; in doing so, however, we should keep in mind that educational objectives and practices are closely connected with an Athenian view of culture. And since this culture was subject to change and to progress, there are different, perhaps nearly discrete, periods of Athenian education to be treated.

The Athenian Educational Ideal

The goal considered by the Spartans most worth working for was citizenship. This basic value permeated all of Spartan life and institutions. The ultimate goal for Athenians can be identified by using the same word—citizenship; but citizenship did not mean for the Athenian exactly what it meant for the Spartan. And education in Athens—something quite different from preparation for a trade or a profession and from traditions or rules and prescriptions pertaining to prudence and morality—aimed at fulfilling the ideal of what man ought to be rather than, as in Sparta, training him to achieve set standards in conduct, skill, and virtue. In terms of the practical, it is not difficult to say what man ought to be, and in an uncomplicated society the process to achieve this objective can be devised rather easily and conducted in an orderly manner; if the ends of education are simple and easily understood, the means to achieve these ends can also be simple. But when what a man ought to be is taken out of a narrow practical context and is viewed in terms of his capacities, his needs, and the creativeness with which he is endowed, then the process becomes less simple. The complaint may be made that it is lacking in direction, or that the breadth of the educational process should be constricted to the point where everyone can see immediately what it is achieving.

Athenian education was not without its critics. Had formal education claimed to be able to do all that needed to be done to bring man to the threshold of culture, then it could not be considered successful. But even when Athenian schools were organized, they were never thought to be the sole custodians of either the cultural inheritance or the cultural ideal. They were sharing a role in which many other social institutions had an important place. The speeches and actions in the theater and the political arena, daily contact with life and with men, and the fact that most men accepted the cultural ideal as something worth working for were all circumstances which made the school's objective much easier to achieve. At least the school was not going in one direction while cultural values that were sought went in another direction. And young people who availed themselves of all of the opportunities for self-cultivation were never put in the unenviable position of having to choose between two contradictory sets of values. They sought culture—they pursued the ideal—not with economic or practical values uppermost in their minds, but with the hope that they might become citizens in the fullest sense, broadly educated, refined, sensitive, ethically conscious, civic-minded men.[27]

We must not continue further along this line without pausing to indicate that this broad view of culture was not always held; rather, it was one which evolved.[28] It can be seen most clearly about the middle of the fifth century B.C., and its influence continued to be felt in later Athenian education as well as in the Hellenistic period.[29] But to obtain the best and most complete view of Athenian education, we must examine the three main periods of Athenian energy and influence: early Athenian, later Athenian, and Hellenistic. We shall explore the first two periods in this chapter and the next, the last period, in Chapter 4.

EARLY ATHENIAN EDUCATION

Homer (ca. 850 B.C.) was the educator of the Greeks.[30] It is probably correct to assume that his influence was felt more keenly and had a greater and more lasting effect in Athens than in any other place, although Sparta and other Greek city states were steeped in the Homeric tradition.

To call Homer the educator of the Greeks requires some justification, for in no sense was he a schoolmaster. He was, nevertheless, a primary force in Greek life and thought. Centuries later, the epic poems attributed to him were memorized or read in the schools (the works of Homer were and are the foundation of classical education), but it would be missing the point of Homer's place in early Greek education to assume that his influence was significant simply because his works were known or studied. They were absorbed into men's thinking and living so thoroughly that for two centuries Athenian education was dominated by Homer. This means that the ideals of life expressed and honored in Homer's epics were accepted and followed as the Athenian rule of life. The values of Athens were the values that Homer found in early Greece

[27] Thucydides ii. 40–41. Translated by Benjamin Jowett, Oxford University Press, New York, 1900. See also R. W. Livingstone, *The Greek Genius and Its Meaning to Us*, Oxford University Press, New York, 1915, p. 141.

[28] Woody, *op. cit.*, pp. 285–286.

[29] The Hellenistic period stood between classical times in Greece and the later Roman and Christian world of the West. See pp. 106–110.

[30] Plato and Isocrates called him the educator of the Greeks, and Aristophanes, in *The Frogs* 1034–1036, said that he was divine. It was generally believed that Homer's poetry was especially inspired.

and in his imagination; his art made them appealing to the Greek mind.[31]

Among an aristocracy responsible for political and social control in Athens, Homer was well known. Boys knew the heroes of his tales; they knew what these heroes thought and how they spoke; and they knew what they would do if they were faced with the problems of the Athens of their own time. The main reason for Homer's great influence was that he was a poet and not a historian. Had he been a historian describing a past that was expected to govern the present and direct the future, his fame very likely would not have been great, and his influence on Greek life would probably have been negligible. He was a poet, however, who framed an ideal and captured the imagination of all who knew his works. Life as it was set forth in the great epics had an appeal which could not be contained in any narrow code of action. Homer did not tell the Greeks how to live, nor did he put words in the mouths of the gods that would dictate a course of individual action. Virtue, in the sense of right action, was not part of his poetic message. Without exceptionally generous interpretations on the part of a reader, moral lessons are not to be found in Homer. Still, it is fair to say that it was the Homeric sense of greatness that gained for Homer the position of educator of the Greeks.[32] The Athenian citizen-aristocrat was primed for glory and heroism; the ideal to which he dedicated himself may be described best by saying that it included all that is contained in the knightly and aristocratic notion of the grand exploit.[33]

The relationship between this ideal and education must be made a little clearer. Homeric values were the accepted goals for life in Athens before the sixth century, and they, like the laws of Lycurgus, were perpetuated in oral tradition. Many Athenians claimed to know Homer's *Iliad* and *Odyssey* by heart. Children learned Homer and gained inspiration from his work in much the same way that Christian children in a later era learned their catechism or Jewish children studied the Jewish law. Schools were not needed to formalize the instruction or to clarify the lessons of this tradition. This was done quite well in the child's daily contacts, and as he grew older he had the same lessons taught to him again by all of life around him.[34]

One must not lose sight of the fact that only the Athenian aristocracy was entitled to this inheritance.[35] Because the few were to be educated in such a fashion, education could be informal. The objectives of educa-

[31] Homeric education is treated with excellence and care by Jaeger, *op. cit.*, vol. I, pp. 46–105.

[32] Jaeger, *op. cit.*, vol. I, pp. 76 ff.

[33] *Ibid.*

[34] *Ibid.*

[35] Woody, *op. cit.*, pp. 281–284; and Bury, *op. cit.*, p. 408.

tion and of life were closely associated and were clear and easy to recognize. Education took no circuitous routes; the boy was to become a citizen, a knight, and a soldier; he was to be a credit to his station in life and to the class from which he came. Skills for making a living were unnecessary—more than this, they were servile and below a young aristocrat's position—and literary accomplishments were accorded no special value. The well-educated citizen of the period before the sixth century B.C. knew his Homer, although he probably could not read. He could count, but quite likely he could not add, subtract, or perform other simple mathematical computations. Few people had any special opportunity to master the skill of writing. Of what real use could these skills have been to the warrior whose mind was set on imitating the heroes of legend and epic? And how could schools have served a society which accepted the values dramatized by Homer?

From the time of Homer to the middle of the sixth century B.C. the chief work of the citizen-aristocrat was soldiering, and the activities preparatory to the life of a citizen were essentially military. In many respects during these years Athens and Sparta were similar, although where Sparta gained her ends by regimentation and strict codes, the Athenians were motivated by a strong sense of duty or dedication to the ideal so vividly depicted in Homer's works. Athens lived on the honor, glory, and ethics of the Homeric model, and this model was influential enough to make unnecessary the prescriptiveness of a Spartan rule of life. It could mold Athenian life as long as Athens was content to conduct her affairs according to an archaic system and to restrict the privileges of citizenship to the members of her aristocracy.

But gradually education drifted away from its preoccupation with military objectives. Perhaps one reason for the shift of interest can be found in the changes which were taking place in military tactics. The citizen-soldier, versatile, skillful, self-reliant, and valorous, was characteristic of the age of Athenian chivalry. Such soldiers were not really needed when military tactics began to accept and emphasize a heavy infantry. The technical qualifications of the Athenian soldier-knight appealed to young aristocrats. No doubt there was a bit of romance about the whole business: this was the life for a citizen; it fulfilled most of his dreams. Could the life and duties and skills of an infantryman have the same attraction for the citizen? What special challenge could be found in the routine but highly effective functions of the infantry soldier? And how could the ideals of Homer's world be served in such a menial capacity? It would be difficult indeed to regard the life and work of such a soldier to be the best, or only, preparation for entering the ranks of the ruling class.[36]

[36] On this point, see Marrou, *op. cit.*, pp. 37–38.

Along with tactical progress in military affairs, the city state was growing commercially. It was not easy any longer, and not always pleasant or gratifying, to live by the rules that had governed men's lives and affairs in the earlier period. Young men of means and position began to see and to respond to enticing opportunities in the economic world of affairs. More than this, the comforts and securities of the aristocracy could not be guaranteed in the new Athens, and military efficiency and knightly ideals were next to useless in the social order that was just coming over the horizon.[37]

Democracy in Athens, however, was only on its way; it had not yet arrived. It was during the years when the aristocratic tradition was having fused to it a number of democratic tendencies that Athens began to encourage schools. A word should be said now about the new ideals that began to shape the foundation for Athenian life and institutions.

The New Ideals in Education

The general picture of Athenian education from the time of Homer to the early sixth century has been described. The reader should be reminded that such an education was conceived in the broadest terms; it could be judged as being the equivalent of life itself. Although broad in the mission that it was to perform, it was narrow in that it bestowed opportunities on very few. The landed aristocracy was entitled to guard and govern; tradition gave it this role. A broad and informal education was directed at preparing gentlemen to exercise the special privileges of their class.

Paternalism was the main operative principle of government, and wealth and position were what made the principle work. How does one prepare himself to govern when these are the conditions which surround him? Mainly, no doubt, by preserving his position of privilege, wealth, and respect. But preparing himself to guard the state was another matter. Possibly it mattered little to the humble shopkeepers, artisans, and peasants whether or not one class of governors was exchanged for another. An aristocracy of wealth and an aristocracy of power may differ greatly on the level of leadership, but for those who are irrevocably committed to a life of doing what they are told, the difference really matters very little. Nevertheless, men will not surrender easily what they value highly. Athenian aristocrats willingly fought to keep what they had; they protected the city state from both foreign and domestic foes. The training which would enable the state's guardians to function well would aim at military excellence, and we have already said that military excellence was closely bound up with the activities of a knight. He had

[37] J. P. Mahaffy, *Social Life in Greece,* St. Martin's Press, Inc., New York, 1913, pp. 57–62.

to have strength, courage, and skill in weapons and horsemanship. More than these attributes was an immovable devotion and dedication to the knight's or the aristocrat's code. Strength and skill could be developed; courage and devotion could be inculcated. But without exercises and without challenges these highly prized virtues would surely rust like an unused sword in its scabbard.

How to maintain a high level of efficiency was therefore both a military and an educational question; in a larger sense, it was a social and political question, too. For years sport had been used to keep the citizen-soldier-knight fit. Interest in and devotion to sporting events and contests of all kinds are attested to throughout Athenian history. The Olympian games, perhaps the best known of organized sporting contests, were generously supplemented by less-known, though nonetheless seriously approached, state and local games. All of the elements of skill and spirit essential to the knight-soldier were served and perfected by sport. Besides, because sport required leisure, which in turn demanded wealth, competitive games were activities more or less naturally restricted to the aristocracy.

The Athenian people's emphasis on sport might be taken as evidence that they were frivolous, impractical, play-loving, and irresponsible. This would not be a fair characterization of them or of their motives in engaging in sport. But whether or not their addiction to physical competition was born of the highest ideals, their exclusive and fashionable sporting world could not withstand the assaults it had to endure from the changing military picture, the broadening economic opportunities, and the sensitive social philosophy indigenous to the times.

These changes did not mean that sport was given up or that it had a less attractive position in Athenian life. Its practical value was, in a military sense, much less clear, but justifications for bodily excellence to be achieved by sport were not slow in appearing nor were they ignored. Where sport had been exclusive because it was expensive in time and money, a new and productive economy opened the doors of leisure to many who previously could not have afforded this luxury. What had been an exclusive preserve for the aristocracy was now being invaded by many who by birth, at least, were not to be numbered among the elite.[38] Since common merchants now had wealth and leisure to engage in most athletic activities, sport became a popular pastime; in a sense it became democratic. Even paid or professional athletes appeared on the Athenian scene, to the great disgust of those who continued to cling to the aristocratic tradition.[39]

[38] On the Athenian sporting tradition, see E. Norman Gardiner, *Athletics of the Ancient World,* Oxford University Press, New York, 1930; and Forbes, *op. cit.*

[39] Plato *Laws* vii. 793–794.

It was natural for aristocrats to feel disturbed and displaced by this turn of events. Society was readying itself for democracy, but the aristocracy was not ready to accept such a society. Without exclusive privileges, nobility seemed to be less attractive. The major changes in early Athenian education, that is, the new direction away from sport and toward intellectual pursuits can be found chiefly in the desire on the part of members of the old aristocracy to protect and preserve their position. They did not have to give up sport, but they felt compelled to find something else which they could reserve for themselves and which would identify them, by its distinctive character, as members of an elite class. If physical prowess was no longer to be the mark of their class, they could turn to intellectual cultivation. And this could be done with relative safety, because the tactics of war no longer depended so much on the varied skills of the individual soldier. What common merchant or artisan could afford the luxury of mental cultivation for its own sake?

Homeric Athenians as a class had been neither illiterate nor unlearned, but they had devoted little attention or energy to mental development. Now, however, the preservation of an aristocracy's identity stood in the balance; this class had all the tools for a successful invasion of the worlds of scientific and spiritual wisdom.

The Organization of Schools

Allegiance to the great deed was not so different from devotion to the noble thought. Heroism and courage could be displayed in connection with things of the mind, as in the past they had been demonstrated on the fields of battle. Yet, despite the validity of this new application of time and talent, Athenians could not turn their backs on centuries of respected tradition, and all of the physical virtues were obviously part of this tradition. Neither athletics nor competition dropped out of the Athenian system of values. What happened was that the system of values was broadened in order that new ideals and new practices could be introduced without interfering with or excluding those already deeply ingrained in Athenian life.

The new concept was that mental training could now be accepted as a distinctive element in the preparation of an Athenian citizen. Physical development and sport, as we have suggested earlier, were retained as part of an honored Greek ideal, but to them was added a program for intellectual development which included the Athenian literary inheritance. A broader conception of aristocratic education was being realized. It should be observed that the evolution of these ideals and practices proceeded much more slowly than our brief account of them would indicate. At first the new education—that is, the combination of mental and physical training—was as closely associated with the aristocracy as sport had been in former times. But drastic adjustments were made until physical and mental formation was universally regarded in Athens as the kind of education necessary for all freemen.[40]

The definition of the freeman was originally one that restricted this broader concept of education to the Athenian aristocracy. However, with progress on all sides, the new education could not be retained for the few only because the political definition of the freeman became more liberal. Although education in Athens at this time could not be called popular, evidently more and more people were in a position to enjoy its advantages. The demand for education, therefore, contributed to the formalizing of instruction. There is hardly any explanation for the rise of the Athenian school other than that of popular demand for the organization of such an institution. The creation and development of schools is one of Athens' most significant contributions to the history of education.[41]

Before the appearance of the school—and no one knows the exact date of the establishment of the first such institution—the new educational objective was being achieved by means of individual tuition. Families of means could care for their children's education by employing teachers for their private use. Popular desire for education, however, was a serious challenge to this practice, and in time a collective principle won out; schools were organized and made available to the children of freemen. This is not to imply that tutorial arrangements for education were given up or that the old aristocracy looked with favor on the practice of distributing more generously what was thought to be an aristocratic education. But whether or not these changes were approved by the few, the picture of the tutor teaching a boy of the privileged class alone in his home was changed to that of Athenian boys leaving their homes in the custody of a pedagogue on the way to schools where teachers were waiting. At this time and for centuries following, educators and philosophers have argued over the advantages and disadvantages of public (collective) and private (tutorial) education. It would appear, however, that the method accepted in Athens at this time gained permanent favor in educational practice.

The studies undertaken by children in these first Athenian schools are clothed in some mystery. And they, too, like the schools themselves, were in the process of developing. When this kind of education was mainly aristocratic and private, the processes and their expected outcomes were two in number: physical training to develop the body and

[40] Isocrates *Areopagiticus.* In Loeb Classical Library, Harvard University Press, Cambridge, Mass., 1927–1929, vol. II, pp. 131-133; Plato *Protagoras* 326.

[41] Freeman, *op. cit.*, pp. 52 ff.

prepare the youth in athletic skills for competitions; and musical training for spiritual, intellectual, and artistic development. Stress on physical training indicated the Athenian allegiance to Homeric tradition. The first schools, therefore, organized a curriculum which gave generously of its time to physical formation, and evidently there were special teachers for this kind of instruction. Musical training was probably less literary and artistic than we have usually been led to believe. Musical education of the schools of early Athens has been commonly represented as being like musical education in the Hellenistic period, that is, primarily studies in literature and acoustics. Actually the school's name, music school, and the course of instruction therein should be taken a bit more literally. Athenians were music-minded; their amusements and their serious culture required musical ability. Perhaps the music school's first duty during the early period was to prepare boys in vocal and instrumental music. This did not mean that poetry, literature, and possibly some mathematics were ignored completely. But the school was preparing boys for life in their social circle, and life's needs—in music harmony, dancing, choral singing, and accompaniment—could not be ignored. The civilized and educated man was, even in Plato's view, one who could fulfill his social role, and this meant, among other things, that he had to be able to sing, dance, and probably play the lyre.

Literature could hardly have occupied as important a place in these early Athenian schools as it did, for example, in the Hellenistic schools two or three centuries later, because poetry still existed mainly in an oral form. Much of it was Homer committed to memory, though some was from the less-known poets of the age. In any case its purpose, as the Greeks interpreted it, was largely moral. We should probably think it moral in transmitting the permanent ideals of the Greek tradition; the Greeks perhaps thought it moral in the narrower sense of being didactic literature.[42]

All of the education just described could be given in school or in a series of schools or by a private teacher, without depending too much, if at all, on the conventional literary skills of reading and writing. In time, of course, writing became an important element in Athenian life—all educated men in classical Athens could write—but it is interesting to observe that the skills or tools of learning which all modern education places first in the lists of goals to be achieved were placed last in the Greek system. Schools for reading, writing, and calculating, or lessons in these subjects in existing schools, were slow to come into being in early Athens. This order of learning should not surprise us too much, however, if we remember that Athenian boys were not being educated for literary or commercial pursuits. It might be worth remarking here, too, that this

[42] Woody, *op. cit.*, pp. 303–305; Freeman, *op. cit.*, p. 229.

somewhat unorthodox order of arranging school subjects did not last beyond the Persian Wars (ca. 479 B.C.), for from about that time onward the three R's became important skills in Athenian life.

It was at about this juncture in the history of education in Athens that the most articulate as well as the most artistic critics of Athenian education spoke out. Their criticisms seem to have been motivated by nostalgia. The aristocratic order, with its educational commitment to the musical rather than the literary and to the athletic rather than the intellectual, was beginning to pass, and its passing was being mourned. Yet those who were criticizing the new education could not have failed to observe that education was not utility-centered; it was still designed for the leisure which only an aristocracy could afford.

One last word needs to be said about these first schools. We have not tried to describe levels of instruction or types of schools, because to do that for the early period would be to engage mainly in guesswork; for later periods such descriptions would have greater validity. But the note that we want to add has to do with the balance, the near-perfect harmony which has been claimed for the two parts of early Athenian education, the physical and the musical.[43] When, in the earliest years, musical education had to do with music in a narrow sense, there was little occasion for conflict between music and athletics. As time went on, however, some critics began to voice their protest against the attention being given to intellectual formation. This was being done, they insisted, at the expense of physical development and bodily beauty and grace. A good deal of hostility developed over the relative importance of musical and physical education as the whole process became more formal, and no real evidence exists of the harmony some historians have found between the two. Aristophanes, a firm friend of the old education and a violent critic of the new, gives us plenty of evidence in *The Clouds* for believing that even in Athens physical and intellectual education made rather strange and uncomfortable bedfellows.[44]

Athenian Society as a Background for Education

Social organization in aristocratic Athens had its basis mainly in kinship, that is, in families, tribes, and clans. Land was owned either by the family, the tribe, or the clan. Land ownership, subject later to even greater restrictions, was the mark of an individual's social and political importance.

Throughout most of the period before the Persian Wars, government

---

[43] L. A. Whibley, *Companion to Greek Studies*, Cambridge University Press, New York, 1905, p. 510.

[44] Aristophanes *The Clouds* 1009–1014. Translated by B. B. Rogers, Loeb Classical Library, Harvard University Press, Cambridge, Mass., 1924.

in Athens was monarchical, although the powers of the king were limited somewhat by a council of nobles and a popular assembly. In the course of time the custom of private property was emphasized and realized, and land ownership drifted gradually from the family and clan into private hands. After the mid-eighth century B.C., the noble-landowner class gained greater strength and brought about a further lessening of the powers of the king, to a point where the monarchy became little more than a symbol. Political affairs in Athens were controlled by the aristocracy, and the state was ruled by nine archons together with the council of the Areopagus. The old popular assembly (ecclesia), to the extent that it still existed, functioned in a largely routine manner. In this aristocratic regime the social classes could be defined as follows: the eupatridae, or ruling nobles, whose estates were in the process of growing larger; the geomoroi, or smaller landowners, whose property was being absorbed into the holdings of the nobles; and the demiourgoi, or artisans. The last two classes, although their members were regarded as free citizens, were without political rights. By the mid-seventh century B.C., Athens became something of a timocracy; that is, property and income now became the chief qualifications for the exercise of civic rights. As a sign of another remarkable change, farmers and artisans now served in military units; however, since the advent of infantry tactics in warfare's methods, no particular glory attached to this service, nor did it bestow any political privileges on those who served. The social structure to which we have made brief reference fostered resentment and dissatisfaction; both became stronger until a climax was reached and reforms had to be initiated. These were achieved in the appointment as lawgiver of Solon (638–559 B.C.), an aristocrat with sympathies for the poor and the politically disenfranchised. Solon's reforms included a cancellation of debts, a freeing of many enslaved people, and a limitation on the amount of land any one individual could own. These reforms tended to give some direction to the first real steps toward democratic or popular government. The old social classifications were retained, but added to them was a fourth class: the *thetes*. An assembly of free but heretofore underprivileged and unrepresented Athenians was created, and a council of four hundred citizens chosen by lot was formed under the direction of Solon. Later, under Cleisthenes (ca. 577 B.C.), all resident freemen, whether native or foreign-born, became citizens, and the council of four hundred was transformed into a council of five hundred members with fifty drawn by lot from each of the ten tribes that were still distinct in Athenian social organization. Athens thus became a fairly well-organized democracy. Under this form of political control she rose to a position of unrivaled leadership among the Ionian states.

At the close of the fourth century B.C., the population estimated for the city state was made up of 21,000 citizens, 10,000 resident aliens, and 120,000 slaves. Because the slaves were committed to all the drudgery of life, Athenian citizens were free to devote their time to civic enterprises. These activities may have included attendance at a public assembly or law court, but they could just as easily have included anything that the citizen undertook to do.[45]

A Child's First Years

The birth of a boy child was an event of considerable import to an Athenian family. Among other signs of rejoicing, the home was decorated, and an unmistakable air of festivity surrounded the entire household. The birth of a daughter, on the other hand, though not actually a cause for mourning, was surely not an event to be celebrated. Whether the child was a boy or girl, its rearing was optional for the father; he had absolute power over its life. If he decided not to keep the infant, he could dispose of it. This was done in any one of a number of ways, there being no prescribed rule governing such early disinheritances. Possibly he would put the baby in an earthenware vessel and leave it either in or near the temple or in some other place in the city where it could be found. Anyone who found such an infant could claim it, care for it, and number it among his slaves. How common was it for Athenian fathers to refuse to accept their own offspring? This is difficult to say, and the answer is not especially important to us. What we should observe in such a custom, especially in considering the relation of the individual to the state, is the parent's authority. The Athenian state, contrary to the practices common in Sparta, did not interfere with, or presume to make, such fundamental decisions for its citizens.

Generally the birth of a child, male or female, was a happy occasion which called for some ritual or feast to pay homage to the gods. The Athenians were not a particularly religious people, but it was the custom to do the gods honor, and the Athenians were very tradition-minded. Commonly a festival was arranged after the birth of a child; and on the child's seventh day he was named. Then a sacrifice was offered to the gods, the mother was purified, and gifts were brought to do the youngster even further honor. The child was now an official member of the family, though not in any legal sense a citizen, and he was placed under the care of the gods with whom the family had some special affiliation.

[45] For extensive discussions of Greek society, see J. P. Mahaffy, *Greek Life and Thought*, The Macmillan Company, New York, 1896; G. Glotz, *Ancient Greece at Work*, Routledge & Kegan Paul, Ltd., London, 1926; and M. Rostovtzeff, *The Social and Economic History of the Hellenistic World*, Oxford University Press, New York, 1941.

The State and Education

In general, one may say that Athenian education was not state-supported, although it is, of course, a fact that five gymnasia situated just outside the city were built and maintained by the city. They were the Academy, Lyceum, Kynosarges, Diogeneion, and Ptolemeion. In addition to the capital and operating costs of the gymnasia, it would appear that their chief teachers, or supervisors, were paid public servants. The support of these establishments is pertinent to our discussion. What was done at a gymnasium was considered not just an important part of Athenian education; it was for many years the essential part, and the physical development promised by gymnastics was, if not the sole, at least the primary goal of secondary education.

Even on other levels, both higher and lower than gymnastics, it would be hard to insist that the city state did not contribute some support; public buildings were often the scene of the schoolmaster's activities, and *paidotribes* (teachers of physical education) were accustomed to using public land and publicly owned equipment. But the point to be emphasized is this: As a rule of tradition, if not of law, the individual was responsible for obtaining his own educational means. Beyond permitting teachers and learners the use of gymnasia, theaters, and temples, public resources were not used to provide the places where instruction or training could take place. And apart from the custom adopted by the city state of supporting the educational ventures of sons of fathers who were killed in battle, the support of education in Athens was an entirely private matter.

Yet we cannot assume that simply because the state does not support education, it is therefore deprived of authority to supervise teaching and learning. Certainly the traditions of Athens could not have argued for stringent supervision over something as personal as physical, mental, and moral preparation. On the other hand, the state looked to its citizens for protection, and during those years when constant dangers threatened Athens' way of life, a firm but not inflexible custom came, at least theoretically, into operation: The state was vested with authority to supervise education. However, in actual practice, the state was reluctant to use this authority.

Certain regulations concerning schools in Athens were attributed to Solon.[46] At that time in Athenian history, it is reported, the state enacted regulations concerning the length of the school day, passed laws restricting entry to school premises to authorized persons, framed legislation governing physical competitions, and established a code having to do with the age of teachers. There is a hint that something resembling compulsory-attendance laws was passed, but beyond the clearly recog-

[46] Freeman, *op. cit.*, p. 57; and Marrou, *op. cit.*, p. 382.

nized and ancient custom that a father was to educate his son if he expected support from his son in old age, the details of such legislation, if it existed, are little known. And it could be argued that the state action mentioned above and said to have been initiated by Solon was not really an attempt to control education. Remembering the level of personal morals in Athens, we may easily believe that such legislation was intended to protect the morals of the young.

With respect to the role of the state in Athenian education, the following conclusions seem accurate: The state did not support education; this was an individual matter; the state did, however, have authority to control or supervise education, but this authority was rarely exercised.

THE SCHOOLS OF ATHENS

Educational practices were not as rigidly adhered to in Athens as in Sparta. It would be a mistake, however, to suppose that in Athens so much freedom of action and thought prevailed that educational practices were in a state of constant flux. Tradition was the main guardian of educational orthodoxy. A system or plan for education that was once generally accepted as customary continued in force as if it had been decreed by the mightiest of kings. During the years before the Persian Wars, when the school and then a system of schools came into existence in Athens, a plan for education either evolved or was designed. It became the permanent, underlying plan for Athenian education, and in form, at least, there were no major changes throughout the course of Athenian history. The education of the early period gained acceptance as conventional Greek education. It is this Greek education that many writers refer to with admiration; it is this plan for education that Plato accepts as preliminary to the higher studies for the wisest men of the state.[47]

Conventional Athenian, or Greek, education was not, as we have implied, restricted to the school. There was no intention to allow some of the many sides of potential human culture to remain underdeveloped, but neither was the school or the schoolmaster expected to assume responsibility for the forming of a complete man.

Before a boy was sent to school his education had already begun. The period of home training began at birth and continued until the youngster was about seven years old. This entire period, though by no means invaded by formal instruction, was considered to be exceedingly important, not only to later instruction but to later life as well. These were the years when the foundation of the boy's moral character was laid. One could almost say that these infant years were reserved for moral education. It would not be easy, however, to give the details of

[47] Plato *Republic* ii. 376; vii. 521d.

the educational work of these first seven years. The child was told innumerable stories, each with a clear-cut moral; he was supervised in his nursery by carefully selected nurses or by his mother. When boys got a little older, perhaps close to seven years of age, a pedagogue became their constant companion and guide. Of course, the poorer families could not afford a pedagogue at all; wealthier families may have had one for each boy in the family; families whose means placed them somewhere between the poor and the rich may have had one pedagogue for all of the boys in the family.[48]

It is not quite accurate to discuss the pedagogue under the general heading of "the schools of Athens." The pedagogue, despite the present connotation of the term, was not a schoolmaster at all. His duty was not to teach letters, although he may have heard lessons, but to inculcate manners and morals. He was the boy's constant companion before he began attending school and during his period of school attendance. In one sense the pedagogue was a member of the family; surely he was being trusted with the family's most precious possession. More accurately, however, he was only a member of the household. In nine cases out of ten he was a slave and a servant; but his role was far greater than his position, for he was a moral master, and as such he occupied an important place in Athenian education.

This pedagogue was usually a man of comparatively old age, unfit for other active work. He was selected to guide a boy because he was thought to have the qualities for such a role. And the fact that the pedagogue was a slave did not mean necessarily that he was uneducated. Many Athenian slaves were captive people who had enjoyed positions of worth and wealth prior to their captivity. Nevertheless, it was not learning that concerned the pedagogue most, but care. When the boy went to school, the pedagogue walked behind carrying the schoolbooks, musical instruments, or writing tablets. Wherever the boy went, the pedagogue was responsible for his conduct. At home the pedagogue watched the boy's manners, seeing to it that he used his left hand for bread, his right hand for other food, kept silent in the presence of elders, rose from his seat when elders entered, sat erect, etc. For infractions of the manners-morals code the pedagogue might scold or punish, although in punishing he had to be careful that he did not inflict a degrading kind of punishment on a freeborn lad.[49]

The Primary School

The primary school, probably the last of the elementary schools to be developed in Athens, was concerned with teaching the elements of

[48] Forbes, *op. cit.*, p. 82.
[49] Freeman, *op. cit.*, pp. 66–69.

literary education.[50] Reading and writing were clearly part of its curriculum; arithmetic and drawing may have been studied in the primary schools kept by more advanced masters or in schools which arranged a program of studies for more advanced students.

Because education in Athens was really a private affair, the primary schools varied greatly as to standards, teachers, and instructional accommodations. Primary schools, which the children of the poor Athenian citizens attended, were small and inadequate. As often as not, it would seem, the scene of such a school was an unrented shop or a corner in a public building. The schools which attracted the children of wealthy Athenians were usually in separate buildings and were more appropriately appointed. When school was kept in a separate building—and this, of course, would depend on the resources of the schoolmaster—there were usually only two rooms to the building, one for instruction and the other for the pedagogues who waited for their charges.[51]

Materials and tools of instruction were quite limited; the master's techniques were largely routine. As a preliminary to instruction in reading, the names of the letters of the alphabet were taught, after which the pupils were instructed in combining consonants with vowels to pronounce words. In the next phase the boys learned the forms of letters, perhaps by tracing them, and at this point they may have learned reading and writing by the same process. They were then taught the component parts of a sentence, although it should be noted that Greek grammar was not highly developed and that therefore the scientific approach to grammar, so common to elementary schools of the later centuries, found little place in the early Athenian primary schools. Reading was taught, not because it was a liberal pursuit but because it was useful: by the time this type of school achieved general recognition in Athens, literacy was necessary to success in life.[52]

Still, the extension of literacy did not preface any literary movement. Books were extremely scarce. Boys did not read poetry; they simply committed it to memory. Learning to read may have meant the attainment of some skill in understanding the written word, but in the actual teaching of reading, much more time was devoted to the learning of a few literary pieces by heart than to preparing the boys to enrich their experience through general reading. The reading school produced boys who were able to recite long passages from Homer, Hesiod, Simonides, and the gnomic poets. In addition, they could read public placards and

---

[50] It was the last type to be developed because it was concerned with literary education. For another discussion of primary education, see *ibid.*, pp. 79 ff.

[51] Woody, *op. cit.*, pp. 300–301.

[52] Marrou, *op. cit.*, p. 42.

commercial documents. These outcomes were neither higher nor lower than what was expected from such schools.

Writing and reading were learned in the same school. Usually the master instructed his pupils in reading one day and in writing the next. Three styles of writing were common in Athens about this time, and all of them may have been included in the writing syllabus: the formal hand, consisting of separate capital letters, usually taught to children; the cursive hand, examples of which are preserved in Greek papyri; and the short hand, the typical writing technique of copyists, clerks, and scribes. One can be reasonably sure that the first two types of writing were taught in the primary school. There is some doubt, however, that Athenians in a position to send their children to schools would have encouraged them to learn the short hand, which was really the skill of a trade. That such a writing technique became popular in the second century B.C. is not open to any real question, but that it formed a regular part of the early elementary school program is doubtful.

Writing was practiced on wax-coated tablets made of wood; the central panel was surrounded by a flat, raised edge, which served to protect the wax coating of the panel. Several tablets could be fastened together on strings passed through holes bored in the edges. For a writing tool the boys had an instrument called a stylus, with a sharp point on one end suitable for making marks and a flat surface on the other to be used for erasing. In the course of time, ink and the reed pen became common implements in the schools.

Pupils just beginning their instruction in writing traced outlined letters made by the teacher.[53] This practice was not abandoned until the boys were capable of writing letters with only the assistance of parallel lines. Letters were written in horizontal and vertical lines so that letters fell beneath one another. No stops or accents were inserted, and there was no space between words. The writing master ruled both vertical and horizontal lines for his pupils. After the boys acquired facility in writing, the master dictated simple words and then passages from the poets to be copied. Various elaborations both in speed and beauty of writing were customary for the more advanced pupils.

In some schools masters were paid to teach their pupils arithmetic. For the most part, this study involved nothing more than simple counting.[54] In Athenian intellectual circles the distinction between arithmetical skill for practical computations and the study of number or quantity and its properties—mathematics in a more proper sense—was made very

[53] Plato *Protagoras* 326.
[54] See D. E. Smith, *History of Mathematics*, Ginn & Company, Boston, 1925, vol. 2, pp. 196–202; and Thomas Davidson, *Aristotle and Ancient Educational Ideals*, Charles Scribner's Sons, New York, 1901, pp. 77 ff.

easily. Possibly the same distinction was not made by people in general or in the elementary school, but this was because little or nothing was known of mathematics in a higher sense. The schoolmaster, who limited his instruction in numbers to counting, did not need to make the distinction. A glance at the mathematical characters the Greeks used, however, will quickly disclose how cumbersome they were; Greek letters were used to do what we do with our common Arabic numerals, and their use involved complexities even greater than those met with in the use of Roman numerals in the Latin schools of the Roman world. It is unlikely that many Athenian schoolboys could either add or subtract. They were taught to count. Not even this was simple, although Athenians counted with their fingers and with their hands.[55] Learning to count from one to one million was the only achievement parents of the day could expect of their sons. The system may have been something like the following: the student held his hand with fingers erect and palms facing outward; by moving his fingers and his hands he could indicate numbers. To put the method in the form of directions: On the left hand, for one, half close the fourth finger only; for two, half close the third and fourth fingers only; for three, half close the second, third and fourth fingers; for four, half close the second and third fingers; for five, half close the second finger; for six, half close the third finger; for seven, close the fourth finger; for eight, close the third and fourth fingers; for nine, close the second, third, and fourth fingers. The same operation on the right hand indicated thousands from one to nine. Numbers from ten to ninety were also shown by the left hand: for ten, put the tip of the forefinger at the base of thumb; for twenty, hold the forefinger straight; for thirty, join the tips of forefinger and thumb; for forty, put the thumb behind the knuckle of the forefinger; for fifty, put the thumb in front of the forefinger; for sixty, hold the thumb as in fifty, but bend the forefinger to touch the ball of the thumb; for seventy, rest the forefinger on top of the thumb; for eighty, hold the thumb on the palm; for ninety, close the forefinger completely. The same motions on the right hand were used to show hundreds from 100 to 900. This is not the complete counting system, but it does suggest what the student was expected to learn and something of the challenge that faced him.[56]

For some pupils in some schools the uses of the abacus were taught. The simplest abacus had beads on wires. Ten beads on the top line counted as one each, and added together made ten; the ten beads on the second line counted as ten each, and added together made one

---

[55] Aristophanes *The Wasps* 656. In Loeb Classical Library, Harvard University Press, Cambridge, Mass., 1924, vol. I, p. 473.

[56] Freeman discusses the system of counting and the use of the abacus, *op. cit.*, pp. 104–107.

hundred; the ten beads on the third line counted one hundred each and added together made one thousand. One may suppose that the use of the abacus was mainly commercial and that practice in its use was not a regular elementary-school exercise.

Drawing and possibly painting completed the primary school program of instruction.[57] Such exercises were part of the curriculum because the Greeks wanted to lay a good foundation for aesthetic judgments. The details of this part of the program seem unnecessary here.

A final word should be added concerning the teachers of these schools. From a glimpse of the teacher's place and status we may obtain a better idea of the value that Athenians placed on their primary schools. There were no qualifications, other than being able to read, which teachers had to meet. For this reason elementary teaching was generally despised and, in addition, was regarded as a servile occupation unworthy of a freeman. Few good teachers were motivated to stay in Athens and conduct primary schools or to come to Athens to open such schools. Many of Athens' elementary teachers turned to teaching because of a lack of other employment rather than because of special fitness for teaching.[58]

Physical Education

In early Greece a boy's first somewhat formal preparation for assuming his role as a complete citizen consisted in perfecting physical skills. In the olden days these skills were, as we have already seen, closely associated with the art of war. But later, even without any real need for the skills of the soldier-knight, Athenian boys were encouraged to perfect their bodies and achieve grace and harmonious movement. These were highly prized accomplishments. Nowhere was the influence of the archaic system of values more thoroughly felt than in the area of physical education.

Physical education achieved a regular place in Athenian formal education. It was not simply a program in a school; it rated a school for itself. This was the palaestra. Either following the primary school and preceding the music school, or being conducted simultaneously with the other types of elementary schools, the palaestra concentrated on exercising the body. The school was under the direction of a *paidotribe*. He was supposed to know something about training the body, and some of the more highly qualified paidotribes had an elementary knowledge of the art of medicine. He conducted a program which consisted of simple exercises, games, dancing, swimming, wrestling, and throwing the discus and the javelin. The last-named skills were approached in their intro-

[57] Aristotle *Politics* viii. 3.1.
[58] On this point, see Freeman, *op. cit.*, pp. 81–83.

ductory phases. No building or play yard was set aside for the work of this school; almost any open space would do, and on rare occasions the paidotribe took his charges to one of the gymnasia.[59]

Paidotribes were private teachers, who, while earning a living by keeping a palaestra, were preparing for and aspiring to a position in one of the city-operated gymnasia. One may guess, however, that since these men were doing a kind of work which through custom and tradition had won a great deal of admiration, they fared better than others who accepted a teacher's role in elementary education.

The Music School

The music school was also a part of elementary education. During the two centuries before the Persian Wars, the music school was probably mainly a place where instrumental and vocal music was taught. The place of music in Greek life must be emphasized if one is to understand why a special school should have been established for teaching music.[60] But as time moved on, need for literary education increased, and the traditional values of Greek life began to give way. Dancing, choruses, accompanied singing, all began to decline in importance. If we look forward several centuries, we shall find the music school without music— music instruction had been converted into an acoustical study—but the recession of music was gradual and slow. In the Athenian education of the old style, the content of the music school was reading, writing (continued from the primary school), poetry, singing, and playing the lyre or oboe.

Some music schools could boast of only one teacher. To him, therefore, fell the task of teaching everything that was to be taught. In better music schools, at least two teachers shared instructional duties: the grammatist and the citharist. The former was the literary master, or more exactly, an elementary teacher of letters. The latter was the choirmaster and the lyre master.

In conventional Athenian education the music school really concluded formal literary and musical education. At about the age of fifteen a boy was excused from further study of letters and music.[61] An Athenian boy had, however, been exposed to a great deal more of the social and literary inheritance than we in the twentieth century think appropriate for elementary schools. His instruction had been both individual and collective; he had copied and composed on wax tablets; and he had memorized a good part of Homer. But this was not all; the poetry of Hesiod, Solon, Alcman, Tyrtaeus, Pindar, Aeschylus, and Euripides

---

[59] Plato *Protagoras* 325–326.
[60] Plato *Laws* ii. 654.
[61] J. P. Mahaffy, *Old Greek Education,* Harper & Brothers, New York, 1881, p. 25.

was part of him, and the fables of Aesop were as familiar to him as his route home. He had enough skill in singing and playing to adapt himself to the society in which such skills were respected. One is entitled to assume that in the absence of any known criticism of the conventional music school, its work was thorough and complete. The Athenians must have had confidence in it, for before the Persian Wars no other educational level or school tried either to duplicate or to complete the work of the music school.

Athenian Secondary Education

It is possible to find a counterpart in modern education for every ancient Athenian school except the gymnasium. To the extent that the gymnasium was a school in the conventional sense—and this could be open to debate—it occupies a unique role in educational history. What has been said about the gymnasium applies to its status during the years before the Persian Wars. There is no question that after the Persian Wars the gymnasia became more and more literary and intellectual and less and less centers of physical training. But in the early period, the three Athenian gymnasia then in existence—the Lyceum, Academy, and Kynosarges—reflected both the aristocratic and the archaic conceptions of Greek education better than any other educational unit. These conceptions, as we have seen, were intimately connected with the ideal of the noble deed. Nobility of action and grace of movement were probably the real objectives of these schools.

Gymnastic training was, of course, securely established in Athenian traditions; when such training was formalized and when it was organized and supervised by state-supported institutions is not easy to say.[62] Surely the Lyceum and the Academy were quite ancient, and the Kynosarges antedated the fifth century B.C. Partly because of their venerable age, these places were prone to reflect aristocratic educational and social ideals. At first the Academy and the Lyceum were open only to free-born Athenian youth, and the Kynosarges was reserved for the sons of Athenian fathers and foreign-born mothers. No gymnastic training was available in these institutions for boys who did not meet these qualifications. But as we move forward in history toward the Persian Wars and the democratic influences that they released, we see the gymnasia discarding some of their exclusiveness.

We have said that these gymnasia were state-supported institutions.[63] The statement is accurate if we keep in mind that such support applied only to the construction and maintenance of the gymnasium as a physical plant. Activities taking place in the gymnasium were not sponsored and

[62] Gardiner, *op. cit.*, p. 41.
[63] Xenophon *Constitutions of Athens* ii. 10.

paid for by the city. Even the *gymnasiarch*, the chief teacher or trainer, was not employed by the state. It is true that his position was state-appointed, but it was, in fact, one of honor rather than of employment. His role in controlling and supervising the activities of the gymnasium may not have been very demanding. Under his nominal supervision were a number of gymnasts and paidotribes who had actual contact with the boys who came to train in the gymnasium.[64]

In general, the gymnasium was open only to those who were able to pay the fees. The course of instruction occupied, two, three, or more years; actually its length depended almost entirely on the boy himself. Boys who were unable to pay but who had some special ability to recommend them could have been selected by the gymnasiarch for gratuitous training. One of the most common recommendations for receiving gratuities of this sort was that the boy had lost his father on the field of battle.

It would appear that Athenian gymnasiarchs were left in their position of honor as long as the gymnasium which they superintended maintained a record of excellence in the many intracity and intercity competitions. To protect his position the gymnasiarch was constantly on the alert for Athenian boys of strength and agility who could contribute to the gymnasium's record. When these boys could not afford the fees, they were trained for nothing.

Considering the social pressures involved—there was no question of legal compulsion—few well-born Athenian boys were willing to place their futures in jeopardy by not attending a gymnasium. As the number of eligible, aspiring Athenian youth increased, the number of gymnasia increased also. There were in all five public gymnasia in Athens, although probably only three were in existence before the Persian Wars. In addition to the three mentioned above, there were the Diogeneion and the Ptolemeion, both public, and several private gymnasia. It might be mentioned, however, that private gymnasia really belong to that period of Athenian educational history when gymnastics were no longer the important content of secondary training. Intellectual formation was the principal objective of these later private gymnasia.[65]

Of the training and kinds of exercises prevalent in the gymnasium during the years before the Persian Wars, little need be said. The elementary physical skills introduced in the palaestra were continued and perfected. Beyond these, such things as riding and driving were practiced. We even hear of some instruction in Athenian law, but there are no detailed accounts of this kind of teaching in the gymnasia of the early period. It is hard, indeed, to think of the gymasium as a school;

[64] Freeman, *op. cit.*, pp. 224 ff.; and Woody, *op. cit.*, pp. 311–312.
[65] Freeman, *op. cit.*, p. 125.

perhaps it will be even more difficult to do so when we see something of the physical dimensions of the place.

Possibly there was no typical architecture for the gymnasium. Despite this, we can have a general idea of the gymnasium. It was, first of all, an enclosed stadium with a large playing field, probably about the size of a modern football field, and a race course. The field was surrounded by places for spectators to sit or stand and buildings in which the athletes could rest, exercise, or converse. There were rooms for wrestling, bathing, massaging, eating, praying, and just talking. There were gardens and groves and walks. Living quarters for servants and attendents were provided on the premises. The gymnasium was an inspiring multipurpose plant. Its total area approached 360,000 square feet.[66]

Ephebic Training

Ephebic training was the last step on the Athenian educational ladder. We have so far resisted the temptation to speak of the ephebic school, because it is not entirely clear that such training was ever organized into an institution that might properly be called a school. Whether in school or not, there is no doubt that ephebic education was intended to prepare boys for the major responsibilities of citizenship. During certain historical periods, such preparation meant training boys in the art of war; in other and later periods, ephebic education was fairly conventional intellectual training. Thus in later periods it is hardly necessary to speak of ephebic training, for it could not really be distinguished from any other kind of education. Even in the early years of Athenian educational history, ephebic schooling and the so-called ephebic college are clothed in considerable mystery.

Some educational historians have credited organized ephebic training with great antiquity; others have claimed that the ephebic system had its origin in the post-Persian War period. Wherever the truth may lie, one can be fairly certain that archaic values were reflected in the ephebic system.[67] One can be confident, too, that the demands made on the citizens for military service required that there be some means available for gaining skill and proficiency in the military arts. As the tendency grew for institutionalizing many things that had been left to individual Athenians, ephebic preparation was probably subjected to some social control. But just when this took place is not known. Neither Plato, Xenophon, nor Isocrates mentions the ephebic college. Aristotle alone

[66] *Ibid.*, pp. 127–130; and Woody, *op. cit.*, pp. 312–315.
[67] Freeman, *op. cit.*, pp. 127–130; Marrou, *op. cit.*, pp. 105–106 and 382; and Mahaffy, *Old Greek Education*, pp. 73 ff.

paused to describe ephebic training, and he recognized it as the entrance to citizenship.[68]

In Aristotle's time citizenship was open to all Athenian residents born of Athenian parents. The conventional path to citizenship took one through ephebic training. At the age of eighteen or so, the boy applied for it. And this application was no mere formality. His age and parentage were examined by a council or a committee charged with this function. If the candidate was found to be younger than the law required, he was rejected; if his parentage was subject to question, the commission could bring charges against him for falsely claiming the right of citizenship. These charges were heard before the court of the city state, and the verdict was final. It could take one of two courses: A verdict against the boy meant that he would be sold as a slave; a favorable verdict enabled him to enroll in the ephebic course without further obstacle.[69]

Once in the ephebic course, boys received military training. As military science and tactics changed over the years, it is reasonable to assume that the course of training for ephebi changed too. In Aristotle's day this military training was of a year's duration. Then, in public ceremonies, those who were judged successful received the shield and the spear, and at the same time an oath of allegiance—the ephebic oath—was taken. Before Aristotle's time, we are told, the ephebic oath may have been administered to the boys when they enrolled for ephebic training, or the oath taking may even have been deferred until the complete course of three years or so had been finished.[70] Whenever this oath was taken—it was first introduced, tradition says, by Solon—it was always a pledge to honor the laws and traditions of Athens:

I will never disgrace these sacred arms, nor desert my companions in the ranks. I will fight for the gods and home, both alone and with many. I will transmit my fatherland, not only no less but greater and better than it was transmitted to me. I will obey the magistrates who may at any time be in power. I will observe both the existing laws and those which the people may unanimously make in the future, and if any person seeks to annul the laws or disobey them, I will do my best to prevent him and will defend them both alone and with many. I will honor the religion of my fatherland, and I will call upon the gods [he names them] as my witness.[71]

The ceremonies of the arms and the oath were followed by two years of active service in the Athenian military organization. The period of preparation, which included training in the use of the implements of war

[68] Aristotle *The Constitution of Athens* 42.
[69] *Ibid.*
[70] *Ibid.*; and Woody, *op. cit.*, pp. 318–320.
[71] Quoted in Woody, *op. cit.*, p. 319.

and which also may have included some instruction in Athenian law, was over. Ephebic schooling lasted one year. Now the boys were journeyman citizens. There was nothing inevitable about being admitted to the ranks of full citizenship. Such promotions depended upon the soldier's performance and his dedication to the state, and many obstacles faced young men during the two-year period of military service. Not the least of these obstacles was actual warfare. Young men had to prove that they could uphold the oath they had taken and that they were worthy of citizenship. Even aside from combat and the real trials all brave men face in battle, these two years were most rigorous; discipline was extremely severe, and much physical exertion and skill were demanded of the men in the contests, games, and military maneuvers.

The earlier the period of Athenian history, the greater the likelihood that the soldier-citizens were the men in the military ranks or, at least, the men who would actually be engaged by an enemy in battles or skirmishes. But as armies became larger and as military conditions changed, these soldier-citizens tended more and more to be the officer class. The leaders were the citizens, or prospective citizens; those being led were mercenaries or noncitizen conscripts.

Possibly along with such changes or because of them, the ephebic training usual in the time of Aristotle was modified. This modification may have been due, also, to the declining fortunes of Athenian military power. In any event, ephebic training, instead of emphasizing or giving sole attention to physical and military development, accepted an intellectual function. In time a library was collected for the use of boys in the ephebic course, and with the acceptance of literary and intellectual objectives, ephebic training came to be identified as the ephebic college. It is doubtful that ancient Athens ever really relinquished the practice of ephebic preparation; when citizens no longer needed to be military men or military-minded, the scene of ephebic training shifted from the public gymnasia and the battlefield to the courts, the public arena, the schools, and the libraries.

LATER ATHENIAN EDUCATION

Beginning around 479 B.C., a date which marks the end of the Persian Wars, Athenian society was subjected to a number of remarkable changes.[72] The success of Athens in defending herself against Persia led her to a position of leadership among Greek city states. It would seem that this advantageous political position was employed to further Athenian economic interests which added to the wealth of an already

[72] I am anxious to acknowledge my indebtedness in this section, as in previous sections, to Jaeger, *op. cit.*, vol. 1, pp. 286–332.

flourishing economic community. More important for us, however, were the internal innovations which seemed to be generated by the favorable political climate and which seemed also to nourish the state's political stamina. If cause and effect are hard to isolate in history, they were likewise troublesome to unravel in the Athenian social order. To put it briefly, life was becoming very complicated. In the old days citizens were prominent. Now, as a result of the conscription practices used during the Persian Wars, many noncitizens who had fought in the defense of Athens—a role previously restricted to citizens—asked for the rights they had fought to protect. Their demands were honored.

This was a political and social change with far-reaching effects. The democratic tendencies in politics were consolidated in practice. All free inhabitants became citizens, and, in the age of Pericles especially (459–431 B.C.), these citizens practiced their newly found privileges. Here, of course, is where education was affected: the old education had given its attention to making citizens; the new education did not need nor did it fully understand such a purpose. In place of the objective of citizenship—service to the state—the ideal of individual development was substituted. Where the old goal was society-centered, the new goal was individual-centered. In this atmosphere the honored virtues of the past were replaced by individualism.

The form of education was not changed. The same schools remained as symbols or as remnants of an honored but unneeded and unheeded past. Their content was modified only to the degree necessary for making them primarily literary institutions: this was accomplished on all levels. The schools of Athens became centers for preparing citizens to take advantage of their newly found freedom. Education flourished because it was regarded simply as a means to be used to speed up the process of social assimilation. But the schools of Athens, especially in the first years after the victory over Persia, were in the position of being able only to whet the intellectual appetites of the people. They contained little or no opportunity for higher training or intellectual formation. It was in this ferment, or from it, that a new class of teachers—the Sophists—came into prominence. It is the Sophists, along with the great philosopher-teachers—Plato, Aristotle, Isocrates, and others—who play the leading roles in the history of later Athenian education. These roles will be discussed in Chapter 3.

SUMMARY

Ancient Greece contained many city states, the most famous of which were Athens and Sparta. Each of the Greek states had some provisions for education or training, but the prevailing educational systems supported or encouraged in Greece tended to follow the practice either of Athens or of Sparta.

Sparta's plan for education was founded on those values which Spartans found most useful to them. The paramount objective of the Spartan education or training system was citizenship. The goal was conceived in a narrow sense; it meant training Spartan boys in military craft. It may be fair to say that Spartans were owned by the state and that in Spartan history we can find some of the best examples of political and educational totalitarianism.

In Athens the goals of education were also expressed by the single term citizenship. But here the term's meaning was somewhat more complex, for the citizen of Athens was not merely a fighter; he was a man too. In this broader conception, the individual was formed in such a way that he knew, revered, and defended the traditions of the state. Such formation was thought to be the development of virtue—or laying the foundations for knightly and aristocratic conduct and eventually for the great deed. For decade after decade, Athenian education was informal. But with schools or without them, the goals of education were preserved with a surprising constancy. Possibly this was because education was quite exclusive; its opportunities were not generously distributed. Even when schools became common in Athens, the honored preferences in education were not greatly disturbed. Despite the adherence and devotion to practices and ideals of the past, Athenian society could not resist change. The most memorable changes took place after the Persian Wars. In earlier years education had been concerned with forming men; now it became concerned with training boys to become effective and successful. To aid in the achievement of this new goal, the Sophists made their way into Athens.

Questions and Exercises for Study and Discussion

1. What evidence do you find from your outside reading that the history of Western education began with the Greeks? Try to find some examples of influences on Western educational thought and practice that are not Greek.
2. Why should we study Spartan education? Did Sparta influence Athenian education? How did Plato react to Spartan education? Do you see any relationship between Spartan education and education in totalitarian states of the modern world?
3. Can you justify Sparta's relative neglect of the education of women? Compare the status of women in Sparta and in Athens.
4. Both Spartan and Athenian education accepted citizenship as their primary objective. How, then, could Spartan education and Athenian education differ so greatly?

5. Describe the steps in the education of a Spartan boy.
6. If you were to be educated in ancient Greece, would you choose the system in Sparta or in Athens? Why?
7. Since Homer was not a schoolmaster, in what sense is it proper to call him the educator of the Greeks?
8. Why did military training occupy such an important role in ancient Greek education?
9. Describe the role of sport and music in the life of an Athenian gentleman. Do their respective roles have any special significance for education?
10. Compare the experience of a boy in Athenian schools with the experience of a boy in contemporary elementary and secondary schools.
11. What was the status, the preparation, and the reward for teaching in the schools of Athens? What was the state's relationship to education there? Did the state control or support education?
12. What is the justification for distinguishing early from later Athenian education? Did the levels of schooling change? Did the content or the purposes of education change?

3

Greek Educational Thought

SOPHISTS

In Chapter 2 we saw how and for whom the Greeks provided educational opportunity, and what they regarded education's objectives to be. We have noted, too, the marked change which took place in Athens after the Persian Wars and have mentioned a new class of teachers, the Sophists, who arose to revolutionize educational practices for all time. Not again until the Renaissance of the fourteenth century does history record the same restlessness of men's minds or picture a tireless spirit of inquiry comparable to that of the post-Persian War period. This was an era of great intellectual ferment; it was a time for great minds and great men. We can study, naturally, only a few of the outstanding educational thinkers and actors. But before turning to the men whose ideas laid the foundation for educational theory, we should consider in what way preparations had been made for building such foundations. It may not be too much to say that in voicing their opinions of political and social conditions in the new Athens, Socrates, Plato, Isocrates, and Aristotle began a theoretical tradition in education.[1] The individuals most responsible for creating the environment in education and schooling to which the figures just mentioned took quite definite exception were the Sophists.

So much has been said about the Sophists in histories of philosophy, politics, and education that one may wonder how much needs to be added here. It is true, of course, that no group of teachers has ever

[1] Werner W. Jaeger, in his *Paideia: The Ideals of Greek Culture,* Oxford University Press, New York, 1945, vol. I, pp. 298–321, discusses the origins of educational theory during these years of intellectual quickening.

been more thoroughly maligned by generations that followed them than the Sophists. In modern terminology the word sophist expresses opprobrium.[2] It may be easy to conclude that the Sophists were ignorant, evil, irresponsible, pretentious, greedy men, and that they led Athens down the road to intellectual decadence. There is some respected testimony to support such a view.[3] There is, moreover, the long tradition of disbelief in sophistic worth; the tradition is made up, it would seem, of both fact and caricature.

Before the Sophists are cast into a specially prepared academic limbo, it would be well for us to recall that what we know of them comes mainly from their enemies. The principal witness is Plato, and, generally speaking, he loses no opportunity to show them in a most unfavorable light. It is doubtful that Plato's criticisms are entirely fair, for on this point he may not have been an objective reporter.

Whatever Plato may have thought of them and whatever we may think of them, we cannot ignore the Sophists. They deserve careful attention in the history of education. They may need little space in the history of thought, for they accomplished little in increasing man's understanding of truth, but they were teachers. As teachers they cleared avenues for educational progress; they have been called the inventors of modern secondary education. Being teachers principally, they have a legitimate place in the history of education.[4]

After the Persian Wars the Sophists attracted a great deal of attention in Athens, but they were known throughout Greece as well. In answering the question as to why they attracted attention we are led nearer the explanation of their important role in education's long history. First, they contracted with their students to teach whatever the students needed for success in life. In their teaching they employed what has been called the simultaneous method. Second, because their fees for this kind of teaching were not inconsequential, they found it necessary to advertise their skill. They gave themselves a good deal of publicity, and possibly some Sophists were inclined to exaggerate their talents. Finally, the Sophists attracted attention by attempting to accelerate education in Athens to the point where it could reach the level of contemporary Athenian culture. Before examining these points in greater detail, we might explain that the Sophists did not form a cohesive school with a defined doctrine; a Sophist was an independent teacher. Although

[2] This was not always so. See Isocrates *Antidosis*. In Loeb Classical Library, Harvard University Press, Cambridge, Mass., 1927–1929, vol. II, p. 235.

[3] Thomas Davidson, *Aristotle and Ancient Educational Ideals*, Charles Scribner's Sons, New York, 1901, p. 101; and G. A. Grote, *A History of Greece*, J. M. Dent & Sons, Ltd., London, 1906, vol. VIII, p. 316.

[4] On this point, see Jaeger, *op. cit.*, vol. I, pp. 286–298.

we may think of him as a member of a community of teachers, generally he did not acknowledge any such membership.[5]

The motives which operated on individual Sophists and led them to offer their services as teachers must remain forever unknown to us. We may guess that some of them were deeply dedicated to the work they sought to perform; others may have been interested only in the income to be derived from their teaching. We have been led to believe that every Sophist taught for fees and that he tried to teach several students at one time because such a technique was more profitable. We have also been led to believe that taking fees for instruction was a striking innovation and that it was out of keeping with Athenian practices. It is said that because the Sophists charged for their instruction and because their fees were extraordinarily high, they were despised in Athens and in many other Greek city states. If the Sophists were the objects of derision in Athens one wonders why they were so successful and so popular there. The point is this: Since no one knows definitely what the Sophists' reception was in Athens, we may assume that they were welcome and that their services were much in demand. In any case their practice of taking fees for teaching was nothing new in Athens,[6] although their custom of asking for payment in advance may have had a touch of the novel and the unorthodox about it.[7] Athenians had for dozens of decades been accustomed to paying their teachers for services rendered. They paid the teachers of the lower schools, and they paid the teachers of the higher schools. Some of history's most respected thinkers were teachers who taught for compensation. The innovation in educational practices introduced by the Sophists was to contract with students for a course of instruction which may have lasted as long as three years. Such practical agreements between students and their Sophist-teachers, though not altogether orthodox procedure in Athens, were nevertheless accepted without noticeable objection from the general population.[8]

The fees that Sophists charged were high when the demand for their instruction was great and low when they were in need of students. It would seem that by resorting to such business practices the Sophists might have disclosed some superficiality in their approach to learning; what they had to offer was worth whatever the traffic would bear. In a society with a long tradition for appreciating value, such a cavalier

[5] Kenneth J. Freeman, in *Schools of Hellas*, 3d ed., The Macmillan Company, New York, 1922, pp. 157–209, has an illuminating discussion of the Sophists.

[6] See pp. 55–56, 61.

[7] Sophists made the unequivocal promise to teach virtue. If they had any real trust in their teaching, why did they have to demand payment in advance?

[8] It is recognized, of course, that Plato, Aristotle, Isocrates, Aristophanes, to name only a few prominent Athenian figures, took decided exception to the Sophists' practices.

attitude might have stimulated statements of reproach. And of course it did.[9] But such reprimands went largely unnoticed by the Sophists' clients, because it was in the new Athens that sophistry flourished— where men wanted the knowledge the Sophists claimed to have—and not in archaic Athens where men valued the traditional ways of thought.

Besides being accused of fraudulence in teaching, Sophists were sometimes held in disrepute because they were thought to have enriched themselves in their profession. A few had, no doubt. However, it is not easy to see the justice of such a charge. Isocrates, for example, although he is not usually classified as a Sophist, became very rich as an Athenian teacher, and the bulk of his income was derived from his teaching.[10] Despite this, Isocrates' reputation seems to have been unsoiled. One might guess that most Sophists were not wealthy men.

The Sophists moved from place to place in search of students; so-called "stationary teachers"—Plato and Aristotle would be good examples— waited for students to come to them. It is reasonably accurate, there- fore, to think of Sophists as wandering teachers. But when they suc- ceeded in contracting with a number of students, they tried to give their lectures and carry on other teaching practices in halls or build- ings,[11] and thus there was some expense attached to their instructional program. Taking this expense into account—and the Sophists were always eminently practical men—they usually tried to lecture to a full house. And as the number of teachers increased, they were forced more and more to compete for the students' fees and even to resort to publicity campaigns in order to attract students. Without modern ad- vertising media, they were forced to carry on their recruitment pro- grams in person. The picture so often drawn of the Sophist is of a man moving about the city or from city to city, disputing, arguing, and taking advantage of every opportunity to display his learning, his versatility, and his wit. Too often we stop here and conclude, possibly erroneously, that this was the extent of the Sophists' teaching. It was not uncommon for Sophists to have a few of their students accompany them on such excursions to round up students. On these occasions we get a glimpse of sophistic display. We are less fortunate, however, in that few examples of regular sophistic instruction have been preserved.

We should hardly be surprised to learn that the Sophists would advertise their product or that they would exaggerate their abilities as teachers. And we may want to pause for a moment before con-

[9] As only one example from among many that could be cited, see Isocrates *Against the Sophists.* In *op. cit.,* vol. II, p. 3.

[10] R. C. Jebb, *The Attic Orators,* Macmillan & Co., Ltd., London, 1893, vol. II, pp. 28–29.

[11] Freeman, *op. cit.,* p. 158.

demning them, since most educational institutions and many teachers down through history have been guilty of the same kind of pretensions. This is not to say, of course, that because others were guilty too, the Sophists somehow become guiltless, but it seems unfair to single them out for special condemnation when others who resorted to the same techniques of exaggeration generally escape even mild criticism, or, what is worse, are praised for behavior that merits blame.

Nevertheless, much of the unenviable fame which attaches to sophistry had its origin in the recruitment procedures. And when the masters of the permanent schools began to lose students to the popular Sophists, these masters generated a resentment for their rivals which, though it may not have interfered with the Sophists' schools of the day, found its way into history to label the Sophists scholastic fakes and academic cheats.[12] This is a reputation which they do not entirely deserve.

After the Persian Wars, Athens could boast, among her other claims to respect, of being a cultural center. This was no idle boast, for the Athenians had made real and significant cultural progress. Their traditional vision of culture was near realization. However, culture in Athens, that is, her high level of art and thought far outran systematic education. The Sophists' chief work was to close this gap between education and culture.[13] It was the existence of this gap which brought such a class of wandering scholars to Athens in the first place.

In a very real sense the Sophists responded to demand, at least, to opportunity. They appeared on the Athenian scene in the fifth century B.C. at a time when society was ready for them. At this time in Athens, it will be recalled, a system of elementary schooling extended through the music school. Beyond this there was sport, with training for games of all kinds, but there were no schools for broader and deeper intellectual formation. With cultural progress so far in advance of elementary intellectual education, it is no wonder that Athenians welcomed a class of teachers who promised to disseminate the latest advances in Athenian culture and wisdom. Apparently the belief that Sophists were somehow involved in a democratic or democratizing movement in the city state is in need of revision. Whoever could pay the fees could be instructed by a Sophist, but the Sophists were not elementary teachers—they appeared to have no interest at all in teaching the basic tools of learning—

[12] Plato *Sophist* 222–234.

[13] Between elementary education on the one hand, and a sharing in the cultural attainments and intellectual adventures available in Athenian life on the other, was an educational no-man's land. Reading, writing, counting, music, and gymnastics may have been basic skills for the society of that time, but they did not provide a ready entry into the arena of intellect and culture. The Sophists attempted to offer educational opportunity which would bring the level of educational accomplishment and culture closer together.

nor were they committed in any sense to educating the recently en-
franchised men of Athens. Such men, of course, would have been instructed, providing they had the money to pay the fees and possessed
the elementary skills upon which the Sophists' teachings could be based.
Yet there seems to be little doubt that the students who sat at the feet of
the Sophists were aristocrats in search not so much of political goals as
of cultural formation. The latter goal may have, of course, included
political virtue. In any event, the point to be made is this: Sophists were
involved in the mission of preparing leaders for society, and they were
not interested in instructing simple men so that they might be able to
vote or merely participate in discussions of public issues.[14]

Leading Sophists and Their Critics

Of all the Sophists who came to Athens, the most famous and probably
the most respected was Protagoras (481–411 B.C.). He was, it appears,
the first to refer to himself and others like him as Sophists, teachers of
wisdom, an occupation that in Greece of his time enjoyed some respect.[15]
His name is famous, of course, as the inspiration for Plato's *Protagoras*,
the great philosopher's only tribute to the worth of the body of itinerant
teachers who invaded Athens. *Antilogies*, Protagoras' book, has been lost,
but in it he is known to have contributed to the refinement of the
Greek language. To some degree he is responsible for making the Greek
language a suitable vehicle for conveying scientific and philosophical
thought. Protagoras is said to have been the first to recognize the genders
of nouns and the moods of verbs. His chief importance, however, lies
in the introduction of subjectivity to ethical thought and in giving this
subjectivity philosophical respectability. His famous pronouncement,
"Man is the measure of all things, of those that are, that they are; of
those that are not, that they are not," led to a revolution in ethical
thinking that was not resolved in his time and has not even yet been
completely settled. Courage is a trait that usually generates respect. It
must have taken something more than ordinary courage for Protagoras
to declare that he was an agnostic, that he did not know whether or not
the gods existed. Even though the Athenians themselves may have had
some doubts about the gods, their reverence for at least an orthodox
tradition led the assembly to banish Protagoras. The assembly went on to
order that all Protagoras' writings were to be surrendered to public
officials, who were to burn them. Protagoras died shortly after he was
expelled from Athens.[16]

Gorgias of Leontini (ca. 483 B.C.) gained a reputation as an orator in

[14] See Plato *Protagoras* 317.
[15] Freeman, *op. cit.*, pp. 164–167.
[16] *Ibid.*, p. 230.

Sicily. He was commissioned by the people of that country to represent them as their ambassador to Athens. He became famous in Athens after delivering an address in which he urged the Greek states to unify in order to defend themselves more effectively against threats that came from the direction of Persia. This fame, it would seem, led him to assume a role as a teacher—a Sophist. Actually nothing is known of his teaching, although his skeptical thinking is fairly clearly set forth in his book, *On Nature*. It contains three especially interesting propositions: "Nothing exists beyond the senses; if anything existed beyond the senses it would be unknowable, for all knowledge comes from the senses; if anything suprasensual were knowable, it would be uncommunicable, since all communication is through the senses." After achieving considerable success as a teacher in Athens, Gorgias retired to Thessaly where, it is reported, he lived to be more than one hundred years old.[17]

Hippias of Elias, another well-known Sophist, was a contemporary of Socrates. It is claimed that he was a man who had encyclopedic knowledge.[18] Among the subjects he is reputed to have mastered were astronomy, mathematics, geometry, literature, politics, and music. There would not be, of course, any way of checking this claim of unusual erudition. But besides all of this he was an envoy of his government, an orator, and a historian. He knew so many crafts and trades that he was able, so the tale goes, to make all of his own clothing and personal ornaments. It is reported that Hippias boasted that he could make an extemporaneous speech on any subject before the Athenian assembly. Such a boast, set in the context of our own time, does not impress us much, yet it had the desired effect on the people of Athens. The criticism that was directed at Hippias—a criticism that was, in fact, directed at most Sophists—was that he sought to train his students in oratorical effectiveness without giving them any depth in knowledge. If it is true, however, that Hippias' accomplishments were not grossly exaggerated, then it is hard to see why such a man—generally educated, cultured, and versatile—would not have been an excellent teacher.

Minor Sophists include Producus, the grammarian, Antiphon, the materialist, Thrasymachus, and many others for whom there is no space here.[19]

What did the Sophists' contemporaries think of them? Many were

[17] F. Ueberweg, *History of Philosophy*, Charles Scribner's Sons, New York, 1893, vol. I, pp. 112–129; Jebb, *op. cit.*, vol. I, pp. cxx–cxxv.

[18] Frederick Eby and Charles F. Arrowood, *The History and Philosophy of Education: Ancient and Medieval*, Prentice-Hall, Inc., Englewood Cliffs, N.J., 1940, p. 315.

[19] Grote, *op. cit.*, vol. II, p. 67, and vol. VIII, pp. 18–76, 327, and 335.

uncertain of the direction of their glib oratory, and others were disturbed by their claims and their promises. Some Athenians, especially those of aristocratic backgrounds, believed the Sophists were undermining an established way of life. Despite the distrust of their elders, students with aristocratic backgrounds were the ones who flocked to the Sophists and sat at their feet.

Xenophon, the soldier, aristocrat, and historian, uttered a common criticism of the Sophists in his *Memorabilia*. In a discussion between Socrates and Antiphon, the former says: "Those who offer it [wisdom] to all comers for money are known as Sophists, prostitutors of wisdom, but we think that he who makes a friend of one whom he knows to be gifted by nature, and teaches him all the good he can, fulfills the duty of a citizen and a gentleman."[20]

Isocrates, in the *Antidosis*, questions the basic merits of sophistic instruction.

Some say that the profession of the Sophist is nothing but sham and chicane, maintaining that no kind of education has ever been discovered which can improve a man's ability to speak, or his capacity for handling affairs, and that those who excel in these respects owe their superiority to natural gifts; while others acknowledge that men who take this training are more able, but complain that they are corrupted and demoralized by it, alleging that when they gain the power to do so, they scheme to get other people's property.[21]

Isocrates, a wealthy man at the time the *Antidosis* was written, was especially sensitive to sophistic arguments that might be used to deprive him of some of his property. When he was called upon to fit out a ship for the military purposes of the city state, he went to court to prove that he did not have the wealth to accept such an invitation. In *Antidosis* Isocrates used every device that he knew to explain his position in society as well as his educational views. It is by such defensive arguments that the place of the Sophist is brought up for analysis. In addition to the *Antidosis*, Isocrates speaks of the Sophists in his *Against the Sophists*, an oration that was intended specifically as an advertisement for his school. In it he goes to great pains to show that he is not another Sophist; he wants the people of Athens to know what the opportunities for education are in his school. He criticizes the Sophists in this way:

More than that, although they set themselves up as masters and dispensers of goods so precious, they are not ashamed of asking for them a price of three of four minae. Why, if they were to sell any other commodity for so trifling a

---

[20] Xenophon *Memorabilia*. In Loeb Classical Library, Harvard University Press, Cambridge, Mass., 1923, vol. IV, p. 7.

[21] Isocrates *Antidosis*. In *op. cit.*, vol. II, pp. 297–299.

fraction of its worth, they would not deny their folly; nevertheless, although they set so insignificant a price on the sole stock of virtue and happiness, they pretend to wisdom, and assume the right to instruct the rest of the world. Furthermore, although they say they do not want money, and speak contemptuously of wealth as "filthy lucre," they hold their hands out for trifling gain and promise to make their disciples all but immortal.[22]

Isocrates is especially bitter toward the Sophists' policy of demanding the fees for their teaching in advance. He felt that they were exaggerating their abilities when they claimed to be able to sell wisdom to any who could buy it. His conception of formal education was that it makes students more skillful and resourceful in discovering the nature of things. It teaches them, he would hold, to take from dependable sources that information or knowledge that they would otherwise obtain only in haphazard fashion. Yet formal education is powerless to shape into successful debaters or excellent writers men who are without natural aptitude. Education can lead such men to some self-improvement, and it can open up a number of intellectual avenues for them, but it cannot remake their natural capacities.[23]

The Sophists' method of teaching—often criticized for the novelties that it contained—was held up to ridicule by Aristophanes in the dialogue between Euripides and Aeschylus in *The Frogs*.[24] Later, in *The Clouds*, Pheidippides, whose father has been attracted to sophistic theories of justice to the extent of arguing his creditors out of their due, beats his father. The father protests that the son is lacking in filial duty and respect. Pheidippides, who had been trained well in equivocation, a mark of many Sophists, offers to debate the question with his father and boasts: "I mean to say, we argue up or down—Take which you like—It comes to the same end."[25]

It would appear that Plato had a special dislike for Sophists who taught disputation without ethical considerations. More importantly, he was critical of them for trying to teach students virtue without first offering them a fundamental intellectual education. The consequence of such superficial teaching would appear to have been a marked preference for teaching verbal tricks rather than concentrating upon soundly argued philosophical inquiry. Such emphases resulted in an interest in contest and strife for its own sake rather than the determination of the truth and the cultivation of a vision of wisdom.

Aristotle objected to the sophistic technique of giving precise, unequivocal answers to any questions that were asked them. Such methods,

[22] Isocrates *Against the Sophists*. In *op. cit.*, vol. II, p. 165.

[23] *Ibid.*, p. 173.

[24] Aristophanes, *Plays*, E. P. Dutton & Co., Inc., New York, 1922, p. 52.

[25] *Ibid.*, p. 167.

according to the Aristotelian view, actually interfered with the promotion of scholarship and the development of clear and incisive thinking.

Many modern writers find the Sophists less worthy of censure. It would seem to be a fair judgment that the Sophists were popular not only because there was a need for instruction in the fields of knowledge in which they claimed skill and for training in the arts of rhetoric and disputation, in which they were expert, but also because they fulfilled a role that society had actually created for them. In fulfilling this role they pushed back the boundaries of formal education and laid the foundations for secondary schooling. Finally, Plato, Aristotle, and others rose to meet the sophistic challenge, and in their refutations of sophistic thought and practice important and lasting contributions were made to the methods of inquiry and to the content of our philosophic inheritance.[26] If the Sophists had done nothing more than stimulate rebuttal by thinkers and philosophers, their contributions to later generations, though largely negative, would have been extremely worthwhile.

SOCRATES (469–399 B.C.)

If one is discussing philosophy or education, it is unlikely that the origins of either discipline will receive much attention before the name of Socrates is mentioned. His reputation has not suffered from wear; the excellence of his thought and the effectiveness of his teaching methods are everywhere the objects of praise. He enjoys the peculiar advantage, not shared by his most illustrious pupil, Plato, of not having recorded his thoughts for posterity. In this way Socrates gained enviable immunity from criticism. Despite almost phenomenal popularity from the time of his death, Socrates, it should be remembered, was condemned to die because of the content and the manner of his teaching. This was the published charge: "Socrates is guilty of crime in refusing to recognize the gods acknowledged by the state, and importing strange divinities of his own; he is further guilty of corrupting the young."[27] There is evidence that the charge against him was trumped up and that the real reasons were personal; the enemies of Socrates used drastic means to secure their revenge.

In any event, the substance of the litigation concerned the effect that Socrates' teaching was having on the youth of Athens. This was a remarkable, if not an unbelievable, accusation. There was little in the demeanor of the Athenian citizen of that day to suggest that Athenians were fearful of the influence teachers might have on youth. The city

[26] On this point, see Jaeger, *op. cit.*, vol. I, pp. 291–292.

[27] *The History of Xenophon*, translated by H. G. Dakyns, The Tandy-Thomas Company, New York, 1909, vol. III, p. 231.

was full of Sophists, many of whom had poor, if not bad, reputations for personal morality. The charge against Socrates, therefore, had many earmarks of vindictiveness. It is of course true that his constant questioning irritated many people and embarrassed others. His "gadfly" tactics may have led to his being called a revolutionary at a time when the people of Athens were tired of all kinds of disturbances. Besides this, Socrates was no democrat; he defended the doctrine of "aristocracy of ability" in a city state where the disillusionment with oligarchy was nearly complete.[28] He criticized democracy and appeared to be opposed to its principles and its practices. Such stands did not make him popular among those who were committed to the democratic experiment. Besides, Socrates was accused of being an atheist—of not believing in the Greek gods and goddesses—at a time when atheism was a popular, though not entirely an orthodox, view in Athens. But the important point would seem to be that Socrates was put to death not because of what he taught but because he refused to acknowledge the right of his accusers to dictate to him. He declined to recant or to admit that his investigations were without solid foundation or that they led to heterodoxy. In this way he provided succeeding generations with a moving example of the importance of freedom of thought and freedom of inquiry; Socrates died as a martyr to both.[29]

Ends are often more auspicious than beginnings. Socrates was born of poor parents. He learned to read and write, probably from a primary schoolmaster, and thereafter, instead of attending the elementary schools in Athens—the palaestra and the music school—he followed the trade of his sculptor father. No doubt his apprenticeship in this trade was completed with the attainment of sufficient skill to place him among the masters of the guild, although there is neither testimony nor evidence to document this belief. In time, either because of other interests or because he just tired of his trade, Socrates turned away from sculpture and became a teacher.

Because he embraced the teaching occupation, Socrates was called a Sophist by some of his contemporaries. It is possible that in the Athens of his day he was so regarded, but if Socrates was a Sophist, he was not an ordinary one. He did not seek students; they sought him. His teaching involved no fees, no contracts, no lecture halls, no advertising campaigns, no promises of success. He did share the sophistic interest for preparing leaders for politics and society, though not according to any formula, and for accelerating education to the point where it would more nearly approximate Athenian culture. One would probably

[28] Grote, *op. cit.*, vol. VI, pp. 28–49.
[29] See Plato's *Apology*.

not be wrong in thinking of Socrates as a fairly important figure in the origin and development of secondary education.

Socrates was no spirit; he was a man. And the reader may be wondering how Socrates supported himself, his wife, Xantippe, and his family without an income from his trade as a sculptor or from his art as a teacher. Evidently he was not a good provider, and one can sympathize with his poor wife. His income was small and irregular; its source was the patronage of people who encouraged Socrates to lead a life of inquiry and dialectic.

Patrons of the arts are not usually pure philanthropists. Their altruism is tempered with a desire for value received; in other words, they sensibly support a man whose capacity for making valuable social and intellectual contributions is recognized. What did Socrates' patrons see in him? And what of the generations of students and scholars who followed Socrates? Did they find merit in his views? How did Socrates invigorate and enrich thought and learning?

An evaluation of Socrates must always remain somewhat tentative. He wrote nothing. Plato, Xenophon, and others who have left accounts of Socrates' life and thought were among his closest admirers. From Plato we have obtained almost everything we know about Socratic thought, to Xenophon we are indebted for most of the details of his life. In Plato's works it is hardly possible to see where Socratic thought stops and where Platonic thought begins. And Plato was under no obligation to make any such distinction in his writing. In fact we may with reason ask whether or not Plato in his dialogues was merely using Socrates as a literary device. It seems entirely possible that Socrates may never have held the views attributed to him by Plato, or that he may be credited with insights and interpretations which were beyond his interests or his abilities. There is no reason for anyone to go out of his way to tarnish his reputation; yet one should know that a great deal of myth and legend attaches to the name of Socrates.

Despite myth and legend, an educational history must try to deal, at least briefly, with the products of Socratic thought and method. Before the time of Socrates Athenians had avoided searching analyses of man's nature or speculations on the principles governing his conduct. Pre-Socratic speculations had usually centered on nature, with the result that early Greek philosophy was really physics. Why the Greeks avoided a study of man is hard to say. They may have, as some claim, thought that such speculations belonged to the practical order (the illiberal) rather than to the theoretical order (the liberal). For this claim to have much validity one would have to maintain that pre-Socratic distinctions on such matters were clearly drawn and that the allegiances of the time definitely committed the Athenian Greeks to the doctrine of liberal pursuits. These conclusions would not be easy to accept. In any event, the presumption remains that ethical theorizing was stimulated greatly by the activities of Socrates. One aspect, then, of Socratic thought was ethical, and since this thought had some relevance to educational theory, we must give attention here to its ethical content. In addition to this, we must know something about the method of Socrates. It seems to have been novel; and for centuries it has been praised as teaching's most effective technique. We should understand both the method and the principles on which it rests.

Socratic Thought and Method

The breadth of Socrates' interest is difficult to measure exactly. Clearly he was interested mainly, if not only, in man and his actions. He was surely concerned with ethics, and basic to ethical principles are values or evaluations of worth. It was these values or goods that really commanded Socrates' attention: justice, temperance, courage, gratitude, and friendship. He never wearied of discussing topics related to any of these values. And apparently Socrates was never fully satisfied that he or his colleagues completely understood the meaning of these virtues. It was this prying, inquiring attitude that led Socrates into difficulty and eventually to prison and execution.

If we are to understand Socratic pedagogy, we must see that the dialectical techniques flowed naturally from the Socratic definition of intuition. In the Socratic interpretation as we understand it, achieving knowledge was not a discursive process. Teaching was therefore not a matter of implanting or pouring in. Knowledge, according to the Socratic view, is intuitive; that is, it is already in the mind, and the teacher's mission is simply to bring it out. What better technique than dialectic could be devised to open avenues to free, or let out, this knowledge?

Seeking knowledge, for that matter the entire educational process, was not an end in itself. It is not easy to see Socrates as an ardent defender of the doctrine of liberal studies; on the other hand, he showed no great interest in utilitarian studies. He did, it is true, approve of geometry when it was taught for practical application; astronomy had value too, for with it the seasons could be forecast; and arithmetic was useful for business. Despite Socrates' approval of these subjects, it is clear that he thought much more highly of studies that led one to self-knowledge and to an understanding of, and a tendency to, right action. How, he would ask, could a man be just if he did not know the meaning of justice? And what was just in the eyes of one might not be just in the eyes of another. The central issue was to arrive at clear concepts in the field of ethics. Once these concepts were formed and ideas about the meaning of virtue were clarified, one would have some basis for hoping that men might lead a more orderly and efficient ethical life. For Socrates, no doubt, the job of the thinker, the philosopher—the lover of wisdom—was to clarify, to fix general concepts, to introduce precise thinking into intellectual inquiry; the job of the teacher, or more generally, the mission of education was to bring these discoveries to all men. This knowledge would lead them, Socrates maintained, to a more virtuous life. The identification of knowledge and virtue has for centuries been known as the "Socratic fallacy."

As we have said, the Socratic method followed very naturally and very logically the Socratic conception of knowledge. Socrates never implied that teachers were to convey truth to their students. The teacher's place was to stimulate thought, to encourage investigations, and to challenge students to think for themselves. Moreover, truth was something which Socrates did not claim to have. In the dialogues in which Plato depicts Socrates as being unable to give answers, it is not because Socrates, for pedagogic reasons, does not want to give them, but because he does not know the answers. The Socratic method is essentially a method of probing the unknown. The dialectic was an investigation, a quest for knowledge, and not, as those who try to imitate Socrates sometimes claim, a pedagogic technique.

Finally, it should be mentioned that Socrates was no hearer of lessons. We do not mean to imply that he would have found such educational practices unacceptable; he did not use them simply because, on the level of his teaching, such techniques were not at all appropriate. Although it may be true that Socrates had a lasting influence on secondary education, Plato shows him at work on a much higher plane. In actual fact there is little in the Socratic method that could be used without drastic modification on the lower educational levels. Most modern teachers would be wasting their own and their students' time if they were to confine themselves to the method of Socrates. Socrates himself would probably not have used this method if he had been a teacher in the Greek music school.

PLATO (427– or 429–347 B.C.)

Of all who admired Socrates, none did as much as Plato to write an indelible record attesting to the greatness of the man. Plato was Socrates' friend, a more or less constant companion, and his student. Plato shared many of the older philosopher's views, and he, more than anyone else, preserved Socratic thought for posterity.[30] Plato, however, was much more than a witness to the mental acumen of his illustrious friend. In his own right he was one of the world's foremost, philosophers

[30] See pp. 94–95.

—perhaps *the* foremost. Coupling philosophical insight with artistry of presentation, Plato's works are without equal in the history of thought. No one doubts Plato's prominence in the history of philosophy. His place in the history of education should be just as certain and as clear. He was a teacher and an educational philosopher. In his thought and work he organized and promoted a philosophical approach to education. This approach has had the approbation of many educators the world over for more than twenty centuries.[31]

We have relatively incomplete knowledge of Plato's boyhood and his early education. He came from an aristocratic and wealthy family, and quite likely his educational opportunity was the best that wealth and circumstances could provide.[32] He had, moreover, the time and resources to travel and the leisure to study and think. His contacts with Socrates served further to stimulate an already active and extremely able mind.[33] The death of Socrates, under trying circumstances for all his friends and for all who respected truth, was, we are led to believe, a powerful force in shaping Plato's future. It may have been a strong stimulus for Plato to carry on the work of his master. Despite the importance of this tragic event in consolidating Plato's dedication to the search for truth, it should be underlined and emphasized that Plato was much more than a disciple of Socrates. In other words, he did not merely carry Socrates' message to all who would listen; he had an important philosophical message of his own which he disseminated vigorously and artistically. Whatever the long-range effects of Socrates' execution on Plato, its immediate effect was to drive him from Athens. Although there may have been other reasons for his departure, the main one was that Plato's life or liberty was in jeopardy. He remained away from Athens for about a dozen years and then returned to his native city, where he established a school.[34]

The school was called the Academy, because it was located near the Athenian gymnasium of the same name. In this school Plato formulated many of the philosophical positions that have become famous and wrote

[31] There are many analyses of Plato as an educator. The following are especially illuminating: J. E. Adamson, *The Theory of Education in Plato's Republic,* Swan Sonnenschein, London, 1903; Richard L. Nettleship, *The Theory of Education in the Republic of Plato,* University of Chicago Press, Chicago, 1906; and H. I. Marrou, *History of Education in Antiquity,* Sheed & Ward, Inc., New York, 1956, pp. 61–78 (an excellent chapter on Plato).

[32] E. Norman Gardiner, *Athletics of the Ancient World,* Oxford University Press, New York, 1930, p. 128.

[33] T. Gomprez, *Greek Thinkers: A History of Ancient Philosophy,* Charles Scribner's Sons, New York, 1901–1912, vol. II, pp. 250 ff.

[34] Freeman, *op. cit.,* p. 180, is of the opinion that Plato's school was first conducted in Plato's home.

a number of the philosophical treatises that have had such an impressive influence on political and educational thought down through the ages.[35] Plato was primarily a philosopher, and secondarily a teacher. The reader should resist the inclination to draw a mental picture of Plato as an ordinary schoolmaster. In concert with his disciples, who were also his friends, he tried to refine thought so as to ascertain solutions to the universal problems of mankind. But instead of giving his students the answers to the searching questions, and instead of drawing conclusions of his own about the topics under consideration, Plato tried to lead his students through pertinent thought processes.[36] The exact nature of Plato's teaching techniques is not completely clear to us. It is possible that he employed the method of Socrates, for surely his writings prove that he was a master of dialectic. There are good reasons for believing that Plato had greater interest in developing in his students the methodology of learning than in having them deal with the results of this process. It would appear that Plato did on one occasion lecture in the Academy, but the lecture was not popular, and most of his audience left before he had finished. They were unable to follow him. He preferred to use informal discussion for teaching, and these discussion periods were graced with good humor and, we hear, with refreshments—always imbibed moderately—which contributed, no doubt, to the cordial atmosphere of the school. We have so little dependable information on the daily activities of the school, however, that were it not for the *Republic* and the *Laws*, Plato's great political proposals, it would be difficult to give a very thorough picture of Plato's educational doctrines.

Educational Ideals

The statement has been made that Platonic thought shows an extraordinary and unnecessary preoccupation with education.[37] It is true that education is given a great deal of attention. However, it would seem that in his concern for politics and the ideal state, Plato had no alternative but to deal in detail with the formation of the citizens of such a state.[38] When we understand Plato's purpose, we realize that his interest in education is not something tangential to his major purpose, but an integral and essential means for its attainment.[39] We may conclude, then, that Plato did not miscalculate education's relevance to politics; history

---

[35] Marrou, *op. cit.*, pp. 67–68.
[36] On Plato's teaching technique in the Academy, see Freeman, *op. cit.*, pp. 196–199.
[37] Jaeger deals with this charge. See *op. cit.*, vol. II, p. 200.
[38] *Ibid.*, vol. II, pp. 208–211.
[39] *Ibid.*, vol. II, p. 200.

has proved him right time after time. On the other hand, Plato's emphasis on education was not strikingly new. Sparta offered a good example
of education's function in the making of a state,[40] and Plato knew the
Spartan system thoroughly; Athenian practices in statecraft, though different from those of Sparta, gave the formation of the citizen a central
place in all educative activities. Plato, then, should not be regarded as
an idealist or a visionary on this important point. It is true that he
formed a political ideal and worked out means to attain it by using his
imagination, but a number of concrete examples of statecraft could have
influenced his thought.

Plato's principal educational objectives did not differ from those accepted in early Athens or, for that matter, from those considered orthodox in Sparta. He aimed at good citizenship. Even Plato's school—
attended only by carefully selected students—was a place for preparing
citizens. But the identity of objectives did not mean an identity of
means, for in the Athens of Plato's time military service was not regarded
as the citizen's primary duty as in earlier times. Now competence in
civic affairs was given first place. Citizenship was the possession of those
who had a proper system of values, profound knowledge and understanding leading to wisdom, and an ideal of service to their fellow men
and to the state, and who exemplified leadership in politics and society.
Civic ability, therefore, was an outcome of education; it could be
achieved as the end product of a process of intellectual formation. There
is, nevertheless, a clear preference for the elite to be detected in Plato's
choice of those who could be educated, and he, like the Sophists, committed himself to the preparation of citizens who would become
leaders.[41]

The first, and for Plato surely the most important, use to which the
products of education could be put was service to the state, or more
generally service to society. As we have indicated, such a view created
an unavoidable preference for the education of leaders. The few, not the
many, were favored. Perhaps even this had a solid basis in reality, although much modern democratic thought would try to resist all aristocratic tendencies in education. Nevertheless, Plato's proposed curriculum,
though most beneficial in the preparation of leaders, surely had its uses,
too, for citizens who were not destined for high position. Yet it is difficult to accept Platonic educational views as the theoretical foundation
either for so-called traditional liberal education—the education of
gentlemen—or for popular education in its twentieth-century form.

In connection with popular education, Plato was quite willing that
everyone in the state be trained, but he would have made the more ad-

---

[40] See pp. 31–39.
[41] Plato *Republic* viii. 558.

vanced levels of education special places for students with unusual
talent. With respect to liberal education, we cannot state his position in
such clear-cut fashion. This is because the expression, liberal education,
is subject to many interpretations. From Plato's time to our own, few
educators have agreed on what it is and naturally enough, therefore, on
how it is obtained. Plato knew what liberal education meant in his time:
It was the education given to a leisure class for the leisurely life they
were leading and would continue to lead. Such education did not meet
with Plato's approval; a life of useless leisure—useless, at least, in a
social sense—could not have had anything to recommend it. Surely the
highest virtues to be developed could hardly be squared with fifth-
century B.C. practices in education. Yet it is impossible to see Plato as a
utilitarian. Fortunately, the practical and the theoretical are not separated by the same dichotomy as the utilitarian and the liberal.

Plato's objective, to put it another way, was universal truth. The
sophistic doctrine, "Man is the measure of all things," when put in the
hands of the orators who had been trained by the Sophists, was interpreted to mean that "what appears to be true, is true." It is only a
short step from this position to the pragmatic doctrine that only results
count. Plato, of course, was far from being uninterested in outcomes; he
was careful, however, to insist that truth should be based on critical
processes whereby false and superficial opinions can be detected and discarded, leaving a core of sound knowledge. Plato's emphasis on truth—a
truth that is unique, fixed, and eternal—had important consequences for
the curriculum.

State Control

There seems to be little doubt that Plato willingly, almost anxiously,
accepted the traditional Greek view that a citizen's training should prepare him to act for the public good. The individual counted for very
little. Perhaps he was but a tool to be used by the state in the attainment
of civic ends. That Plato accepted what was a more or less traditional
Greek view—one which made the individual's good regularly subordinate to that of the state—is clear from the ideals portrayed in the
Republic and the *Laws*.

Plato was not a democrat, even though it is possible to find some
democratic tendencies in his writings. The supreme good may not have
been the state, but in order that the highest good might be achieved,
state unity was essential. Only by careful regulation of individual action
and by instilling in all citizens, from birth on, an exacting dedication to
the state, could this unity be obtained and preserved. It is unlikely that
Plato was a state worshiper. Rather, he saw the state as the most effective instrument that could be devised and employed for leading men to

the higher life in the realm of ideas. If there appears to be an inconsistency in the idea that men must be slaves first before they can be free, we must not forget the Christian message that men must first lose their lives in order to find them. The Platonic view on state unity may well be interpreted to mean only that men must sacrifice lesser ends for greater. At any rate, whether Plato's views can be defended or not, it is important to know that the principle of state unity, a unity to be achieved principally by education, was basic to his thought. Once this is understood, the inflexible legalisms in Plato's system are not so likely to drive us away from him.

There are unquestionably a number of paradoxes in Plato's writings, and here, in his emphasis on the rigid control which the state is to exercise over education, we find an important one. For though state authority was to be exercised over these matters, still, free and liberal minds capable of apprehending truth wherever it may be found were to have been the products of such an authoritarian system. To call Plato's view somewhat paradoxical does not mitigate the obviously unnatural relationship between authoritarianism and freedom. Nevertheless, it may well be that this is but another of Plato's predictions of things to come—prophetic anticipations of later educational systems—for throughout a great deal of Western man's history, compulsion rather than freedom has been characteristic of his educational practices.

It is not hard to find examples of Plato's theory regarding state control. Book II of the *Republic* contains many references illustrative of Platonic thought on this point. The *Laws*, too, present the same theme. They attest also to the fact that in half a lifetime Plato had not changed his mind. If anything, he had become more explicit in his views; he seemed to be entirely sure of himself when he wrote in the *Laws* that the state should take an active and controlling role in superintending education.

There remains the minister of the education of youth, male and female; here, too, the law may well provide that there shall be one such minister, and he must be fifty years old, and have children lawfully begotten, both boys and girls by preference, at any rate, one or the other. He who is elected, and he who is the elector, should consider that of all the great offices of state this is the greatest; for the first shoot of any plant, if it makes a good start, has the greatest effect in helping it to obtain its mature natural excellence; and this is not only true of plants, but of animals wild and tame, and also of man. Man, as we say, is a tame or civilized animal; nevertheless, he requires proper instruction and a fortunate nature, and then of all animals he becomes the most divine and most civilized; but if he be insufficiently or ill educated he is the most savage of earthly creatures. Wherefore the legislator ought not to allow the education of children to become a secondary or accidental matter.

In the first place, he who would be rightly provident about them, should begin by taking care that he is elected, who of all the citizens is in every way best; him the legislator shall do his utmost to appoint guardian and superintendent. To this end all the magistrates, with the exception of the council of prytanes, shall go to the temple of Apollo, and elect by ballot him of the guardians of the law who they severally think will be the best superintendent of education. And he who has the greatest number of votes, after he has undergone scrutiny at the hands of all the magistrates who have been his electors, with the exception of the guardians of the law, shall hold office for five years; and in the sixth year let another be chosen in like manner to fill his office.[42]

Thus in the *Laws* Plato provides for a minister of education, whose duty it shall be to manage all of the schools of the state. He will dictate the regulations concerning discipline in the schools; all matters pertaining to instruction in the schools and gymnasia will be within the ambit of his authority. Even the "going to school" of boys and girls, by which Plato may have meant school attendance at appropriate ages as well as the rather obvious physical movement to and from school, would be under his control. Finally, the minister of education was to control school buildings and everything that went on within them. While the law was explicit in many of its demands, it was nevertheless true that the minister of education could do many things at his own discretion. No wonder that Plato implored the legislators to look for the best man for this position, to choose the most superior of all. Besides making a judicious selection of ministers of education, the legislators were admonished to create a fabric of law within which ministers of education could be prepared and which would be a guide to them, once selected, in the performance of their duties.

But how can our law sufficiently train the director of education himself; for as yet all has been imperfect, and nothing has been said either clear or satisfactory? Now, as far as possible, the law ought to omit nothing that concerns him, but to explain everything, that he may be an interpreter and tutor to others.[43]

As a final word on this matter of state control, and in fairness to Plato, it should be said that he had visions of a state wherein law's place would eventually be preempted by widespread culture. Whether a completely and competently educated citizenry would make even the most fundamental law unnecessary is to be doubted; for fundamental law may find an even more secure foundation in oral tradition than it does in statute. But it would seem that Plato did see education as a substitute for regimentation and extremely detailed legal codes.

[42] Plato *Laws* vi. 766.
[43] *Laws* vii. 809.

If our citizens are well educated, and grow into sensible men, they will easily see their way through all these, as well as other matters which count, such, for example, as marriage, the possession of women, and the procreation of children.

Thus educated, they will invent for themselves any lesser rules which their predecessors have altogether neglected. I mean such things as these: when the young are to be silent before their elders; how they are to show respect for them by standing and making them sit; what honor is due parents; what garments or shoes are to be worn; the mode of dressing the hair; deportment and manners in general.[44]

The Education of Boys and Girls

Social as well as educational traditions had regularly recommended various kinds of training for girls. Females, however, according to the same tradition, were not thought to be equally capable as boys in mastering the intricacies of education. Accepted Greek practice, whether in Sparta or Athens, placed girls on a different level from boys. In Sparta, as we have seen, some of the games and contests intended especially for little boys were entered by little girls.[45] However, this type of cotraining did not continue for the Spartan girl; by the time she was eleven or twelve years of age she was no longer welcomed to the boys' exercises. The Spartan code, nevertheless, demanded certain competence from the woman; she was to be trained or groomed for motherhood. Yet with all of this attention to important details of female education, there was hardly ever any suggestion that the sexes were equal.

In Athens girls were somewhat less well off than in Sparta. It was the exception, not the rule, to find Athenian girls prepared in much of anything beyond those domestic arts informally communicated or directed by mothers or domestic servants. With these examples of the treatment of women Plato was thoroughly familiar. In addition, he knew of, and referred to, other approaches to the education of women common to countries outside the Greek world.

But what is important to us here is the theory advanced by Plato concerning the education of girls. He proposed that boys and girls be educated in separate elementary and secondary schools.[46] Plato believed that boys and girls should be educated alike, although he probably did not consider a woman to be a man's equal. From the age of six to the time when students entered higher studies, girls were to follow the same educational program as boys, but they would have their own schools. This was a kind of dual system. Had Plato thought that woman's nature was different from that of man, he would unquestionably have provided

[44] *Republic* vii. 425.
[45] See pp. 32–33.
[46] *Laws* vii. 804.

for schooling consistent with these natural differences. Coeducation was approved in whatever may have been done before children reached the age of six. Advanced or higher studies attracted only the best minds; these higher studies were available to the best minds, regardless of sex.

It seems clear, however, that little explicitly and formally educational could take place before the age of six. At the other end of the scale, so few would have been involved that the matter of coeducation in higher studies could not have had any great effect. Thus Plato was really advocating parallel education, but he was doing so largely for social and moral and not for intellectual reasons. Within this utopian system, however, either a man or a woman with the capacity to do so could rise to the highest position that the state could offer.

Elementary Education

Students who came to Plato's school, the Academy, were fortified with the best foundation traditional Athenian elementary education was able to give them. This small, highly selective school could be very demanding in its entrance requirements. It was really a school for leaders. The remarkable thing about all of this, however, is not that Plato was conscious of the need for solid preparatory education (this could be assumed), but that he was willing, even in his literary utopia, to accept with only a few modifications the pattern of elementary education that had been traditional in Athens. Though no statement in his writings expresses his satisfaction with elementary education, yet by indirection he does give it his approval. At the same time, it should be remarked that Plato spends little time in discussing the lower levels of education.[47]

From what he does say, it appears that Plato would have made some slight revisions in conventional elementary education. For example, he would have made greater use of educational games and toys during the years of three to six. This learning by play would form part of the pre-school preparation. But of even greater significance than mere skill was the inculcation of a love of excellence; the pleasure of excelling was never to be minimized, and a favorable attitude toward it was to be cultivated principally by employing amusement. Plato may not have introduced pleasure and amusement as motives to education; no doubt they were around long before his time. He did, however, recognize the multiple uses to which they could be put. Despite this, there is no suggestion at all that Plato shared the illusions of later educators who were unwilling to regard education as a demanding discipline or to give it due respect. Even though details of educational theory and technique may not be totally ignored (and Plato did not ignore them), he wrote that

[47] *Republic* ii, iii; *Laws* vii.

"the most important point of education is right training in the nursery."[48] This may not sound highly philosophical, or, indeed, Platonic, yet it is Plato speaking.

With the end of the nursery period—about the age of three—Plato proposed that the children receive further preparation for formal education. It should be noted that the Greeks had always considered the years before seven a period in which the child was preparing for schooling. All that Plato was adding were a few details with respect to this preparation. We may follow his thought with his own words:

Up to the age of three years, whether of boy or girl, if a person strictly carries out our previous regulations and makes them a principal aim, he will do much for the advantage of the young creatures. But at three, four, five, and even six years the childish nature will require sports; now is the time to get rid of self-will in him, punishing him, but not so as to disgrace him. We were saying about slaves, that we ought neither to add insult to punishment so as to anger them, nor yet to leave them unpunished lest they become self-willed; and a like rule is to be observed in the case of the freeborn. Children at that age have certain natural modes of amusement, which they find out for themselves when they meet. And all the children who are between the ages of three and six ought to meet at the temples of the villages, the several families of a village uniting on one spot. The nurses are to see that the children behave properly and orderly,—they themselves and all their companies are to be under the control of twelve matrons, one for each company, who are annually selected to inspect them from the women previously mentioned, (i.e. the women who have authority over marriage), whom the guardians of the law appoint.[49]

Education proper began when the child was seven. And following the traditions of Athens, this education was to consist of gymnastics for the body and music for the soul. We have discussed these components of Athenian education in Chapter 2; here we shall try to indicate the principal changes that Plato wanted to adopt. At the same time, we should not forget that this traditional Athenian elementary education of which we speak was classical education in its original form, and that by accepting it, although dictating some revisions, Plato strengthened classical education's claim to man's allegiance.

The basic literary skills that we assume were taught to most Athenian boys during their first years in school seem not to have commanded Plato's attention. There would be no good reason for Plato to tamper with reading and writing, the basic elementary instruction of the day. In another area of the elementary school's program—counting—Plato did prescribe some reorientation. Calculation was added, for, as Plato said,

[48] *Laws* i. 643.
[49] *Laws* vii. 793 ff.

all branches of instruction which are a preparation for dialectic should be presented to the mind in childhood. Plato was convinced that everyone who could reason could share in mathematical knowledge, at least, up to a point.[50] There is no evidence that Plato led any city-wide campaign for upgrading the teaching of arithmetic in the Greek schools, but in the *Republic* and in the *Laws* he does suggest a revision and some rethinking of elementary mathematics.

In physical training, too, Plato wanted some changes. He was somewhat disturbed at the unwillingness of his fellow citizens to continue the old tradition of gymnastics for the body and music for the soul. The two had at one time been inseparable. But Plato saw how some men became preoccupied with music to the extent that they grew soft and cowardly; other men pursued gymnastics so exclusively that they became insensitive to culture and were little better than savages. He was concerned especially with the place of dancing and wrestling in Greek schools. But here again Plato shows less concern for the actual skills in the dance or in gymnastics generally than he does for the spirit with which they are taught and practiced and the environment in which they are imparted. Plato never objected to excellence in any form. Gymnastic training or any other discipline which aimed at excellence was sure to obtain Plato's approval. But training for superiority was another thing. A boy might wrestle in order to achieve all the values that the sport offered, and Plato would commend him for it, but if he wrestled, not for inherent values but in order to defeat an opponent in a contest, his action would not be entirely meritorious. Plato did not speak out violently against competitive sport, but evidently he did not entirely approve the professionalism that was finding its way into sport.

It is true that Plato's views on elementary instruction and physical training did not mark any sharp break with traditional education in Athens. But in asking for a state-controlled, state-financed system of elementary education, with state-approved teachers, Plato was surely setting himself apart from the past. Despite the theoretical relationship that the state had to education, instruction of the young in Athens had been largely a family affair. Consistent with his ideal of state unity, Plato would have had education on all levels subject to closer control and teachers on all levels recognized as public officers. It would no longer have been possible for an unqualified person to open a school. By taking this stand Plato may have offered teachers their first glimpse of professional status.

There were other departures. Since Plato believed that good music

---

[50] In the *Republic* vii. 526b, Plato speak of mathematics as "a something which all arts and sciences and intelligences use in common, and which every one first has to learn among the elements of education."

was heaven-born, he advocated the enactment of laws that would have prevented, or at least deterred spontaneity in music. When modes of music change, he said, the state changes with them. This thought may be put another way: Music, according to Plato, was primarily a vehicle for the inculcation of morals, and tested procedures for developing character should not be tampered with. Finally he argued for a strict censorship of literature.

Higher Education

The generalization that Plato accepted traditional Greek elementary education—even though this generalization cannot be applied uncritically—must not be extended to include higher educational levels. What is distinctive in the thought of Plato as it applies to the content of instruction in the schools is to be found in his prescriptions for the curricular organization of secondary and higher education.

Few readers are unaware of the long course of studies through which Plato would have put the best minds. Fifty years is a long time to spend in education. But although we should not ignore this aspect of his program, we should not overemphasize it. The important thing is that the end of such a long and exacting course of study is the attainment of truth. Above all else Plato was interested in truth. It should be made clear that the Platonic conception of truth included at least a realization that truth does not lie in our sensations, for all senses are deceptive. The search for truth, moreover, is an occupation for mature men; it is not for the dull, the slow-witted, or the young, for it has, in addition to all of its promise, a certain danger: opinion may easily be mistaken for sound knowledge. We cannot appreciate Plato's educational thought unless we first understand that his objective was always to push back the boundaries of knowledge. His students were to be frontier thinkers.

Before the time of the Sophists and Plato the Greeks had made no clear distinction between elementary and secondary education except in physical training. The palaestra was a school for elementary physical education; the gymnasium may at least be called a secondary experience, for it is not easy to refer to it as a school in the ordinary sense of the term. Music was taught on the same level of relevance to life as were reading and writing and counting. The absence of a literary type of secondary education may be somewhat surprising, but in view of the traditions of Athens it is not too difficult to understand.

The Sophists were among the first, if not the first, secondary teachers. Plato followed them and improved on their work; or perhaps it should be said that Plato reacted to the Sophists and perfected what they had begun. He was the first to devise both a theory and a content for secondary education. Once the young minds were exposed to the primary skills of reading, writing, and arithmetic in the initial and formal educational experience, Plato would begin secondary education. This would be at about the child's thirteenth or fourteenth year. Few details concerning such things as school buildings or teachers' qualifications are known to us, nor do we know whether or not Plato spent much time considering these points. Secondary education would be made up of music, literature, and mathematics. Music would be both instrumental and vocal; it had a social as well as a moral value. Literature, with the same limitations and cautions that Plato had previously imposed, would be carried into secondary education. As always, Greek literature, with expurgation or without it, was an artistic articulation of the exploits of a mythical hero. Mathematics was the innovation: numbers, geometry, and arithmetic were in the program.

Judging from Plato's references to the age of students,[51] we have defined for us for the first time the nine-year secondary school. Such a school was of course no stranger to the modern period in educational history (1500 to 1900); its model was classical. Plato's proposals concerning secondary schooling were, perhaps, the first to be made on the level of theory.

As an aristocrat steeped in the traditions of Athens, Plato could not forget gymnastics. He did not always approve the direction taken by the gymnastics of his day, but he could not exclude them from some place in education. However, since his concern was neither with popular education nor with keeping boys in school who preferred to be elsewhere, he could keep gymnastics as a part of Greek life or culture or of education in the very broadest sense, and at the same time separate them from the school. He could also recognize the possibility of using gymnastics as a device for screening; that is, for discovering the young men most suited for advanced studies.[52]

When the nine-year secondary school curricula were completed, a boy would undertake to fulfill the requirement regarding gymnastics. Plato's view may be given here as it is expressed through the person of Socrates. Socrates is asked at what age young men ought to be inducted into the course of higher studies. He replied:

At the age when the necessary gymnastics are over: the period whether of two or three years which passes in this sort of training is useless for any other purpose; for sleep and exercise are unpropitious to learning; and the trial of who is first in gymnastic exercises is one of the most important tests to which our youth are subjected.[53]

[51] *Republic* vii. 536.
[52] *Laws* vii. 810; *Republic* ii. 377, x. 595.
[53] *Republic* vii. 298.

After the two- or three-year period of compulsory physical training, the young men returned to their studies. They were now about twenty years old. From among those who had proceeded this far up the educational ladder, the best would be selected for ten additional years of study. Arithmetic, which would sharpen the intellects of the bright and even improve the minds of the dull, geometry, which needed no recommendation to the Greeks, music and astronomy, both approached in their theoretical aspects, were the fundamental subjects of this curriculum. Plato can again speak for himself:

After that time [after gymnastic training] those who are selected from the class of twenty years old will be promoted to higher honor, and the sciences which they learned without any order in their early education will now be brought together and they will be able to see the natural relationship of them to one another and to true being.[54]

This ten-year course enabled the student to cross the threshold of philosophical studies.

Such was the long course devised by Plato for making a philosopher. But it was not yet complete. For fifteen years following their formal preparation, the students of philosophy would take an active part in the government of the city. We may go to the *Republic* again for Plato's description of his program.

And how long is this stage of their lives to last? Fifteen years, I answered; and when they have reached fifty years of age, then let those who still survive and have distinguished themselves in every action of their lives and in every branch of knowledge come at last to their consummation: the time has now arrived at which they must raise the eye of the soul to the universal light which lightens all things, and behold the absolute good; for that is the pattern according to which they are to order the State and the lives of individuals, and the remainder of their own lives also; making philosophy their chief pursuit, but, when their turn comes, toiling also at politics and ruling for the public good, not as though they were performing some heroic action, but simply as a matter of duty; and when they have brought up in each generation others like themselves and left them in their place to be governors of the State, then they will depart to the Islands of the Blest and dwell there; and the city will give them public memorials and sacrifices and honor them, if the Pythian oracle consent, as demigods, but if not, as in any case blessed and divine.[55]

Plato's Influence

Before going any further we should say that Plato's plan for higher education was nowhere completely put into practice. In the Academy,

[54] *Ibid.*
[55] *Republic* vii. 302–303.

where future political philosophers were educated, it was possible for Plato to translate many of his theories into policies and procedures to guide teaching and learning. But regardless of the inner consistency and the general logical structure of the studies in Plato's famous school, the system practiced there was partial and inchoate when compared with the theoretical model provided in the *Republic* and the *Laws*.[56] Plato's was a utopian plan, sincerely proposed, but never fully tested.

Plato's influence as a teacher must have been great, although we cannot call many witnesses to support this assumption. His influence as a molder of later theories and practices seems to be universally recognized, and it was quite profound. We cannot claim that Plato's thought has always been predominant in the educational systems and schools of the Western world, but we should be unrealistic not to recognize that in some way Plato has affected all of them. No literary utopia has ever wielded more practical influence than Plato's; yet it remains true that Plato's ideal of the search for truth in education has frequently been rejected in favor of utility-centered curricula and objectives.

ISOCRATES (436–338 B.C.)

A good deal of the tradition regarding the life of Isocrates must be accepted with caution. The available biographies are, for the most part, late compilations in which it is most difficult to distinguish fact from fiction. All of them must be measured against the standard drawn from Isocrates' autobiographical statements.

Isocrates was born in 436 B.C., five years before the Peloponnesian War. He died in 338 B.C. His father, it is said, was a manufacturer of flutes. This business must have been profitable, for the family, according to Isocrates' own testimony, lived in comfortable circumstances. Isocrates received a good education at the hands of the most prominent teachers Athens could boast.

The details of his formal education are little known. The biographers claim that he profited from the established education of Athens as well as from the Sophists, who had only recently arrived in Athens to prepare the Athenians for citizenship and practical success. It has been suggested that Isocrates sampled the teaching and the wisdom of all the renowned Sophists who taught in Athens.

The teachers from whom he is said to have gained most were Gorgias of Leontini, a famous Sophist,[57] and Socrates. From Gorgias Isocrates

---

[56] The point should be made that the views in the *Republic* and in the *Laws* do not always agree. Neither document can be considered as a complement to the other. Of course, the *Republic* was a work of Plato's youth, the *Laws* of old age.

[57] See pp. 73–74.

may have gained much of his devotion to oratory, a devotion that remained with him to the day of his death. What influence can be assigned to Socrates is a more involved question. Socrates, as reported by Plato, says that Isocrates had brilliant qualities of mind and that his future as an orator or philosopher was promising. Whether or not Isocrates would become prominent in philosophy, Socrates goes on to say, would to some extent depend on how far "some divine impulses" led him.[58]

Either these "divine impulses" were lacking or somehow they escaped Isocrates, for although he did not ignore philosophy, he never gave it a place of any special significance in his school. As a matter of fact, he may have regarded the teachers of philosophy as his competitors. He generated an extreme dislike for philosophical professors and denounced them on various occasions. He denounced Plato, too. Actually, Isocrates and Plato were competitors. This need not mean that their views never coincided or that they never realized the possibility of mutual accommodation of ideas, but it does mean that Plato pursued one objective, Isocrates, another. Plato hoped to lead his pupils toward intellectual research and a life that would enable them to search for truth. Isocrates tried to inculcate the principles of practical life; his teaching was meant as a preparation for success in society and politics.

Still, and even admitting the fundamental dichotomy just referred to, Isocrates carried over into his thought and work many of the intellectual, political, and moral positions generally attributed to Socrates. The similarities do not prove that the teaching of Socrates had a permanent influence on Isocrates. On the other hand, we may suppose that in certain areas of thought and action Isocrates was at least a partial disciple of Socratic thought.

1. The *Antidosis,* a treatise in which Isocrates defends and justifies himself to the people of Athens, is strikingly similar to Socrates' defense before these same people. It is considerably more detailed than anything reported for Socrates by either Plato or Xenophon, yet it is constructed in such a way that the indebtedness to Socrates is apparent. The tone of the *Antidosis* alone seems to place Isocrates in an ideological fellowship with Socrates, for both, it appears, were completely, if unfortunately, misunderstood by their contemporaries.

2. Isocrates shared the Socratic aloofness and disdain for public life.

But I thought as he said these things, and I think now, that they would be of all men the strangest and most perverse who could take offence at being told that I hold myself at the service of Athens in discharging the liturgies and performing any public duty she enjoins, and yet do not ask to have any part in the allotment of the offices nor in the distribution of the gifts she doles out

[58] The comment is made at the close of Plato's *Phaedrus.*

to others, nor in the privilege of prosecuting or defending cases in the courts. For I have prescribed this course for myself, not because I am rich or have any false pride, nor because I look down on those who do not live in the same way as I do, but because I love peace and tranquillity, and most of all because I see that men who so live are looked up to both in Athens and in other parts of the world. Moreover, I consider that this kind of life is more agreeable than that of men who are busy with a multitude of things, and that it is, besides, more in keeping with the career to which I have dedicated myself from the first.[59]

3. Isocrates was most critical of Athenian democracy, and his criticism, though it brought no retribution like that inflicted upon Socrates, did not endear him to the democrats of Athens.

And yet how can we praise or tolerate a government which has in the past been the cause of so many evils and which is now year by year ever drifting on from bad to worse? And how can we escape the fear that if we continue to progress after this fashion we may finally run aground on rocks more perilous than those which at that time loomed before us?[60]

4. Isocrates' contempt for some of the Sophists reminds one of Socrates' disdain.

Indeed, who can fail to abhor, yes to contemn, those teachers, in the first place, who devote themselves to disputation, since they pretend to search for truth, but straightway at the beginning of their professions attempt to deceive us with lies.[61]

5. Although Isocrates resided in a borderland between philosophy and politics—he was neither a philosopher nor a statesman in the Platonic sense—and in oratory engaged in a kind of fence sitting that Socrates would probably not have admired, he did, nevertheless, share with Socrates his emphasis on ethics. This is evident, of course, only when we keep our eyes on the prudential morality of the Socrates of Xenophon and not the idealistic morality of the Socrates of Plato. But Isocrates did more than just share Socrates' interest in moral philosophy; he added to it an oratorical dimension which is displayed in the following quotation:

There is no institution devised by man which the power of speech has not helped us establish. For this it is which has laid down laws concerning things just and unjust, and things base and honourable; and if it were not for these ordinances we should not be able to live with one another. It is by this also that we confute the bad and extol the good. Through this we educate the ignorant and appraise the wise; for the power to speak well is taken as the surest index of a sound understanding, and discourse which is true and lawful

---

[59] Isocrates *Antidosis*. In *op. cit.*, vol. II, pp. 150–151.
[60] Isocrates *Areopagiticus*. In *op. cit.*, vol. II, p. 115.
[61] Isocrates *Against the Sophists*. In *op. cit.*, vol. II, p. 163.

and just is the outward image of a good and faithful soul. With this faculty we both contend against others on matters which are open to dispute, and seek light for ourselves on things which are unknown; for the same arguments which we use in persuading others when we speak in public, we employ also when we deliberate in our own thoughts; and, while we call eloquent those who are able to speak before a crowd, we regard as sage those who most skillfully debate their problems in their own minds. And, if there is need to speak in brief summary of this power, we shall find that none of the things which are done with intelligence take place without the help of speech, but that in all our actions as well as in all our thoughts speech is our guide, and is most employed by those who have the most wisdom. Therefore, those who dare to speak with disrespect of educators and teachers of philosophy deserve our opprobrium no less than those who profane the sanctuaries of the gods.[62]

Despite the claims that may be made for Socrates' influence on Isocrates, it should be remembered that sharing ideas need not imply borrowing them. Thinking men may have much in common and still be original. Originality, moreover, is not the only road to intellectual or philosophical glory. It is entirely possible that the most lasting and profound influence that was exerted on the great Attic orator by Socrates was a sobering one which touched his life and thought deeply. It was this influence which may have led Isocrates to try to be a statesman and a philosopher without really committing himself to the extremes of either. He would have shared with Socrates the thought that one good man—a gentleman in the aristocratic meaning of the term—is worth much more than a learned scholar, because the gentleman could be a man of action responding only to the attractions of a single goal, while a scholar could easily become confused in examining the conflicting aims or claims of contending positions. So Isocrates, covering himself with a cloak of neutrality and seeing the dangers which may befall the enthusiastic man of action, tried to compromise. He manifested his philosophical turn of mind by working out certain moralisms; he attempted statesmanship, without ever holding any public office, by issuing political pamphlets from the friendly confines of his study. In his own life these compromises between action and thought were not especially successful. Yet the Isocratic judgment which endorses such compromises became a fairly constant and even a respected tradition in the history of Western culture.

Isocrates the Schoolmaster

Isocrates has been called the most famous schoolmaster of antiquity. Whether or not this claim can be supported is not our special concern here. Certainly, few teachers ever conducted a more stable school—one that was in continuous operation for nearly fifty-five years. Isocrates

[62] Isocrates *Nicocles*. In *op. cit.*, vol. I, pp. 79–81.

opened his school in his own home when he was about forty-two years old; he was still teaching when he was ninety-seven. Unfortunately his fame does not shed any light on the levels of education with which he dealt. Was his school a secondary or a higher institution? This question must go unanswered. The whole issue is complicated by the fact that the course in his school lasted for only three or four years. This was too short a period in which to cover a secondary and a higher curriculum, yet Isocrates is always talking about the content and the objectives of both levels.

When Isocrates opened his school, he advertised its existence by preparing a pamphlet to be read by the people of Athens. This was his *Against the Sophists*. The title has more than passing significance. Isocrates was promising the people of Athens that his school would teach them what they needed to know. This promise and the assumptions necessary to make it put Isocrates in the position of having to distinguish his school and his practices both from the Sophists and from the stationary teachers of Athens. The following were the points which Isocrates thought important enough to refer to especially:

1. In order to distinguish his school from that of Plato (Plato's school, the Academy, was opened in 387 B.C., and Isocrates began his teaching career in 393 B.C.), Isocrates emphasized the democratic features of his school. They were mainly that the students could come from any walk of life and find the environment of the Isocratic school inviting and friendly, and that what they studied there was to form them in such a way that they could reenter general society, not the society of the elite or of the aristocrats. Here, perhaps, Isocrates was reflecting not only his convictions with respect to the formative function of education but his own social and class inheritance as well. Isocrates, unlike Plato, did not spring from aristocratic or noble blood.

Isocrates attempted to place a democratic aura over or around his school; yet in practice the school fostered a strange kind of democracy. It is true that it was open to all who cared to, and could afford to, attend. But the charges for instruction at the Isocratic school, although one cannot be precise about them, were far from being moderate. Without visible means of support other than the income from the school, Isocrates became one of Athens' richest men.

Instructionally, the Isocratic democratic ideal was supported by the oratorical ideal of good speaking. Isocrates never tired of telling his readers (and, we may suppose, he told his students too) of the great expectations he had for oratory. All the culture and education of antiquity, he said, could be transmitted most effectively by holding firmly to the oratorical idea.[63] Here again Isocrates is calling attention to the essential

[63] *Ibid.*

difference between his school and the schools conducted by the philosophers. Despite this difference, Isocrates maintained that he was teaching true philosophy, and that he himself was an authentic philosopher: not a dreamer, who neglects what is practical and essential, but a man who studies subjects that will enable him to manage domestic and civic affairs. That which is of no immediate use either for speech or for action, Isocrates said, does not deserve the name of philosophy.

2. If Isocrates was anxious to show the people of Athens that his school was not a mere imitation of Plato's, or a school devoted to an unreal or misunderstood ideal of truth, he was just as anxious for the people to know that he was not another Sophist, or better, because the Sophists enjoyed some respect in Athens, that his school was superior to those conducted by most Sophists. And here the differences seem to be not so much on the level of theory or of essential content but on the level of emphasis and methodology. When Isocrates does not want to be confused with the Sophists, he does not say that he disapproves their objectives. He rebukes them instead for their failures in achieving, or even respecting, these objectives in the practical order. Isocrates had, in fact, much more in common with the Sophists than he had with Plato. Sophists who claimed to teach the exact science of a happy and successful life and who then in practice indulged in captious wordy contests which had no relation to life came under his personal ban, but not for what they said they would do but for what they actually did, or failed to do. Other Sophists promised to teach the art of oratory to anyone who could learn the alphabet; but the "art," in the sophists' system, consisted in following a few simple rules and in memorizing a few clever catchwords and phrases. Here again Isocrates approved the objective, although he had piercing denunciations to make respecting the method and also the degree to which the ideal was actually attained.

If one is to judge from the successes enjoyed by the schoolmaster, Isocrates, it may be said that he advertised his school convincingly in his treatise *Against the Sophists*. It may be said also that he remained relatively true to the original definition of his mission; a half-century later in *Antidosis* he is able to refer to and quote from *Against the Sophists* with every evidence that his earlier views had not been changed in any important way.

We know the practices in schoolmastering to which Isocrates objected, and we know his devotion to oratory. We know something less, however, about the actual methods of his school. Like Plato, he was apparently willing to take conventional Greek elementary education as he found it.[64] To the lower level he added both the secondary and the higher. Secondary education was in Isocrates' hands a study of grammar and

---

[64] Isocrates *Panathenaicus*. In *op. cit.*, vol. II, p. 389.

literature, which, along with a smattering of mathematics, would prepare students for studies in rhetoric.

Isocrates' higher education gave a very special place to rhetoric, it is true, but, according to the famous master himself, in addition to good style and composition, its primary objective was teaching morals. Isocrates' claim for his school and for his kind of education was that it formed the gentleman. This is my definition of the educated man, he says: (1) He is capable of dealing with the ordinary events of life by selecting the right course of action; (2) he is always correct and proper, and he treats everyone with whom he comes in contact with fairness and gentleness; (3) he is always the absolute master of his thought and deed; and (4) he is not spoiled by success.[65]

Isocrates was interested in teaching rhetoric, but he was always aiming at something beyond it. This aim was to be achieved by following the course of studies he proposed. He advised students to study those things that would lead them most directly and most quickly to prudence or practical wisdom. But study alone, Isocrates was quick to see, is not enough; it must be supplemented by practice. And so we find the students debating and deliberating. They wrote and recited their own speeches on topics of contemporary interest or on subjects drawn from history, philosophy, or political science. In all of these speeches style was given constant attention, and to this end models were always readily accessible. The models were the speeches of the great orators and the orations that Isocrates himself had written.

The Influence of Isocrates

In recording the history of thought it is extremely difficult to be precise about influence. The effect that the thought of others had on Isocrates can be guessed at and reported, but the influence that he exerted on later educational theory can be evaluated and communicated only very uncertainly. It may be possible to call him the "father of literary humanism." Certainly he felt a commitment to the culture of the past and held that a principal purpose of education was to transmit this culture. The most excellent as well as the most sublime vehicle to be used for this purpose was oratory. Isocrates may have had a naïve and uncritical attitude toward the past, but he had nothing but respect for the poet's skill in making the past a living experience for the student. All of life's most fundamental experiences could be, and were, according to Isocrates, manifested in the great classics. It was the educated man's conversance with these fundamental experiences and the basic ideas to be drawn from them, joined with cleverness and elegance in expression, that impressed Isocrates most; and whether by coincidence or design,

[65] *Ibid.*, p. 519.

this mark of culture impressed secondary education and secondary educators from Isocrates' time down to the end of the nineteenth century.

Isocrates prized words, although it would be grossly unfair to call him a narrow pedant. Words were vehicles for thought, much of it ethical thought. Distilled in the classical tradition, thought was the content and finally the outcome of humanistic scholarship. No thinker or teacher in the history of education was more influential in giving to secondary education both its content and its form than this most famous schoolmaster of antiquity.

ARISTOTLE (384–322 B.C.)

Aristotle's theory of education, as it has come down to us, does not appear as complete as that of Plato or Isocrates. In the seventh and eighth books of the *Politics*, Aristotle touched on the educational questions that were of most interest at the time: whether education should be public or private and what education's proper function was. It is obvious to anyone who reads the *Politics* that Aristotle was sensitive to the role education should play in a state; yet we have no explicit educational theory from the pen of the great philosopher. He may have produced one—he did promise to do so—that has been lost.

Aristotle was a teacher and a scholar with nearly universal interests. As a teacher he conducted one of Athens' famous stationary schools, the Lyceum. This was an undertaking which occupied his time after he had dissolved his association with Plato's Academy. As a scholar, philosopher, and scientist he laid the foundations for, and advanced progress in, a number of academic and scientific fields. Any one of his contributions to human knowledge would be sufficient to win for him a lasting place in the history of thought. Here we are interested in Aristotle as a representative of Greek educational thought, and we may begin by admitting that his role in this area is somewhat subordinate to that of either Plato or Isocrates. Nevertheless, such an assessment leaves plenty of room for Aristotle. What were the principal educational views of this great man? Possibly the one that belongs first is the Aristotelian position that "all art and education aim at filling up nature's deficiencies."[66] The capacities of the individual to be educated—and these would include intellectual, moral, and physical qualities—are the foundations on which all education rests. Added to these more or less natural endowments are the habits that are formed through care and exercise. All else, says Aristotle, is the province of instruction. "We learn some things by habit and some by instruction."[67]

[66] Aristotle *Politics* vii. 17.
[67] *Ibid.*, vii. 13.

Education's general function is to take men toward happiness. There may be all kinds and descriptions of happiness, but a utilitarian or materialistic view of happiness never quite seems to fit into the Aristotelian mold. There is also, of course, the question of the meaning of education. And here, one may be sure, Aristotle is thinking of it in its very broadest sense.

The setting for education should be social. Aristotle called into question the common practice among Athenians of caring for the education of their children by providing them with tutors. Here he agreed with Plato, and incidentally with the Spartans, when he wrote that the education of the young required the special attention of the lawgiver.[68] This lawgiver should concern himself especially with education's public nature and with educational uniformity and opportunity. This would be done, not to control citizens or to deprive them of freedom, but to fit them with the best possible character.

The Influence of Aristotle

Despite Aristotle's well-deserved fame as a philosopher, his influence on education down through the ages has not been great. Many of his books were used as texts in the schools of the Middle Ages, and his philosophical ideas stimulated all kinds of intellectual activity among medieval men. Yet on the level of educational theory and practice he was almost entirely ignored. Under the circumstances, this is not surprising; Aristotle, at least in his extant writings, never gave the same kind of attention to education that was given by the theorists who dominated educational thought and practice almost down to modern times, Plato and Isocrates.

XENOPHON (430–355 B.C.)

There is a vast difference between the intellectual inheritance Plato bequeathed and that left to later generations by Xenophon. The latter could be ignored, and no great harm would be done to the history of educational thought or to the student's understanding of it. Yet Xenophon was not an entirely unimportant man, either for his own day or for our own. He reflects best the essential conservativism of mankind. Plato, Isocrates, and Aristotle were all devoted to reform and progress; they did not disregard the past, it is true, but they were critical thinkers with an eye on the unknown future. Even the Sophists had estimable dynamic qualities to recommend them. Xenophon, however, was willing to look to the past not just for guidance but for control, and with one exception

[68] *Ibid.*, viii. 1.

his interest in education was to restore and consolidate archaic educational practices in Athens.

Xenophon was a writer of history and biography; he was not a philosopher, nor did he pretend to be one. Perhaps his greatest single contribution was his *Memorabilia*, a biographical account of the great Socrates. But in educational thought his voice was the voice of the past. His views on education were clothed in an interesting fictional account of the education of a Persian prince, Cyrus. The work is entitled *Cyropaedia*. He begins by assuming that of all living things man is the most difficult to control, and he finds some evidence to support this assumption in the various types of social and political organization with which he was familiar. But he discovers that there is one place—Persia—where men are not difficult to control. His mission in *Cyropaedia* is to find out why. The result is that Xenophon is able to recommend a kind of education that is remarkably like the Spartan system and one, too, which could resemble in some of its features the education of archaic Athens. There are three points from the views of Xenophon that should be singled out for special mention:

1. Education is not for the good of the individual but is intended exclusively for the common good.

2. The curriculum should be geared toward military goals.

3. A literary curriculum should be given no place in formal education.

There is nothing in any of these views of Xenophon to suggest progress or to recommend attention. On one other point, however, Xenophon did show some independence: He thought that the contemporary opportunities for the education of women were about what they should be, that is, none at all. A general evaluation of Xenophon's educational position may be coupled with a general evaluation of his educational writings; they are interesting but not very influential.

SUMMARY

The Sophists came to Athens to offer Athenians an opportunity to pursue culture by means of secondary education of a literary type. The cultural inheritance of Athens was great; the actual accomplishments of the large majority of her citizens were low. The people wanted to raise themselves in order to be closer to the cultural ideal. Thus the Sophists came to Athens because they were invited and because good opportunities for profit and fame awaited them there. The picture of a group of hated Sophists invading Athens to teach an unwilling people what they did not want to learn needs to be redrawn.

Once the Sophist came to Athens, he offered his services to all, that is, to all who could pay the fees that he charged. And he offered to teach whatever his students wanted to learn. He assumed that they would have had an elementary education, although in actual practice few Sophists seem to have worried about the backgrounds of their students. The Sophists' objective was to teach their students how to be successful.

Plato, a stationary teacher in Athens, disapproved of the Sophists. He disliked their methods, and he deplored their purpose. Plato's general educational view was to subordinate everything to truth. He followed this ideal in his own school, the Academy, and he followed it, too, in the plans that he drew for education and presented in literary and artistic form in the *Republic* and the *Laws*. Throughout his long life Plato never ceased to support a kind of education which was predominantly philosophical, scientific, and mathematical.

Standing somewhere between the Sophists and Plato is Isocrates. Here was the most famous schoolmaster of all antiquity, and he, like the Sophists, emphasized eloquence as the goal of formal education, although the oratory that he approved was somewhat more responsible than that of the Sophists. The Isocratic educational theory was built around the theme that the right word is the sure sign of good thinking. Building on this theme, education became literary or literature-centered, and Isocrates is credited with being the father of literary humanism.

Aristotle and Xenophon fill out the picture of Greek educational theory.

Questions and Exercises for Study and Discussion

1. Evaluate the role of the Sophists in Athenian education. What effect, if any, did their teaching have on the history of education?
2. It has been said that the Sophists were teachers, not thinkers. What is the meaning of this distinction? Is it valid?
3. Why were the Sophists so frequently opposed by the stationary teachers? What did Plato, Isocrates, and Aristotle think of them? Was Socrates a Sophist? What is your evaluation of the Sophists?
4. What was elementary education like in Plato's time? What proposals did he make for revisions in elementary education?
5. Plato is sometimes called as a witness to support an educational program in which intellectual and physical goals are to be achieved side by side. Is Plato a good witness?
6. Gymnastics for the body, music for the soul: this was a dictum that received nearly universal support in Athens. What was Plato's reaction to it?
7. Compare Plato's educational plan as it is set forth in the *Republic* with the educational program attributed to the Sophists.
8. What was Isocrates' definition of philosophy? Do you think Isocrates was really a teacher of philosophy, as he claimed to be?
9. If you had the choice of attending Plato's Academy or Isocrates' school, which would you select and why?

4

Greek Education in Transition

THE HELLENISTIC ERA:
THE SPIRIT OF EDUCATIONAL INQUIRY

In the Hellenistic era the education of Greek antiquity was given its historical form. As a preliminary to any discussion of the significance of the age in the history of education, we must place it in time and indicate the general nature of Hellenism. In a way it was a hybrid age and one which was responsible for producing a novel educational species. From about the middle of the fourth century B.C., or about the time the Athenians were defeated by Philip of Macedonia in the Battle of Chaeronea (338 B.C.), to A.D. 529, when a few of the pagan schools were closed in Rome and Athens by a government decree, the Hellenistic influence was strong. Some scholars claim that the age lasted almost a thousand years. Although the outlines of Hellenistic influence were never entirely obliterated during this long period of time, the Hellenistic period proper was somewhat shorter. Without altering the date given for the beginning of the period, about the middle of the fourth century B.C., we might move the closing date back to about the end of the second century A.D., at which time the last of the Hellenistic-Roman schools came into existence and after which the Roman genius for educational organization began to appear more clearly. From this point on, though a remarkable fusion of Greek culture and Roman application still remained and though nothing had yet appeared that could be thought of as an autonomous Roman culture, Hellenistic influences were somewhat diluted.

It must be made clear at the outset that the long Hellenistic, or "Greeklike," period was not restricted to Rome in either setting or influence, although without Rome the effects of Hellenistic education would probably have been quite restricted.

A general, uninformed impression is that the classical tradition had its origin in Greece and Rome. But it is doubtful that Rome may share a place with Greece as the birthplace of such an inheritance. The Romans looked back for their intellectual inspiration, but, generally speaking, they looked back not to classical Greece but to Hellenistic Greece, which was so much closer to them. In turn, the localities, municipalities, and principalities that had sprung up around Asia Minor looked back to Athens and tried as best they could to continue her traditions and to emulate her achievements as they had discovered them from their study of the more ancient Greek institutions.

Hellenism, following in the footsteps of many cultures that had preceded it, began by living in the past. One of the first cultural objectives that grew out of this examination of the past was the acceptance of an aristocratic character for classical education. This character was securely identified with education in early Athens,[1] and it is a character that classical education, even in contemporary times, has not completely lost. Aristocratic education in classical Greece had never given any amount of thought to perpetuating its kind. Somewhat naïvely, no doubt, it assumed that what was good for the Greek citizen would never really change and that no external supports were needed to maintain these values. This confidence might have been well founded in archaic Athens and in classical Greece, for then the structure of society and the tone of culture supported the kind of education dedicated to the ideal of the heroic deed.[2] But the communities that sprang up outside of Greece, where Hellenism received its greatest impetus, had no such structures or social or cultural traditions to rest on. What they found in classical ways of living could not be left to a living or an oral tradition. Formal communication of these traditional values seemed essential, and to do this job the school became more important than ever before. Moreover, the job seemed to require literary abilities. Not only did the school become important, but the school as a literary agency gained nearly universal recognition. The Greeklike feature remained, of course, for this was the very heart of Hellenism, but it existed in the new era more on the level of inspiration than of established fact. Athens had had schools from perhaps the sixth century B.C., but these schools were not especially important for communicating the culture of Athens, and they were not truly literary institutions. The chief outcome of Hellenism in the history of education was to commit the school primarily to literary objectives.

Yet this was not an immediate outcome of Hellenism, for the traditions

---

[1] See pp. 49–51.
[2] See pp. 42–43.

of the past had to do a good deal of unfolding before this came about. The clearest goal of what was then called classical education was superiority in sport. It is true that sport was criticized, even condemned, by philosophers and educational theorists in Athens,[3] but excellence in sports persisted with only slight deemphasis as the true mark of the gentleman right down to the time the first Hellenistic settlement was incorporated. From that time on, however, although the gymnasium did not disappear, sport began to decline. Its place was occupied by literary instruction.

This emphasis on literary education was neither precisely Athenian nor traditionally Greek. It was the outstanding feature of Hellenistic education. So true is this, that what for the past four hundred years has been called classical education had its more exact model in Hellenistic schools. It is the education that achieved definite form in the two or three centuries preceding the opening of the Christian era. It was the basis for teaching and learning in later Rome, and its fundamental contribution is clear, in spite of Latin features that are apparent when one examines Roman schools. These Latin features were attached to essential features, and these essential features were not distinctly Roman. This, too, was the kind of education that became attractive to the Christians when Christianity reached a stage in its development that seemed to demand an intellectual basis for its creed. And finally, this Hellenistic codification and amalgamation of educational thought and practice was what passed for and still passes for classical education in modern and contemporary times. We need not be critical of this mislabeling; perhaps we should hardly expect that the authentic classical ideal or the educational informalities of early Greek times, with sport as their center and heroism as their most prominent objective, would have made much of an imprint on modern educational practices. Yet the roots of classicism were not found in Hellenism, but in the Greece of antiquity. This is an important point to remember. Hellenism synthesized more than it generated; it symbolized more than it created; but in doing so, this age stood at an intellectual crossroads and accepted, integrated, embodied, and passed on the classical tradition. In some respects this age is more important to the history of education than Greek education itself.

If the age was important to education, it is no less true that education was immensely important to the age. Alexander the Great had carved out an empire, and he and his successors carried out a policy of establishing Greek communities throughout the Hellenistic kingdom. The kingdom exercised general administrative control, and though it intended to maintain its ultimate authority, it was always willing to delegate a certain amount of control and responsibility to the cities

[3] Plato *Laws* 795–796.

which it had created or reanimated. It was always made clear, however, that whatever functions these cities performed, they were functions delegated to them. The autonomous city state of Greece could make definite and fundamental policies and, depending on its strength and the opportunities of the day, attempt to carry them out. This the Hellenistic city could not do. Despite appearances of independence and the kingdom's encouragement of the city's assumption of control over machinery for the administration of political life, the city had no real authority.[4] It lacked the legal and the moral power to discipline, not its citizens, but its inhabitants. (The inhabitants of the city were citizens of the kingdom.) The city did not have the authority to demand allegiance from the people or the stature to merit it. Whereas the municipal organization in Greece had been of a city-state type, which carried with it the implication of organic character, the Hellenistic urban center was a mere municipality and no real heir to the ancient city state.

The moral and political sterility of the Hellenistic city was a weakness, to be sure, but it was not a total loss. Had the larger political unit—the kingdom—supplied and imposed the moral authority and the fundamental political discipline that classical Greek cities had themselves supplied, the city's position would not have been improved, but at least a norm or a standard of action would have been provided as a guide and control for the lives of the city's people. This, however, the larger political unit did not do, and it did not permit the city to exercise a degree of autonomy necessary to exercise the control itself. At this point the importance of education to the Hellenistic city becomes a little clearer. It would indeed be surprising to find that the interest in education was not rooted in real life. Education became important to the Hellenistic man and to the society he lived in because it alone could supply the moral bases on which individual and social discipline could be built. Could an objective for education be more practical than this?

In time the Hellenistic educational objective grew broader; the citizen of the later period became enamored of the Athenian humanism of the golden age of Pericles, and he began to look toward education to find the key to the building of a complete personality. One can hardly express his desire without becoming poetic, for the idealistic hope for human perfection calls for poetry to capture and convey its thought. It revolves about the commitment to make complete and perfect use of all of nature's endowments. This was the fundamental principle behind Hellenistic education. With such high ideals inspiring their educational enterprises, we can hardly understand why these Greeks of

[4] M. Cary, *The Legacy of Alexander,* The Dial Press, Inc., New York, 1932, pp. 270–272.

the Alexandrian empire missed the mark in accomplishment by so much, unless, of course, their ideals were unrealistic rather than high. They were unrealistic, not in aiming at human perfection, but in assigning to formal education the primary goal of the complete intellectual and cultural improvement of man. This was not the same thing as the "education of the whole man" that our contemporary educators speak of, for Hellenistic schools had few physical and fewer moral commitments. In trying to follow earlier educational practices too closely, Hellenistic educators misinterpreted some of them. They thought classical education had accepted a total cultural commission, whereas, in fact, it had not.[5]

Wherever the Greeks settled, as they spread throughout the Mediterranean world, they met with peoples not Greek in origin; probably the majority of the inhabitants of the Hellenistic cities were not Greek. Though all of them, the Greeks and the non-Greeks alike, could admire and try to absorb the culture of the past, they could never really achieve their ambition simply through the medium of schools. Nevertheless, the idea of perfection and devotion to the Greeklike things of life dominated their thought, inspired their hopes, and consolidated their interest in education.

EDUCATIONAL THEORY

Not only was Hellenistic man more interested in the cultural function that schools could perform than any of his ancestors, but he was also much more interested in creating a theory for education, not as a corollary to political theory, but as a separate or independent doctrine leading to culture. The age, then, among other things produced an educational theory of an easily recognizable kind. Plato, Isocrates, Aristotle, and others of the Greek world proper had not overlooked the significance of education, and in many respects what they had to say about it was superior to any pronouncement made in the Hellenistic age, but they did not single out education for independent analysis and treatment. This was done by Hellenistic philosophers and writers.

Aristippus (ca. 435–350 B.C.), who belongs to the very early fringe of Hellenism, wrote a book entitled *On Education*. Clearchus of Soloi, who lived in the third century B.C., was the author of another book, *On Education*. Theophrastus (ca. 370–286 B.C.), often recognized as a disciple and interpreter of Aristotle, was the author of a work entitled *Of the Education of Kings* and of another called *A Polemical Discussion*

[5] Werner W. Jaeger, *Paideia: The Ideals of Greek Culture*, Oxford University Press, New York, 1945, vol. I, pp. 298–321.

on the Theory of Eristic Argument. Aristoxenus, who belongs to the third century B.C., produced a treatise on the *Rules of Pedagogy.* Cleanthes (ca. 331–232 B.C.) is credited with *Of Education, Of Usages, Of Dialectic, Of Moods or Tropes,* and *Of Predicates.* Zeno (ca. 333–261 B.C.) was the author of two works on education, one entitled *Of Greek Education* and the other *A Handbook of Rhetoric.* Cleomenes of the second century B.C. wrote a book *Concerning Pedagogues.* All of this activity gives evidence of considerably more professional interest in education than earlier times could exhibit. With this activity and the good omens suggested in it, the historian can get the first glimpse of a willingness, if not a desire, to separate education and learning from life. Perhaps the separation was implicit in the cultural doctrines and ideals of thinking men of the time. They may have wanted to remove education from the market place, or they may have been unaware of the force that they were creating—a force which lasted several hundred years and which was, unfortunately, especially instrumental in keeping education impotent. This judgment is in no way intended as a criticism of the theories of education proposed at this time or as a denunciation of the techniques and methods of teaching and learning that were only then in the process of evolvement. Singling out education for special theoretical and practical attention was probably inevitable in the context of the times and was in some ways a step forward. The science of education profited from the literary and theoretical specialization, but the place of education in the life of a growing man—the relationship between learning and life—took a backward step. If Plato and Isocrates generated a dilemma in educational theory and bequeathed it to the educators who followed them, the educators of the Hellenistic age seem in their turn to have created a dilemma with learning on one horn and life on the other.

Hellenistic educational theories were successful in bestowing on formal education an importance that it never had enjoyed before. Men became professional intellectuals because of the value they saw in learning and because of inner motives that are not subject to scientific or historical analysis. But there was an added motive: Accomplished men of letters and learning received special reverence. The cultured mind became a goal worth seeking. The most direct road to culture was formal education.

Both Plato and Aristotle had emphasized the need for state control over education, if the state was to succeed in achieving the highest ends.[6] Neither had made much of a mark on educational practice in Athens: the Greeks went right on leaving education in the hands of the in-

[6] See pp. 85–88 and 102–103.

dividual.[7] No doubt some control of an indirect and indefinite kind was imposed by custom or tradition, but this was obviously not the kind of public control that the philosophers had written about. In the matter of regulation by the state, Sparta seems to have been the model. In Hellenistic cities, however, education ceased to be a matter reserved exclusively for private initiative—the theories of Plato and Aristotle were now being heeded—and generally speaking, education was subject to the control of the public. State legislation over education became the normal thing. Instead of attributing this practical innovation to Rome, as is so often done, historians should recognize and emphasize its rightful place of origin in Hellenistic Greece.[8]

It may not be too much to maintain that in early Greece not only were girls not educated, but educational theory, apart from Plato's tongue-in-cheek prospectus, which could have made room for girls, made no plans for their participation in instructional programs. In this transitional age, however, educational opportunity was distributed a good deal more freely than heretofore, and girls as well as boys could attend the schools. Girls were even permitted to go to the palaestra and the gymnasium.[9]

EDUCATIONAL OPERATIONS: GENERAL ORGANIZATION

The organization of education in the age that stood between the earlier Greek and the later Roman systems must always remain something of a mystery. This is so because each of the cities, functioning as a free agent in about the only area left for such freedom of action, organized its educational institutions to suit itself. There was no one, unified program. We must trace not one but many discrete systems of educational organization. For reasons we have already discussed, the Hellenistic towns were most anxious to follow their own private plans

[7] Thomas Davidson, *Aristotle and Ancient Educational Ideals,* Charles Scribner's Sons, New York, 1901, pp. 198 ff.; A. S. Wilkins, *National Education in Greece in the Fourth Century B.C.,* Stechert-Hafner, Inc., New York, 1911, pp. 160 ff.; and Jaeger, *op. cit.,* vol. III, pp. 197–212. The statement that neither Plato nor Aristotle had made much of a mark on educational practice in Athens should not be taken to mean that their work as schoolmasters was inconsequential. The point is that neither was able to get the city state to follow his educational views.

[8] M. Rostovtzeff, *The Social and Economic History of the Hellenistic World,* Oxford University Press, New York, 1941, pp. 1059–1061. It is possible, of course, to become overenthusiastic about this view. State legislation or municipal laws concerning education may well have varied from one Hellenistic city to another. (See Cary, *op. cit.,* p. 270.)

[9] E. Norman Gardiner, *Athletics of the Ancient World,* Oxford University Press, New York, 1930, p. 113; Clarence A. Forbes, *Greek Physical Education,* Appleton-Century-Crofts, Inc., New York, 1929, p. 135.

for education. School models did not come from Greece, but ideals of humanism and liberalism did. Each city was anxious to show its independence, so far as educational structure was concerned, but at the same time it wanted to demonstrate its dedication to the cultural values of Greece.

Largely by default, then, education came to be a local responsibility. The kingdom was content to leave the cities alone in this area of activity. Yet despite the Hellenistic allegiance to individualism, some common bonds can be discerned in institutional practices and content of teaching. It is true that individualism served by diversity was characteristic of patterns for education both in organization and administration. And while no Hellenistic city would have been entirely indifferent to education, even the policies of interest or devotion were apt to show variety.[10] But it may well be that the similarities from city to city are of more value to us in understanding Hellenistic education than the differences that may be found in organization, the titles of various officials in the educational units, or the specific relationships that may have existed between schools and cities.

It is generally assumed that every Hellenistic city had a gymnasium. This assumption, if valid, would justify the view that the lines of inspiration remained open between Athens and the Greek world around her. There is, however, a good deal less certainly about the nature of the Hellenistic gymnasium. Possibly the municipalities that sprang up on the fringe of the Greek world were loyal to names and not to essential natures of Greek institutions. In addition to the gymnasium, every Hellenistic city seems to have had an ephebeum.[11]

The ephebic system in Athens had a twofold purpose, military and civic. Its military purpose was to produce soldiers; its civic purpose was to form citizens. This may have been a needed combination at one time in Athenian history, and to some extent the ends that were now sought formally had been obtained informally in the past. But ironically enough, at the point in history when Athens no longer had any special need for citizen-soldiers, because Athens was no longer a free city, the system to produce them was most highly developed. Civic leadership in the political arena was no more needed in Athens, when ephebic training reached its highest point, than a civic army. When autonomy was lost, military training and civic virtue became a mere display. It should be understood that it was this paradoxical idea pattern of civic and military

[10] Rostovtzeff, *op. cit.*, pp. 1084–1095.

[11] A. H. M. Jones, *The Greek City from Alexander to Justinian,* Oxford University Press, New York, 1940, pp. 220–225; Rostovtzeff, *op. cit.*, pp. 1059–1060; and M. Rostovtzeff, *The Social and Economic History of the Roman Empire,* Oxford University Press, New York, 1957, pp. 186–188.

education that was transplanted from Athens to the Hellenistic towns. But here we must insert a word of caution: This was the transplantation of an ideal not of a practice. On the level of practice, this ideal of the Attic ephebea had as little meaning in the Hellenistic world as it had in Athens.[12]

Ephebic training was so unrealistic that change was inevitable. The changes were made first in Athens, and then the departures from the ephebic ideal began to take shape in the Hellenistic ephebic institutions. Although there were pockets of anachronism or ultraconservatism in the Hellenistic area of influence, where young men went right on following the original curriculum with its strict military and political orientation, the Athenian revisions were usually quite acceptable, and Hellenistic ephebea lost no time in adapting them to their use. New objectives were substituted for the old; civic education aimed not at leadership in public affairs but at the perpetuation of an aristocratic way of life; military training was conveniently redirected toward sport. The glory of the ephebeum was that it could transform hope into reality; in it the Hellenistic boy could be immersed in Greek culture, and from this immersion ensued an even greater consolidation of the position of the aristocracy. Aristocracy was made the equivalent of civilization, and it was judged that culture, not position or wealth, could distinguish Greeks from the other inhabitants of the city. The distinction was important, for, as Rostovtzeff has shown so clearly in his monumental study of Hellenistic life, the city was a place for many allegiances and many races. Cultural homogeneity for the Greeks was possible only when it was cultivated with extreme care.

Schools of the Hellenistic World

Apart from the ephebic schools, which along with most gymnasia were maintained at public expense, there was no state system of publicly supported schools in the Hellenistic cities. It was true that all the schools felt the state to some degree, for in this period the injunctions of the philosophers like Plato and Aristotle with respect to state control of education, were beginning to be heeded.[13] Still, in practice, the control fell short of the ideal presented by the philosophers. Of course it was in the general organization of schools that the state made its influence felt most effectively, and not in the day-to-day operation of educational institutions. Perhaps the largest single factor that militated against any greater assumption of authority over education by the city was the fact

[12] Rostovtzeff, *The Social and Economic History of the Hellenistic World,* p. 810, says that the majority of younger citizens were unaccustomed to military service.

[13] See pp. 85–86 and 102–103.

that schools did not receive regular support from municipal governments. The structure of municipal government was too fragile to permit the kind of revenue vehicles that would have made such support possible. Ephebea were supported to some extent, as were gymnasia, but the support was probably neither generous nor regular, although it very probably did include provision out of the public treasury for the site of such institutions, the buildings, and other necessary physical facilities. As ephebic institutions attuned their objectives more and more to those of Attic ephebea, and as such places began to join in their curricula both sport and literary education, the costs tended to be considerably lower than before. But even in the days when the ephebea were inclined to hew closely to the line of original purpose and when total costs were higher, these costs were borne largely by the young men who attended. This was still the established practice in most Hellenistic cities. In spite of these private contributions, the ephebic school may be considered a state school. Apart from the ephebic school, there were, strictly speaking, no other state schools.

Other schools that existed in these cities were either endowed or instituted by private venture.[14] In either case they were private schools, and from this distance in history the points at which public authority touched them are not especially visible. Most schools in the Hellenistic world were conducted by enterprising masters, who saw an opportunity to make teaching and learning pay, and some of these masters were able to make an especially handsome profit from their endeavors. Profits aside, these private school teachers, most of whom were conducting elementary schools, were seldom accorded much, if any, recognition for the relatively important work they were doing. The fact that their work was socially important and even necessary did not result in any improvement in the teachers' status. The main reason for the low estate of teachers may be found in the generally accepted custom of permitting anyone who wanted to teach to do so; he would need only to open a school. There were many teachers without any real qualifications for teaching. An occupation which apparently requires no special knowledge or skill would naturally not be held in reverence, and teachers would not be accorded any special social esteem.

Another source of school support, apart from state support and student fees, was the public-spirited, wealthy citizen. From very early classical times down through the Hellenistic period, tradition recommended that men of wealth endow some enterprise of public worth. Some schools were founded or maintained in this way.

[14] Frederick Eby and Charles F. Arrowood, *The History and Philosophy of Education: Ancient and Medieval,* Prentice-Hall, Inc., Englewood Cliffs, N.J., 1940, pp. 468–472.

SCHOOL PROGRAMS

So far we have concerned ourselves with those features of schools and education that may be called extrinsic. But whatever the value these organizational forms may have had for succeeding generations (and we are inclined to think that they had considerable value), the really important and distinctive thing in Hellenistic education was not how schools were organized or supported but what they taught and what students learned. In other words, we have every right to suspect at this point in our study that the content and purpose of Hellenistic programs of study were important to all later education. This was a transitional period, but it was also anticipatory, if not actually prophetic, of later educational values. We do not want to become one-sided in an analysis as complicated as this, but even with this caution in mind, we find it difficult to recognize any other period in the history of education so influential in the formation of a permanent content for education and in its direction toward stable values. But we must not deal in generalities on such important questions. There is some evidence available for our examination.[15]

Physical Education

Perhaps one of the most striking features of early Greek education was the attention given to physical training.[16] Physical training, though in later times it was developed to include drill, health studies, and scientific methods, was, throughout the Greek period proper and for at least the early part of the Hellenistic period, nothing more than athletics. There was no period of youth in which athletics were given special attention; every age, from early youth through ephebic preparation, was liberally provided with athletic opportunity. At one time athletic activities were apparently meant for the social elite, but this type of discrimination was shortly replaced by a more moderate kind; certain types of sport were thought to be appropriate only for the upper classes. Riding was one of these aristocratic sports.[17]

In spite of various undemocratic attitudes that were part of Greek

---

[15] Again I want to acknowledge my indebtedness to H. I. Marrou, *A History of Education in Antiquity.* His thorough and searching study is the best available. It was written first in French (1948); an English translation by George Lamb (Sheed & Ward, Inc., New York, 1956) made this unusually fine volume accessible to many more readers. My own treatment of Hellenistic education follows Marrou closely. See Marrou, pp. 102–226.

[16] Kenneth J. Freeman, *Schools of Hellas*, 3d ed., The Macmillan Company, New York, 1922, pp. 118–120.

[17] *Ibid.*, p. 143.

life and were applied naturally enough to sport and recreation, physical education was nearly universal. Physical education was sport. Sport was traditionally one of the means employed for inducting the young of the city into the life of culture and leisure. And with the Hellenistic dedication to all that suggested the Greece of old, physical education was a staple in a broadly conceived educational program. Every Hellenistic town had some opportunities for physical education. It has already been mentioned that the Hellenistic cities, favorably disposed as they were to Greeklike institutions, readily established gymnasia where boys and girls could exercise and where they could begin to obtain the fundamental athletic skills which were universally prized.

There is no question but that physical education was well-established in Greek and Hellenistic education. But the modern reader, familiar possibly with extracurricular programs of intramural and interschool athletics, should not be misled; Hellenistic schools did not conduct or supervise such athletic activities. Nevertheless, they were educational in a broad sense. No true citizen of the Hellenic world could grow to manhood without the social graces and physical benefits to be derived from athletics.

What the Hellenistic youngsters did in physical education may not be too different from what young people do today. The curriculum of physical education is curtailed by the limitations that nature places on the human body. Yet what was done was sufficiently distinctive to warrant brief notice. Hellenistic physical education included running, jumping, throwing the discus and javelin, wrestling, and boxing.[18] There were other physical skills or abilities common to the life of the day that were not part of this more or less formal physical training program. The most obvious exception was swimming. Most Hellenic people could swim, as most people in early Greece had been able to swim. Yet swimming was not part of the formal training program.

Elementary Education

Before the onset of the Hellenistic age the various levels of formal education that have been accepted in later times almost everywhere were not always easy to recognize. We may be sure that the logical order of regular procession from the simple to the complex was not neglected in the earliest schools, and instruction in any field would demand certain prerequisite learning. Prerequisites, however, stand out more clearly when one has literary education in mind. Although we can be easily convinced that literary education has occupied a dominant place in all modern societies, as a matter of fact it is just one stage—though surely a broad one—in the evolution of education. Education

[18] *Ibid.*, pp. 131–142.

has not always been predominantly literary. In the Hellenistic educational systems, however, we see the literary side of education making its first definite moves toward scholastic supremacy. Actual supremacy of literary studies in education was a long time in coming, and possibly it was not achieved on the elementary or primary level during the Hellenistic age. Other studies claimed attention in the elementary school.

But studies would be only part of the story. There was no general view that the school should be given responsibility for all education, including moral and physical education, and, indeed, the elementary school may have been given somewhat less attention and responsibility than it rightfully deserved. What was included in the school's curriculum was really only a relatively small part of elementary education. As we have seen, physical education was considered important, and the whole matter of moral formation had to be attended to also. Physical education was carried on outside of the elementary school, although there was something formal and even school-like about physical education programs. As for moral education, this was something far too important to be left to the direction of the teacher. It was considered the work of the nurse, the pedagogue, the family itself. There were, then, really three parts to elementary education—literary, physical, moral—and only the first of the three was the clear responsibility of the school.

Hellenistic elementary education included drawing, instrumental and vocal music, dancing, reading, writing, and counting.[19] What of the first three—drawing, music, and dancing? If these were not clear responsibilities of the elementary school, where would they be handled? The development of drawing as a school subject is difficult to trace. Apparently it occupied a more prominent position in the schools of early Greece than it did in the schools of the Hellenistic era.[20] There were drawing masters, nevertheless, who found customers for their teaching in all Hellenistic centers. Even in higher studies, instruction in drawing might have been included. Yet it would seem that drawing as a subject of formal instruction was on the decline. Though the historical picture here becomes somewhat confused, we may suppose that drawing was in the curriculum of some elementary schools and may have been taught by some elementary schoolmasters.

Music, too, sometimes found a place in the lower school. More commonly music was taught by special masters. Masters, we say, because instrumental and vocal music were not taught by the same teachers. In spite of what would appear to have been a somewhat unrealistic specialization in the teaching of music, music continued to retain a fairly secure position in Hellenistic culture. Music had been so firmly woven into the

[19] Marrou, *op. cit.*, pp. 133–159.
[20] Aristotle *Politics* viii. 1337.

fabric of Greek life that it would have been strange indeed to find that the Hellenistic age rejected music while retaining such a wholehearted attitude of acceptance toward most Greeklike institutions and the bulk of Greek culture. Though we may doubt that music had a permanent and an important role throughout the Hellenistic age, we may be sure that it retained a role that was always and everywhere superior to that of drawing. Yet it, too, declined. The Hellenistic age was able to retain a general devotion to Greek culture and at the same time allow music to become less important both in education and in life. Literature crowded music out of the school's curriculum; acoustical studies invaded music itself and changed its course. These are the most obvious illustrations of how music began to lose its hold on Hellenistic culture. By the end of the Hellenistic period, music as it was known in Athens of the fifth century B.C. no longer existed.

As traditional concerns of elementary education were gradually lost, the primary school was left with reading, writing, and counting. These subjects were taught with little imagination and with less skill. No thought was given to adapting the materials of instruction to the nature of learning. This was so, no doubt, because the masters knew little of the nature of learning and almost nothing at all about the arts of teaching. As we have said, anyone who could read could teach in these schools. There was no alternative for the child; he had to put up with such teachers.

The teaching of reading began with the alphabet. Here the child's attention was directed at learning names; there was no concern for sounds. A great deal of time was spent on learning the alphabet. From the alphabet instruction moved to syllables, and from them to words and then to texts. Recitation was mainly memorization, and writing was taught with the same lack of imagination as reading. In general, children learned to write by copying. Counting completed the elementary school program, and it was conducted according to the same involved counting system that had been common to the schools of Athens.[21]

Elementary schools could be found throughout the Hellenistic world, and all free children were expected to attend such schools. In some cities girls and boys were enrolled together and were engaged in learning the same things. Yet in spite of their fairly vital interest in primary education, Hellenistic cities did not see fit to set aside or construct any special buildings for schools. A school was kept wherever a vacant room could be found. It needed no equipment other than a few chairs or benches on which the children could sit.

Children in the elementary schools that present-day educators ap-

[21] See pp. 57–58. For details of elementary instruction, see Marrou, *op. cit.*, pp. 150–158.

prove have no reason to envy the children who attended lower schools in the Hellenistic cities. Instruction was poor, and progress was slow. An elementary school child would probably not be able to write his name after three years in school, and even simple addition would have been beyond the ability of the child who had spent five years there. Another feature may be added to the generally unattractive portrait of life in these schools: children were treated brutally. Corporal punishment was used for both prevention and cure, and fear was the only motivation in which the schools had confidence. Tradition decided what was to be taught. The teacher's ability or inability determined the how of teaching. Learning under such conditions could hardly have been other than painful.

Secondary Education

Literary and scientific secondary education developed rather slowly. Both had existed in theory much more than they had in practice in the pre-Hellenistic years.[22] The Athenians, of course, had had a secondary level, but the emphasis on this level (we are thinking of the gymnasium, of course) was on physical rather than literary training. In some other places the emphasis may have been artistic rather than literary. The claim that the secondary school with a definite commitment to literary education had its real beginning in the Hellenistic period may be given a sympathetic hearing. Prior to this time, the organization of a content for literary studies of the secondary type would have encountered some difficulty. The great Greek classics existed mainly in oral tradition. This oral tradition was part of elementary education, although not necessarily a part of the elementary school's curriculum. The classical willingness to leave to informal transmission the literature and the literary inheritance that were prized so highly may well have worked to retard the development of literature as a school subject. The place of literature in formal education was one of many questions; others involved grammar and science.

Hellenistic teachers accepted the Greek classics as part of the content of secondary education, and in doing so they went one step beyond their classical ancestors. To these studies in literature they added an ever-growing body of scientific and mathematical knowledge. Finally, the science of language—grammar—arose, and this, too, was added to the content of the secondary school. There were, then, three principal curricular areas: literature, science, and grammar. They were not, however, of equal value in the eyes of the Hellenistic man of culture.

Literature. Hellenistic schools made the classics a formal part of

[22] It would be hard to ignore Plato's theory of secondary education. See pp. 92–95.

secondary school education. Few innovations in the history of education may lay claim to greater permanence than this: from secondary schools that operated before the Christian era down to those being conducted today, classical studies may still be found. And more than this, some of the classics read, studied, and explained then are still being read and studied today.

As we have said, Homer had a solid reputation for being the educator of the Greeks. Not only Athens, but all of the Greek world felt his influence. The Homeric impress on early Greece was unquestionably great, and its influence was not limited to Greece, for the most popular of all of the ancient poets to be accepted in Hellenistic intellectual circles and in the school's literary curriculum was Homer. The preeminent literary works were the *Iliad* and the *Odyssey*. But other epic poets were studied; Hesiod would be an outstanding example. Lyric poets and dramatists were also read and studied. One would surely hesitate to try to draw up a complete list of the literature studied in these schools, for the classical heritage was rich.

Although the curriculum with which the teachers of literature had to work had rare quality, the teachers were not disposed, or perhaps were not able, to take full advantage of it. Instead of directing their students in a search for literary taste and appreciation, they turned them toward the superficialities of literary study. Analysis of the text and searching for unusual words or expressions were all preliminary to reading a poem or drama. Sometimes the student hardly had time to read the literature that he was studying.

Grammar. It is safe to assume that literature preceded grammar and science in secondary school studies. Literature had existed in a fuller and more complete form for a much longer time than either grammar or science. How far back would one have to go to find the origin of literature in the Greek world? At least as far back as the time of Homer—seven or eight centuries before Christ. Grammar as a body of knowledge about the structure of language was developed in the first century B.C. by Dionysius Thrax of Rhodes.[23] Dionysius produced the first book on the subject, a book that was used as a text and reference in the teaching and study of grammar for centuries. This sixteen-page work was still found in use in the later Middle Ages.

In Dionysius' *Grammar* we have the beginnings of a new subject for secondary schools. From this time on, that is, from about the first century B.C., secondary schools that followed the Hellenistic model included literature and grammar in their curricula. Dionysius defined grammar as the practical knowledge of the usage of writers of poetry and prose. He dealt with accent, letters, syllables, and parts of speech.

[23] See Eby and Arrowood, *op. cit.*, p. 482.

The book concluded with a brief treatment of the declension of nouns and the conjugation of verbs.[24]

In actual practice in the schools, grammatical study not only included the scientific, abstract, and arid approach to language that had been introduced by Dionysius (which must have turned many a student away from serious study because of the obvious implication that learning and life had little in common), but included an introduction to composition as well. Composition, however, was not stressed in the secondary school, for both oral and written compositions belonged to the sphere of higher education.

Science. Science or science study did not begin with the secondary schools of the Hellenistic world. Yet the age did give science a larger role in formal education than any earlier age had given. Excepting the scientific investigations conducted by men engaged in higher studies or by scholars commissioned for such purposes, scientific study and mathematical study of this period attained a degree of formalization not found in earlier educational history. The Hellenistic age had, of course, the benefit of theoretical justification for treating science as a secondary school subject. Both Plato and Isocrates had agreed that such studies had a great deal of merit for formative and cultural purposes. Such support, coupled with the advances being made in scientific and mathematical knowledge and man's natural curiosity about the world in which he lived, made the inclusion of science in the curriculum almost inevitable. In their ardent desire to be Greeklike, Hellenistic people often did not distinguish between the real nature of Greek institutions and the ideal picture, given by Plato, Isocrates, and Aristotle, of what they ought to have been. By putting science in the secondary school, Hellenistic educators were surely not following classical practice. But this is not too important a point, because classical Greek secondary schools were not literary institutions at all. Science in the secondary school curriculum may or may not have been a sign that Hellenistic people wanted to be better Greeks than the Greeks themselves had been. Without further speculation on these obscure matters, we should touch quickly on what the study of science in these schools entailed. A broad curriculum probably contained geometry, arithmetic, astronomy, and music. Geometry, as it was studied in these schools, had its beginning and end with Euclid. It was not intended, moreover, to be a subject with entirely liberal objectives.[25]

Arithmetic in Hellenistic schools differed very little from Greek arithmetic, a fact which helps us to understand why it was studied in

[24] *Ibid.*

[25] See D. E. Smith, *History of Mathematics,* Ginn & Company, Boston, 1925, vol. I, p. 271.

the secondary schools. Today we find schoolboys and schoolgirls laboring over their addition, subtraction, multiplication, and division problems, and for the most part they meet these problems in the elementary school. Hellenistic arithmetic study was neither commercial nor practical; it was a study of the theory of numbers—the Greek notation made any other approach most impractical—and far too complicated for elementary school students.

Music was, in a sense, an adjunct of mathematics. In Athens and in other Greek cities from the sixth to the third century B.C., music had probably been an elementary school subject. In what was the generally accepted definition of secondary education, music had no recognized position. Usually school subjects start on a high level and sink. In other words, the normal development has been that subjects are introduced in higher schools, and when a subject becomes generally accepted as a part of organized knowledge, it drops to the secondary school curriculum and from there to the elementary school. Music, at least as far as Hellenistic education is concerned, provides us with the rare example of a subject going up the educational ladder rather than down. Yet it should be pointed out that music itself had changed, or rather, that the subject that was brought to the secondary school was a different kind of music from what had been or even what was then accepted as a cultural tool. This was the kind of music that declined in value as a part of Hellenistic life. The force of this decline was such that both instrumental and vocal music, the kinds of music that had occupied an integral part of Greek life before, declined too. Despite these trends, conventional music did not disappear completely from the schools of the Hellenistic world. Music could still be found in the curriculum of some of the schools of later Rome.

The place of astronomy was similar to that of geometry. It was studied as a liberal rather than a practical subject.

Higher Education

We have drawn a general picture of the lower schools that flourished in the Hellenistic world.[26] It would probably be a mistake to maintain that a high degree of uniformity was attained in the various elementary and secondary schools, but certainly there was much more unity of purpose than could be found on the level of higher education. Of course the lower schools had a so-called liberal commitment: They wanted to transmit Greek culture. The same purpose was accepted, though not as an exclusive objective, by some of the schools of higher education. Higher schools that directed their energies at cultural transmission were

[26] The general picture to which I refer is given in detail in Marrou's *History of Education in Antiquity*.

the schools of rhetoric and philosophy. In time, however, if we read the history of these two parts of higher education correctly, both rhetors and philosophers began to show less and less interest in culture and greater and greater interest in building an academic domain of their own in which rhetoric or philosophy became pretty much an end in itself. The other side of higher education—if one side was ostensibly cultural—was professional. The line to be drawn between professional and technical higher education is almost always quite thin, and one hesitates to be too positive on such delicate and elusive matters. Yet the Hellenistic age seems not to have had what we should call technical higher education. This omission was intentional, for a definite attitude prevailed which questioned the worth of every study that appeared to be illiberal. At the same time, some obvious inconsistencies marked this skeptical spirit. For example, Hellenistic people loved the architectural design of their ancestors and hoped to imitate their capabilities in construction. If they had been realistic, they could hardly have dismissed the need for advanced technical education. Still, we have no clear evidence of provisions made for technical higher education either in existing higher schools or in special schools created for technical progress.

Ephebic institutions could still be found, and because they had drifted away from their original purposes or because they could no longer achieve them, they found room for general cultural studies. In addition to the studies in the ephebea, there were two kinds of programs in higher education, medical and scientific. With respect to the first, it is probably not accurate to talk about medical schools, because young men who aspired to the profession of medicine received their professional training not as students in schools but as apprentices. Some scholars turned to a systematic formulation of scientific knowledge, and this was an educational development of great significance for the future of grammar, rhetoric, medicine, geometry, and many other areas of human knowledge. Now scientists had an institution—the museum—which gave them a place to experiment and study. Men of skill and wisdom were appointed to their offices and were supported in their research and study. They were not required to use their energy or their time in making a living. With these enviable subsidies, whose source was royalty, government, and men of wealth, scholars tried to systematize and advance knowledge, but in doing so they did not always retire from public view. Sometimes they invited the public, or specially interested people including students in the higher schools, to the museum or to the library or laboratory attached to it to view or to hear of new discoveries or interpretations of a scientific nature. At other times they offered their knowledge to the public in prepared lectures. In addition to providing scholars with facilities for study, the museum, although it was never a school in a complete sense, may well have generated the inspiration and a general model for higher education in later centuries. At the very least, it showed what dedicated scholars could do in an atmosphere which welcomed inquiring minds and offered them the liberty and the leisure to pursue their studies without interruption or interference.[27]

So Hellenistic higher education can be classified as cultural and professional. Its subject matter can be further classified into four divisions: rhetoric, philosophy, medicine, and science. The first two deserve a little more attention here.

Rhetoric. We have previously referred to the exceptional interest that educated men in the Hellenistic world took in rhetoric or oratory. Their attitude is the more surprising because oratory could not have been an art that had much real value at this time. When rhetoric flourished in Athens in the time of Isocrates, it was a useful tool for the citizen who engaged in public affairs. Now, however, political activity was an avenue almost completely closed to citizens. Nevertheless, rhetoric was studied as if nothing had happened to change the political climate, and it was studied with great care. Oratorical skill was as highly prized as ever. We can go further and claim that at no other time in the history of education have teachers tried to train their students in the art of oral expression with such formality and such thoroughness.

There were three parts to rhetoric: information, style, and delivery. Each was approached with meticulous care, although style, both in oral and written composition, ranked first in importance. Informational aspects of the rhetorical study could not be overlooked, for the orator needed a memory well stocked with knowledge; but it was usually assumed that secondary education had supplied the future orator with the bulk of his knowledge. In the realm of higher study, just the finishing touches were needed. By placing the major responsibility for the informational aspects of the study on the secondary school, rhetors were free to turn their attention to style and delivery. Style was cultivated by going to the tested classical orations and using them as models; delivery was perfected by following an exacting and detailed set of rules and by constant practice.[28]

Philosophy. Although philosophy could lay claim to a secure and permanent place in Hellenistic higher education, it did not have the popular appeal of rhetoric. Philosophy, despite Isocrates' definition of it as a practical study, could not have been popular because it was too demanding. By this time the various philosophical doctrines were highly

[27] H. L. Jones (ed.), *The Geography of Strabo*, Loeb Classical Library, Harvard University Press, Cambridge, Mass., 1932, vol. III, p. 35.
[28] The details of rhetoric as it was taught and studied in the Hellenistic age are interestingly portrayed in Marrou, *op. cit.*, pp. 197–205.

differentiated. A student could hardly be interested in philosophy without being aware of the four prominent contemporary schools of philosophical thought. These schools, which usually had their beginnings in Athens, had disciples throughout the Greek world. They were the Platonic, Aristotelian, Epicurean, and Stoic schools. Together they formed an imposing philosophical tradition, yet their systems of thought were never studied together. Each school had its own adherents, and each school attempted to recruit its own students.

When a student was finally recruited, he faced a formidable program. Probably philosophical teaching began with a few general ideas about the nature and value of philosophy. This first part of the philosophical course may have been nothing more than an advertisement, an attempt to attract students to the school. No philosophical commitment was necessary in order for students to enroll in the next part of the program, the survey or introductory courses. In these courses the teachers of philosophy tried to do two things: They made a sincere effort to instruct their students in the first mysteries of philosophical knowledge, and they tried to elicit from them zeal and devotion to the school of thought the teachers themselves embraced. One could say, then, that teachers of philosophy were not only teachers; they were missionaries too. Despite the philosophical proselytism which found its way into this stage of teaching, the real purpose of the instruction was exploratory. The next step took students directly to the school's doctrines. This was a rather straightforward presentation of the positions taken in the school's fundamental views, but the teaching did on occasion approach what we might call comparative philosophy. In other words, although the real objective was to teach a belief, this end was often more easily achieved by seeing the preferred belief in relation to other less desirable philosophical doctrines. Now students were led through the works of prominent members of the philosophical school of thought. For example, students in a Platonic school would read and discuss the dialogues of Plato. In addition to this rather formal phase of the philosophical curriculum (one which teachers would not tamper with), students were given the benefit of their teacher's own philosophical views. The branches of philosophical study that received most attention were logic, physics, and ethics.

SUMMARY

Hellenistic education provided classical (early Greek) education with its historical form. Had it not been for the Hellenistic period, it is doubtful that many of the classical views and practices in education would have been preserved. For the most part, what we today call classical education is really Hellenistic education.

The distinctive quality of Hellenistic man was his devotion to Greek culture. Preserving the glory and the traditions of classical Greece seemed more important to him than anything else. For this reason Hellenistic cities were much more conscious of the need for schools than the classic age had been. To some extent education at this time became a municipal concern. Schools were organized on all levels. Even physical education was not ignored. Elementary schools taught what elementary schools usually teach, although in this context we see music slipping out of the school. Secondary education—the grammar school—was totally different from what it had been in classical times. For the first time there was a definite commitment to literary studies, and the secondary school was given the assignment of carrying out this commitment. Higher education was served mainly by schools of rhetoric and philosophy. Of the two, the age prized the former more highly.

Questions and Exercises for Study and Discussion

1. Describe the main features of classical education. Where was it devised, or where did it evolve? In what ways principally was Hellenistic education related to the classical world? Why deal with Hellenistic education at all?
2. In what way did the educational theory that was formulated in the Hellenistic world differ from the theories of Plato and Aristotle? Was Hellenistic educational theory simply a corollary of their political-philosophical doctrines?
3. What was the political and military role of the inhabitant of the Hellenistic city? Did this role have any effect upon his education?
4. Study the athletic program of the gymnasium in the classical period. What program was followed in the Hellenistic gymnasium?
5. Classical elementary education had been literary, musical, and physical. How would you characterize elementary education in the Hellenistic schools?
6. What changes took place in secondary education after the appearance of Dionysius Thrax's *Grammar?* What did secondary school students study at that time?
7. Today the museum is a place where rare and valuable articles are preserved. What was the Hellenistic museum, and what was its relationship to the future of higher education?
8. Investigate and report on the content of rhetoric as a school subject. Why do you suppose rhetoric was assigned such an important place among the Greeks in the Hellenistic cities?
9. Describe the teaching of philosophy as part of Hellenistic higher education. Was philosophy intended to be a cultural or a practical study?
10. Teachers of rhetoric and philosophers often competed with each other.

Why should this have been? If you had been going to college back in this era, would you have chosen rhetorical or philosophical studies?

11. Discuss the status, security, preparation, and skill of Hellenistic schoolmasters.

12. What were the opportunities for education in Hellenistic cities? Did boys and girls attend schools? Were the schools coeducational? Were the experiences in the schools valuable? Was discipline severe?

5

Roman Educational Thought
and Practice

EDUCATION IN EARLY ROME

It is fairly common to speak of Roman education as an extension of
Hellenistic education. Such a generalization, although it has a good deal
to recommend it, nevertheless errs in a number of important respects.
It seems to forget that there was a purely Roman education in Rome
before the onset of Hellenism and long before the literary qualities of
classic culture, screened through the values of the Hellenistic world,
could have permeated Rome. The inauguration of education in Rome
coincided with the elemental organization of Roman society. Rome's
education could not have been a mere extension of the education in the
Hellenistic world. Yet we cannot deny that Rome was influenced tre-
mendously both by Greek and by Hellenistic educational thought and
practice. In considering this question of influence, we must not overlook
the complexity of man and the social institutions he creates, or try to
put the various thoughts and practices of education in a neat chronology.
In the context in which we are now working, we must keep two things
in mind: We must recognize that Roman education, though possibly
not Roman culture in a literary and aesthetic sense, was at one time
autonomous, and we must also realize that the major movements in
Roman education (movements recorded late in Rome's educational
history) had their inspiration in Hellenism or classicism. We shall not,
then, overemphasize the original autonomy, but we shall understand that
Roman education was never a mere duplication of Greek or Hellenistic
education. It could not have been, for it had its own traditions, and
usually, considering the Roman mentality and allegiances, there was no
other choice but to honor them.

129

What were these traditions and how did they manifest themselves in education? We are thinking now of a time between the sixth and the fourth centuries B.C.

First of all, the early Romans were a rural people. They lived on the land, and they tilled it themselves. Even the Roman aristocrats were devoted to agricultural and rural pursuits. Their language, their buildings, and their values reflected solid, common origins. They had few illusions about education. There was no talk of liberal education, because it would not have meant anything to anyone. These people were for the most part farmers, and they expected very little from education; all they asked was that it initiate the young into contemporary society, that is, give them an understanding of the Roman way of life. This may not have been as easy a commission as it sounds or as the Roman people thought it, but at least it was less complex than the demand sometimes made upon education by other ancient societies. For example, the Greeks in Athens could ask education to perform the initiatory function and at the same time attempt to attain important cultural and literary objectives. Early Roman life was neither complicated nor pretentious; the traditions were solid and clear; Romans looked not for great or heroic deeds but for easily recognized and fundamental virtues. Society was simple. Education could therefore be simple and clear and still perform a role that was vital and essential. Its principal constituent was custom or tradition, and the typical Roman of the early days never tired of confirming the belief that what was good enough for his ancestors was good enough for him and for his successors. This was a view from which Romans were not likely to stray.[1]

Such a philosophy of education—and who would doubt that it was a philosophy, albeit in a somewhat raw form—allows no place to the school. The relationship between theory and practice could be quite close and consistent; schools were not essential and were, therefore, rarely found. The family was the chief educational agency; it was the best, if not the only, school of the early Roman period.[2]

The Greeks, whose cultural and educational development was about two centuries ahead of the Romans in 600 B.C., could have taken a theoretical stand alongside the Romans on this matter of family education; but the Greeks hardly ever put their theory into practice. While emphasizing the importance of the family and its influence on the formation of youth, a Greek father could turn his son over to the care of a nurse or a pedagogue.[3] Greek philosophers could argue about the moral

[1] Aubery Gwynn, *Roman Education from Cicero to Quintilian,* Oxford University Press, New York, 1926, pp. 11–33.

[2] M. A. Cary, *A History of Rome down to the Reign of Constantine,* St. Martin's Press, New York, 1938, p. 14.

[3] See pp. 54–55.

training of children and insist that it was far too important a matter to be left to the schools; they could and did establish it as a family responsibility. Yet, in fact, the family seldom assumed the responsibility. For the Greek such questions were too often just academic. For the Roman family, education was not a matter of theory; it was a natural thing, to be realized in daily life.

While children were still quite young, they were under their mother's care. At this time and with the mother as the teacher and guide, the child's moral foundations were laid, and he was taught reading, writing, and elementary arithmetic. As the child grew older, the father's place in domestic education became more important; now he was his son's principal teacher.

For the boys—and here we come upon the most distinctive aspect of Roman education—there was nothing to replace the much maligned and often misunderstood technique of learning by doing. This was probably the most fundamental principle of learning in the early Roman period. The boy was educated by doing what his father did, by following in his father's footsteps. The phrase should be taken literally: Wherever a father was, there his son would be also.[4]

The Roman ideal of family education was never allowed to be put on an impractical level; it was confirmed in practice and clearly accepted in the performance of duty. The sense of duty knew no hills or valleys. Its constancy was typical of Roman character. Yet the emphasis on duty did not mean that these Roman fathers assumed prudish attitudes in the care and education of their sons. No doubt a Roman boy could be found at the banquet table or in the gaming room or at other places where more sensitively moral people would think a boy should not be, but when he was at these places he was with his father. Education and care were not equated with austerity or insistence upon self-denial. Education under these paternal auspices could be fun; it could even on occasion seem to be frivolous. But its result was always intended to be moral excellence and a high sense of duty. The father who could not achieve these objectives in the education of his sons found that society accepted few excuses. A father's standing in the community was affected by the impression his sons made.[5] No wonder, then, that the sense of duty was unwavering; its reinforcements were too imposing to ignore.

One more side of family education should not be overlooked, even though the modern age finds it somewhat difficult to understand or approve. It had to do with instilling pride in the family traditions along

[4] Thomas Woody, *Life and Education in Early Societies,* The Macmillan Company, New York, 1949, p. 515.

[5] H. W. Johnston, *The Private Life of the Romans,* Scott, Foresman and Company, Chicago, 1932, pp. 29–33.

with the family's good name. Of course, the idea of family was as broad as its physical make-up, and this was very broad. Such a far-reaching concept of family, however, added to, rather than detracted from, the bulk of lore concerning family backgrounds. Here we come very close to the Greek ideal of the noble deed, an ideal that played an important role in early Greek education. In Rome, however, the ideal was far more social than it had ever been in Greece; and this social feature, we may insist, was distinctively Latin. As far as educational practice was concerned, this objective of instilling reverence for the family and its traditions was achieved through example and precept. Every Roman family was eager to build a fine and even enviable family tradition or to add to one already founded. In this respect Roman families were usually quite successful. It becomes apparent, now, how Roman education, in spite of its negligible intellectual content, could have had such an important influence on the essential fabric of Roman society.

Education and the Public Man

Even though Roman education in its nascent years was not distinctively intellectual, it was not, on the other hand, nonintellectual or anti-intellectual. There was nothing conscious or planned about the relative absence of mental training. Its inconspicuousness seems natural enough when we remember that early Roman culture itself was not very intellectual. Nevertheless, education and culture were not narrowly familial. The family was the starting point, but the goal was the attainment of many virtues, one of which was absolute and unquestioning devotion to the community or the state.[6] This high goal could not be left to chance; it was the end to be achieved in public education.

One element in this preparation of a young man for public life was Roman law. Later in Roman history we see the evolution of a body and a philosophy of law and a system of legal education, but throughout most of Rome's early history law meant the laws of the Twelve Tables, and knowledge of the law meant memorizing the edicts. There is no need here for details on the laws of the Twelve Tables. Generally speaking, they were intended to regulate the social intercourse of the two major classes in Roman society, patricians and plebeians. Because these laws could claim to be an integral part of Rome's traditions and because a knowledge of law is an obvious and necessary part of the equipment of a public man, boys who were serious about a public career tried to achieve as complete an understanding as possible of the laws of the Twelve Tables. As to the laws themselves, the time of their origin is indefinite and has been ascribed to various periods from the early fifth century B.C. to the late third century B.C. Traditionally, the Tables were at first

[6] Gwynn, *op. cit.*, pp. 13–33.

ten in number; two were added later. It has been maintained also that the laws were really Greek and that they were borrowed by the Romans. None of these esoteric items need delay us. We are interested in the content of the education of young men who were preparing for public life; the Twelve Tables formed part of that content.[7]

The boy's preparation for public life was not neglected by his father (whose supervision of his son's education never really diminished), but when a boy became sixteen, several important changes took place in his training. Now he was to spend some time preparing for public life. This preparation was analogous to the general education program which a modern boy follows in college before he goes on to a professional school. The Roman boy was undergoing a kind of professional schooling when he received his proximate preparation for public life. Here are a few of the details of his training.

When a Roman boy was about sixteen, he went through a ceremony reminiscent of some tribal initiations. He was leaving the period of life when family education and the family's immediate control over him had been dominant. This departure seemed to deserve a ceremony. The boy took off his toga, which had marked him as a lad, and put on the *toga virilis*. Now a great future was open to him. He was a citizen and eligible for military service. At this stage young men found themselves on the threshold of public life. There was no question, of course, of a sixteen-year-old boy embarking immediately on a public career. Preparation was necessary. This preparation had two more or less formal phases, the first of which was intended to take about one year.

We have already said that the Roman father never really relinquished basic authority over the education of his children. But he could no longer occupy the center of the stage in the conduct of his son's education, and it was now normal for him to step aside. We discover that he was not moving out of the educational picture, but simply moving over to make room for some other guide who would help him prepare the boy for public life. The new figure was an old friend or possibly a relative.[8] In either case, he was a man of standing and sagacity. The program followed in this preparation for public life was set in a context that continued to respect the principle of learning by doing. Rather than follow his father—although it was not impossible for a father to prepare his son for public life at this stage of training—the boy now accompanied the public man who had agreed to take him under his wing. We are not too sure of all the details of this kind of apprenticeship. Where did the

[7] E. C. Moore, *The Story of Instruction: The Beginnings*, The Macmillan Company, New York, 1936, vol. I, pp. 313–318.
[8] H. I. Marrou, *A History of Education in Antiquity*, Sheed & Ward, Inc., New York, 1956, p. 233.

boy live? Were there any expenses involved in his training? These are but two examples of inquiry that indicate how little we know about this kind of education. It is true that one or another historical figure has left an account of what happened to him as he passed through this educational period, but the accounts can hardly be taken as typical.

The next step in the preparation of the public man was military service. Possibly other societies regarded the attainment of military status as tantamount to citizenship and civic stature, but the Romans apparently did not. A young man became a citizen at sixteen. The Roman boy did not have to wait until his tour of military service was over, as the Athenian youth did, to have citizenship conferred upon him. However, while Athenian citizens were public men in every way that society wanted them to be by virtue of their citizenship, the Roman boy followed a long route toward this objective.[9] One step along the way was military service.

Although a good deal of information is available on the Roman military system, the details of the discipline of arms as it pertained to public education are not well known. Distinction in military service, especially in war, was the most certain path to greatness and to positions of honor and power in the state, and we may assume that young men pursuing public education were exposed to a period of military service of somewhat indefinite duration, in which they learned warlike ability, physical steadfastness, discipline, unflinching courage, and obedience. With the termination of a tour of military service, a young man was ready to take his place as a public man.

After this preparatory period—long or short, as the case may be—the young Roman was on his own. All his ideals had been shaped in such a way that service to the state belonged among them.[10] But whether or not he became a public man or an exceptionally efficient public servant was up to him as well as to the fickleness of opportunity. In any event, the education we have described led young men up the ladder of public service. We cannot be certain that there were exact counterparts for this Roman practice in other early societies.

One more point ought to be mentioned in connection with education in early Rome. Whether boys were preparing for public life or looking forward only to the care of their own property, they were interested in physical fitness and sport. Of course the Romans liked to think that whatever games or events they participated in had practical worth, and usually their play was useful to them in some way. Still, it would be a mistake to think that the Romans were not sport-minded. Roman

[9] Woody, *op. cit.*, pp. 520–526.

[10] M. Rostovtzeff, *The Social and Economic History of the Roman Empire*, Oxford University Press, New York, 1957, p. 47.

children began with the usual games that all youngsters play, and as they grew older they took part in ball games, wrestled, ran, jumped, hunted, and rode horseback. Some of these sports were conducive to the skills needed in military activities, it is true, but we can suppose that sport was sometimes pursued simply for the sheer enjoyment of it.

Swimming was almost as important as walking; every Roman boy or girl knew how to swim. Dancing and music, though chiefly associated with religious cults and funeral processions, could be considered enjoyable in themselves. The Romans, however (and this may be why they are often thought to have forsaken sport), refused to give much public attention to competitive games; for them recreation was mainly a private matter. Despite this firmly held view, certain public games can be traced back to a very early period in Roman history. Sport in Rome was not essentially different from what it was in Greece, although the Romans had no gymnasia, and in sporting events they would not expose their bodies.

LATER ROMAN EDUCATION

Built on the secure foundation of Roman tradition, later Roman education never forgot its past. This means that although the native traditions may have become pretty thoroughly interspersed with Greek influence and Roman innovation, they were still occupying an essential directive function. Romans did not want to betray their past. Yet Rome was in no position either socially or psychologically to escape the cultural influences that were appearing on her borders. Even had she wanted to, she could not afford to ignore them. Of these influences, along with a variety of internal circumstances that pleaded for change and updating, the most pervasive, permanent, and effective emanated from Hellenistic Greece.[11] Despite an indigenous teaching tradition, Roman education underwent drastic changes, inspired by Greek models. And despite the existence of an autonomous and rural culture in early Rome, before this distinctive culture could be brought into reality and Rome thus extricated from barbarism, all kinds of classical and Hellenistic influences had descended on her.[12]

Perhaps the picture of Hellenistic influences descending on Rome is not as accurate as it should be. What actually happened was that the

[11] It should be remarked here that the Romans were not trying to isolate themselves from the world around them. They were already committed to extending their sphere of authority, and in attempting to do so, they were brought in contact with a variety of cultures, many of which seemed to them to be superior to their own. Rome's political, military, and economic history, however, lies outside the ambit of this book.

[12] Gwynn, *op. cit.*, pp. 34–69.

Roman Empire was being extended. With each new acquisition of territory, Rome met with cultural forces that affected her deeply. Undoubtedly a number of stages of Greek influence could be isolated, but their enumeration and analysis belong to other histories, and we shall content ourselves here with the conclusion that when Greater Greece surrendered to Rome at Tarentum in 272 B.C., and when Rome became a bilingual empire with the annexation of Greece and other Macedonian and Asiatic provinces, these outside influences really began to be effective.[13] This is the beginning of a period of adaptation; it marks also the first steps in a Roman adoption of Greek culture.

Greek Influence on Roman Education

Important and interesting as they are, cultural evolutions cannot be traced in this book. We want to deal with only one part of that immense subject—educational evolution. When Greece made her educational conquest of Rome, both the content and the form of Roman education were changed in a number of important respects.

While remembering that Greek influence may always have had some role to play in Roman education, we must look for a really decisive influence. Perhaps we shall find it in the Greek slaves who were brought to Rome and made teachers. The earliest example of this custom is to be found in the teaching of Livius Andronicus, a Greek captured at Tarentum, who was finally emancipated after he had finished teaching his Roman master's children. With his freedom secured, he stayed in Rome and for the next sixty-five years functioned as a teacher and writer.[14]

This begins a strange and often contradictory period in Roman education. Though old customs and traditions were still an object of reverence, the new education was sought with eagerness and enthusiasm. Not enough teachers of Greek could be found. Greeks captured by the Romans had nothing to fear now. Whether or not they were teachers or might possibly become effective teachers, they were highly prized. Greeks brought exceptional prices in the slave market. However, not all Greek teachers were slaves. Some free Greeks, seeing the enormous opportunities open to them in Rome, simply immigrated and accepted a teacher's role.

Why did the Romans want Greeks for their teachers? First of all, we must remember that Rome could boast of little in the way of a literary tradition. But a more complete answer is to be found in what may be called a Roman educational awakening; tired of being thought bar-

[13] Theodor Mommsen, *The History of Rome,* Charles Scribner's Sons, New York, 1903, vol. III, p. 136.
[14] *Ibid.*

barians, Romans wanted, more than anything else, to learn Greek. And yet even while this enthusiasm was being displayed, there were elements in Rome who wanted nothing to do with Greek-inspired education. Whenever they gained the power to do so, they proscribed by law not only the teaching of Greek but the teaching activities of Greeks in Rome.[15]

Elementary Education

Though, as we have already said, Roman education was probably always affected to a certain degree by Greek models, apparently a point was reached in Roman educational history when the Greek influence became decisive. Even then Rome tried to be loyal to her past, and rather than let schools of a Greek type dominate all of education, she developed a plan whereby dual systems of schools were organized. If the systems were not always distinct, they were at least responsible for schools in which two educational objectives were accepted. Alongside Roman schools in which Latin was taught and which were committed to the traditional Roman values, were the Greek schools. What we have now in historical focus is really a dual system—one Greek and one Latin. The development of dual systems was evidently slow, so slow, in fact, that all of the levels of education may not have been touched by the movement.

Elementary schools in Rome, which must have come into existence around the seventh century B.C., were caught up in the whirl of Greek influence before they could get a good start on their own. Reading and writing—the essentials of literary training—were skills that had come indirectly from the Greeks.[16] This web of direct and indirect inheritance that was woven around elementary education in Rome, though it brought with it the traditions of a great culture, did not succeed in making elementary schools popular institutions,[17] although by the third century A.D. they could be found throughout the Empire. It may have taken three hundred years before they were fully accepted as part of Roman life.

What were Roman elementary schools like, and what did they teach? First of all we might mention that the term used by the Romans to designate an elementary school was *ludus*. Literally *ludus* meant sport, play, or game, but it would hardly be correct to assume that the boys and girls who attended Roman *ludi* were there to play games. Rome had a long tradition of elementary literary and reckoning instruction; mothers had taught children their letters and their sums long before elementary

[15] Woody, *op. cit.*, p. 575.

[16] *Ibid.*, pp. 477–482.

[17] A. S. Wilkins, *Roman Education*, Cambridge University Press, New York, 1914, p. 43.

education was institutionalized. This was important work, for which the mother was praised in those early years; it was no less important now when the teacher was the *litterator* rather than the mother.

The teacher, the *litterator*, was responsible for teaching reading, writing, and calculation in the school. Moral education, too, formerly the special prerogative of mothers and fathers, now seemed to be in the hands of the pedagogue. We have met the pedagogue before when he accompanied Greek boys to and from school; and now, largely because of the influence of Greece on Rome, we meet him again. If the Roman family had not actually relinquished its responsibility for the moral formation of children, it had at least delegated this important duty to the pedagogue. Whatever his relationship to the family, whether slave, servant, or trusted freeman, the pedagogue had at least a tangential relationship to elementary education, for he was concerned with his charge's manners and morals.

Elementary schooling began when boys and girls were about seven years old and lasted until they were about twelve. The site of the school was a porch or a booth, and no great effort was made apparently to isolate the school from the traffic and distractions of everyday life. The discipline of the school was such that the young scholar had better not permit the outside world to distract him from his schoolwork. The first elementary schools were not well equipped, and books, maps, handbooks, etc., were not used. In the elementary schools of the Republic, however, books are said to have been plentiful. Thus, we have a dim view of the Roman elementary school with the teacher on his raised platform and the students sitting on the floor. They were ready to begin the work of the school day, which consisted of reading, writing, and elementary calculation. Neither the techniques employed in teaching these subjects nor the content of the subjects themselves were sufficiently distinctive to command our further attention.

Secondary Education

Boys and girls who had finished with the *ludi magister* in the elementary school and who were privileged to aspire to secondary schooling enrolled in the school of the *grammaticus*. Here a strange and probably new literary world unfolded for them. This was a grammer school, and in its essentials it did not differ from the grammar schools of the Hellenistic world.[18]

The school the youngsters entered now differed in some important respects from the schools with which Roman boys and girls presumably were familiar. There was still no separate building, but the room in which classes were kept had an academic appearance. Even the teacher

[18] Woody, *op. cit.*, p. 581 ff.

—the *grammaticus*—wore a cloak whose attractive ornamentation added some color to the educational setting. Unfortunately the teacher had to take his compensations where he could find them; an ornamented cloak was one of them, and there were very few others. He was not well paid. Undoubtedly he was better off than the elementary teacher both in his income and his place in society. Yet his income was not appreciably greater than that of a tradesman, if, in fact, it was as great. To add insult to financial instability, society did not accept him, and parents did not trust him. The age-old question rears its head again: How is society to obtain and keep the services of good, effective, and trustworthy teachers if it refuses to reward them? Without just rewards for character if not for quality, too many secondary school teachers lacked the stature to command respect. And because parents did not respect these teachers, they did not bother about being prompt in paying them the fees they owed. Teachers were almost powerless to collect the money due them.

Such conditions are, of course, always deplorable wherever they are found. Yet it is possible to understand why the Romans may not have thought very much of their elementary teachers. They demanded very little from them and, of course, did not ask such teachers to have any academic or scholarly qualifications. Anyone could have been an elementary school teacher. But could the same be said of the *grammaticus?* Could anyone do what he did? It was not enough for him to know how to read and to be able to compute in whole numbers and fractions. The secondary school teacher had to know grammar and literature. Any able teacher had to have some kind of academic background, for the content of the grammarian's teaching was something that had to be learned; it did not come from living. There was a certain inconsistency in seeing a Roman parent send his child to school, eager to have the child introduced to learning and culture, prizing them both highly, and yet refusing to value in any proper or realistic manner the work of the *grammaticus.*

We must always remember that there was no such thing as secondary education in Rome before the Greek slave-teachers brought a content to form it. Secondary education in Rome was Greek, and consisted largely of the study of the Greek classics. And if Roman youth were to study Homer and other accepted Greek authors, it is easy to see why schools were established for learning the Greek language.

Yet what appeared at first to be a decisive victory for a secondary education of a Greek type was subject to some cultural and educational annotation. Greek classics were translated into Latin. Livius Andronicus translated the *Odyssey*—in about the year 250 B.C., it is said—to begin a secondary education of a Latin type.[19] Homer's epics were not a national

[19] Woody, *op. cit.*, p. 608; W. C. Lawton, *An Introduction to Classical Latin Literature*, Charles Scribner's Sons, New York, 1904, p. 19.

literature for the Romans; yet their hesitation in accepting them as a fixed content for secondary education could be moderated somewhat, because now, at least, the literature was in their own language. If they had had to depend on a national literature for the rise of secondary education, then Roman secondary schools would have been delayed for another century. Yet no one can be sure that this employment of Greek literature translated into Latin did not retard the growth of Latin literature. As it was, when Virgil and Horace and other Latin writers appeared on the scene, the system of Latin secondary schools was ready to provide Roman secondary schools with an authentic Latin literature. Even then, secondary education in Rome did not become exclusively Latin. The dual approach was still accepted, and Greek literature was still studied.

The other side of secondary education—grammar—was a little slower than literature in making its Roman debut. Of course literature had a long head start on grammar. The former began with Homer; the latter waited for Dionysius Thrax. Dionysius was known in Rome very shortly after his work on grammar appeared, and was still as closely studied in Rome at the time of Virgil and Horace as he had been in the Hellenistic grammar schools. Although the grammar of Dionysius was not studied in Greek—it had been translated into Latin by Varro (116–27 B.C.)—in its essentials it was Greek grammar, and it was not accompanied by any transition to strictly Latin teaching. The great grammatical works of Donatus, Servius, and Priscian followed the grammatical path that Dionysius had blazed. The first textbook on Latin grammar, written by Remmius Palaemon, did not appear until the first century.[20]

When grammar seemed unreal, as it often did, literature made some effort to rescue learning from the pedantry into which grammar led it and to put it in a Roman, lifelike context. This was possible only after Rome had obtained a literary tradition and a literary content of its own, for before this was accomplished the Greek classics that were studied in the original or in translation were the only literature worthy of the name. For understandable reasons the Romans were most anxious to have their own literature. And once they had a literature of their own, they were impatient to study it, that is, to get it into the school's curriculum. So Latin works became part of the secondary school literary study even during the lifetime of their authors. This was an extremely unconventional innovation. Even in our own day, the serious study of living authors seems to be a bit unorthodox or unseemly. Because the Romans were thus disposed to take their Latin literature where they found it, there was a good deal of variety in the content and quality of the literary pieces that found their way into the schools. Yet what began

[20] Frederick Eby and Charles F. Arrowood, *The History and Philosophy of Education: Ancient and Medieval*, Prentice-Hall, Inc., Englewood Cliffs, N.J., 1940, p. 541.

as an ephemeral content did not remain in a state of flux. The giants in Roman literature began to assume their proper places, according to their tremendous literary strengths, and in time we find Virgil, Terence, Sallust, and Cicero the accepted and immovable authors of the Latin classics. It was at this point that the evolution of Latin literature came to a halt. From this point on, humanistic education chose to look backward and defended the assumption that the content of these classics could never be improved upon; it could only be imitated.

Literary scholarship and the science of grammar were approached among the Romans much as they had been among the Hellenistic teachers and students. Their content was so little changed that we need only refer the reader to the previous chapter, where the studies in the Hellenistic grammar schools were discussed. One could hardly find a more apt characterization of the motives behind grammatical teaching and learning than the one made of them by Marrou: "a lust for learning," a dedication and devotion to erudition itself and for its own sake.[21]

Higher Education

The first steps in higher education were taken with Greek models in mind. For a long time much of higher education in Rome remained quite thoroughly Greek in its content and objectives. This was especially true of philosophy and science. Neither ever really became Latin. Latin rhetoric, though somewhat different from Greek, was unquestionably based on Greek rhetoric. The difference, nevertheless, is important. Where Greek rhetoric was conservative and completely content to continue its own teaching of rules and academic ritual, Latin rhetoric was more practical; it tried to find its problems and its questions in the real social and political world.

In medical education the Romans were, for years, dominated by the Greek medical inheritance. In later Rome medical teaching became more practical and more distinctively Roman. The updating of medical knowledge and technique tended to leave Greece in the past. Besides modernization in professional studies, the Romans were responsible for the development of a new professional study—law—and for the general upgrading of technical or utilitarian higher education.

Dualism in Roman Education: Adding to the Classical Tradition

What began as a commitment to dualism in education—one system of schools for Latin education and another system of schools for Greek—tapered off in time to the point where schools accepted a dual function: One part of this function was achieved by teaching Latin; the other was

[21] Marrou, *op. cit.*, p. 281.

attained by teaching Greek.[22] Some emphasis should be given to the compromise, because in accepting this dual function Roman schools began what has since been regarded as real classical teaching. In other words, the classical inheritance was contained in and communicated by both Latin and Greek. The man who was fully educated would know both Latin and Greek.

This was an attitude which would come to be associated with classical teaching of a later period; it was not necessarily a natural outgrowth of classical thought, and it was obviously not a part of classical method. As a matter of fact, it is almost impossible to imagine the Hellenistic Greeks using Latin as a cultural instrument. They regarded Latin as inferior, not only because it was inadequate for communicating subtle scientific and philosophical ideas, but because it had no respectable cultural or literary traditions behind it. Only in one area of study had the Greeks accepted Latin; this was in the study of law, but law was hardly ever regarded as a study with cultural value. We know how the Greeks defined the word *barbarian;* their inflexible attitude as to the intrinsic superiority of the Greek language never changed. Bilingual classicism did not originate in Greek lands, and it never had Greek approval.

Rome took the heart of classical education and without changing it in any essential respects, preserved and transmitted this education to later generations. With Rome the classical influences became a glorious and revered heritage. How did this happen?

As Roman political influence was dispersed more and more widely, it became necessary for Roman officials to know many languages. In time most of these officials, who had to be prepared to go anywhere in the service of the Empire, achieved considerable fluency in Greek. There were obviously practical reasons for having Greek taught in the schools. But they were not the only or the real reasons. Romans were moving up in the world. They could look at their magnificent political and military accomplishments with approval. Where did Rome have a peer? Was beaten Greece, a country without military power or political influence, really Rome's equal? The practical-minded Roman could see that Greece was a conquered land, but when the Romans came in contact with the people, it was evident to them that the Greeks had a culture and a view of the world which the Romans could not claim. Even their language was a vehicle which could convey thought far better than the Roman tongue could. This seeming superiority of Greek gave the proud Romans feelings of inferiority with respect to their own language. As far as literature was concerned, they knew there was no argument. What Roman writer had Homer's stature?

[22] S. S. Laurie, *Historical Survey of Pre-Christian Education,* Longmans, Green & Co., Inc., New York, 1895, p. 338.

If the Romans thought so highly of Greek, why didn't they simply adopt it as their own language? Such a question is too complex to answer here. Of course, it would have been entirely impractical to forsake Latin in favor of Greek. At least half of the Roman Empire was Latin. Romans had many allegiances, one of which was to their own language. Latin was the official language in most of the Empire, and was used in public documents and official proceedings. It is true that the public officer who could meet the people in every corner of the Empire and converse with them in their own language was equipped for political effectiveness. This was a clever technique; but the official's linguistic skill was never an acknowledgment that any other language could take the place of Latin.

Multilingualism was not found frequently in Rome, but bilingualism was common. Its evolution began with a political or administrative motive and finally became a matter of cultural integration. During a time in Rome, marked out roughly by Cicero's lifetime (100–43 B.C.), this cultural integration was at its climax. The two languages seemed to be entirely natural tools in the hands of an educated man. Cicero could write and speak and think in Greek as easily and as naturally as in Latin. And Cicero's excellence may well represent the apogee of this integration to which we refer. Before Cicero, culture was so tied to Greece that the Greek language was indispensable. Only a fool would claim to be an educated man unless he had all of the classical tools, and the classical tools were still Greek.

Virgil and Horace changed this attitude. Roman education never ceased to be bilingual, because it was believed that there was something culturally superior about having a second language, and also, perhaps, because the Romans, like us, used another language to help in learning their own. But it was no longer necessary to study Greek literature in Greek and the new Latin literature in Latin. Translations were not necessary either; Latin literature was enough. Greek began to decline.[23]

The decline of Greek is evident after the time of Cicero. The Greek culture that seemed so natural to Cicero became for his successors little more than affectation. But the evidence of a decline does not explain it. Latin was more and more valued as a means of communication, and by the time the Christian Church adopted Latin as its official language, probably sometime in the early third century, the day of Greek had pretty well passed. Greek never recovered its position of superiority.[24]

---

[23] Theodore J. Haarhoff, *Schools of Ancient Gaul: A Study of Pagan and Christian Schools in the Last Century of the Western Empire,* Oxford University Press, New York, 1920, pp. 230–231.

[24] On this whole issue of bilingualism in Rome, see Marrou, *op. cit.,* pp. 255 ff.; and Rostovtzeff, *op. cit.,* pp. 33, 113, 191, 211.

ROME AND THE FUTURE OF EDUCATION

We are prone to yield to the temptation to look for ways in which Rome made original contributions to culture and learning, for generally speaking, we find it hard to separate high historical significance and creativity. Rome, however, was remarkably uncreative. The fact in no way destroys or even minimizes her historical worth. In spite of our categorical statement, we should not make the mistake of insisting that the Romans were never able to create anything. This would be a monstrous claim, and under no circumstances could it be justified. In culturally significant areas, however, though Rome was a great assimilator of culture and a great agent in spreading the culture she absorbed from others, she was not creative.

Rome excelled in administration. As she pushed her military authority into the Alexandrian world, she adopted and adapted. Rome was precocious, and what she learned so quickly and so easily she retained in her national memory. When she turned to other lands to conquer, she spread the culture she had absorbed. Although this appears now to have been a simple and easily executed policy of Romanization, it was really quite difficult. Even with the genius of Roman organization and executive ability, complete Romanization of "barbarian" lands was impossible. In the sense that success is a relative thing, the Romans succeeded, that is, they won more often than they lost. Yet they were not even successful in having Latin adopted as the general language of communication in all of the lands over which their jurisdiction reigned. This goal was never fully achieved, although the Christian Church came closer to establishing Latin as a universal language than imperial Rome ever did.

The Roman schools of which we have spoken above were found in Rome proper. In republican days they were rarely found outside the city of Rome. The Empire enlarged their scope, but the Empire never succeeded or hoped to succeed in establishing a complete system of Roman schools everywhere in imperial Rome. Although the influence of Rome, both political and cultural, was ubiquitous in the Empire, formal education was not. Yet some schools could be found in every part of the Roman world, and by the time educationally minded emperors came into power in Rome, the Empire was ready for their policy of distributing education more generously throughout its extent.

In the early years, the Roman state had what we may call a laissez-faire policy with respect to education. This policy did not change materially until the Empire came into being. Hellenistic Greeks thought they saw the first signs of Rome's barbarism in her apparent indifference to education, but in this matter they read signs poorly. Although Rome had no official policy of providing for education, the state's laxity in establishing schools did not mean that the Romans did not value education. If we may depart a little from our main theme here, we can call attention to the cultural blindness of the Hellenistic Greeks and the weakness they shared with many states—and individuals—in interpreting all values in the light of their own and in evaluating all social functions by the part they played in them. Had the Hellenistic world been only a little more alert, it would have seen that classical Greece pursued the same noninterventionist policy in education that republican Rome accepted.

Throughout a great part of Rome's history, she had neither a plan for compulsory education nor a system of schools supported by the state. From time to time a man of some importance and wealth would help establish a school and prevail upon the public treasury to share some of the cost with him. But a few schools of this type do not make a system and would not justify the conclusion that the Roman state had entered the business of education. Late in the Republic, the state became more active in encouraging education. Under Augustus education was given even further encouragement: In a decree that proclaimed the banishment of all foreigners from Rome, teachers and physicians were made exceptions. Vespasian, though he had banished philosophers from Rome, lent his support to rhetoricians and established a professorship of rhetoric, to which the first appointee was the great Quintilian. Besides, the emperors built libraries and collected books; they subsidized teachers and exempted them from taxation and military service; and finally they endowed chairs of teaching outside Rome and made grants to the various cities and towns to establish schools.

In return for its generosity, the Roman state demanded considerable control over education. When teachers' salaries were paid from the public treasury, the emperor wanted his agents to have a decisive voice in appointing teachers; when teachers of rhetoric and philosophy were awarded honors and money, the emperors wanted them to sacrifice some of their freedom of thought and liberty of expression. Thus public or state assistance to teachers and schools was not an unmixed blessing; control followed the funds. Eventually, because state control over education in Rome moved steadily forward, the state assumed that it could suspend, direct, or completely proscribe all teaching whenever it saw fit. Two emperors, Theodosius and Valentinian, forbade the opening of schools without the state's prior approval, and Justinian issued his notorious edict in A.D. 529, closing the schools of philosophy and law in Athens and all higher schools in Rome, save those engaged in the teaching of law.

EDUCATIONAL THEORY IN ROME

Every culture, when it begins to want schools to transmit its most essential elements, formulates educational policies that are intended to give direction to these schools. This is the initial point of contact for educational theory and educational policy. Yet educational theory, conceived in somewhat broader terms than school policies, must exist in every culture long before schools come into existence. This was true in Rome. Basic educational theory was very old, and spelling out of the theory was the work of many minds. Still Romans did not distinguish themselves in theoretical areas, and education was no exception; the list of Roman educational theorists, though respectable, is not long. In a sense, Rome had only one finished and fully accomplished educator, Quintilian, but she produced two educational theorists who made an impression on education that was deeper and more permanent than that of any other two figures in all of Western history: Cicero and Quintilian.

Marcus Tullius Cicero (106–43 B.C.*)*

Marcus Tullius Cicero exerted a greater influence upon Roman education during the latter part of the Republic than any other man of his time. He was Rome's leading orator and statesman. He was exceptionally proficient both in rhetoric and philosophy, and wrote much on those subjects as well as on politics and education. Cicero was not an educator. Even his educational writings did not express the point of view of an expert in the subject, but sprang from a knowledge of the fundamental place that education must occupy in society and of the demands that society makes on educated men. Thus *De Oratore* (The Orator), in which most of his educational views are to be found, is an expression of the ideas of an educated man about the purposes and methods of a system of education through which he himself had passed; it is an expression, moreover, of his convictions as to education's practical results. His writings on education are often in the nature of reflections, and they should not be taken as descriptive accounts of the conduct of the schools during this period of Roman history.

Cicero was the son of a Roman knight. His family was relatively new. In Rome he received an excellent education in Greek rhetoric and was also well educated in law. At seventeen he served in the army. He became a pleader in the courts at twenty-five, but ill health forced him to retire from this line of work for two years. During this period of inactivity he studied philosophy in Rhodes and Athens, then returned to Rome and resumed his legal career. He became the greatest of Roman orators and one of the outstanding writers of the golden age of Roman literature. His influence is felt even today.

De Oratore, published in 55 B.C., contained the basic principles which Cicero felt were necessary for an orator's education. He distinguished between technical training and general education, or liberal culture. He insisted that the orator needed a broad, well-rounded, and general education in the liberal arts as a basis for the higher professional education of oratory. This liberal education was also considered necessary for success in professional and public life.

The branches of study that he included in this well-rounded education were grammar, literature, logic, geometry, astronomy, music, physics, history, civil law, philosophy, and rhetoric. Cicero claimed that philosophy gave substance to rhetoric. He was the first Roman theorist to endorse history as a valuable study, especially national history. He wrote that "if an orator knew not history, he remained always a child." A well-rounded education should be supplemented with wide experience, upon which the orator could always draw. In addition, it was Cicero's constant claim that the purpose of study was for usefulness in public and private life and not for knowledge alone.[25]

Marcus Fabius Quintilianus (A.D. 35–97)

Quintilian was born in Calagurris in Spain about A.D. 35. He was educated as a public man in Rome and returned to his native Spain when he was about twenty-five years old. In Spain he practiced the arts of oratory. About the year 68 he was invited to return to Rome, where he acted as a pleader in the courts and as a teacher of rhetoric, and in both activities enjoyed more than usual success. In A.D. 76, when Vespasian arranged for teachers of rhetoric to receive salaries from the public treasury, Quintilian became a public teacher. He retired from teaching about the year 88, and devoted himself to study and writing. In A.D. 96 he published his famous book on the education of an orator, *Institutio Oratoria* (Institutes of Oratory). Quintilian was able to write from his eminent position as Rome's most cultured and successful teacher with more than twenty years' experience. His theories on education were responsible for setting the pattern that Latin grammar schools followed for centuries.

Institutio Oratoria consists of twelve books. The greater part of the work is a technical discussion of rhetoric and the role that rhetoric should occupy in secondary and higher education. The goal of this kind of education was the making of an orator, a public man, and Quintilian's treatise was intended to give direction to schools and schoolmasters for educating young men for oratory. Book I and Book II are devoted to details of educational methods, content, and organization of schools.

---

[25] For more extensive treatment of Cicero's place in Roman education, see Gwynn, *op. cit.;* Wilkins, *op. cit.;* Woody, *op. cit.;* and Eby and Arrowood, *op. cit.*

Books III through VII are concerned with the study of the rhetorical device of invention. Books VIII through XI contain Quintilian's views on elocution, memory, and pronunciation. Book X contains what is probably the first formal list of "great books." Book XII turns its attention to the orator himself and asks what kind of person he should be and what moral stature he should have. Considering both the breadth and the attention to detail of Quintilian's *Institutes* it is not surprising that this work came to be the final and standard book on the theory and practice of Roman oratory, and that it is universally recognized as the most elaborate and most complete treatise on Roman education ever written.

Quintilian's general concept of education is the same as Cicero's; both maintained that the aim of education is to produce the orator. In Cicero Quintilian honored Rome's greatest orator and education's best model. The education described by Quintilian is a formal and institutionalized process. Instruction was to be given in school, preferably in public schools, and the content of this kind of education was to be largely grammatical and rhetorical.

According to Quintilian, the orator should be a good man. He should be a master of the liberal arts and skillful in the art of speaking. The public interest should be his special interest and he should seek to serve it at all times. The orator was defined as "a good man skilled in speaking."

The following is a summary of the main educational ideas expressed by Quintilian: He believed that the great object of instruction was to create or stimulate the student's mental activity. Teaching had to be accommodated to the ability of the student. Quintilian recognized the fact of individual differences, and he advised teachers to adjust their methods and the forms of study according to the special qualities of the students. Knowledge could not be acquired easily, and it could hardly be acquired at all unless the process of acquisition was logical. Education's main function was to correct the weak points of nature. Quintilian never tired of advising that the first years of life were the foundational years and therefore the most important. During these early years, he said, all kinds of mental work must take the form of amusement. Young children learn with ease, and the whole course of their education will be determined by what is done in their infant years. Therefore the very best teachers should be assigned to the education of the young. On this lower level especially, but perhaps on all levels as well, a variety of subjects should be taught simultaneously and not in succession. Variety in study, this great Roman teacher argued, promoted activity; and the capacity of the young for congenial work, he wrote, is very large. At the same time, since relaxation and amusement are necessary, periods for play and rest are essential. During these noninstructional periods a great deal can be learned about the child by observing him. Quintilian always advised against corporal punishment. He felt that it disgraced the student and that it did not lead him toward greater performance. The true motives for good work are competition, commendation, affection for the teacher, and interest aroused by the subject itself. These were the things that were to be attended to, not fear and punishment. The usual child, Quintilian maintained, is eager for knowledge; he is intelligent and curious about the world in which he lives. It is the fault of the teacher if he loses this interest or this curiosity. Public education (by which Quintilian meant education in common) is better than private education (by which he meant tutorial arrangements), and large classes of students stimulate both teachers and students to do better work. The best teachers, he said, prefer to teach large groups of students. In such public teaching the students learn from one another and develop friendships which are lifelong.

Quintilian cautioned teachers about overteaching, about needlessly intervening between the student and his studies. He noted that attainment is always lower than the goal aimed at, and for this reason he advised all educators to set their goals very high. As far as teachers themselves were concerned, he wrote: Ability and learning are desirable on all levels; teachers must be strictly moral; they must be friendly, clear, patient, generous, and ready to give praise.

The surest sign of a child's ability is the power of his memory. The next is his power of imitation. Quintilian advised that students be spurred on by praise, for success delighted them, and failure made them lose their drive for learning. The student must be made to realize that revision of written work is every bit as important to the excellence of the final copy as the initial steps in writing.

Finally, we may say a word about the curriculum Quintilian proposed for the schools that would educate orators. Since this curriculum is not novel, we need only say that it would consist of the following: (elementary) correct speech, writing, reading, Greek grammar, Latin grammar; (secondary) correct speaking, literature and literary criticism, astronomy, philosophy, geometry, music; (higher) literature, history, composition, rhetoric, logic, ethics.[26]

SUMMARY

Rome had a teaching tradition of her own. During the early years of Roman education, probably before the third century B.C., the practical

[26] For Quintilian's educational views the student should consult the *Institutes of Oratory*. One of the finest commentaries on Quintilian's educational plan is W. M. Smail, *Quintilian on Education*, Oxford University Press, New York, 1938.

orientation of the Romans comes through quite clearly. Their education was organized in such a way that young people would be prepared to take their place in society. Since literary achievements were not generally recognized in society, they found little recognition in the educational program. During this early period the child—usually a boy—was trained or educated first by his mother, then by his father, and finally by a relative of position or a public man of trust. Then he fulfilled his debt of military service to the state. By that time he was a citizen, and he was well on his way to becoming a public man.

This kind of education was changed somewhat when the Greek influence began to invade Rome. The change was not so drastic, however, that it did away with archaic practices. Rather, it added something to the Roman educational model that was not there before. What was added was the Greek school. Thus, side by side, the Roman school and the Greek school enjoyed the confidence and the patronage of the Romans.

Finally, the Greek educational influences became so strong and the parallel system of schools so unwieldy that the Romans adopted an educational organization that provided for only one school, which offered both Greek and Latin studies. At first the Greek studies predominated because of the greater reputation of Greek literature. Yet when Latin literature (Virgil, Horace, Cicero) gained status, its place in the school was equal to that of Greek literature.

In the later period the Romans took the educational organization and program of the Hellenistic Greeks, adapted them somewhat to their own needs, and continued that type of education in a system of schools that lasted as long as the Roman Empire lasted. When the Empire died, the schools died with it.

Rome's chief importance in the history of education may be that she preserved the education of the Greek and Hellenistic worlds and spread it throughout the Greek-Roman world.

Questions and Exercises for Study and Discussion

1. Describe Roman education before it was affected by Greek models. Was Roman education at any time completely independent of Greek education?
2. Who were the teachers of youth in early Rome? Did the Romans have pedagogues? If they did, was their position a sign of Greek influence?
3. Much has been made of the role of the Roman father in the education of his son. Is this emphasis justified? Do you think the father's influence in education had good or bad results?
4. What were the laws of the Twelve Tables and how were they related to education?
5. Describe the steps through which a boy would go if he wanted to prepare for public life. Evaluate this kind of education.

6. Why were Romans interested in Greek culture? Did they have a culture of their own? Did the Romans have a national Latin literature?
7. Did Romans share the Greek attitude concerning barbarism? Why did Romans become bilingual?
8. Who was Livius Andronicus and what role does he occupy in Roman secondary education?
9. In later Rome—late Republic and early Empire—the pattern for education showed signs of Greek and Hellenistic influences. Discuss these influences.
10. Did the Roman state and its emperors have any interest in education? Discuss the relationship between education and the state in Rome.
11. Was Cicero's impress on education significant during his lifetime? What place would you assign to Cicero in the history of education? Read some of Cicero's *The Orator* and compare its tone and content with the first books of Quintilian's *Education of the Orator*.
12. Who was Quintilian and why is he still remembered in a history of teaching and learning?

6

Early Christian Education

THE MEANING OF CHRISTIAN EDUCATION

This chapter should begin by calling attention to the distinction between a Christian education and a Christian school. During the first three or four centuries of Christianity, such a distinction was no mere literary figure of speech. In fact, during the first three centuries after Christ there was no such thing as a Christian school. There were schools that were attended by Christian boys and girls, schools in which Christians taught, and schools—if we may call them that—in which prospective Christians were prepared for entrance into the Church. But none of these, individually or together, fulfilled the modern sense of the word school.

The early Church did not have schools of its own. One reason was that the Church did not want them, either because she did not think they were important or because she did not have the time or the energy to look after them. The Church regarded her mission as being on a level that was certainly supraschool and maybe even supraeducational. That this was a general view is not debatable, nor is there any real dispute as to why it was held: Christians did not expect the world to last very long. Naturally they were much concerned with putting first things first. In spite of this, they were laying foundations for Christian education in teaching the principal Christian message. But where was the chief work being done in laying these foundations?

First and foremost, the child's Christian formation was a parental responsibility. The apostolic message is clear on this point. It is unnecessary to refer to anything more than the admonitions of St. Paul to convince the reader that this was the general Christian position.[1]

[1] For example, see Eph. 6: 4; Col. 3: 21.

The family was the first and possibly the best instrument for inculcating Christian education, and it was the natural place for moral and religious teaching to begin. In Roman lands (and of course the Church made some of its greatest progress in areas where the jurisdiction of Rome was felt) this Christian view of parental responsibility was accepted without question as being the only reasonable way to prepare a family for life in the world. Romans, though by this time committed to schools, still continued to accept their traditions on an intellectual level long after they had discarded them in practice, and the Roman tradition of family education had some effect in solidifying the early Christian view. But it should not be thought that Christians simply adopted a Roman way of doing things. The Christian family was the center of the Christian educational structure because it was natural for the family to have this position and because at this time the family was the most effective instrument available to promote Christian education. The Christian practice had something more to it than Roman tradition. Yet it may be overgenerous to Christian beginnings to maintain that familial education was without precedent. The Jewish model for family education looms much too large to be ignored here; and it was a model that was very apparent to the Christians. The Christian practice was not, however, a mere duplication of firmly established Jewish practices either. There is a noticeable element of autonomy about Christian education in parental hands.

Christian education started and continued with the family, even when parental training was supplemented in important ways. Very early it became clear that in addition to being formed with a Christian mind and Christian heart, a child was to be prepared for Church membership. To be a member of the Christian Church one had to know something of its rules and rituals, and neophytes had to be inducted formally into the Holy Church. The induction was the sacrament of baptism; the preparation for the sacrament was catechumenal instruction. With baptism, this phase of Christian instruction came to an end. In fact, the so-called catechumenal school had a relatively short life. Its importance to the early Church under persecution cannot be overemphasized, it is true, but the time came quite soon when Christianity's foothold was so sure that it was possible to dispense with the more or less formal catechumenal teaching. There is no very clear evidence that the catechumenal school lasted much beyond the end of the second century. There was, however, no end to religious training.

Was catechumenal instruction an example of purely Christian education, separated from secular training, or was this instruction part of the work of a Christian school? By this time in educational history we have a right to restrict the name "school" to those institutions in which a literary training was given or to institutions which made use of literary skills in pushing back intellectual horizons. The catechumenal endeavors had no interest whatever in literary education, and if they did not actually reject the literary inheritance that was so eagerly accepted in contemporary culture, it may have been because they were indifferent to it. The luxury of indifference was something later Christianity could not afford. But in its earliest years Christianity was not even aware of the relevance of culture to the Christian's mission. It is possible to make the claim that catechumenal instruction was a mere extension of Christian education and that it did not contain the germ or the prototype of later Christian schools. Despite this claim, it must be acknowledged that this catechumenal instruction evolved into highly developed and extremely efficient religious education. The course, in its final and finished form, lasted about three years. To guide the teachers who conducted the course, a theory of religious instruction was produced whose architects were teachers, deacons, priests, and bishops. This theory remained in vogue for several centuries; in a rather disguised form some of the elements attached thereto may be found even today.

We remarked above that Christians' indifference to culture became a luxury which they could not afford. With growth and expansion the Christian Church had to face all kinds of new problems. The natural development of the Church, its preaching and teaching, and its continued permeation of all of life made imperative the establishment of an intellectual foundation for its creed. As Christianity became more and more an intellectual religion, education became more and more an important adjunct. The time soon came when the Church could not ignore the school.

THE DILEMMA OF CHRISTIAN EDUCATION

Many Christians were prepared to ignore schools and all literary skills, fearing that they would bind them to paganism. The fact that the Christian Church needed learning may have been recognized; but it was quite another thing to get such a fact acted upon even when it was recognized. Apparently Christianity was faced with a dilemma: She could not get along without learning and she could not seem to get along with it.

A great deal has been made of the division of Christianity into Eastern and Western camps. According to some views, the Eastern camp was favorable to learning and culture and sought to incorporate both into the Christian message, or, at least, to clothe the message with their semblance. To what extent is this an accurate appraisal of Eastern Christianity's approach to pagan learning? Of course we cannot know what the average Eastern Christian thought on this question, if, indeed, he thought about it at all; but among the leaders in the East there was hardly any attempt to bring about an integration of culture and faith. Most Eastern Christians had been brought up in a cultural context that was full of pagan learning. They were able to accept the content of their traditions as an instrument, and though they made no attempt to reconcile the irreconcilable, they did not make many charges against pagan learning or deny its worth to them. Even if they had thought it possible to do without pagan learning, how were they to purge themselves of their personal intellectual inheritances? But their acceptance of the fact of pagan learning—what may be called classical education—did not mean that they also accepted the culture it represented. In other words, Eastern Christians could talk like educated pagans and use all of the tools of pagan learning and at the same time specifically reject pagan cultural ideals. If they had not been able to do this we should have plenty of grounds for doubting their orthodoxy. As it was, they were under constant surveillance by their more sensitive and generally less learned Western brothers. Sensitive we say, not only because certain Western Christians seemed to have made a business of sniffing for heresies, but because they shared the human tendency to fear things that are not understood.

In the West Christianity remained, at least for a time, somewhat more primitive. The West had neither the cultural awareness of the East nor the need for vehicles of cultural progress. Christians could venture among barbarian peoples and communicate with them on a nonintellectual level. They could make converts without putting into service many of the tools of learning. It was true, of course, that the Christian message required intellectual foundations and intellectual assent, not merely emotional attraction, if it was to have any kind of permanence. For general progress, for uniformity of doctrine, and for discipline, Christianity needed the aid that a refined intellectualism could give it. Soon this need was recognized in practice, as Christians came to see that they lacked schooling or learning. At the same time they wanted, paradoxically, to deny that they needed schools, and wherever it was possible, they avoided establishing them. Only in those lands where some learning was absolutely essential to the continued success of the Church and where there were no schools in actual operation, did Christians set about establishing what we could call Christian schools. But these exceptional undertakings resulted from the demands of practical expediency and not from a clearly defined policy.

So, generally speaking, Christians used the schools that Hellenism and paganism had built. They used them not without premonitions of danger or without protests that the elements of Christianity were being sacrificed to the gods of pagan learning. Christians were regularly cautioned about the dangers that lurked in such schools, and they were encouraged to make their own Christian education—that broad education given by the family—so strong that the pagan literature and the pagan learning could not undermine it. With these cautions and warnings in mind, Christians continued to accept and use the classical schools.

It is a wonder that they were able to do so in view of the continuing hostility to what was called pagan learning. Thus, at least on the theoretical level, the dilemma remained unresolved. St. Basil, although at one time a friend of learning, was able to write in his later years that he was spending all of his time with the scriptures and with other similarly motivated writings. To his old teachers, the classics, he could say: "If ever I learned anything from you, I have forgotten it."[2] This was the man who earlier had written the well-known essay, *On the Reading of the Profane Authors*, for the guidance of Christians in their use of heathen authors. If this essay is read correctly, it turns out to be advice to well-advanced students on how to avoid the dangers in such authors, advice which is quite different from a general endorsement of them.[3] And this is the same man who, to confound the picture even more, had written to the celebrated Sophist, Libanius: "What fruits do they not gather, who spend even a short time with you?"[4] So St. Basil's writings on this question may be used to prove almost anything, and finally they resolve nothing. St Basil's position was really not very different from that of any other Eastern Father.

Was the story any different in the West? Only in the sense that Western Church Fathers were ready to display even greater hostility toward classical schools and education than any Eastern divine had shown. Tertullian, Tatian, Augustine, and Jerome certainly did not seek any alliance between Christianity and Greek learning. Tertullian expressed the most uncompromising view. He had little or no confidence in reason, and he claimed that Greek learning—especially philosophy, "which really treated nothing"—was only a network of contradictions. He would have nothing to do with anything but faith: "With our faith, we desire no further belief. For this is our palmary faith, that there is nothing which we ought to believe besides."[5]

---

[2] St. Basil, *Letters and Select Works.* In Philip Schaff (ed.), *A Select Library of Nicene and Post-Nicene Fathers of the Christian Church,* 2d ser., The Christian Literature Publishing Company, New York, 1895, vol. VIII, p. 322.

[3] H. I. Marrou, *A History of Education in Antiquity,* Sheed & Ward, Inc., New York, 1956, p. 322.

[4] St. Basil, *Letters and Select Works.* In Schaff, *op. cit.,* vol. VIII, p. 325.

[5] *The Writings of Q. S. F. Tertullianus,* translated by Peter Holmes, T. & T. Clark, Edinburgh, 1870, vol. II, p. 10.

It is fair to claim that Tertullian is not the best representative of the Christian position, for his orthodoxy may be questioned. Yet his view was only a little more extreme than the general view of the time. St. Augustine (354–430) in his *Letters*[6] and St. Jerome in reporting his dreams[7] took the same stand. Even Pope Gregory the Great at the end of the sixth century opposed liberal culture and considered it dangerous and unnecessary. Although Jerome's and Gregory's positions on this question, though not the same, were quite consistent, Augustine sometimes followed Ambrose in seeing that pagan learning and the forming of Christian character were complementary. In his *Of Christian Doctrine,* Augustine was able to praise the liberal arts and write introductions to them, and he seemed to suggest that all of the arts be integrated in the crown of all studies, theology. But in his *Retractions,* where he again discussed the question of the arts, Augustine was not so sure of the value of arts and the power of theology to integrate them. He concluded that he had gone too far in praising them and withdrew some of his previous endorsement in a charming and pithy statement: "Many saintly men know them [the arts] not, and some who know them are not saintly men."[8] This goes pretty far, but it does not go far enough to take away all the props that stood under classical learning.

There is another side to the question, the side that sees a closer correlation between learning in pagan hands and Christian truth. It is not the partially humanistic position of a St. Jerome, who could see the classics and their literary implements as necessary instruments for Christians. It is, rather, a recognition that truth is truth wherever it is found, whether in philosophical dialogues or in scriptural commentaries. We do not find such a view expressed too often, and it is doubtful that any Western Church Father shared it. But we should know that the liberal attitude existed. We find it expressed best in a delightful dialogue called *Octavius,* written by Minucius Felix. E. K. Rand has called this work "the first monument—or at least one of the first monuments—of Christian Latin literature."[9] *Octavius* is a report of a conversation between two friends, one a Christian and one a pagan. The latter claims to be an orthodox Epicurean. The conversation begins with a number of charges which the pagan makes against the Christians' practices and beliefs. He goes on to become involved in a philosophical monologue that appeals for its authority to Epicureanism and skepticism alike.

[6] *Letters of St. Augustine.* Translated by J. G. Cunningham, T. & T. Clark, Edinburgh, 1875, vol. II, pp. 192–193.

[7] F. A. Wright, *Select Letters of St. Jerome,* Loeb Classical Library, Harvard University Press, Cambridge, Mass., 1933, vol. XVI, p. 127.

[8] In Edward K. Rand, *The Founders of the Middle Ages,* Harvard University Press, Cambridge, Mass., 1928, p. 228.

[9] *Ibid.,* p. 43.

Finally, he concludes his diatribe. Now it is the Christian's turn. Being a gentleman, he presents his case for the Christians with courtesy and care. He does not say everything that can be said, but only enough. He does not argue or even recognize his friend as a philosophical adversary. He uses reason to show why there must be one God and that He is the God whom the Christians adore. But this is all incidental to the main point, the Christian's conclusion of the discussion: "I have set forth the opinions of well-nigh all the philosophers of more conspicuous renown, who denote the one God with diverse names. One might well conclude that either Christians today are philosophers, or the philosophers of old were Christians."[10]

What is the answer? Where did the early Christians stand on the educational question? Was there one Christian answer? We can be certain only that there was no one answer and no official stand taken by the Church. The relationship between learning and Christianity was an open question. And it was not answered on the level of theory, although on the practical level the children of Christians and Christian teachers could be found in most of the pagan schools that were spread out over the Roman Empire. It is impossible to find the connection between the views expressed by various Church Fathers and the actual educational practices of the day.

Christians in Classical Schools

Possibly the real reason why educational theory and practice were so far apart in the early years of Christianity was that the theoretical expressions were directed not at learning in the schools, which was a preliminary kind of training, but at the formation of an intellectual life, which was something quite beyond and different from school learning. At any rate, there were Christian teachers and students in the classical schools. It may be interesting to see what they were exposed to and how they got along.

We can hardly believe that the Church was opposed to learning as such. Back in the years of the early Church, it became more and more apparent that some learning was an essential tool for the faithful. But how to get the pagan skills without getting pagan impiety and immorality along with them was the big question. Children in the pagan schools began with their letters, then moved on to reading and writing, and, if they went beyond the primary school, continued with the study of grammar and literature. Literature contained myths involving the gods and poetry that was unquestionably out of keeping with Christian morals. But there was no law that children should remain away from such schools, although there were canons which enjoined bishops and

[10] *Ibid.*, p. 47.

priests from spending their time with the profane authors. In this matter the law is stricter for the cleric than for the layman—and understandably so. The Church wanted clerics to be attending to their business and not engaging in literary pursuits. The determination of the Christian, as this objective was illuminated for him by the Church, was to superimpose religious truths on humanistic education.

A Christian adult could be a teacher in pagan schools almost as easily as a Christian youngster could attend such schools. A general injunction advised teachers who were able to do so without depriving themselves of their livelihood to give up teaching the secular sciences. This was a mild and tolerant proviso, and the view it expressed was to become more rather than less tolerant as time passed.

By the year 362 there were Christian teachers on all of the educational levels. This does not mean that teaching became a primary objective for Christians, but only that the Church's attitude was sufficiently relaxed to allow Christians to become teachers, and that the non-Christian attitude was sufficiently tolerant to allow Christians the freedom of pagan schools. The date 362 is one to remember. It was in that year that the Emperor Julian became concerned about Christian teachers occupying the important professorships in the pagan schools. He decreed that all teachers would have to be approved. He was especially interested in their morality, and by morality he meant that teachers who taught the classical poets would have to believe in the gods. To teach the poets and not to believe in the gods was, according to Julian, a kind of fraud and therefore immoral. This ban did not remain in force for any great length of time; after two years the order was rescinded. Christians went back to the schools.

In the meantime Christians had reacted to Julian's measure. They refused to be deprived of a literary inheritance or to be excluded from the art of teaching. They began to experiment with a school that had a real religious mission and whose content was derived from Christian sources. Such experimental schools were probably not immediately successful; actually they had too little opportunity to develop. Nevertheless, in their unfinished state, these schools that were organized as a result of the Julian edict were the first Christian schools.[11]

Although the Church could accommodate to classical education, and Christian teachers could teach and Christian students could be taught without too much evidence of discrimination, the Christian teacher let pass few opportunities for giving the Christian message. This teaching of the Gospel was done unofficially as an aside or as a bonus. Perhaps one of the conditions that the Church laid down for teachers who were to

[11] Geraldine Hodgson, *Primitive Christian Education*, T. & T. Clark, Edinburgh, 1906, p. 222.

teach in pagan schools was that they seize every occasion to strengthen Christian beliefs. Yet in spite of this, formal education, especially on the highest levels, was apparently not affected to any extent by the teachings of Christianity. Christians and pagans got along well; there are many accounts of Christians having studied under pagans and of pagans having studied under Christians, and as far as we can judge, religion did not intrude on the highest studies. The Church seemed content to emphasize Christian education in the traditional sense and leave the pagan schools relatively undisturbed. Even when Christians were in the majority, they do not seem to have made any exceptional efforts to introduce Christian teaching into the schools' syllabus. All of this would suggest that the Christian influence on the school was slight.

LAYING THE FOUNDATIONS FOR A CHRISTIAN EDUCATIONAL TRADITION

Questions of origin are usually interesting to historians and to students of history, but they are often quite complex. We usually wonder where to begin. Christianity itself and Christian education present no such problem. They began with Christ; no other origin was possible. Of course the historical setting which antedated Christianity could not be ignored, but the explicit Christian mission was independent of this historical background. Christ's teaching was directed at the salvation of souls and the institution of a new order or a new ethos. Justice was the basis of the old law; charity was the basis of the Christian code. In a real sense Christ and his disciples were revolutionaries. We should not be surprised, then, that the established order treated them as subversive men. The fundamental Christian doctrine could not be separated from Christian educational views. Early Christianity showed little interest in formal schooling—we have seen some of the reasons for this[12]—but there were educational positions implicit in Christian doctrine that were waiting to be made explicit.

Christ himself was a teacher.[13] Some would maintain that He was the world's greatest teacher; others would reserve this honor for Socrates. There is no sure way of demonstrating which was the greater teacher, that is, which was the better pedagogue, and we are forced into this neutral position if we think of teaching only in the sense of communica-

[12] See pp. 152–153.

[13] We are not going to go into any of the details of Christ's teaching methods. For a discussion of them, see Frederick Eby and Charles F. Arrowood, *The History and Philosophy of Education: Ancient and Medieval,* Prentice-Hall, Inc., Englewood Cliffs, N.J., 1940, pp. 584–588; and Patrick J. McCormick and Francis P. Cassidy, *History of Education,* The Catholic Education Press, Washington, D.C., 1953, pp. 171–174.

tion and formation—a high type of schoolmastering. In the broader sense
of teaching—influencing, reforming, capturing men's minds and loyalties
—Christ had no equal. In a way, the comparison of Christ and Socrates
as teachers is a comparison that misses the greatness of both and betrays,
besides, a lack of understanding of the missions that each set out to accomplish. Christ was no schoolmaster, although He was called rabbi,
and Socrates was not God. Only on the level of methodology is there
a possibility of comparison, only in a limited way. We should know
by now, however, that methodological similarities mean very little and
methodological differences may mean even less.

Despite the fact that Christ was not a schoolmaster, He was the
originator of the Christian educational tradition. What He inaugurated
was carried on by His apostles. We are not, of course, dealing with
specific educational doctrines or practices; obviously neither Christ nor
His apostles were educational philosophers or thinkers in any professional or limited sense. Nevertheless, an educational theory was implicit
in the body of Christian doctrine—the same theory that is still in the
process of being developed and understood—and it belonged to the
tradition that was begun by Christ and was preserved by the apostles
and by the Church that Christ founded. It is important for us to see how
Christianity resolved the educational issues that faced it, issues which
were both theoretical and practical. Here the question of where to begin
is somewhat more difficult to answer. One could look to the Church
Fathers and other Christian writers, but there were many such writers
of varying importance. Yet we can isolate the early Christians who were
most responsible for shaping the Christian educational tradition. They
were: Clement of Alexandria (ca. 150–215), Origen (ca. 185–254),
Jerome (331–420), Ambrose (340–397), Chrysostom (344–407), and
Augustine (354–430).

Clement of Alexandria

Not all scholars believe that Clement of Alexandria was the first
Christian to deal with educational theory. Such a claim has been made
for St. Justin Martyr (ca. 100–165). It is said that he was the first to
develop a Christian theory of thought.[14] In addition to this, in his
Apologies, Justin was supposed to have explained Christian thought to
the pagan world.[15] Despite what may have been unusually successful
efforts on Justin's part to explain the reasonableness of Christianity to the
pagan world, it is hard to see why one should make claims for him in the
realm of educational theory. Admittedly, it is not easy to isolate educa-

[14] *Ibid.,* p. 179.
[15] J. E. Sandys, *A History of Classical Scholarship,* Cambridge University Press,
New York, 1906, vol. I, p. 332.

tional theory at any time, and in this period it was even more difficult, but Justin was surely not alone in trying to explain Christian beliefs to the pagans. This was a preoccupation of many Christian writers and it had nothing to do with the formulation of Christian educational theory. In this field Clement was a pioneer.

Clement of Alexandria, was one of the first Christian thinkers to be really aware of a theory of education. We mean, of course, a theory of education in a formal and general sense, for, broadly conceived, Christianity itself might be understood as a theory of education. In recognizing and attempting to develop a theory of education more fully, Clement was somewhat different from his Christian associates. He was different in two ways mainly: He showed some understanding of the need for learning itself, and he was cognizant of the role intellectual culture could and should have in spreading and consolidating the Christian message. While no one seemed to give a second thought to his interest in learning purely as a human ability, his apparent championing of the cause of liberal culture as a handmaiden of higher Christian thought and action came in for a good deal of criticism. Whether or not this phrase was used in his own time, his contemporaries were prone to look upon him as a "liberal Christian." Still, his so-called liberalism could not have been especially flagrant or offensive, for in many localities for many centuries Clement was called a saint. Popes Clement VIII and Benedict XIV, however, found reasons for excluding his name from the Roman Martyrology. Here we are interested in his educational ideas and his place in educational history and not in the claims made for or against him in the matter of his having been a saint.

In general, it seems safe to say, no one really disagrees with the conclusion that Clement was a great teacher or that the plan for his school in Alexandria was a noble one; or that his support of liberal culture in the Church was good; or that in seeing Christianity in its relation to the whole field of human thought he was traveling the road of orthodoxy. Nevertheless, he has been charged with gnosticism and heresy, an indictment which we have the commission neither to prove nor to disprove. But in his own day, when Christianity was viewed as a progressive doctrine, Clement's views may have been a bit too conservative. The Christians of the early centuries fully expected the Savior to return for a final accounting of mankind within a few short years. For the most part they saw no good reason, at least no compelling reason, to firm up their faith or their basic beliefs with intellectualism. They saw no need for theology in a formal sense, less need for philosophy, and no need at all for using pagan literature or any models from pagan learning, represented best in grammar and rhetoric, to convey or strengthen Christian doctrines. In addition, they found it difficult or impossible to distinguish between the arts and sciences of the pagans and the pagan view of life. In passing through pagan hands, or in coming from pagan minds, all of these things were tarnished. Even if the early Christians had thought that pagan literature had utility for Christianity, they would have avoided using it. In this sense some early Christians were progressive. They turned their backs on the past; they felt that they did not need the past; and they were understandably suspicious of any of their brethren who showed signs of conservativism. Clement was the object of some of these suspicions, as were others with whom Clement may have found some intellectual fellowship. His fame as a teacher may have created more fears concerning his complete orthodoxy than it allayed. But whatever his values, they were less subject to criticism in his own time—probably because of the inevitable lag in communication and the unsettled and generally unorganized state of Catholic orthodoxy—than they were two or three centuries later. But with all of this Clement could count himself fortunate, although he did not recognize his good fortune, for had he lived during the time of Gregory the Great or later and held the same so-called liberal views, his influence might have been stifled and his place in history denied him.

Clement was not born into the Christian religion. Although accounts of his life differ, the Alexandrian teacher became, it appears, a Christian in his early adult years. Perhaps he experienced an intellectual conversion; if he did, little account of it is left in his writings. Apparently he found little or nothing painful about the religious experience which brought him to accept the Christian doctrine; and possibly he had to give up little from his former actions and beliefs in order to participate fully in the Christian Church. A life of leisure and learning were the most obvious features of his pre-Christian life. He became in turn, then, a Christian, a priest, and finally the most famous of teachers for his place and time.

It would be a mistake to think of Clement as an academician in any narrow sense. It is true that his fame is that of a teacher, and the institution with which history most closely associates him was a catechetical school. Yet Clement was not only a teacher; he was a pastor and, in his later years, a writer. His school, which was left in his care by Pantaenus, was hardly a school in the ordinary modern sense. More like the Academy of Plato or the Lyceum of Aristotle, it was a well-appointed home with a good, possibly an excellent, library, which the youth of Alexandria who came from good families might attend. It bears in historical writing the name of catechetical school, though it was considerably more than the usual run of catechetical schools of that or any period. Christian doctrine was explained, the scriptures were prominent in all of the teachings, and a wide range of learning was undertaken.

Nevertheless, the boys who had the good fortune to attend the school were not always Christians, and those who were did not, for the most part, have any vocation for or interest in catechizing. In other words, the school was a kind of study club in which young men approached Christian teachings for personal reasons, either religious or liberal. The impression that this school over which Clement presided was a Christian teachers' institute represents a narrow and inaccurate view.

There are three areas, then, in which to carry out an investigation of Clement's place in the history of educational theory: the nature and objectives of the school he conducted, his work as a teacher, and his writings. Of his school's nature we have probably said enough, except to add that during Clement's stewardship it was not subject to ecclesiastical control. It was independent of this kind of supervision for several reasons. Clement's work was well known and admired in Alexandria. His appeal to the more highly placed people of the city was recognized by the men who occupied the episcopal chair in Alexandria. The bishops of the city during the period of Clement's educational activity there were favorably disposed to a cultural approach to Christian teaching. Possibly, also, Clement's activities were not clearly understood, so that what at later times and in other places was to be represented as a real dichotomy, that is, liberal learning versus Christian beliefs, did not attract attention. Possibly Clement's stature was unassailable. Whatever the reasons for the freedom of the school, it was independent while Clement remained in charge of it. When he relinquished his headmastership because he was forced to leave the city, the school passed to the management of Origen, under whom it was controlled by the authorities of the Church.

Of Clement's work as a teacher, only a little is known with any accuracy, and most of our impressions of his ability must be inferred from his fame as a schoolmaster. Enduring fame as a teacher—not merely the accolades of a few satisfied students—is the honor history has given Clement. Clement's academic morality and his stature as a scholar have been the objects of severe criticism,[16] but no one has challenged his place as a great, perhaps the greatest, of early Christian teachers. He is represented as a mild, thorough, learned man. While little fame attaches to his originality in scholarship and less distinction to his literary ability, as a teacher he was well prepared to direct and guide students on intellectual adventures. He was both widely read and broadly educated, and his life was devoted completely to learning. This devotion may have been the real source of his success with students, whom he no doubt inspired by his example and who are said to have shown many evidences of the excellence of their education. Apart from whatever fine qualities

[16] There is the general, though undocumented, charge that Clement was a plagiarist.

the man may have had as a learned and inspiring teacher, it may be that the bold course he charted for his school was the real source of his fame. He aimed at no less than a synthesis of knowledge and faith—of reason and revelation. In its earliest years Christianity was not a doctrine which had great appeal to the learned or the sophisticated. There was even some antagonism to learning among Christians; the classics, for example, with their false gods and their immoral tales were often proscribed and pagan thinkers were subject to condemnation and the vehicles of their thought to ridicule. Still, here was Clement—not alone, to be sure, but in a minority—who with mildness but firmness retained and defended his background of learning in the classics when he entered the Church and went on to seek a reconciliation in his teaching between the world of ideas and the world of faith.

Clement may not have been an iconoclast, though there was a stubborn independence about him, but he was no starry-eyed intellectual either. Any portrait of him which neglects his acceptance of scripture as the final authority would be unjust. He did not put reason on one stool and faith on another and abstract from both in order to put something new on a third stool. Rather, he tried to move the two stools so close together that both could be used to support any weight that fell on either. Analogies, however, are often either dangerous or unsatisfactory, for here one might assume from the image used that Clement regarded revelation and reason as equals. He did not. Not for a moment did he show any doubt as to the superiority of revelation. On the other hand, he showed no inclination to discount the worth of reason and the outcomes of its employment. Where much of early Christian educational theory was anti-intellectual, Clement went out of his way to defend the role of reason. By this we do not imply that he was interested in glorifying Greek learning or even secular learning, for Clement gives us many examples of his apprehensiveness concerning the real or spurious knowledge then available to man. Nor was it expurgation that he was working for, but something far more significant than taking an editor's pencil and striking out whatever was offensive to Christianity. He was defending reason, and in doing so he was saying that revelation could be made more meaningful by using reason to explain it. In addition, all human knowledge, being the product of reason, could and should lead man closer to God. Clement was not undertaking a defense of secular knowledge, for if he is understood correctly, he is saying that there is no such thing as secular knowledge. On the other hand, Clement was no rationalist either, though he did defend reason against numerous castigations by many early Christians.

As a writer, Clement leaves a picture which is somewhat less precise than that left by the oral tradition which portrays his role and success as a teacher. The liberal thought claimed for him in his instruction shows through rather dimly in his writings. He wrote toward the end of his life, preparing his writings for publication in the twilight of his career. Always his pronouncements were mild and noncontroversial, and possibly this feature became even more evident in his writing. Bold conclusions and straightforward demands for reform are characteristic of youth, not old age. By the time Clement was ready to write, he may have become even more moderate in his manner of expression than he had been in earlier years. It may have been, also, that his published works were delivered originally in the classroom, where mind in contact with mind brought greater clarity in purpose and greater unity of meaning.

Then, too, it must be acknowledged that Clement was not a polished writer of prose. Either he cared little for style, or he did not have the skill of an accomplished writer. His work is ponderous. His thought is usually simpler than his words. It is not that his eloquence conceals commonplace ideas, because Clement is hardly an eloquent writer. He seemed to try to find and adopt the most difficult manner of presentation for an idea. He carried into his compositions the intentional verbosity of many of his classical predecessors, and at times he came perilously close to being unintelligible. It has been said that Clement was not repudiated as a heretic in the fifth and sixth centuries because he was not understood.[17] And if his unintelligibility were not enough to discourage many readers, he added to their confusion by filling his works with quotations from a variety of sources, usually the Bible, and he did not use sources well. There was, of course, no good reason why Clement should not have proceeded in this way, because it was a style that was both accepted and approved in his time. Still it must have caused hearers and readers a good deal of difficulty. He is hard to follow. But since sources extant in Clement's library were neither generally known nor generally accessible, by the generous employment of quotations Clement was really doing his readers a favor. Yet the modern reader cannot help but wish that Clement had made use of footnotes. His purpose would have been served just as well, and he would have spared the reader the agony of following his thought through a maze of quotations and interjections. Too often the quotations seem to obscure rather than to illuminate Clement's thought. Clarity and unity have always been praised as qualities of good writing. It seems undebatable that a writer's chief purpose is to communicate. If he does not do this, he has failed. If he does not have something to say to his readers, he should not write at all. The subject of a written discourse may not be simple; it may not be possible for

[17] E. Molland, *The Conception of the Gospel in the Alexandrian Theology*, Oslo, 1938, p. 5.

a writer to write what is on his mind, even though he does so in the clearest manner, and yet be understood by everyone who may pick up his book. Though Clement understood this, he tried, apparently, to cultivate intentional obscurity. At least he wrote for those who were among the intellectual initiate, and he tried to write in such a way that comprehension would not come easily. He may have confused obscurity with profundity; he may have written as he did hoping to contribute to the expansion of the reader's mind and not merely to fill it; or, fearing criticism if he put his thought too clearly, he may have resorted to obscurity as a protective measure. It is more likely, however, though we may try to pick our way through the alternatives mentioned above, that this excellent teacher was simply a poor writer.

And this brings us to a point not usually understood, that is, the difference between classroom teaching and academic writing. It raises, too, the problem of the degree of responsibility a writer must assume over and against that of a teacher. The teacher's audience is limited, and he knows something about his pupils. If they raise questions or objections, the teacher is there to explain, elucidate, or defend his views. The relationship between the teacher and the learner is important; it is and must be one of superior to inferior, for the teacher must know, or he cannot teach, and the student must be seeking knowledge, or he would not be under the tutelage of the teacher.[18] This is not true of the author. He does not know his readers, and they do not know him. They can assume little background for judgment or evaluation. The writer expresses himself and must rest his case and his reputation on what he has written. Emendations cannot be made easily, if at all; critics must be heard to be answered. The author, then, in Clement's view, needs both greater courage and greater confidence than the teacher. He is unable to avoid responsibility for what he has written; he must have confidence in his convictions and the courage to express them. Yet, as Clement wrote, he did "not imagine that any composition [could] be so fortunate as that no one [would] speak against it." He continued with considerable self-assurance:

But that is to be regarded as in accordance with reason, which nobody speaks against, with reason. And that course of action and choice is to be approved, not which is faultless, but which no one rationally finds fault with. For it does not follow, that if man accomplishes anything not purposely, he does it through force of circumstances. But he will do it, managing it by wisdom divinely given, and in accommodation to circumstances. For it is not

[18] The superior to inferior relationship is intended to be interpreted only in an academic sense: no discrimination of any kind is being endorsed.

he who has virtue that needs the way to virtue any more than he that is strong needs recovery.[19]

What he seems to be saying here, and this is a good example of his indirectness, is that the author who is reasonable and careful has nothing to fear from critics who are also reasonable and careful. Perfection need not be demanded, only prudence and care.

One more point concerning Clement's writing should be touched on— the reason for his having written at all. From his tone one gathers that he preferred not to write, but that he felt some obligation to do so because of the message he had to give to others who wanted to know more of Christianity. But apart from what may have been missionary zeal, there was another and quite prosaic reason: His memory was dimming with the passing years, and he recorded his thoughts in order to have something on which to rely when his memory failed even more. In a sense, then, what we are reading when we read some of Clement's works, especially *Stromateis*, are his lecture notes, organized a bit and perhaps enlarged somewhat, but his notes nevertheless. This statement does not seem to apply to *Paidagogos* and surely not to *Protreptikos*, perhaps the most charming of his writings and a work which represents Clement at his very best.

These three works must be studied especially to discover Clement's theory of education: *Protreptikos* (*An Exhortation to the Greeks*), *Paidagogos* (*The Instructor or Tutor*), and *Stromateis* (*Miscellanies*). It has been claimed that Clement planned these three books as a trilogy on Christian education. Certainly no one who has read them could think that Clement was writing a theory or philosophy of education in any formal sense; his theory is incidental to other main ideas, particularly to his exposition of Christian doctrine. Moreover, educational theory was more practical in Clement's day than in ours, and the subjects with which he might deal quite appropriately seem rather foreign to modern educational theory. The big questions of Clement's day revolved about the *what* of education. There was no dispute about the *why*, and it was still much too early to think in scientific terms about the *how*. *Why*, of course, is the question of why man should be educated. For the Christian in Clement's time, the answer was obvious. The eternal view was dominant; educational objectives were all made to subserve man's final end. No Christian thinker from the early Christian period to the beginning of the modern period even remotely questioned this conclusion. But if no consideration was given to the possibility of a variety of educational objectives, both temporal and eternal, primary and secondary, the

[19] Clement of Alexandria, *The Writings of Clement of Alexandria,* in *The Ante-Nicene Christian Library*. Translated by Alexander Roberts and James Donaldson, T. & T. Clark, Edinburgh, 1870, vol. I, p. 359.

question of *what* should be taught became more acute. It is with this
question that Clement deals, and, of course, it is an important and recur-
ring question in the history of education. The question of content was
central in educational theory from the time of Clement to the time of St.
Thomas Aquinas. And from this central question flowed a number of
additional significant questions: for example, the whole matter of whether
education was to be made available to everyone or only to a few, and
whether those privileged to obtain the advantages of education were to
be clerics and prospective clerics only or laymen. But much of this is
anticipatory both of Clement's views and of the views of others from the
early Christian period through the Middle Ages.

What is considered to be the first work in Clement's trilogy on Christian
education is *An Exhortation to the Greeks.* It has usually been evaluated
as a rhetorical plea to the Greeks to look at Christianity more closely;
it is surely not an apologetic work. The two later works, it has been
suggested, are the ones that really deal with educational questions. No
doubt both *The Instructor* (or, as it has been rendered, *Christ, the
Educator of Children*) and *Miscellanies* have a great deal of educational import in them, but many people believe that the basis of
Clement's educational theory is really found in the *Exhortation.* Let us
examine this plea to the Greeks more carefully.

Clement is obviously not assuming the role of an educational theorist
in any limited sense. His object is to call to the attention of the Greeks
the beliefs they had so long accepted and to point out to them the
wisdom of looking at these beliefs a little more critically. He does not
say that they are or have been ignorant, but he does say that the "extremes of ignorance are atheism and superstition, from which we must
endeavor to keep."[20] He is suggesting that they strip themselves of superstitious beliefs and look at the gods they have honored. He recommends
that they observe honestly and carefully and then in all candor arrive at
a reasonable conclusion. Reason is the human ability on which man must
depend, and for reason to be effective it must be informed. Clement puts
it this way:

Then, he that is uninstructed in the word, has ignorance as the excuse of
his error; but as for him into whose ears instruction has been poured, and
who deliberately maintains his incredulity in his soul, the wiser he appears to
be, the more harm will his understanding do him; for he has his own sense
as his accuser for not having chosen the best part. For man has been otherwise constituted by nature, so as to have fellowship with God. As, then, we
do not compel the horse to plough, or the bull to hunt, but set each animal
to that for which it is by nature fitted; so, placing our finger on what is man's
peculiar and distinguishing characteristic above other creatures, we invite

[20] *Ibid.,* vol. II, p. 34.

him—born, as he is, for the contemplation of heaven, and being, as he is, a truly heavenly plant—to the knowledge of God, counseling him to furnish himself with sufficient provision for eternity, namely piety. Practice husbandry, we say, if you are a husbandman; but while you till your fields, know God. . . . Your means and substance you squander on ignorance, even as you throw away your lives to death, having found no other end of your vain hope than this. Not only unable to pity yourselves, you are incapable even of yielding to the persuasions of those who commiserate you; enslaved as you are to evil custom, and, clinging to it voluntarily till your last breath, you are hurried to destruction: "because light is come to the world, and men have loved the darkness rather than the light.["][21]

Then Clement exposes the Greeks to a little of the basic Christian doctrine, not apparently to convince them of the truth of these beliefs or to defend the Christian point of view, but simply to give them some information on which to ponder. Neither the Greeks nor other readers are led to believe that reason as it is represented in classical philosophy and literature is the sure or steady road to faith and salvation. Clement admits that some of the non-Christian philosophers had glimmerings of truth; and he charges that many of the pagans had devised pernicious, evil systems of philosophy and had disseminated literature that both injured and ignored morality. He says, though his language is somewhat equivocal, that the learning of the classical sages cannot be accepted as a beacon for truth:

Wherefore, since the Word Himself has come to us from heaven, we need not, I reckon, go any more in search of human learning to Athens and the rest of Greece, and to Ionia. For if we have as our teacher Him that filled the universe with His holy energies in creation, salvation, beneficence, legislation, prophecy, teaching, we have the Teacher from whom all instruction comes; and the whole world, with Athens and Greece, has already become the domain of the Word.[22]

This passage would be easy to misinterpret. It would not be entirely fair to Clement to take him at his word here, for he really does not mean what he seems to say, and the context of the quotation is actually broader than the *Exhortation to the Greeks* itself. Clement does not mean to say that learning is unimportant and that the Greeks have nothing which the Christian learner might seek. He is saying that the human learning of Greece that was seeking after ultimate causes is no longer necessary, for the First Cause Himself has already given man the information he needs. And he is not saying that Christ is going to give, or has given, man all of the information and instruction he needs in every avenue of human activity. He means that with God-given ultimate

[21] *Ibid.*, vol. II, p. 92.
[22] *Ibid.*, vol. II, p. 100.

answers, man needs to search no longer for these hidden, basic truths. He implies elsewhere, though he does not say it here, that there are many kinds of questions, not all of them of ultimate concern, and that man must try to use the reason God has given him to understand the world. In this way man will come, Clement maintains, to a fuller and more complete knowledge of God.

If the three works mentioned above are a trilogy on Christian education, then the first, the *Exhortation to the Greeks,* is really the foundation for the trilogy. In it Clement demonstrates his meaning better than he explains it. He is asking the Greeks, as he would ask all men, to use their reason. Reason is man's supreme endowment, and its cultivation leads to human truth, which in turn gives man a larger vision of divine truth. Had not reason's place been established by Clement here, both the *Paidagogos* and the *Stromateis* would surely lead many readers to wrong conclusions. This trilogy must be studied as a unit, for it has an internal unity, and each part rests somewhat on every other part. Having established reason as the foundation for human development in the first treatise of the so-called trilogy, in the other works Clement is able to go directly to the points he wishes to discuss—moral training in *Paidagogos* and a variety of intellectual matters in *Stromateis*—without stopping each time to remind his readers that he is willing to give allegiance to man's intellectual abilities. It is on man's rational nature that Clement's theory of education rests. Without this foundation Clement becomes a mere eclectic or a pious tinkerer in Christian pedagogy.

In *Paidagogos* Clement displays remarkable breadth of vision, because he treats that part of human formation without which an educational theory would be inadequate or incomplete. *Paidagogos* is not simply a sermon on the moral formation of youth. To consider it as such would not recognize its special distinction or recommend it to the attention of readers interested in the formative years of Christian educational theory. An assertion of the importance of character formation in the molding of men has unquestioned value. But this is not the same thing as integrating moral and intellectual formation and ascribing to each its proper role in man's life as he moves toward his ultimate destiny.

Paidagogos is made up of three books. Book I contains thirteen chapters, Book II, twelve, and Book III, twelve. The first book is of the greatest value to us, though Books II and III were probably especially valuable at the time they were written. For example, they treat of subjects from conduct or manner in eating to bodily exercises for the sake of health. Today they have a puerile character, but Clement's advice concerning deportment at the public bath was not superfluous or puerile when it was given. It is axiomatic that the past should not be judged by the present.

In Clement's view, Christ is both the example and the teacher. There is no suggestion at all that one is superior to the other. In *Paidagogos* Clement is dealing only with morality or the inculcation of virtue. He is not ignoring learning and intellectual virtue, but in this work he is simply not considering Christ's wisdom and knowledge.

Moral formation is far too important a subject to be left to schools. There are many reasons for this opinion: School life is deferred to a time when many of the child's most basic moral habits have already been formed; moral education is too broad a responsibility for the school, which has the child under its care for only a relatively brief time; moral formation cannot be solely a function of the school, because there are too many experiences over which the school has, and can have, no control, that are instrumental in shaping character. Clement's discussion of moral education is not intended for schoolmasters. It is a fine piece of pedagogical writing that is intended to have universal appeal. It is directed toward all Christians, whether they are parents, teachers, or merchants, for all of them, when it comes to moral formation, are teachers of the young. But even taking into account the universality of its message, we must conclude that Clement's treatise probably had greater meaning for teachers of his day than of our own. Schools were both schools and homes then. Christian teachers often accepted very young students and cared for them from their late infant years until they were ready to stand alone in the world. Clement's own school, while never a nursery, was a place for living as well as a place for learning, and it was, according to his own pedagogical creed, a place for moral as well as intellectual formation.

Stromateis, a book which critics say was written before *Paidagogos,* has a character that is not easy to describe. Some of the *Miscellanies,* it appears, have been lost. However, of those which remain only a few of the 193 chapters in the eight books have a direct bearing on educational theory, although all of them are really concerned with mental culture. The difference to be noted, though, is that some of the chapters take up the problem of intellectual formation in and for itself, while others contain only the content which students of that day might have used for intellectual cultivation. More than any of Clement's other works, *Stromateis* has a lecture-note character; notwithstanding Clement's caution that he has only hinted at some things and left other things out altogether, the reader of *Stromateis* may be pardoned if he concludes that Clement often left out too much.

Stromateis, as we mentioned above, is made up of eight books, comprising in all 193 chapters, some of which are very short. No one book, let alone the entire work, displays the kind of unity that would enable one to summarize either its purpose or its contents. It is surprising, indeed, and somewhat disappointing, that in the work which Clement reserved for a discussion and analysis of intellectual education, he is at his worst as far as style and design are concerned.

Clement's educational thought is not elaborate; nowhere does it wander very far from fundamentals. In his *Stromateis* it is possible to find the foundation for all subsequent Christian schools and educational systems. Clement's contributions notwithstanding, it may be observed that the fundamental issue with which he dealt still continues to be an issue in Christian schools and in Christian educational theory. Although Clement did not have to raise the question in this way, it is possible to interpret him as asking: What is the primary function of a school? Admittedly this is a somewhat narrower problem than the one with which Clement dealt, but it was surely, though implicitly, contained in the larger one which faced him. We have stated above that the problem which vexed Christian thinkers involved the relative position and worth of reason and revelation.

No Christian disputed the preeminence of revelation, but some in accepting revelation degraded reason to the point where intellectual effort was both useless and dangerous. Instead of leading man to virtue and salvation, it was often maintained that cultivation of reason would lead to eternal destruction. Clement, in a moderate, perhaps oversanguine manner, expressed the view this way:

> Some, who think themselves naturally gifted, do not wish to touch either philosophy or logic; nay more, they do not wish to learn natural science. They demand bare faith alone, as if they wished, without bestowing any care on the vine, straightway to gather clusters from the first. Now the Lord is figuratively described as the vine, from which, with pains and the art of husbandry, according to the word, the fruit is to be gathered.[23]

Origen (ca. 185–254)

Clement set the pace. He was the first but by no means the last to work toward a reconciliation or a compromise between classical and secular learning and Christianity. He was followed in this work by Origen. It is not easy to see how Origen surpassed his teacher, Clement, although such a claim is made with monotonous regularity. As a matter of fact, Origen and Clement had somewhat different interests, and to compare the two men is not altogether fair. Clement was a teacher and an educational thinker; Origen was a scholar.

Origen cultivated fields that had been only explored by Clement and others. He was interested in teaching and writing; he was attracted to secular and divine subjects; and he had the instincts of a scholar. There is a story, apparently authentic, to the effect that Origen owned an ex-

[23] *Ibid.*, vol. II, p. 379.

ceptionally fine library, one that may have been left to him by his father, who was a teacher of rhetoric, and that he sold the library for an annuity that amounted to about ten cents a day for the rest of his life. If this seems an unusual act for a scholar, it must be remembered that Origen was seeking leisure and freedom from economic cares, both of which are indispensable to the man who wants to lead the life of a scholar and devote his best energies to learning. Yet giving up a library would be sacrificing the scholar's most valuable tool. But Origen apparently arranged to sell his books and have them too, for the agreement that brought him the annuity also permitted him to use the collection of books and manuscripts that formerly had been his property. If we have established Origen as a man of learning and common sense, we have done him simple justice. We have yet, however, to establish him as an outstanding figure in the history of educational thought.

He was one of the most famous of the early Christian teachers. The Alexandrian Catechetical School was never better known or more influential than when Origen was its master. When he was forced to leave Alexandria, the stature of the school diminished at once. The testimony of his own time, that is, of fellow teachers and students, plus his acknowledged influence on later generations would be enough to justify his reputation. But many of his writings are extant and bring his thought directly to us.

Briefly, what was the educational position of Origen? Following the lead of Clement, although without any acknowledgment of indebtedness, Origen continued to seek a means for bringing sacred and secular subjects closer together. It seems unlikely that Origen respected secular subjects for what they were or that he saw secular knowledge as an end in itself; he probably regarded secular subjects as mere means for understanding or confirming Christian beliefs. St. Jerome expressed this opinion of Origen's position when he wrote of his genius and praised his spirit and his skill. Students, he said, came to Origen in large numbers for instruction in all subjects including secular literature. "These he received in the hope that through the instrumentality of secular literature, he might establish them in the faith of Christ."[24] In other words, secular subjects had value only in so far as they could advance or illuminate the Christian cause. Origen himself seems to confirm Jerome's view in a letter to Gregory of Thaumaturgus, who, along with his brother, was one of Origen's most prized students at the school in Caesarea. In this letter Origen urged young Gregory to devote all his strength to the Christian cause. This devotion might, in part, be shown by extracting "from the philosophy of the Greeks what may serve as a course of study or a

[24] Jerome, "Lives of Illustrious Men," in *A Select Library of Nicene and Post-Nicene Fathers of the Christian Church*, 2d ser., vol. III, p. 349.

preparation for Christianity, and from geometry and astronomy what will serve to explain the sacred Scriptures, in order that all that the sons of the philosophers are wont to say about geometry, and music, grammar, rhetoric and astronomy, as fellow helpers to philosophy, we may say about philosophy itself in relation to Christianity."[25] Origen's advice is an express recognition of the value of secular subjects and secular learning but only as instruments to a more sublime goal. In spite of this evidence, some scholars maintain that Origen freed Christian education from its narrowness and opened to it all of the prospects of liberal culture. But if Origen was not an unwavering friend of liberal learning, he was certainly not an uncompromising enemy. By the time Origen finished his work Christian education had made considerable progress, and it had left behind the untenable stand that secular subjects were to be avoided altogether.

As a last word on Origen, we may say that he seemed to have a deeper understanding of the nature of education than most of his predecessors or his contemporaries. He tried to inculcate in his students motives for learning that were not based on fear. His school was a workshop in which character and mind were formed. And as a general evaluation we may add that he was an excellent example to help disprove the shibboleth that scholars always make poor teachers.

St. Jerome (331–420)

A certain contradiction between the actions and the expressed attitude of Jerome had a good deal to do with the reception Christians were to give classical learning. We have seen that various points of view, some expressed in extreme form, either commended Greek learning or condemned it. The Christian was often not able to say exactly where he stood on the matter. Should he turn his back on all secular learning? Should he accept pagan learning as an instrument? Should secular knowledge be accepted as valid and valuable for Christians? Christians looked toward their leaders for guidance. How much help was Jerome to them?

It seems unnecessary for us to concern ourselves here with the details of Jerome's life or even of his career. But we must not overlook the fact that he was Christianity's first great scholar. The *Vulgate* alone attests his scholarship, although Jerome's Biblical commentaries and his *Lives of Great Men* are added evidence. Jerome was a scholar, and he provided an excellent example of scholarly competence that his fellow Christians might emulate. Even when he was experiencing the trials of the ascetic life in mountain caves or on desert sands, Jerome continued his studies.

[25] *Ante-Nicene Christian Library,* vol. X, p. 388.

He could arrange, it seems, to have his library with him wherever he went.

Often, however, Jerome did one thing while he preached another; he was a scholar but he did not endorse classical scholarship for his companions in Christianity. It is true that he became a schoolmaster for a few years. He had founded and conducted a boys' school in Bethlehem. But the most lasting impression that Jerome created, though not necessarily the most effective, was that scholarship should be feared and learning avoided. When Jerome was on the desert, having deserted civilization to find salvation, he had a dream which he reported vividly.

I could not altogether give up my library, which I had collected at Rome with much zeal and much labor. And so, poor wretch, I would fast in preparation for reading Tully. After the long vigil of the night, after the tears which the remembrance of my past sins drew from the depth of my heart, I would take Plautus in hand. If I ever recovered my senses and tried to read the prophets, their uncouth style rubbed me the wrong way; and because with my blind eyes I saw not the light, I deemed it the fault not of my eyes, but of the sun. While thus the old serpent was beguiling me, one day, about the middle of Lent, a fever flooded me to the very marrow and wracked my weary body. Pausing not—incredible as it may sound—it so fed on my hapless limbs that I could scarce cleave to my bones. Meanwhile they made ready for my obsequies. The vital heat of my soul, of my breast, in a tiny spot, was still tepid—when, of a sudden, I was caught up in the spirit and hailed before the judgment seat of God. Blinded by its light and by the brightness of those who stood about it, I fell prostrate to the earth, not daring to look up. When the voice asked me concerning my condition, I replied that I was a Christian. "Thou liest," answered he that sat upon the throne. "Thou art a Ciceronian, not a Christian; for where thy treasure is, there shall thy heart be also."[26]

If this is not a hostile attitude toward pagan learning and scholarly excellence, it is at least a warning that such learning does not have a high place on a hierarchical scale of Christian objectives. Did Christians accept the implications contained in Jerome's dream and leave Cicero alone? Perhaps they did not go quite that far. Yet it can hardly be argued that Jerome's words would lead Christian minds toward learning or the intellectual life.

Another point might be mentioned before we move on. Jerome expressed his principal views on education in his many letters. In them we find that he had something to say about the education of Christian girls. In doing so he shaped much of the policy on women's education for the next thousand years. His advice on the education of girls may be found mainly in two letters, one addressed to the noble mother, Laeta,

[26] *Selected Letters of Saint Jerome,* translated by F. A. Wright, Loeb Classical Library, Harvard University Press, Cambridge, Mass., 1923, vol. XVI, pp. 125–127.

concerning the education of her daughter, Paula, the other to Gaudentius, advising him about the education of his daughter, Pacatula.[27] In general, the girls' education was to be pointed toward Christian service, and was to be almost entirely religious. There were, nevertheless, some tools that Jerome would have the Christian girl use and she could learn their use best by following this prescription:

> Have letters made for her, of boxwood or ivory, and let them be called by their names. Let her play with them, and let the play be part of her instruction. She must not only get the right order of the letters and memorize them in a song, but now and then mix the alphabet, last with the middle and middle with first, so that she may tell them by sight as well as by hearing. But when she begins with trembling hands to draw the pen through the wax, either let her elder's hand guide her tender finger joints, or let the letters be graven on the slate, that the marks she traces be confined within the edges of these furrows and not stray outside. Let her learn to join syllable to syllable by the inducement of a prize—something very acceptable to that tender age. She should have companions in her task of learning, whose accomplishments she may envy and whose praises may spur her sense of shame. Don't scold her if she is slow, but arouse her ambition by praise so that she may delight at victory and smart at defeat. Above all, don't allow her to hate her studies, lest the bitterness of them, acquired in childhood, may last to her mature years.[28]

Jerome was certainly aware of approved techniques in teaching and of the psychological principles that supported such techniques. Even so, we can call him an educator only in a rather tangential way.

St. Ambrose (340–397)

The position of St. Ambrose in the history of education is not as clear as that of Jerome or Clement. He was not a teacher, except in the episcopal sense, and he was not engaged in building a theory of education. Yet his name ought to be mentioned in any general account of the evolution of Christian education, because he committed himself to a definite acceptance of scholarly content and form for Christian literature. The old indecisiveness with regard to classical scholarship and its intellectual standards, an indecisiveness that left the individual Christian in a quandary, was resolved by Ambrose. Christians could still hear a certain amount of declaiming against learning and arguments that intellectual formation was an obstacle to salvation. Nevertheless, the works of Ambrose, principally *The Duties of the Clergy* and his works on theology, originated a Christian educational tradition or at least reinforced the tradition started by Clement, with exemplary Christian determination.

[27] *Ibid.*, vol. XVI, pp. 363–365.
[28] *Ibid.*, vol. XVI, pp. 345–347.

Even more than any of his predecessors, Ambrose accepted and supported the full utilization of man's mind and the intellectual instruments the ages had refined. The eminence of St. Ambrose, who was a great bishop of Milan and a powerful theologian, forestalled criticism. His reputation was not adversely affected by his stand in favor of intellectualism or by the fact that he was himself a thorough Greek and Latin scholar. St. Ambrose stands at the historical gateway to the Middle Ages as one of the principal inspirational sources for the intellectual energy of that era.

St. John Chrysostom (344–407)

Along with Clement of Alexandria and Origen, St. John Chrysostom, a Church Father of the East, reacted to the educational questions of the day. The most important question that the Christians had formulated concerning education was: What, if any, use could be made of classical learning? Except for St. Ambrose, the Western Fathers were strongly inclined to proscribe classical learning. That they did not always do so may testify to their prudence rather than to their willingness to accept the content of pagan culture. Of course, the mere use of the vehicles of classical learning did not imply any acceptance of the culture itself. Some, however, did not understand this; and others, understanding it, still saw danger in any employment of pagan learning. But the Fathers of the East, who had been closer to the classical culture and who often had been nurtured on it, were able to see ways of using classical literature and all of the implements of classical learning without allowing the non-Christian spirit that permeated them to cloud Christian thought. Some of the Fathers of the West did not have this advantage of familiarity with the classics, although it would not be fair to say that the opponents of the use of the classics were the Fathers who were most ignorant of them. We have already said enough about this problem.[29] In a way though, it is this same problem that alerts us to the work and influence of St. John Chrysostom.

He advised parents to see to the Christian education of their children. This meant to him, as it had to earlier Christians, that parents were responsible for the moral and religious formation of their offspring. He told parents that this was their first duty, and as the times did not make possible any ready delegation of this function, one that had to be fulfilled personally. Certain elements in education could be delegated, and Chrysostom had no intention of turning parents into schoolmasters; but the parent who sent his son or daughter to the schools to be trained in the skills of learning had to be sure that the school would not undermine the moral and religious foundation already laid. This impor-

[29] See pp. 154–158.

tant responsibility was placed squarely on the shoulders of parents. Was it really possible for parents to know what the dangers were that lurked before their children in the schools of the day? St. John seemed to be convinced that parents who could direct the Christian education of their children would be equal to the task of detecting and evaluating dangers in formal instruction.

Instead of firing a broadside at the classical schools of the day or declaring them out of bounds with a sweeping condemnation, Chrysostom wrote:

If you have masters among you who can answer for the virtue of your children, I should be very far from advocating your sending them to a monastery; on the contrary, I should insist upon their remaining where they are. But if no one can give such a guarantee, you ought not to send children to schools where they will learn vice before they learn science and where in acquiring learning of relatively small value they will lose what is far more precious—their integrity of soul. . . . Are we then to give up literature? you will exclaim. I do not say that; but I do say that we must not kill souls. . . .

When the foundations of a building are sapped we should seek rather for architects to reconstruct the whole edifice, than for artists to adorn the walls. . . . In fact, the choice lies between two alternatives: a liberal education which you may get by sending your children to the public schools, or the salvation of their souls which you secure by sending them to the monks. Which is to gain the day, science or the soul? If you can unite both advantages, do so by all means; but if not, choose the more precious.[30]

Chrysostom undertook a more systematic treatment of educational questions than any of the other Church Fathers, and came closer to being an educational thinker than any of his contemporaries. It has been claimed, and with good reason, that he produced the finest educational treatises of the period. They were scattered among his many works (722 are credited to him)[31] and remained uncollected until John Evelyn translated them and grouped them together in one volume called the *Golden Book of St. John Chrysostom*.[32] The most complete of St. John's single works on education was *Concerning the Education of Children*.

In his various writings on education Chrysostom touched on most of the educational topics that are today considered to be of greatest significance. He concerned himself with theories of child development and child psychology; he dealt with home training and with certain aspects of vocational guidance; he treated the problem of cultivation of the senses and the powers of observation; he was interested in incentives

---

[30] Quoted in Hodgson, *op. cit.*, p. 223.

[31] McCormick and Cassidy, *op. cit.*, p. 186.

[32] William Upcott (ed.), *The Miscellaneous Writings of John Evelyn*, Henry Colburn, London, 1825.

for particular goals as well as general questions of motivation. To this catalogue of broad interests must be added his theory and method of sex instruction. In brief, the idea was to prepare young men and women for marriage. This instruction was to begin early and was to continue over a long period of time. Little was left to chance, for Chrysostom could see no sense in neglecting to prepare for one of life's most important vocations, and the training was approached with meticulous care.

Chrysostom was an effective champion of Christian education. All of his writings and all of the provisions he would make for education had Christ at their center. The world and everything in it could be used to educate young people, but young people should always be educated toward Christian wisdom. In his own words Chrysostom reflects this view very clearly: "This is the very sum and top of all wisdom, that he be not taken up with impertinent and childish vanities. Teach him therefore that riches avail nothing, worldly glory nothing, power nothing, nothing death, nothing this present life. Thus he shall indeed become a wise man."[33]

St. Augustine (354–430)

In the history of the Church St. Augustine has few equals. He was a powerful ecclesiastic in his own time, and his disciplined and astute mind was a source of intellectual inspiration for many centuries. The impression he made on theology and philosophy was significant. Augustine is generally recognized as the father of early Christian philosophy. Yet despite his renown in philosophy and theology, we must pass over these areas of thought to ask: Where does Augustine stand in the history of education?

To begin with, we find fairly orthodox educational attitudes reflected in Augustine—orthodox, at least, for Western Church Fathers. He had been thoroughly schooled in the classics, although it appears that while his accomplishments were outstanding in Latin they were only a little more than ordinary in Greek. In spite of this generally acknowledged excellence in classical learning, Augustine's judgment about the place of the classics in the education of Christians is somewhat equivocal. It is only fair to say, however, that he was neither more nor less indecisive on this question than most of his eminent contemporaries. Augustine would probably have supported the stand that the classics and all of pagan learning could be used, with proper precautions, as instruments of Christianity, even though he several times made some strong statements which indicated that he might place a severe limit on the value of the classics and their use by Christians. On occasion, in the heat of controversy or in dealing with particular problems, he denied the worth of

[33] *Ibid.*, p. 136.

most, if not all, secular knowledge. But these polemics are probably not typical of his general attitude.

If the following excerpt from Augustine's *Of Christian Doctrine* may be accepted as representative of his position, then he apparently conceived of knowledge as arranged on a hierarchical scale. Some kinds of knowledge were more valuable and therefore more desirable than others.

Moreover, if those who are called philosophers, and especially the Platonists, have aught that is true and in harmony with our Faith, we are not only not to shrink from it but to claim it for our own use from those who have unlawful possession of it. For, as the Egyptians had not only the idols and heavy burdens which the people of Israel hated and fled from, but also vessels and ornaments of gold and silver and garments, which the same people when going out of Egypt, appropriated to themselves, designing them for better use, not doing this on their own authority, but by the command of God, the Egyptians themselves, in their ignorance, providing them with things which they themselves were not making good use of; in the same way all branches of heathen learning have not only false and superstitious fancies and heavy burdens of unnecessary toil, which every one of us, when going out under the leadership of Christ from the fellowship of the heathen, ought to abhor and avoid; but they contain also liberal instruction which is better adapted to the use of the truth, and some truths in regard even to the worship of one God are found among them. Now these are, so to speak, their gold and silver, which they did not create themselves, but dug out of the mines of God's Providence, which are everywhere scattered abroad and are perversely and unlawfully prostituted to the worship of devils. These, therefore, the Christian, when he separates himself from the miserable fellowship of these men, ought to take away from them and devote to their proper use in preaching the Gospel. Their garments, also, that is, human institutions such as are adapted to their intercourse with men, which is indispensable in this life, we must take and turn to Christian use.[34]

Although it may be said that all of Augustine's writings have educational implications—for what philosophical and theological works do not?—those that are of especial interest to the educational historian are: *Confessions, The City of God, Of Christian Doctrine, Catechizing the Uninstructed,* and *De Magistro.* In most of his writings we find sections that deal with the liberal arts, for in spite of some serious reservations, Augustine was still deeply interested in liberal learning.

The *Confessions* are autobiographical and include many comments on Augustine's own education as well as unusually fine insights into psychological problems, especially problems of learning. *The City of God*

[34] *A Select Library of Nicene and Post-Nicene Fathers of the Christian Church,* 1st ser., vol. II, p. 554. On the general question of the classics in Christian education, see Gerald L. Ellspermann, *The Attitude of the Early Christian Latin Writers toward Pagan Learning and Literature,* The Catholic University of America Press, Washington, D.C., 1949.

is an expression of a philosophy of life and as such is basic to a Christian philosophy of education. Although this work is primarily inspirational, its instrumental value should not be discounted completely. In *Of Christian Doctrine* we find Augustine explaining how scriptural study should be approached and also how rhetoric, philosophy, and classical literature might be used in conjunction with divine studies and for the end of divine studies. *Catechizing the Uninstructed* was intended to be a guide for teachers who directed the religious instruction of those about to enter the church. This work has been interpreted as a guide to the program of the so-called catechumenal schools, but by the time Augustine appeared on the scene the catechumenal school was rarely found and had not been in general use for more than a century. This work was effective, nevertheless, for though catechumenal schools were hard to find, religious instruction was still given, and the Church was very much interested in converting people who were still outside the Christian communion. Augustine's own conversion may have contained experiences which he felt could be useful in illuminating the whole matter of instruction for religious neophytes. But we must remember, too, that Augustine was the bishop of Hippo, and had a definite obligation to direct the religious education of those who had just embraced Christianity. Finally, there is *De Magistro*. This work voices general ideas about the teacher and teaching, and deals with the fundamental conceptions which make up an ideal of the instructor's art. It is well worth studying but not with the expectation of finding a full exposition of a philosophy of education. It was never intended to be anything other than what it is: a discourse on the authority and general function of the teacher. Augustine's *De Magistro* has often been regarded as anticipatory of the *De Magistro* of St. Thomas Aquinas.

Before we leave St. Augustine, we should admit the difficulty of weighing the significance of his educational influence. On the one hand, he seemed to stimulate learning both by his excellent scholarly example and by precept; on the other, he cautioned against the excesses of intellectual activity. There is little wonder, then, that the Christian writers of the day were somewhat confused. They found it hard to discover just what the Christian's position should be with respect to classical or pagan learning. The relative unwillingness to accept or to pursue secular knowledge was due primarily to the Christians' lack of trust in the intellect. They took the following words of St. Augustine as a warning to them to beware of too much intellectual activity, and generations of Christians who followed Augustine did not easily forget or ignore his caution:

Accordingly, I think that it is well to warn studious and able young men, who fear God and are seeking for happiness of life, not to venture heedlessly upon the pursuit of the branches of learning that are in vogue beyond the pale of the Church of Christ, as if these could secure for them the happiness they seek; but soberly and carefully to discriminate among them. . . . But for the sake of the necessities of this life, we must not neglect arrangements of men that enable us to carry on intercourse with those around us. I think, however, that there is nothing useful in the other branches of learning that are found among the heathen, except information about objects, either past or present, that relate to the bodily senses, in which are included also the sciences of reason and of number. And in regard to all these we must hold by the maxim, "Not too much of anything."[35]

Some commentators maintain that Augustine was instrumental in retarding scholarship and freedom of activity in learning.[36] There may be some truth in this accusation, for he was surely devoted to authority and discipline and to the Church's primary teaching function. Other scholars insist that he helped to construct an intellectual framework for Christian thought and educational activity that lasted almost to modern times.[37] There may be some truth in this claim also, for it is not hard to identify the influence of Augustine in both the early and the late Middle Ages. In spite of these categorical statements, and in spite of the scholarship that has been devoted to Augustine's work and influence, it seems impossible now to give an exact or accurate evaluation of his place in the history of education. He has had his admirers and his detractors. Augustine's educational work will bear further study.

THE FIRST CHRISTIAN SCHOOLS

We have already expressed the doubt that the first organized efforts by Christians to instruct either the faithful or those who were aspiring to Church membership could be called scholastic. Christian schools with a formal, literary-centered curriculum were slow in coming. We have already explored a number of reasons for the delay. In any event, the monastic school seems to have been the first Christian school.

There was Christian-centered instruction before the monastic school appeared, but little of this instruction went beyond religious teaching. Though the monastic school was primarily religious in purpose, its curriculum was not always made up exclusively of a religious content; in other words, it often fulfilled the first requirement of what we now call a school—an institution with a literary curriculum and with literary objectives. These early efforts to consolidate and spread the Christian faith are worth examining. They were directed mainly in catechumenal, catechetical, and cathedral or episcopal centers of teaching.

[35] St. Augustine, *Works*, vol. IX, *Of Christian Doctrine*, T. & T. Clark, Edinburgh, 1875. Book II, chap. 26.
[36] Eby and Arrowood, *op. cit.*, p. 648.
[37] McCormick and Cassidy, *op. cit.*, p. 194.

Catechumenal Schools

Catechumenal instruction was intended to prepare a prospective Christian for the sacrament of baptism. We know little about the beginning of such instruction, but we may assume that in the early Church some preparation was always needed as an essential preliminary to baptism. In the most general sense, then, catechumenal instruction began with the Church itself and lasted until infant baptism became common—about the ninth century. But in a more specific sense, the catechumenal school belongs to the first two centuries of the Christian era. Thereafter, though religious instruction continued and became much more thorough and more carefully graded, the catechumenal school did not keep its institutional form. It may be argued that the catechumenal school did for non-Christians what the Christian family did for its younger members; that is, it inducted them into a Christian moral climate and a Christian way of thinking and indoctrinated them with Christianity's basic precepts. The reason why the catechumenal school did not last much beyond the second century is to be found mainly in its principal objective. There was a social environment which assumed much of the educational work that the school had done in earlier years.[38]

The catechumenal schools were conducted by Christians who were known for their steadfastness and their allegiance to the Christian religion. Teachers in such schools did not need the qualifications of schoolmasters, for the instruction given probably never went outside the realm of Christian history, doctrine, and practice. In the catechumenate's most infant years the teachers or leaders were clerics, usually bishops or priests. But this was only natural, considering that the Church was just getting started. Shortly thereafter the guidance of prospective Christians was entrusted to minor clerics or to laymen. Although the bishops began to delegate this important work, they continued to show great interest in it and to supervise it with considerable care.[39] The course of instruction was probably neither detailed nor extensive, but the time required to pass through the course was long. Possibly three or five years elapsed before a candidate was baptised and thus finished his course in the

[38] It should be mentioned here that there is some difference of opinion as to the duration of the catechumenal school, but this may be only a difference of opinion as to what the catechumenal school really was. Although the statement is made here that the catechumenal school did not last much beyond the second century, other historians think that it was a going institution well into the Middle Ages, up to the ninth century.

[39] Much of the Christian literature of the period dealt with the proper means and methods for preparing candidates for induction into the Church. For the most part, this literature was the work of episcopal authors.

catechumenal school. One final word may be added in connection with the internal functioning of these schools. The favorite, perhaps the only, method employed in instruction was the question-and-answer method. The doctrines of the Church were learned by catechizing, and this was the method that continued to be used—and is still used—in instructing children in catechism classes. The method of the catechumenal school outlived the educational level that produced it by many centuries.

Catechetical Schools

If we hesitate to acknowledge the catechumenal schools as the first authentic Christian schools, surely the catechetical schools filled the bill. The fame of the Alexandrian catechetical school under the mastership first of Clement and then of Origen ought to satisfy any skeptic. If this is not enough, then the catechetical schools of Caesarea, Antioch, Edessa, Nisibis, and Rome may be cited. There is no doubt that they were outstanding centers of learning. But were they Christian schools?

First of all, the teachers in the schools just mentioned had no commission to teach Christian doctrine as had the teachers in the catechumenal schools. It is curious but true that the Christian leaders of this period saw fit to appoint teachers to communicate elementary points of Christian doctrine to the uninitiated, but saw no similar need to commission teachers to teach Christian doctrine on higher levels. The teachers in catechetical schools of the type that flourished in Alexandria may have been Christians, but they were not in any full sense Christian teachers. Usually they were laymen who taught on their own responsibility and authority. The Church could, of course, interdict their schools but otherwise could exercise no authority over them. And it was the unusual catechetical school that made any attempt to integrate religious and secular knowledge. The well-known catechetical schools were of a type that emphasized secular knowledge. It was the main, if not the only, constituent of the curriculum and the principal reason for the school's existence. Such schools were the pagan schools all over again, except that Christians taught in them and that in some schools a course of religious instruction was added for those who wanted it. Perhaps it was only in this additional instruction that these schools differed from pagan schools, for we know that Christians had been teaching in the pagan schools all along. If these schools were the best representatives of catechetical instruction, it may be necessary for us to revise what is often a first impression in the history of education: that catechetical schools were authentic Christian schools. But there were other types of catechetical schools.

The schools that evolved in the larger urban centers were answering

a need. An ever-increasing number of Christians began to show enthusiasm for secular knowledge, and the schools were a natural consequence of demand. Or possibly a Christian who was prepared as a
teacher, and had no other way of making a living, opened a school. Still
this is only part of the picture. There were a number of inchoate institutions, roughly classified as catechetical schools, that were intended to
continue the religious formation of the Christian convert in his post-
baptism years. Thus clerical and lay teachers may have continued a
course of instruction that was devoted exclusively to Christian doctrine.
Such catechetical schools differed from catechumenal schools only in a
matter of degree and also, of course, in that their students were professed Christians. These were the catechetical schools that were probably
most influential in the early Christian period. Little is written about
them; little is known of them. They were impermanent and their teachers seldom achieved any fame.

There may have been still another type of catechetical school, one
that acted as a minor seminary and gave early instruction and guidance
to boys who aspired to holy orders. Such instruction was preparatory to
the course of training offered in episcopal schools. Schools with this objective could not have been very numerous, for clerical training was for
the most part nonacademic and noninstitutional. It was apprenticeship
training pure and simple. A preparatory school does not fit very neatly
into such a picture.

Catechetical schools may have been of three types, no one of which
filled all the requirements of a Christian school. The types were these:
places for secular education and quite advanced learning; institutes for
the religious instruction and formation of practicing Christians; and
preparatory schools for boys aspiring to the Christian priesthood. The
first of these types concerns us most, because it was the academically
centered catechetical school that promised most for the future of
Christian education and schooling, although this promise was not fulfilled until a time well after the catechetical schools had passed out of
existence. We return again to Alexandria, where the most famous
catechetical school of all was conducted and where Origen, its famous
master, began his teaching career.

Under Clement, the Alexandrian school was nonintegrated; that is, its
masters were Christians, but the main content of its curriculum was
secular. Religious studies were "extras" or almost on the same level as
the extracurricular activities of the schools of the mid-twentieth century.
This was hardly a Christian school in the most complete meaning of the
term. Yet when Origen gained control and became its chief teacher, the
content of studies was divided. Under this new leadership the Alex-

andrian catechetical school became a school for advanced theological studies[40] as well as a school for the study of mathematics, literature, and philosophy. The latter studies, which could perhaps be called liberal, were pursued on a secondary level of teaching; the religious studies were accomplished on the level of higher education. So there were actually two schools, one for secular knowledge and another, separate from the first, for higher, specifically religious studies. What this type of educational organization might have produced if it had been cultivated is hard to say. It did not last very long.

Catechetical schools were not permanent fixtures in the Christian educational system; they disappeared rather quickly. There were different reasons for their disappearance just as there were different types of schools. The catechetical school that had an academic orientation depended too much on a few men to keep it going. When these men died or were otherwise prevented from maintaining an association with the school, the school either declined or disappeared. There was not enough interest in the kind of learning that these catechetical schools offered to keep them alive, vital, and permanent. Even the Church Fathers who expressed interest in education in their writings and in their sermons made no effort to create or preserve the catechetical schools that were committed to clear-cut academic objectives.[41]

Catechetical schools for advanced instruction in catechism disappeared when religious teaching of this type became a definite function of the Church. Such teaching had always been the Church's responsibility, but the Church saw fit to delegate the actual teaching to trusted Christians. When the Church distributed this commission less freely, the catechetical teachers decreased in number. This did not happen, however, until other types of Christian schools had appeared on the scene.

Finally, the few ecclesiastical catechetical schools disappeared when the training of future clerics was regularized. The kind of education that this type of catechetical school purported to give was offered in an educational adjunct, or annex, to the cathedral or episcopal school. But this was a development some distance in the future, as we shall see shortly. The basic reason for the anemic career of schools of this type was that what they proposed to do was done in part by the pagan schools—the teaching of elementary literary skills—and in part by the clerical ap-

---

[40] See pp. 173–174.

[41] One of the interesting features of the catechetical schools was that so many heretics were associated with them either as teachers or headmasters. One is led to wonder why the incidence of heresy was so high among the learned, when everyone in the early Church was his own theologian. That so many learned men were declared heretics may have lent credence to the belief that learning was a threat to faith. It was obviously a threat to orthodoxy.

prenticeship system. In other words, there was no real need for such schools during most of the early Christian period.

Cathedral Schools and Episcopal Schools

In the time of the early Church, boys who had some aspiration to clerical life were educated in the regular, pagan schools and were then apprenticed to a bishop. They learned to be priests by living and working with the bishop. He taught them what he thought they needed to know and what experience had taught him, and when he felt that they were ready, he ordained them. This informally organized training led to the formation of the cathedral school. Actually, it was not a school in any complete sense of the word. However, as time went on, the bishops may have offered the young men attached to them a more formalized course of instruction or one more highly specialized in doctrine and theology. The bishop was still the teacher, and because the teaching was done in or near the cathedral, the name cathedral school came into common use. Probably the bishops engaged in this kind of instruction never thought that they had organized a school in any formal sense.

Apprenticeship training built on a foundation of classical education could lead a young man to holy orders. A continuance of classical education beyond elementary studies was not thought to be necessary; in fact, it was sometimes studiously avoided by clerics themselves, who had known the Church to proscribe clerical use of the classics. But some of the elements of learning did seem to be essential, and in the absence of any Christian schools on the lower educational levels, the classical or the pagan schools were about the only places where these tools of learning could be obtained. As long as they were available, the pagan schools were used. But the whole climate of education changed when the Roman political and social system collapsed, for the classical school collapsed with it.

Now a new dimension was added to clerical education. Boys who were to become priests went to the bishop when they were mere lads seven or eight years old, and they took their complete education from him or from the teachers he appointed, in what was called the episcopal school. From the teaching of the most elementary skills of learning through the classics and through specialized training in theology, the whole gamut was the work of the episcopal school. The chief and sometimes the only teacher in such a school was the bishop himself.[42] The

[42] The question may be asked with good reason: Why were the classics included in the curriculum of the episcopal schools? Were the classics now in good standing among Christians? By the time the episcopal school appeared, much of the sharpness had worn from the debate over the value of the classics, and also there was much less doubt about the value that a trained mind could have for the Christian

episcopal school was a real Christian school, although what we have called the cathedral school was not. But the episcopal school did not arrive on the educational scene until the early sixth century.

Parish Schools

With the spread of Christianity, the Church's organization expanded also. The urban centers had had their cathedral churches and their bishops to care for Christian souls, but now that parishes were formed in the rural areas, there was a greater and greater need for priests. Ordained priests were encouraged to perpetuate their class. It was in the Church's need for priests and in the relatively barbaric environment that surrounded rural parishes that the parish schools were born. Classical schools had not penetrated the rural areas, and even the most elementary schools in the Roman system were not to be found in every village. The parish school was a village school conducted by the parish priest mainly with the object of giving an early education to boys who might become priests. These schools were, of course, only elementary, but they were the first step in a system which seemed to extend all the way up to the episcopal school. By assuming responsibility for the elements of literacy, parish schools relieved episcopal schools of some responsibility for teaching their students how to read and write. In a real sense the parish schools were an extension of the educational idea which brought episcopal schools into existence.

The origin of parish schools is far from clear. Little is said of them either in the historical accounts of the early Church or in official Church documents. It is usually assumed, probably with reason, that parish schools were more or less regularly found after the fifth century, and that from that time on one of the important functions of the pastor of the parish was to supervise education in his parish, or if need be, to accept the duties of a teacher.[43]

Monastic Schools

We come now to the schools that were probably the first permanent Christian schools; they were schools that had exclusively religious purposes, but they had at least the name of literary institutions too. Despite

---

cause. In addition, the classics had been given something of a new look in the hands of Boethius and Cassiodorus. There is still another point: What other curricular materials were there? Classics may well have been inserted in the curriculum of the episcopal school because such curricular material was traditional for secondary and higher schools.

[43] Various Church councils made reference to parish schools at different times. Their pronouncements, however, do not provide entirely adequate sources for the general history of such schools.

the schools' definite literary commitment, the classics were neglected; more than this, positive efforts were made to forget them. These were the monastic schools that made their first appearance in the West about the fourth century.

Eastern and Western monasticism had placed little value on learning. We know that most early monks were not priests. In fact, it was often thought that learning—even mere literacy—stood in the way of holiness. The Eastern monks tried to escape from the world, and certainly the monastic ideal did not require them to be in the world. It is doubtful that they ever thought of their monasticism as having any general educational function. They had, of course, made a number of provisions for inducting the novice into monastic life. The rules even of the Eastern monastic groups had a "bookish" side to them. Although it may not have been necessary for the monks to read, it was expected that they should know a number of Psalms and some Epistles. Those who could not read were expected to learn by heart what they had to know.

But what may have been acceptable in the early centuries of Eastern monasticism did not always remain acceptable. St. Basil's *Rule,* for example, required that young boys who were admitted to the monastery be taught to read. Nothing was said about a thorough education since none was needed, but literacy seems to have been an unavoidable minimum. St. Jerome, too, although his views on education and its relationship to monastic life belong to the West, prescribed a completely ascetic education—one intended for girls who were to become nuns—for Paula and Pacatula.[44] Even the great Chrysostom had advised parents to send their children to the desert for their education. He thought a ten-year stay would do them good.[45] Whether or not Chrysostom expected that boys so educated would become monks is not the point to be considered here; at least they would have been under the direction and guidance of monks, and their education would have been a monastic one to the degree that it would have been useless for boys who were to return to the world. It may have been that Chrysostom had in mind what many Eastern rules had prescribed: that no boy was to be admitted to the monastic internship who was not committed to a life in the monastery. He came, in time, to acknowledge the imprudence of sending a boy away from the world in order to learn to live in it. As a result of his changed view, he endorsed family religious training (a practice that in actual fact was associated with all Christian education) and secular and literary education in the classical schools.

In general, Eastern monasticism did not engage in education because it did not have to. The relatively high standards and the fairly general

[44] See pp. 176–177.
[45] See pp. 179–180.

distribution of education in the East absolved the monasteries from engaging in work for which they had not been designed in the first place.

What we have said of Eastern monasticism and its general unawareness of education and educational problems cannot be said of Western monasticism. Almost from the beginning, the monasteries of the West accepted the elements of learning as essentials to the full monastic life. Monks did not have to be learned and not many of them were, but they had to be able to read. The same was true of the convents; rules for religious women were very nearly uniform in their demand that all the nuns were to learn to read. If the ability to read was important for women, it was obviously more important in this day and age for men. Many rules that preceded the *Rule* of St. Benedict (ca. 525) had emphasized the importance of studying the written word, but the *Rule* of St. Benedict consolidated the practice and gave reading an unassailable place in the monk's life and duty. The Benedictine *Rule* did not, as other Western rules before it did not, assume that boys would come to the monastery already educated. Therefore it was necessary to have a system of education for young men who applied for admission to the monastery. In spite of the exclusiveness of most early monastic schools—they were intended specifically for novices and often the admission of any others was prohibited—these schools were both Christian institutions and schools in a proper sense. And more than this, during the dark years that were about to envelop Europe, the monasteries, largely because of their educational features, were true homes for Christian culture.

SUMMARY

The first Christians showed relatively little interest in establishing systems of schools that would continue the classical literary tradition. There were two principal reasons for this lack of interest. One was that Christians felt they had no real need for such as intellectual inheritance, and even if they had felt the need there would have been no reason for them to establish such schools, because a well-established system of classical schools was already in operation. The other was that the educational goals they sought to achieve were of such a nature that they could be obtained more satisfactorily in a family plan for education. Christian education meant family education. The values of the Christian life and the moral habits to sustain these values were to be communicated in the home. Thus those Christians who chose to turn their backs on classical learning could do so without endangering the kind of human formation they considered most valuable. And the Christians who decided to imbibe the classical tradition could do so without creating any special schools under Christian auspices.

It would be a mistake to think that Christians were not aware of classical or pagan learning. They were very much aware of it. Few of them, however, were inclined to embrace it. Yet many Christians did see the need for a substantial intellectual foundation for their faith. While the dangers of learning were often emphasized, the values of learning were regularly, if not popularly, promoted. Christianity found itself in a dilemma in regard to the classics and generally in regard to the content of the pagan schools. Time saw a slow but gradual resolution of this dilemma.

The resolution was not attained without painful effort. Yet throughout most of the early Christian period, it was entirely usual to find both Christian teachers and Christian students in the classical schools. At the same time, Christian thinkers and teachers gave their views on the educational questions of the day, and in so doing they laid the foundations for a Christian theory of education. The most prominent of these figures were: Clement of Alexandria (ca. 150–215), Origen (ca. 185–254), Jerome (331–420), Ambrose (340–397), Chrysostom (344–407), and Augustine (354–430).

Although a system of Christian schools was not to be found during the early Christian period, some Christian institutions were operated which came close to being schools with specifically religious objectives. These were the catechumenal, catechetical (of three types), and cathedral institutions.

After the Roman system of schools had pretty well collapsed, Christians organized parish and episcopal schools. The first true Christian school, created around the fourth century, was the monastic school.

Questions and Exercises for Study and Discussion

1. Compare the attitudes toward family education that were common in conventional Greek and Roman culture with those of the early Christians.
2. What does Christian education mean today? What did it mean to the early Christians?
3. Can you justify the Christians' indifference to general culture and things of the mind? Couldn't early Christians see that learning and culture provided an essential framework to which the core of Christian teaching could be grafted? If not, why not?
4. Why didn't Christians open literary institutions of their own? Did they use Roman (pagan) schools? What was the Roman reaction to Christian teachers and students in their schools?
5. What was the dilemma of early Christian education? Who were some of the Christians who helped either to construct the dilemma or to resolve it?
6. One of the educational issues that faced the early Christians continues to present itself to Christians everywhere. It is the issue of content—what

to teach and for what purpose. How did early Christians handle this issue? How do present-day Christians handle it?

7. Prepare a brief report summarizing the principal educational views of Clement of Alexandria, Origen, St. Jerome, St. Ambrose, St. John Chrysostom, and St. Augustine.

8. List and explain the purposes of the first Christian schools. How did these schools differ from the classical schools? How did they differ from Christian schools that followed them?

9. What commitments, if any, were made to education in Eastern and Western monasticism?

10. If monasticism was religious-centered and if monks were not highly educated, how was it possible for the monasteries to affect education? Describe the educational work of European monasteries.

7

The Development of Christian Educational Doctrine

THE COLLAPSE OF THE CLASSICAL SYSTEM

Slowly but surely the Christian movement proceeded through the Roman Empire and spread beyond it whenever missionaries found the means to carry the gospel of Christ that far. By the time of Constantine's reign (306–337) the Christian strength, although by no means overwhelming, was remarkable. In 313 the decree of Milan promulgated by Constantine had ended the persecution of Christians and had extended to them the civil rights enjoyed by followers of other religions or of no religion. At the same time Constantine showed great interest in education, and the schools on all levels and almost everywhere in the Empire flourished under the emperor's favor. This was especially true of higher studies in Constantinople, where scholars were encouraged in their studies and rewarded generously for their work. Almost everywhere teachers were attracted to the schools with the lure of high salaries and privileges and immunities that were hard to find elsewhere.

During this time Christian teachers in even greater numbers than before found their way into the schools. Unfortunately, educational prosperity of this magnitude was not permanent. The edict of 362, to which reference has already been made,[1] was published by Julian. From this point on the classical school, which continued to be the school of the Empire, was in a state of flux. It enjoyed periods of prosperity but also had to endure long periods when the professed interest in education was not too evident in practice. These schools were pulled in two directions as occasional attempts were made to reform them. The

[1] See p. 159.

Christians, understandably enough, were never completely satisfied with them. On the other hand, a number of influential people in Rome had a nostalgic yearning for the pagan-centered classical schools of years past. Julian, representing this position, made one last desperate effort to revive pagan culture. He failed; yet classical schools surely did not disappear when Julian's scheme did not succeed. Classical schools never disappeared completely, as the modern and contemporary educational eras can attest.

Students of the history of education, when they meet the subject of early Christian education immediately after they have studied the chapter in their textbook that treats of Roman education, often assume that the Roman schools simply disappeared from the face of the earth and that a new educational order came into being. They have not been told how the Roman schools were disposed of. Possibly they have an erroneous impression that the Christian school conquered the classical school and in doing so was left in command of the educational field. We have seen that there was no Christian school worthy of the name until about the fourth century, and that this monastic school had neither the will nor the strength to engage in any struggle for survival. The classical school system of Rome had begun to decline before Christianity received its tremendous boon in the edict of Constantine. The collapse began in the outskirts of the Empire.

It will be recalled that one of the established policies of the Empire was the support and control of education. Although the efforts of the state were partial, possibly even sporadic, the policy of the Roman state was clear. This policy led to the decline of private schools and private tutors. Either private masters found it hard to compete with the state schools, or they were motivated for financial or other reasons to become part of the public system. There is no question here of educational doctrines or purposes or of theories of curriculum; public schools were just as classical as private schools had been. But in tying themselves to the Roman political system, the schools became utterly dependent on that political system. It was their life's blood; when it died, they died with it.

The branches died and fell away long before the trunk was afflicted. The Anglo-Saxons had shattered Roman Britain by the early fifth century. Its political system was replaced by violence and its educational system by the vacuum of barbarism. But the fifth century was late in the history of educational collapse. In Gaul decay had begun in the third century, and by the early fifth century Roman dominion over Gaul was a thing of the past. Perhaps decay is the wrong word, since it connotes internal weakness or rot. Although the Gallic schools may have been weak, it is far more significant that Germanic barbarians crossed the Rhine River in 276 and that from then on Gaul became an insecure appendage of the Roman system. What happened in Gaul and Britain happened also in the other continental outposts of Roman influence. There were exceptions, for example, Africa. Here the Roman influence remained fairly secure for another two centuries and then was challenged by the Arabic invasions: another kind of barbarism from another source. Italy was the last great stronghold of the Roman system and thus of classical education. Classical education on all levels was found in the Italian cities, and some of the cities—Milan, Ravenna, Pavia, and, of course, Rome—were great university towns for a hundred and fifty years after the Roman system had collapsed in Britain and three hundred years after it had started to collapse in Gaul. The force of the early barbaric invasions had not been great enough to push all the way into Italy and disrupt an established way of life. Italy's time was yet to come. By about the middle of the sixth century the Lombards swarmed down on Italy and laid waste almost all of the culture that stood before them. The political system was destroyed; the social system was badly disrupted; culture and learning were given little or no chance. For a hundred years or more—it was close to the end of the seventh century before a revival of culture was seen—Italy was subjected to the same fate that had been visited on Gaul and Britain. The great traditions, social, political, cultural, and intellectual, were buried by the barbaric hordes from the north. When they finished overrunning the country, Italy was intellectually barren. The educational slate was not wiped clean, but there remained only dim outlines of past vitality, excellence, and glory.

What was left to take the place of the classical school? There were few Christian schools, and of them the most important was the monastic school. The educational problem that faced the few surviving schools and the newly created Christian schools was the problem of what to teach. The old hostilities to pagan literature still existed. Some of these hostile attitudes never actually left the Christian school or what by now can be called Christian education. But this is not a point of history, although some historical dimensions may be involved. There stood the monastic school, but it, too, was insecure. What was it to teach, and to whom? We have already touched on the first point;[2] with respect to the latter, it is fairly clear that many monastic schools could not or would not accept children of the world; that is, they could not accept students who had not committed themselves to the life of religion. This ban had its origin in the canons of the Council of Chalcedon and apparently remained in full force for some time.[3] Christians were required to face once more the problem that had faced them so often before, the problem of content for their schools.

[2]. See pp. 189–190.
[3] See H. I. Marrou, *A History of Education in Antiquity*, Sheed & Ward, Inc., New York, 1956, pp. 337, 341.

CONTINUING AND CONSOLIDATING
THE CHRISTIAN TRADITION

By the time the Middle Ages were ready for the universities, a fairly definite theory of education had been worked out, and Christians were quite certain what schools ought to teach.[4] But these decisions were the final result of a long and sometimes painful process of educational evolution. Our object is to try to establish some of the foundations of a teaching tradition that culminated in the medieval university.

Boethius (ca. 480–525)

Too often Boethius is just a name in the history of thought. One writer may say that he was the last of the ancients, another that he was the first of the Scholastics, a third that he was both. We should not like to believe that the only claim for the man is based on authority, for surely his relevance to history should be made clear, or his name should be dropped from the catalogue of famous men who helped shape our intellectual inheritance. Is it not possible that Boethius, like Martianus Capella (ca. fifth century), has been given far more credit than he deserves? Or has Capella's significance been overstated?

Martianus Capella, along with Cassiodorus and Boethius, is said to have been responsible for what the Middle Ages knew about the liberal arts. Since knowledge of the liberal arts was pretty well disseminated in that period, this is saying a great deal. The claim made for Capella contains much truth. Nevertheless, it is hard to evaluate his position in the history of education. His work, *The Marriage of Philology and Mercury*, was written in Carthage in North Africa in the early fifth century. Cole has called it the most successful textbook ever written.[5] Yet despite this claim, even despite Capella's tremendous popularity in later years, we may wonder if it is accurate to refer to this book as a text. It was either allegory or fiction.

According to the story, Mercury decides to take a wife. After looking over the field, he selects Philology. At the wedding Mercury presents his bride with a number of appropriate gifts, the most elaborate of which was introduced by Apollo. He brings forward seven maid servants. As each is introduced she steps forward, is described, and then goes on to explain herself. The seven maids are the seven liberal arts, by now— or by Capella—reduced from eleven or nine to seven. Thus the encyclopedia of the arts, for this is what the *Marriage* was, had nine books: one for each of the arts—grammar, rhetoric, dialectic, arithmetic, geom-

[4] See pp. 249–254.
[5] P. R. Cole, *Later Roman Education*, Teachers College, Columbia University, New York, 1909, p. 16.

etry, astronomy, and music—plus two introductory books. Capella's book was not the only means that later ages had for understanding the nature and function of the arts that classical culture had seemed to prize so highly, but it was a very popular source of information. So in a way Capella's book was a textbook, for it contained many of the things that students of later times, especially of the Middle Ages, studied. The trivium and the quadrivium were there, although Capella did not introduce into his description of them the fine distinctions that were made by later thinkers.

Boethius must share the stage with Capella. Even if Capella's part is a big one, the principal actor is still Boethius. He, like Capella, transmitted culture, but he did even more: he placed the content of this culture in a Christian frame of reference, and he made it intellectually and doctrinally palatable for Christians.

Here was a man of good standing, who married well and became an important political figure. But he fell into the pitfalls of politics. He spent his last years in prison and was executed for political crimes. The great work that came from Boethius' pen in his most mature years and the one which had a lasting and profound influence on European thought structure was the *Consolation of Philosophy*. As Rand has said, this was prison literature.[6] Even so, in general estimation it seemed to stand above Capella's *Marriage of Philology and Mercury* and Cassiodorus' *Divine and Human Readings*. It was more generally accepted than the former because of the reputation that Boethius had for being a Christian saint, and it was more thorough and satisfying than the latter because much of Cassiodorus' work is simply based on the *Consolation*. Professor Patch gives high praise to Boethius' book:

> The work was quoted verbatim in almost every connection, and, it is perhaps fair to say, thousands of times, if we may judge by the instances that have been listed. From casual reference and extensive borrowing, Boethius is everywhere recognized as an authority, fully as eminent as one of the Church Fathers, but more versatile than most of them. . . . One must call the roll of practically everyone of account in the Middle Ages if one is to include those who showed indebtedness to him.[7]

The *Consolation of Philosophy* was one of those books that no educated man left unread. It was, probably to a greater extent than Capella's fictional account of the arts, the textbook of the Middle Ages and, though unconventional, one of the most successful of all time. But Boethius wrote much beside the *Consolation*. He was engaged in

[6] Edward K. Rand, *The Founders of the Middle Ages,* Harvard University Press, Cambridge, Mass., 1928, p. 159.

[7] Howard Rollin Patch, *The Tradition of Boethius,* Oxford University Press, New York, 1935, p. 24.

scholarly endeavors long before he fell victim to political chicanery. He wrote some pastoral poetry; he prepared an arithmetic book based on the earlier work of Nichomachus; and he began a tremendous project which involved translations of and commentaries on both Plato and Aristotle. His commentaries on Porphyry's *Isagoge,* an *Introduction to the Categories of Aristotle,* brought logic up to a point where Christians could begin to regard it more favorably. Eventually they adopted it as an instrument for building their own intellectual system. Boethius offered, in addition to writings on philosophy and education, treatises on theology and music and many commentaries on the works of classical authors. If we find difficulty in accepting Boethius as the first of the Scholastics we can at least call him the schoolmaster of the Middle Ages in the same sense that we called Homer the schoolmaster of the Greeks.[8] Students who look to Boethius for solutions to practical educational problems—problems such as Quintilian tried to solve—will look in vain. Boethius' importance does not lie here.

It is worth the risk of repetition to emphasize the significance of Boethius. He was an inspiration to Christians in that he could integrate a tremendous wealth of classical learning and pagan philosophy with a healthy and apparently orthodox Christian faith. He led the early Middle Ages to the doorstep of philosophy, and, although the times were anything but encouraging for building intellectual foundations, provided budding Christian philosophers with a content and a terminology, and with the inspiration for moving ahead. More than this, he constructed a bridge between the classical years, with their high culture and their profound accomplishments in the arts, and the Christian Middle Ages, with their spirituality and their motivations for reconstructing the social order. The material for the bridge which Boethius built was the content of education, mainly the arts and, as they came to be known, the seven liberal arts.

St. Benedict (ca. 480–546)

A contemporary of Boethius and a builder with him of Christian tradition: this is an apt characterization of St. Benedict. Yet it does not begin to tell the whole story. St. Benedict, it is said, was not much affected by learning or art. His biographer has described him as one who was "sagely ignorant and wisely uneducated."[9] How unlike Boethius he must have been! However, the really important question for us is not whether or not St. Benedict was learned, but whether or not there was a place for liberal arts in the monastic establishments that he founded.

One conclusion might be that in following the monastic traditions

[8] See pp. 41–44.
[9] Rand, *op. cit.,* p. 239.

with their usual hostility toward classical learning, the Benedictine monasteries turned their backs on the liberal arts.[10] Yet we know that Christianity had now developed to the point where the written word was indispensable to it. There are not too many steps between this emphasis on the written word and a definitive Christian literature and the liberal knowledge to subserve it. In the *Rule* of St. Benedict a certain amount of sacred reading was prescribed.

There are some other alternatives. It is possible that liberal studies did find a place in Western monasticism; otherwise how is it possible to explain the learning that emanated from many of the monastic houses of Europe? Or it may have been that the secular schools were expected to provide the learning preparatory to sacred studies or to higher schools of theology. Benedict himself had attended a classical school which purported to offer studies in the liberal arts.

If the liberal arts were given a place in the Benedictine system, this place was usually well concealed. However, we do consider the monastic schools the first Christian schools in the proper sense, and we know that they evolved from an elementary to a higher stage. It may well be a mistake to look at the first monastery in order to find what we have really no right to expect for several centuries yet to come. We shall probably be making extravagant claims if we think that St. Benedict contributed to Christian culture and education in the same way that Boethius did, or that Boethius influenced the education of every peasant in the early or the later Middle Ages, or that the monastic schools were such a great force in education that they caused it to be widely and generously distributed. Benedict's contribution was that he laid the foundation for the Christian institutions in which Christian thought could revitalize and redirect classical culture. Here was the opportunity to breathe a Christian soul into pagan literature. From an educational point of view, the monasteries of the sixth century are of much less importance than those of the ninth and tenth centuries. Yet the later monasteries could not have reached their importance had it not been for the monastic beginnings of the West in the sixth century.

In a way, the cultural demeanor of Boethius and the Christian rusticity of Benedict are both mutually hostile and complementary. Although modern historians may have taken too literally the self-acknowledged ignorance, or preference for ignorance, of men like Benedict, it is safe

[10] For a further development of this point, see William Boyd, *History of Western Education,* 6th ed., A. & C. Black, Ltd., London, 1952, pp. 101–107. It should be mentioned again that the monastery was primarily a place where monks sought the salvation of their souls. The essential idea of monasticism neither included nor excluded literary culture. The monk was expected to be a holy, not necessarily a learned, man. Very few monks were ordained priests.

to assume that Benedict would have had some reservations about the direction of Boethius' learning. We must admit that the monastic ideal was originally frankly hostile to culture. On the other hand, we cannot ignore the Benedictine definition of the monastery as "a school for the service of God." The complementary role of monasticism was to be found, therefore, in the preservation of culture in the monasteries when it most needed to be rescued from oblivion, and in the monks' cultivation of the intellectual inheritance when they found a place for the liberal arts in their system.

Most of the strength of the secular schools had been lost by the sixth century. It is not likely that Benedict or his immediate followers had any thought of building on the educational foundation of the secular schools, nor is it likely that they thought of the monastery as a step on the educational ladder. We have already seen how the monastic schools had to provide for the most elementary literary training of their novices, if they preferred not to have them illiterate. They would not have been teaching the fundamentals if the public schools, the educational remnants of the Roman system, had been available to do the job.

Thus Benedict's contribution to the intellectual development, or redevelopment, of the West is to be discovered, apart from its relevance to spiritual improvement, in the type of monastery that he founded and the rule that he devised for it. It became the principal agency for the preservation and advancement of learning and culture during the period from the sixth to the twelfth century. Cultural foundations are constructed out of many things: eminent writers and thinkers are only two elements in such foundations.

Cassiodorus (ca. 480–575)

There are different opinions as to date of Cassiodorus' birth. Some scholars think he was born as early as 480; others move the date forward as far as 490 or 491. Research seems to bring agreement on the fact that Cassiodorus died when he was ninety-five years old, but it cannot clear up the uncertainty about the exact date of his birth or death.[11]

Flavius Magnus Aurelius Cassiodorus Senator[12] was born into a distinguished family. For generations the male members of the family

[11] In its length and industry the career of Cassiodorus as a statesman and scholar is almost without parallel. Here we are concerned with a sketch of his life and work, and his influence on the education of the Middle Ages.

[12] The word Senator is part of Cassiodorus' real name and is not a title as is so often assumed. See Cassiodorus Senator, Flavius Magnus Aurelius, *An Introduction to Divine and Human Readings,* translated, with an introduction and notes, by Leslie Webber Jones, Columbia University Press, New York, 1946, p. 4.

had held important and powerful positions in the service of rulers, and Cassiodorus followed in the footsteps of his illustrious forbears.[13] After being educated in rhetoric and philosophy—not an unusual education for a young man of his class—Cassiodorus began his public life as an assessor. This was only the first step up a ladder of public service that was to take him almost to the top. At the end of his public career he held the highest office that the state had available for citizens without royal blood.

His official duties kept him in touch with letters, and he, like Boethius, coupled his public duties with scholarly interests and accomplishments. Yet not until Cassiodorus left the public service did his life assume a dimension that was to have a great effect on the learning and culture of succeeding generations.[14] While still an important public official he wrote a *Chronicon,* an abstract of the history of the world from the Flood down to his own day,[15] and the *Gothic History* in twelve books. Neither work would stand too searching a critique, but they had, nevertheless, a certain respectability, and for that day and age were certainly nothing to be ashamed of. In addition to being a writer of books, Cassiodorus was, as so many other public figures often were, an inveterate writer of letters. These letters, both public and personal, showed an unusual sense for the historical. Cassiodorus kept copies of many of the letters he wrote. Toward the close of his public career his literary interests came to have a definite religious orientation. The outcome of this interest was to be felt, first of all, in a treatise in twelve books entitled *On the Soul.* The author himself seems to have regarded *On the Soul* as a philosophical work, but it is really a book on religion. It may be considered a sign of things to come during the last part of Cassiodorus' life; it shows his continuous interest in religion.

Some time earlier, probably in the 520s or 530s, Cassiodorus had proposed the establishment of a theological school in Rome. The plan did not come to realization, although it appears that Pope Agapetus favored the idea of creating a school in which the liberal arts would have been taught as preliminaries to sacred learning. Sacred learning, theological and scriptural, would have been given a new and more formal place in the mind and life of reason. Agapetus died in 536, and the plan was given up, but Cassiodorus did not forget the need that

---

[13] Rand says, "Next to Boethius, Cassiodorus was the most important figure at the court of Theodoric" (*op. cit.,* p. 240). Cassiodorus was destined throughout most of history to take second place to Boethius, and not without reason.

[14] Cassiodorus retired from public life when he was about sixty or sixty-five. This left thirty-five or thirty years for him to devote to other interests, both religious and scholarly.

[15] Cassiodorus Senator, *op. cit.,* p. 12.

Christianity had for a higher type of divine learning.[16] In place of a school he founded a monastery, in fact, two monasteries, on his own ancestral estates. They may not have been monasteries in the then conventional sense, because one of their chief objectives was scriptural study, and in the context of the day such an objective was somewhat out of keeping with the monastic ideal.

Was Cassiodorus a monk when he founded the monasteries or did he ever become a monk? Since it was not at all unusual for a layman to found a monastery in those days, commentators who argue that the founder of the double monastery at Scyllaccum must have been a monk have a rather weak case. But he may have entered the order, either when he founded the monasteries or later. Some authorities maintain positively that he was a monk; others are just as sure that he was not. After painstaking research, the most recent conclusion is that it is not possible to say definitively whether Cassiodorus was ever a monk or not.[17]

We move on now to the matter of Cassiodorus' influence on the Middle Ages. Did this influence have its source in his own writings or was it to be found in the monasteries that he brought into existence? If in the latter, what was the relationship between the monasteries of Cassiodorus and those of St. Benedict? Beside these two questions that need answers are others: What were the effects of Cassiodorus' monastic enterprises on the general monastic ideal? In other words, where did the monasteries go from there? Did they continue to be spiritual hermitages, or did they take on the appearance of spiritual houses with important educational and intellectual functions to perform? What was Cassiodorus' attitude toward the liberal arts? Was he a follower of St. Augustine, or did he advocate a certain independence for the arts? Finally, what did the book, *An Introduction to Divine and Human Readings,* for which he is so famous, contain? Have its value and significance been given an inflated estimation?

[16] It is claimed that the idea for the higher type of Christian school came to Cassiodorus from the Jewish theological schools with which he came in contact when he was in Constantinople. His own testimony ought to be interesting here. In the preface to *An Introduction to Divine and Human Readings* he wrote: "Perceiving that the schools were swarming with students because of a great longing for secular letters (a great part of mankind believed that through these schools it attained worldly wisdom), I was, I confess, extremely sorry that the Divine Scriptures had no public teachers, since worldly authors were rich in instruction beyond doubt most distinguished. I strove with the most holy Agapetus, bishop of the city of Rome, to collect subscriptions and to have Christian rather than secular schools receive professors in the city of Rome, just as the custom is said to have existed for a long time at Alexandria and is said even now to be zealously cultivated by the Hebrews in Nisibis, a city of the Syrians, that thereby the soul might obtain eternal salvation and the tongue of the faithful might be adorned with a holy and completely faultless eloquence." (Cassiodorus Senator, *op. cit.,* p. 67.)

[17] *Ibid.,* p. 24.

Postponing the question of influence on the culture of the Middle Ages, we may begin by examining the matter of Cassiodorus' relationship to St. Benedict. First of all, there is no evidence to suggest that Cassiodorus adopted the Benedictine plan. The general idea of monasticism was well known, and there were a number of special monastic plans that may have been followed. Besides, St. Benedict's famous Monte Cassino was not yet solidly established or generally known at the time Cassiodorus began his foundations. It must be remembered that Cassiodorus and Benedict were contemporaries. In fact, this may explain why scholars have been unable to find obvious threads of influence running between them. In any case, according to L. W. Jones, "there is no doubt whatever that the pains taken by Cassiodorus for the instruction of his monks distinguish his monastery quite clearly from Benedictine foundations."[18] Even though we may want to accept this point of view, we should not forget that there were clear and definite differences between monasticism of the East and monasticism of the West. While the monks of the East could be holy and illiterate and no one would despise the ignorant monk, Western monasticism was never completely oblivious of the Christian literary tradition that was being built and of the need to perpetuate it.[19] In other words, the Christian religion was becoming more and more a literary, if not an intellectual, creed, and Western monasticism was completely aware of its character. The monks of the West seemed to need simple skills of literacy, although they may not have needed or wanted the skills and motivations for scholarship. In spite of a necessary and natural affinity that the work of St. Benedict had for the monastic foundations of Cassiodorus, the latter made some fairly sharp departures from monastic conventions.

Cassiodorus has been called the "father" of literary monasticism. This is a wonderful tribute and we have no wish to deprive him of it. Yet we are not quite sure what this literary monasticism was that Cassiodorus fathered. As far as the practice of reading and writing was concerned, it would be impossible to claim that either was introduced to monastic life by Cassiodorus. St. Pacomius had prescribed both reading and writing as a daily practice for the monks who lived under his rule. St. Pacomius died in 346. And, in addition to this, many copyists did their work in the monasteries that followed the rule he had devised. There were copyists in other monasteries too. St. Jerome's monastic experiences did not foreclose literary endeavor or scholarly accomplishment. Still, there is really little reason to doubt that, though literary monasticism may have preceded Cassiodorus—if we mean by that simple reading and writing—Cassiodorus brought about an innovation in em-

[18] *Ibid.*, p. 23.
[19] See pp. 190–191.

phasis. In the two monasteries that he founded, writing and study were regular and important parts of the discipline of the monastery.

Literary monasticism as it appeared in the monasteries of Cassiodorus was more than mere copying. There was a scriptorium in the monastery, a place where monks copied the scriptures and the writings of the Fathers, and where, on occasion and perhaps with special permission, they would also copy the classics. Today we should think of the scriptorium as a printing shop or a small publishing plant. In connection with it, of course, there was necessarily a library of some kind. The library was the source of the copyist's material, if not his inspiration. This scriptorium was a well-organized and important part of the monastery. Instead of tilling the soil for a livelihood, a monk might take his pen in hand and prepare manuscripts. Despite the importance attached to copying manuscripts and the ancillary skills that went with copying—bookbinding, illuminating, minuscule, ink manufacture, paper making—literary monasticism involved something more. The other side of it, as Cassiodorus envisioned it, was a scholarly approach to scriptural and theological study. Perhaps this phase of literary monasticism was not too highly developed in the monasteries of Cassiodorus, but that it was developed at all or even provided for indicates Cassiodorus' insight into the problems of his day as they impinged on the Church and also into the problems that the Church might expect to face in succeeding ages.

At this point it is natural to ask the question: Was Cassiodorus' interest confined to divine studies only? What was his attitude toward the liberal arts?

The surprising thing about Cassiodorus is not that he was engrossed with divine learning, but that he was as liberal as he was. After all, he was a product of his age. And this was an age, as we have seen, that was somewhat unsure of its attitude toward classical learning. There were some precedents for accepting classical authors, but generally speaking, it was safer and more popular to avoid them. The praises of the arts that we find here and there in the writings of Cassiodorus, though genuine, are somewhat reserved; and understandably so, for Cassiodorus, along with St. Augustine and most of the Western Church Fathers, was sincere in his conviction that the arts were simply aids to the study of theology. All liberal culture and all profane science were thought to be contained in scripture or derived from it. With this view—one which actually made scientific and cultural studies unnecessary—the surprising thing is not that profane knowledge was neglected but that it was studied at all. This was the general position taken at the time, and it was representative of the age. There is no reason to believe that Cassiodorus did not endorse this position. Yet he could act like a scholar at times. He had some of the scholar's habits and interests. He would neither encourage nor forbid the reading of the classical authors, but he did encourage—possibly even prescribed—the reading of the Bible for the monks in his monasteries. This in itself was remarkable.

The Introduction to Divine and Human Readings. In the preface to this work Cassiodorus explained his motives for writing a guide to divine and human literature and, in a manner of speaking, an educational syllabus for the intellectually inclined monks of his monasteries. After referring to his abortive plan for a Christian school of higher studies in Rome,[20] he goes on to say:

> But my ardent desire could in no way have been fulfilled because of the struggles that seethed and raged excessively in the Italian realm, inasmuch as a peaceful affair has no place in anxious times, I was driven by divine charity to this device, namely, in the place of a teacher to prepare for you under the Lord's guidance these introductory books, through which, in my opinion, the unbroken line of the Divine Scriptures and the compendious knowledge of secular letters might with the Lord's beneficence be related—books not at all fluent, perhaps, since in them is found, not studied eloquence, but indispensable narration; to be sure, they are extremely useful, since through them one learns the indicated origin of both the salvation of the soul and secular knowledge. In them I commit to you, not my own learning, but the words of men of former times, which it is right to praise and glorious to proclaim for future generations, for whatever is said about men of former times by way of praise of the Lord is not considered hateful display. Add to this the fact that one is pleased with a venerable teacher if one consults him frequently; moreover, whenever one desires to have recourse to such teachers, one will find no harshness in them.[21]

This then is his purpose: to instruct his monks in what ought to be studied. The work is divided into two books. Book I is concerned with *Divine Letters* and is arranged into thirty-three chapters. Despite the promise implicit in the book's title, this is hardly a compendium of divine learning. In print, Book I is not more than seventy-five pages long.

In Book I Cassiodorus describes the contents of the nine codices which make up the Old and New Testaments. He names the chief scriptural commentators. He discusses the various methods of understanding the scriptures and adds a caution that editors, commentators, and scribes should be conservative in their handling of sacred texts. He devotes one chapter to the cosmographers—those who explained the nature of the world—and one to ecclesiastical commentators. Then he urges his monks to pursue learning and cultivate it, not for its own sake, but as a means toward better knowledge of the scriptures. This is how Cassiodorus phrases his advice in Book I, Chapter 27:

[20] See pp. 202–203.
[21] Cassiodorus Senator, *op. cit.*, pp. 67–68.

We have decided that you ought to be cautioned about this matter too: since we can understand much in sacred literature as well as in the most learned interpreters through figures of speech, much through definitions, much through the art of grammar, much through the art of rhetoric, much through dialectics, much through the science of arithmetic, much through music, much through the science of geometry, much through astronomy, it is not unprofitable in the book which follows to touch briefly upon the elements of instruction laid down by secular teachers, that is, upon the arts and sciences, together with their divisions, in order that those who have acquired knowledge of this sort may have a brief review and those who perhaps have been unable to read widely may learn something from the compendious discussion. Beyond any doubt knowledge of these matters, as it seemed to our Fathers, is useful and not to be avoided, since one finds this knowledge diffused everywhere in sacred literature, as it were in the origin of universal and perfect wisdom. When these matters have been restored to sacred literature and taught in connection with it, our capacity for understanding will be helped in every way.[22]

If there were monks in the monastery who by reason of lack of intellectual capacity were unable to profit from the studies that Cassiodorus had outlined up to this point in *Divine Letters,* they should, according to the instructions contained in the volume, turn to the manuscripts that had been written on the subjects of farming and gardening. Cassiodorus notes that he had stocked such manuscripts in the libraries he had collected for the two monasteries. He does not, however, dwell on this phase but returns quickly to literary matters. The monks are encouraged to copy the manuscripts that they find in their libraries, and they are admonished to copy them with care. His interest in the work of the copying monk may be seen in the following passage:

I admit that among those of your tasks which require physical effort that of the scribe, if he writes correctly, appeals most to me. . . . Happy his design, praiseworthy his zeal, to preach to men with the hand alone, to open tongues with fingers, to give salvation silently to mortals, and to fight against illicit temptations of the devil with pen and ink. Every word of the Lord written by the scribes is a wound inflicted on Satan. And so, though seated in one spot, with the dissemination of his work he travels through different provinces. . . . A sight glorious to those who contemplate it carefully.[23]

From here our author turns to orthographical rules for the monk-scribe to follow and then to bookbinding. The latter is treated briefly but with more than usual care. Finally, there are instructions on the use of mech-

---

[22] *Ibid.,* p. 127. It may be noted that this quotation from chap. 27 represents more than half of the chapter. Thus the reader may obtain some idea as to the length of Cassiodorus' thirty-three chapters.

[23] *Ibid.,* p. 133.

anical devices that were provided for the monastic scriptoria, a brief discourse on medical works, an admonition to the abbot and the monks to be honorable and faithful, and a prayer. So ends book I of *Divine and Human Readings.*[24]

Book I was the book that counted, for it, according to Cassiodorus and many of his contemporaries, discussed the essential components of all knowledge. Yet Cassiodorus did not stop with Book I. His investigation of secular knowledge, though it does not imply the enthusiasm of an advocate, does suggest, at least, that he was more liberal than many of his Christian contemporaries. Yet because he was fundamentally conservative, the Christians of his own day and those who followed him felt that they could trust him. Thus they turned to Book II, *Secular Letters,* to find their way through the labyrinth of liberal knowledge. What did they find?

They found, first of all, a preface and a conclusion. To these were added seven chapters, which contained brief accounts of the seven liberal arts: grammar, rhetoric, dialectic, arithmetic, geometry, music, and astronomy. In all, the second book takes up no more than sixty-seven or sixty-eight pages.

Cassiodorus' treatment of secular letters is no more original than was his treatment of divine letters. Of course, Cassiodorus never claimed that he even hoped to be original. And as we have said before, originality is not the only stepladder to fame or influence. He was indebted, as most writers are, to many authors who preceded him, and though he may have tried to follow them faithfully, he did not always do so satisfactorily. In spite of whatever shortcoming this second book may have had, it was one of the chief sources to which medieval teachers went when they wanted to know something about the liberal arts. They hardly ever went to the authors of whom Cassiodorus spoke as follows:

And, moreover, we shall not fail to reveal the authors, both Greek and Latin, whose explanations of the matters which we discuss have become famous, in order that those who desire to read zealously may more lucidly understand the words of the ancients after having first been introduced to them in abridged form.[25]

It is hard to believe that Cassiodorus ever intended his work to be anything more than a guide to study; at least, he never made the suggestion that it be a textbook or *the* textbook for the schools.

We have already heard a good deal of the relation of liberal learning to education. Throughout most of history this topic seems never to have lost its freshness. But in spite of all the interest, it is sometimes said that

[24] For the complete table of contents of the first book, see *ibid.,* pp. 73–74.
[25] *Ibid.,* p. 145.

before Cassiodorus the number of the liberal arts was never clearly recognized. Cassiodorus is thought to have fixed the number at seven, possibly because he echoed the ancient claim of mystical significance for this number. This is how the claim was set forth in the beginning of Book II:

One surely ought to know that the Sacred Scripture frequently expresses by means of this number [seven] whatever it desires to be understood as continuous and perpetual, as David, for example, says, "Seven times a day I have given praise to thee," though he elsewhere vows, "I will bless the Lord at all times; his praise shall be always in my mouth," and Solomon says, "Wisdom hath built herself a house, she hath hewn her out seven pillars." In Exodus as well the Lord said to Moses, "Thou shalt make seven lamps, and shalt set them to give light over against it." Revelation constantly mentions this number in various applications. And this number leads us to that eternity which can have no end; with justice, then, it is always used whenever perpetuity is indicated.[26]

As a final point with reference to Book II, this question may be raised: Was Cassiodorus' *Secular Letters* used as he had intended it to be used? Did he look forward to the time when it would be followed by learned men and used as a textbook by students who were intent upon probing the world's secrets? Neither Book I nor Book II was ever intended for the learned. These were not manuals for scholars. Their language alone is enough to suggest a less ambitious purpose. The treatise taken as a whole was a literary prescription for the monks at Vivarium and Castellum and not a tool for the schools or the universities. Of course, Cassiodorus had no control whatever over the use that later ages made of the *Introduction to Divine and Human Readings*. Let us turn to that question now: What was the influence of Cassiodorus on the culture and the education of the Middle Ages?

Cassiodorus did not introduce to the monastery either the scriptorium or the study of the scriptures. They had been established before his time. But Cassiodorus did succeed in integrating the work of copying manuscripts with daily monastic life and in transforming the monastery into something resembling a theological school. This was a remarkable service. His systematic approach to literary or scholarly monasticism had important consequences.

Cassiodorus' influence permeated the Middle Ages in a number of ways. It would not be easy to supply documentation for all the claims that have been made for him, but in three areas it is possible to be quite definite: (1) The *Introduction to Divine and Human Readings*, especially Book II, which contains the outline for the seven liberal arts, was used as a bibliographical guide for several centuries, and in it librarians,

[26] *Ibid.*, p. 144.

masters, and students found inspiration and guidance for their work. (2) Book II took its place alongside the works of Martianus Capella, Boethius, Priscian, and Donatus as one of the important schoolbooks of the early Middle Ages. It made no difference whatever that Cassiodorus' manual had not been intended as anything more than a guide for the monks' study. (3) Finally, because Cassiodorus made a commitment to literary monasticism, both his monasteries and others were encouraged to collect selections of the Church Fathers and the ancient Latin authors. Monastic libraries became depositories for early medieval culture. The fact that they performed the function of preservation when no other agency was prepared or inclined to do so should hold all of Western culture in their debt.

Gregory the Great (540–604)

Again we meet a question that has faced us so often before. Now it is Pope Gregory (590–604) who weighs the merits and demerits of the education of the past; it is the Church's highest officer who gives his views on classical education. Here was a man whose education comprised the secular as well as the divine arts, and who was in turn a political official, a monk, an ecclesiastical officer, a papal emissary, and a pope. Gregory was in a position of authority; his stand on the question of the content and purposes of education was bound to make a great impression on Western and on Christian minds. It would not be unreasonable to suppose that Gregory's influence was great enough to last for centuries. What direction did this influence take?

It is evident that St. Gregory was interested in education as well as in church organization, administration, and discipline. But he did not show any sympathy for the education of the past. He was willing, it seems, to turn his back on the past, to reject the heritage of Greece, to repudiate the foundations of his own education, and to start anew. More exactly, St. Gregory was committed to a practical Christian education that would find its ultimate goal in eternity and its most fundamental curricula in Christian doctrine and morals. We must not forget that Gregory would have permitted the liberal arts to remain, though in a subordinate position and only to the extent that they might be useful instruments for understanding the scriptures and the commentaries on them. The liberal arts became stepchildren who were not really loved or wanted but were being put up with. In a real sense, moreover, these arts could no longer be very liberal.

Although Gregory has his apologists with reference to his stand on the liberal arts, we cannot overlook his often-quoted utterance to Bishop

Desiderius of Vienne: "For the same lips cannot sound the praises of Jupiter and the praises of Christ."[27]

Christian bishops were expected to be doing something more important than holding discussions or seminars on the classics, and Gregory was, in one sense, simply reminding one of the shepherds of souls of this higher duty. Yet, in another sense, Gregory the pope is setting classical learning out of bounds. This is no mere monk speaking. Just what apology can bring classical learning back within bounds and make it a worthy objective for Christian people? The answer to this question is far from clear. Gregory was not given to looseness of speech; he usually said what he meant. The conclusion seems unavoidable: Liberal learning and the Christian ideal were separated by an impassable gulf. Is there not evidence of this gulf in the following quotation from Gregory?

> Wherefore I have scorned to observe all art of style, in which pupils are drilled in schools of the outer training. For, as the tenor of the present letter makes evident, I shun not the collision of M's; I avoid not the disorder of barbarisms; I despise a conformity to constructions and moods and cases of prepositions. For I deem it exceedingly inept to fetter the words of the Heavenly Oracle to the rules of Donatus.[28]

In Pope Gregory we find official recognition of a new kind of education, a Christian education. It is one that goes far beyond the earlier conceptions of Christian education to which reference has already been made.[29] It included home training and moral formation on the most elementary levels, but it rejected any accommodation of the Christian view of life or goal to the secular schools and the classical education that made up their curricula. Finally, though it did not create the institution for this new education, Gregory's plan came to be a clear endorsement of the monastic school. In other ways and at other places he had already given his unqualified approval to monasticism of a Benedictine type. With Gregory's educational plan, the past loses much of its significance for Christian schools. Gregory was no humanist, and he held no brief for humanism. He looked forward, and he demanded that education should look forward too. One word may be used to characterize his educational theory: practical.

It was in this setting, where a practical Christian education received praise and encouragement, that the *Introduction* of Cassiodorus and the *Etymologies* of Isidore of Seville achieved their great fame and exerted

[27] St. Gregory *Epistle* xi, 54. In Migne, *Patrologia Latina*, LXXVII, 1171c.

[28] This passage is from Gregory's prefatory letter to his moral exposition of the book of Job (Migne, *Patrologia Latina*, LXXV, 516b).

[29] See pp. 152–154.

their most pervasive influence. Though Gregory and Cassiodorus could not have agreed on all points of educational theory, Gregory's program for educational reform did create a climate wherein Cassiodorus' brand of Christian humanism, in which the arts were made subservient to divine learning, could take root and grow.

Isidore of Seville (560–636)

On the important educational questions of the age, Isidore stood somewhere between Cassiodorus and Gregory the Great. He was less liberal and possibly even less learned than Cassiodorus. He was only slightly less critical of classical and secular learning than Gregory. No qualification was inserted, apparently, when he wrote that Christians are forbidden to read the lies of the poets, although it is not clear just where this proscription came from.

Isidore is not remembered for his writing on theory. He presented no ideal for education, although by his work, principally the *Etymologies,* he served the tone or the ideals which had already been set. He wrote a voluminous thesaurus or encyclopedia that purported to contain all knowledge, at least, all knowledge that was worth having. This was the *Etymologies,* which was used as a standard reference and text from the seventh through the eleventh century. It is difficult to overestimate, and almost unhistorical to depreciate, the worth of a book that was used regularly and in some places exclusively for four centuries. Isidore was credited with being the most learned man of his time, and he may have been. Yet it is possible to recognize such a credit as an index of the general retrogression in learning. Isidore was probably the most widely informed man of his time. Expressions of praise for his learning reveal how great the intellectual darkness must have been to make Isidore appear so brilliant. His writings, though they do attest to the fact that Isidore knew many of the earlier authors, some of them classical authors —he had copied verbatim from some—disclose that his mind was quite willing to accept the conclusions of authority without any question whatever in all areas of knowledge, even in some into which authority should not intrude.

Isidore's *Etymologies,* because it was such a popular schoolbook, warrants our further attention. It is divided into twenty books, which treat the following topics: grammar, rhetoric, logic, arithmetic, geometry, astronomy, music, medicine, law, time, books of the Bible, laws and worship of the Church, God, angels and believers, the church and the sects, languages, races, empires, warfare, citizenship, kinship, alphabetical lists of words, men, monsters, animals, the universe, the earth, buildings, fields, stones, metals, agriculture, war, games, sports, ships, clothing, food, drink, and utensils. The variety of topics in the work is intriguing, and its breadth is imposing. The remarkable thing about this schoolbook was that the contents which the boys studied were not very clearly related to life. This irrelevance did not seem to bother anyone. Perhaps it was not possible for education to turn its back on the past as Gregory would have liked and thus give its undivided attention to the practical matter of education for salvation. But it was possible, apparently, to shut off education from life and to make it practically meaningless. We have seen how Hellenistic grammarians and rhetors devitalized their learning,[30] and we see Christians of the early Middle Ages engaged in the same process. If formal education must have an indebtedness to the past, if it is not possible to exclude all but divine learning, then the thing to do is to deprive this secular learning of significance. Its lack of significance and relevance to life's real problems is well demonstrated in the way it was organized and presented in the work of Isidore.

Despite the limitations of Isidore's "textbook" and the valid criticisms that can be made of the book's contents and the author's methods, it would be unfortunate if we were to neglect another side of Isidore's influence. As Bishop of Seville, Isidore exercised authority over schools, monasteries, churches, and the clergy. Though he used this authority in many legitimate ways, one way in particular has especial interest for us here. He attempted to upgrade the education of the Spanish clergy. Isidore was adamant on the point that illiterate men were not to be made priests. So Isidore was more than a writer of a famous and much-used textbook for the early Middle Ages; he was a spiritual leader, who directed that the educational standards of clerics in Spain be raised. Andrew West writes of him:

Isidore stands last on the list, closing the development of Christian school learning in the midst of a barbarism that was extinguishing not only learning but civilized society in Western Europe. The darkness that followed his time for over a century was profound and almost universal. Rome itself had become barbarian, and only in distant Britain and Ireland was the lamp of learning kept lighted, not to shine again on the Continent until brought thither by the hand of Alcuin.[31]

IRISH EDUCATION (FROM THE SIXTH THROUGH THE NINTH CENTURY)

When the framework which held education together, schools and general culture, disintegrated, education itself became all but extinct.

---

[30] See pp. 125–126.

[31] Andrew F. West, *Alcuin and the Rise of the Christian Schools,* Charles Scribner's Sons, New York, 1892, p. 27.

There is little reason to doubt that culture and learning on the Continent had fallen to a very low level; it would be a mere waste of time to try to prove that the Dark Ages never really existed. Only in one place in the Western world, for reasons that are sometimes obscure, did learning flourish. This was in Ireland.

Ireland was never part of the Roman Empire, and its education, therefore, was not directly affected by what was happening to the Empire in the early sixth century or by the erosions that had been wasting it for three hundred years before. On the other hand, standing as it did on the fringe of the classically oriented world, Ireland was in a position to absorb some of the main components of ancient learning, though what passed for classical culture in Ireland was a reasonable facsimile rather than the real thing. Of course no sort of cultural fraud was involved or intended in the Christianizing of the content of classical culture so as to make it more acceptable to the people who had responded enthusiastically to the preaching and missionary work of St. Patrick. In spite of St. Patrick's tremendous influence for good in Ireland, it would be a mistake to attribute the improvement of scholarship to him.

The precise state of culture during pre-Christian times in Ireland is difficult to determine. There seems to have been a Celtic literature, and there were Celtic scholars—bards or druids—who conducted schools that preserved and cultivated the Irish literary inheritance. And there was a native script—ogam or ogham—a peculiar invention of the Gael and found only where he had his settlements. If Ireland was barbaric, it was so only in the original and strictest meaning of the word. All the evidences of culture, a native literary tradition, a written literature, schools and teachers, scholars and higher schools, could be found in Ireland before Christian scholars migrated there from a Continental environment that was neither conducive nor friendly to learning. Perhaps these scholars did not come in great numbers, but it is said that they came before the time of St. Patrick.[32]

In spite of the existence of Irish scholarship and culture before Ireland was Christianized, we can be certain that the Irish became the schoolmasters of the West and that they molded the connecting link in the chain of learning only after the advent of the Christian period in Ireland. Irish schools, of course, were not the sole factor in preserving learning for later ages, though they played a leading role. The school that rates first place in this consideration was the monastic school. It may be added, in fairness to the excellence of pre-Christian Irish culture, that there was no real need for the schools of the pre-Christian period to engage in any principal mission of preserving culture. Evidently the cul-

[32] James J. Auchmuty, *Irish Education,* Hodges, Figgis & Co., Dublin, 1937, and George G. Harrap & Co., Ltd., London, 1937, pp. 7–18.

tural commitment to progress was so clear that little or no attention was given to preserving the past.

We have seen something of the monastic schools on the Continent,[33] but Irish monasticism and Irish monastic schools were somewhat different from their Continental counterparts. What were the chief features of these Irish monastic schools, the schools in which the culture of the West was kept alive for two or more centuries?

Before answering this question we should mention that monastic schools in Ireland did not replace the bardic schools which antedated them. In actual fact, there was a dual system of education in Ireland, the lay or bardic schools formed one system, the monastic schools the other. Early in the period when this dualism was current in Irish education, perhaps in the seventh century or late in the sixth, the lay schools assumed a responsibility for instruction in military science, law, and general literature. The first two were professional curricula; the last was what one might call a curriculum of general or liberal education, and became a professional curriculum only when used as a preparatory school by young men who were looking forward to admission to a religious community. Incidentally, this was not an uncommon professional use. But whether these schools were exclusively devoted to higher studies, leaving lower education to the monastic schools, or whether they provided opportunity for elementary and secondary education is a point that is obscure and cannot be answered here. At any rate, monastic schools were interested in elementary and secondary education, and they rarely went into the professional areas, except for studies in theology.

Late in the seventh century the value of the bardic schools was questioned (for what specific reasons is doubtful), and they were nearly eliminated from the Irish educational scene. The number of such schools was drastically reduced. What was called a reform in Irish education suppressed all but a half-dozen or so of the bardic or lay schools. And with this suppression we have, it would seem, the first signs of some decay in Irish scholarship and cultural values. It may be true that the destruction of the Irish educational system was due to invasion and a physical wrecking of the means for education, but it is hard to believe that the suppression of bardic schools was not a sign of internal decay or at least of lessening interest in the kind of education that these schools had to offer. It was also an indication of a shift away from cultural values once quite firmly held. Yet the reduction in the number of the bardic schools did little or nothing to tarnish the reputation these schools had for unmatched quality. The teachers were laymen who were following in the footsteps of fathers, grandfathers, and great-grandfathers. Teaching in the Irish bardic school was a family vocation passed on from genera-

[33] See pp. 189–191.

tion to generation, an intellectual inheritance that was kept vital as it was bequeathed from one generation in a family to the next. That such a practice was followed should not surprise us too much, for we are familiar with it in many of the trades and crafts. Yet it is a tradition not often met in the history of education.

But to return to the monastic school: First, it has been thought that education in Ireland was purely an ecclesiastical affair. We have seen that such an idea is erroneous, for much of Irish education, especially professional education, was in the hands of laymen. It has been intimated, also, that Irish monastic schools were narrow religious institutions which, though they may have cultivated a kind of catechetical learning, left the elements of general culture completely alone. This criticism, too, is erroneous, as we shall see.

The monastic school handled the elementary and secondary levels of education, which are often thought to be the most important to an individual's formation. Under the most favorable circumstances, then, lay and monastic schools complemented each other, for the lay schools built on the foundation that the monastic school had laid. The most distinctive feature of the Irish monastic school, however, was that it was principally, though not entirely, a school for externs; that is, monastic schools were in the business of education, not only for the preparation of boys who were seeking the clerical life, but for all children who came to them. The monastic school was a school in a proper sense; it was not, as on the Continent, merely a necessary but perhaps unwanted adjunct to the monastery. It was far from unusual to find a layman teaching in the monastic school (although we know nothing of the working conditions or the professional status accorded him), and it was not extraordinary to find monks studying in the lay schools. Girls, apparently, were not excluded from opportunity for education, although little is known of the details of their studies. And foreign students, if not actually recruited, were, at least, welcomed to the Irish schools.

It was these Irish monastic schools that brought about a new flowering of the culture of antiquity as interpreted through Christian eyes. Science, too, though of course without experimental or observational techniques, had a place in the curriculum. In short, the monastic school in Ireland became a preserve for the seven liberal arts. Despite its protection of the liberal arts and a certain relative breadth in the curriculum, the aim of the Irish monastic school was frankly religious.

Besides supporting schools that grew out of Irish monasticism, the monasteries themselves acknowledged a literary ideal which had, as we already know, the emphatic endorsement of Cassiodorus. In nearly every monastery in Ireland there was a scriptorium and a library.

Within the borders of Ireland flourished the "school of the West." The

Irish cultivated and preserved learning until the end of the eighth century, when the Danes invaded the Emerald Isle and, with a special fury directed at instruments of literature and religion, destroyed thousands of manuscripts by fire or water. But by this time Ireland had been able to perform a work of transmission. The culture that had first of all been imported to Ireland was returned to the Continent by Irish monks and scholars, and though in itself this was not enough to produce a renaissance, it was the basic material out of which the renaissance of the ninth century was fashioned. Ireland had been the university of the Western world in the seventh and eighth centuries. This is a title of which she can be truly proud.

THE MOHAMMEDANS AND LEARNING IN THE WEST

Learning and culture in Continental Europe declined to the point of near extinction. The decline must be understood, for it is relevant to a number of later historical developments. That a revival was possible at all was due to the ability of the people in other lands to communicate their learning effectively when Continental Europe was ready to accept it. Thus we may say that Continental Europe's cultural revival was possible because in a number of places outside the Continent culture did not decline. But this is not the whole story. We cannot neglect the truly important preservative function that the monasteries on the Continent performed, and we should not try to insist that there were neither cultured nor educated men on the Continent during the three-hundred-year period following the sixth century. We have already seen something of two of three important factors that contributed to the renaissance of the ninth century: monasticism on the Continent of Europe and the Irish reservoir of learning and culture. The third was Moslem learning.

These Moslems, sometimes called Arabs, were the followers of Mohammed (569–632); they accepted the religious doctrines that he preached and the holy book he left for them, the Koran. The religious doctrine and the Arabic language were central elements in a culture that included music, science, architecture, literature, and philosophy. This culture, which may be called Arabic civilization, was picked up by the Mohammedans as they moved their conquering armies westward from Arabia all the way to northern Africa and across the Mediterranean to southern Spain. If these Arabs were barbarians, they were surely something more than mere barbaric collectors. They did not carry culture as a veneer but used it to good advantage, not only to themselves but indirectly to the advantage of all the Western world. What significance did Arabic arts and learning have for Western education?

In the first place, the Moslems came along about the time when classical learning was in danger of being lost in the West. They took the philosophy and science of the Greeks and grafted them to their own ideas as well as to ideas borrowed from others, especially from India and China. The Moslems were anything but provincial, and though they were selective, they did not turn their backs on anything that might be of value to them. They were philosophical and scientific scholars. But in another way the Moslems performed a service of nearly inestimable value: They preserved the writings of the Greek scholars and thinkers— of Aristotle, Euclid, Galen, Ptolemy, to mention only a few of the authors for whom the Moslem scholarly community had great reverence. Even though the hazards of translation canceled out some of the worth of the works that antiquity had produced, it is true that for a time during the first years of the later medieval period, all that was known in Europe of the classical writers was known through Arabic preservation, translation, or transmission. The Arabs were responsible for reintroducing the learning of antiquity to Western Europe, it is true, but they did more. The Arabic notation and algebra were their contribution and invention respectively. The former was a contribution that served to make arithmetic a standard school subject. Before the advent of the Arabic notation, as we have seen,[34] arithmetic was really a theory of numbers rather than an art of computation, for neither the Greek nor the Roman numerals had the characteristics necessary for the development of arithmetic. With the exception of elementary school children, who find no joy in doing the fundamental operations or who resist the attainment of skill in arithmetic technique, the Western world is inclined to thank the Moslem for his notation.

In the practical arts the Moslems were both skillful and imaginative. Among the many practical achievements that may be credited to them, one stands out especially because of its relation to learning: the manufacture of paper. This was an art that the Arab had learned from the Chinese. He perfected it with results that were everywhere apparent. It was a tremendous achievement and a great contribution to the cause of learning and cultural progress.

There is one last area in which the influence of the Arab was productive of results, not in that he created something new but rather in that he stimulated Christians to be more creative. This creativity was displayed particularly in the field of theology. The religion of Mohammed was a challenge to Christianity, and Moslem scholars furnished persistent, pertinent, and often effective opposition to Christian theologians. In order to defend Christian doctrines and Christian theology, to give them greater strength in the face of Moslem assaults, Christian theologians perfected and elaborated their own system. As a result of the Moslem

[34] See pp. 56–57.

threat, real theological scholarship arose, possibly for the first time. It may even be possible to argue that the principal impetus for the establishment of the Christian university of the medieval period was given by the challenge of Mohammedanism. If this is an extravagant claim, we can at least say that the Mohammedan ideological threat was one of many contributing factors in the creation of the greatest of medieval institutions, the university.[35]

MODIFYING EDUCATIONAL THOUGHT AND REVIVING EDUCATIONAL INTEREST

We come now to the first revival of learning—to be followed by two others, both of which were stronger—that was inspired by Charles the Great (768–814) and guided by Alcuin (ca. 735–804). This first renaissance was a vital step in the evolution of modern education. Had it not been for this first though admittedly relatively weak revival, neither the renaissance of the twelfth nor the renaissance of the fourteenth century would have been possible.

This revival of learning was indebted to the sources to which reference has already been made: monasticism, Irish learning, and Moslem culture. These must be considered indispensable sources even when we admit that the leadership of Charlemagne and Alcuin exercised the most direct force in bringing a revival of learning to fruition. Nor can we forget that other men and institutions continued the work they started.

At this point we should make some mention of Christian scholarship in England in the seventh and eighth centuries. England's role in the revival that was generated in the late eighth and early ninth centuries may not be easy to assess, and we can make only the general claim that England was a cultural bridge between Ireland and the court of Charlemagne. The finest products of English scholarship were Alcuin of York (even though much of Alcuin's formal education had been obtained in Ireland) and the Venerable Bede (ca. 673–735). The former, perhaps not as great an ornament of English learning as Bede, was, nevertheless, the man who rekindled the flame of liberal learning on the Continent of Europe.

Before we turn to the great renaissance of the ninth century, we should

[35] We have not touched on the subject here because it is not relevant to our study, but we should note that the Arabic revival was not confined to Europe. Moslem civilization brought about a great enrichment of learning and life in and around the capital of Eastern Mohammedanism. The cultural progress most typical of this enrichment was both profound and permanent. See F. J. C. Hearnshaw, *Mediaeval Contributions to Modern Civilisation,* George G. Harrap & Co., Ltd., London, 1921, pp. 107–148; and E. M. Hulme, *The Middle Ages,* Holt, Rinehart and Winston, Inc., New York, 1929, pp. 214–237.

touch on a few points that belong to the educational history of this
earlier period. Royal patronage of education was to enjoy its finest hour
in the court of Charles the Great, but there were other evidences of royal
or princely interest in learning about this time.[36] Partly because of this
royal interest (superficial though it often was) and partly for other
reasons, the Church, especially the monastic foundations, took another
look at education. What the Church saw was slightly different from the
prescriptions of Gregory the Great. The result of a more searching and a
more realistic look at education was that under the guidance of Alcuin
and others who shared his general view, ecclesiastical education became
considerably more liberal. One of the clearest evidences of this laterali-
zation of policy and practice is that for the first time the seven liberal
arts were given a secure and permanent place in the curricula of
cathedral and episcopal schools. The echo from the past that denied that
the praises of the classical poets and the praises of Christ could be sung
by the same voice was no longer heard so distinctly.

Chivalry, too, belonged to this era, and it continued to be an important
vehicle for individual formation. The steps of training from page,
through squire, to knight did not neglect education. Yet it is not possible
to claim that chivalry, as an educational force, had very broad effects.
Very few young people were touched by it, and education under its
auspices seldom had any literary orientation.

Finally, we must mention the education of women. The seventh or
eighth centuries did not provide much opportunity for their training, nor
was the renaissance of the ninth century much more interested in the
subject. The kind of education that women of this period did receive
was not unique in any sense; it was simply domestic training. And
domestic training was about all the ordinary woman, even the extraordinary woman, could have hoped for at this time.

Charles the Great

The remnants of learning that remained evident, though unpopular, in
the Frankish Empire were the spark that ignited the Carolingian revival
of the late eighth and ninth centuries. This spark was fanned by Charlemagne, and the implements he employed to start the fire and keep it
going were principally Alcuin, a trusted and scholarly lieutenant, and
the learning that could be had for the asking in the Irish and Moslem
cultures. Who was this man Charlemagne?

Charlemagne, or Charles the Great, is generally recognized as a
leader of rare quality. He was a soldier and a king, but he was an
organizer and administrator of considerably more than ordinary ability,
and apparently he was something of a humanitarian too. At any rate, he

---

[36] On this point, see Boyd, *op. cit.*, pp. 117–118.

promoted cultural and educational projects, and it is in this phase of his work that we are most interested here. Had he not been an emperor it is almost certain that he would not have had any opportunity to leave his mark on the history of Europe. Before 800 Charles was the king of the Franks and the Lombards; after 800, the year he was crowned as the successor to the ancient Roman emperors of the West, Charles was recognized as the ruler of the Continental German-Roman world. He had all the authority he needed to establish or restore learning and culture to a place of importance. But, what is more important, under Charles Europe enjoyed a period of peace, and in such an environment of relative tranquility the arts and sciences had a greater opportunity to flourish than before. To credit Charlemagne with having created conditions favorable to learning is to tell only part of the story of the Carolingian contribution to educational history. Charles himself took an active interest in education and literary culture. He wanted greater and better opportunity for the education of children, and he demanded improvement in the standards that governed the education of the clergy. This latter demand led to liturgical and literary advancement in the Church and in ecclesiastical circles.

It is possible to discover something of Charlemagne's attitude toward education by seeing what he did for the education of his own children and what course he followed in developing his own mind, by examining the provisions he made for education in his own court, and by understanding what he did to stimulate education in his empire.

Charlemagne's attitude toward the education of his own children is reported as follows by his biographer:

The plan that he adopted for his children's education was, first of all, to have both boys and girls instructed in the liberal arts, to which he also turned his own attention. As soon as their years admitted, in accordance with the customs of the Franks, the boys had to learn horsemanship, and to practice war and the chase, and the girls to familiarize themselves with cloth making, and to handle the distaff and spindle, that they might not grow indolent through idleness, and he fostered in them every virtuous sentiment.[37]

Of his own education, we can say that he liked to listen to music and that a good deal of his leisure was taken up by having readers read to him. The works of St. Augustine are said to have been his favorite literature. He spoke both Latin and German, and, according to some authorities, was fairly well versed in Greek. In addition, he was a patron of the arts and sciences, supporting scholars who worked in these fields. He also attempted to reform Frankish law and to improve the Frankish language.

[37] Einhard, *Life of Charlemagne,* translated by S. E. Turner, Harper & Brothers, New York, 1880, p. 51.

Some of this work of scholarship and of legal and linguistic reform was carried on at the court of Charlemagne. Here Charles was not only the patron but a student as well. He was not, so it is said, too great or powerful in his own eyes to sit at the feet of a humble scholar. Although Charles may not have been able to write, he encouraged the writer-scholars of his court, and the literary output therefrom was noteworthy both in quality and quantity.

The patronage of scholars and schooling was not foreign to the royal courts before or during the time of Charlemagne, but both were advanced considerably as a result of his interest in education and culture. Palace or court schools in the Frankish Empire, following the example of the king's court, became important educational forces. They provided opportunity for learning, of course, but they also gave leadership and example to the monastic schools and other schools on the Continent.

Although what has been said up to this point about Charles and his educational interests is not without relevance to the cause of education or learning in general, we can point out a more direct and perhaps more effective way that Charles took to bring about a revival. He issued edicts, decrees, or capitularies—letters of advice—which called on secular and ecclesiastical officials to promote education. Besides this, he made appointments of bishops and abbots as well as of secular officials that were consistent with the high value that he placed on education.

In 787 Charlemagne issued the following capitulary to all abbots and bishops of Frankland, in which they were encouraged to promote learning and teaching in the religious communities subject to them:

During recent years we have often received letters from different monasteries, informing us that at their sacred services the brethren offered up prayers on our behalf, and we have observed that the thoughts contained in these letters, though in themselves most just, were expressed in uncouth language, and while pious devotion dictated the sentiments, the unlettered tongue was unable to express them aright. Hence there has arisen in our minds the fear lest, if the skill to write correctly were thus lacking, so too would the power of rightly comprehending the Sacred Scriptures be far from fitting, and we all know that if verbal errors be dangerous, errors of the understanding are much more so. We exhort you, therefore, not only not to neglect the study of letters, but to apply yourselves thereto with perseverance and with that humility which is well pleasing to God, so that you may be able to penetrate with greater ease and certainty the mysteries of the Holy Scriptures. For, as these contain images, tropes, and similar figures, it is impossible to doubt that the reader will arrive far more readily at the spiritual sense, according as he is better instructed in learning. Let, therefore, there be chosen for this work men who are both able and willing to learn, and who are desirous of instructing others, and let them apply themselves to the work with a zeal equaling the earnestness with which we recommend it to them. It is our wish that you may be what it behooves the soldiers of the Church to be—religious in heart, learned in discourse and eloquent in speech.[38]

In 802 Charlemagne was responsible for the issuance of another capitulary which, though perhaps somewhat less well known than the one of 787, may have had a much greater effect on bringing about a revival of general learning. In it a practice that had been instituted about four hundred years earlier was recommended and reinforced with imperial authority. The practice was one that we noticed before of having parish priests instruct young children in the elements of learning.[39] Charlemagne's minister of education, Theodulf, prepared an order that read, in part, as follows:

Let the priests keep schools in the villages and towns, and if any of the faithful wish to give his little ones to learning they ought willingly to receive them and teach them gratuitously, remembering what has been written: "They that are learned shall shine as the brightness of the firmament; and they that instruct many to justice, as stars for all eternity." And let them exact no price from the children for their teaching, nor receive anything from them save what the parents may offer voluntarily and from affection.[40]

Alcuin

The educational work of Alcuin was incipient and premonitory, and the outcome was greater than the plan. This is a fair, though not an especially flattering, way to introduce the master of Charlemagne's palace school. Andrew F. West's evaluation, which may be taken also as an introduction to our study of the man, is even more severe:

While he must be refused all the credit that belongs to a courageous mind which advances beyond what has been known, he must yet be highly esteemed for the invaluable service he rendered as a transmitter and conserver of the learning that was in danger of perishing, and as the restorer and propagator of this learning in a great empire, after it had been extinct for generations.[41]

Alcuin was educated at the cathedral school of York, a famous school that had been founded by Egbert, the Archbishop of York, in 732.[42] He remained at the school as a student and master until 782. In that year he left York at the invitation of Charlemagne and with the permission of the Archbishop of York, and became the master of the palace school

---

[38] Quoted in J. Bass Mullinger, *The Schools of Charles the Great and the Restoration of Education in the Ninth Century*, Stechert-Hafner, Inc., New York, 1932, pp. 97–99.

[39] See p. 189.

[40] Quoted in Patrick J. McCormick and Francis P. Cassidy, *History of Education*, The Catholic Education Press, Washington, D.C., 1953, p. 222.

[41] West, *op. cit.*, p. 90.

[42] Mullinger, *op. cit.*, pp. 49–52.

at Aachen. Besides being the schoolmaster of the palace, he became the "schoolmaster" of Frankland and the chief educational adviser to Charles the Great. Thus in the capitularies that are of educational import and are rightly attributed to the Emperor, we see the hand of Alcuin.

The reputation of Alcuin was such that Charles was, first of all, anxious to have him associated with his court, and, second, more than willing to listen to the advice that Alcuin could give on educational practices and on the need for a revival of learning. The palace school that Alcuin was called upon to manage was already in operation when he arrived at the court and had apparently been conducted for several years, but during all of those years it was probably little more than an elementary school, and not an institution that could have added anything to the illustrious name of Charles the Great. Alcuin made it a school in the full sense of the word. In addition to this, the court of Charles gained the reputation of being something of an intellectual center. No doubt there was an element of show about all of this; having a fine school in a royal court was something like having an unexcelled stable of horses. Yet in spite of a natural inclination toward royal ostentation, Charles was genuinely interested in education, and the energy that he put into his support of the school and of Alcuin himself indicates that he was not interested only in display. Alcuin stayed at the court of Charles for about fourteen years. He returned to York after retiring from the mastership of the court school, but he was recalled by Charles to quell a theological controversy that had arisen on the Continent, and then, though only a deacon and not a monk, he was appointed abbot of the monastery at Tours.

In the history of education Alcuin should be remembered for three things especially: (1) the widespread reform of education initiated by Charles and guided by Alcuin; (2) a number of fairly worthwhile books on education that contributed to the educational consciousness and understanding of his own age; and (3) the cultivation of a closer relationship between liberal learning and spiritual knowledge.

Since we have given enough of our attention to the first point, we shall turn to the second and shall at least mention the educational writings that have over the years added some luster to the name of Alcuin. It may be remarked at the outset that as a writer Alcuin was rarely original. He was an able compiler and adapter and, at times, a literal transcriber of the works of others. West wrote that Alcuin "adds nothing to the sum of learning, either by invention or by recovery of what has been lost. What he does is to reproduce or adapt from earlier authors such parts of their writings as could be appreciated by the age in which he lived."[43] However, it may take some special insight or ability to under-

[43] West, *op. cit.*, p. 90.

stand what one's own age will appreciate, and Alcuin should be given credit for having had this ability. If he was not an original or highly illuminating writer, neither was he an original thinker and philosopher. He may have been nothing more than a grammarian.[44] But labels are of relatively little significance to us now, and surely a grammarian could have been a broad and profound man or even a frontier thinker. The source of the charge that Alcuin was not a philosopher may be found in the fact that he never identified himself with a philosophical school; he was neither a Platonist nor an Aristotelian. But this is slender evidence on which to base a charge that he did not have a philosophical mind. A better source for such a claim is that Alcuin, generally speaking, did not deal with philosophical questions or treat questions in an approved and appropriate philosophical manner.

We have said that Alcuin followed other older and respected writers. Who were they? In his theological works he followed Augustine, Jerome, Ambrose, and Gregory the Great. His principal sources were Latin; apparently he did not know Greek. For his educational writings he depended mainly on Isidore, Bede, and Cassiodorus. He knew something of Boethius but used him only indirectly. Martianus Capella is never mentioned in any of Alcuin's writings. We might here point out the tendency of medieval writers to exaggerate the acquirements of the teachers among them who had good reputations for scholarship. We might remark, too, that later, even modern, writers have often accepted these exaggerations and added to them. Of course it is unfair to judge every age by our own, but it is also unhistorical to magnify a very slender acquaintance with a branch of learning into a mastery of the subject. Alcuin was a great man in his day; he was a product of his age and the best that his age could produce. What he would have been in any other age is an entirely meaningless question.

The following are the writings of Alcuin that have the greatest relevance to educational history: *On the Virtues and Vices* and *On the Nature of the Soul* (really theological works, although they do have some educational implications); *On Grammar, On Orthography, On Rhetoric and the Virtues, On Dialectics* (here Alcuin dealt with a technique that, like most Christian writers, he feared); *Disputation with Pepin, De Cursu et Saltu Lunae ac Bissexto* (a treatise on astronomy); *On the Seven Arts, A Disputation for Boys,* and *Propositions of Alcuin.*[45]

The most important of the works listed above is *On Grammar.* It is divided into two parts. The first part is a general discussion of ends and methods in education, and deals also with the duty of the student, or his

[44] See Mullinger, *op. cit.,* p. 74.

[45] It should be mentioned that the last three works may be attributed to Alcuin only with some doubt.

obligation as a Christian to study the liberal arts. The second part of the treatise is an exposition of grammar proper. According to West, " . . . Whatever is excellent in any way in his Grammar ought to be credited to Donatus, whom Alcuin follows. Isidore also furnishes him many a definition, but wherever this happens the treatise is apt to be childish."[46]

How did Alcuin cultivate a closer relationship between the liberal arts and divine learning? This is an accomplishment for which we have already given him credit.

From the Western Church Fathers to Alcuin it is almost impossible to find an acceptance of the liberal arts for what they were in themselves or a commitment to them in anything that might be called a Christian theory of learning. Although the liberal arts were used for one reason or another throughout the early Middle Ages, they were always regarded as instruments of temporary value that might be used to advance divine learning. There was the suggestion, at times the clear announcement, that the arts would one day lose even this element of usefulness, and some Christians may have looked forward to the day when any semblance of the arts might be dispensed with. Alcuin led an assault on this attitude.

For Alcuin the arts were seven in number. What earlier writers on the arts had usually advanced as conjecture Alcuin accepted as indisputable fact. For him, the arts were the necessary steps to higher wisdom, and the higher wisdom was always to be found in scriptural studies. The outcome was that what others had regarded as being merely useful to the scriptural investigations and to divine learning, Alcuin considered indispensable. His support gave the liberal arts a new lease on life, and Alcuin, although his ideas on the subject may have been clothed in simple, even childlike, language or rhetoric, emphasized the need Christians had to value their scanty learning and to advance it, not for vulgar ends but for the love of God. For the first time liberal learning could hold up its head without shame, and on the level of theory could take the place prepared for it in the syllabus of the better schools. Alcuin himself saw to it that the liberal arts were not neglected in the monastic schools over which he had either influence or authority.

The Influence of Alcuin. Alcuin was the leader of a movement that had lasting effects on the history of education. Christian education today is unquestionably indebted to him. Here, at this point, we are interested in the impression he made on the minds of intellectual leaders who followed and continued to cultivate the soil he had tilled. Of many names that might be mentioned, four are especially important in the context of this book. They are: Rabanus Maurus, John the Scot (Erigena), Alfred the Great, and Gerbert.

[46] West, *op. cit.,* p. 101.

Rabanus (also Hrabanus) Maurus (776–856), a student of Alcuin and later head of the monastic school at Fulda, the abbot of Fulda, and the archbishop of Mainz, carried on the work that Alcuin had begun and in some ways improved on it. The scene of his teaching and personal influence was Germany, although as a result of his writings—and he was a prolific writer—his influence went far beyond the German boundaries. He was called the first teacher of Germany, and his students were to occupy important civil and ecclesiastical positions in that country. Of the many books that Rabanus wrote, the one that is of most interest to the educational historian is *On the Instruction of the Clergy*. In this book Rabanus counseled—some would say prescribed—an educational syllabus for clerical students. The syllabus was to be built around the liberal arts and included the following: " . . . the unadulterated truth of history, the derivative modes of speech, the mystical sense of words, the advantages growing out of the separate branches of knowledge, the integrity of life that manifests itself in good morals, delicacy and good taste in oral discourse, penetration in the explanation of doctrine, the different kinds of medicine, and the various forms of disease."[47] Rabanus goes on to say that anyone who is unfamiliar with all of this is not really able to care for his own welfare and is, therefore, obviously unable to care for that of others.

John the Scot (Johannes Scotus Erigena, ca. 810–ca. 877), although his system of thought was condemned by Church authorities, broke ground for reason. He may have been, as he is sometimes called, the first Scholastic. In any event, Erigena was a liberal, who based his intellectual position on the thesis that authority emanates from reason, not reason from authority, and that reason needs no authority to support it. This was a bold position. Regardless of its acceptability or orthodoxy, it blazed a trail that led some scholars and some teachers into profitable but unexplored intellectual territory. Erigena initiated a spirit of inquiry, which is an essential, even though at times unpopular, spirit in the advancement of the cause of learning and culture.

Alfred the Great (848–900), the king of Wessex, made his court a center of teaching and learning. He helped to build feelings of pride in Anglo-Saxons. And in order to give these embryonic national feelings an opportunity to motivate productive effort, he built monasteries, sponsored scholars, supported translations of important books, and encouraged court schools. He was a friend of learning, and he initiated an attitude toward learning and culture that the British have never really lost.

Finally, there was Gerbert (ca. 950–1003), or as he is also known, Pope Sylvester II (993–1003). He was a teacher, a scholar, and a builder

[47] Quoted in F. V. N. Painter, *Great Pedagogical Essays*, American Book Company, New York, 1905, p. 160.

of libraries. He saw the liberal arts and sciences in the same light in which Alcuin had seen them, and he reinforced the traditions that had their clearest support in the work and theories of Alcuin. As a scholar-pope and the most learned man of the tenth century, Gerbert contributed immeasurably to the consolidation of liberal or secular learning in the Christian educational and intellectual structure.

SUMMARY

When the political structure of Rome collapsed, the schools collapsed with it. Over a period of years the Roman state had shown greater interest in education and had come to exert greater control over it. The support of schools was partly, at least, a state problem. Thus the schools became dependent on the state, and the state's role in education tended to drive out private-venture teachers. The result was that when the state lost its force, the schools, too, found their energies depleted. With the Roman schools gone, nothing was left to take their place. The decline in the fortunes of the Roman Empire, noticeable first on the outskirts of the Empire, began to set in as early as the second century. The movement of decline continued until the sixth century, when Italy, the last stronghold of the Empire, was overrun. For at least the next hundred years the stature of culture and learning on the Continent was low.

The classical-Roman system of education had generally made it unnecessary for Christians to create their own schools. Now, however, they were forced to establish them or do without. The large question that faced them when they began organizing schools was: What content should make up the school's syllabus? This was not a novel question but was, nevertheless, a question that was now being asked in a novel context. To continue and to expand what might be called the infant traditions of Christian education, a content for the schools had to be supplied. This was done first by Boethius and then by Cassiodorus and Isidore of Seville. Boethius' *Consolation of Philosophy,* Cassiodorus' *Introduction to Divine and Human Readings,* and Isidore's *Etymologies* were used for hundreds of years as textbooks in the schools.

The goals of Christian education were refined by Gregory the Great. St. Benedict, the father of Western monasticism, provided the institution —the monastery—which education used as a vehicle during the early Middle Ages. In Ireland, especially, the monastic establishments made extraordinary contributions to education and culture. Ireland, moreover, performed the additional function of preserving a great deal of the West's intellectual inheritance.

The Moslems absorbed, clarified, and preserved learning. The West learned from them, no doubt, but the West was also challenged by them.

The values of the Christian West stood in peril before the intellectual and ideological assaults of the Mohammedans. Learning and culture, a total intellectual system, became indispensable weapons for the Christians in their contest with Mohammedanism.

The great revival of learning in Europe was sponsored and guided by Charles the Great and Alcuin. Charles, the king, and Alcuin, the teacher and scholar, succeeded in creating the renaissance of the ninth century.

Questions and Exercises for Study and Discussion

1. Was there ever a period in the history of Europe when learning and culture were almost blotted out? If there was a dark age, show how it came about.
2. Is it entirely fair to say that the collapse of the Roman system and of its schools was due to internal decay? Explain.
3. Boethius is sometimes called the last of the ancients and the first of the Scholastics. What significance does this statement have? If it is accurate, what, if any, are the implications for education?
4. Prepare a short biography of Boethius.
5. Explain the connection between Martianus Capella's *Marriage of Philology and Mercury* and the liberal arts.
6. Prepare a biographical report on Martianus Capella. Was his treatment of the liberal arts original?
7. St Benedict is often called the father of Western monasticism and Cassiodorus, the father of literary monasticism. At what points did their educational views touch? In what ways were they different?
8. Prepare a brief report on Cassiodorus' life and career.
9. Summarize Cassiodorus' *Introduction to Divine and Human Readings.* Discuss its adequacy as a general text for secondary and higher schools.
10. Do you see literary monasticism as an important step in the direction of a complete Christian theory of education?
11. Explain the role of St. Gregory the Great and St. Isidore of Seville in the construction of a Christian plan for education.
12. List and explain Ireland's contributions to, and influences on, education in Western Europe. Give special attention to the Irish monastic school. Is there any justification in calling the Irish the schoolmasters of the West?
13. Show how the education of the Christian West was indebted to the Moslems.
14. Who was Alcuin? Is it true that Alcuin's role in educational history has been grossly inflated? Discuss this question.

8

Medieval Education

The impetus and direction given to education by Charlemagne was forceful enough to last until the stronger revivals of learning in the eleventh and twelfth centuries. There were pockets of darkness in Europe, places where the revival had not penetrated or had not had lasting effects, after the work of Charles and Alcuin came to an end. On the other hand, new leaders with new enthusiasms for education and scholarship, Bruno, for example, the brother of Otto the Great, an illustrious successor to Charlemagne, served to keep the renaissance of Charles effective. We might even claim that Bruno was as active in the interests of education as his famous ancestor, Charlemagne, had been. He is said to have restored the palace school to a position of excellence equal to its former high estate; to have searched for and collected classical texts; to have supported capable scholars and teachers and encouraged the higher clergy to enlist in the cause of educational reform. There were peaks and valleys of enthusiasm and support, it is true, but through all vicissitudes the renaissance of Charlemagne was kept alive.

In spite of this continued support, education had a long way to go, and the road was often treacherous and troublesome. Desire for culture, demand for learning—these were only one side of the coin; the other was the political disorder and unrest that were felt in the Empire and that led to its dismemberment. Out of the disorder arose the separate nations of France, Germany, and Italy. Parts of Western Europe were under attack from invaders more or less regularly from the eighth through the tenth centuries—from the Norsemen, the Moors, and the Magyars. It was not until the eleventh century that the threat had passed, and Europe could look forward to the future with some feeling of security. The Dark Ages were over; the renaissance of Charles the Great had done its work well in spite of most difficult conditions: and Europe was ready for an intellectual awakening. The year 1000 marks roughly the beginning of a new era in Europe.

The sources of this awakening were civic, religious, and educational. Surrounding all of these is the latent strength of the culture that had come into being through the efforts of the Church and the state to build a society from the remnants of the Roman Empire. Yet the civilization of the eleventh century in Europe was vastly different from that of the eighth, and the schools were different too. The source of the eleventh-century inspiration and intellectual quickening on which our interest centers here was educational. As a first step toward understanding the medieval educational awakening, we must turn to the medieval schools.

MEDIEVAL SCHOOLS

Of all the schools that were conducted during the medieval period (some of which may have been founded at another time), those that have attracted most attention were the universities. They formed the educational crown of the Middle Ages. While most of the other schools that flourished at this time were dwarfed by the stature of the universities and are hardly now remembered, the universities are often given credit for being even greater than they were.[1] Despite the prominence of the universities, we do not want to overlook the lower and less famous schools of the period.

The Medieval Monastic School

The medieval monastic school achieved a higher educational status than any of its predecessors, with the possible exception of the monastic school in Ireland. Even if this exception is valid, the Continental medieval monastic school was still a ground breaker for the universities. This is an enviable distinction that should do much to remove any doubt regarding ecclesiastical interest in education, and it is a distinction which the Irish school cannot claim.

The impetus for educational development in the monastery came largely from ecclesiastical laws and royal proclamations. Charlemagne may well have been the chief mover. Yet it is not during the time of Charlemagne but after the year 1000 that we begin to see the educational outlines emerging in the monastery. Almost from the beginning of monasticism in the West, the monasteries had a literary character. In spite of their desire to avoid learning, nearly every monastery found it necessary to conduct a school in which the religious novices could be prepared for the life they were to lead in the monastery. This commit-

[1] We have in mind exaggerated claims of quality for these medieval institutions as well as inflated enrollment figures.

ment, however, should not be thought of as educational in any proper sense. The monastery could not avoid becoming a teaching agency, but it may not have relished these educational duties, although they were certainly elementary and largely nonliterary in character.

The medieval monastic school was established on a sound basis. There were regular teachers, who may or may not have been monks, and a regular and fairly broad course of studies that included the seven liberal arts. Some of the monastic schools may have gone beyond these curricula to offer studies in law and medicine to the more advanced and interested students. We may safely assume that there were not many such schools.

The seven liberal arts were still believed to have little, if any, value in themselves. But following the position taken by Alcuin, most early medieval teachers regarded the arts as indispensable to the study of theology. The liberal arts were classified into the trivium and the quadrivium. The subjects in the trivium were grammar, rhetoric, and dialectic; those in the quadrivium were arithmetic, music, geometry, and astronomy. Of all these arts, the one studied most carefully and generally thought to be the most valuable was grammar. Grammar at this time lacked the dialectical character given it by scholars and thinkers of the later Middle Ages. It was now principally the study of the Latin language and Latin literature. Language came first and was followed by literature when the student was ready to read the authors.

We should not expect to find at that time a preference for any method of grammatical instruction that would prepare the mind of the student to deal with the problems of the world. Such a method did not appear on the educational scene for some time. Pedagogy was still backward-looking, although it gave a more careful and somewhat more purposeful backward look than had been known for about five hundred years. The grammatical authorities were the honored and respected and usually the ancient names. The grammars of Donatus and Priscian were the popular elementary works, although perhaps most grammar scholars would admit that Priscian's was the more advanced treatment of the subject. Then the treatises—at least those parts that dealt with grammar —of Martianus Capella, St. Augustine, Boethius, Cassiodorus, Isidore, Alcuin, and Rabanus Maurus were used as more advanced texts. In one or two instances the commentaries on the arts by these writers may have been especially illuminating and well worth the student's time, but it is not easy to see how the works of Cassiodorus, Isidore, or Alcuin could have added much to the student's store of information or understanding after he had studied Donatus, Priscian, and Boethius.

From a foundation in language the students went to literature. They studied the classics, especially the works of Vergil and the Christian writers. The Greek classics were generally unnoticed in the educational syllabus of the medieval monastic school. Though these schools had liberal sentiments with respect to what could be studied with profit by Christians, they were evidently not yet liberal enough to admit to their curricula the arts that they thought were distinctively pagan in origin.

The other arts were studied too, although they were subordinate to grammar. Dialectic was approached with caution, for to the Christian as to Plato, its most ardent exponent, it appeared to be a most dangerous thing. Plato, however, regarded it as useful in spite of the possible dangers. Logic, later the subject to replace grammar as the most relevant of the arts in the trivium, did not at this time have an independent position. Later it was to crowd out even dialectic, but in the early monastic school of this period it was not really distinguishable from dialectic, and dialectic was not studied with any great amount of enthusiasm. Boethius' translation of the *Categories*, Aristotle's *De Interpretatione*, and Porphyry's *Isagoge* were the tools of the prospective logician. Rhetoric was studied by using Boethius' works on rhetoric, and sometimes the text of Fortunatianus was supplemental to that of Boethius. Other supplements may have been the rhetorical works of Cicero and Quintilian. For the most part rhetoric was prose composition, and it was often directed toward the preparation of legal letters and documents.

The quadrivium—subjects that Plato had thought belonged to higher studies—were secondary school subjects on a level that was slightly below the trivium. When the subjects of the quadrivium were studied in the monastic schools, the standard texts were by now several hundred years old. Arithmetic probably had the most recent roots, because the Arabic notation introduced about the tenth century had changed the subject somewhat from the arithmetic that the ancients had studied and written about. In spite of the innovation in arithmetic, the text most often used was that of Boethius. Perhaps the most highly developed course in the quadrivium, as it was offered in the monastic school of this period, was music. The Church's interest in music was naturally great, so that the study of music was promoted in church-related schools. Geometry and astronomy were approached mainly for their practical values: Astronomy was useful for computing the liturgical calendar, and geometry was still cultivated for its potential in practical application. This was a carry-over from the days when arithmetic, without a flexible notation, was not used to solve problems which involved measuring and computing. Regardless of motivation, these were the studies of the medieval monastic schools, and they continued to be a part of these schools' curricula until the universities came along to take over much of the work that the monastic schools had been attempting to do.

Here we might with advantage say something more about the Church's interest in education. By seeing the Church's position clearly, we can more easily understand the academic interest of the monastic school. We may be tempted to attribute the Church's interest in learning to the influence of Charlemagne and to find in the renaissance of the ninth century the impetus for her first valid efforts in the cause of more generously distributed education. Such a temptation should be resisted. We have seen how the early Church understood Christian education and how literacy and a degree of learning became essential to Catholic Christianity.[2] We cannot find proof that the Church supported education and sponsored schools to any great extent before the medieval years, but that was because the Church was simply not in the business of education in any formal or literary sense. We may therefore wonder why she so often bears the brunt of criticisms directed at the educational inadequacies of the early Middle Ages. By 1000, however, the Church's educational policy had been formulated, and this policy exhibited a zeal for learning that in time was felt on all levels of education from the elementary schools through the universities. Except in very sparsely settled districts, a boy would not have had very far to go to find a school where he could learn to read and write, become better versed in religion, and learn the Latin language. To say that the years from 1000 to 1200 enjoyed all the advantages of popular education would be saying far too much. Nevertheless, education must have been generally available, for it is evident from tradesmen's accounts that the tradesmen of this period had greater literary skill than their counterparts who lived in the period from 1300 to 1500.

Not all of this opportunity for education came as a consequence of the Church's efforts, although much of it was due to her leadership. Since few of the schools of the time were independent of the Church, we can believe that the church-related schools took the important and deciding direction in education. As early as the tenth century the ecclesiastical laws of England had taken a stand in support of broader and better educational opportunity. The responsibility of the clergy in the process of education may be seen in the following excerpt from an ecclesiastical decree:

Priests ought always to have schools for schoolteachers in their houses, and if any of the faithful wish to give his little ones learning they ought willingly to receive them and teach them gratuitously, remembering what has been written: "They that are learned shall shine as the brightness of the firmament, and they that instruct many to justice, as stars for all eternity." But they ought not to expect anything from their relatives except what they wish to do of their own accord.[3]

[2] See pp. 152–154.
[3] A. F. Leach, *Educational Charters and Documents*, Cambridge University Press, New York, 1911, p. 37.

It may have been that the church legislation went even beyond this to require priests and clergymen generally to direct the training of young men in the manual arts and crafts.

Somewhat later, in 1179, the Third Council of Lateran formalized in its decrees what had been the Church's attitude toward education for about two hundred years:

The Church of God, being, like a good and tender mother, obliged to provide for the spiritual and corporal wants of the poor, is desirous of procuring for children destitute of pecuniary resources the means of learning to read and of advancing in the study of letters, and ordains that every cathedral church shall have a master who will instruct gratis the ecclesiastical students of that church and the poor scholars, and that a grant be assigned him which, by suffering for his maintenance, will thus open the door of the school to studious youths. A free school shall be reopened in the other churches and monasteries. . . . No one may exact any remuneration, either for the license to teach, or for the exercise of teaching, even if his right be based on custom; and the license to keep a school shall not be refused to any person who can demonstrate his capacity for it. Offenders shall be deprived of their ecclesiastical living, for it is meet that, in the Church of God, he who hinders the progress of the churches by selling, from cupidity, the permission to teach, should be himself deprived of the fruit of his labor.[4]

Later councils recognized and renewed the decrees of the Third Lateran Council, which, though hardly a constitution for church-supported popular education, were certainly important stimulants in the cause of greater educational opportunity.

Thus the Church's educational policy was born. Now for the first time the Church entered the field of education, not merely to superintend the preparation of future clerics, but to provide opportunity on a much broader base to all who wanted to study secular subjects. Secular learning was still pretty much what it had been before, but Christian theories of education were in the process of becoming considerably more mature. Because of this policy there arose in Europe educational institutions and schools attached to religious institutions that were to play an important role in European education for centuries to come.

Cathedral Schools

We have already seen how cathedral or episcopal schools were attached to the Church in the early Christian period,[5] and we have understood that they were not schools in any very strict meaning of the term. In the beginning, at least, they were agencies for apprenticeship; the

---

[4] G. D. Mansi, *Collectio amplissima Conciliorum,* vol. XXII, p. 227. See also Patrick J. McCormick and Francis P. Cassidy, *History of Education,* The Catholic Education Press, Washington, D.C., 1953, pp. 306–307.

[5] See pp. 188–189.

bishop was the master and he trained the young men who came to him to be priests. In time, of course, these centers for the training of priests came to have an instructional character and began to admit literary subjects to their curricula. Even then the bishop continued to be the chief, if not the sole, teacher at the place. By the ninth century these cathedral schools (which were really the forerunners of our modern diocesan seminaries) accepted the seven liberal arts, or some of them, as subjects to be included in a course of studies for the intellectual formation of prospective priests. No doubt the cathedral schools of this early period varied in quality, and they must have varied considerably in curricula, just as today's schools may vary in the standards of excellence they achieve and maintain. Not every ninth-century cathedral school saw the need for the liberal arts, and almost all cathedral schools kept them in what was considered to be their place.

From 1200 and for three centuries thereafter the cathedral schools played an increasingly important role in spreading educational opportunity throughout Europe. There were great numbers of cathedral churches and collegiate churches to which schools were attached. The former were bishop's churches—in a sense the headquarters of a diocese—to which many priests were usually assigned. These priests were organized into chapters and lived under a rule or a canon. Hence they were called canons. Each chapter had a dean—the chapter's superior, a precentor—the cleric in charge of the cathedral's music, a treasurer, and a schoolmaster. The latter was called the *scholasticus* or the chancellor. It should probably be mentioned that the chancellor was the cleric who was in charge of the educational activities of the cathedral or collegiate church and not merely the teacher of the school organized there. It is safe to say that most of the members of the chapter were engaged in teaching in the church's school. Apart from cathedrals, there were churches that had large congregations and as a consequence had a chapter or a college of canons assigned to them. These were called the collegiate churches. They, too, were engaged in teaching.

The teaching that was conducted in the cathedral and collegiate institutions covered broad areas; the schools that were operated may have extended from the most elementary level to the highest; and the curricula of these schools may have begun with the most rudimentary forms of learning and stopped only after the most abstruse points of human knowledge and thought had been tackled. It would be difficult indeed to be either positive or precise about the details of these schools. Yet a general statement pertaining to their work may be made: Cathedral and collegiate schools were the eleventh-, twelfth-, and thirteenth-century centers in which the fine and the liberal arts were taught and studied. When the monastic schools' interest in higher learning began to wane, sometime in the eleventh century, the cathedrals became the principal centers of thought and assumed many of the educational, scholarly, and intellectual burdens that the monasteries had been bearing for two or three hundred years or more.

These cathedral schools offered instruction in a variety of subjects. The greatest cathedrals had schools with more or less complete courses of study. Their curricula included theological courses or institutes that were presided over by the chancellor himself. Large and important cathedrals sponsored and supported schools that offered students a number of enviable opportunities for study that would carry them all the way through the subjects of the quadrivium: arithmetic, geometry, music, and astronomy. Of course, all of the cathedral schools that amounted to anything at all offered courses of study in divinity that led students up to ordination. Smaller cathedral churches and relatively insignificant collegiate churches had courses of study built around the trivium: grammar, rhetoric, and dialectic. Such courses may have been the equivalent of twelfth-century secondary education. It should also be mentioned that most of these ecclesiastical-centered schools had song schools attached to them. There is, however, some doubt as to the function of the song school. It may have been a school that devoted its attention entirely and solely to music.[6] It may, however, have been a school that accommodated the liberal arts in addition to the choral and musical instruction that was needed to prepare boys to take part in divine services.

Monasticism might point to Bec and Cluny and claim that they had fathered centers both for intellectual and moral quickening. The cathedral schools had their finest examples in the institutions of Chartres and Laon. These were famous classical centers, renowned throughout Europe for the quality of their instruction and for the great scholars that were assembled in their chapters. The educational historian hesitates to mention the name of Chartres and its famous school without mentioning also the names of John of Salisbury and Bernard of Chartres.[7]

The Courts

We have seen some of the features of the monastic schools and the cathedral schools that made them centers for intellectual culture. Along with the schools that were associated with the greater cities, the municipal schools, they provided the foundation on which the universities could be built. However, there were court schools that shared some of the responsibility and the credit for providing a higher quality

[6] James Mulhern, *A History of Education*, 2d ed., The Ronald Press Company, New York, 1959, p. 254.

[7] See pp. 252–253.

of educational opportunity. Such schools may be thought of as the secular contribution to a blossoming medieval intellectual life.

Since the courts had sponsored schools for some time, the medieval court school does not appear as a novelty at all. It was almost always necessary for governments—and these royal courts were the seats of government—to have literate men, or scribes, to conduct the work of civil administration, and it was not unusual for nobles to seek to distinguish themselves by gaining the skills of literacy. Then, too, courts were often in competition, and when education became something that the courts could compete about, each court tried to outdo the others. The fact that the largest courts had the advantage of greater resources did not deter the smaller and less wealthy from trying. Pride alone and not a real or sincere interest in education led many princes to organize schools. In the larger and richer courts the scholars were patronized much in the same way that a stable of fine horses might be cared for and cherished. Regardless of the motives of their sponsors, the scholars, the poets, the physicians, and the scientists were able to use their time to good advantage. The entourages of princes became intellectual centers.

On a lower level, the courts often maintained elementary schools for the children of nobles and also, perhaps, for the training of clerks and other civil servants. Yet at their best these schools were exclusive establishments; no one has ever claimed that they hastened the arrival of popular elementary education. On a much higher level, schools were conducted in some great courts in which students could pursue medical, theological, or scientific studies. The court school of Henry II, king of England from 1154 to 1189, was a notable example.

There is still another type of education in which the courts were engaged and another school that they conducted. This was the school of the knight, an institution characteristic of the age of feudalism. Knights were mounted troops who provided the lord or overlord with military strength. He in return gave these knights estates or fiefs. In the age of chivalry the knight was an important figure.

How did a young man become a knight? At this point education enters the picture. A regular system of training led through the steps of page and squire to knight. Although we may admit that the knight's preparation had little immediate relevance to intellectual advancement in the period, we cannot ignore one of the most important actors on the stage of medieval life. And who could claim that the knight was not educated? In the broadest use of the term education, when we make it nearly identical with life itself, the knight was educated beyond his contemporaries. The ideal knight was, according to the code of his class, "to protect the Church, to fight against treachery, to reverence the priesthood, to defend the poor from injustice, to keep peace in his own province, to shed his blood for his brethren, and if necessary, to lay down his life."[8]

It should be clear that courage, loyalty, allegiance, fidelity, manners, and generosity, in addition to horesmanship and skill in the use of arms in combat, were highly prized virtues and accomplishments. Their inculcation and development could not be left to chance.

In spite of the high value that the medieval age placed on chivalry, it is not easy to see how chivalry contributed in any important way to intellectual culture. Chivalry was a culture of courtesy, not of intellect. Still, the knights were often quite literate; they were admonished from the earliest years of their training to listen to good and true men. At times some of them are pictured as philosophers and theologians, and these pictures, even when obviously overdrawn, do contain elements of truth. According to the standards of the day the knights were educated men, although they may not have been either scholarly or learned. What the knights did for intellectual culture is a question that can be answered in a negative way by saying that they did nothing to retard the growth and distribution of intellectual values and culture. But in another way they did make an indirect contribution: All who shared in the chivalric ideal became the subject matter for the literature of chivalry. So in addition to requiring from the poets a few romantic verses that might, at opportune times, be quoted to their ladies fair, the knights provided the literary men with attractive subjects about which to compose epic or romance.

To some degree the courts must be given credit for all of this. They had, besides, a kind of education which fitted the nobles and their ladies to manage their estates, but since this kind of education had such limited application and influence, nothing more need be said of it here.

Private Schools

There has never been a time in the history of education when private-venture schools or opportunities for education did not exist. Some of history's most famous schools were privately organized and supported. Plato's Academy and Aristotle's Lyceum are notable examples. The medieval period was not an exception. It, too, had its private-venture schools, although no one of them achieved anything approaching everlasting fame.

In the United States today private-venture schools would not be differentiated from church-related or any other private schools. They are all called private, that is, nonpublic schools. In the medieval years, however, when there were no state systems of schools, the church schools were the closest thing to the public school systems of contemporary

[8] L. F. Salzman, *English Life in the Middle Ages,* Oxford University Press, New York, 1926, p. 190.

times. Private-venture schools were conducted by private persons; with only relatively few exceptions they were operated for gain. Sometimes the schools were really nothing more than tutorial arrangements; sometimes they were fully organized educational institutions that instructed young scholars in the arts of reading and writing and in other elements of education. These schools seldom went beyond elementary teaching. A few private-venture schools may have given elementary education to girls.

One feature may be associated with all medieval private-venture schools: They charged fees for instruction. Teaching was the schoolmaster's means of livelihood. Aside from this common practice, we know very little about such schools, except that they flourished and that they contributed to a fairly high degree of literacy in the population of medieval Europe.[9]

Municipal Schools

Beginning about the twelfth century, an important new emphasis was added to European education. Hitherto the tools of learning had been normally reserved for the clergy. The keeping of accounts or the computation of simple problems required the literate hand of a cleric. This was obviously a cumbersome and inefficient arrangement both for laymen and clerics. The growth of city life, the development of the medieval free town, the increasing importance of guilds, the expansion of commercial enterprises—all of these motivated laymen to seek some of the advantages which literacy could give them. There are no signs that any concerted efforts were made to wrest control of education from the Church; on the other hand, there is no evidence that the Church wanted its lay members to remain illiterate and uneducated. Generally speaking, the chancellor was the church officer through whom all educational questions had to pass and from whom all decisions relative to education came. Nevertheless, lay participation in the educational establishment was just beginning to see the light of day. The strengthening of the lay hand would not necessarily mean the proportionate weakening of ecclesiastical control. Yet in the long run this was the result, even though no one may have meant to bring it about. In its simplest terms, lay participation in the affairs of education meant that ordinary men and sometimes women wanted to be able to read and write. The Church and the church schools had never actually denied this skill to them at any time in the past; they had simply not had the facilities or the resources to give people what they wanted. And now such schools were not nearly plentiful enough to fulfill the demands

[9] See Friedrich Paulsen, *German Education, Past and Present,* translated by T. Lorenz, Charles Scribner's Sons, New York, 1912, pp. 29 ff.

of a public newly awakened to the values of literacy. So the schools that came into being were, at least at first, supplemental to the church schools that were already in operation.

According to the legal climate of the day, it was in the power of the church authorities to proscribe these new ventures in education, for no school could operate and no private teacher could instruct without the Church's permission. Although there is no evidence to support any conclusion that the Church either opposed or forbade, as a matter of policy, the establishment of these supplemental educational institutions, namely, the town schools, it is true that individual chancellors did at times outlaw lay-inspired educational ventures. Such procedures, however, were exceptional, for the Church had no reason to oppose the creation of broader and better opportunities for the education of the people. The new schools came to aid, not to replace, the cathedral, monastic, and parish schools that the Church was sponsoring.

Because of the Church's authority even over the schools that were established by towns, the municipal school movement cannot be considered the beginning of public control over public education. The initiative for municipal schools, it is true, did not come from the Church; yet, although lay officers had some authority over these schools, the Church's fundamental control over education, which had been exercised for about five hundred years, was not altered in any way by the rise of municipal schools.

The Kinds of Town Schools. A variety of interest is reflected in the kinds of schools that were established under municipal auspices. This variety would seem to be evidence that the town school movement had broad support, that is, support from the common people who would benefit from such schools. Regular Latin grammar schools (secondary schools) were established in and by the towns; reading-and-writing schools (elementary schools) were opened; private-venture schools were permitted.[10]

Latin grammar schools that arose under municipal sponsorship were intended for the sons of the commercial class, but in no other way did these schools differ from the Latin grammar schools that the Church had been directing for many years. In methods of instruction, in curriculum, possibly even in general objectives, these schools were patterned after the church schools of the same type. This would seem to be some evidence to support the view that the municipal school movement did not intend educational reform. If we are surprised that the town fathers saw no need to make their schools different from the church Latin grammar schools, we must remember that these men really did not feel competent to consider questions relative to the internal functioning of an

[10] See p. 239.

educational institution. In the absence of any sign of change in church educational policy, the town fathers merely created copies of already existing Latin grammar schools. Such an attitude would hardly inspire educational revolution, nor would it seem to be consistent with any efforts to wrest control over education from the Church.

If the town fathers saw no need to modify the secondary schools or to bring their purposes closer to the needs of life in society, they did, at least, see the need for creating a system of schools in which the common people could learn to read and write. We have already said that the people were most anxious to achieve these literary skills, and, of course, the grammar schools were ill-adapted to such purposes. Town reading-and-writing schools, which were almost always vernacular schools, came to be quite popular and offered some elementary instruction to almost anyone who wanted it.

These town elementary schools were really supplements to parish schools, and of course the parish schools had a long history of conducting their instruction in the vernacular. In spite of the parish school's long life and its honorable record in elementary education, it was not so popular a school, that is, not so regularly found, as the ecclesiastical Latin grammar school. In any event, the real significance of the parish school is the proof it provides that the Church had not forgotten the need for elementary training in the vernacular. It was an ever-present need, and to some extent it was always fulfilled.

Some towns, particularly in France and Germany, did make a real break with tradition in that they opened elementary schools for girls. In addition to receiving some instruction in the vernacular language, the girls were exposed to Latin. Anticipating contemporary coeducation in public and private schools, some town schools were opened to both boys and girls. This practice was quite unusual, however, and in some towns or localities coeducation was outlawed.

The road that town schools traveled was not entirely free from hazards. Perhaps it was inevitable that there should be clashes between town and church authorities. The lines of authority were so thinly drawn on some of these questions of educational control, and the position of the church officials often seemed to be so arbitrary, that varying interpretations were bound to result in charges that one side or the other was intruding on rightful authority or infringing upon legitimate rights. In the German states, especially, there were many bitter struggles between town officers and the chancellor of the diocese, and some of these conflicts lasted for years. When compromises were worked out, they usually granted the right of municipalities to establish schools and make provisions for their support but retained the right of teaching for the Church. In practice this meant that priests or church-appointed instructors were to be the teachers in the town-supported schools. Although such compromises had special meaning for the grammar schools, churchmen hardly ever insisted on exercising the right claimed for them as teachers in the reading-and-writing schools.

No doubt the town schools brought about a heightening of interest in education, and this alone was worth a great deal. We may also suppose that the competition generated between church and municipal schools probably served the interests of educational quality, but this is in the realm of conjecture.

As a final word on the municipal schools, we should suggest that they may have made some contribution to the founding of the great medieval universities. It has even been claimed that their contribution was the definitive one, but again proof is difficult. In the great cities great municipal schools were developed, and in this somewhat forced evolution no effort was spared to have the finest schools manned by the most erudite scholars. Their excellence was a matter of municipal pride, and this pride, coupled with the real desire and opportunity for learning, may have led towns to support schools so generously that they could induce Europe's best scholars to come to them. Such opportunities in teaching may have motivated scholars to band together to form guilds and to offer their services to the town that made the most attractive offer. If this is what happened—and we are led to believe that it was—then some of the seeds that germinated and matured to become medieval universities may have been planted in the municipal schools.

Guild Schools

Guilds were associations of persons who joined together to advance the interests they had in common. In the medieval age there were guilds of all kinds, not even excluding guilds of teachers and students, who came in time to form the educational corporations that we recognize in history as the universities. It is not with these regular educational guilds that we are concerned here, however, but with guilds that were formed among craftsmen and merchants. Although no guild except the scholars' guild was organized with the primary purpose of looking out for the literary education of its members or of those who came to it for training, on the other hand, no guild of any kind or description was indifferent to education. One of the central values to be protected by the guild was the quality of the commodities its members produced, and this protection was always achieved most effectively by the careful training of prospective guild members. The theory was that it was easier to prevent poor craftsmanship than to correct it. It must be admitted that every guild was vitally concerned with education in a broad sense. The steps a boy would take in preparing himself for the craft he had chosen, passing from apprentice and journeyman to master, need not detain us here. The guild prescribed the steps involved and super-intended the quality of the training. The purpose in all of this was obviously to produce good craftsmen and in so doing to protect the guild's reputation and safeguard the public interest.

There are other, and probably more direct, ways in which guilds became associated with education. One way was through the philanthropy they extended either to schools or schoolmasters; some guilds became bene-factors to schools and, without attempting to control them, contributed generously toward their support. Another way in which the guilds made an impression on medieval education was in the schools they created for their own members and their families. Guild membership included apprentices, of course, and many of these apprentices were young boys to whom the masters had a definite and legal educational responsibility. Articles of indenture—the contract which bound an apprentice to his master—required the master to provide food, clothing, and shelter for the boy, to care for him and treat him well, and to teach him his craft and all things belonging to it. This latter came to mean literacy, for after the twelfth century no master could have been efficient and illiterate. Then, too, the guild was often disposed to provide educational opportunity for the children of guild members. Guilds created schools, usually of the elementary type, and employed schoolmasters to conduct the school. Often the schoolmaster was a priest, possibly the guild's chaplain.

Although there was no suggestion at all in the guild school movement that it represented any kind of threat to ecclesiastical control over education, the guilds' schools provide us with still another example of lay participation in the enterprise of medieval education. But this point has no real relevance to the guild schools or their influence. Their greatest significance lay in the fact that through them the opportunities for edu-cation in the medieval years were considerably broadened.

Chantry Schools

A chantry was an endowment for masses. The endowment supported the priest who was to sing the masses, and it also supported a chapel or a special altar in a cathedral or parish church in which the masses might be offered. The endowment was assigned to the chantry priest. In addition to saying masses for the dead and possibly some other prayers, the endowment usually required the priest to perform certain works of charity, among which was regularly included the teaching of poor children. Thus we have the chantry school, usually an elementary school, but one that could on occasion rise to the challenge of preparing a gifted boy for higher studies. The chantry school could trace its origin to philanthropy, and it benefited from charity more than any other school. It was most popular in England, where there were more than three hundred chantry schools at the time of the Revolt and Reformation. They could be found on the Continent too, although they were not especially popular there. Some other charitable schools of the time, though they may have made but a slight mark on history, were, nevertheless, custodians of important educational opportunities of their own day.

SCHOLASTICISM

The chief intellectual movement of the medieval period was Scholasticism. Late in the eleventh century, when medieval scholars were heir to the bulk of the knowledge accumulated by the ancients, the medieval mind turned toward literacy and education, and from education to intellectual culture. A point which we have made before is worth underscoring: A combination of circumstances and causes motivated medieval man to undertake an almost insatiable quest for learning. How else can the schools that were associated with cathedrals, monasteries, towns, and guilds be explained? But our interest here is not principally in the causes of the intellectual movement called Scholasticism, since we have already seen some of its major antecedents,[11] but rather in its essential character and its effect on schools and education.

In a general way Scholasticism may be characterized as a means for employing reason in the search for truth. As a means, it was responsible for most, if not all, of the intellectual accomplishments attributed to the medieval period. It was a movement, of course, in that it spread its influence throughout the intellectual centers of Europe, but it was a method too, and Scholasticism as an intellectual movement could never have been very vital had it not been productive and effective as a method.

Why did intellectuals of this period want a new method? The answer is that they wanted progress and were dissatisfied with what had gone before. Their own age had problems that demanded answers, problems that were philosophical, theological, and scientific, to say nothing of social and human. There was a determination to solve these problems. It is a bad caricature of the medieval scholar—say a St. Thomas Aquinas or a Peter Abelard—to depict him as a thinker or a writer for the edification and education of future generations. These scholars were writing and thinking for their own day and not for ours. They tended to be forward-looking, progressive thinkers, but they saw their responsibility for trying to answer the huge questions that their own age posed. Out of the

[11] See pp. 230–231.

ferment of thought and study a method developed in which reason, using logic as its tool, was employed to search for truth. This method gave reason a position that it had not usually enjoyed before, except of course among ancient thinkers. The compilations and encyclopedias, which were so familiar to the early Middle Ages and which were thought to contain everything that was worth knowing, had certainly discredited reason. In restoring reason to its rightful position in the pursuit of truth, Scholasticism may be credited with the following achievements: (1) It developed deductive logic to the highest point in the history of thought; (2) it devised a terminology which facilitated scholarly communication; (3) it trained a large body of critical thinkers, who set the intellectual tone for years to come; and (4) it produced a large body of scholarly works, especially in the fields of law, philosophy, and theology.

The early Scholastics—Roscellinus (d. 1106), Anselm (d. 1109), and Abelard (d. 1142)—were interested mainly in the problem of universals, a philosophical and theological problem that had been posed as early as the time of Boethius. The implications of this problem, however, had far-reaching effects that may be seen most clearly in the two principal solutions that were offered, nominalism and realism. Although we cannot here go into the details of a philosophical dispute, we may find it worth our while to point to the effects that such disputes could have had in the field of education. Nominalism, it would seem, in addition to posing a challenge to traditional Christian beliefs by its ultimate claim that there were three Gods not three persons in one God, would have reduced learning to a quest for uncertainty. Individualism and complete empiricism were its cornerstones. These interpretations arose out of the central nominalistic thesis that there is no substance which forms the real essence of objects or persons.

Realism, however, was based on the central doctrine of substance and accident. Universals were accounted for, not on the basis of what they were called, but rather by the doctrine that substance had no separate existence. Substance may occur in many individual existences and in varying degrees therein. The differences between individuals are accounted for, then, by the fact that substance may appear in different degrees and that accidents—nonessential features—may differ. But these are abstruse philosophical points that should be pursued elsewhere. As far as education was concerned, the realists' position seemed to have had this meaning: Knowledge was one; it had an essential unity, and essential meanings were to be found in theology, thus elevated to the queen of science. This had the effect of placing all nontheological branches of learning in a subordinate, an almost unrespectable, position. It may also have had the effect of depreciating the kind of knowledge that comes from observation and investigation, because of its contention that in obtaining such knowledge the observer is in contact with accidents and not with essences. On the level of method, the Scholastic movement elevated logic to an extremely lofty position and in so doing tended to break ground for rationalism. On the level of content, the Scholastics came to be preoccupied with an abstract reality, thus making an approach which once again seemed to separate life from learning. But these points all indicate that the Scholastic movement, like most other movements in the history of thought, had about run its course and was losing its principal significance and sense of mission. The movement had its glorious years of high contribution before it went into decline. A few of Scholasticism's most illustrious figures are Abelard, Peter Lombard, Albert the Great, and St. Thomas Aquinas.

Peter Abelard (1079–1142)

Perhaps one of the most famous teachers of the medieval age, if not, in fact, the most famous, was Peter Abelard. His life and especially his association with Héloïse has made him the subject of debate, discussion, and dramatic presentation by academicians and nonacademicians alike. As a teacher he attracted students from all over Europe; as a scholar he tackled the question that the age thought most important, the question of universals. Abelard's method of presenting philosophical questions, illustrated in his well-known *Sic et Non* (Yes and No), was adopted by other writers and scholars of the later medieval period. In its most refined form, it is often thought to be the philosophical method itself. This may be too strong a statement, however, for Abelard simply arranged theological issues in two classes, affirmative and negative, and then found authorities to support both sides. The Scholastic method is represented more adequately by the work of Peter Lombard.

One great achievement of Abelard, for which he should be remembered in the history of thought and education, was the emphasis that he put on reason as the avenue to truth. The rationalism of Abelard was possibly too extreme, but from his time forward, in the Scholastic movement and outside it, no one could be an advocate of education without at the same time being a champion of reason.

There are few educational theories or techniques of teaching that can be attributed to Abelard, yet his name continues to be illustrious in the history of education. Why is he remembered? First, as a brilliant teacher, Abelard stimulated dialectical studies. His teaching had considerable effect in popularizing the study of theology, and in his hands it gained an eminence that twelfth- and thirteenth-century literary and scientific studies could not match. Abelard's approach gave theological study a more objective basis in formal education. In spite of his contribution of a method to theological study, Abelard himself had no special reputation as a theologian. Second, Abelard's influence, through the unmatched radiance of his teaching, was great enough to promote the popularity of higher education. The University of Paris owed a great deal to him, for because of his presence Paris became a prominent center of higher learning. Somewhat less directly other European universities stood in his debt.

Peter Lombard (ca. 1100–1164)

Though the work of Peter Lombard did not have the dramatic appeal of Abelard's brilliant arguing, its influence may have been almost as great. Where Abelard provided this age of intellectual quickening with the inspiration for scholarship, Peter Lombard provided it with the method. In organizing and presenting the views of the authorities on crucial topics, he employed a method that was accepted in future times as distinctive of Scholasticism. This system is seen at its best in Peter's work in his *Four Books of Sentences*, a treatise that set the tone in theological and philosophical studies for years to come. The treatise was divided into topics; each topic, in turn, was set forth simply and clearly; the solution or conclusion to any question involved in the topic was offered, and the authorities supporting such a conclusion were cited along with the chief reasons for their support. Finally, the author presented a summary, restating the problem or the topic and repeating the conclusion. Because this method became so firmly attached to Scholasticism, it could not escape having an effect on education everywhere in medieval Europe.

Albert the Great (1193–1280)

Albert, the teacher of the famous Thomas Aquinas, broke ground for St. Thomas by using the philosophy of Aristotle as a foundation for his own system of thought. He was, in addition, a botanist and a geographer, who prepared practical books and manuals for the schools. It was as a philosopher, however, that he made his mark on educational thought, and it is for his pioneer work in relating Greek philosophy to Christian thought that the history of education reveres him.

St. Thomas Aquinas (1225–1274)

St. Thomas occupies a monumental position in the history of philosophy and theology. The world has known few minds that were the equal of his. He was educated by the Benedictines at their famous Italian monastery, Monte Cassino, at the University of Paris, and at the great Dominican house of studies in Cologne. Albert the Great was his principal teacher at the two latter institutions. St. Thomas joined the Friars Preachers, the Dominicans, and became their most famous scholar.

He taught at the University of Paris and at Rome. Thus it can be said that as a living teacher he helped shape the minds and the thoughts of students, and that because of the permanent influence of his work and thought, he is still the great teacher in Catholic schools. In addition to this, although it would not be accurate to say that so-called Thomistic philosophy is the official philosophy of the Catholic Church, nevertheless, the philosophy of St. Thomas has a privileged position in all Catholic colleges and universities as well as in ecclesiastical institutions.

The impact of St. Thomas on Christian scholarship is unmistakable. His work permeated all Catholic educational thinking, and in his own day his leadership continued the emphasis that Abelard had given to reason as a means for attaining truth. Yet St. Thomas was not an educational philosopher in any professional sense. In spite of his *De Magistro* (The Teacher), in which the place of the teacher in the educational process is discussed along with that of the principal agent in the process, the student, we should look in vain for a systematic and explicitly stated educational theory. St. Thomas accepted the prevailing educational theory, and though he may have sharpened it at certain points, he did not go beyond it. This in no way dims the glorious memory or the scholarly lustre of the patron of all Catholic schools. The great monument to St. Thomas's prolific scholarship, a living monument, is the *Summa Theologica*.

What position, then, does the educational historian set aside for St. Thomas? Though he was a teacher and apparently a very effective one, his fame rests not on his ability as a master but on his contributions as a scholar. Yet one must not forget that St. Thomas established the pattern for philosophical studies that was generally accepted for centuries, a pattern that is still considered to be valid among philosophers who are Catholics.

MEDIEVAL EDUCATIONAL THEORY

We have seen that medieval educators were indebted to the ancients on a number of points, but we have seen also that medieval educational practice and theory differed considerably from what it had been in antiquity. The chief difference is to be found in the answer to the question: For whom was medieval education intended? It was intended mainly for clerics. Since classical education had known no priesthood and had set its objectives for laymen, the influence of ancient educational theory on medieval educational theory could not have been direct. We must wait for the Renaissance before we see again the direct application of ancient educational theory. Beside the difference between those who were to be educated in the two periods, another important distinction was made: Whereas ancient educational theory had provided for the education of citizens of this world, medieval education and the theory behind it were unquestionably otherworldly. Despite the generally high rates of literacy among the people of medieval Europe and the more and more generous opportunities for training in the arts of utility in the later years of the Middle Ages, the emphasis in education was definitely clerical. It aimed to equip men for their journey to heaven rather than for their exploration of the ways of this world.

During the Middle Ages a number of works appeared that were concerned primarily with the education of clergymen. Chief among them were the treatises by Cassiodorus,[12] Isidore of Seville,[13] Rabanus Mauras,[14] Thierry of Chartres, Hugh of St. Victor, Conrad of Hirschau, and John of Salisbury. All of these authors wrote before the thirteenth century. The effect of their work was cumulative in pointing medieval educational theory in one direction, the direction that has already been indicated, and for a number of good reasons, the direction was not changed.

In the sixth century, Cassiodorus, an able and versatile figure, composed his *Introduction to Divine and Human Readings.* Anyone who has read the work of Cassiodorus might hesitate at first to assign to it a place of importance in the history of educational theory or to think of it as a charter for medieval learning. Yet this is the precise role that it fulfilled. For three hundred years after the *Introduction* appeared there was really no other justification for the study of the arts than the one it presented. Beside this, the work contained the basic elements necessary for the construction of a theory of education. It dealt with the questions of who was to be educated, why education was necessary, and what was to be used as a means in the educational process. It must be admitted that the theory of Cassiodorus had not been refined, and much of the content in the *Introduction* was certainly not original. Cassiodorus' fame comes in part from the fact that he was the first to present the material, but it comes, too, from the fact that he was successful in adapting the theories, plans, and curricula of the past to the needs of the Christian era. There was no question of simple transfer. Although on the level of theory transfer could have been made with a fair amount of ease, on the level of practice it would have been simply impossible to apply the answers of the ancients, without considerable revision, to the educational questions that were being asked by Christians. It should be pointed out that the question of application here would not have been nearly so difficult if the educational theory of Cassiodorus and those who

[12] See pp. 201–210.
[13] See pp. 212–213.
[14] See p. 227.

followed him had been somewhat less limited in its scope, that is, if lay-men had been considered as well as clerics. Whether or not the work of Cassiodorus was entirely satisfactory is a question we need not at-tempt to answer. It was, at least, acceptable, and it commenced a Christian tradition in learning, perhaps even a Christian theory of educa-tion, that was continued throughout the medieval years and possibly longer.

Isidore, the archbishop of Seville, appeared on the scene in the seventh century. He was devoted to the promotion of clerical education, on which subject he composed several works. The most important of his writings, the *Etymologies*, was a concise encyclopedia of universal knowl-edge that, if it did nothing else, attested to Isidore's familiarity with about 150 authors from whom he took extensive quotations. In *Etymologies* he discussed the seven liberal arts, in their capacity as useful instruments for advancing the cause of divine learning. As far as educational theory is concerned, Isidore apparently followed, repeated, and reinforced the position that had been taken by Cassiodorus. The *Etymologies* became the standard reference book for the Middle Ages and, though often defective, was nevertheless instructive and generally useful.

Rabanus Maurus appeared in the ninth century. This is the man who had studied under Alcuin and had learned from Alcuin that the seven liberal arts were not just useful instruments for studying divine subjects but that they were indispensable. Rabanus, who was a famous schoolmaster in his own right, subsequently abbot of Fulda, and finally archbishop of Mainz, was in a position to make his views on education felt. These views were probably considerably more liberal than those of a Cassiodorus or an Isidore, although they certainly belonged to the tradition that these men had either begun or continued. It may be argued, however, that Rabanus was as much indebted to the Carolingian renaissance and to Alcuin as he was to older theorists, when he com-posed his *On the Instruction of the Clergy*. In this work he discussed secular learning and divine learning separately. His liberal outlook may be seen in his view that grammar was to include literature, a part of grammar that had been sacrificed by many an early medieval teacher in the interest of studying the structure of language without distractions. Of course this academic method had had the effect of separating grammar, or language, from life itself. Rabanus praised logic as an instrument to be used in the search for truth; he regarded arithmetic as a practical as well as a disciplinary subject; he maintained that geometry had something divine about it, that astronomy was practical, first of all, but was ornamental too, and that music should be appreciated for its importance to life in general as well as for its place in the proper performance of Christian church services. There is no doubt that

Rabanus was willing to take the seven liberal arts and use them. But use them for what? His work, after all, was a prescription for the education of clerics. A prescription of this type was badly needed, but it did have the effect of reasserting the importance of clerical education at the expense of education for the layman. As a schoolman and a leader of schoolmen, Rabanus may be considered an even more important figure than Alcuin. From the ninth through the twelfth century he dominated the educational thinking of central Europe, and because of his vital role in the education of that region he has been often called the teacher of Germany.

The works of Cassiodorus, Isidore, and Rabanus had the effect of stimulating educational thought. By the twelfth century scholars were ready to speculate about education, and from this time it is possible to speak in a proper sense of educational theory. The twelfth century has been called the golden age of medieval educational speculation. In the course of this century four important works on educational theory appeared, written by Thierry of Chartres, Hugh (or Hugo) of St. Victor, Conrad of Hirschau, and John of Salisbury.

Thierry of Chartres was a teacher both at the University of Paris and at the famous school at Chartres, where he succeeded his brother, Bernard of Chartres, as chancellor. His influence on the school at Chartres must have been great. His work on education is regarded by many as especially important; certainly it was the largest work up to that time devoted to the subject of education, and filled two large manuscript volumes. The title of the work was *The Heptateuchon* or *A Library of the Seven Liberal Arts*. In this work Thierry took up each of the arts, pointed to its significance, and dealt with the way it was to be employed in practice. The place of the arts in education was surely becoming recognized; yet there is no reason to believe that Thierry modified the clerical frame of reference in which these arts were to be taught and studied.

In the same century Hugh of St. Victor (1096–1141) wrote a prospectus for the education of clerics. He entitled his treatise *The Didascalicon de Studio Legendi* or *The Pursuit of Learning*. Once again we meet the division of knowledge or learning into the secular and the divine. But we find in Hugh of St. Victor an inclination to emphasize the unity of knowledge, and this emphasis, it must be admitted, had not been especially apparent in educational theory before this time. As a first step in bringing about a unification of knowledge, Hugh placed all organized learning under the heading of philosophy. Under this general heading he tried to coordinate the various branches of knowledge; or, in the terminology of contemporary education, he tried to integrate knowledge. Although we can hardly make a definitive evaluation of his work, we can say that Hugh of St. Victor was dealing with vital pedagogical questions and with questions necessary to any theory of education. His work is so easily recognized as the production of a man interested in educational theory that he is sometimes called the only educational theorist that the Middle Ages ever produced.[15] Although this must be an exaggerated claim, it serves, nevertheless, to emphasize the stature of Hugh of St. Victor as an educational thinker. In spite of taking fairly advanced pedagogical positions in his thought, he gives little or no attention to the education of laymen, and we can hardly assume that he meant to include them or their educational problems in his treatise. The frame of reference is still clerical education.

Another of the great twelfth-century educational works was the *Dialogue on Authors* or *Dialogus super Auctores sive Didascalon* by Conrad of Hirschau. This work was prepared while Conrad was teaching at the Cluniac Benedictine Abbey school of Hirschau in Germany. It contains lists and discussions of the authors to be read and studied in the monastic course of grammatical and rhetorical studies. It is thus directed at the education of clerics, although in his treatment Conrad includes standard classical (pagan) works as well as those by Christian writers.

The most famous and perhaps the most effective of the twelfth-century educational theorists was the illustrious humanist, John of Salisbury. John has still an excellent reputation for many things in the scholarly arena. In educational theory, his important work is *Metalogicon*, which, as John himself says, is a defense of logical studies. But the title should not be taken too literally; though John is defending logical studies, which include logic, he is by no means elevating logic in the school's syllabus at the expense of the humanistic studies to which he was so completely devoted. *Metalogicon* consists of four books. The purpose of the work is to refute the arguments of those who would curtail the trivium (grammar, logic, rhetoric) and give additional attention to the science-oriented quadrivium (arithmetic, geometry, music, astronomy). It is more than a defense of the trivium; it is an attempt to enhance the position of the studies belonging to the trivium and to cast from them certain appearances of inferiority. In spite of his humanism, we cannot discover that John distinguishes himself from other theorists of his day by giving attention to the education of laymen.

It is true that during this period no one gave much attention to formulating a theory that would make room for the education of laymen. One must not forget, however, that there were some works of

---

[15] McCormick and Cassidy, *op. cit.*, p. 265. See also Hugo of St. Victor, *Didascalicon: A Medieval Guide to the Arts*. Translated with an introduction and notes by Jerome Taylor, Columbia University Press, New York, 1961.

a theoretical nature that centered their attention upon laymen and their training. The most outstanding were *On the Education of Noble Children* by Vincent of Beauvais, a Dominican friar, and Egidio Colonna's *On the Governance of Rulers.* Both of these works seem to anticipate Renaissance educational theory, and it would not be difficult to transfer them to that period and not incur too much criticism for having done so. In both works the authors discuss the cultivation of literary tastes, natural science, ethics, economics, political science, and philosophy, with the intention of making the subjects available to the lay student. They bring up for consideration such things as marriage instruction, religion's place in the education of laymen, moral training, and physical and military training. Finally, and this should come as something of a surprise, they discuss the education of girls. Both writers say a good deal about the domestic training that girls need; but the important thing is not that they do or do not resolve the question of how women should be educated, but that they bring it up at all. It is true that Vincent touches on the education of girls only in an appendix. Yet the mere fact that girls' mental development was discussed ought to change some conceptions of what medieval education was all about. The surprising thing is not that it was indebted somewhat to classical education but that it was as liberal as it was, since its general objective was the preparation of clerics. We have not intended to give the impression that opportunity for laymen in education was entirely lacking from the fifth to the twelfth centuries, only that their education was underemphasized during this period, in spite of the attention that it had received in the Carolingian revival. Laymen had to wait for the Renaissance of the fourteenth century before much attention was given to the theory that supported educational opportunities for them.

THE MEDIEVAL UNIVERSITY

The universities constitute the greatest achievement of the Middle Ages in the sphere of the intellect. "Their organization and their tradition," says Rashdall, "their studies and their exercises affected the progress and intellectual development of Europe more powerfully or (perhaps it should be said) more exclusively, than any schools in all likelihood will ever do again."[16] These universities were the products of what was highest and best in the Middle Ages, and their rise and growth is necessarily bound up with all the history and the contributions of the times.

During the twelfth century a great educational revival—an intellectual

[16] Hastings Rashdall, *Universities of Europe in the Middle Ages,* new ed., Oxford University Press, New York, 1936, vol. I, p. 512.

quickening—manifested itself in Western Europe. For some time men of learning had been available as teachers, but now students from all over Europe flocked to them, and the teacher and the scholar became important men. There was a new enthusiasm for logic and philosophy, prompted no doubt by the greater respectability that the arts had achieved, and a more thoroughgoing and productive approach to theology. A scholastic fever began to spread all over Europe; even those who did not live and work in the academic community were affected by it. Some men were willing to make extraordinary sacrifices of home and family, wealth and possessions in order to pursue knowledge. Both young and old were motivated to participate in this fascinating exercise, and they did not stop with one teacher or one school. By the time they had absorbed the intellectual offerings of one school, they were ready to move on to the next, where they hoped that new horizons would be opened for them. John of Salisbury, for example, followed the route to learning that was taken by so many of his contemporaries, a route which took him from school to school and from teacher to teacher. One of his teachers was the famous Abelard, the most fascinating and brilliant academic figure of the time, who did a great deal in the way of starting students up the path of learning. As more and more great teachers began to appear, students began to crowd into the old schools, and as the process of learning received greater refinement the age of the universities began.

New thought was finding its way into the intellectual structure of the university. It came from Constantinople, Syria, Sicily, and Spain. In all these places more texts of the ancient sciences and philosophy had been kept than in the West. The Byzantines had kept the old manuscripts in the original Greek; the Saracens had translated them into Arabic. The Saracens had also a considerable inheritance from the Orient. All of this ancient learning was now rapidly becoming available to the Western scholar, especially through Spain, which was the center of the translation of ancient texts into Latin. Aristotle's works, *Physics, Metaphysics,* and *On the Soul,* were now available to all who could read and understand Latin. Greek mathematical, medical, and philosophical works were introduced to Europe by Arabic scholars, and it was not long before they found their way into the curricula of the schools. We can hardly overemphasize the magnitude of the enrichment brought to teaching and learning. Men gained new knowledge, new material for individual reflection, and new stimuli for thought and progress.

The desire for higher learning and the determination to push back the boundaries of knowledge form only a part of the picture which eventually became the medieval university. The universal dominion of the

Catholic Church had by this time created a spiritual European commonwealth. The scholarly tendencies of the universities and the efforts at association made by their masters would probably have resulted in nothing of great consequence had it not been for the friendly cooperation accorded the universities by ecclesiastical authorities. From the beginning the papacy gave them protection and aid. One after another, the popes gave the universities their most cordial support and, in addition, published bulls chartering universities and establishing or confirming certain privileges for the institutions or their masters.[17]

As early as the eleventh century the Church had formulated a policy on education, as a result of which some famous and successful monastic, cathedral, and collegiate schools developed. In time several of these schools became the *studia generalia* (what we today would call universities), and students flocked to them from all parts of Latin Christendom. Popes, bishops, and abbots sponsored schools and promoted and fostered scholarship in them. The intellectual revival of the twelfth century and the rise of the medieval universities took place under the watchful eye of the Church.

But the Church was not alone; influential schools were founded and patronized by imperial authority. The emperors of Germany, the kings of France, and other princes often undertook to establish universities in their own areas. Besides the growing favor of Scholastic philosophy, the reputation of individual teachers, and the actions of imperial and ecclesiastical authorities in founding and supporting schools, there were other reasons why the universities flourished. Men now began to attach great significance to the subjects that interested them most and that were most essential to their welfare as members of society. With this new interest in secular subjects, a demand arose both for breadth and for specialization in educational institutions. The curriculum could no longer be mainly clerically centered, and even the clerical students began to show greater interest in specialization than ever before. Thus we find that the universities came to offer studies in four faculties: arts, law, medicine, and theology. It should be said that few of the medieval universities offered all of these curricula, although all of them did offer arts. Rather they specialized in one of the so-called superior faculties: law, medicine, or theology. In order to be recognized as a *studium generale* (a university) a school would have to have at least one of the superior faculties in addition to the inferior faculty of arts. This specialization drew vast numbers of students to noted centers of study: Salerno for the study of medicine, Bologna for law, and Paris for theology.

[17] On this point, see J. G. Compayré, *Abelard and the Origin and Early History of the Universities,* Charles Scribner's Sons, New York, 1893, p. 36.

Organization of Universities during the Middle Ages

During the Middle Ages there was a great movement toward association; everywhere guilds of various kinds were formed. There were guilds of burghers in the same town, guilds of men engaged in the same crafts, guilds of journeymen, of merchants, of actors and artists, of soldiers, even religious guilds. The medieval universities, too, were formed on the same basis and were an expression of the same movement.[18] They were guilds of masters, or students, or both: associations of men of like mind, purpose, interests and responsibilities, united and organized to defend their common interests and to secure recognition of definite rights and privileges which belonged to them as corporate bodies. The relationship and similarity between universities and guilds, especially craft guilds, is generally recognized in the system of apprenticeship, leading in both to the stage of journeyman or candidacy for mastership, and culminating in the granting of the license to teach or practice the craft after a final examination before the masters of the association and the presentation of a masterpiece.[19] The name university, *universitas*, meant a corporate body of persons, usually a guild, and what we call a university, the *studium generale* or simply *studium* or *schola*, was only one kind of *universitas*.[20]

In the pages that follow, our attention will center upon the University of Paris. The reason for this is that Paris was the most renowned university of the Middle Ages and the model upon which most of the others were organized.[21] We read in the charters of other universities[22] the provi-

[18] Pierre J. Marique, *History of Christian Education*, Fordham University Press, New York, 1924–1932, vol. II, p. 188.

[19] Lynn Thorndike, *The History of Medieval Europe*, Houghton Mifflin Company, Boston, 1917, p. 390.

[20] Any academic institution was a *studium*. The addition of *generale* meant that students from other countries attended. The term *studium generale* came later to be applicable only to *studia* which possessed a higher faculty—law, medicine, theology —and a plurality of masters. (See Dana Carleton Munro, *The Middle Ages, 395–1272*, Appleton-Century-Crofts, Inc., New York, 1922, p. 368.)

[21] Nathan Schachner, *The Medieval Universities*, J. B. Lippincott Company, Philadelphia, 1938, p. 56.

[22] For example, in the charter of Heidelberg, issued October, 1386, by Rupert I, Count Palatine of the Rhine, it is decreed "that the University of Heidelberg shall be ruled, disposed, and regulated according to the modes and manners accustomed to be observed in the University of Paris." The Papal bull of 1385 (Urban VI), which had approved the foundation of the university, had specifically enjoined that it be modeled closely after that of Paris. (Frederick A. Ogg, *A Source Book of Mediaeval History*, American Book Company, New York, 1907, p. 346.) All the German universities followed the model of Paris. (See Friedrich Paulsen, *The German Universities: Their Character and Historical Development*, The Macmillan Company, New York, 1895, pp. 146 ff.)

sion that they should follow in their organization the model of Paris. Hence, what is said about Paris is true, with little modification, of the universities that followed her. Bologna, too, became something of a model, and those *studia generalia* that did not follow Paris tended to follow Bologna. In fact, the Middle Ages produced two different types of university organization: the masters' university, like that of Paris, and the students' university, like that of Bologna. In the former type the masters controlled the school; in the latter type the students were in complete charge of all academic policies. The first was the only type found in England and Germany; the second was found more generally in Italy, Spain, and southern France. Since Oxford and Cambridge, though similar to Paris, differed in some important points, these, too, will be given some special consideration here.

The Nations

Before or after students gathered at a center of learning they grouped themselves according to the nations from which they came. Youths from foreign parts found themselves among strangers and subject to various impositions. Out of necessity they formed themselves into associations for mutual protection. The English students at Paris, for instance, would form a kind of club, as would students from other foreign countries. In time these "clubs" amalgamated into larger and more formal organizations called "nations."[23] Each nation elected one or more councilors or proctors who were entrusted with the interests of the student body and were the official spokesmen for their fellows of the nation. Other officers were the receptor, or treasurer, and a number of outside beadles, who were general assistants, messengers, and heralds. A council of proctors or procurators of the nations represented the student body collectively.[24] The number of nations varied at the different universities and even at the same place at different times. At Bologna, about 1219, there were two distinct *universitates,* although closely allied, the *citramontane* (or cisalpine) and the *ultramontane* (or transalpine) universities, each made up of a number of nations, three in the first and fourteen in the second.[25] At Paris there were four nations—the French, the Normans, the Picards, and the English. Orleans had nine nations—France, Germany, Lorraine, Burgundy, Champagne, Normandy, Touraine, Guyenne, and Scotland.

[23] For what may well be the definitive account of the nations, see Pearl Kibre, *The Nations in the Mediaeval Universities,* Medieval Academy of America, Boston, 1948.

[24] Rashdall, *op. cit.,* vol. I, p. 311.

[25] Brother Azarius, *Essays Educational,* D. H. McBride and Company, Chicago, 1896, p. 59.

Nations were often subdivided into tribes; the French nation at Paris had five such tribes—Paris, Sens, Rheims, Tours, and Bourges.[26]

In the early years of the medieval universities, the nations were organizations or guilds of students, and at the student universities they continued along these lines. But at Paris and at many other masters' universities, the nations came to be composed of masters. Although this may have changed the internal functioning of the nation somewhat, its external image was not altered. Each of the four nations at Paris continued to have its own hall and its own rights and privileges as a corporate body. It had its own seal distinct from that of the university, its common purse, its patron saint, and its masses.[27]

University Administration

The general administration of the university varied also according to the place. In the south, at Bologna and the universities modeled after the organization there, the control of university affairs was in the hands of a student council. The guild of students constituted the university. The students determined the fees to be collected, the salaries to be paid to the professors, the conditions preceding and leading to graduation, the time when lectures should begin and end, and all matters of a similar nature.[28] The position of the professor was not an enviable one. Indeed, professors were granted little more than the status of covenanted servants. In the northern universities the control was in the hands of the masters, and the guild of masters made up the university. The explanation of this peculiar variation in administration lies in the constituency of the schools. The bulk of those attending Bologna were law students who had completed the arts course—very likely at some other school—many of whom were well along in years and well able to administer their own affairs. In the northern universities, on the other hand, the great majority of students were quite young and still in the arts course.

At any rate, whichever type of organization had control, whether that of students or teachers, it had to oversee the university's relations with the town and ecclesiastical authorities and to deal with questions of fees, rents, conduct, and discipline. The universities, when finally they received their charters and formal legal rights, received them from the Church or from the state. Thus the charters were either papal or royal.

[26] Robert Goulet, *Compendium Universitatis Parisiensis,* Toussains Denis, Paris, 1517. English translation by Robert B. Burke, Universitiy of Pennsylvania Press, Philadelphia, 1929, pp. 37 ff.

[27] Rashdall, *op. cit.,* vol. I, pp. 315–320; Brother Azarius, *op. cit.,* p. 59.

[28] Schachner, *op. cit.,* pp. 147 ff.; Munro, *op. cit.,* pp. 368–369.

With such charters scholars and masters enjoyed immunity from civil jurisdiction and were answerable for their behavior only to fellow members.[29] As we shall see, even the jurisdiction of local ecclesiastical authorities was gradually curtailed to the point of becoming mainly honorary. Medieval universities were free from all outside control. The University of Bologna, for instance, by the statutes of 1317 had complete civil jurisdiction over its members. By 1411 it had criminal jurisdiction over them as well.

The administration of purely scholastic matters was by faculties. Originally the term "faculty" meant a subject of study, but gradually it came to designate a body of professors in a given subject, and it is in this sense that the word is used here. Eventually four distinct faculties developed: arts, law, medicine, and theology. A student had to complete the course in arts before he could advance to any of the other faculties. The arts course was an expansion of the trivium and quadrivium. Not every university had all four faculties; in fact, such inclusiveness may have been unusual. All, of course, had a faculty of arts. Law as a university subject developed at Bologna and included both civil and canon or church law. Medicine as a subject for study in higher education originated at Salerno and Montpellier, while theology began at Paris. Bologna added the medicine and theology faculties in the fourteenth century; Montpellier added law in the thirteenth century; Paris added canon law gradually to its arts and theology faculties and in the course of time acquired medicine also. Each superior faculty—law, medicine, theology—elected a dean for its own internal administration and academic leadership, and this dean represented the faculty in the university councils. The faculty of arts, however, although this special example is from Paris, was made up of the four nations, each of which had its own councilor or proctor (sometimes even called rector) to represent it in university affairs.

While the importance of the faculties varied at the different universities, in the government of each university the faculty of arts was apt to be the strongest, because it was the largest (having the greatest number of students), and especially because a student had to become a master of arts before he could proceed to further study. When he received the mastership, he was required at many of the schools to take an oath to obey the decrees of the faculty of arts. Consequently that faculty was usually able to control the university.[30] Each nation, moreover, had its own vote at congregations of the entire university. Thus the arts faculty had four votes to one each for the other faculties.

The deans of the faculties, together with the council of the nations,

[29] Goulet, *op. cit.*, pp. 51–52.
[30] Munro, *op. cit.*, p. 369.

usually elected a rector, who was the head of the whole university. In the south of Europe the rector was frequently a student. At Paris the rector of the faculty of arts, elected by the four nations, was also recognized as the rector of the whole university.[31] By about 1300 the faculties of law and medicine had become subject to the rector of the four nations, and about 1350 the faculty of theology came under his jurisdiction also.[32]

The position of rector at Paris became one of great honor, magnificence, and power. A man's elevation to the post was celebrated by a solemn procession, in which even the communities of religious orders of the neighborhood joined. The rector had supreme jurisdiction, extending to all schools, officers, and trades of the university. He was held in great honor and esteem, was called into the councils of the king, and in procession walked side by side with the Bishop of Paris as his peer.[33] He was custodian of the treasury and the archives and controlled the Pré-aux-Clercs (Meadow of the clerks). He gave letters of scholarship to masters and students, conferred on them the privileges of the gown, and received from them in return the oath of perpetual obedience. He was addressed as *Amplissime Rector*, or *Vestra Amplitudo*. However, his term of office was short, a new rector being chosen four times a year. The rector's revenue came from the sale of parchment, over which he had a monopoly.[34]

The Church had its representative at the university in the chancellor, the representative of the local ecclesiastical authority. The Church was considered to have the first right in education and for many years had possessed a monopoly in it. The right was derived from the pastoral office, the commission by the Savior to "teach all nations," and by her superior dignity. The right to teach, then, was in the beginning granted by the Church to the university, or at least was recognized by the Church when the right was granted by the emperor or some other civil authority. Canon law had previously asserted the principle of church control over education. In the gradual evolution from lower schools to universities, the right of conferring degrees was given to that member of the chapter who had for long been an ex officio director of education, the chancellor. At Bologna by a bull of 1219 of Pope Honorius II, all promotions to degrees were conditioned upon the consent of the archdeacon, who in that chapter ranked next to the bishop.[35] Thus, for a time the chancellor was the real head of the university, and possessed the sole right to grant the license to teach, or the degree. Gradually,

---

[31] Goulet, *op. cit.*, p. 40.
[32] Rashdall, *op. cit.*, vol. I, p. 325.
[33] Goulet, *op. cit.*, pp. 77–82.
[34] *Ibid.*, pp. 44–53.
[35] Rashdall, *op. cit.*, vol. I, p. 223.

however, the chancellor's powers passed into the hands of the rector, and the former's position in the university became largely honorary.

The office of chancellor was originally purely ecclesiastical, being that of secretary of the cathedral chapter in a diocese. Since the secretary had to be a man of learning, it was natural for the bishop to designate the chancellor as the director of education in the cathedral school. He had long claimed the responsibility for the selection of teachers for the schools of the diocese, and when the universities came into existence, he tried to extend his control over them as well. At Paris, the teachers or masters in the university's first years sought a teacher's license from the chancellor of Notre Dame. Up to the beginning of the twelfth century, his control over the university was nearly absolute. Not only did he dispense licenses, but he was also the students' civil and religious judge, and he wielded even the power of excommunication.[36] It was not unusual for some chancellors to abuse their great powers, and as the universities grew stronger, their officers were not always willing to accept the sometimes arbitrary directions of the chancellor. In the inevitable dispute between the university and the chancellor, appeals were sometimes made to Rome. It came to be a papal policy to decide such disputes in favor of the university, and thus the independence of the university was gained at the expense of a limitation on the chancellor's powers. Gradually the chancellor's tyranny was broken down. Innocent III in 1208 authorized the teachers to be represented by a syndic; in 1209 he bestowed upon them the right to take oaths to observe such rules as they deemed proper and useful to impose upon themselves as a body. Most important, in 1213 he restricted the judicial powers of the chancellor of Notre Dame by forbidding him to refuse the degree to anyone who had been recommended by the masters. This amounted to granting the university its first charter. In 1219 Pope Honorius III forbade the chancellor to excommunicate masters and students in a body without the authorization of the Holy See.[37]

Another very important circumstance that restricted the chancellor at Paris was the possibility that the masters and their students might obtain their licenses by crossing the Seine to its left bank outside of Notre Dame's jurisdiction and within that of the cathedral (later on the abbey) of Ste. Geneviève, which had its own chancellor.[38] In 1216 a school was opened under the jurisdiction of the chancellor of Ste. Geneviève. The chancellor of Notre Dame regarded this as a violation of his rights and refused to regard as valid any degree or license signed

[36] *Ibid.*, pp. 304–312.
[37] Charles Thurot, *De l'organisation de l'enseignement dans l'Université de Paris,* Dezobry, E. Magdeleine et Cie, Paris, 1850, p. 12.
[38] Rashdall, *op. cit.*, vol. I, pp. 340–341.

by the chancellor of Ste. Geneviève. Upon appeal to the Holy See by the masters, Pope Honorius III ordered that any licentiate of the chancellor of Ste. Geneviève be admitted to teach upon the same footing with the licentiate of the chancellor of Notre Dame. Thus the chancellor of Notre Dame could not absolutely monopolize the power of conferring degrees to teach or practice, since what he refused might be obtained, by crossing the Seine, from the chancellor appointed by the abbot of Ste. Geneviève. In this way the University of Paris came to function under two distinct chancellors.

Inasmuch as all scholars were considered clerics, and the chancellor was the representative of church authority, it was his office also to try scholars and any laymen subject to the university and "to sever from the University wandering, rebellious, forward, and incorrigible scholars, also to restore the penitent and free scholars and masters from the hands of violence."[39]

The chancellor at Oxford had a somewhat unique position. By the papal ordinance of 1214, the bishop of Lincoln was empowered to appoint a chancellor over the scholars at Oxford. Since Oxford did not have a cathedral, there was no cathedral chancellor at hand, and the chancellor of Lincoln was too far away to play an effective role in university affairs. Although the chancellor technically was the bishop's representative at the university, he was not, as the chancellor of Notre Dame was, an outsider, but came to be a real officer of the university. He was, in fact, elected by the masters from among their own number,[40] although this election had to be confirmed by the bishop. His office combined the duties which at Paris would have been assigned to the chancellor and the rector. Deriving his authority from the bishop, he had jurisdiction in trials, and could enforce his decisions by excommunication or deprivation of magisterial license, or by imprisonment in the king's prison or the prison of the town. He had the authority to supervise the schools also. As he moved up to the position of head of the university, he gradually became more and more independent of the bishop, yet retained his episcopally derived authority. The chancellor at some other schools, notably Montpellier, had a similar position.

The Colleges of Medieval Universities

At many of the universities, *hospitia,* or halls, were set up to provide food and lodging for students, usually the poor students. Ordinarily these halls were endowed and provided their facilities gratis or at very moderate cost. In the beginning, at least, the students in the halls managed their own affairs, that is, they took care of all the activities that

[39] Goulet, *op. cit.,* p. 60.
[40] Rashdall, *op. cit.,* vol. I, pp. 41–42.

had to do with the house, hall, or hospice in which they lived. This place was also called a college. It should be noted that the name college for such a hall did not imply that any instruction was conducted there. At first the colleges had no interest in giving instruction to the university students who lived within their walls, and certainly no facilities to do so. Eventually, however, instruction was introduced on a tutorial basis, especially for students who were preparing for their final examinations; this, in time, expanded to the point where in the early modern university all of the instruction at a university was given in the colleges.

The most noted of the colleges of the Middle Ages was one that gives us a good example of this type of academic institution—the Sorbonne, founded by Robert of Sorbon about 1257. This was a building where the students roomed and had their meals and where they were under the charge of a master. Probably because this college was for very young boys, the students recited their lessons to the master, dined in common, and formed a compact body. The number of scholars at the Sorbonne was restricted to sixteen; in order to be admitted, a scholar had to have the academic objective of theological study. This type of academic foundation suited so well the needs of the time that elsewhere others followed the example of Robert, and endowed colleges were soon established in all of the leading universities of Europe. It may be mentioned that by 1500 there were seventy-nine *studia generalia* (universities) in all of Europe.

The primary object of these first colleges was simply to afford scholars shelter and protection. They were derived from the hostel in which certain licensed masters used to keep students at moderate terms, offering freedom from extortion and a residence where quiet could be ensured and some discipline maintained. The college principal conducted the students to the lecture hall of the university professor and led them back to the college in a body. Gradually, with the aid of assistants, he came to superintend their studies, started disputations, occasionally heard scholars recite, and thus profitably filled that part of the day that was not taken up in attending lectures. Recognizing that this passing back and forth from the college to the lecture hall took up a good deal of time and often led to some disorder, the principals, or masters, as soon as students in a college became numerous enough, began to give private lectures. Somewhat later these lectures were given official recognition in the university, and eventually they replaced the university lectures entirely. As the colleges increased in number and size, they superseded the university at some places, notably at Oxford and Cambridge, where they took over most of the teaching and disciplinary functions that had previously been the work of the university. Indeed, the colleges became the university and the university became a kind of academic superstructure.

Methods of Teaching

The chief methods employed in teaching and learning at the medieval universities were lectures, repetitions, and disputations. Lectures were of two types, ordinary and extraordinary. The ordinary lecture was given by a master on the subject of one of the texts that had been selected for presentation. Extraordinary lectures were given by masters or advanced students on subjects that may have been of general interest; or they may have been special explanations or interpretations of the text that had been dictated in the ordinary lecture. The ordinary lecture, it should be understood, was usually nothing more than a dictation. The master read from his text, and the students copied. This was one of the ways the age hit upon for providing prospective teachers with some of the tools of their art. Printing with movable type had not yet been developed, but both students and teachers needed texts with which to do their work; thus, the technique of the medieval lecture, where the master simply conducted an exercise in dictation. It should be said that in some of the universities the masters' guild legislated that the ordinary lecture could be nothing more or other than an exercise in dictation. Yet at the same time other guilds permitted their masters to "gloss" the text, or make commentaries or interpretations of it as a supplement to the matter that was dictated. It may well be true, however, that commentaries, interpretations, and explanations were usually reserved for the extraordinary lecture.

The repetition may have been a detailed discussion of a course of lectures that had been given. If so, the master who had delivered the lectures in the first place would assemble his students and give them every opportunity to probe those avenues of thought that had stimulated their intellectual curiosity. Here, with the friction of mind on mind, teaching and learning was at its very best. On the other hand, there was no guarantee at all that the repetition would take this form, and it could have been nothing more or less than a rereading of the lecture that had been given before. Under such circumstances the students would have the opportunity to check their text for inaccuracies or for incompleteness, but such an experience could hardly have been highly stimulating.

The disputation method has been given a good deal of attention. It was surely one of the university's important exercises in learning. Disputations came to be regular techniques in the university because they provided opportunities for clearing up difficulties that masters and students may have faced in their studies. Such exercises also provided students with practice in dialectic, and it would be hard to say which was thought to be the more important, explanation or skillful arguing. Two methods were employed in conducting disputations. One person might take up a thesis and examine both sides of it, that is, argue one side and then the other and finally try to come to some conclusion. Or two persons, scholars or masters, might engage in debate, one taking one side of the thesis presented for discussion and the other, the other. Normally, such formal disputations and their theses were publicized well in advance, in order that those who attended could be prepared to ask questions or offer arguments from the floor. Even outside the university, usually in ecclesiastical circles and sometimes in the pulpit, the form of the disputation was adopted. Medieval man was about as interested as his Hellenistic ancestor had been in disputing or listening to disputes.[41] In addition to the disputations that formed a regular part of the university's instructional process, a master might organize disputations for his own classes. These would not be given university or public recognition but would merely be ways which a master might devise to enrich the educational experience of the students under him. Of course skill in disputation was considered to be important. The student who took a degree from a medieval university had to furnish evidence that he had taken part in a certain number of disputations, usually six.

Students and Teachers

Student life at the medieval university is not easy to describe in general. Some students came to the university with plenty of money to care for their wants; others came with meager or limited funds and had to supplement their resources by begging or by seeking scholarships. There is no evidence to indicate that many, or any, of the medieval university students worked their way through school by productive labor.

They lived in the houses that the university and town authorities approved, and they took their meals at local taverns. When they were not engaged in their studies—and they found many good reasons for not studying all the time—the students looked for fun. Often they had to make their own amusement, and this sometimes led to trouble. Many of the most serious disputes, to say nothing of armed conflicts, between town and gown arose out of the exaggerations of sport in which the students sometimes engaged.

Perhaps the most unusual characteristic of the medieval student was his willingness to move from university to university. There were no academic obstacles to such transfers; all that was necessary was physical movement from one place to another. The student would move when his favorite teacher moved or when he believed that some other university held out greater prospects for academic adventure.

The medieval master, who could be called professor or doctor, was first of all a member of a teaching guild. As a member of the guild he had a voice in all the details and policies that surrounded the conduct of

[41] See p. 125.

academic affairs. He was admitted to the guild, not by the rector of the university or by a faculty dean, but by the masters who were already established members. He earned his income from student fees paid directly to him. The rates for teaching were set by the guild, and the individual teacher could neither raise nor lower them if he wanted to retain his membership in the guild. Most of the masters were clerics as were the students, for the medieval intellectual world did not offer many impressive invitations to laymen. Incidentally, present-day academic costumes are derived from the clerical dress of the medieval masters.

Despite the definite clerical orientation of the university, medieval universities played a significant role in the development of European culture and education. The university had a direct and most pervasive influence on education. It sent out large numbers of fairly well-equipped teachers at a time when they were badly needed, and it compelled the lower schools to improve their quality in order that their students might enter university studies. Most significant of all, the university performed a great service for mankind by placing the administration of human affairs in the hands of educated men. It is easy to detect the quickened pace of social and scientific progress and of human freedom after the university became a securely established institution. Modern and contemporary institutions of higher learning clearly owe a great deal to their medieval forebears.

SUMMARY

The schools of the Middle Ages were more solidly founded than the Christian schools of earlier periods. The monastic school, the first Christian school, was still in evidence, and by this time it had broadened its curriculum to include the liberal arts. Cathedral and collegiate schools were important educational centers from 1200 to 1500. Court schools tried to perform the dual function of educating the sons and daughters of nobles and of training some young men for clerical positions in civil government. Courtly training included the steps which led selected young men to knighthood. Municipal schools were founded to supplement the educational opportunity offered in church schools. For the most part, these schools were identical with church schools in all respects save their sponsorship. In some parts of Europe chantry schools were quite popular; and in England, especially, they made a deep impression on elementary education. Finally, there were guild schools. These schools were intended mainly for the sons and daughters of guild members and for apprentices or others for whom masters had a legal responsibility.

It was during this period that Scholasticism arose and produced a large body of critical thinkers and an impressive array of scholarly works.

Abelard, Peter Lombard, Albert the Great, and Thomas Aquinas were among the brightest stars of the period.

In the realm of educational theory the names of Thierry of Chartres, Hugh of St. Victor, Conrad of Hirschau, and John of Salisbury were most prominent. Medieval educational theory remained within a rather narrow framework of educational thought; in its view, education was intended mainly for clerics, and its purpose was largely otherworldly.

Of all the educational works for which the medieval years are most famous, the universities attract the greatest attention. The foundations for modern higher education were laid in these universities.

Questions and Exercises for Study and Discussion

1. Did medieval monastic schools differ from those that grew directly out of the plans of St. Benedict and Cassiodorus? Explain.
2. The seven liberal arts are always referred to whenever medieval education is discussed. What were they, and where had they come from? What was their relationship to the schools?
3. How did medieval cathedral schools differ from the cathedral schools of the sixth century?
4. What was the collegiate school, and how was it different from a cathedral school?
5. If the Church dominated medieval education, how was it possible for private schools to exist? What were these private schools like?
6. Do you see the municipal school movement as a challenge to the authority the Church claimed over education?
7. Why were the guilds interested in education? What role did the guilds play in medieval life?
8. Show how Scholasticism affected education, and summarize the work of the men most closely connected with Scholasticism.
9. Identify the main features of medieval educational theory. How did it differ from classical educational theory? In what ways had it grown away from earlier Christian educational theory?
10. Describe the day of a young man in a medieval university. Who were the medieval masters, and what was their preparation for their professorships?

9

The Classic Renaissance
and Education

THE RENAISSANCE

The intellectual quickening of the twelfth century was a movement that never really subsided. Its effects were probably not seen as clearly in the fourteenth century as in the thirteenth, but they were there, and they were renewed dramatically in an intellectual movement that is called the Renaissance. The Renaissance was a number of things: It was a renewal of contacts with classical Greece and Rome; it was an emphasis on humanness; it was a collecting of manuscripts, and a criticism and dissemination of their contents; in part, it was a disregard for the centuries that had intervened between the close of the classical period and the onset of the Renaissance (1350); and finally, it was a heightening of the spirit of individualism among men.

In spite of the fact that contacts with classicism had never been completely lost during the medieval period, the Renaissance can be rightly called a movement which had as its central preoccupation the reestablishing of closer and firmer contacts with the classical past. It might be pointed out that the medieval interest in the classical period had been practical in nature. Both Latin and Greek were used in some church services; ancient architecture was used for many churches and public buildings of the medieval world. We note, of course, that the medievalist had added something to classical culture and remolded it, but even with such additions or modifications, an authentic classicism had continued to exist during the medieval period. Classical writers—Vergil, Caesar, Cicero—were fairly well known and generally cherished; Aristotle was used by the medieval Scholastics in constructing a philosophical system that was entirely Christian in its orientation. Aristotle's influence on medieval philosophy was incontrovertible, even though the system of thought that evolved from medieval speculations about the world and man was quite different from the philosophy which Aristotle had proposed. When medieval scholars turned their attention to scientific investigations, crude as they were, they found that in this area, too, classical scientific thought had furnished a basis for their own conclusions about the world. Yet when the Christians of the Renaissance turned to the classics, they did so not so much because they wanted to confirm what they already believed about the universe or themselves, but because they found their form beautiful and their content provocative.

The Renaissance mind looked both forward and backward. It looked backward for inspiration; it looked forward to the time when a better life would be available to men who had used their talents to produce such a better world. The idea of progress was no more foreign to the Renaissance than was the idea that life could be a good deal more humanly enjoyable than it was. The place that education could occupy in such a world view was by no means insignificant.

Renaissance Educational Theory

We have seen something of the effects that medieval educational theory had on the educational patterns of that age. Theory provides a foundation on which educational institutions and opportunities are built. The theory that supported Renaissance education, we feel certain, would be different from medieval educational theory. Let us see whether this is true.

Some historians argue that the educational theory of the Renaissance was constructed out of the remnants of educational philosophy that the classical theory of education had left behind. They usually claim that the theory and the practice of education during the Renaissance were revolutionary, that theorists took a dramatic leap back over a thousand years to the theoretical foundation that had supported classical education, that this theory was adopted as a governing agent for Renaissance education, and that in practice the educational models that were imitated were those that had been common either in the classical or in the Hellenistic period. Proof of the revolutionary nature of Renaissance education, they claim, is to be found in the great number of allusions and quotations that Renaissance writers on education incorporated in their works. We cannot read very far in any of the works of Renaissance educational theorists without being convinced that they did lean rather heavily on classical writers. Yet such references would constitute proof that the medieval writers on education knew classical authors about as well as the Renaissance writers did. In the fifty-one chapters of Vincent of

Beauvais's *On the Education of Noble Children,* a medieval work that may have anticipated Renaissance educational theory, there are over nine hundred quotations. Although most of them are from scripture and from the Church Fathers as well as from some Scholastic authors, about one-third are classical in origin.[1] It would be difficult to convince anyone that Vincent was leading an educational revolution.

Another position may be taken: that the educational theory and practice of the Renaissance were really the end products of an evolutionary process. In such a view, medieval education is not regarded as a cultural outcast. Its pedagogy, evidently agreed on many points of more or less importance with the educational theory and practice of the ancients. Medieval education, then, becomes a direct descendant of ancient education, and Renaissance education is a direct descendant of the medieval. To say it another way: The precedents for Renaissance educational theory and practice were present either implicitly or explicitly in medieval education, and it was entirely unnecessary for the Renaissance educator to find a way to ignore the educational impact of a thousand years.[2] This did not, of course, prevent the theorists of the Renaissance from denying their intellectual and cultural paternity, but their denials in no way changed the facts.

Probably the chief influence of classicism on the educational theory that grew to maturity in the Renaissance was in the realm of education for the layman. The medieval program had been less than generous in its provisions for the education of laymen. In centering its attention on the clergy, medieval education had to make some adjustment in the inheritance that it accepted from the ancients, for classical education had been for all who could profit by it. In the Renaissance, however, educators could apply the views of antiquity more directly because they were interested principally in the education of laymen.

Although we may want to give emphasis to the new direction that was taken by Renaissance education—the education of laymen for citizenship —we are forced to recognize that the curriculum of the schools of the Renaissance was little different from what it had been before. Some historians have pointed out that the new education seemed somewhat reluctant to give to its wider group of students the freedom in style and content that had been afforded clerical students in medieval education. But one should not try to make too much of this point. The essentials of education in both periods were very much the same, in spite of their difference in direction. The reform which characterized Renaissance

[1] Arpad Steiner, "Guillaume Perrault and Vincent of Beauvais," *Speculum,* vol. 8, pp. 51–58, 1933.
[2] Daniel D. McGarry, "Renaissance Educational Theory," *Historical Bulletin,* vol. 32, pp. 195–209, May, 1954.

education was directed, not so much at what was to be taught, as to who would be taught and why.

Despite the general validity of our conclusion that humanistic educational theory was concerned with the education of all men for citizenship, we should not forget that a number of specific issues faced educators and theorists that were not on this high level. One issue had to do with the control of education: Should educational control be vested in the Church or in the state? Of course, there was no possibility of settling this question by going back to the ancients, who had not been faced with this particular choice. The problem the ancients had to settle was the question of state or individual control of education. One may recall that Athens generally favored the individualistic approach,[3] while Rome tended to be more collectivistic in its outlook.[4] It is hard, of course, to generalize about Rome, for, though the Romans may never have lost their inclination to regard the collective good and the welfare of the state as superior to the individual good, there is not much evidence that ancient Rome ever had a full-fledged state system of schools.[5] Thus the humanists of the fourteenth century had no ready ancient model to follow, even if they had wanted one. As for models from their own time, it can be said that they were familiar both with church schools and with schools, such as the municipal schools and some universities, that had a public character. One looks in vain for a definitive position that favored either state or church control of education. There were, however, a number of middle positions. If we must draw a conclusion here, we can say unequivocally only that humanistic educational theory supported the view that laymen with genuine skills for teaching and scholarship ought to replace clergymen as teachers, that the Church ought not to dominate education, and that there ought to be plenty of room for institutions not directly controlled or sponsored by the Church.

Humanistic theorists did not spend all their time on this question. There were many others. One was: What value ought to be attached to the classics? While it is no doubt true that the classics were never completely lost, their original purpose was changed by a number of Christian and medieval teachers. They were used exclusively as means or as handmaidens in religious teaching. For the humanists, many of whom had nothing against religious knowledge or religious teaching, this was a misuse of the classics. They saw that they were of far greater value than mere steppingstones to something else. In discussing this question, we must consider the position of the Scholastic method, which had risen to fame and prominence, not to say power, during the medieval

[3] See pp. 40–41.
[4] See pp. 129–132.
[5] See pp. 144–145.

years. We need be in no doubt as to the position taken by the humanists. They maintained that the classics were superior in content to any other literature that might be put into the school's program, and that no other content could inspire youth to develop their God-given capacities in the way that the classics could. They saw in the classics not only literary and intellectual inspiration, but moral inspiration as well. Nowhere else, they said, could one find better directions for the building of character than in the classics. Students were advised to study Plato, Aristotle, Plutarch, Seneca, and many other ancient authors in order to find the best ways of forming character. The humanistic approval of the ethical emphases that they detected in the classics may go a long way toward explaining the unrelenting attention most of the theorists of this era gave to character education when they wrote tracts or treatises on educational theory.

Besides giving inspiration for intellectual formation and directions for building character, the classics were supposed to contain genuine scientific worth; that is, they not only were supposed to contain scientific information of merit but were expected to generate in students a real scientific interest. Although this all may have been true in theory, in practice it would have been hard to find much evidence of natural or physical science in Renaissance education. So taken up were the humanists with the desire to know man, that they found little or no time to pursue nature. They were true followers of Quintilian, who, though he said "No mathematics, no orator" and meant it, could find no time for science in the educational program that he constructed. Although we may understand that the humanists did not find the supreme value of the classics in ornamentation, it is difficult for us to see the precise point at which ornamentation stopped or started and other values took over.

The humanistic educators asked and attempted to answer many other important questions. For example, they concerned themselves with the problem of aim. Should education aim at knowledge or at style? We cannot discover that they resolved this issue or that any of the views they presented contributed to the solution of another problem related to it, namely: Is the end of education discipline or utility? It is of course a fact that the humanists gave more attention to the education of women than their immediate predecessors had; it is quite another thing, however, to claim that this attention led to actual educational opportunities for women that were noticeably richer than they had been before. And considering all the veneration that the humanist educator had for the past, we may find it somewhat surprising that he did not give more place to physical education in the school's program. On the level of theory there was no doubt at all that physical development was important; the humanist could see the interdependence of mind and body, and he could understand and appreciate the ancient educators' interest in physical formation. Yet it must be repeated that except for a few examples furnished by exceptional schoolmasters—Vittorino was one[6]—the humanists of the Renaissance period were quite willing to leave physical education to the schoolboys' periods of free play and recreation. The same generalization would apply to music, dancing, and drawing,[7] though we should point out that the humanist was always ready to defend the value of these things. Music was often thought to be an appropriate skill for women, and the humanists believed that it might prove to be an instrument that could lead them further along the road to an appreciation of the finer things of life. But we cannot attempt to write a very full history of the educational opportunities that women enjoyed at this time; the task would be almost futile.

There is almost universal agreement that the early humanists did not think much of the vernacular. They considered it a vulgar tongue and evidently shared the general prejudice against it. Perhaps the distinction should be made between a language to be used for culture and one to be used for everyday speech. The language for culture—the Sunday language, so to speak—was Latin; Latin was considered the language of learning, and no doubt it had to be. The various vernacular languages were employed every bit as fully as they are today for common speech and ordinary communication, but the weaknesses of a vernacular were real enough, and it was more than mere prejudice that kept the speech of the people from becoming the language of learning in the fourteenth century. Of course, the Latin that was prized so highly was not the living medieval Latin, but the classical Latin of the time of Cicero. In time Cicero was to become the model in both language and literature. But to return to the vernacular for a last word: Its major weakness was that it did not contain either the vocabulary or the structure necessary to a medium of communication that was to be an instrument of learning. As the native languages developed (and some developed more rapidly than others, English being especially tardy in its development), they came to occupy a place of greater prominence in the schools, especially in the higher schools. We should state quite clearly that it was not prejudice that kept the vernacular languages out of the halls of learning, but their own deprivations. Later, no doubt, the inertia of tradition or preferences for the medium already in use tended to block the progress of the vernacular as a tool in learning. Whether or not the vernacular should be used in the schools was never a matter for debate in the early Renaissance; it is not until the fifteenth century that we witness the beginning

[6] See pp. 285–289.

[7] The reader may be reminded that music, drawing, dancing, and physical education were staples in the program of classical education. See pp. 47–49.

of the struggle between the vernacular and Latin in the field of education. And it is safe to say that when the vernacular turned the tables on Latin and became the popular medium for all communication and instruction, its popularity was not due to a new and more pervasive feeling against Latin. There were other reasons. Chief among them was the growing nationalism that demanded not only a national language but a national literature as well.

Humanists did not avoid history. They did, it is true, take a relatively dim view of the thousand years that separated the Renaissance from the classical period and were usually willing to ignore them. This attitude toward the past did not mean that the Renaissance was antihistorical. As a matter of fact, the humanist had a better sense of history than his older medieval brother, and had the humanist theorist had his way entirely, he would have insisted that history occupy an important, even a central place in the school's instructional program. In addition to glorifying ancient civilization, history could be expected to uphold sentiments of patriotism as well as to present literary and artistic values. There may have been some good reasons for the decided preference that the humanists had for Roman classical history. The great national heroes about whom the Romans wrote were real historical figures; the heroes of Greek literature had reality only in the imaginations of the authors. For all their cultural idealism, the humanists were realists too.

What was to be done with pagan literature—the classics? This was surely not a new question. It had given educational thinkers and writers a good deal of trouble for some centuries. From the time of Alexander the Great to the time of Alcuin of York there was always some doubt as to just where the classics should stand in Christian culture.[8] By the time the humanistic movement attained maturity, no one doubted the merit of the classics as instruments of study, and few humanists expressed any fears with respect to the impression the classical authors might have on the formation of Christian minds. Christian humanism had come a long way in a short time. There was still a kind of pagan humanism, of course, which, while emphasizing the intellectual values in the classics, refused to acknowledge the authenticity of the Christian message or the Christian mission.

We come now to the chief weak points in the humanistic movement as it applied to education. They need not be discussed in detail, but they ought to be mentioned. In the organization of schools, in building a systematic curriculum, in psychological and methodological approaches to teaching, the humanists were weak almost to the point of negligence.

---

[8] The place of the classics and their relationship to Christian education have been discussed in some detail before. There is no need to repeat that discussion here. See pp. 154–158.

With all their concern for education, with a revolutionary or at least a liberal outlook toward education, the humanists seemed to be unable to see that order and discipline in the schools were essential to any degree of excellence. If we maintain that the theory of the humanists represented progress in education, then we should admit that the humanists were almost unbelievably weak in transferring their theories to the schools in which teachers were teaching and students were learning.

HUMANISTIC SCHOOLS AND SCHOOLMASTERS

Humanism, often another name for the Renaissance, exerted an influence on many of man's activities. The effects of humanism were felt deeply in the schools. We turn now to study the evolution of humanistic education in Europe.

Humanistic Education in Italy

One aspect of the Renaissance in Italy was the attention that was paid to a revival of learning. As a matter of fact, so important was this phase of humanism in Italy, that it is not uncommon to think of the revival of learning as having been the Renaissance itself. Of course, the Renaissance was more than this, but it was notably a general reawakening to the importance of learning, and it became a movement motivated by a passionate desire to recapture ancient Greek and Roman literature, learning, and culture. Perhaps it was natural for the interest in the classics to be generated in Italy, for the Italians were certainly aware of the glories of their past, if they were not in fact conversant with the things that had contributed to that glory.

Given the ideal, the stuff out of which the ideal could be constructed could be obtained. In Italy, the great revival of learning had as its forerunners two important names in the history of literature and in the history of thought: Dante Alighieri (1264–1321) and Francesco Petrarch (1304–1374). We cannot, of course, think of Dante as a schoolman or a schoolmaster or claim that he has a part in educational history. But the historian experiences very little difficulty in presenting Dante as a figure who contributed by the spirit of his writings to the humanistic movement and the educational awakening that accompanied it. The fact that he was the first layman since Boethius to gain a reputation in literature and to be recognized as one of the most learned men of his day was in itself important to humanism. And finally Dante showed that a broad culture could be conveyed by the vernacular as well as by classical languages. The ultimate importance of Dante's use of Italian cannot be overstressed, as we consider the broad sweep of educational history. Yet we must admit that the vernacular was not esteemed by confirmed Italian humanists and that little use was made of it for some time, except, of course, as a medium of informal communication among the unlearned and unlettered.

The fact that Dante's *Divine Comedy* was not written in Latin but in Italian did very little to stimulate interest in vernacular languages. Dante did, however, generate interest in the classical past because in his great work he quoted from and referred to the classical authors hundreds of times.

Petrarch's importance as a forerunner of humanistic education is a little easier to recognize. He took the steps that other humanists were to follow in emphasizing the significance of classical language and literature as a basis for all education. As a scholar, he made many of the classical works available to students. He was responsible for the establishment of a center for humanistic or classical studies at the University of Padua, and for a long time it was from Padua that the inspiration for continuing the humanistic movement came. From this university Petrarch set out on his journeys in search of classical manuscripts. He and his colleagues left few stones unturned, few libraries untouched, in their efforts to collect classical manuscripts.

We might mention, at this point, the status of Greek in the program of humanistic education. The Greek language had not been completely forgotten in Europe during the Middle Ages. It is unthinkable that the knowledge of Greek could have been stamped out completely all over Europe. Yet it is true that few people knew very much about the language or were able to read or write it with any skill. One of the major points of emphasis in this reawakening and revival was the value of reading the Greek classics in the original. It was not enough to capture their humanness in translation; it was necessary, too, to taste their sweetness and observe their beauty in the original. The attitudes on this point were so contagious that Greek was subject to a rather significant revival on the Continent. The man who played a central role in this revival, both in the stimulation of interest in Greek and in the development of skill to use it, was Emmanuel Chrysoloras (1350–1413). In 1397 Chrysoloras, who had come to Italy as a diplomat, accepted the chair of Greek at the University of Florence, and with him the revival of Greek in Italy really began.[9]

With this preparation the humanists of Italy were ready to enter the educational arena proper. The first to do so was Peter Paul Vergerius (1370–1445), the author of a work entitled *On Noble Character and*

[9] See John Addington Symonds, *The Renaissance in Italy*, The Modern Library, New York, 1935, vol. I, pp. 379–381. For one account of the work of Petrarch, see J. H. Robinson and H. W. Rolfe, *Petrarch: The First Modern Scholar and Man of Letters*, G. P. Putnam's Sons, New York, 1909.

Liberal Studies. The work of Vergerius is usually recognized as the first example of humanistic educational theory.[10] In it Vergerius advocated the teaching of Latin literature as part of liberal education; and he directed the attention of educators to the needs that certain noble laymen had for learning. His work was considered to be entirely orthodox by church authorities. There is evidence, moreover, that Vergerius was familiar with a number of classical authors; Plato, Cicero, Aristotle, were all known to him in one form or another. He could not have known the classical educational writers very completely because the bulk of their works had not yet been unearthed.

Whether or not Vergerius knew any of the ancient authorities on education, his own views were worth a good deal to the teachers of his day. It is claimed that the greatest teacher of the Renaissance, Vittorino da Feltre, was indebted to Vergerius.[11] In his work on *Liberal Studies,* a treatise that was intended as a practical guide for the education of Ubertino, the son of Francesco Carrara, the lord of Padua, Vergerius touched on the following topics that then, as now, had considerable relevance to education and educators: the training of children in manners, motivation for study, the relation of capacity to accomplishment, rewards and punishment for success and failure, and the interest of the teacher in the student as a person and not merely as a learning machine. It should not be overlooked that this work was intended to guide the education of a young prince, and though its precepts might well have been applicable to children who were not of noble birth, the context in which it was offered would seem to have somewhat limited its influence.

The work of Vergerius appeared about 1393. Within a quarter of a century later, work had been done and discoveries had been made in connection with the ancient educational writers that had important consequences for humanistic educational theory. In 1411 Guarino da Verona translated Plutarch's *On the Education of Children.* Having Plutarch's work in their hands in usable form, the theorists were now in closer touch with antiquity. It has been suggested that over the years the accomplishment of Guarino and the effects of Plutarch's work cannot be overestimated. Such a claim, however, might be in itself an example of overestimation. Of considerably more import than the translation of *On the Education of Children* was the discovery of a complete text of Quintilian's *Institutes of Oratory.* Poggio, a man renowned for his ability to ferret out old manuscripts, found the *Institutes* at the Swiss monastery of St. Gall in 1416. A few years later Cicero's *The Orator* was found at Lodi. Thus men who were interested in dealing with education

---

[10] William H. Woodward, *Vittorino da Feltre and Other Humanist Educators,* Cambridge University Press, New York, 1905, p. 94.

[11] *Ibid.,* p. 25.

on the level of theory had available to them four of the most important theoretical works on education ever written. These works were: *The Republic* of Plato, *Politics* of Aristotle, *The Orator* of Cicero, and Quintilian's *Institutes of Oratory*. From a study of these authors and from a study of the ancient forms of education, humanistic theorists were able to construct a theory of education which made possible a new order of schools. The greatest and the best known of these schools was conducted by a man who was, and is, acclaimed as the foremost schoolmaster of the Renaissance, Vittorino da Feltre. Before we turn to the work of Vittorino, it might be well to review the theoretical contributions of some of Vittorino's contemporaries and in this review provide the reader with some sense of direction in following humanistic educational practices. The educators to whom we turn now are: Leonardo Bruni D'Arezzo (1369–1444), Aeneas Sylvius Piccolomini—later Pope Pius II (1405–1464), Leone Battista Alberti (1404–1472), Battista Guarino (1434–1515), Mapheus Veglus (1405–1458), Matteo Palmieri (1400–1475), and Baldassare Castiglione (1478–1529).

Leonardo Bruni D'Arezzo. Bruni was the author of a tract entitled *On Studies and Letters*. This tract, really a letter, was addressed to Baptista Malatesta, a lady who had some reputation for learning. In the letter, he wrote: "The foundation of all true learning must be laid in the sound and thorough knowledge of Latin: which implies study marked by a broad spirit, accurate scholarship, and careful attention to details." And this advice, it must be remembered, is being given to a lady not for her own guidance because that was unnecessary, but as a pattern for the education of women. It might be pointed out that Bruni's reputation as an educational theorist in the humanistic tradition comes mainly from his views on the education of women, although it is difficult to see why these views attracted so much attention. In no sense was his tract a prescription for the general education of women; it was an educational code to be followed by noblewomen. If Bruni's view as to who should be given educational opportunity was narrow, his view of the content of education was not. He wrote:

But my last word must be this. The intelligence that aspires to the best must aim at both. [That is, both ancient and Christian literature.] In doing so, all sources of profitable learning will in due proportion claim your study. None have more urgent claim than the subjects and authors which treat of Religion and of our duties in the world; and it is because they assist and illustrate these supreme studies that I press upon your attention the works of the most approved poets, historians and orators of the past.[12]

Despite Bruni's place among humanistic theorists, one should not overlook his emphasis upon the relationship between certain classical authors

[12] *Ibid.*, pp. 132–133.

and religion, an emphasis that would seem to be more characteristic of the medieval period than of the Renaissance. Actually, it is an expression of Christian humanism, and in no way did it bar Bruni from the company of the other humanists.

Aeneas Sylvius Piccolomini. Sylvius prepared a set of directions for the education of boys. The immediate motive for his work on education was a desire to guide the young. He was in charge of the education of Ladislas, the youthful king of Bohemia. The tract was intended to guide him and others in preparing this boy for the station in life he was destined to occupy. Since the work appeared about 1450, it was possible for Sylvius to have the benefit of classical educational theories in formulating his own educational doctrine. His position in the history of educational thought is not of great eminence. His work *On the Education of Boys* is not distinctive enough to set him off from other Renaissance educators. Yet Sylvius does deserve a bit more attention than some of the others because of the position that he was to hold in the Church and the influence that he may have been able to exert from that position. He became Pope Pius II.

The tract begins with what is a more or less conventional humanistic introduction to educational speculation, which incidentally shows that humanists were indebted to the classical theorists.

In addressing ourselves to the question of the education of a boy in whom we are interested, we must first of all satisfy ourselves that he is endowed by Nature with a good and teachable disposition. Now this is a gift, not an acquirement; although a gift which has not been sparingly granted. For, as Quintilian rightly says, if flying is instinctive with birds, or galloping with horses, so an eager and forward temper is the natural mark of a child. The educator, therefore, is generally entitled to assume a native bent towards mental activity on the part of his charges, although, to be productive of real progress, this innate energy needs to be developed by methodical training and experience; nature, training, practice—these seem to be the three factors of all education.[13]

We have said that these were more or less conventional views of the humanistic educators of this time, and we might also point out that they are still considered to be entirely sound. Perhaps Sylvius made no mark on history for the views that he expressed above. However, in another part of this tract he looks at the opposition which, he must have suspected, came from some churchmen who did not take too kindly to the new emphasis in teaching and learning.

Now I meet an objection. You will be confronted by the opposition of the shallow Churchmen. "Why waste precious time in studying such sources of corruption as the pagan poets?" They will quote Cicero, Plato, Jerome, and

[13] *Ibid.*, p. 136.

Boethius, and will cry out for the banishment of the very names of the ancient poets from the soil of your country. To this your answer can only be: "If this tirade indeed represents the serious opinion of my people, I can but shake off the dust from my feet and bid farewell to a land shrouded in darkness so appalling." Happily, however, there are in Hungary not a few to whom the poets of antiquity are a precious possession. You will have no difficulty in quoting classical precedent for honouring them as they deserve. Nay the Fathers themselves, Jerome, Augustine, Cyprian, did not hesitate to draw illustrations from heathen poetry and so sanctioned its study. Further, if we are to reject the great writers of antiquity for the errors they contain, how shall we treat the masters of theology? From them proceed heresies. Shall we, then, expel them and their writings, as once the Romans banished doctors because they made mistakes?[14]

This was a strong defense for the classics and the extensive use that the humanists made or hoped to make of them in education. And it was an important defence, too, although it must be admitted that the classics were not in an especially precarious position. The stand that Sylvius took with respect to the classics was given even more stature once he became pope. It would, indeed, be hazardous to make extravagant claims for this man or for the impress he had on educational thought. On the other hand, both his work and his influence would seem to merit further study.

Leone Battista Alberti. Alberti was a many-sided, accomplished man. He was a painter, a poet, a philosopher, a musician, and an architect. On at least one occasion he turned his attention to education and wrote a short work entitled *On the Care of the Family,* a treatise made up of four books, each of which deals with a different aspect of family life and education. In part, the views of Alberti are the usual ones that have been attached to Christian education for centuries: He writes of the respective positions of parents and children in the family circle, of the role that the home must play in the moral formation of youth, of the central place of religion, and of the fulfillment of God's plan as the overriding ideal in man's life. On these points Alberti is not original, although the reemphasis that he gave them was remarkable, considering the direction that Italian humanism was often inclined to take. But Alberti did not stop here. He underlined the worth of letters both in forming character and in making the mind keener and more colorful. Besides, he encouraged parents to see that their children learned the vernacular well and that they could use it fluently for all the purposes to which the classical languages might otherwise be put. At this point Alberti departs from some of the more rigid humanists of the day; few of them would even admit that there was such a thing as the vernacular, to say nothing of using it widely.

Alberti belongs to any classification of humanistic theorists, although

[14] *Ibid.,* pp. 149–150.

the evaluation of him might vary from class to class. He has sometimes been called one of the leading educators of the humanistic age.[15]

Battista Guarino. Battista Guarino's short treatise, *Concerning the Order and the Method to be Observed in Teaching and in Reading the Classical Authors,* was written for Maffeo Gambara. The recipient of this humanistic tract on education has no particular place in the history of education. That Battista presented the tract to someone is mentioned only to indicate that he was staying well within the tradition begun by earlier writers on educational subjects. Few humanist theorists used conventional literary vehicles for setting forth their views; they usually selected the letter or the tract to carry their message.

Battista's purpose in writing this tract was, as the title would suggest, to offer guidance to students in their private reading and to masters who were in search of some definite principles of method in teaching the classics. Battista seems to have had the masters chiefly in mind. By the classics Battista meant both Greek and Latin letters, and in his view the outcome of their study would be a thoroughly satisfactory training in literature and scholarship. He has little to say that is novel. Within its humanistic frame of reference, the tract is both conventional and ortho-dox. The nature of the child, the skill of the master, the importance of proper content, the attention to moral formation—all of these are treated as earlier humanists and classical theorists had treated them. Only in one passage, early in the work, where Battista compares the master to the father, are his views especially interesting, if not distinctive. He wrote:

In the choice of a Master we ought to remember that his position should carry with it something of the authority of the father: for unless respect be paid to the man and to his office regard will not be had to his words. Our forefathers were certainly right in basing the relation of teacher and pupil on the foundation of filial reverence on the one part and fatherly affection on the other. Thus the instinct of Alexander of Macedon was a sound one which led him to say that, whilst he owed to his father Philip the gift of life, he owed to his tutor Aristotle an equal debt, namely, the knowledge to use it.[16]

There is no reason to doubt the sincerity of this author when he re-flects convictions as to the importance of the teacher. These were views that had been expressed in Western educational thought at least as early as Plato, and the classical writers on education were obviously sincere when they agreed with him. Yet it must be fairly clear to the reader by this time that theory and practice hardly ever went along hand in hand. While the theorists extolled the virtues of great masters and pointed to the need for skilled and virtuous teachers of the young, the people who

[15] See George Santayana, *Two Renaissance Educators: Alberti and Piccolomini,* Meador Publishing Company, Boston, 1930.

[16] Woodward, *op. cit.,* p. 162.

were in charge of selecting masters—parents, guardians, or public officials—went right on taking anybody they could get. This was especially true on the lower levels of education. The most surprising thing about the humanist educators of the fourteenth and fifteenth centuries is that they either did not recognize this separation of theory and practice when they saw it, or did not consider the separation to be really important. At any rate, we need give neither special blame nor special praise to the work or the influence of Battista Guarino.

Mapheus Vegius. The work of Vegius, *On the Education of Boys and Their Moral Culture,* is the longest and, many think, the most important of the humanistic treatises on education, His approach to the classics is entirely Christian; this Augustinian monk could see the value of the classics, and he never tired of recommending their study. A question has been raised concerning the lack of originality in this work of Vegius.[17] It is no doubt quite accurate to claim that for many of his views he was indebted to classical writers. But need this be a serious criticism? He was certainly a thorough investigator of the classical ideas on education.[18]

Vegius's book is divided into six parts. The first three parts deal with the place of parents and teachers in the total educational process; the last three deal with students in their relationship to God, to their fellow men, and to themselves. Although his work is directed principally toward the education of boys, Vegius does touch on the education of girls, and for them he prescribes a training in household duties.

In one of the finest statements ever written on the worth of knowledge, Vegius sums up what may have been the usual humanistic attitude toward it:

> May the youth of happy disposition seize knowledge and dedicate himself to it, since it has in view great benefits. . . . He receives the best guidance how one may live a modest, earnest, and pious life, how one should love parents and fatherland, reverence God, and avoid evil and despise sensuality. . . . Knowledge furnishes youth the greatest pleasure; knowledge of the changes of fate, of times and peoples and their history has something alluring. The doctrines that it offers us, are not merely of great moral influence, but conduce also to prudent judgments, to ripe reflection upon the mastery over the tasks of life. Scientific studies furnish relief and refreshment in those countless difficulties of which human life is full, and they cause us to forget them. In misfortune of any sort whatever they furnish strong protection; they

[17] See Frederick Eby and Charles F. Arrowood, *The History and Philosophy of Education: Ancient and Medieval,* Prentice-Hall, Inc., Englewood Heights, N.J., 1940, p. 884.

[18] What is probably the definitive study of Vegius was made by Vincent J. Horkan, *Educational Theories and Principles of Maffeo Vegio,* The Catholic University of American Press, Washington, D.C., 1953.

are themselves a support to riches and fortune, in consequence of the extra-ordinary esteem and worth which science contributes. Finally, knowledge is an ornament of mankind.[19]

Vegius's formulation of the objectives of education is both interesting and enlightening. It is easy to see his Christian outlook. He wrote that the ends of education ought to be such that a youth would reverence God, love his parents, be respectful toward strangers, regard the aged, not disdain youth, be friendly with his equals, never swear or lie or slander, be true to friends, courteous to women, gentle to servants, and good to everybody.[20] These are worthy, though not scholarly, objectives. It should be pointed out, however, that some of the means to obtain these ends would have been the usual literary means that were so much emphasized in humanistic educational practices.

Matteo Palmieri. Palmieri, a close friend of Alberti, wrote a work in dialogue form entitled *Concerning the Method of Ruling the Household and the State.* At first glance this may not appear to have any relevance to educational theory. We find, however, that in this work Palmieri discusses in four books the education of a boy from childhood to manhood and the virtues that would enable him to manage the household and conduct the affairs of the state. So this author deals with two kinds of education, domestic and civic, and expects that such education will produce a scholarly man of affairs.

Palmieri himself was a diplomat and a highly skilled and polished man. It is reported that he was sent to the king of Naples as an emissary from Florence. After hearing Palmieri discourse in Latin, Spanish, and Italian, the king is said to have remarked: "What must the Medici be, if this be but a simple citizen-trader of Florence!"[21]

Baldassare Castiglione. The Courtier, Castiglione's celebrated work on education, came rather late in the humanistic period, and tended to reflect rather than to form humanistic educational thought. Thus *The Courtier* was in a position to exert considerable influence on education after the Renaissance. Although written in the sixteenth century, this work of Castiglione's represented the best in fifteenth-century manners and morals, so that those who followed its dictates could be confident that they would be both learned and cultured. It should be mentioned, too, that the prescription laid down in *Il Cortegiano* was for men and women alike. It is clear, however, that this work was never intended to guide the education of the common man. The title betrays the emphasis;

[19] K. A. Kopp, *Mapheus Vegius's Erziehungslehre,* Herder and Co., Freiburg, 1889, p. 219, quoted in Eby and Arrowood, *op. cit.,* p. 892.

[20] Kopp, *op. cit.,* pp. 119–120.

[21] William H. Woodward, *Studies in Education during the Age of the Renaissance, 1400–1600,* Cambridge University Press, New York, 1924, p. 66.

the men and women to be educated were the members of the court or, at least, those who traveled in polite society. The educational doctrine, to be followed by ladies and gentlemen, was a doctrine of courtesy applied to education.

It is only fair to say that the best in humanistic educational theory was broader and more valid than the theories we find in Castiglione, although many of the positions taken in *The Courtier* are entirely responsible and acceptable. Yet in the main Castiglione was reflecting the educational thought of humanism; Renaissance educational theory did emphasize the education of laymen for their role in life. Castiglione narrowed this objective somewhat, but even in a narrower context it is still an outgrowth of orthodox humanistic theory.

Vittorino da Feltre (1378–1446). The humanists we have mentioned above played important roles in the evolution of educational thought and practice during this period. Their impact was considerable, yet compared with the influence of Vittorino da Feltre, it was relatively weak. Vittorino made no mark on the history of education as a theorist. He wrote nothing that could be called a book, although some of his letters have been the subject of careful study. It was as a schoolmaster that Vittorino achieved everlasting fame. One often reads the statement that Vittorino was the most famous schoolmaster of the Renaissance, and there may be only a little extravagance in the claim that he was the greatest teacher of modern times. Both statements are fairly easy to make and almost impossible either to prove or disprove. We make reference to them here simply to indicate that Vittorino was an educator of unquestioned stature and that we can learn much from him.

Little is known of Vittorino's early life. In 1396 he entered the University of Padua as a student. This is an important date in the history of learning, for it was in 1396 that the *studium* of Florence invited Emmanuel Chrysoloras, who was then a professor of Greek in Constantinople, to accept the chair of Greek letters. Thus Chrysoloras became the first professor of the Greek tongue in the West, and to this incident it is possible to relate much that took place in the revival of learning in Europe.[22] At Padua Vittorino was influenced by the spirit of Petrarch, which was still strong although the poet had died in 1376. Vittorino studied under Giovanni Conversino da Ravenna, who had been a close friend and student of Petrarch. He must have breathed in some of the spirit and the restless quest for learning that had motivated Petrarch and his followers.

Neither the details of Vittorino's life nor the course that he pursued at the University of Padua is entirely clear. He began, of course, with the faculty of arts and took his degree in arts. From there he went on, it

[22] See p. 277.

appears, to one of the higher faculties, although to which one is something of a mystery.

He remained at or near the University of Padua for about twenty years. For a short period of time he was a member of the university faculty in the position of master of rhetoric. It is reported, however, that he could not continue in that position because he felt that the discipline of the students was so bad that learning was impossible. Vittorino was a dedicated teacher. He refused to try to teach students who did not want what he had to offer, and he may not have remained a member of the faculty for more than about a year. Both before and after this academic experience he acted as a tutor to university students and conducted a private school for students who were preparing for the university. Thus Vittorino's career as a schoolmaster began early, but it was not at Padua or in Venice, where he also kept a school, but in Mantua that he achieved his great reputation as the finest schoolmaster the Renaissance ever produced.

In 1423 Vittorino received an invitation from the lord of Mantua, Gianfrancesco Gonzaga, to conduct a court school for the children of the Gonzaga family and for the children of the nobles of his court. It was quite unnecessary to seek a man of Vittorino's caliber if the lord of Mantua was interested only in a school; a man with less talent might have been an entirely satisfactory schoolmaster. However, it was usual at that time for rich and influential families to make every effort to consolidate their position and ensure their power. Some families employed painters, sculptors, or architects, thus becoming patrons of the arts whose fame could be spread throughout the country. Since learning and letters were highly prized at the time Gonzaga was looking for a schoolmaster, he decided to secure a man of letters as a teacher, and thus, in addition to providing instruction for the children, he could embellish his own position as a patron of the arts. And who was to say that there could not be justifiable pride or glory in being the patron of and the sponsor for the most reputable school in the region? So much for the motives that may have influenced the lord of Mantua.

Vittorino accepted the invitation extended to him. His teaching career at Mantua began in 1423 and ended with his death in 1446. While he was there he established and perfected what Woodward has called the first great school of the Renaissance.[23]

Vittorino shared the prevalent views on education. When he differed from other humanists on the level of theory it was only in degree, although it is obvious that he was much more of a practical schoolmaster than any of the humanistic theorists whom we have touched on above. He was unquestionably familiar with Quintilian's *Institutes of Oratory*

[23] Woodward, *Vittorino da Feltre and Other Humanist Educators*, p. 92.

and used it as a partial guide for his own educational plans. He knew Cicero's *The Orator* as well. It would be a mistake, therefore, to think of Vittorino as an educator who stood outside the humanistic tradition in learning. Yet it is well worth our while to look more closely at the ideal that motivated all of his work. Vittorino brought with him to Mantua a desire to combine the spirit of the Christian life with the educational apparatus of classical literature. He sought to achieve a genuine integration of the two.

In addition to the Gonzaga children in Vittorino's Mantuan school, other children from the vicinity were admitted, although they were always from the so-called better families. Compared to modern schools, the one conducted by Vittorino would be called small. Its enrollment probably never went beyond forty students, who ranged in age from six to twenty-seven. But before the reader reacts unfavorably to this great range in age, it should be said that Vittorino had a number of assistants, perhaps as many as fifteen, to help him conduct the school.

The site of the school was a villa. It was turned over to Vittorino by the Duke of Mantua and was called "Pleasant House." Like a typical humanist, Vittorino favored an educational setting that was devoid of gloom; he wanted his school to be bright and cheerful, and probably "Pleasant House" was really a house of delight.

The spirit of the school also sounds delightful. First of all, Vittorino considered himself the father of his students, and in a sense he was; the children who attended the school lived there. It was their home and Vittorino's home too. In addition to instructing his charges, he was responsible for their moral formation and their physical welfare. His highest desire, as far as cultural development was concerned, was to create in his students a genuine love of learning. When he was successful in doing this a great part of his task was accomplished.

Though history and ethics formed an important part of the program, the curriculum of the school at Mantua was basically a curriculum of the seven liberal arts. In content the arts were essentially the same as they had been in the medieval period, although Vittorino introduced some change in emphasis. He was conservative also in his teaching of Latin. Imbued as he was with the spirit of humanism and recognizing the requirements of learning, Vittorino continued to make Latin the language of the school. Greek was taught, but probably never on a very advanced level, and could not have been Latin's rival. Perhaps the only time the vernacular was used was when the children were at play.

One of the things that Vittorino attempted to avoid was routine, and apparently he was fairly successful in doing so. The first part of the school day—the total school day lasted about eight hours—was set aside for group instruction and lecturing; the second part of the day was reserved for individual work. Attention to the individual student and his special learning problems was perhaps the distinctive feature of Vittorino's technique. There is an account given by Prendilacqua, an assistant to Vittorino, which tells us that "Vittorino, now well advanced in years, would of a winter's morning come early, candle in one hand and book in the other, arouse a pupil in whose progress he was especially interested: he would leave him time to dress, waiting patiently till he was ready: then he would hand him the book, and encourage him with grave and earnest words to high endeavor."[24] This, the testimony of one of Vittorino's most successful lieutenants, creates a wonderful picture of the great teacher's dedication to the intellectual welfare of his students.

In class, or with group instruction, the technique employed consisted partly of dictation of texts, notes, and translations and partly of oral questioning. The practice of recitation and declamation varied the monotony of the class lecture. Vittorino insisted upon the importance of variety in all of the periods set aside for instruction. There was only one routine exercise—reading aloud. Memorization was as important as recitation. But the outstanding feature of Vittorino's work, to which reference has already been made, was careful individual work. Since the school was amply staffed, the teachers were able to devote time to gaining an intimate knowledge of the tastes, capacity, and industry of each student. Vittorino's readiness to adapt the content of instruction and the techniques used to the students' needs and interests explains in great part the unique success of the school. He had an unaffected pride in his work as a teacher, a keen interest in the progress of each of his students, and, added to this, an unusual insight into the teaching art itself.

Vittorino's fame rests solely on his reputation as a schoolmaster. No one has yet made any claims for his scholarship or for his literary ability. He left no documents explaining either his educational theory or his educational techniques. Yet in actual methods of instruction, so far as our sources enable us to draw any conclusion, we find a definite contrast between those of Vittorino and those of the medieval schools. His attitude toward learning seems fresh and attractive; his school, we are told, was bright and cheerful; his relations with the children in the school were excellent; and he had great hopes for knowledge, which, he believed, could be a great instrument for improving society and for bettering the life and character of the individual man. These are points of emphasis, it is true, but they sharply distinguish the school of Vittorino from the typical school, or better, from the usual medieval attitude toward learning. These distinctions in Vittorino's school are due partly to the influence that humanism had on him; its glow affected him as it affected his age.

[24] Quoted in *ibid.*, p. 62.

But in addition to his humanistic approach, Vittorino had an undoubted genius for teaching; he had a swift intuition of the right method to be used in his art.

Humanism in Northern Europe

The spirit of humanism in the north of Europe was somewhat different from what it was in the south; social rather than individual objectives seemed to dominate its outlook in the north. We shall be interested to see whether or not this difference between the two types of humanism was reflected in the application of humanism to education. In northern Europe a number of important educators belonged to the humanistic camp: in France, Guillaume Budé and Peter Ramus; in England, Colet, Elyot, and More; in the Netherlands, the Brethren of the Common Life. Erasmus and Vives cannot really be claimed by any one country, although Vives was a Spaniard by birth, and Erasmus was Dutch. In Germany, Agricola, Reuchlin, Wessell, and Wimpheling were important humanists. Of all of these northern humanists, the chief figures for the historian of education were Vives and Erasmus. Before we examine their thought, a word may be said about the less important humanists of this region.

The Humanists of France. Guillaume Budé (1467–1540) wrote a book on education entitled *On the Education of a Prince.* This book was not especially important; it expressed orthodox humanistic views on education and directed the greater part of its attention to the formation of the noble child. Still it was different. It was the first humanistic treatise on education to be written in French. Though itself written in the vernacular, the book advocated the study of the classical languages as the most effective means for obtaining a complete education. Budé was especially critical of the University of Paris, which at this time had well-established faculties of philosophy and theology but gave too little attention, so Budé thought, to letters. It would be somewhat unfair to compare Budé's influence with that of Vives or Erasmus; nevertheless, Budé's book was of considerable consequence, and it did a good deal to break ground for humanistic education in France.

Peter Ramus (1515–1574) and François Rabelais (1483–1553) were lesser French humanists. Ramus came rather late in the period, and by his time the direction of humanism was pretty well set. His contribution was mainly that he prepared textbooks with the humanistic content of the seven liberal arts and that he advocated a reform of educational methodology. Ramus's views on the spirit and method of teaching called for a rejection of medieval methods, a freeing of education from the tight grasp of the past, and a broadening of academic horizons on all educational levels.[25] The books that Ramus prepared for student use became extremely popular; some of them even crossed the ocean and were used in American colonial schools.

Rabelais is not the greatest figure in French educational humanism, but we cannot dismiss him as a negativist of the Rousseauistic type. When Rabelais's negativism is taken too literally, the reader, not Rabelais, is being misled. It is quite possible that the influence of Rabelais in bringing about some educational reform in France was greater than is generally believed. The book in which he demanded reform, his *Pantagruel and Gargantua,* is world famous.

The Humanists in England. The English humanists were Thomas Linacre (1460–1524), William Grocyn (1466–1519), William Latimer (1460–1545), John Colet (1467–1519), Thomas More (1478–1535), Thomas Elyot (1490–1546), and Roger Ascham (1515–1568). These men were somewhat more practical in their approach to education than most of their counterparts on the Continent; they were more inclined to work with educational questions on the level of teaching and learning. Some of them were schoolmasters or headmasters, and others were authors of schoolbooks.

The center of English humanism was Thomas More. He had studied under Colet, Grocyn, and Linacre at Oxford and had risen to prominence in public life in England. In addition to this, he was recognized as an important colleague by the leading humanists of Europe. More's *Utopia* was one of the first English contributions to Renaissance literature, and with it English writing took on additional significance and distinction. More was not an educator in any narrow sense, although he had a consuming love of learning and seemed to understand the pedagogical steps that led to its attainment. Despite the absence of any clear marks of the schoolmaster, More may be regarded as the chief inspirer of educational reform and humanistic popularity in England.

One could not mention English humanists without coming sooner or later to the work of Thomas Elyot, *The Boke Named the Governour.* This book has the remarkable distinction of having been the first book on education to be written in English. In it the word "educate" was used for the first time. Elyot's book treats of the proper education for those who are likely to be called upon to occupy responsible positions in government and to exercise authority. This, then, is another prescription for the education of nobles. Besides endorsing the usual humanistic content for the schools, Elyot proposed in the *Governour* that more attention be given to physical education and the social sciences. He entered, moreover, into another question on education that was not often

[25] Ramus was violently opposed to Aristotle. Two books in which he developed his attack on Aristotle were *The Institutes of Dialectic* and *Animadversions on Aristotle.*

discussed at this time: He wrote a book on the education of women, *Defense of Good Women*. Finally, he prepared a Latin-English dictionary. Probably this last-mentioned contribution was his most significant.

A little later in the development of English humanism, Roger Ascham appeared on the scene. He was a professional scholar, who at one time had been the tutor to the Princess Elizabeth of England. He belongs in this company of English humanists because of the work that he wrote late in his life, the *Scholemaster*. This book has been criticized rather severely because, it is said, it contains nothing new about humanistic education. But special merit in writing does not come only from originality, and perhaps it was impossible for Ascham to be bright and fresh on all of the educational matters that humanists had been discussing and writing about for a century or more. He repeated many previously advanced opinions, it is true, but he apparently made a distinctive contribution to teaching by advocating new and positive methods of teaching Latin and Greek. Ascham may be a lesser figure in the history of education than, say, Thomas Elyot, but his significance should not be totally obscured.

The Brethren and the German Humanists. The spread of humanism from Italy and France to the Teutonic world was comparatively slow, perhaps because Germany had not had any strong connection with the classical past. Although by the end of the sixteenth century most of the German universities had been reorganized along humanistic lines, it was not the universities that were most responsible for the growth and spread of humanism in Germany. The real source for humanism here was a community of teachers, thinkers, and religious that had been founded by Gerhard Groot (1340-1384) and was known as the Brethren of the Common Life.[26]

Groot's chief aim was to bring about a reform in the Church.[27] In his opinion the surest and quickest way to reach this end was to train young men, and thus the chief occupation of the Brethren was education. The curriculum of the schools conducted by the Brethren included pagan or classical as well as Christian literature. Grammar, rhetoric, logic, mathematics, and philosophy, subjects all common to the curriculum of some medieval schools, were studied too. The most important of the schools opened by the Brethren were at Deventer, Zwolle, and Münster. From these schools came young men with a good education and with a new and somewhat clearer picture of the role of religion and the mission of

[26] Pierre J. Marique, *History of Christian Education,* Fordham University Press, New York, 1924–1932, vol. II, p. 54.

[27] Albert Hyma, *The Brethren of the Common Life,* Eerdmans, Grand Rapids, Mich., 1950, p. 116.

the Catholic Church. A few of the schools produced young men with truly great minds. One such pupil, who was educated at the school of Zwolle, became the most famous educator of Transalpine Europe, Alexander Hegius (1433–1498).[28]

Though a leading humanist of the late fifteenth century and a serious student of the ancients, Hegius was, like Vives, a believer in the worth of the vernacular. He was also a leader of the movement to introduce new and better materials for instruction into the schools, recognizing, for example, that the textbooks of the schools were badly in need of revision.

During the time that Hegius was its rector, the school at Deventer was one of the chief centers of the German Renaissance. An indication of the strength of this intellectual movement may be seen in the 450 classical works that were printed by the Deventer presses before 1500.[29] By the beginning of the sixteenth century hardly a school could be found in the Netherlands and Germany that had not been influenced by Deventer, Zwolle, and Münster. Under the leadership of the scholars and teachers sent out from these three schools, practically all of the larger schools of Western Germany were reorganized and reformed. The thought and practice of Groot and his followers were spread throughout the land. Hyma writes that even "modern education perpetuates the best features of the reformed education of Groot and [John] Cele and the Brethren of the Common Life."[30] Hegius himself was something more than a scholar and a teacher. In the spirit of his broad humanism, coupled with a deep sense of the truth of Christianity, he influenced several thousand students to carry out the Brethren's reform plans in schools, churches, and monasteries.[31] He is another figure that may be added to the list, a growing list, of Christian humanists.

A few other German humanists, all of whom came under the influence of the Brethren of the Common Life, were Rudolph Agricola (1443–1485), Johann Wessell (1420–1489), Jacob Wimpheling (1450–1528), and Jacob Reuchlin (1455–1552).

Rudolph Agricola was born near Groningen and, under the tutelage of the Brethren, revealed special capacities in the classical languages. He studied at Louvain, where he obtained his master's degree, and at the Universities of Paris and Ferrara. His connections with Reuchlin led him to develop a strong conviction that the Hebrew language was essential in humanistic education as an instrument for scriptural studies. He translated Greek classics into Latin and wrote a number of letters in

[28] *Ibid.*, p. 118.
[29] *Ibid.*, p. 121.
[30] *Ibid.*, p. 126.
[31] *Ibid.*, p. 120.

which he expressed many of his educational views. Agricola's most famous pedagogical work was *On the Regulation of Study*. It had great influence on German education.

Jacob Wimpheling, a product of the University of Heidelberg, a distinguished priest and scholar, was rector of the Heidelberg *studium* in 1482. Wimpheling's most important work may have been the education of a large number of humanistic teachers. He wrote several textbooks and speculated on educational theory. His *Guide to German Youth*, a book which discusses many practical considerations in education, was the first pedagogical treatise in German. As a result of it, we are told, he received the merited title of the "Teacher of Germany." In the work *Adolescentia* (Youth), he expounded his views on the relationship between the classics and moral and religious formation.

Of what use are all of the books of the world, the most learned writings, the profoundest researchers, if they only minister to the vainglory of their authors, and do not or cannot advance the good of mankind? . . . What profits all our learning, if our character be not correspondingly noble, or our industry without piety, or our knowing without love of our neighbour, or our wisdom without humility, or our studying if we were not kind and charitable?[32]

He urged the city authorities at Strassburg to begin a school in which education according to humanistic ideals would be offered. Interestingly enough, he was listened to, and the city fathers founded a school that a generation or so later was to be presided over by the great John Sturm.[33]

Jacob Reuchlin was a layman. He taught at the University of Heidelberg, where he was an exceptional scholar in Latin, Greek, and Hebrew. Perhaps his greatest scholarly achievement was to bring out a Hebrew grammar and dictionary. Throughout his career he advocated greater tolerance for all people, especially the Jews.

ERASMUS

Desiderius Erasmus was born in 1466 and died in 1536. He was a complex, many-sided, talented man. Although some have regarded him as an enemy of the Catholic Church, this view is probably in need of some revision. It is, of course, understandable that his allegiance to the Church might be suspected, for he was a regular and often bitter critic of the extravagances churchmen sometimes condoned or engaged in. He was a man who made many enemies. The details of Erasmus' life are not well known. He was an Augustinian monk, who found life in the monastery so oppressive that he spent as little time there as possible, left

[32] Quoted in Marique, *op. cit.*, p. 56.
[33] See pp. 314–316.

whenever he could, and sometimes did not bother to let his superiors know that he was departing or get their permission for his travels.

Erasmus was the greatest scholar of his age. No doubt he took pride in his own accomplishments, but his real objective was to advance and refine taste, purify morals, promote unity and peace in Europe, and correct ecclesiastical abuses. Education was to be the chief instrument to obtain these ends.

One need look no further than the classical writers on education to find the bases for Erasmus' principal educational views. But where some of the other humanists showed a marked inclination to adopt the form rather than the spirit of Quintilian, Cicero, Plutarch, and others, Erasmus was inspired by their words. This led him not only to criticize many of the contemporary educational practices, but to make some positive contributions to educational methods, especially to the teaching of the classical languages. Erasmus' position in regard to language study was balanced and sane. He considered Latin and Greek means to an end rather than ends in themselves, and he encouraged the study of these languages as tools to deepen man's knowledge of himself. With these tools men could come in direct contact with the generations that had preceded them and, so Erasmus and others believed, learn from the great things that had been thought and said by the great minds of the classical period.

Educationally, the contributions of Erasmus were chiefly that (1) he prepared textbooks that were used all over Europe; (2) he prepared two outstanding treatises on educational theory, *The Right Method of Instruction* and *The Liberal Education of Boys*. In addition and not necessarily in an educational vein, he wrote among other things *The Praise of Folly* and *Letters of Obscure Men*. Both of these books attracted a great deal of attention and were widely read both for their satirical qualities and for the ideas they expressed about the reform of society. But these were the works that brought down upon the head of Erasmus the wrath of many European ecclesiastics.

Before turning to a close examination of *The Right Method of Instruction* and *The Liberal Education of Boys*, we might say a word about three earlier writings of Erasmus which may be classified either as minor educational works or as writings that were incidentally educational. They are *The Manual of the Christian Knight, The Education of the Christian Prince,* and *On Christian Matrimony*. The first is an inspirational and practical work, intended to guide the Christian knight to God. *The Education of the Christian Prince,* written in 1516, appeared only three years after *The Prince* of Machiavelli. Perhaps this work of Erasmus, more than any of his others, would give him the name of a humanistic educator; few educational theorists of this time wanted to pass up the opportunity to write something about the education of a young nobleman. More significantly, *The Prince* of Erasmus is almost exactly opposite in tone and direction to that of Machiavelli. For Erasmus the highest principle of action is not expediency, and the prince is not, like Machiavelli's prince, totally emancipated from the Christian ethic.

The most progressive people of the humanistic period considered a limited monarchy the best form of government. Erasmus shared this view and expressed it in *The Prince*. He believed that the limited monarch was best able to promise good government and therefore to lay the foundation for a more productive, orderly, and effective society. Yet we can detect democratic signs in this work by Erasmus, although we cannot say that it is a genuine charter for political democracy. The prince and his consort are expected to live both in harmony and in contact with their people. There is no charter for aloofness; they should be of the people. Laws are said to serve no other purpose than the welfare of the people; government should be conducted according to law and not allowed to follow the whims of individuals. In other words, Erasmus stood for a government of law and not of men. Such a political environment would provide men with the opportunity to build good lives for themselves and for their families. They could live with a sense of honor and dignity, and their pride would reflect itself in the progress and stability of the nation. Crime should be fought, Erasmus advised, not in a spirit of vindictiveness, not with the idea of punishment foremost in the society that had been injured, but by preventive economic and political and social measures. Still within the context of the preparation of a Christian prince, Erasmus advocated the abolishment of artificial class distinctions. There was no question at all in Erasmus' mind that there are natural distinctions in society among men; what he opposed was the unnatural distinction that was maintained, even encouraged, by law and custom.

Erasmus expressed the opinion that government should take an active part in the economic development of a country. Perhaps he saw more clearly than any of the other humanists the relationship that exists between economics, on the one side, and a strong and healthy society on the other. He showed especial interest in the reform of agriculture, and even went so far as to advocate the government's assistance in the development of a nation's agricultural potential. His measures would have included a reform of the land policy as well as a new and more progressive program of conservation and road building. These unusually advanced social and economic positions would hardly allow us to call Erasmus a conservative. Finally, he took an unequivocal stand against war. The Christian prince, he said, should know that few wars have solved anything and that a war should never be fought unless it is absolutely necessary for the defense of human rights. So much for the syllabus that he prepared for the prince. It may be remarked that this work by Erasmus was almost completely forgotten by European political thinkers, while the work of Machiavelli became a classic.

On Christian Matrimony, written in 1526, was intended to guide and reform the Christian society in Europe. It was designed to do for the common man what *The Education of the Christian Prince* was to do for the nobles. The chapter that is of greatest interest to the educational historian is the one that deals with the education of girls, a subject that was either not mentioned at all by the humanists, or else treated in a perfunctory way. Perhaps Erasmus discussed the subject because there was no logical way to avoid it. How could he write on matrimony without saying something about the woman's preparation for it? Few humanists, Erasmus included, thought that women had sufficient intellectual maturity to be educable, yet Erasmus certainly did not approve of crude inequality in the treatment of women. Possibly the best summary of this chapter would be to say that Erasmus wanted girls educated in such a way that they would be good Christian women who could become loyal and effective wives and mothers. Today's reader may find this position something less than acceptable, but he should remember that even on this point Erasmus was many decades, if not centuries, ahead of his time.

The two chief works that Erasmus prepared for the guidance of educators were *The Right Method of Instruction* and *The Liberal Education of Boys.* In the first, Erasmus is concerned primarily with the right method of instruction to be used in teaching the classics, in interpreting the authors, and in teaching the techniques of composition. It would be difficult to find an educational theorist in the history of thought who attached greater importance to the methods of instruction than Erasmus. Of course, he considered methods something more than mere techniques involved in directing learning activities; he included the choice of material as well as the means employed in imparting it as part of the methodological problem. And he insisted that with the right methods of instruction, boys who under ordinary conditions would be little more than acceptable in their accomplishments in Latin and Greek could rise to creditable standards of scholarship. He even went a little beyond this when he promised that boys of average intelligence could look forward with greater hope for achievement in higher learning if their education on the lower levels was reinforced by the correct methods of instruction. The care devoted to the child's early years in learning was considered by Erasmus to be most important. In this respect Erasmus was following the thinking of Quintilian, who never tired of emphasizing the care that ought to be devoted to the early education of children.

Erasmus was no "mere theorist"—to use a somewhat denigrating phrase—when he wrote of methods. He did not neglect the fact that a technique has meaning only when it is put in the context of all the things that teachers do in directing learning. A method is a tool to be used in guiding and directing the learning activities of children in classrooms and laboratories, and has very little meaning outside this context. Thus Erasmus was on solid ground when he proposed that teachers be trained in a systematic manner especially for their work. He went beyond this: He wrote that churchmen and statesmen alike had a duty to see that teachers were available to educate the youth of a country. This, he maintained, was an obligation and responsibility of a superior order.

Although Erasmus' *The Right Method of Instruction* is an educational document of unusual quality and one that influenced educators throughout much of the modern period, his most mature work on an educational subject was *The Liberal Education of Boys*. Taking these two works together, however, we find that they form a coherent and thoroughly humanistic theory of education. Both works are full of a genuine sensitivity to the need for good teachers; both recognize their responsibilities; and both are definitely superior to the educational writings of the earlier humanists.

In *The Liberal Education of Boys* Erasmus deals with the aim of education. Education's objective, in his view, is to lead men toward knowledge, honesty, and independent judgment. If this is a hierarchy, if, in other words, independent judgment is higher in the scale of educational values than knowledge, then Erasmus is really saying that the essential purpose of education is to lead the individual toward autonomy, both intellectual and moral. Or, to put it in another way, sound education is the essential condition of real wisdom.

The versatility of Erasmus is not too difficult to demonstrate. We have seen that he was a follower of Quintilian. When he touched on wisdom he stepped into the tradition of Aristotle, but his Aristotelian praise of wisdom is combined with the Christian ideal of man. He did not forget Plato. There is evidently a similarity between the view that Erasmus expressed on man's need for education and Plato's words on the same subject. Erasmus put it this way: "It is beyond dispute that man not instructed through reason in philosophy and sound learning is a creature lower than a brute, seeing that there is no beast more wild or more harmful than a man who is driven hither and thither by ambition or desire, anger or envy, or lawless temper."[34] According to Erasmus, it is reason that enables men to unite in a community and to remain therein

[34] The Argument of Erasmus of Rotterdam, "That Children Should Straightway from Their Earliest Years Be Trained in Virtue and Sound Learning," in William H. Woodward, *Desiderius Erasmus, concerning the Aim and Method of Education*, Cambridge University Press, New York, 1904, p. 186.

without destructive dissension. Individual differences were recognized and thoroughly understood by this great humanist. Such differences were found only in achievement; or, as Erasmus would say, they were found according to the degree of a man's participation in the achivements of culture.

Where did Erasmus stand on the questions relative to freedom and authority? We could make a reasonably strong case against Erasmus to the effect that he defied and denied all authority. Yet in spite of the strength of our contention, it would not be valid. Erasmus did not oppose authority, although he did deplore its invasion into areas where it did not belong. He would have considered the misuse of the Church's authority, or of churchmen's authority, as offensive as the misuse of an authority based on the ancient authors. Of course, all that Erasmus was really saying (and it was something that needed saying) was that the will of man does not make truth. He was an ardent and courageous enemy of voluntarism.

To turn now to some clear educational issues: We have seen that Erasmus was something of a reformer, that he would have added a good deal to education, and that he would have removed many things from it. Perhaps he opposed nothing with more vigor than the generally cruel discipline that was associated with most of the schools of the day. He deplored the existence of the cruel schoolmaster:

A poor master, we are prepared to find, relies almost wholly upon fear of punishment as the motive to work. To frighten one entire class is easier than to teach one boy properly; for the latter is, and always must be, a task as serious as it is honorable. . . . Do schoolmasters consider how many earnest, studious natures have been by treatment of this type—the hangman type— crushed into indifference?[35]

Of course, if teachers were to achieve the best results without the rod as a chief tool for instruction, they needed to have far more insight into child nature than most teachers of Erasmus' time were able to boast.

Even though Erasmus' views may not have been entirely original, they were not simply borrowed and then communicated without considerable analysis and modification. On the point of individual progress he said that three conditions determine the progress that a child in school will make. They are nature, training, and practice. By nature Erasmus meant innate capacity for achievement and a natural motivation to attain excellence. By training he meant the instruction and guidance that the student would be able to obtain; the more skillful and careful this instruction and guidance, the better for the student involved. By practice he intended a free exercise by the student of that capacity which

[35] *Ibid.*, pp. 205–206.

nature had implanted and which instruction had shaped, directed, and polished. "Nature without skill training must be imperfect and practice without the method which training supplies leads to hopeless confusion."[36]

Our brief discussion of the educational work of Erasmus may be summarized by pointing to the principal positions that he took: (1) He recognized the worth of physical education, as any good humanist would almost certainly have to do, but he did not give much attention to it in any school program with which he dealt, and this, too, was a typical attitude among the humanists. (2) He acknowledged the rights of the middle class for educational opportunity, and he was generally unwilling to think in terms of a "class to be educated." (3) He understood and respected the individual differences and special talents among children, but he would not have authorized any onesidedness in their education or their training. He prized and proposed the well-rounded, generally educated, culturally competent individual. (4) He maintained that formal education should begin at an early age, but he did not become any more definite about the exact time. No doubt, following all educators since the time of Homer, as well as his own observations of child nature, he would have thought a child should begin formal schooling at the age of seven or thereabouts. (5) The curriculum that Erasmus devised or approved was mainly classical. Yet it had a range that would have surprised the present-day pragmatist. In it, language was emphasized as a tool, a door to experience, Erasmus said, rather than a barrier to shut it out. For the first time in about a thousand years of educational history, we find an educator who is unwilling to endorse the separation between language and life and between learning and life that had become evident as early as the Hellenistic period.[37] (6) Finally, Erasmus was very liberal-minded when it came to understanding the possibilities of adding to the body of man's knowledge. The door of the school was never closed to any subject. The curriculum was open to all legitimate areas of experience, and the schoolroom was a forum in which all questions could be raised and discussed. Erasmus' *Latin Conversations,* a work intended for school use, brought up and discussed many subjects that even the teacher of the twentieth century might hesitate to introduce.

What can be said about the influence of Erasmus on education in the modern world? It was not overwhelming, but it was significant. Some of his worth was swept away, of course, when many of his works were

---

[36] *Ibid.,* p. 191.

[37] See pp. 110–112. For a more thorough treatment of Erasmus' views on learning, see P. S. Allen, *Erasmus' Services to Learning,* Oxford University Press, New York, 1925, and *The Age of Erasmus,* Oxford University Press, New York, 1914.

placed on the *Index of Prohibited Books.* (It should be added that they were all removed from the *Index* by Pope Leo XIII in 1897.) In spite of this very real hazard to popularity, Erasmus' books were extremely popular. He had written a number of textbooks for the schools; many of them were printed in other countries and were used for centuries. He had consistently maintained that Latin was not an end in itself, and he wrote his textbooks to emphasize this doctrine. He wanted boys to learn Latin by dealing with the common objects of life. Erasmus' works were so closely related to instruction in Latin and the place of Latin in the schools, that it is not surprising that they did not survive the decline of Latin study in the curriculum of twentieth-century schools. Erasmus did not make many, if any, provisions for the study of the vernacular language in his school program.

JUAN LUIS VIVES (1492–1540)

Juan Luis Vives was a humanistic educator with a good reputation. This Spanish-born thinker receives our attention not only because of his educational theories, but because he was a student of the Brethren of the Common Life, a student and friend of Erasmus, and the tutor to the Princess Mary of England.

Vives is often called the forerunner of educational realism. By realism we mean the commitment to use knowledge and not merely to seek it as an ornament or adornment. We could not discuss Vives as a humanist, of course, if the term realist better describes him. Yet may it not be true that every one of the humanists was to some degree a realist, and that every one of the later realists—Comenius perhaps—[38] was at least slightly humanistic in his outlook? No theorist, no man, is able to turn his back on every intellectual position save one. This was true of Vives. We may think of him as a realist in a relative sense: He was more of a realist than, say, Castiglione, that is, was more willing to put into the school's curriculum instruments that would furnish the student with skill. He supported useful knowledge. Very possibly Vives thought of schooling as an interlude which might provide students with the opportunity to learn to know something very well and to learn to do something very well. From another point of view, one that begins to introduce a science of education, Vives was much more of a realist than any of his contemporaries. He tried to go to the root of the methodological problem, and he tried to go to the foundations for an understanding of child nature. In this book we should hesitate to attempt to make a comparison between Vives and Erasmus, but we can say that Vives reminds us much more of modern-day educators than does Erasmus.

[38] See pp. 336–346.

Vives, moreover, was something of a pioneer in a number of important educational and social areas; his *De Anima* (*Concerning the Soul*) explored the relationship between learning and psychology. His work in breaking ground in this area is so well thought of that Vives is often called the father of educational psychology. His *De Subventione Pauperum* (*On Poor Relief*) is a vivid illustration of Vives' interest in the plight of the poor and of social problems in general. *On the Instruction of Christian Women* is an early, though by no means the earliest, treatment of the education of women. Because of this work and because of his commission as tutor to the Princess Mary, Vives has often been thought of as the chief mover for greater opportunities for the education of women. The perspective of history suggests to us that the role of Vives in the education of women has been overemphasized. His works, *On a Plan of Studies for Youth* and *Concerning the Teaching of the Arts*, contain the best evidence of his humanism. The latter is unquestionably his most complete as well as his most mature work on education.

Without going into detail on the opinions that he expressed, the following summary may be made of Vives' educational theory:

1. He emphasized the role that parents should take in the education of their children. It is true that Vives, along with his humanistic contemporaries, gave more attention to the school and literary education than was common, say, in the medieval period, but he did not forget that the child is first of all a responsibility of the parent. He did not forget, moreover, that the basic foundation of education considered in its broadest sense is most securely laid in the home during the child's earliest years.

2. He thought that children should be sent to school when they were about seven years of age. Here Vives agrees with the usual humanistic and classical view of the right age to begin formal education. It may be noted, however, that nothing in his view suggests the kindergarten or any other kind of institutional training that might be considered pre-elementary.

3. Vives preferred, as most humanists did, that boys be educated in public schools where there were many boys rather than in private schools which were in reality mere tutorial arrangements. However, if the tutorial system was to be used, Vives admonished parents and others responsible for the education of youth to be certain that more than one student was under the direction of a master. He proposed that at least one companion be provided for every tutored student. Vives' reasons for this position were not, as is often supposed, that the student's morals would be more secure if he attended his lessons with a companion, but that he would enjoy greater opportunities for learning with a companion or in a group.

4. Vives willingly endorsed the inclusion of sport, drama, entertainment, and recreation in the educational program.

5. Instruction was to be adapted to the individual. Of course, Vives did not envision broad commitments to public or universal education, or he could not have taken such an unequivocal stand on this point. Yet within the context in which he operated, he insisted that the students be taught according to their ability to learn. Who could dispute the validity of this position? In order to assure the practical application of the stand he took in theory, he advised that every boy be studied by his teachers for at least two months before instruction was to begin. How could teachers adapt learning procedures to the needs of the students unless they knew their students thoroughly?

6. Vives advocated the public support of education. That is, he regarded education as a public enterprise and thought that the public ought to pay for it. He saw, too, that opportunity in education was bound to be limited if such opportunity had to be provided by private means alone.

7. In keeping with a completely orthodox humanistic view of education, Vives supported the notion that the environment in which teaching and learning take place should be pleasant and generally conducive to learning.

8. He took a firm stand on the value of the classics. He would never have left them out of the school's curriculum. Yet he did reject the absurd imitation of the classics that so many teachers were prone to insist on. Although Vives thought the classics important, he advised teaching the vernacular in the schools and using it as a means for introducing students to Latin.

9. Vives gave his complete support to studies in history and the natural sciences.

10. When he spoke of the education of women, Vives suggested for them a careful study of the vernacular, Latin, religion, and moral precepts. The development of good conduct was much emphasized as was training for the care of children and household management. No mathematics, science, or politics appeared in the school's syllabus for girls. Yet Vives did not agree with the educators of his day in thinking of the education of women in terms of the finishing-school.

SUMMARY

The Renaissance was a renewal of interest in the past. It was an attempt to capture the goals and practices of the classical period, but above all it sought to regain the spirit, the humanism, of classical antiquity. In education this meant not so much a turning away from the practices and theories of the medieval years as an attempt to give them a new direction. The new direction was influenced greatly by the great Roman educator, Quintilian. The curricula and methods of the schools remained much as they had been before, although the humanists did emphasize the education of laymen for citizenship. This change was at least a partial rejection of the medieval plan, which had called for a clerical monopoly of education and a preoccupation with otherworldly objectives for education. Beside this, humanistic educational writers dealt with such issues as the control of education, the value of the classics, the relative claims of knowledge and style, the education of women, the place of physical education, and the use of the vernacular in school.

In the south of Europe the prominent theorists of the humanistic age were Vergerius, Bruni, Piccolomini, Alberti, Guarino, Vegius, and Castiglione. For all their humanism, they showed unusual interest in the education of noble children and a remarkable lack of interest in the education of the common man.

The great schoolmaster of the Renaissance was Vittorino da Feltre. Although in its curriculum his school reflected orthodox humanism, Vittorino, with the intuition of genius, organized and conducted a school that was unique in the method and spirit of instruction.

Erasmus and Vives, in the north of Europe, offered educational views that were somewhat more mature than those of their southern counterparts. The theories of these men and the practices they advanced exerted greater influence on later modern education than those of any other humanistic theorists.

Questions and Exercises for Study and Discussion

1. There were three renaissances: one in the ninth, one in the twelfth, and one in the fourteenth century. Compare the last renaissance with the two earlier ones.
2. Summarize Renaissance educational theory. In what ways was it different from medieval educational theory?
3. Renaissance educators ignored medieval education. Were they justified in doing so? Why or why not?
4. Discuss the Renaissance attitude toward vernacular languages. Were there any exceptions to this attitude?
5. How would you distinguish Christian humanism from classical humanism?
6. Describe the evolution of humanistic education in Italy.
7. Sample one or two of the tracts on education prepared by humanistic educational theorists. What is your candid evaluation of these tracts as documents in education?

8. Quintilian, it is said, had tremendous influence in fourteenth-century education. Do you find his impress on Renaissance educational theory?
9. What was the Renaissance attitude toward the education of women? How could this attitude have been justified?
10. Compare the educational views of Mapheus Vegius with those of Baldassare Castiglione.
11. Prepare a brief report on the life and career of Vittorino da Feltre. Try to be explicit when you deal with his work as a teacher, and show why he is called the most famous of all humanistic schoolmasters.
12. Report on the life of Erasmus and summarize his chief educational views.
13. Compare the educational influence of Erasmus with that of Vives.

10

Revolt, Reform, and Education

We cannot hope for a thorough understanding of either the Protestant Revolt or the Catholic Reformation without taking into account the general development of society in the hundred years before Luther. Great changes were slowly coming over Europe during the fifteenth century. The age was becoming more and more aware of its modernity, brought on by new inventions and the opening of new worlds of science and geography. The traditional view of the Renaissance has been modified somewhat. This traditional view, most characteristic of the nineteenth century, regarded the Renaissance as a dramatic leap back over a thousand years. The contemporary view is inclined to see a closer relationship between the Renaissance and the medieval civilization that preceded it. It might be argued that the Renaissance grew out of the Middle Ages; it might also be argued that the Revolt was as much a reaction to the Renaissance as it was a development from it. The fifteenth century differed from the centuries that preceded it mainly in the evolution of a new political and social environment, in which humanism and human individuality found freer expression.

To give all the credit to the Italian humanists for the achievements and great moments of the Renaissance is to go too far. We might even suggest that their formalism and preoccupation with imitation tended to slow rather than to foster the free play of individual character and natural feeling. It was in Italy that the first signs of humanism were found, and it was there that the humanistic movement achieved its form. In Italy, as well as in southern Europe, humanism was in general quite aristocratic and individualistic in its economic, social, and educational aims. But as the ideals of the humanistic movement spread north, the movement became more religious, moral, and social. Education in the north of Europe, especially in the hands of the Brethren, Erasmus, and Vives, was understood to be a means for social and moral reform and not merely a means for personal improvement and the individual pursuit of culture. To put it another way: The humanism of the Renaissance in southern Europe was intellectual and patrician; in northern Europe it made its appeal to the masses through religious and emotional means. In both the north and the south of Europe the scholars of humanism were somewhat opposed to Scholastic philosophy and its formalistic methods, and in both places the humanists were opposed to authoritarianism. This opposition to authoritarianism, especially in the north, sometimes took the form of protests against the doctrines and practices of the Catholic Church. Often there were demands for a return to simple, uncomplicated, nonritualistic devotions.

The protests did not mean, of course, that humanism bred paganism, for there is no sign of paganism in simple demands for reform; but it did breed a questioning attitude concerning the complexities of Catholic Christian doctrine, and it stimulated ideals of greater religious freedom. Perhaps these outcomes were unavoidable. The conditions of study and thought had been revolutionized by a considerable increase in the number of universities, many of which were intended to promote the humanistic modes of thought, by the invention of printing, by the appearance of the lay scholar, and by the rise of studies that had little direct connection with theology or philosophy. The growing antagonism between Scholastics and humanists was at first little more than a matter of competition for university positions, but gradually humanistic thought sought to refashion the mind of the Church in accordance with the naturalistic standards of classical virtue, laying more emphasis on the natural goodness of man than on his fallen nature. The general revulsion from ascetic ideals was strongly aided by the new ventures of travel and geographic discovery and the pursuit of commercial profit. The spirit of human gratification was found in some of the works of the ancient writers, and this spirit found fertile soil for growth in some humanistic centers.

There was also a general laxity within the Catholic Church itself. This, together with the other conditions present in the society of the time, precipitated the revolt. The more sensitive observers of the day could probably see it coming. The signs were clear: The authority of the pope had been weakened; a great part of the clergy had been caught up in a spirit of worldliness; Scholastic philosophy and theology had lost some of their earlier strength, vitality, and meaningfulness; and serious disorders were evident in political life. To many contemporaries the later fifteenth-century popes seemed intent upon three objects—the consolidation of their political power in central Europe, the continuance of their artistic and literary patronage, and the maintenance of the papal Curia and its financial system. These and other interests resulted in the identification of the papacy with one nation, Italy. Thus the nepotism, worldly life, unscrupulous state policy, and scandal-giving appointments furnished just enough fuel to keep the fire of discontent burning, and it warmed agitators to the task of seeking reforms in the Church. At the same time they were pursuing their own selfish ends, which included the secularization of property and the suppression or elimination of ecclesiastical jurisdiction.

On the eve of the Revolt, then, the papacy, though still in principle accepted as the divinely founded spiritual head of Christendom, had ceased to exercise any real leadership in Europe. Italianized in sentiment and policy, it exerted political power in central Italy and was active as a secular state; but in the world at large, where changing conditions of life and thought were bringing serious religious and intellectual problems up for solution, it was ineffectual. Throughout the entire church organization, office had come to suggest profit rather than duty, and the papacy was losing touch with the people and with the churches in the national states. The Catholic Church was not prepared for the revolt that swept over it. In all of the areas of its activity there was perplexity and confusion. A wealth of inflammatory religious material had been for years in the process of laying a foundation for revolt; the fuse for a huge explosion was set; all it needed was the final spark to set it off. This spark was supplied, and the fuse was ignited at Wittenberg.[1]

MARTIN LUTHER (1483–1546)

The leading figure in the rebellion against the Catholic Church was Martin Luther, Luther, the son of a lower-middle-class miner, was born in Eisleben. His schooling began at Mansfield, where, we may assume, he took his primary education before he went to Magdeburg, where he studied under the Brethren of the Common Life. It is said that he went to school in Eisenach also, but we know little or nothing of this experience. In fact, little is known of his life or his schooling on the preuniversity levels, other than the places where he attended school.[2] At eighteen he began his university studies at Erfurt, a university of two thousand students that was then recognized as one of Germany's finest. In the university he pursued the usual studies of liberal arts and philosophy and studied under masters who had good reputations for

---

[1] See Philip Hughes, *A Popular History of the Reformation*, Hanover House, Garden City, New York, 1957.

[2] *Ibid.*, p. 98.

scholarship. By 1505 Luther was ready to take his master's degree in arts, and at almost the same time he undertook the study of law. This scholastic interest was prompted mainly by his father. It was not, however, a lasting interest, for almost immediately he abandoned it and turned to the monastic life. Luther himself tells of the event that brought about the rather abrupt change in his plans that turned his life from law to religion. He was riding back to Erfurt after a visit to his home and while en route was overtaken by a very serious storm. The dangers he met seemed to him so severe that he thought his life was in peril. He called upon St. Anne to help him and made a vow that if his life was spared he would become a monk. This is supposed to have happened early in July of 1505. Luther entered the Augustinian monastery at Erfurt on July 17, 1505.

Luther's progress in the monastic community was rapid, too rapid. He was ordained a priest on April 3, 1507. This was only a year and eight months after he had entered the monastery and barely nine months after his religious profession. After his ordination he undertook formal theological studies, which he completed in about eighteen months. In the fall of 1508 Luther was transferred to Wittenberg, where the Augustinians had a house, and was appointed to lecture on the ethics of Aristotle. At the same time he continued his advanced studies in theology; that is, he was working for a higher degree in theology.[3] Within a year he was returned to Erfurt, where he was called upon to lecture on theology in the house of studies of his own order. It was while Luther was at Erfurt that he was assigned the duty of going to Rome, accompanied by a companion, to present the case for the Erfurt community of Augustinian Hermits, who wanted to stay a reorganization of the order that had the approval of the pope and the superiors of the Augustinians. Luther's journey took him to Rome in 1510. He returned from Rome in 1511 and was again sent to Wittenberg, where he received a variety of assignments and where in 1512 he obtained his degree as a doctor of theology. The next year he became a professor of theology at the University of Wittenberg.

Luther was without doubt a gifted man. There was no sign in 1513 that he would become a religious outcast by 1517. His duties at the university and the demands for his time in his office of subprior of the religious community were such that he was constantly being challenged. His responsibilities sometimes took him outside the monastery into the affairs of the world, where he found it difficult to fulfill all the religious observances that the rule required. This was an experience that disturbed him a great deal, and he began to have doubts about himself and about

[3] This was a practice that was entirely common at the medieval and early modern university; a master of arts often studied for a degree in one of the superior faculties. Luther's pursuit of advanced work in theology had no special significance.

the life that he was leading. Frustrations and tensions led him into extremes of mortification and penance. Yet he chose not to obey the rules of the monastery or to follow the advice of his counselors. He relied rather on his own strength, upon his own penances, and upon faith. Faith alone, he believed, was enough to save him. Later he was to argue that it was enough to save mankind and that the intercession of the church's officers or her sacraments were totally unnecessary. Luther did not, of course, make any such claim when he posted his ninety-five theses on the church door at Wittenberg on October 31, 1517. He thought, no doubt, that he was doing nothing more than attacking the principal ecclesiastical abuses, but, in fact, this was the deed that led to the great Revolt.

But our interest in Luther has to do with education, not with religion. It must be remembered, whenever Luther's educational views are discussed, that he was a religious, not an educational, reformer. His views on education are found, therefore, not in documents that were written for educational purposes, but indirectly in sermons and writings that had primarily religious objectives. His statements on education, nevertheless, had considerable influence on the direction that education took during and after his time. One general consideration ought not be neglected in this context: In the Germany before the Lutheran Revolt the schools were conducted and for the most part owned by the Catholic Church. There was very little in the way of educational opportunity that was not provided by church-related institutions. At the time of the Revolt, these church-owned assets were confiscated, not by the new religion, but by princes, nobles, and state officers. Some of the schools were destroyed, others were converted to other uses. It is obvious, therefore, that the new religion had little in the way of tools with which to work for better or more generous educational opportunities. The bulk of education and the means to offer it lay in ruin in the wake of the Protestant Revolt. This was physical ruin, and schools could be rebuilt; in time the ruins were changed into wonderful school plants, but this reconstruction was hardly the work of religious revolt or reform. It came, rather, from the impact of nationalism on education, an impact that was not felt until the eighteenth century. In addition to the physical destruction that was visited upon the means of education, a kind of spiritual destruction acompanied the new religious message. Faith alone was needed for salvation. The seed of faith may grow as rapidly and flower as generously in the unlearned as in the learned. What man really needs learning? Besides, the clerical profession, one that had been sought after by many because of the attractive opportunities it offered, was dried up. The clergyman of the Protestants could not look forward to many, if any, of the advantages that clergymen enjoyed in the old order. The clerical orientation in education, one that had been strong up to this point in European educational history, was fast disappearing. Formal education was losing many of the motivations that had previously supported it. Luther was faced with imposing educational problems.

One of his first statements on education—it is said to be the first Revolt document on education—was "A Letter to the Mayors and Aldermen of All Cities of Germany in Behalf of Christian Schools." The officials to whom Luther addressed this letter were reminded of their duty to build schools, to replace those that had been destroyed, to assemble libraries, and generally to assume responsibility for education. In the "Letter" Luther expressed a strong conviction of the spiritual benefits to be derived from education, especially in enabling men to understand the scriptures. Education also provided a strong foundation for civil authority. In this document Luther spoke out against the schools of the Catholic Church, especially the monastic schools.

Luther was undeniably concerned with the education of the young. Every sermon or letter of his seems to touch on education. Yet Luther never developed any systematic view or theory of education. Perhaps the most complete as well as the most mature of his deliverances on education was his last, "A Sermon on the Duty of Sending Children to School." This was prepared and delivered in 1530.

In the "Sermon" we have an example of Luther's honest concern not only for the education of children but also for the dignity of the teacher and the respect that should be given him.

Where were your supply of preachers, jurists, and physicians, if the arts of grammar and rhetoric had no existence? These are the foundation, out of which they all flow. I tell you, in a word, that a diligent, devoted schoolteacher, preceptor, or any person, no matter what his title, who faithfully trains and teaches boys, can never receive adequate reward, and no money is sufficient to pay the debt you owe him; so, too, said the pagan, Aristotle. Yet we treat them with contempt, as if they were of no account whatever; and, all the time, we profess to be Christians. For my part, if I were, or were compelled, to leave off preaching and to enter some other vocation, I know not an office that would please me better than that of schoolmaster, or teacher of boys. For, I am convinced, next to preaching this is the most useful, and greatly the best labor in all the world. . . . My friend, nowhere on earth can you find a higher virtue than is displayed by the stranger, who takes your children and gives them a faithful training, a labor which parents very seldom perform, even for their own offspring.[4]

In addition to expressing his sincere respect for education in this tract, Luther took occasion to point to the two principal reasons why education should be supported. In fact, he divided the "Sermon" into

[4] Quoted in Frederick Eby, *Early Protestant Educators,* McGraw-Hill Book Company, Inc., New York, 1931, pp. 144–145.

two parts. The first part dealt with the spiritual benefits to be derived from sending children to school; the second part dealt with the temporal benefits. In the first part, Luther was pleading with parents under his general religious jurisdiction to send their bright boys to schools where they could be prepared for the Christian ministry. At this point Luther emphasized the need for the study of the classical languages and for other ancient languages in order that the study of scripture might be promoted. This emphasis led him to endorse the Latin schools at the expense of the schools that were being conducted in the vernacular. In spite of Luther's hope that the Bible in the vernacular could be put in the hands of all the German people, the vernacular schools did not receive a great deal of support from him. In the second part of the "Sermon" Luther pointed to the good that well-educated boys and young men could do for the state. "A Sermon on the Duty of Sending Children to School" was intended to be chiefly an admonition to parents and others in charge of children to select the most gifted children and educate them in schools for the elite.

The moving force behind Lutheran education was not Luther but Philip Melanchthon.[5] Luther himself looked at education through the eyes of a preacher and with the mind of a religious reformer. Melanchthon, on the other hand, was an educator by profession and was anxious to act as Luther's educational lieutenant. Luther was willing, it appears, to endorse and promote the views and methods of the Protestant humanist, Melanchthon.

Because the Scholastic universities depended on the philosophy of Aristotle, Luther distrusted the content and methods of their studies. He believed that in them the authority of Aristotle superseded the authority of the scriptures. This attitude stemmed in part from the fact that whereas Luther considered Latin and Hebrew to be essential for the furtherance of biblical studies, the old universities emphasized the study of Greek in order that Aristotle might be understood more exactly. This was, to Luther's way of thinking, a perversion of studies, and he attacked at one and the same time the authority of Aristotle and the authority of the Church, which he believed relied too heavily on the philosophy of Aristotle. By the time Luther appeared on the stage of history, Scholasticism had seen its best days. It had been declining in importance for about a century, and Luther did all that he could to hasten its demise.

Luther turned away from Scholasticism to humanism, at least to Melanchthon's kind of humanism. According to this way of thinking, education should provide suitable preparation for the study of the scriptures. Both Luther and Melanchthon supported the theory that the Bible and the catechism—the Lutheran catechism—should have a cen-

[5] See W. Kane, S. J., *An Essay toward a History of Education*, Loyola University Press, Chicago, 1938, p. 229.

tral place in the syllabus of every school. Yet they willingly included rhetoric and dialectic, for this was an age of controversy, in which effective writing and speaking were important, as were history, natural science, vocal and instrumental music mainly for church use, and gymnastics. History was especially emphasized for the sake of studying moral truth and social institutions. The study of nature was intended to give the students some slight insight into the goodness and greatness of God. Gymnastics were considered to be of value both to the body and to the soul as a means of driving away all care and melancholy from the heart.[6]

On the subject of method, Luther seemed to be mildly anticipatory of the educational realism of the seventeenth century. He suggested that the natural activity of the child be utilized in learning; he tended to oppose any methods that would repress child nature. It is not easy to be sure just where Luther stood on some of these points, for, as we have already said, he was not accustomed to deal with educational questions in terms of school practices and techniques. In the same vein we may suggest that he advocated the use of concrete examples in teaching and that he thought that the grammatical approach to the teaching of languages was somewhat unnatural.

In its first years Protestantism contributed little to higher education. For reasons that we have already discussed, the universities in Lutheran Germany were seriously depopulated. It was not until the University of Halle was founded in 1694 that higher education took a new lease on life, but this new lease had little if any relationship to the Protestant Revolt as such.

PHILIP MELANCHTHON (1497–1560)

Melanchthon was born the son of a sword cutler of Bretten. He had a thorough education which began with a private tutor who prepared young Philip for the university. When he was thirteen years of age he entered the University of Heidelberg and within two years had fulfilled the requirements for the bachelor's degree. He obtained the master's degree, spent a few years at Tübingen, and then became a lecturer in

---

[6] F. V. N. Painter, *Luther on Education*, Concordia Publishing House, St. Louis, 1928, pp. 198 ff.; and Frederick Eby, *op. cit.*, pp. 41–43. One example may be enough to show how definite some of Luther's views were on education. We find him saying this: "But, you say again, if we shall and must have schools, what is the use to teach Latin, Greek, Hebrew, and the other liberal arts? Is it not enough to teach the Scriptures, which are necessary to salvation, in the mother tongue? To which I answer: I know, alas! that we Germans must always remain irrational brutes, as we are deservedly called by surrounding nations." (Painter, *op. cit.*, p. 183.)

Greek at the University of Wittenberg. Luther was at Wittenberg at the same time, and the two became intimate friends.

Through his association with Luther Melanchthon became interested in theology and eventually became a dedicated exponent of the evangelical doctrine. Luther and Melanchthon labored together for the reform of the Church. Yet one should not lose sight of the fact that Luther was the religious reformer and Melanchthon the educator. Melanchthon had great ability as a teacher, administrator, and scholar, and did more than any other Protestant to establish schools throughout Lutheran lands and to reorganize the universities in those same lands. All of the schools with which he dealt were marked with his strong humanistic convictions. In his book, *Visitation*, he laid the basis for the reorganization of the schools in Saxony. This basis proved to be a system of Latin schools somewhat similar to the Gymnasium of Sturm at Strassburg.[7]

Melanchthon agreed with Luther that the Aristotelian system should not be made the foundation for higher education. Since Melanchthon's thinking, it appears, was originally principally Aristotelian, the change in his convictions is an indication of Luther's influence. When Aristotle was removed from education, humanistic learning was admitted. Melanchthon himself would have preferred to make education, especially higher education, Greek- rather than Latin-oriented, but he never succeeded in convincing Luther or of bringing about such an innovation. Although Luther was hardly an ardent exponent of humanism, he accepted Melanchthon's views as a kind of compromise, believing that classical learning in a humanistic context could at least be a preparation for scriptural study. Melanchthon grafted humanistic education onto the Protestant system, and in so doing he gained fame as Germany's most prominent educator. He was called *Praeceptor Germaniae*. But more than this, he took an important role in the establishment and reorganization of Protestant education on all levels, and from the elementary schools through the great universities of Germany his influence was felt. The stature of Melanchthon in educational history is indicated in the following quotation:

When Melanchthon died there was probably not a city in Protestant Germany in which some grateful student did not mourn the loss of the Praeceptor Germaniae. And long after his death he controlled, through his method and textbooks, the instruction in the Protestant schools and Universities. It was primarily due to him that the Protestant half of Germany won the ascendency over Catholicism in the realm of education and culture. There can be no doubt whatever about the final outcome: German philosophy and science, German literature and culture grew up in the soil of Protestantism.[8]

[7] See Kane, *op. cit.*, p. 257.

[8] Friedrich Paulsen, *German Universities and University Study*, Charles Scribner's Sons, New York, 1906, p. 33.

JOHN STURM (1507–1589)

Despite the interest that the Lutheran reformers had shown in education, they had not been able to go very far beyond what were then common practices in schooling. Luther's views on education, as we have indicated, were somewhat sketchy and indefinite.[9] Melanchthon and Bugenhagen were important figures in the school picture, it is true, but they operated on the level of organization and administration of schools and seldom touched directly the problems that teachers faced in curriculum and methodology. A contemporary of Luther and Melanchthon and the greatest of the Lutheran schoolmen was John Sturm. It was under his direction that Protestant humanistic education took a novel and specific form, and it was under his supervision that secondary education achieved a definite status and became almost exclusively classical. It was centered on the Latin authors of classical Rome. The other leading Protestants, especially Melanchthon, had recognized the worth of classical learning, but they tried to maintain this learning in a position that was definitely subordinate to the new religious doctrines. In other words, one part of the Protestant movement as it touched education would have turned back the clock to the time in educational history when the liberal arts or the classics were regarded as useful instruments for divine studies. This might well describe the position taken by Luther and Melanchthon. Sturm, however, did not follow this educational doctrine. He placed the classics in a position of supremacy, unchallenged by the catechism. Yet Sturm tried to support the Protestant position by adding the Lutheran catechism to the classical curriculum he had organized.

John Sturm was a scholar and a teacher. He had received the best education that his age could boast. Elementary studies were made available to him in the court school; he spent three years with the famous Brethren of the Common Life; and he concluded his formal education by spending five years at the recently established and humanistically oriented University of Louvain. He spent a short time on the faculty of the University of Paris, and in 1537 he was invited to become rector of the Gymnasium at Strassburg. He accepted the position offered to him by the town fathers and remained at the school for forty-five years.

When Sturm arrived in Strassburg to assume his duties as rector, he found that the town was conducting three Latin schools. Although these schools were operating according to the humanistic plan for such schools laid down by Melanchthon, they were not as effective as the town fathers thought they should be or as efficient in their methods and precise in

[9] See p. 309.

their aims as Sturm wanted them to be. His first step, therefore, was to reorganize the three schools by consolidating them into one school. This was but the initial step in a long-range plan that Sturm had for secondary education. He spelled out his plan in a book entitled *The Best Mode of Opening an Institution of Learning*. This book was not intended to be anything more than a guide for Sturm and for his teachers in opening and conducting the Gymnasium at Strassburg. It was very detailed and touched on every phase of the school's operation. Not only was it detailed, it was also final. Once Sturm decided on the direction that his school would take and the means that should be used in it, he was unwilling to allow any deviation from the plan. Throughout Sturm's long association with the school in Strassburg there were remarkably few changes in its structure. Perhaps the main change from the original plan was the substitution of a nine-year program for the ten-year course that had been originally projected. It was as a nine-year school that the classical Gymnasium became the supreme model for all modern secondary education. In addition to drawing up the formal plan for the conduct . of an institution of learning, Sturm often wrote letters to the teachers in the school, giving them directions and advice.

What was the goal that Sturm held up for his thoroughly classical education? What were the chief means for achieving this goal? The goal for teaching, Sturm held, was threefold: piety, knowledge, and the art of speaking. Piety could hardly be accepted as a clear-cut objective of the school, although it might rightfully be an object of teaching. With this in mind, Sturm assigned to the school the work of achieving knowledge and eloquence. "Knowledge and purity and elegance of diction should become the aim of scholarship, and toward its attainment both teachers and pupils should sedulously bend their every effort."[10]

The aim of Sturm's teaching was knowledge and eloquence. To achieve these objectives would not be easy, nor would the time consumed in their pursuit be short. Assuming the effort, then, what were the means? Sturm was convinced that only through Latin would knowledge and eloquence be achieved. He demanded that the boys in the school learn Latin in their first years and grieved only that Latin was not their mother tongue. The Latin that he liked, the only Latin that he would allow in his school, was pure Ciceronian Latin. This Protestant schoolmaster, more than any other schoolmaster of his time, advocated a return to the classical style. And on this level Sturm established the standard for secondary education for many years to come.

The curriculum which Sturm organized for his school aimed directly at the realization of the supreme goal, oral and written eloquence. He

[10] Henry C. Barnard, *German Teachers and Educators*, Brown and Gross, Hartford, Conn., 1878, p. 195.

refused to allow the vernacular to be taught. As a matter of fact, the only way the vernacular could get into the school was as a vehicle for learning the Lutheran catechism in the elementary years. Greek and Latin language and literature formed the core of the curriculum; the scriptures were read in Greek and Latin; and the teaching of logic involved a knowledge of Latin. No mathematics, geography, history, or science was given attention. The school's curriculum was narrow and the goals precise. The curriculum, although narrow, was carefully organized and graded. Each of the classes had its work, the accomplishments of the lower grade leading to the next higher grade. In other words, the grades were tightly integrated. Students were promoted from one grade to another when their achievement warranted such promotion, although the actual movement from one grade to another was made only once a year. In the grade, excellence in achievement was recognized by premiums of various kinds. Two premiums for scholarship were awarded to each class.

The success that Sturm's school achieved was almost unbelievable, and with success came fame and imitation. All over Europe and in America, too, the kind of secondary education that Sturm organized took a firm hold. In England and in America Sturm's formula for secondary education was applied to the Latin Grammar Schools.

OTHER DEVELOPMENTS IN PROTESTANT EDUCATION

Standing behind Luther, Melanchthon, and Sturm as educational reformers in the Protestant tradition were such men as John Bugenhagen (1485–1558), John Brenz (1499–1570), Valentin Trotzendorf (1490–1556), Ulrich Zwingli (1484–1534), and John Calvin (1509–1564). In general they accepted the basic religious doctrines of the Revolt and at the same time saw the need for revising or reorganizing the existing system of education in order that it might serve the ends of religious reform more explicitly. Bugenhagen, for example, achieved considerable repute as an organizer of schools in northern Germany. In addition to the Latin schools which formed a part of the system that he created, he became interested in the schools in German for certain children of the lower and middle classes. Despite the general indifference of Luther and Melanchthon to vernacular schools, Bugenhagen forged ahead with his plans for them and to some extent succeeded. At least, the vernacular school became somewhat better known as a result of his work. Brenz and Trotzendorf were minor figures, who organized schools in various parts of Germany and tried to introduce more practical teaching methods in them.

Neither Zwingli nor Calvin made a great impression on the education of his own or later times. Zwingli was a religious reformer who approached his task with all the zeal of a Luther but with a far more practical attitude. He made haste slowly and in the end had severed all connections with the Catholic Church. Zwingli's interest in education was more practical than Luther's. He turned almost at once to the improvement of schools, and instead of talking about the need for better schools that might provide a steady supply of ministers for the churches, he saw to it that these schools were established. Moreover, he saw to it that they were closely supervised and that they held to their original aim. Their purpose was, of course, to teach a greater knowledge of God, for the schools were really professional divinity schools. The curriculum of these schools, in addition to the religious studies, which were central, was largely humanistic. Most of Zwingli's views and attitudes on education may be found in his *Christian Education of Youth*, which appeared in 1523.

This work of Zwingli's adds very little to the body of knowledge about education; even in his own time it was not thought of as a forward-looking document. Perhaps it did not have to be. In any event the educational career of Zwingli was interrupted by an untimely death, and his work was carried on by John Calvin. Calvin did not alter the educational plan that had been proposed by his predecessor. Schools and colleges were established on the basis of Protestant religious doctrines and humanistic educational theories. Though Calvin is remembered as a great religious organizer rather than as an educator, he did have a short career as a teacher when he taught for Sturm in Strassburg. His greatest impact on the world of the mind was made by his *Institutes of the Christian Religion*. It was in this work that the Calvinistic doctrine of predestination was clearly set forth.

Apart from the men who were involved in the Protestant educational movement, what can be said of the movement itself? What were the outcomes of this movement? It may be said, first of all, that the municipal schools that had been in existence from the first years of the medieval period were subjected to some reorganization. These schools had been careful imitators of the church schools.[11] Now, however, they tended to strike out in a new direction. They became to a great extent vernacular schools and occasionally admitted girls to their student body. It made little difference that most of the leaders of the Protestant movement would not have thought highly of these new departures. Protestantism breathed a new independence into the souls of the municipal schools. At the same time, this independence led to greater favor from the town, so that eventually such schools could look to the town treasury for their support. In a very real sense many of these municipal schools

[11] See pp. 240–243.

became free schools; it should be remembered, however, that they did not open their doors to all the children of the town, but only to the off-spring of the so-called better classes. In the light of this exclusiveness, it is hard to see such schools as the precursors of free public education.

In England the Revolt, led by Henry VIII, took its toll of schools and colleges. Both in Britain and Ireland the monasteries had had exceptionally close ties with education and for many years had offered the greatest opportunity for schooling. England's break with the Roman Catholic Church led to the abolishment of these monastic institutions and to a confiscation of their property. In addition, the chantries, which had been so popular in England for many years, were closed; their bequests were claimed by the crown; and the chantry schools that were conducted in connection with them were cast into oblivion.[12] Nobles had for some years conducted schools at their palaces, and bishops and other ecclesiastical dignitaries had secured schoolmasters to teach selected students. The court school or the palace school, which dated at least from the time of Charles the Great,[13] was swept away by the tide of Henry's religious revolt. It is easy to see why Henry should not have allowed the ecclesiastical schools to continue to operate, but it is almost impossible to understand why the schools connected with the courts should have disappeared too. Perhaps Henry was attempting to make a clean break with the past, although the essentials of Henry's proposed reforms in religion did not argue for a clean break. At any rate, the instructions that were given in religion following the English Revolt were quite generally given in English, and the tools of such instruction were catechisms and primers that were written in English. This move had some indirect consequences for education, in that it assumed that the vernacular should be given a principal position as a language of instruction. Though this is by no means an innovation, it is, however, a significant emphasis.

The funds that were confiscated from schools and religious houses and the property that was taken over by the crown were used in any way the king wanted to use them. When the spirit moved him he endowed some schools and colleges. Latin schools and the especially favored colleges of Oxford and Cambridge received most of these endowments. How large the endowments were is not as important as the fact that the action taken by the monarch in supporting schools and colleges established a precedent for further state or royal patronage of education. And in the context of these times in Henry's England, the schools and colleges lost some of their independence every time they accepted a favor or grant from the king. On the level of higher education, Scholasticism was ushered out and humanism was given free entrance. Grammar and

---

[12] For the place of the chantry school in medieval education, see pp. 244–245.
[13] See pp. 220–223.

literature, good humanistic subjects, took the place of dialectics as the most prominent study in the curriculum. On the lower levels, where there was little disposition to leave such matters as the determination of school policy and the selection of schoolbooks to the teachers of the local schools, the state began to assume an important role in shaping educational policy. In time, especially under Elizabeth, not even the universities were exempt from state surveillance; the crown exercised strict supervision over all of the schools and licensed or accredited the teachers who taught in them. It was during this period, too, that the great English public schools came into existence. These were the schools that achieved such enviable reputations for preparing young Englishmen for public life.[14] Despite the excellence that these and other English schools attained in later years, the period of Revolt was a time when both in quality and in quantity education in England deteriorated. Many of the schools and colleges were forced to close; educational opportunities for everyone, but especially for women, declined sharply; and Catholics were obliged to send their children abroad if they wanted to be sure that they would not be schooled with danger to their faith.

CATHOLIC REFORMS AND EDUCATION

The Church attempted in a number of ways to bring about the reforms that were recognized now as necessary. Most of these, of course, had to do with the religious side of revolt and reformation, but from a strictly educational point of view, two reforms had special significance. One was the legislation of the Council of Trent, the other was the creation of the Society of Jesus. Not only did the Council of Trent deal with matters of doctrine which were of a superior order, it dealt also with the matter of discipline and order in church-related education. Most especially this point of reform touched on the education of the clergy. Discipline for the education of the clergy was reestablished. It was decreed that every diocese should have its own seminary for the preparation of priests. Codes were established regarding the qualifications of teachers in these seminaries. Thus, all over the world the education of priests and the standards required of prospective clergymen became more or less uniform. The Council also admonished bishops and pastors to give greater encouragement and support to the parish schools. In a word, the Council of Trent gave its complete endorsement of the revival and revitalization of Catholic education. It supported the idea that free schools should be opened for the poor and that colleges should be made more accessible,

[14] Nine "great public schools" were recognized by the Clarendon Commission of 1864. They were Winchester, Eton, St. Paul's, Shrewsbury, Westminster, Rugby, Harrow, Merchant Taylors', and Charterhouse.

and it rejected the notion that the Catholic Church had anything to fear from education or learning.

The Society of Jesus

The Council of Trent was a specific Catholic reaction to the Protestant Revolt. A renewal of interest in education and the management of schools was a reaction shared by many of the existing religious orders; and two new religious groups, the Jesuits and the Ursulines, appeared on the scene to promote Catholic causes generally and to advance the fortunes of Catholic education. These two new groups, it should be emphasized, were only two among many that labored in the field of Catholic education, but by their work they achieved a reputation that was the envy of the educational world.

The Ursulines, the first teaching order of women established in the Church, were founded by St. Angela Merici in 1535. Long before she entered the religious life, St. Angela displayed a vital interest in education. She conducted a school for girls in her home when she was only twenty-two years old. When she was sixty-two, St. Angela, with the help of twelve companions, founded the Ursulines. This community of religious women was followed by many other orders and communities that have done important educational work down through the years.

Religious associations of men were generated in this age also, and they, too, turned their energies to the work of educational and religious reform. Among these religious communities, then only recently formed, were the Oratory of Divine Love, the Theatines, the Capuchins, and the Jesuits.

Throughout the history of education, probably no group of teachers has gained greater fame than the Jesuits. The Sophists may be more widely known, but we cannot claim for the Sophists either the uniformity of educational practice or the devotion to purpose that was distinctive of the Jesuits. The Society of Jesus, moreover, was carefully and closely organized; this, of course, could not be said of the Sophists.[15] Many other religious orders within the Catholic Church performed outstanding services for the development of Catholic education, and lay groups of Catholics and individual masters were often exceptionally successful in conducting schools of high quality in an environment of traditional Catholicism. Yet for all the excellence that may be claimed, for example, for the Brethren of the Common Life, the Jesuits occupy a unique position. No one should assume that they have not had their detractors over the centuries—both within and without the Church—but even their enemies have found it difficult to ignore the successes of the Society of Jesus during the three centuries following the Revolt. It was in the six-

[15] See pp. 68–77.

teenth, seventeenth, and eighteenth centuries that the educational reputation of the Jesuits was established.

Before entering upon a detailed discussion of their work, particularly
of their method of study, a word should be said in general about the
reasons for their phenomenal success. Why could their work extract almost universal acclaim from Europe? Why did they succeed so marvel-
ously where others had failed so miserably? The first reason is that the
Jesuits had a dedicated group of teachers. They had been carefully educated over many years; they were trained to teach with the same careful
attention that had been directed at forming their minds; and they were
motivated by the zeal which their society generated. This does not
indict the character, devotion, mind, or skill of the other teachers of
these or preceding centuries. It would be both unhistorical and unflatter-
ing to maintain that the Jesuits were so good and so successful because
other teachers were so bad. The second reason for the success of the
Jesuits was that they developed a uniform plan for education. We shall
have something more to say later about the *Ratio Studiorum*, the plan to
which all Jesuit schools conformed. The plan included certain educa
tional practices that today are taken for granted, for example, the grading
of students and an organization of the curriculum to fit their ages and
maturity. No Jesuit school neglected these steps. Finally, the Jesuits engaged in gratuitous teaching. The Jesuit institutions of Europe were
founded with endowments of sufficient size and scope to enable them to
conduct schools and charge nothing at all for the instruction that was
given. Fees could have been charged, and sometimes were charged, for
food and lodging, but no charges were made for the actual costs incurred
by teaching.[16]

St. Ignatius of Loyola (1491–1556), a Spanish nobleman and soldier,
was the founder of the Society of Jesus. Ignatius' military career was
interrupted in 1521 when he was wounded at the siege of Pampelona.
While he was recuperating from his wounds his mind turned to religion,
and he decided after much mature thought to become a soldier in the
army of Christ. His original intention seems to have been to become a
missionary in order to combat the influence of the Mohammedans. When
he had recovered his strength, he went to Jerusalem with a small band
of followers—the Society was not yet formed—where he hoped to convert the Mohammedans or at least to blunt their effectiveness. Within

[16] The student may be interested to know that this feature of gratuitous teaching in
the Jesuit system is based in the Constitutions of the Society and that the Constitution and this part of it are still in force. Under certain circumstances Jesuit schools
may be permitted to accept tuition. (See Edward J. Power, *A History of Catholic
Higher Education in the United States,* The Bruce Publishing Company, Milwaukee,
1958, pp. 161–165.)

a relatively short period of time he realized that neither he nor his followers had the missionary skill or the fundamental religious education
to accomplish their purpose. Ignatius returned to Europe and began
to prepare himself for the work to which he was now dedicated. Among
other schools, he studied at the University of Paris. This period devoted
to study must have lasted about six years, for in 1534 Ignatius and a few
loyal followers formed a society. This was not yet the Society of Jesus,
but it was the germ of what was to come. In 1540 the Society of Jesus
was duly organized and recognized by Pope Paul III. At that time the
membership of the newly formed society was limited to sixty, but this
was a restriction that was removed within three years.

The objectives of the Society of Jesus were all based on the central
idea of strengthening and spreading the Church of Christ. The Jesuits
became the pope's special task force, and they vowed to go anywhere
and do anything to protect the life of the Church. Yet in actual practice
their principal work embraced or came to embrace three things: preaching, confession, and education.

Jesuit Schools. The Jesuit position on education and their organization
of a system of pedagogy are subjects of extreme interest which reward
investigation.

1. Generally speaking, the Jesuits were not interested in and did not
engage in elementary education. Whether this was due to the circumstances of the time, to the increasing popularity of secondary education
as a result of Sturm's influence on it, or to a natural desire on the part
of the Jesuits to use their talents on educational levels where they could
be expected to do the most good is not entirely clear. The Jesuit tradition would lead one to believe that the last interpretation is the most
valid. At any rate, the Jesuits opened elementary schools only when they
found such a procedure unavoidable, and they relinquished the schools
for children at the earliest opportunity. Jesuit teachers were hardly ever
found in elementary classrooms. Yet when they were in missionary
countries, for example, during the colonial years of North America, they
never hesitated to do what needed to be done.

2. The Jesuit system of education was highly organized and intimately
related to the fundamental foundations of a religious society. No thought
was given to any plan for teaching that did not assume that Jesuits
would be the teachers. In other words, laymen did not figure promi-
nently, or at all, in the Jesuit system of education. This emphasis on the
society's teaching function was entirely natural and was in no way restricted
to the Society of Jesus. Other religious orders made no provisions for
lay teachers in their schools either, but simply followed the medieval
practices that were based on the concept of a clerical monopoly in education. The principal roles in teaching, among the Jesuits and other

orders or congregations, were assigned to clerical teachers. Surely one of the reasons why the Jesuits were as successful as they were was that they had a devoted body of teachers; the dedication that the Society demanded could hardly ever be found outside the ranks of the Jesuits.

3. The schools of the Jesuits were humanistic schools. They took the content of Christian humanism, organized it carefully, and presented it according to the best teaching techniques they could devise or discover. Consistent with the humanism of Europe, this meant an emphasis on Latin. So far as the place of Latin in the school was concerned, there would be little to chose between Sturm's Gymnasium and the schools of the Jesuits. In the teaching of Latin grammar and Latin literature, the Jesuits sought to achieve, as Sturm had, knowledge and eloquence. In their teaching methods they used a practice revived from Hellenistic pedagogy, the practice of prelection.[17] Although prelection in the hands of Jesuit teachers became an important technique and, in the evaluations made of Jesuit pedagogy, their most significant contribution to method, it is easy to overestimate its importance. The great fame that attaches to Jesuit education could hardly be attributed to prelection, a technique in teaching that was in regular use at least sixteen or seventeen centuries before the Jesuits appeared on the stage of history. Not prelection alone, but prelection carefully organized and integrated with other techniques, such as the technique of repetition and the wise use of prizes, rewards, and premiums, brought the Jesuits their great fame as schoolmasters.

4. The early years of modern education under other schoolmasters were harsh years from the point of view of discipline. The earlier lament of St. Augustine could be applied again. (He had said that if he were given the choice between death and returning to the primary school, he would choose the former.) The educated opinion of the day chose to accept the view that a schoolmaster who taught without severity was simply worthless. Into an educational world that honored this attitude almost without question, the Jesuits introduced their code of mild discipline. They tried to avoid chastising the students put under their care, and if a boy could not be led they refused to drive him. Young men who did not fit into the practices of the Jesuit schools were released. They were not beaten and forced to conform in either an intellectual or a physical sense.

5. After the time of Comenius[18] the educational world was to hear a great deal about the advantages that could be gained for learning if classes were very large. Yet from the beginning and throughout most of their history, the Jesuits kept their classes small. They were also rather selective, for they believed that their efforts were better spent in teach-

[17] See pp. 120–121.
[18] See pp. 336–346.

ing bright boys than in teaching the average or the slow. With the policy of gratuitous teaching, economic obstacles hardly ever stood in the way of the education of a talented youth in a Jesuit secondary school or college.

The Ratio Studiorum. The heart of Jesuit pedagogy is to be found in the *Ratio Studiorum.* This is the instrument that guided Jesuit schools and Jesuit teaching and brought fame to both.

On December 8, 1584, a board of six Jesuits was convened by the Jesuit General and commissioned to examine the record of Jesuit schools and to make recommendations concerning the future course and philosophy of Jesuit education. This board continued to meet for about two years, examining all the evidence that it could gather from the forty-odd years of Jesuit educational history. In the summer of 1586 this board was ready with its report and recommendations. They constituted the first draft of the *Ratio Studiorum.* This first draft was offered as nothing more than a point of departure; it was sent to all the Jesuit provincials with instructions that it be examined and discussed. As a result of the discussions in the provinces, certain recommendations for revisions of the draft or criticisms of it were to be made within a six-month period. These were to be sent to Rome, to the Jesuit General, where they would be examined and where some of them would be incorporated in a new document: This document, the second draft of the *Ratio,* appeared with the force of law late in 1586.[19]

The 1586 edition of the *Ratio* dealt with the following general topics: the organization of the curriculum and a separation of the humanities from philosophy and theology; the selection of teachers for the courses in the humanities; the establishment of standards for the selection of grammar texts; the consideration of the place of Greek in the curriculum; the invention of exercises and methods for stimulating study, and for studying Latin and Greek; and finally the determination of policies with regard to promotions, vacations, discipline, and the inculcation of piety.[20] Though the *Ratio* was to be followed by Jesuit teachers and had an unquestioned official status in Jesuit schools, the document was not regarded as definitive. In other words, it was to be a growing, evolving document that would change as time and new ideas required. Yet it was not to be so flexible that Jesuit schools in different countries could con-

---

[19] The basic idea for such an order of studies was probably the earlier work of James Ledesma, a Jesuit. In his *De Ratione et Ordine Studiorum Collegii Romani,* Ledesma attempted to draw together the Jesuit classroom practices, appraise them, and advance beyond them in constructing a *ratio* that would be complete in detail and universally applicable. (For an exhaustive examination of the background of the *Ratio Studiorum* of the Jesuits, see Allan P. Farrell, S. J., *The Jesuit Code of Liberal Education,* The Bruce Publishing Company, Milwaukee, 1938.)

[20] *Ibid.,* pp. 228 ff.

duct substantially different educational programs or even follow a course that was locally attractive, and still claim to be within its boundaries. The *Ratio* changed a great deal over the years, and the changes, for the most part, came from the schools or were inspired by them. It was a successful educational instrument because it was realistic; it was a philosophy and practice for education that came from the hands of teachers. And, though it had undoubtedly a long-range flexibility, the *Ratio* had also what might be called a short-term rigidity. The total nature of the *Ratio* was demonstrated to some extent in an appeal that came from the German Jesuit schools to permit the addition of a course in German history to the curriculum. The appeal was not regarded with favor. In refusing to permit the addition of a course that seemed to be good for certain schools in certain areas, the Jesuit authorities were simply applying a basic principle in their theory of education. A well-known Jesuit scholar has put it this way: " . . . for the principle animating the Jesuit system was not so much the communication of information from many fields of knowledge as the formation of intellectual habits and literary expression."[21]

A new edition of the *Ratio* appeared in 1591. In it were incorporated the lessons that had been learned from the use of earlier editions. Although the 1591 edition was binding on Jesuit schools, it was not intended to be the final document codifying Jesuit pedagogy. It was expected and planned that another and possibly a definitive edition would follow the one which appeared in 1591. In 1599 the third edition of the *Ratio Studiorum* was ready.

The third edition was the product of approximately a half century's work. The first thirty or more years were spent in gathering, testing, adapting, and experimenting. The reports from the schools, the impressions gleaned from visiting schools, and the actual teaching experiences in the classroom played a large role in giving final form to the *Ratio*. But there were other important influences too: Nadal's 1551 plan for Messina, Ignatius' fourth part of the *Constitutions*, the *Ordo Studiorum* of Nadal, and *De Ratione* of Ledesma. These were works that stood out especially as the Jesuit educational tradition was being shaped. The final ten or fifteen years of this half century of preparation were spent in sorting, revising, and codifying everything that had been gathered or learned during the earlier period.

Though we cannot make an extensive analysis of the Jesuit *Ratio Studiorum* here, we think it important to give a brief summary of its essential points. The section in the document of 1599 that dealt with the administration of schools was clearer than that in the earlier editions. It defined the offices in education and set the limits of responsibility

[21] *Ibid.*, p. 249.

for school officers. In methodology, the most elaborately developed section in this edition, a twofold aim was achieved: helping the new teacher adjust to the system and perpetuating educational policies and practices that guaranteed universally high quality in the schools. The section on curriculum concerned itself with the relative importance of the humanities, philosophy, and theology in the order of studies. The basis of all studies was formed out of the classical languages and literature. This, of course, was in line with what was then accepted as a theory of cultural transmission. Mathematics and science were given a subordinate position as mere adjuncts to philosophy, and the vernacular, though its use was not forbidden, was given only slight attention. Both Latin and Greek were taught, though Greek had a position in the curriculum inferior to that of Latin. Its relative unimportance followed the orthodox humanistic tradition. Spiritual growth among the students was given high priority on the Jesuit scale of educational values, yet very few classes in religion found their way into the curriculum.

The section on discipline was remarkable for its moderation, considering the standards of discipline common to that day. The Jesuits looked not to corporal punishment or to fear for good order. Good example, the hope for honor, and the fear of blame were the motives that dominated the policies on discipline.

Remarkable unity was established through a definite declaration of aims, the centering of all studies around the classics, the use of uniform texts and techniques in the classroom, uniform entrance and promotion requirements, and the consistent insistence on attainment of eloquence in both oral and written work, regardless of the matter studied. Purpose and organization stand out in the Jesuit system. According to Allan Farrell, "In the last analysis, that which made the Jesuits the schoolmasters of Europe for nearly two centuries was organization."[22]

The Jesuit system of education was interrupted when the Society was suppressed by Pope Clement in 1773. At that time the Society had 865 schools. After forty-one years, in 1814, the Society of Jesus was restored. In 1820 a general congregation of the Order requested a modernization of the *Ratio* and suggested that such a modernization follow the same pattern that had been followed when the *Ratio* was born. A committee was appointed to begin the work in 1830; by 1832 it had completed its task of adapting and revising the *Ratio* of 1599. The new edition ushered in few changes, the only noticeable alterations being in curriculum. In the nineteenth century it was not so possible to reach agreement on curricular questions as it had been in the sixteenth century. Yet the changes in curriculum, or the liberalization of Jesuit policies toward it, did destroy the essential unity which the older orders

[22] *Ibid.*, p. 191.

of study had possessed. The new edition was directive rather than mandatory; at least, this was the official position until 1853, when another attempt was made to revise the *Ratio*. Neither this attempt nor the one made in 1906 was successful. The status of the *Ratio* was explained as follows by a Jesuit historian: "Only by a decree of a General Congregation of the Order is this sanction possible. Such a decree, however, was not passed; consequently, the revised *Ratio* has not the force of law in the Society, but is merely to be considered as a regulation of the General. So much liberty is left to Provincials that the teaching in Jesuit colleges can be adapted to the educational needs of all countries."[23]

When it seemed impossible to draw up a new *Ratio* that would be binding on all Jesuit schools everywhere in the world, a kind of compromise was effected. Each province was to draw up its own course of study, based, as far as possible, on the previous editions of the *Ratio* and the educational traditions of the Society, and submit it for approval. This compromise has lasted to contemporary times, and while it allows the Jesuits to continue many of their fine pedagogical practices in schools of the modern age, they operate their schools without the unity that they once enjoyed from the guidance and direction of the *Ratio Studiorum*.

SUMMARY

The Protestant Revolt and the Catholic Reformation had important consequences for education. Neither was an educational movement in any narrow sense, yet both were movements that looked to education for the fulfillment of their ideals.

Protestantism, as evidenced by heresy and schism, had been brewed in Europe before the time of Luther, although Luther was the religious leader who gave it its most definite and lasting form. The new religious doctrine that Luther preached needed the support of education, and many of Luther's sermons and letters attest his interest in the schools. In spite of Luther's interest in the education of the people, his program never provided the breadth of educational opportunity that was available in the years that just preceded the Lutheran movement. Often the education of the common man was badly neglected, and schools with a program in the vernacular were never really supported.

Protestant leaders in education—and followers of Luther—were Philip Melanchthon and John Sturm. To Melanchthon goes the credit for being an organizer and administrator of schools in many Protestant lands. These schools, however, were always Latin schools for students of the

[23] Robert Schwickerath, S.J., *Jesuit Education: Its History and Principles,* B. Herder Book Company, St. Louis, 1904, p. 198.

elite. Sturm was a schoolmaster, the greatest of Protestant schoolmasters and quite possibly the greatest schoolmaster the modern age produced. He organized and conducted the Gymnasium at Strassburg, which formed the model and provided the tone for all modern secondary education.

Catholic reforms which touched on education were led by religious orders and congregations, both for men and women, and by the great Council of Trent. The Council breathed new life into Catholic action and discipline. All the religious orders showed a renewed interest in education and tried to reorganize and reestablish it on a sounder basis. To the Society of Jesus, however, goes the chief credit for leading a Catholic educational renaissance. The Jesuits became the best known schoolmasters of Europe. They developed the famous *Ratio Studiorum,* a guide to their aims and practices, and were more successful than other groups of teachers because they organized their educational program and devised their educational method with greater care. In addition, the Jesuit schools could count on a dedicated group of teachers, a uniform method of instruction in the hands of carefully trained Jesuit school-masters, and the best students of the land, for Jesuit schools were free schools, and economic obstacles never stood in the way of talent that needed to be developed in them.

Questions and Exercises for Study and Discussion

1. What were Martin Luther's principal views on education?
2. What influence did Luther's views on education have on Protestant educators who followed him?
3. It has been claimed that the beginnings of national systems of education in which popular education was given a sympathetic hearing grew out of the Luther-led Protestant Revolt. Evaluate this claim.
4. Report on the life and works of Philip Melanchthon.
5. Describe Sturm's secondary school. How did it differ from the classical schools of Rome? In what sense was it a Christian school?
6. Show in what principal ways Sturm's educational plan affected all later secondary education.
7. Jesuit education, it has been argued, is simply the educational plan of Sturm with a Catholic bias. Compare the two systems—the Jesuits' and Sturm's—and, if possible, refute this statement.
8. Prepare a brief report on the educational practices and accomplishments of the Ursulines.
9. Explain the nature of the Catholic educational reforms of the sixteenth century.
10. Why were the Jesuits so successful as secondary school teachers? Isolate those features in their system that contributed especially to their success.

11

Realism in Education in the Seventeenth Century

REALISM

The first schools that men founded were intended to do what could no longer be done easily without them. In its original form the school was a kind of extension of the home, and the basic opportunity that it offered was practical, as the opportunities for training in the home had been practical. We have seen something of the evolution of schools and their purpose and the means used to attain the ever-changing aims of formal education. We have observed that the schools became less and less utility-minded and that they gradually turned their attention almost exclusively to literary objectives. We have seen, moreover, how these literary objectives were fashioned and refashioned and how they became less and less relevant for the man who wanted a preparation that would fit him for life in society. We have noted the increasing separation of learning from life, a tendency whose origin we first detected in the schools of the Hellenistic world.[1] Medieval schools were realistic and eminently practical in relating their programs to their religious orientation and ultimate concerns, but it was this orientation and these concerns that the modern world was often to find unacceptable. Humanistic schools and humanistic educational theorists revived classical goals of learning, which in their own day had had great utility. But in the long run these schools did not close the gap between life and learning, and the theories that the humanists proposed did not do so either, because classical schools and classical theories simply tended to widen the gap. Neither the Revolt nor the Reform tried to bring about basic alterations

[1] See pp. 112–114.

in educational theory or policy. The reforms in the Catholic world were not without real educational significance, but it can hardly be argued that these reforms changed the direction that Catholic education had been taking for some centuries. By the time we reach the seventeenth century, we find that the world is ready for a number of innovations; the seventeenth century is the threshold of the modern world. The general movement in this century of great significance was realism. Realism permeated the century and changed men's outlook upon life in many ways. Its effect upon education was deep and far-reaching.

Realism wanted to return the schools to their original utilitarian character. Essentially, then, the movement was conservative. According to this view, the school was to have a curriculum based on real knowledge— knowledge that could be tested by the methods that the seventeenth-century scientists were then devising or authenticated by observation or experience—and a methodology arrived at as a result of the scientific study of the nature of learning. Beyond this, the school's purpose was to prepare men and women to step into the world, the world that could be sensed and seen, and to enable them, as a result of this preparation, to make the world a better place to live in. Realism, then, was both an educational and a social reform.

Realism took different forms, or, to put it in another way, emphasized different aspects of life. There was social realism, which put the emphasis upon social reform as well as upon the real knowledge of society that might be obtained from the newly-formed social sciences. There was also humanistic realism, in which the emphasis was upon the real knowledge that might be found in the humanities, although its proponents probably did not claim that the humanities could be a substitute for the facts that were then being revealed by experimental techniques. There was, finally, sense realism. In its extreme form sense realism did not recognize the validity of any reality that could not be tested by an empirical method.

The seventeenth century started with realism; it ended with empiricism. The outstanding educational exponent of the former was John Amos Comenius; the name that belongs to the latter is that of John Locke.

Before we turn to the work of Comenius, which, from an educational point of view, was the most significant in realism proper, a word should be said about some other contributors to the realistic movement: Francis Bacon, René Descartes, and Wolfgang Ratke.

Francis Bacon (1561–1626)

It is hard to say where the scientific movement really began. Perhaps we might assign its origin to Sir Isaac Newton (1642–1727) and his *Principia,* which appeared in 1687. Yet it should be understood that the scientific movement was really an outgrowth of realism. Realism ante-dated the scientific movement. In that movement Francis Bacon was, if not the "father of realism," at least an important figure. We should recognize at the outset, however, that Bacon was not an educator. He was neither a teacher nor an educational theorist, and in methodology he was content to endorse the work of the Jesuits. Bacon belongs to that class of practical scientists who were determined to use the secrets of nature to the advantage of mankind. There are two things for which Bacon ought to be remembered in the history of education: (1) the emphasis that he gave to inductive methods as means for achieving verifiable knowledge, and (2) his determination that knowledge should be used. We should not forget that it was Bacon who interpreted and popularized the idea that knowledge is power. "Human knowledge and human power meet in one."[2] Apart from these emphases, we cannot attach too much significance to Bacon's name. He was not really a scientist; at least, he left no important scientific work. He was not a philosopher. He was not an educator. Yet, despite what may be regarded as weaknesses in the Baconian image, Bacon influenced the realistic movement and helped to bring in the modern age. His works that are most often referred to by educational historians are *Novum Organum* and *New Atlantis*. The first was intended to replace the *Organon* of Aristotle. In it, as we have said, Bacon promoted the inductive method, a method that has since unquestionably become the method of science. *New Atlantis* was a utopian plan, in which Bacon pointed to the social values that could be served by the proper employment of knowledge. In *New Atlantis* Bacon tried to give a word picture of the power that can come from knowledge, especially of the great good that can be done in society if men cooperate in seeking and using knowledge.

René Descartes (1596–1650)

Descartes was not an educational theorist or a teacher, nor was he especially interested in distinctively educational questions. His philosophy, however, as well as the emphasis that he gave to reason and the scientific method did create a new frame of reference in which man and his educational problems could be viewed. Descartes belongs indirectly to the family of historical figures who shaped educational thought and practice.

The goal for which Descartes searched was certainty, and in this context his thought affected education. He was impressed with the certainty that could be achieved in mathematics, and he was no less impressed with the power of the human minds. As a result, he turned

[2] M. T. McClure, *Bacon Selections,* Charles Scribner's Sons, New York, 1928, p. 280.

his attention to mathematics and was able to make notable achievements in this field of knowledge. In geometry, especially, he made lasting contributions to man's knowledge and technique. Using the method that brought results in mathematics and accepting the power and force of reason, Descartes applied his method to other fields of thought and to the nonmathematical problems of mankind. The impelling motive behind Descartes's work was his desire to lay a solid and certain foundation for human knowledge. This, of course, opened a broad and complicated philosophical problem. The outcome of Descartes's thinking, so far as education is concerned, was rationalism. Apparently Descartes concluded that ideas are innate, and that the development of knowledge depends only on the drawing out of these innate ideas. This was an abrupt about-face for the seventeenth century. The principal intellectual movement of the century, the one that really counted, was realism; and realism, for the most part, depended upon the inductive method, which was then as it is now the distinctive method of science. But Descartes all but tossed induction out the window; deduction, for him, became the supreme method. It had to be, for once the basic position of Descartes was accepted, no other method could have validity. And this method was given a place in learning that it had never occupied before. Here was the beginning of rationalism, a narrow and unreal movement that has affected so much of education and thought since the time of Descartes. Besides laying some foundations for rationalism, the work of Descartes made room for scepticism and for psychophysical parallelism. These three positions have affected education down through the years; they may even be seen in a number of contemporary issues that command the attention of educational philosophers.

Wolfgang Ratke (also Ratich) (1571–1635)

It would be a very liberal interpretation of the meaning of the term "science" that would permit its use in connection with the work of Ratke. But to some extent Ratke's work does represent a development in the same direction that the exact sciences were taking. He advocated the use of the vernacular in formal education, a recommendation that was by no means original with him. He gave attention to what he called the natural method of learning. Following the natural rules of learning, some of which were faintly implied in his work, students might be expected to be able to learn twice as much in half the time. This, of course, opened the door to pansophic emphases in education that were added by Comenius and others, but in the work of Ratke the motivating force was not encyclopedic knowledge—something that he approved—but natural learning. To develop this natural method of learning was the motivating purpose behind all of Ratke's endeavors. Thus he began, somewhat awkwardly, it is true, the development of an educational method which in its more polished phases is associated with the names of Comenius, Locke, Rousseau, Pestalozzi, Froebel, and Herbart.

Ratke was one of the most unusual men ever to concern himself with education. Apart from all else, the thing that stands out about the man and his work is that he hoped to keep his methodology secret. Almost from the beginning, his work had something mysterious about it. The contradiction in his methods (for how could educational reforms really be brought about if the reformer refused to put his means for reform in the public domain?) revealed a basic and perhaps an indelible contradiction in the man. Born at Wilster in Holstein, Ratke attended the Hamburg Gymnasium and afterward studied philosophy at Rostock, a university of some repute. He pursued a theological course, for he had long aspired to the Lutheran ministry, but a speech impediment forced him to turn to some other type of social work. Perhaps his interest in education was developed quite naturally, or possibly it was a kind of second choice. At any rate, Ratke undoubtedly possessed admirable tools for the trade of a teacher, and was especially well schooled in languages. He was a linguist who spoke and wrote with considerable facility in Hebrew, Arabic, Latin, Greek, and German.

Ratke made his first appearance on the educational scene when he proposed to Prince Moritz of Orange a new method of teaching, a method which he claimed to have invented. In general terms—and this is the only way in which Ratke ever discussed his novel method—his proposition to the prince claimed that (1) the languages—Hebrew, Greek, Latin, and others—could be taught to young and old more effectively and in a shorter time than ever before; (2) a school could be established in which all the arts and sciences could be taught more effectively than ever before; (3) a single language could be adopted in the principality, a measure which would facilitate the administration of civil affairs; and (4) a single religion could be accepted, a simple procedure which would promote domestic and spiritual peace and tranquility.

The prince was apparently not convinced that Ratke could perform up to the level of his promises, and he showed little or no interest in the universal method of instruction that Ratke claimed to have at his command. The most important part of this method, at least at this time, was the provision that all instruction would begin with the vernacular and would move upward and onward from there. Since this idea was not cogent enough to secure employment for Ratke, he took his method and left Orange. We meet him again in the city of Frankfort, where he presented himself to the city fathers and offered to use his universal method in the city's schools. This was about 1612. Before anything could come of the proposition, although it has been said that some money was given to him by the city as a retainer and that an offer was made to provide his venture with the physical facilities that were needed, Ratke left Frankfort and went to Augsburg. Apparently the city of Augsburg had invited Ratke to establish a school there, although in actual fact we know nothing of the way he spent his time in Augsburg. He returned to Frankfort in 1617. Again he approached the city fathers and asked them to appoint an agent to whom he might explain his educational plan. The city council did appoint such an agent, with whom Ratke had several meetings. Eventually the agent made his report to the council, and the council, in turn, informed Ratke that he had its permission to apply elsewhere for an educational position.[3]

Ratke's big chance was not long in coming. In 1618 he was invited by Ludwig von Anhalt Köthen to undertake the work of educational reform in his principality. On April 10, 1618, Ratke arrived in Köthen to begin the work that he had promised the prince he would do. Special buildings, assistants, printing presses, and all the things that Ratke had requested for his work were either ready and waiting for him or were soon put at his disposal. Ratke was apparently given a free hand in bringing his schools into existence. He was, moreover, given every assistance in setting up a school that was to operate as a training school for teachers in his method. As an interesting sidelight, it might be mentioned that the prince was so confident of the work that Ratke could do that he promulgated a miniature compulsory-attendance law. If Ratke's method was any good, the prince was not going to have it wasted.

The schools that Ratke established were six-class schools; the first three classes—perhaps the first three years—were conducted in the vernacular, and the vernacular language was included in the curriculum as a subject of instruction. Beginning with the fourth class, Latin was introduced. From then on it was the main subject of instruction, although Greek was introduced in the sixth class.

The actual workings of Ratke's schools are little known. There is no question but that he ran into some difficulty, for in October of 1619, about a year and a half after coming to Köthen, he was imprisoned by the prince. He remained in prison until about the middle of 1620 and was released only after he had signed a declaration that he had "claimed

---

[3] For further study of Ratke's place in the history of education, see R. H. Quick, *Educational Reformers*, D. Appleton & Company, Inc., New York, 1897; O. Browning, *Educational Theories*, Kegan Paul, Trench, Trubner & Co., London, 1881; John W. Adamson, *Pioneers of Modern Education*, Cambridge University Press, New York, 1905; and Henry C. Barnard, *German Teachers and Educators*, Brown and Gross, Hartford, Conn., 1878, pp. 321–342.

and promised more than he knew or could bring to pass."[4] Whether or not the real reasons for Ratke's fall from favor can be found in the educational plans and practices he espoused cannot be answered definitively here. It may be suggested, however, that the reasons were not wholly educational. Ratke was a strong, uncompromising Lutheran; the principality in which he was working was committed unequivocally to the Calvinistic Reformed Church. The religion that was taught in Ratke's school was, in doctrine and form, the religion in which he himself believed. This was a kind of arrogance that the citizens of the place, to say nothing of the prince, would not long accept. It was hinted, also, that the discipline of the school was somewhat less rigid than the citizens of that time and place thought they had a right to expect, and they complained that there was too much time being wasted on recreation. In addition, they opposed the speed which was one of the cornerstones of Ratke's educational plan. He had, after all, promised to do twice as much as had normally been done in only half the time. Speed was of the essence. This commitment to speed, however, led, it is said, to passing students too quickly from one level of instruction to another without being certain that they were ready to take the step up. There were complaints, possibly rumors, that the students did not write well. The real reasons for Ratke's difficulty may not have been educational so much as personal.

In spite of the trials that Ratke was prone to bring on himself, he remains an interesting figure in the history of education. If a novel, a play, or a movie script were to be written around some person in the history of education, Ratke would be a "natural."

After his bitter experience in Köthen, Ratke wandered around Europe. It seems unlikely that he ever again obtained a favorable position as a teacher or director of education. Nonetheless, he was a fairly good publicity agent for his own cause. He spread the word that he really did have a secret method of teaching, one that was far more successful than anything yet invented; but he refused to let anyone know what this method was. Even the great Comenius wrote to him, asking for some of the details of the method, but to no avail. Perhaps it was not as secret as he thought. From his actual teaching experiences and from the emphasis which he made in pedagogy, we can reconstruct fairly well his principles of teaching. The recommendations which Ratke made, or implied that he would make, may be inferred from his general outlook.

1. A natural method of learning should be followed. Though Ratke nowhere spells out what this natural method is, we should not be too severe with him for what is apparently only an oversight. He had an

[4] Frederick Eby, *The Development of Modern Education*, 2d ed., Prentice-Hall, Inc., Englewood Cliffs, N. J., 1952, p. 165.

intuition that there was a natural method of learning, but he was unable to go much beyond this. Much of modern pedagogical thought begins with a similar intuition.

2. Only one thing should be learned at a time.

3. Repetition is necessary for impression. Ratke accepted a principle of learning here, repetition, that has almost always been accorded a position of importance in any hierarchy of learning principles.

4. The natural method of learning that Ratke suggested prompted him to begin all instruction with the vernacular. When the students undertook Latin, they did not study Latin grammar first. Rather, they gained a knowledge of the Latin tongue by reading and speaking, and later learned grammatical structure by its application to what they had read. This innovation in the teaching of a language is certainly a part of the general realistic outlook, and may well have been Ratke's most important contribution to the history of pedagogy.

5. Motivation was to come from the desire or interest of the student to learn something about the subject that was put before him. Ratke was violently opposed to compulsion and harsh methods in teaching, and the discipline in the schools that he managed was always mild. But this refusal of his to accept fear as the most effective motive for learning often led not to praise but to severe criticism of his work.

6. Rote memory was little employed as a technique for learning in Ratke's plan or in the schools that he operated. He aimed at understanding. This, too, is a sound principle, which today is accepted by all teachers.

7. Finally, it may be said that Ratke had such complete confidence in the method that he had devised that he claimed everything should be taught according to it. Of course, if Ratke did discover a natural method of learning, it would be hard to see why it should not be applied to all learning experiences.[5]

We have suggested above that it is difficult to evaluate the merit or the influence of Ratke's so-called secret method or his educational plan. In spite of this, we can say that Ratke broke ground for Comenius and that his most important contribution to the history of education was that he prepared the way for a greater man.

JOHN AMOS COMENIUS (1592–1670)

The accepted customs of mankind cannot be changed overnight. Human behavior can best be altered through a logical presentation of truths and by a process of evolution involving not years but generations.

[5] On some of these points, see Quick, *op. cit.*, pp. 109–118.

The European situation in the seventeenth century, following centuries of unrest and of the inhumanity of man toward man, was critical in matters of religion and politics.

The period of the Reformation saw an attempt by certain devout Christians, angered at the laxity and even worldly arrogance of the Roman Catholic clergy, to branch out on their own in the foundation of religious sects which would provide for their salvation. Salvation, at this time, was not only concerned with the period of life after death, but with the salvation of the earthly dignity of man and with materialistic success leading toward the ultimate, heavenly reward.

Not only were these new religious sects lacking in true, international leadership and organization, they were also subject to the political vagaries of the rulers and princes of the independent states of Europe. The resultant conflicts which arose were, therefore, both political and religious. A Catholic prince was able to secure the assistance of the militant Jesuit order, and with the Jesuits' more unified chain of command and authority, was better able to rout the Protestant forces struggling for recognition and survival in his country. A Protestant ruler, on the other hand, oppressed his Catholic opposition by both political and military action, occasionally securing the assistance of sympathetic, neighboring princes.

The so-called "Religious Peace of Augsburg," in 1555, did little to alleviate the situation. The effect, really, was to legalize these religious divisions by placing final authority for the determination of a state's religion in the hands of the ruler of each state. Under such authority no freedom of religion, as it is known today, existed in many countries.

John Amos Comenius was a Protestant with definite convictions against the claims of the papacy in Rome. To Comenius the only authority for the religious guidance of mankind lay in the interpretation of the Bible, the only true source for the word of God. The pope was the anti-Christ, and the Catholic clergy representatives of a group seeking only secular power. So firmly was Comenius convinced of his stand that he even urged the Jesuits to see the error of their ways and follow him.

The sect to which Comenius belonged was known as the Unitas Fratrum, or Unity of Brethren. The Unity had been in existence since 1467, at which time "over sixty delegates met in a small village and chose three laymen as candidates for the priesthood. These were ordained by the laying-on of hands by the assembled group. But the youngest of them, having been chosen by lot the chief among the three, later received an additional ordination to the episcopal office; this ordination was performed by the priest Michael, who possessed Roman Catholic ordination to begin with. . . . Thus originated the most truly national of the Bohemian religious communions—the Unity of Brethren."[6] With this un-orthodox procedure for ordination to the priesthood, the Unity repudiated its belief in the apostolic succession formerly adhered to. The die was cast, and the struggle for survival of this new sect began. The conflict between Protestant and Catholic forces continued in Bohemia under wavering rule, culminating in the Thirty Years' War, which broke out in 1618. Although the irate Protestants expelled the Jesuits for "all time" from Bohemia at the start of this religious war, the tide of battle turned in 1620 with the defeat of the Czech-Moravian forces at the Battle of White Mountain. Emperor Ferdinand II, with the help of the Jesuits, forced Roman Catholicism upon the entire Czech nation. The nobility had the choice of becoming Catholic or leaving; the peasants had no choice. Comenius, whose aversion to the Catholic Church was well known, was forced into hiding and later into exile from his native land.

To many who have studied the history of education the name of John Amos Comenius is that of a pioneering educational theorist. He has been called an educational reformer and the father of modern educational theory and practice. His best known work is *The Great Didactic*, in which many of his ideas on education are set forth. Initially he makes proposals for a standardized, thorough, and humane system of teaching and learning. Many stop with this general concept, or view the attempts of Comenius as a chapter of the past containing some "good ideas." A more detailed analysis of this man's work seems warranted out of deference to his influence in the whole field of education.

To know Comenius, we must first understand the basic principles of his philosophy. Although he is thought of primarily as an educator, this aspect of his life and work was really secondary. Primarily John Amos Comenius was a man of God. His life motivation was to serve God. He realized this ambition when, in 1618, at the age of twenty-four, he was ordained a priest in the Unity of Brethren. He was not lacking in educational experience, however, for he had been teaching at a school of the Unity for two years prior to his ordination.

In addition to being a religious man and an educator, he was a humanitarian. He had suffered enough under political and religious persecution to know some of the needs of mankind. In his early schooling he had experienced the rigors of the heartless, inefficient methods of the time. To complete his qualities, he was an idealist. The combination of all the above facets of his personality made him a potential force for the good of mankind through education. His travels while in exile added an international approach to his proposals for educational reform. Although his first loyalty was to his own group of Brethren, he continued

[6] M. Spinka, *John Amos Comenius: That Incomparable Moravian,* University of Chicago Press, Chicago, 1943, p. 10.

to work in exile for the betterment of mankind in many countries and unselfishly gave the benefits of his wisdom wherever and whenever he found a receptive ear.

Comenius was born in 1592 in Nivnitz in Moravia. Moravia, located in the center of today's Czechoslovakia, was then, as it is now, in the heart of a troubled sector of Europe. Comenius' early education had been strictly religious. At the age of twelve, after having lost his parents, he lived with an aunt and attended an elementary school for less than two years. The methods in the school were painful and crude. At sixteen he went to a Latin school run by the Unity of Brethren, and there his love for learning was kindled. A nobleman, Count Zerotin, aided the young Comenius in his studies, urging him to continue to the priesthood.

After a brief visit to Amsterdam in 1612, Comenius began to study his life's work, theology, at the University of Heidelberg in 1613. Here he started the ambitious project of a Czech-Latin dictionary, which was to take him forty-four years to complete. In 1616 he obtained a position at a school in Prague, where he taught for two years prior to his ordination in 1618. Almost at once after becoming a priest, Comenius was made pastor of a parish in Fulnek, which was an especially troubled area in the year that marked the beginning of the Thirty Years' War. Fulnek was ravaged in 1620, and Comenius went into hiding. His parishioners and friends were able to hide him for eight years. But in 1628 he gave up his life of concealment and left his native land for the city of Leszno, Poland, which was to be his second home until 1656.

Throughout his life Comenius was a prolific writer. In addition to the Czech-Latin dictionary, on which he spent forty-four years, he wrote his *Labyrinth of the World* in 1612, in which he chided the pseudoscholars of the day for their claims to be teaching the seven liberal arts. In 1614 he wrote *A Theater of All Things*, a sixteen-volume encyclopedia in Czech. This work, the first of its kind, was written by a twenty-two-year-old university student. Two years later he published a small but complete Latin grammar, because he was not entirely satisfied with the grammars that were then in use. While in exile, from 1628 to 1631, he wrote the *Janua Linguarum Reserata* (Gate of Tongues Unlocked), which made him famous throughout Europe for his shifting of the approach of Latin instruction from words to things. This book employed the Baconian principle of an inductive, scientific method of study and led to the proposal of a lifetime dream, the pansophic college.

Whenever Comenius was in exile, and this was often and for extended periods of time, he never gave up the desire to live in his home country. His travels throughout Europe included stays in England, Sweden, and Hungary, where he gave the benefit of his knowledge and ideas to any who requested them. In England, his close friendship with Samuel

Hartlib was due to the great encouragement Hartlib and others gave to his pansophic theories. In keeping with his humanitarianism, Comenius yearned for the establishment of a pansophic college which would be of benefit to the whole world. In such a college the universal knowledge of the centuries, compiled by the best scholars of the day, would be amassed for the betterment of mankind. The breadth of such a task is easy to appreciate. No such dream has ever been realized. It is little wonder that the troubled era in which Comenius lived did not see its attainment.

With his exile in 1628 Comenius had additional time to spend on educational reform. The followers of the Unity were widely dispersed, but Comenius looked forward to the time when they might return to Moravia and began to prepare the way for them by writing his greatest treatise on education, *The Great Didactic*. He finished this work about 1632. That it did not make much impression on the educational world at that time was probably due to the fact that the work was written in Czech. In 1657 it was translated into Latin, and from that time on it was somewhat better known. The original Czech manuscript was discovered in Lissa in 1841 and was printed in 1849. The first complete English translation was made in 1896.

Into *The Great Didactic* Comenius poured his soul, with the firm conviction that all men could be taught all things to make them learned, virtuous, and pious. The firsthand knowledge Comenius had of the crude educational methods of the time, together with his devotion to God's work, demanded of him that he be instrumental in correcting the faulty ways of mankind through an infallible system of teaching and learning. Comenius wrote:

> Didactic signifies the art of teaching. . . . We venture to promise A Great Didactic, that is to say, the whole art of teaching all things to all men, and indeed of teaching them with certainty, so that the result cannot fail to follow; further, of teaching them pleasantly, that is to say, without annoyance or aversion on the part of the teacher or pupil, but rather with the greatest enjoyment for both; further, of teaching them thoroughly, not superficially and showily, but in such a manner as to lead to true knowledge, to gentle morals, and to the deepest piety . . . that we may lay the foundations of the universal art of founding universal schools.[7]

The thoroughgoing character of Comenius' aspirations is apparent from the above quotation. He realized that the proposal of such a method would be met by many doubts or, even worse, would be ignored. Invoking God's help, as he does throughout the work, Comenius appeals in his "Dedicatory Letter" to the leaders of human society—rulers, pastors, and

---

[7] John Amos Comenius, *The Great Didactic*, translated by M. W. Keatinge, A. & C. Black, Ltd., London, 1896, in the "Greeting to the Reader."

parents—to realize the sacred trust which has been given to mankind in the form of little children. Scripture points to the command of God that elders must be "as little children" to attain salvation. Children must, therefore, be given their rightful place in the world. Children are the future older generation, and great care must be taken of their education in order that the corruptness of mankind may be remedied.

To the persons and agencies concerned, Comenius recommends the use of teaching as an art. Parents, schoolmasters, students, schools, states, churches, and heaven itself, would derive the benefits from this system. The attainment of this ideal through education would, in Comenius' view, provide mankind with knowledge, morals, and piety, so that they would live happily on earth and, ultimately, in heaven.

The purpose of education is logically presented by Comenius in the first chapters of *The Great Didactic*. Scripturally, man is seen to be the most excellent of things created by God. Reason, given to man, permits him to know that there is a life beyond this life and that existence on earth is therefore merely preparatory. For life in accordance with God's will man needs erudition, virtue or seemly morals, and religion or piety. These primary aims of life—learning, virtue, and piety—must be attained, and the surest way to attain them is through education.

That man is capable of being educated is evident by the presence of the sense organs, through which the rational soul can perceive everything in the universe. In one of his many analogies Comenius compares the brain, the workshop of thought, to wax, which either receives the impress of a seal or furnishes the material for small images. This comparison is similar to the *tabula rasa* concept later proposed by John Locke.[8] Further analogies between the making of objects from materials and the formation of the intellects of men are used by Comenius to explain the necessity of education. Education is compared to the tools applied to inanimate objects to perfect them. He refers to the adage, "As the twig is bent the tree's inclined," in stressing the necessity for education from the child's most infant years.

Comenius' foresight can be detected in his proposal to educate both boys and girls of all social classes in common schools. The inability of parents to educate and train their children is taken for granted by Comenius, as is the need for wise and generous teachers. All men are formed in the image of God, and according to Comenius all men have a common destiny. The same commonness should apply to education. Although Comenius stresses the universality of education, he does not claim that all men should be taught identically. Only that which concerns man as man should be taught to all, for in later life some things will be of more use to one man and other things to another. Again

[8] See pp. 360–361.

Comenius returns to his theme: Knowledge, virtue, and piety must be acquired in order to serve God and oneself.

Following the admission that children differ and that education need not be identical for all, Comenius describes the conditions prevalent in the imperfect schools up to and including those of the seventeenth century. Schools, heretofore only for the rich, must be made available to all, and teachers must adopt an approach that will make learning more pleasant. Comenius acknowledges the differences in the intellectual capacities of children, and would have a brighter student assist in the instruction of slower ones. The instructor must recognize individual differences. Following this, the proposal that schools must be run with clocklike precision appears to many to be a contradiction in Comenius' plan.

Having laid the groundwork for the establishment of reformed schools, Comenius outlines, in the last half of *The Great Didactic*, the requirements for the methods he proposes for teaching and learning. A statement of first importance is that the subjects being taught should be geared to the ability and maturity of the students. In addition, examples of the application of what is to be learned should precede the memorization of mere rules, and subjects should be integrated and graduated for more thorough comprehension. Other prime requirements would be readiness and perseverance on the part of the pupil and the proper environment of the school itself. With the realization of these requirements, many of the conditions necessary to the development of wisdom, virtue, and piety are also realized.

Methodology was very important to Comenius. He considered it to be so crucial a factor in teaching that he declared one "right method" should be used for all teaching. This, no doubt, was the natural method of which we heard so much from Ratke. Ideally, one method of teaching applied to every subject would simplify the task of the teacher and make learning somewhat easier for the student. Unfortunately, the hope for achieving such a method is based on invalid assumptions about learning and knowledge. Perhaps Comenius did not really intend to go as far as to say there should be only one method for teaching; perhaps he was only striving for greater organization in teaching during a chaotic period in education's history.

The principles of thoroughness in teaching advanced by Comenius in *The Great Didactic* seem to be quite sound. He admonished teachers to teach only those subjects which would be of some use to students, maintaining that useless subjects could never be defended, and he directed that they be taught without interruption and only after careful preparation or cultivation. Later learning was to be based on previous learning, and subjects linked within and among themselves. Lesson plans were required of all teachers.

Many have questioned the size of classes proposed by Comenius. He seemed to believe not only that large classes were necessary at that time from a social point of view, but that they were also desirable educationally. He wrote that teachers would be more attentive to their work if their classes were large. By large classes he meant possibly as many as two hundred students. Of course, in order that anything at all should be accomplished under such conditions, systematic sectioning of students was required, with key students supervising and tutoring perhaps twenty others.

Utilizing many of the foregoing principles, Comenius explained the application of the senses in learning the sciences. A student must keep the eye of his mind pure and see that the object is brought near to it. He must pay attention and proceed from one object to another, using a suitable method. In the matter of learning the arts, the proper use of materials can be acquired only through practice. For the teaching of the arts Comenius prescribed the use of models, and the instructor, he insisted, must teach by demonstration and practice instead of by words alone.

Comenius was never opposed to the languages. He was convinced that they needed to be in the curricula of the schools, but he objected to making the study of language an end in itself. He saw the languages as tools or instruments for learning and communication and was unwilling to isolate them from the real problems of life and living. For this reason he was often critical of the language teaching of his day; he was especially critical of the aridity of language study and of its irrelevancy. In his own system, which he set forth in the textbooks he prepared, words were joined to objects—Comenius was the first to illustrate a Latin-grammar text—and a language was learned only as thoroughly as was considered necessary. In such an academic context the vernacular was given a place of primary importance; Greek, Latin, and Hebrew followed it. Only one language was to be learned at a time.

Comenius' Levels of Education

Proceeding from his understanding of human nature, Comenius outlined a distinct series of schools that was designed to take a student from birth to maturity with the proper organization, gradation, and integration of studies. The first of these four six-year schools was the Mother School, covering a period from birth to the age of six. With the mother as the tutor, the child was to learn by association of things with words. Of course Comenius could see from firsthand experience that few mothers were ready to assume the responsibility for launching their children on their educational careers. Yet whether they were ready or not, they had been starting their children's education for centuries and would continue to do so. Taking a realistic position in the matter, Comenius decided to help mothers prepare themselves. He wrote a book called the *School of Infancy,* in which he tried to give directions to mothers on how to educate their youngsters during the first six years of their lives.

During the second six-year period, boys and girls would attend the Vernacular School. Here proficiency would be developed and to some extent perfected in reading and writing the mother tongue, and skill would be developed in counting. Singing was to be taught, as were various hymns and Bible stories. The principles of morality were to be taught by the use of rules and by practice in the art of living. Economics and politics were to be taught on a rather elementary level; that is, they would never go beyond the assumed needs of the students. General world history, covering the creation, fall, and redemption of man, was to be presented, along with geography and topography. At this point in Comenius' educational plans we note the emergence of a "theory of education for life," for here in the Vernacular School the curriculum was to provide opportunities for study of the mechanical arts. This is one way in which Comenius acknowledged the natural differences among students. This level of education, the Vernacular School, was to have been the last formal education for many of the students in it; girls would always cease to pursue formal education at this level, as would boys who lacked real academic interests or abilities. The boys who were anticipating higher studies would proceed to the next level, the Latin School, for a term of six years.

The curriculum of the Latin School was designed to produce grammarians, dialecticians, rhetoricians, arithmeticians, and geometricians, musicians, and astronomers. In addition, the boys were to be physicists, geographers, chronologers, historians, moralists, and finally theologians. Boys who followed such a course of studies in the Latin School would be considered to have a solid foundation upon which their final training in the university could be built. The last level was, of course, the University School, a school which was open to the highly qualified and which, in addition to its teaching function, recognized the university's function in research.

Classes in the Vernacular School were to be held for two hours in the morning and for two hours in the afternoon. Each year of the six would be set aside for a specific class, and each class would have its work assigned to it. It was only after much study and deliberation that Comenius arrived at the right order of study. He tried to determine what the students' previous experiences would permit them to study with the greatest benefits. He decided finally that the grammar class should be held during the first year of the six, to give the students further basic foundations. The class in natural philosophy was next, followed by classes in mathematics, ethics, dialectics, and lastly rhetoric. In connection with the work of each of these classes, Comenius decreed that history should be studied, in order that every student might have a thorough knowledge of the events of the world, from ancient times to the present.

Writing on the universal and perfect order of instruction, Comenius attempted to justify his assurance of the future success of his methods by a comparison between the student being taught and a piece of paper on which print is impressed. Originally documents had to be hand-copied by many for distribution to the few. With the invention of the printing press, this situation was changed, and printed materials could be prepared by the few for distribution to the many. Not only would the new system of printing be faster, but it would also be more accurate. Once the type was set, the finished products were identical, and this identity was due to standardization. The analogy drawn by Comenius is easy to understand. The point where it touched education, particularly on the question of a single method, has been the subject of much discussion and, over the years, has led to a great difference of opinion. For his part, Comenius believed so deeply in the good that could be accomplished by the use of his standardized methods that he wanted the world to start using them at once. Their use, he wrote, would assure that "the entire youth of both sexes, none being excepted," would "quickly, pleasantly, and thoroughly, become learned in the sciences, pure in morals, trained to piety, and in this manner instructed in all things necessary for the present and for the future life."

Comenius has been called a realist. He knew that his educational theories were somewhat advanced for the world in which he lived and that they could be applied only with great difficulty. He realized that surprisingly few teachers were prepared in such a way that they could follow his pedagogical advice. Even if qualified teachers were available, Comenius might well ask how the towns and villages were going to support them. Another obvious obstacle was the inability of children on the lower social and economic level to attend school. Usually they had to work at home or in the shops. If these obstacles were not enough, there was the opposition that came from the accepted educational opinion of the day. This opinion found expression among educators and politicians who did not want the world to change; they were entirely content with society as it was, and they wanted to keep it that way.

Yet one hope for making some inroads on the established opinion and practice of the time lay in the preparation and distribution of specially prepared textbooks. These were the products of Comenius' work and ideas. If they were used as tools in the schools and used with success, then the application of other more advanced ideas might be looked for with greater hope. Perhaps it was in this area, the preparation of textbooks for the schools, that Comenius made his greatest mark on his own time. Certainly the total effect of the work of Comenius for seventeenth-century educational reform was not great. The majority of the reforms that he advocated were destined to lie dormant, only to be put into effect one by one as men in changing times demanded, and to some extent obtained, educational reform. Free and universal education, open to all and compulsory for all of both sexes, is now a reality in the world's most advanced countries. Comenius' ideas for preschool home training surpass even the most advanced modern ideas of the kindergarten's role in public education. Instruction in the native tongue of the pupil, graded subject matter, psychological adjustment to the maturing student, all are accepted without question in today's school programs. Parents and educators are willing to consider the nature of the child's mind and to correlate thoughts and things. History, geography, drawing, and manual training are now being given without any doubts as to their need or their worth, and schools try to gear their programs to bring life and learning as closely together as possible.

As we said before, the accepted customs of mankind cannot be changed overnight. John Amos Comenius was aware of this. *The Great Didactic* proposed a reform in the field of education that must have appeared to the author, at times, to be little more than a dream. He knew it was possible to realize the fulfillment of this dream in a limited way and in particular localities, but he was enough of a realist to know that his voice was not strong enough to turn the educational tide in favor of the realistic views that he advocated. Nevertheless, in the face of great odds against him, he spoke out for educational reform. His voice was heard, but not until many years later, for it was the nineteenth rather than the seventeenth century that benefited most from the educational views of Comenius.

RELIGIOUS EDUCATION IN THE SEVENTEENTH CENTURY

Of all of the movements that promised to remake modern education, two of the most important attempted to keep religion and education close together. One was the work of the Brothers of the Christian Schools (the Christian Brothers), whose founder, St. John Baptist de la Salle, may be regarded as one of the pioneers of modern education; the other was Pietism, as it was applied to education by August Hermann Francke.

The Christian Brothers

The Institute of the Brothers of the Christian Schools was founded by St. John Baptist de la Salle in 1684. The system of schools which the Brothers developed under the guidance of their saint founder was one which evolved naturally from the needs of society, especially of children, in seventeenth-century France. The Brothers' schools began as humble institutions. For the first several years of the existence of the Institute, it was not known outside of three dioceses in central France. During this time when their schools were confined to the three dioceses, the Brothers devised a new type of education, which, while not losing sight of wider meanings, related instruction to the needs of the children who came to the schools. The courses that were pursued by humble boys in the Brothers' schools fitted them for life, and although the schools were not by any means simple trade schools, they provided the particular educational equipment that future artisans, shopkeepers, and tradesmen would have to possess if they wanted employment and a reasonable expectation of success in their work. When the schools of the Institute broadened the base of their operations, when they became national and then international in scope, they still found time for further progress along these practical lines. In fact, the Brothers provided the general model for the type of elementary school that spread throughout the United States in the early nineteenth century—the common school, a primary school of a higher type that was intended to provide the student with terminal school experience.

The Educational Accomplishments of the Brothers. The original and fundamental idea that surrounded the work of the Brothers of the Christian Schools was that educational opportunities were needed for poor boys. The Christian Brothers came to be committed to the elementary education of these children. It was this commitment that led to the rather natural development of the course of instruction that has been referred to above, a course broad enough to meet a boy's basic educational needs and narrow enough to prepare him for the things that he would have to do in the real world in which he was destined to live. Considering this admirable purpose and the very real success that the Brothers had in achieving the goals they set, we cannot wonder that John William Adamson in his *Pioneers of Modern Education* counts the Brothers of the Christian Schools as the most successful innovators in modern education.[9] In making his evaluation, Adamson weighs the accomplishments of the Brothers against such educational movements as

[9] Adamson, *op. cit.*, p. 212. For a recent account of La Salle's life and work, and his commitment to the education of poor boys, see W. J. Battersby, *St. John Baptist de la Salle,* The Macmillan Company, New York, 1957.

are to be found in realism, the Protestant Revolt, and the Catholic Reform.

Along with the idea that opportunity for elementary education needed to be more generously provided in seventeenth-century France, in fact, as a central part of that idea, was the conviction that the education offered should be in the vernacular. The work of the Christian Brothers was essentially that of providing elementary education in the vernacular for poor boys. The opposition that was generated to the Brothers' plan came mostly from the members of the Catholic hierarchy in France. Of course, education in France and elsewhere on the Continent had for many centuries been mainly classical. The Church's authorities had too frequently regarded education in terms of the preparation of boys for the priesthood; they could not understand and could not, therefore, approve of a school that did not have Latin in its curriculum. Overcoming opposition to the vernacular school was one of the most difficult tasks that La Salle had to perform. In time he was able to make the bishops see that for most of the boys who came to the Brothers' schools, instruction in Latin was not a very valuable educational asset. It was not until many decades later, and generally outside of France, that the Brothers accepted responsibility for secondary education. In America especially they have achieved an enviable reputation as secondary school teachers, and the Brothers' schools are among the finest in the country.

One of the first weaknesses that La Salle detected when he turned his attention to education and tried to work out a plan for elementary instruction was that the teachers were generally poorly prepared or not prepared at all for the kind of work they had to do in the schools. Some provisions may have been made for the preparation of teachers for higher and secondary schools, but little thought was given to the preparation of teachers for the elementary levels. This led La Salle in 1687 to establish a normal school, a teachers' training college, for the preparation of Brother teachers who were to conduct the schools of the Institute. We have no clear record of any teachers' training school earlier than the one founded by and for the Brothers of the Christian Schools, although such projects were surely speculated about long before this. In 1439 a training center for grammar school masters was proposed at God's House, Cambridge, by William Byngham. Even before this, there are evidences that the formal preparation of elementary school teachers was considered, but apparently no practical outcomes were achieved.

In addition to the regular schools conducted by the Brothers, schools were opened for young people who for one reason or another could not attend the regular schools. These were the Sunday Schools or the Continuation Schools of the Christian Brothers. Such schools did a great deal of good work, but they never became principal considerations in the educational work of the Brothers.

One of the things for which La Salle and the Christian Brothers are remembered is class or group instruction, sometimes called simultaneous instruction. It has not been uncommon to credit La Salle with having founded, discovered, or invented class methods of teaching. Actually, the practice of having one teacher teach several students at the same time is much older than the seventeenth century. It would be difficult, if not impossible, to assign either a date or an inventor to this method of teaching, for it goes back to the beginnings of formal education. But in the hands of the Brothers the method was thoroughly exploited and skillfully employed. The great Comenius was perhaps the most thoroughgoing advocate of simultaneous instruction, but it was the Christian Brothers who were most successful in developing it as a modern educational technique. They used it with skill for a hundred years while teachers in other elementary schools were using the conventional technique of individual instruction, a method which made the teacher a mere hearer of lessons. Without a method such as the Brothers perfected, popular elementary education would never have been possible.

Along with the application of the technique of simultaneous teaching, the Brothers made greater and more effective use of monitors than had been made before or since in the history of education. It should be pointed out, however, that the Brothers never used monitors for instruction, an omission which made their employment of monitors essentially different from the system devised in later years by Joseph Lancaster and Andrew Boll.[10]

The Work and Influence of La Salle. There is little reason to doubt that La Salle was a pioneer of modern education. Yet it was as a man of action, as an organizer and administrator of the Institute's schools, rather than as an elaborator of theories that he made his mark on education. We look for signs of La Salle's influence in deeds rather than in written words; we find them in institutions more than in books.

During the course of forty or more years in which the Saint was connected with education, there were a number of times when he was called upon to set down his thoughts on paper. These thoughts may be found in his letters and in some of his devotional works, as well as in the *Rule* of the Institute itself. His principal writing with a strict pedagogical character was the *Conduct of the Schools,* a document which may be thought of as the *Ratio Studiorum* for the schools of the Brothers. Though the book was extremely useful to the Brothers who later established schools all over the world, its content illustrates the nonliterary character

[10] See pp. 373–374.

of La Salle's educational efforts. It was not until after the Saint's death in 1719 that any known printed edition of the *Conduct* appeared, in 1720.

Despite the tardy appearance of the work in printed form, in its essentials it had been in existence from the earliest years, when the Institute was but a small and little-known diocesan association. At Rheims the founder of the Christian Brothers had drawn up a set of directions for the Brothers to follow, and each of the Brother teachers had a manuscript copy. Since the *Conduct* cannot really be separated from the *Rule* of the Institute itself, we may assume that every Brother was especially familiar with the teaching directions that made up the *Conduct*. As the educational work of the Brothers recommended itself to other dioceses, the *Conduct of the Schools* grew more detailed in content. The experience of the Brothers at Paris and elsewhere, but especially at Paris, led to a more rapid development of their special teaching technique, and this technique found a definite and permanent expression in a more complete edition of the *Conduct*, prepared by La Salle in 1695. This was still a manuscript edition, privately circulated. Even when the *Conduct* appeared in printed form, it was not given wide circulation. It was and is regarded as a teacher's manual for the Brothers of the Christian Schools to follow. This does not mean, of course, that it is not a pedagogical classic in its own right.

In any event, the *Conduct* is still, as it was in the seventeenth century, a living instrument for guiding teaching. It is not a stereotyped document that does not admit of addition or modification; La Salle himself made many changes in the *Conduct* during his own lifetime. As the educational needs of the world have changed and as we have come to know more and more about the science and art of education, the *Conduct* has been modified by the faithful followers of La Salle.

The 1720 edition of the *Conduct* helps us to picture the schools of the Brothers as they were conducted in the seventeenth century. Its contents disclose both the organization of classes in the schools and the course of study that was pursued. If we try to summarize the contents of the *Conduct* in bold strokes, we might say that the great aim of the Brothers was to teach religion and to inculcate piety in their charges; that a secondary but still important aim was to give boys the kind of educational experience that would be valuable to them in the kind of world they were living in; and finally, that the means to achieve all of this, as grasped by the founder and through him by the Brothers, was the effective use of the simultaneous method for teaching large classes of children.

Of all the movements in modern education, none stands out as being of greater import than the one initiated by St. John Baptist de la Salle and perpetuated by the Brothers of the Christian Schools.

Pietism

How can one convey the meaning of Pietism as it found expression in Germany in the seventeenth century? Perhaps we may call it realism with a soul. The realist educators were looking for the content of education and the inspiration for it in the real world, the world that could be experimented with, the world to which the inductive method could be applied. The Pietists were realists, too, at least in a way, for they tried to find in the message of Christ the content of education and the inspiration to preserve and extend it. The Pietists made their mark on religious history because of their opposition to authority and externalism. They emphasized the inner workings of faith and religious feelings. In education, the Pietists, following the lead of the illustrious Francke (1663–1727), tried to subordinate all learning to a vital faith in the principles of Christian life. Some Pietists may have gone so far as to assume that all learning is due to divine illumination. When this view was emphasized, that is to say, when it became fairly commonly believed that truth would come to one as a result of inspiration or of intuition rather than by the hard work of discursive learning, the movement began to lose both force and significance. But as long as it remained within the limits of a method that tries to promote efficiency in obtaining natural knowledge and in applying that knowledge for the good of the individual and mankind, Pietism accomplished a great deal of good.

August Hermann Francke was a thoroughgoing exponent of Pietism. Although he may not have been its religious leader, he was without question the greatest of Pietist educators. His fame rests mainly on his achievements in the field of educational opportunity; he opened schools and prepared teachers. He started a small school for the poor in 1695 and later added a boarding school, an orphanage, and an elementary school. In addition, he founded an institute for training teachers about 1700. It is estimated that, in all, the institutions that came into existence as a result of the influence or the direct work of Francke numbered more than two thousand. Anyone who was responsible for the establishment of that many schools must be given a place of some prominence in the history of education.

The central idea in all of Francke's schools was that emphasis was to be placed on the religious, the useful, and the realistic. Everything was viewed and studied in the context of its relation to God and of man's relation to God. The dominant purpose of Francke and of the Pietists generally was to make religion a living and vital thing in the life of every German child. This was the school's chief mission. With such a purpose the school was of course not humanistically oriented, although its curriculum may have included some of the subjects that would have been proper to a classical course of studies. In a Pietist school the New Testament was considered to be vastly more important than the Greek or Roman classics.

But it was not only in religious education that the work of the Pietists was important. In other areas, too, they stimulated interest in education and were largely responsible for the development of a German system of schooling. The Pietists and Francke, then, played no small role in the development of modern education.[11]

JOHN LOCKE (1632–1704)

The seventeenth century began with realism and ended with empiricism. The great Comenius was the prophet for realism; Locke performed this role for empiricism. John Locke was born in Wrington, England, where his father was an attorney. Locke received an excellent education at Westminster School, one of the famous English public schools, and at Christ Church College, Oxford. He turned out to be a perpetual student, for he entered Oxford when he was about twenty years old and was still there, working on a studentship, when he was fifty. During this long academic career Locke studied Greek, rhetoric, and ethics and completed his formal education with the study of medicine.

Locke's fame ranges far beyond the field of education. His written works disclose his interest and ability in such fields as government, philosophy, economics, education, and religion. It is sometimes said that he is the only philosopher England ever produced. *Two Treatises on Government* is probably his best-known and most influential work.

Locke's Educational Works

Having been directly involved in education throughout most of his life, John Locke had a good background from which to propound his view to a listening world. He carried with him from his studies at Oxford at least the germs of most of his ideas on education. He made an application of them in his work as a tutor and a counselor. In the families of friends, especially the family of Lord Shaftesbury, Locke undertook a close study of children and observed their intellectual development with scientific care.

Despite the apparent contradictions that often crept into his theories, Locke's educational writings reveal many valuable and progressive ideas. In Locke's time teachers strove for great intellectual progress on the part

---

[11] For more thorough treatments of Francke's role in modern education, see D. G. Kramer, *A. H. Francke's pädagogische Schriften*, H. Beyer & Söhne, Langensalza, 1885; Barnard, *op. cit.*; and Eby, *op. cit.*, pp. 244–260.

of their students, while the physical side of education was almost totally neglected. Locke had very clear notions about this neglect and voiced his opinions quite boldly. His insistence on the necessity of looking after the body if the mind were to be trained properly was possibly his most audacious departure from the educational practices common to the day. He gave popularity to the now-universally accepted theory: a sound mind in a sound body.

As an educational theorist, Locke's fame rests mainly on *Some Thoughts concerning Education,* published in 1693, and the incomplete and unrevised *Of the Conduct of the Understanding,* which first appeared in the posthumous edition of Locke's works published in 1706. This latter short work was composed to be used as a manual of self-instruction for a young man. The *Conduct* is complementary and in many ways supplementary to *Some Thoughts* and is important to an adequate understanding of Locke's theory of education. His *Some Thoughts* is mainly concerned with the physical, moral, and intellectual training of the child, while in the *Conduct* the one big problem is how best to cultivate the rational element in man, a problem with which Locke believed neither the schoolmaster nor the tutor had much concern.[12]

The genesis of *Some Thoughts concerning Education* is interesting. A friend of John Locke's, Edward Clarke, wanted some advice concerning the education of his son, and realizing that educational questions were often foremost in Locke's mind, sought his help. In answer to Clarke's request, Locke wrote a series of letters. The letters, naturally enough, were written in the style one usually employs in friendly correspondence. A few years later, however, after the contents of the letters became more generally known, Locke's friends convinced him that he should collect the letters and publish them in book form. In the dedication of the printed work to Clarke, Locke declared that the only thing different from the original letters was their order and a slight refinement in the style, designed to make it less intimate.[13] Locke did not have the time, or did not take the time, to publish his views on education in a carefully organized book on the subject. As a literary work, *Some Thoughts* suffered from its hurried publication; the work as a whole is highly repetitious.

In reviewing Locke's *Some Thoughts concerning Education,* we must keep in mind: first, that Locke had no thought of writing about the education of ordinary people, since he makes clear that the letters are intended as guides to the education of young gentlemen; and second, that Locke's methods were intended for an individual system of in-

[12] John W. Adamson (ed.), *The Educational Writings of John Locke,* Cambridge University Press, New York, 1922, pp. 12–13.

[13] Benjamin Rand (ed.), *The Correspondence of John Locke and Edward Clarke,* Harvard University Press, Cambridge, Mass., 1927, p. 27.

struction and not for the teaching of large numbers of students in a classroom.[14]

Locke's educational aim is threefold: (1) vigor of body, (2) virtue of the soul, with its manifestations in good breeding and wisdom in conduct, and (3) knowledge, or mental acquirements. Knowledge, the last of the three-point aim, is also subordinate to the two former points.

Keeping Locke's aim before us, let us turn to a closer look at his *Some Thoughts*. Being a medical doctor and, in addition, hampered by a frail constitution, Locke naturally devotes his attention first to the care of the body. Yet he is quick to acknowledge that this attention is only a first step; it should not stop here. In order to fashion the body into a strong and vigorous organism, nature must be given full scope of action: "It seems suitable both to my reason and experience," Locke wrote, "that the tender constitutions of children should have as little done to them as is possible and as the absolute necessity of the case requires."[15] He warns parents against spoiling their child's constitution, claiming that strength of the physical organism can be secured only by accustoming it gradually to the endurance of hardships encountered in the course of life. His main theme is that a person can bear anything to which, from the beginning, he has become habituated. In line with this, Locke advised that children be taught to tolerate temperature change by not dressing too warmly either in summer or winter; to spend as much time as possible in fresh air; to bathe in cold water; and to sleep on hard beds. He insisted, moreover, and at great length, on simplicity and frugality of diet; bread, milk, and gruel would be sufficient nutriment for childhood. Reason must control the appetite, and a child should not be given anything to eat or drink simply because he wants it but only when it is needed for subsistence. He cared nothing about regularity in eating habits, although he was quite sure that children ought to get plenty of sleep on a regular schedule. If this regimen seems disagreeable to human nature, it is not because Locke wanted life to be painful and disagreeable. Rather, he had the sincere conviction that physical hardness was a prerequisite to the attainment of self-denial and self-restraint, both of which would become essential attributes in the life of a gentleman. Locke's own words may be interesting: "Plenty of open air, exercise and sleep, plain diet, no wine or strong drink, and very little or no physic, not too warm or straight clothing, especially the head and feet kept cold, and the feet often used to cold water, and exposed to wet."[16]

[14] Sister Mary Louise Cuff, *The Educational Theory of John Locke: Its Limitations for the Christian Teacher*, The Catholic Education Press, Washington, D.C., 1923, pp. 28–29.

[15] Quoted in *ibid.*, pp. 15–16.

[16] John Locke, *Some Thoughts concerning Education*, edited by R. H. Quick, Cambridge University Press, New York, 1934, sec. 30, p. 26.

Having strengthened and disciplined the body to ensure its obedience to the dictates of the mind, the educator may turn to the next task, which is to set the mind in right order. In the refinement of the mind, Locke attaches far more importance to the formation of virtuous habits and even of those social qualities which go by the name of "good breeding" than to the mere inculcation of knowledge. In Locke's view, a sound mind need not mean necessarily a well-informed mind. A pupil may be well schooled in language, philosophy, and literature, and yet be badly educated. Character, virtue, wisdom, and breeding are the marks of a sound mind; learning is secondary.

Locke discovered all virtue and moral power in the achievement of the ideal: " . . . that a man is able to deny himself his own desires, cross his own inclinations, and purely follow what reason directs as best, though the appetite lean the other way."[17] A multiplicity of rules and principles of good behavior does not produce right conduct. The fewer the regula tions that children must learn, the better, says Locke. Once habits are settled, they tend to operate naturally, and therefore no precious time should be wasted. From infancy a child must be made to realize that there are things he may and may not do and things he may and may not have. Locke does not argue for the breaking of children's spirits by excessive rigor in discipline. He would have the child at ease and free. The perfect solution in raising children is to allow them freedom but at the same time to direct them away from those things they naturally crave toward those things which are somewhat less attractive to them.

Most expedient in the formation of good habit and virtue is the early recognition of parental authority. In the early years of the child's life the motives for this recognition would stem from awe and fear. These sources of motivation ought to change as the child grows older. Yet for holding children on the road to duty, rewards and punishment are unavoidable. Pains and pleasures of the body are not what Locke has in mind; in fact he rejects them. "Esteem and disgrace are, of all others, the most powerful incentives to the mind, when once it is brought to relish them. If you can once get into children the love of credit and apprehension of shame and disgrace, you have put into them the true principle which will constantly work and incline them to the right."[18] Constant reference to parental authority may ensure good behavior when the child is young; but unless the reason is carefully guided from the earliest years, the child may wander from duty and virtue when he has left home and school. A calm insistence on what has been determined as

[17] *Ibid.*, sec. 33, p. 27. It may not be going too far afield to indicate that in these views Locke has something in common both with Spartan ideals and Christian asceticism.

[18] *Ibid.*, sec. 56, p. 39.

proper to reason, once implanted in the child's mind, will expand in power as he progresses.[19]

Example is an excellent teacher of virtue. A child more readily comprehends what he sees in others than what he hears, and therefore those about him should be careful in their actions. This brings out the need of proper environment. Locke opposed public education and favored private or tutorial arrangements. He argued that in a public school teachers exert less influence on the character of a child than fellow students do:

> For let the master's industry and skill be ever so great, it is impossible that he should have 50 or a 100 scholars under his eye any longer than they are in school together; nor can it be expected that he should instruct them successfully in anything but their books; the forming of their minds and manner requiring a constant attention and particular application to every single boy, which is impossible in a numerous flock, and would be wholly in vain, when the lad was left to himself, or the great prevailing infections of his fellows the greatest part of the four-and-twenty hours.[20]

It can be put in another way. Locke wanted children to remain at home under the care of their parents as long as possible, for he believed it foolish to sacrifice virtue for a little Greek and Latin.

If we turn to consider the special virtues that Locke held to be most necessary for young gentlemen, we see that he emphasized the social virtues and the social side of virtue. He recognized the supernatural sanction of virtues by referring them to God, "the independent Being, Author, and Maker of all things, from whom we receive all our good, who loves us, and gives us all things."[21] Locke seemed to regard this reference to God as sufficient to establish a religious basis for morality. This is a slim foundation compared with the one that he constructs for rational, social, and utilitarian virtue. On the level of theory he does take into account divine ratification of virtue, but on the level of practice he is content to accept something less: This is natural virtue.[22] He values breeding, good breeding, and everything included in that expression, as the best and surest sign of a gentleman. With all its limitations and its misplaced emphases, Locke's theory is really one of moral education. He is quite definite in placing moral formation above intellectual formation in the hierarchy of educational purposes.

At any rate, Locke places his discussion of intellectual education last in *Some Thoughts*. The outstanding feature of his discussion of this phase of education is his almost total disapproval of the prevailing system

[19] Cuff, *op. cit.*, pp. 21–23.
[20] Locke, *op. cit.*, sec. 70, p. 53.
[21] *Ibid.*, sec. 136, p. 116.
[22] *Ibid.*, sec. 135, p. 115.

in regard to both matter and method. He thought contemporary education was out of date. His most pointed criticism was directed at the
classical languages. He did not reject outright the real beauty, value, and
importance of Greek and Latin literature for the gentleman. Rather,
Locke questioned the emphasis that was placed on Latin and Greek
grammar, rhetoric, and memorizations, which, he declared, would be of
little benefit in future life.[23]

Although Locke placed greater emphasis on moral education than
he did on intellectual formation, he would not delay the beginning of
intellectual education. As soon as the child begins to talk, the teaching
of reading should begin. The start should be in the nature of play, and
a few letters should be introduced at a time until the child has command
of the entire alphabet. Letters should then be turned into syllables and
before long into words, although the whole process should be like a
game. When the child begins to read he should be given simple, pleasant
books, such as Aesop's *Fables*; when facility increases, Bible stories may
be added. Reading should be followed by writing.

In all schooling, the mother tongue should be given first attention.
Locke was fairly sure that the weaknesses of the vernacular—especially
English—were due to the overcrowding of the curriculum with the
classical languages. He would have brought greater prominence and
respectability to the vernacular by having gentlemen carry on their oral
and written discourse in the vernacular language. Once the vernacular
was securely learned, another language might be undertaken, and in the
usual course of events this would be rather early in the child's educational career. The second language for English youngsters, who seemed
to be Locke's only concern, might be French, and it should be started
early, as we have said, because in early life children's organs of speech
are very pliant, so that the formation of sounds is relatively easy for
them. After French, Latin could be introduced. The method of instruction for all foreign languages would be the same—conversational. A
child would never be troubled, if Locke had his way, with the grammar
of a language until he had developed the facility to speak it. And then
grammar would be a subject of study only for those students who wanted
to make a critical study of the language. Normally, grammatical studies
would not be undertaken until the student was quite mature. If it
appeared that a young man's business might in later years require a
foreign language of him, then Locke would have him learn the grammar
of that language.

Locke spoke out against the practice, then common, of having children
compose themes and verses in Latin on topics with which they were

[23] Cuff, *op. cit.*, pp. 29–30. This is a point that should be remembered in connection with Locke's position on formal discipline (see pp. 361–362).

almost totally unfamiliar. He was no less critical of the practice of having children learn long passages by heart. He was certain that memorization served no useful educational or cultural purpose. Greek, save for the student who aspired to the life of a scholar, had no place in the curriculum.

Added to the study of language were arithmetic, geometry and history. These were especially important to the gentleman who was engaged in business. It is fairly clear by now that the gentleman of whom Locke was thinking was a different man from the courtier of whom the humanists of the Renaissance were thinking when they prepared an educational program for him.[24] Locke considered arithmetic "the easiest and consequently the first sort of abstract reasoning, which the mind commonly bears or accustoms itself to. Hardly anything in life and business can be done without it. A man cannot have too much of it or have it too perfectly."[25] The method prescribed is that of counting, addition, and subtraction. When the students have mastered these processes, they advance to geography by learning the meridians, latitude, and longitude, and finally go on to astronomy. All of this is to be taught gradually, placing one part on the other so as not to confuse but rather to illuminate the understanding. Once the child is acquainted with these matters, a little geometry may be introduced, perhaps the first six books of Euclid. Beyond this point Locke does not believe it is useful to go. Yet if the student is truly fascinated by the subject, Locke would not stop him. Thus the measure of each subject's worth seems to be its utility.

The study of civil law would be quite appropriate in the curriculum of the young gentleman. A study of politics and government would provide a good foundation for such a study. For logic, however, Locke has no time. He does not condemn the science itself, but he does condemn the stilted formalism in which the study of logic was clothed. If the use and end of right reasoning is the formation of correct judgments and the ability to distinguish between truth and falsehood, then he strongly advises parents not to allow their children to be schooled in the art of disputing. This method, Locke claimed, produces a wrangler, or one who is concerned only with contradicting and victory in argument. Truth, the real end to be sought in reasoning, is, Locke said, too little considered in the formal study of logic.

Other less formal accomplishments could be added to the personal equipment of the gentleman, and these would be gained by exercise. Locke mentions dancing because it cultivates graceful movement and confidence; fencing and riding, which he considers such necessary parts of good breeding that it would be impossible to omit them; and exten-

[24] See pp. 284–285.
[25] Locke, *op. cit.*, sec. 180, p. 157.

sive travel. We should find it hard to select the accomplishment in which Locke placed the greatest faith, but he surely thought a great deal of travel. It would broaden and mature the gentleman, he thought, in a way that nothing else could. Finally, Locke speaks of gardening or carpentry as pursuits that would be of considerable value to men who go into business, for either one would divert the mind from the usual cares of the day and promote bodily health.

The program of studies that Locke proposes for the young gentleman is to be finished when he is about twenty-one. At this age, it is assumed that the young man will marry, and then he will have no time for studies.

After examining Locke's curriculum for the young gentleman, we conclude that his criterion of fitness and suitability is utility. Nonessentials should be ignored unless the young man has very special talent; for instance, Greek would be appropriate for the scholar. When we examine the whole range of subjects whose worth and method are discussed by Locke, we come to the conclusion that history, civil law, English law, foreign language, and a command of the mother tongue, together with what is implied in these or found necessary as preparation for them, constitute Locke's idea of a desirable curriculum for the student. Added to these, perhaps as extras, we find the books of Euclid, accounting—for every man of good standing must be able to care for his finances—astronomy, and French. There is no suggestion that the student should have expert knowledge of all this. Locke asks only that the educator try to inculcate a love and esteem of knowledge and that he put the student in a proper frame of mind so that he will want to improve himself. He makes no demand for depth of knowledge; he asks only that it be sufficient for the student's needs.

Locke's Methodology

While Locke insisted on making the curriculum more meaningful, he was equally demanding in the matter of methodology. He wanted teaching to be more efficient, and at the same time he wanted compulsion removed from all learning and teaching techniques. Learning must never be a task or a burden, nor must a child be kept at it until he is tired. Above all, children should never come to associate the idea of punishment with learning. In learning, as in discipline, he strongly opposed the use of punishment, for a child cannot learn, Locke argued, when he is emotionally disturbed, and a mind filled with terror has little room for other impressions. Learning should be made attractive and pleasant. The introduction of games and play in the school in connection with lessons to be learned would do away with the drudgery and boredom.

Another salient point to be observed in his methodology is a strict order of learning beginning with the simple and moving to the complex.

The learner must first grasp an elementary idea before moving forward to another simple idea, which the teacher proposes because it comes next in the total pattern. With such gentle and sensible steps, confusion is avoided and understanding is opened and extended. The tutor should accustom the pupil to order and show him the advantages to be gained by clear thinking. Inductive and deductive reasoning should be exercised, and, with their repeated use, the student will see what methods are proper for gaining different ends.

Locke recognized the need for diversity in methodology. No two children have the same temperament, background, and capacity, and therefore no two children can be taught effectively by using the very same method. Here Locke is setting forth a pedagogical principle which today is universally recognized; education must adapt itself to the learner.

The criticism that Locke leveled at contemporary education was not entirely negative or destructive. When he rejected something, he was always ready with something to put in its place. His most general criticism was that education relied too blindly on the past, but when he rejected the authority of the past, he called upon parents and tutors to use their reason and ingenuity in directing the education of youth.

Locke's Principal Educational Views

From the foregoing we can summarize certain of Locke's educational views that have made the greatest impress on modern education.

1. Locke rejected the doctrine of innate ideas. This doctrine, which had been respected for centuries, held to the belief that certain abstract propositions—or even the idea of God—are innate. Locke argued that if there were innate ideas all people should have them in common. This, he claimed, was not so. The only source for ideas was experience. He put it this way: "Whence has it [the mind] all the materials of reason and knowledge? To this I answer in one word, from experience; in that all our knowledge is founded; and from that it ultimately derives itself."[26]

2. From the rejection of innate ideas it was but a short step to a theory that captured the imagination of modern educators, although it may have done very little to change their academic practices. This was the *tabula rasa* theory. According to Locke's theory, man's mind is passive and, like a wax tablet, can receive only the impressions made on it. He wrote: "These simple ideas, when offered to the mind, the understanding can no more refuse to have, nor alter, when they are imprinted, nor blot them out, and make new ones itself, than a mirror can refuse, alter or obliterate the images or ideas which the objects set before it do therein produce."[27] As a result of the *tabula rasa* theory, two new emphases were given to

[26] John Locke, *Essay concerning Human Understanding*, Book II, chap. 1, p. 2.
[27] *Ibid.*, p. 25.

modern education. These emphases may not have flowed immediately from Locke's pronouncement of the theory, but they are, at least, indirectly related to it. One was the increased attention given to environment and the experiences that it engendered, for Locke's theory could lead one to say that environment makes the man. The other was the doctrine that all men are created equal. It is true that Locke made room for individual differences. One child might have a larger piece of white paper or a larger wax tablet on which impressions might be made, than another, but in the beginning, at least, both were equal, because neither had any impression on his mind. The doctrine of equality of men had great political implications, and in education the doctrine of equality of educational opportunity could find a theoretical base in the *tabula rasa* theory. It would be going too far, however, to maintain that Locke was a champion of equality of opportunity in education. With all his talk about the equality of men, his schools were intended only for the upper classes.

3. Locke advocated private rather than public education. He was so sure that the purpose of education was moral that he would not have the students about whom he was concerned exposed to the danger of education in common. In his view, education was for the elite, and with this restriction it was easy for him to ignore the turn of events that eventually brought popular education into reality.

4. From all that we have said concerning Locke's views about the curriculum, it is plain that he wanted the student to study the subjects that would be of use to him when he left the schoolroom. And from what little we have said about his philosophical and psychological views, it is clear that he believed experience was the only source of knowledge, the only avenue leading to ideas. This single-minded attachment to experience confirms our belief that Locke left modern education a legacy of empiricism.

5. Locke did not take a clear and definite position on the matter of formal discipline. Despite what has been written for many years, Locke can hardly be called the father of formal discipline. In some of his writings, it is true, he maintained that habit of mind was more important than the contents of that mind. He distinguished between a sound and an educated mind.[28] The implication in this distinction was that strength of mind, perhaps an ability to think, to reason, or to judge, was more important than knowledge. On the other hand, he never tired of measuring the validity of a curriculum, of judging whether or not it was adequate, by referring to criteria that were surely utility-centered. Looking next at his thoughts on the memory, most educational theorists now agree with Locke in his disapproval of the common practice of his time

[28] See p. 355.

of taxing children's minds with the rote memorization of their lessons. Furthermore, he did not believe that the memory could be improved by exercise, for he states that a good memory is due to a "happy constitution." Here he brings into the discussion his peculiar conception of the soul, which is but a *tabula rasa*, an empty and inert capacity, and not a collection of living forces that can be strengthened by exercise. He rejects the idea that any faculties are capable of growth and development. Learning pages of Latin grammar or literature by heart does not fit the memory for the retention of anything else.

On the other hand, the major aim of Locke's pedagogy was to qualify the pupil to use his reason and to subject all his actions to its guidance and control. He did not expect that any of the students who were educated according to his plan would become experts. Rather, he wanted them to have an acquaintance with certain areas of knowledge, or an inclination to travel the avenue that led toward them. Locke sought mental power and activity rather than knowledge, and it was as part of his search that he wrote *The Conduct of the Understanding*. In this work he elaborated many principles for the development of the reasoning process, and described many common-sense methods for ridding the mind of defects which stand in the way of better reasoning. But at the same time he could define education as a practical pursuit which should aim to prepare youth for social living.

As an educational theorist Locke has been variously classified. He has been called a humanist, a realist, a utilitarian, an empiricist, and a disciplinarian, and there are grounds for each designation. It is better not to try to label him, for labels sometimes stand in the way of understanding. Locke was too many-sided to fit into a neat classification.

SUMMARY

The seventeenth century was just about the most active hundred-year period in the history of education. All the educational developments of the century centered around realism. In education, realism meant putting curricula, methods, and students in direct contact with reality for the purpose of preparing young people for the world as it existed in their century, not as it may have existed in the mind of some classical writer.

The greatest educator of the century was John Amos Comenius, a clergyman, a schoolmaster, and an educational theorist. His famous work was *The Great Didactic*. Before him, as ground breakers for philosophical ideals that supported realism, were Francis Bacon and René Descartes. A contemporary whose work constituted an awkward beginning of many of the educational techniques of the nineteenth century was that curious teacher, Wolfgang Ratke. Despite Ratke's real contributions to realistic education, his so-called secret method has probably kept his name in the history of education.

With all the emphasis on realism in education, there is a tendency to forget religion. The two seventeenth-century educational movements that were intimately related to religion were Pietism, with its champion, August Hermann Francke, and the Brothers of the Christian Schools (Christian Brothers), with St. John Baptist de la Salle.

Finally, there is John Locke, a many-sided thinker, who by the end of the century had converted realism into empiricism. He endeavored to center the educational process about the child by noting individual tendencies and capacities, and in this way he foreshadowed the doctrine of individual differences. He is most often remembered for his *tabula rasa* theory, for his views rejecting the doctrine of innate ideas, and for his connection, or supposed connection, with the doctrine of formal discipline.

Questions and Exercises for Study and Discussion

1. How did realism differ from humanism?
2. Distinguish the three types of realism called sense, social, and humanistic.
3. In what ways were the educational doctrines of Francis Bacon and René Descartes alike? How did they differ?
4. Ratke is described as one of the strangest men ever to show an interest in pedagogy. Do you find anything especially strange about his plans and practices?
5. Prepare a brief report summarizing *The Great Didactic*.
6. Report on the life and teaching career of John Amos Comenius.
7. What was Comenius' principal impact on modern education?
8. Compare Comenius' school plans—that is, levels of education—with the plan followed in the United States in the twentieth century.
9. Did Comenius' school of infancy break ground for the kindergarten movement? Explain.
10. Prepare a report on the life of St. John Baptist de la Salle.
11. Discuss the educational accomplishments of the Brothers of the Christian Schools.
12. Compare and contrast the educational positions of John Amos Comenius and John Locke.
13. Why is John Locke called an empiricist?

12

Naturalism in Education in the Eighteenth Century

EDUCATIONAL CONDITIONS

The seventeenth century—the century of the great Comenius—was important for the advancement of educational theory and plans. On the level of practice not a great deal was done. It is true that the Brothers of the Christian Schools instituted their schools in 1682 and, properly speaking, the plan of La Salle belongs to the seventeenth century. Yet the fulfillment of the plan and its prophecies for popular education had to wait until conditions were riper than they were in the last twenty years of the seventeenth century. The practical achievements of the Brothers may be found principally in the eighteenth and later centuries. It was the seventeenth century that gave birth to Pietism and its plans for education. Yet in spite of the eminent worth of Francke and the schools that he founded, no educational revolution took place, and people of the lower and middle classes knew of few opportunities for education. In some ways the eighteenth century, for all the theory and speculation of the earlier period, was not in as good a position to provide educational opportunity as the seventeenth had been.

The schools of the eighteenth century were severely criticized by men who were sensitive to their weaknesses. It was charged, and with plenty of reason, that the elementary schools of this century were generally inadequate. In a nominal way the curricula of these schools included reading, writing, and arithmetic. In practice, although this century, like every other, could boast excellent teachers of skill and dedication, the great majority of schools were conducted under the worst possible conditions. Of course, most of the common people received no education at all.

Teachers were poorly prepared or totally unfitted for their work. They accepted a teaching position when they could find nothing else to do, or they accepted the obligations of a teacher and tried to fulfill them along with their regular occupation or trade. Classes were ungraded; boys and girls, if girls went to school at all, were herded into the same schoolroom and studied whatever the teacher wanted to teach them. The maturity of the student and his scholastic achievement did not give many of these teachers pause; everyone was treated alike. By the time the ordinary child was twelve, if he went to school at all, his educational career was over. What he had been exposed to in school was not evaluated by society, although, in general, he should have been receiving some kind of preparation for life. One wonders if the kind of educational opportunity offered at the advent of the eighteenth century was a preparation for much of anything.

Elementary schools were bad, and the grammar or secondary schools were not much better. These schools may have been able to claim that their teachers were somewhat better prepared than those of the elementary schools and that their curricula were more orderly and more carefully designed. Yet, in spite of this, the schoolwork did not have much relevance to the life in society that young people were expected to lead. Secondary schools were classical schools, and it was claimed almost universally that they were of very low standard. It was said, too, that regardless of its theoretical quality, a classical school could not offer a meaningful educational experience. The pitiful inadequacy of the elementary and secondary schools was duplicated and, in a way, reinforced by the inadequacy of the higher schools—the colleges and universities. It was not unusual or surprising that men of ability, who under ordinary circumstances would want to be associated with institutions of higher learning, refused to have anything to do with the universities.

The picture of education at the beginning of the eighteenth century was a bleak one. The saving feature in all of this, however, was that the people were not deluded by the educational drama that unfolded before them. They were fully aware of the major inadequacies of their schools. It was this consciousness that led them to bring about improvements, and it was these improvements, in practice and theory, together with the popular awareness of the importance of education, that prepared the way for the revolutionary advances in the nineteenth century.

Reference has already been made to the new light that was shed on elementary education by the plans and practices of the Brothers of the Christian Schools. Their program was, perhaps, the real beginning of popular education, at least in France. But the Brothers were not entirely alone. In England the charity school movement was begun. Its purpose was to teach reading, writing, the catechism, and prayers to all who could use the opportunity its schools offered. Also in England, and especially under the auspices of the Church of England, the Society for Promoting Christian Knowledge was organized in 1698. The most obvious purpose of the schools of the society was to promote Christian knowledge by teaching the catechism, but the schools that came into existence—more than two thousand of them in England and Wales—offered instruction in the elements of education as well. Somewhat later in the eighteenth century, England inaugurated the Sunday school movement. This effort to achieve educational reform and greater educational opportunity was undertaken principally by Robert Raikes in 1785. The idea of the Sunday school was to offer instruction in reading, writing, and religion to children who could not come to school during the week.

The educational institutions that resulted from the inspiring work of August Hermann Francke—elementary schools, boarding schools, teacher-training schools—have received brief notice before.[1] Their direct influence upon German education should not be minimized. But they had also an indirect force that was of considerable consequence for the future of education in Germany. Largely as a result of the favorable impression made on him by the Pietistic schools, Frederick William I, the king of Prussia, came to appreciate the need that the common people had for education. In the example that these schools provided he thought he saw a practical way to offer the common people some educational opportunity. In 1717 he promulgated a decree that made attendance in the elementary schools compulsory in Prussia. And later, in 1763, Frederick the Great issued the General School Regulations, which made attendance in school compulsory for all children between the ages of five and fourteen.

We do not need to go into any detail here concerning these school regulations, but we should stress the fact that Prussia's example had far-reaching effects in Europe. It provided the historical foundation and some of the political justification for state control of education.

Not only on the level of lower schools was this precedent for state control effective; the higher schools felt its impact too. The tendency to reform higher schools, the colleges and the universities especially, was of course much less in evidence than the efforts to alter the existing patterns of elementary and secondary education. Higher education touched so few people that reform movements within its institutions naturally lagged considerably behind reform directed at other parts of the educational enterprise. Yet what was done on the level of higher education in Prussia shaped the direction and the tone of higher education for centuries to come. In the first place, the curriculum of the universities in Germany became broader. The change was due largely to the realistic

[1] See pp. 351–352.

movement, and the new curriculum was permeated with the spirit and method of science and modern philosophy. This was an important step forward. More important, however, was the development and finally the acceptance of the doctrine of academic freedom. In the German university, for the first time in the history of higher education, the principle of research and freedom—the freedom of the teacher to study and teach and of the student to study and learn—was accepted as a fundamental foundation for university life. The principle was recognized and affirmed by the government. In the third place, the method of the university was altered radically. The old university, following the medieval model, had honored the practice of lecturing on standard works. The new method was to present the facts and interpretations of scientific findings in lectures, and in seminars to help the students to consolidate what they had learned and to find inspiration for the continuation of their study and research. Finally, the modern university, following the German model, began to serve the rising spirit of nationalism; all the lectures in the modern university were delivered in the vernacular. The whole spirit of modern higher education centered around independence and progress. The university's purpose was to serve mankind, not knowledge.[2]

On the level of secondary education—and still in the German states—we find that the *Realschule* was established. It was a practical school in the sense that it prepared boys for the various vocations in life and did not confine its goals, as the classical schools had done and were doing, to the preparation of boys for the established professions. Johann Julius Hecker (1707–1768) was the man who advanced and implemented the idea for a secondary school with a practical orientation. He established such a school in Berlin in 1747.

EDUCATIONAL IDEALS

Except for a relatively few privileged people, the chances for schooling in the eighteenth century were, as we have seen, not appreciably better than they had been in the seventeenth. The common man or even the middle-class man was in no position to lead theoretical or practical movements to bring about much-needed reforms in education. We have seen a few of the practical changes that were inaugurated. But the theorists were not inactive, and actually the changes in educational theory had their effects not only in the eighteenth but in later centuries as well. There are big changes and big names in this century. The eighteenth century, no less than the centuries that preceded and followed it, was a time of educational ferment.

[2] Friedrich Paulsen, *German Education, Past and Present,* translated by T. Lorenz Charles Scribner's Sons, New York, 1912, pp. 122–123.

In the eighteenth century Germany stands out as the country in which practical educational reforms were most widely and actively instituted. Yet Germany is not the country that attracts our attention when we look for the national home of theoretical reforms in education. This honor belongs to France. More than any other place, France was the home of the Enlightenment.

The educational effects of the Enlightenment are notoriously difficult to assess. It would be hard to find a document of the Enlightenment that was distinctively educational, or to find any leading figure in the movement who could be called an eminent educator. In spite of this, the educational ferment of eighteenth-century France was certainly generated principally by the Enlightenment. We may ask, of course, if there was not something in its doctrine that could explain its influence over education. But the answer would have to be that the doctrine of the Enlightenment is almost undiscoverable and practically inexpressible. In the main, the Enlightenment was a revolt against the established order; it was critical and destructive and individualistic. What did the men of the movement have in common? Such a question either has no answer or else has so many answers that both the question and the answers lose their meaning. Yet we may suggest that the bond which held the men of the Enlightenment together in a kind of loose relationship—not a bond of friendship but an affinity of ideas—was the rejection of authority. It could be called antiauthoritarianism. Nothing that could not be recommended by reason or common sense was accepted; the Enlightenment was coldly and critically rationalistic. And as a reaction to this movement the reformer of the century appeared. He was Jean Jacques Rousseau.

The Enlightenment, with the Encyclopedists as its guardians in France, had glorified reason and had rejected authority. Rousseau was willing, even anxious, to go one step beyond this: Not content with rejecting authority, he rejected reason itself, or, at least, he attacked it with such force that skepticism was the logical outcome. So Rousseau became a reformer who was to reform the reform. He could not agree with the Encyclopedists, however much he might have wanted to see established the reform that they also wanted. Rousseau's position was made quite clear in his *Discourse on the Sciences and the Arts*. It may be said that Rousseau's educational interests began with the *Discourse*, for in it, as elsewhere in his later work, he emphasized the nobility of man and the freedom that ought to be extended to him. With Rousseau we see the first clear signs of the conflict that marked the educational thought of the eighteenth century. On the one hand are the theorists, of whom we shall see more later, who stressed the social objectives of education and the control that the state ought to exercise over it to ensure the attainment of those social objectives. On the other hand is Rousseau, who expressed a doctrine entirely acceptable to a great many common people, that the only justifiable purpose of education was to produce a man. Not a political man or a social man or any other special kind of man, but just a man. On this fundamental level the conflict rested: Are the goals of education social or individual? One attempt at compromise that was offered in the eighteenth century and that has been more or less honored since, was the conclusion that the social and political man can be formed as a by-product when man is educated as man. Another idea which is sometimes accepted is the converse of this: The perfect man may be produced by aiming first at the preparation of a good citizen and a good or worthy member of society. Although these statements were the bases for later disputes in education, they were not the only theoretical positions that were taken. In addition to the educational work of Rousseau, of which we shall see more later,[3] Condillac and Helvétius contributed to the ferment that characterized this century.

Neither Etienne Bonnot de Condillac (1715–1780) nor Claude Adrien Helvétius (1715–1771) achieved any special eminence in eighteenth century educational thought or practice, and neither is much remembered in the history of education. That they have been somewhat neglected is no great historical crime. Yet the full picture of the restlessness of the eighteenth-century educational world would not come into clear focus without a word or two concerning their theories. Both expressed what have been called sensationalist views on education. In a way, both are indebted to the philosophical and psychological thought of John Locke.[4]

In his *Treatise on the Sensations,* a psychological-philosophical work written in 1754, Condillac attempted to develop the suggestion that he had gleaned from Locke's writings that man's senses are not immediately useful to him. In other words, it is necessary for a child to learn to see, to hear, to smell, to taste, and to touch. Condillac was apparently laying a foundation for a formal training of the senses. But he did not follow through on this line of thought. Rather, he proposed the theory that the senses are developed not as detached faculties but as a result of understanding; their development and more complete usefulness follow the evolution of judgment and the improvement of understanding and insight. The first goal of the educator must be, then, not the training of the senses but the awakening of understanding and judgment. At the same time, Condillac's position was that the instruction to which young people were exposed should be graded to fit their intellectual maturity, for their sensitivity to experience depended upon this instruction much more

[3] See pp. 381–388.
[4] See pp. 352–362.

than it depended upon the senses. His ideas, which were not without merit, were more fully developed in a work that appeared in 1775, with a dedication to the grandson of Louis XV, under the title of *Course of Instruction*.

Claude Adrien Helvétius, while he belonged to the same general sensationalist company as Condillac, made an application of his views to education which was quite different from anything proposed by Condillac. In his book *On the Soul*, which appeared in 1757, he set out to prove that all of man's faculties have their foundation in the senses. Observable inequalities among men are not due, he maintained, to the differences that are supposed to exist in innate capacity, for there are no such differences. There are differences in men's experiences, and it is these experiential differences that account for the variations among men. The mind, as Helvétius said in his last book, *On Man, His Intellectual Faculties and His Education*, is nothing more than the sum total of all of a man's experiences. When one mind is better than another, this excellence is due to the quality and quantity of the experiences it has had. Any other interpretation, especially one that would maintain that qualitative differences among men are due to varying gifts from nature, he deplored and rejected. He would even go so far as to say that if two men were educated in the same way and exposed to the same environment, then their minds would be exactly the same.

Although philosophers may say that the writings of Condillac and Helvétius had no great impact on psychological thought—excepting possibly on Behaviorism—or philosophical speculation, we should be mistaken if we thought that education was in no way affected by their views. Almost from their time forward, educational philosophers began to think more and more of the influence the social environment was having on the formation of mind and character. Another view, also, came in for wider acceptance, namely, that there is a common mold from which all men are made and that the development of men depends primarily upon opportunity. Whatever we may think of these ideas, we can hardly disassociate them from the democratic movement in education in the nineteenth and twentieth centuries. There is still one other line of thought that might be mentioned in this connection: If men are really the products of their environment, then society is in a position to control its future by carefully controlling the education that it offers. Here, of course, we see the foundation being laid in the modern world for education as an instrument for social reform. Who can doubt that this was not a sharp departure from the role that pre-eighteenth-century education was expected to play?

The eighteenth century offered a framework in which Condillac, Helvétius, and Rousseau could express their views on education. But these men were not alone. A year after Rousseau's *Emile* appeared, another book on education was published, which was to be especially influential in the last forty years of the eighteenth century. This was the *Essay on National Education* by Louis-René de la Chalotais (1701–1785).

La Chalotais's name is one that is associated with the expulsion of the Society of Jesus from France. This was done in 1764 largely as a result of the unfavorable report that he drew up against the order. This report, entitled *The Constitutions of the Jesuits,* was prepared over the years 1761 and 1762 and appeared in the latter year. Basically, La Chalotais was opposed to political and religious privilege. It was safer to oppose the Jesuits and religious privileges in the eighteenth century than it was to oppose the monarch and political privileges. Yet La Chalotais did not object to the Jesuits because they were a religious society, but because they had almost complete control over French education. The bill of particulars that he made against them was an imposing one. He argued that the Jesuit system of education was inefficient, and he did not pause to consider the testimony—and ample testimony it was—that would contradict this part of his view. He admitted that the boys who studied in Jesuit schools learned Latin, but he insisted that it was bad Latin. Beyond this, his contention was that such scholars knew nothing of the principles of religion, little of the elements of composition—not enough, he said, to write a good letter—and nothing of the fundamentals of right reasoning or argumentation. These charges were made in spite of the reputation for excellence that the Jesuits had in these very areas of instruction. He also called attention to the Jesuits' way of life, their isolation from the real world, and declared that men in such circumstances were unfit to prepare boys for their role as citizens. It was not that their methods were ineffective, for La Chalotais could not really have feared the Jesuits if this were so, but that they placed the Jesuit system—the individual Jesuit, the Society, and its Constitutions—above citizenship, the rulers of the state, and the state itself. With such dedication and devotion, he claimed, the Society could not be trusted to educate the youth of the French nation. We need not pause to examine the authenticity of the charges that La Chalotais leveled at the Society of Jesus. They were effective charges quite apart from whether or not they were true.

The two works of La Chalotais are simply two parts of the total picture that he was drawing. *The Constitutions of the Jesuits* was instrumental in depriving the Society of its opportunity to do educational work in France; the *Essay on National Education* was really a document that seconded all of the charges made in *The Constitutions* and added that with the vacuum created in education with the departure of the Jesuits, a national system of education was needed more than ever. In his plan for a national system of education, La Chalotais did not exclude clerical or religious teachers. It is true that he did not place education in the hands of the religious or of the Church—this was the main point of his opposition to the current state of educational affairs—yet he would not have driven clerical teachers from the schools. He left no room for doubt when he said that clerics who were prepared to teach might teach, or when he called attention to the work of the priests of the Oratory for whom he had a good deal of admiration, or when he demanded that a system of education which was intended for the national good be controlled by the people of the nation, and that laymen, who were the first citizens of the state, should have the first claim on teaching in such national schools. In other words, it is possible to detect both an anticlerical bias and a pro-lay bias in the views of La Chalotais. Considering the near monopoly that the clerics had over education in France, it is not at all surprising that sensitive Frenchmen who were devoted to the spirit of reform should have taken such a stand.

If we were to stop here with a summary of La Chalotais's work and writings, our impression of the man would be quite incomplete and could lead to inaccurate judgments. Perhaps La Chalotais was right when he demanded that education be controlled by the people rather than by members of the clergy or religious orders. He may have been on solid ground when he argued that laymen should play a larger role in shaping the educational future of the French nation. Yet, as we read on in the *Essay on National Education,* we find that he is not unequivocally an educational reformer committed to progress: La Chalotais did not want to extend educational opportunity any more generously than the current practices allowed. As a matter of fact, he would have been in favor of curtailing some of the educational opportunities that the children of France then had. He believed that France had too many students and too many schools. He opposed the educational work of the Brothers of the Christian Schools, not because he did not commend their methods or recognize their successes in teaching poor boys, but because he was convinced that educating people beyond their needs was both dangerous and unnecessary: dangerous for the common welfare and unnecessary for the happiness and welfare of the people involved.

After having settled the questions of who should teach and who should be taught, at least to his own satisfaction, La Chalotais turned to the problems of what should be taught to the privileged few who did attend the schools. Only a word need be said about this phase of La Chalotais's work because, in the first place, it has little to do with the national education theme for which he is so well known and, in the second place, what he had to say on the subject is not very significant. Perhaps the most remarkable thing about his excursion into the realm of practical education was that he completely ignored Rousseau's writings on education. Although he relied heavily on other authorities—Locke, Milton, Bacon—for he was no expert in this area himself, he chose to turn his back on the advice that Rousseau had given. And this is all the more surprising because of the sense of urgency which surrounds the advice of Rousseau and the need for urgency of action which permeates the outlook of La Chalotais. It is said that La Chalotais despised Rousseau and was unwilling to give him any further recognition by an endorsement, or even a mere mention, of any of his proposals. In spite of this antipathy, it is clear that in their attitude toward sense education—what we call sensationalist psychology—Rousseau and La Chalotais had much in common. But there were important differences too; the most important, it would seem, lay between La Chalotais's complete approval of an academic and a classical curriculum and Rousseau's advocacy of natural methods of teaching and learning.

National education is a big subject, much larger than La Chalotais, although he gave it much of its direction and impetus. Behind national education itself there were many pressures for the reform of education, but in themselves these proposals for reform were just recommendations and were in no way patterns for educational revolution. Even the views of Rousseau cannot be called revolutionary, although on one point, the point of control, they contained revolutionary features. And, of course, it may be argued, many of the reform recommendations were made within the context of hope for changes in the administration of education. Thus, behind all of the changes that were proposed for education in eighteenth century Europe, especially in France, was the radical idea that the control of education should be vested in the nation. Although this was a new, and in some respects a revolutionary, concept, it was accepted quickly in many European countries. It found ready acceptance in Germany; its application in France was somewhat slower. Even in England, where very little in the way of a national system of education was established in the eighteenth century, the proposition was viewed with more than mild interest.

Perhaps the greatest change that occurred in the thinking of the people interested in national education was that La Chalotais's contention that the common man does not need education was rejected outright. Its place was taken by the claim that of all the people who need education, the common man is the most important. He must be considered first. He was given this primacy of consideration, logically enough it would seem, for he was the one person in society who could not provide for his own educational needs, even assuming that he was in a position to judge what they were.

In England the nearest thing to a national system of education that evolved in the eighteenth century was the plan for monitorial schools that was devised and put into effect by Joseph Lancaster (1778–1838) and Andrew Bell (1753–1832). This system of monitorial or mutual instruction may have been a step in the right direction, although it was neither high in quality nor generous in the opportunity that it provided. The idea was, of course, that one teacher would be able to instruct very large classes of elementary school children (Lancaster himself taught one hundred youngsters) at an extremely low cost. This would be done by following a plan whereby the teacher would teach the older children and they in turn would teach children younger than themselves. These monitors—student teachers of a sort—would work on down the instructional line until all the children were exposed to some elementary instruction. The only instructional cost would be the money that had to be paid to one teacher.

It may be said that this plan, proposed and developed independently by Lancaster and Bell, had some merit, even though it was largely negative. That is, it demonstrated that large numbers of children could not be given educational opportunity of good quality unless there were adequate administrative controls, financial backing, and instructional personnel and facilities. Yet, the historian would probably have to admit that it was not its inadequacies that caused the plan of mutual instruction to come to a somewhat unceremonious end. Though the other schools of Lancaster were not committed to the teaching of any sectarian doctrines, those of Bell were set in the context of the Established Church and taught her doctrines. In England in the eighteenth century these approaches pleased almost no one, and the dissatisfaction with the way monitorial schools handled religious teaching spelled their failure in England. The schools were not representative of what one could look for in a national system of education, but they marked the tentative beginnings of such a system in Great Britain.

Although England was slow in moving forward, Germany made considerable progress in establishing national education in the eighteenth century. Germany, of course, had something of a head start. We have already seen how as early as 1619 the Duchy of Weimar had required the attendance of boys and girls in school, and how Frederick William and Frederick the Great had accepted this practice and applied it to Prussia.[5] In the eighteenth century, however, the possibilities of national education were even more fully realized in Germany; the moving force at this time was Johann Bernard Basedow (1724–1790).

The educational ideas of Basedow were apparently formed out of a kind of amalgamation of the views of Rousseau and La Chalotais. Basedow was impressed by Rousseau's belief that men learn through natural

[5] See p. 366.

experiences and he made every effort to convert Rousseau's theory into practice by suggesting methods for teachers. These reformed theories and techniques of learning were to be set in the context of a national system of education, like that which La Chalotais had proposed, although Basedow was not very favorably impressed with La Chalotais's commitment to limiting educational opportunity to the privileged classes.

Despite Basedow's profound and long-standing interest in education, it was not until about 1768 that he was able to translate his interest into action. In that year he wrote a book that contained the bases for all of his later educational theories and practices. This book had the rather imposing title of *Representations to Philanthropists and Men of Wealth regarding Schools and Studies and Their Influence on Public Well-being*. Two ideas seem to dominate the work: one is that all education should be approached as if it were play;[6] the other is that the state should create administrative machinery for the control of education. Subsumed under these central ideas is the view that there ought to be two systems of schools constituting a dual system. Separate provisions would be made for the common people and for the upper classes. Also, although religion was not a subject that could be dealt with in summary fashion, Basedow proposed that it should not be taught in the schools of the dual system.

Basedow's first book was followed by two shorter works that dealt with the practical business of managing a school; one was called *The Elementary Book*, the other *The Book of Method*. Neither was intended to reflect Basedow's final attitude or opinion on the questions with which he dealt. In 1774 he published a full length book that purported to integrate and perfect the contents of the two shorter works mentioned above. This new book was entitled *The Elementary Work*. Its purpose was to set forth Basedow's ideas on what should be taught, especially in elementary schools, and on how it should be taught. Thus we may accept this book as being a treatise on curriculum and a treatise on method.

The presentation of material in *The Elementary Work* suffers from lack of order. Some would say that the book is a chaotic expression of Basedow's confused ideas on education. This would be a bit too strong. In spite of the book's defects, it gained a good deal of attention and quite general approval. It contained Basedow's plan for operating an elementary school.

Basedow's ardent wish to open a school of his own was finally realized in 1774, as a result of the munificence of patrons who believed in his work. This school, located in Dessau, was called the *Philanthropinum*. In it he divided the students according to their stations in life and taught them those things that most befitted their positions. The cur-

---

[6] This was a position that John Locke had taken. See pp. 359–360.

riculum had some common features for all children. There were certain things, Basedow said, that all children should know; there were things that were appropriate for middle-class children; finally, there were things that "students" should know.[7] The curriculum was constructed in such a way that the children would get experience appropriate to their various social levels. At the same time, Basedow employed his "playlike" approach to learning. And he never tired of calling to people's attention the need for public support and public control of education. By 1784 Basedow had severed his connection with the Dessau *Philanthropinum*, for reasons that were both personal and professional. Yet Basedow's departure did nothing to dim the popularity of the institution he had fathered. It served as a model for many others, and as the fame of the *Philanthropinums* spread, they could be found all over Germany. Even in other countries pedagogical enthusiasts were able to bring a few into existence. But it was in Prussia that Basedow's influence was felt most, and there the cause of national education was served best. The figure that ought to be mentioned in this connection was Baron von Zedlitz. He was appointed head of the Prussian department of instruction by Frederick the Great and served in that capacity for eighteen years, from 1771 to 1789.

The name of Von Zedlitz is an important one in the history of education. As minister of education in Prussia, he advanced the doctrine of national education far beyond anything that had been seen or heard before. He was responsible for the reorganization of the classical schools (the German Gymnasia that had their origin with Sturm) and for the promotion of the scientific study of education. As a result of the encouragement from the minister of education, the first university chair of pedagogy was established at the University of Halle in 1779. And if this was not enough, he added to the luster that his name enjoyed by bringing into being a Supreme Council of Public Instruction (the *Oberschulcollegium*) that was to superintend all education in Prussia. This council came into existence in 1787. Ten years later an additional step was taken—almost a conclusive step for Germany—when a law was passed that made all colleges and schools of every kind state institutions. With this law, the establishment of a national system of education was almost complete. Only one thing remained to be done and that was to deal with the problem of sectarianism. The schools of Germany had been confessional schools, that is, they had been established to accommodate the various religious preferences of the people. The child from a Catholic home would acknowledge (confess) his religious preference and would be assigned to a Catholic school. The child from a Lutheran home would

[7] When Basedow spoke of students he meant those children who were especially qualified to continue up the educational ladder.

indicate his religious commitment and would be enrolled in a school with a Lutheran religious climate. The sectarian relationship that had for some time been permitted, even encouraged, to exist in Germany came to an end in 1803. A law was passed which eliminated the confessional school.

Other countries lagged behind Germany in the creation of a system of national schools. In most of the countries of Europe the nationalization movement did not become a reality until the next century, and France, as we have said before, did not make any great progress except on the level of theory. We have seen the work and some of the influence of La Chalotais. He was followed by Rolland, Rousseau, Helvétius, Turgot, and Diderot, all in the eighteenth century. All of these men had one thing in common, namely, their convictions that the state alone should be responsible for the education of future citizens and that teachers should be laymen. Rolland expressed this view in his *Report;* Rousseau's ideas on the subject were contained in his *Considerations on the Government of Poland;* Helvétius followed suit in his *On Man,* Turgot in his *Memoirs,* and Diderot in the *Plan for a University,* which he prepared for the Empress of Russia. In spite of the ferment in France, very little of a practical nature was accomplished. Educational theorizing did not lead to effective action. With the outbreak of the French Revolution, inertia was uprooted and the influence of conservatives was destroyed. In 1789 educational reform and reorganization could begin to see some hope. Yet the educational reforms of the Revolution itself were abortive, whether they were initiated by Mirabeau, Talleyrand, Condorcet, Lakanal, Lepelletier, Robespierre, or any of the other revolutionary figures. The numerous educational schemes contained all kinds of ideas, ranging all the way from the most conservative to the most radical. Yet out of the new framework for society that the Revolution devised, the French system of national education took its form. The chief mover was the Marquis de Condorcet (1743–1794). He prepared a *Report* on education for the French Assembly and presented this *Report* to it in 1792. More than any other document, the *Report* was responsible for bringing a national system of education into existence in France.

JEAN JACQUES ROUSSEAU (1712–1778)

Jean Jacques Rousseau, who became a controversial figure, appeared, as many great thinkers do, at a time in history when what he had to say needed to be said. These men of ideas seem almost to vocalize a ferment and desire for reform which exists unexpressed in the people's subconscious mind. Right or wrong, for good or bad, they have inflamed the people and the times in which they lived. Because a man achieved popularity with humanity for what he said at one time, does not mean that his words had universal value or even that they have any validity for later periods. He may have merely possessed a volatile eloquence, while the ideas he thus made attractive may have rested on a fallacious philosophical assumption.

This inflation is especially prevalent in the field of education, where so much has been said and written by so many for so long a time. It is, therefore, constantly necessary to reevaluate an educational thinker to determine what actually his influence was in his own times, what it has been in subsequent periods, and what it should be for the present and the future. This reviewing is important because if he was a great expounder of verities, he should be constantly studied for what he has to offer to teachers in educating the young. If he was not a thinker of consequence, then it would be better to put him out of the main stream of educational history. It would seem, at least at this point in history, that the work and the words of Rousseau cannot be put aside.

The Man

Jean Jacques Rousseau was born in Geneva, June 28, 1712, of French Protestant parents. His family was middle-class, his father being, at the time of Rousseau's birth, a watchmaker by trade. His mother died when he was born. The absence of maternal influence in Rousseau's early childhood affected his life considerably, and the lack of maternal care resulted in his extolling motherhood and its responsibilities, almost excessively, in Book I of *Emile*.

Very early, then, Rousseau was placed in the guardianship of a paternal aunt. Her care did not seem to be a substitute for that of a real mother, as it might have been if she had been affectionate by nature. W. H. Hudson suggests that "under the aunt's care, the precocious boy learned nothing of restraint, obedience, self-denial, but rather conceived against all rule that deep aversion which was to mark him through life."[8]

Indeed, this lack of respect for authority seems to have been further engendered by Rousseau's father, who possessed no sense of responsibility himself, either in regard to money or family. It is interesting and perhaps important to note that, possibly by imitation, the boy developed the same attitude. Jean Jacques venerated his father throughout his life, no matter what he did or how he felt toward his son. Considering his disorganized childhood, we cannot find it surprising that Rousseau received no formal education. He claims later that his progress in spite of this neglect is one argument against institutionalized education. He is convinced that his personal natural education enabled him to develop

[8] William Henry Hudson, *Rousseau and Naturalism in Life and Thought*, T. & T. Clark, Edinburgh, 1903, pp. 4–5.

into a natural mature adult. Romain Rolland is sure that "his greatest teacher was not any book. His master was nature . . . nature imbued his whole being. . . ."[9]

His interest in reading was stimulated by association with his father, whose reading preferences were not commendable. They read cheap French romances which emphasized the sensational and the sensual. This led to a premature stirring of passion in the lad, hardly on the level of the ideal. Early family life was, of course, hectic under these conditions. There seems to have been a "lack of any sense of home ties and duties [which] was part of that general spirit of vagabondage which seemed a tradition in the Rousseau family."[10] An older brother, characterized as a scoundrel, ran away from the family and was never heard of or from again. Indeed, the father himself was forced to flee, because of a quarrel and resulting legal trouble.

Subsequently Rousseau was placed under the care of his father's brother-in-law, Gabriel Bernard. Later he was boarded in a minister's home for two years, where certain moral restrictions were developed. It was here, at Boissey, that young Rousseau's passionate love of nature and country pursuits was nurtured, possibly as an escape from any responsibilities which might be imposed upon him. Later Rousseau returned to his uncle in Geneva and occasionally visited his father.

Between 1725 and 1728, he was articled to a notary, who discharged him for his ways, and apprenticed to an engraver, who, Rousseau felt, mistreated him. In 1728, when he was sixteen, he finally, and one might add almost inevitably, ran away. Falling in with an elderly curé during his wanderings, Rousseau was given a letter of introduction by this man to a Mme de Warens, a recent convert to Catholicism. These associations seem to have continued the pattern of unusual life experiences begun as early as his infancy. This Mme de Warens exercised "a despotic force [in] the life of the shy yet sensuous youth, who had accidentally drifted under her spell."[11] Under her influence, Rousseau was sent to a monastery at Turin, where he was baptized a Catholic. This conversion was apparently not an affair of the soul but only an expedient means of getting along at the moment. It is interesting to observe that later he became a Protestant again. The monastery gave him some money and secured employment for him as a lackey in the household of the Comtesse de Vercelles.

Rousseau, while still in this position, was accused of stealing, lied to protect himself, and placed the blame on a young servant girl. His result-

[9] Romain Rolland, André Maurois, and Edouard Heriot, *French Thought in the Eighteenth Century*, David McKay Company, Inc., New York, 1953, p. 7.

[10] Hudson, *op. cit.*, pp. 7–8.

[11] *Ibid.*, p. 14.

ing unpopularity prompted him to move to the household of the Comte de Gouvon, where he was taught Latin and Italian by a young son of the family. Here it was that he was influenced by a Savoyard ecclesiastic, who served as a pattern for the Cicaire Savoyard in Book IV of *Emile* in his presentation of a natural, deistic religiosity.

Eventually Rousseau was dismissed from this position. He wandered for a while and then returned to Mme de Warens. But this association and some of the others that he struck up were short-lived. We find him next in Paris, on his first visit to the great French city. His reaction to Paris was unfavorable, and rather than live in the city he took refuge in the countryside, where he encountered the peasants and where, it is said, he gathered some of his ideas for social reform. R. L. Archer maintained that "his youthful wanderings brought him into contact with the French peasant and convinced him that French society rested on a wrong basis."[12] Whether or not this short visit to Paris and its environs had a decisive effect on Rousseau's social ideals cannot be determined. In any case, he did not remain near Paris long, but returned to Mme de Warens in 1732. He was ill for a time, worked intermittently at odd jobs, and in 1740 tried tutoring, unsuccessfully, for a very short period of time. Though this was his only encounter with an experience in teaching, he seems to have gained enough insight into pedagogical method to comment on it at great length in *Emile*.

Shortly after this, in 1741, he returned to Paris and tried to make a place for himself. After trying to do several different things with indifferent success, he became secretary to the ambassador to Venice. But this position did not suit him either, and in 1743 we find him back in Paris again. At this time in his life Rousseau met and formed a lasting association with Thérèse de Vasseur. Several children were born of this union, and all of them were abandoned, for which cruelty Rousseau blamed society, which did not provide him with the wherewithal to support them. Once again we see his refusal to accept responsibility and his habit of absolving himself from all blame. Cassirer suggests that "the fact that Rousseau confesses to abandoning his five natural children at a foundling home does not affect the merits of the educational plan in *Emile*.[13]

Meanwhile Rousseau became the intimate companion of people of social and literary prominence. Among them may be noted Richelieu and Diderot, for whose encyclopedia he wrote an article on music. A certain

[12] R. L. Archer (ed.), *Rousseau on Education,* Edward Arnold & Co., London, 1928, p. 8.

[13] Ernst Cassirer, *The Question of Jean-Jacques Rousseau,* translated and edited by Peter Gay, Columbia University Press, New York, 1954, p. 15. This observation is unquestionably valid; yet Rousseau's educational theory is often condemned simply because Rousseau did not provide an adequate environment for his own offspring.

notoriety attached to Rousseau from these activities, as well as from the essays which he wrote for contests sponsored by the Academy of Dijon. One dealt with the effect of the progress of civilization on morals; it was in this article that Rousseau proposed the paradox of the superiority of the savage state. The other included a discussion of "The Origin of Inequality." Archer believes that "the question propounded for a prize essay by the Academy of Dijon, whether the progress of the arts had contributed to human happiness, suggested to him the further stage in his thought that modern civilization was not wrong merely by accident but in virtue of its inherent character as civilization."[14] These were views that seemed to appeal to that portion of society which Rousseau had under attack. This society did not take him seriously, but it liked to play with dangerous things, and his ideas seemed to have an element of danger in them.

This brush with fame was terminated for Rousseau by another period of illness, which caused him to retire for six years, from 1756 to 1762, to the Hermitage, a place secured for him by a patroness. It was here that he became involved, in 1756, in an argument in writing with Voltaire over the social significance of the catastrophic Lisbon earthquake. Here, also, he published his major writings: *Julie, ou la Nouvelle Héloïse* (1760), *Le Contrat Social* (*The Social Contract*, 1762), and *Emile* (1762). The publication of these works and the subsequent public reaction brought an end to his stay in the country in 1762. *Emile* was banned by the Parliament of Paris; the book was also banned by Catholics and Protestants alike for its rejection of institutions and authority and for its decided deistic bias. Because of imagined or real persecutions, Rousseau fled first to Geneva, then into asylum granted by Frederick the Great, and, finally, to England, under the auspices of the philosopher, David Hume. In 1770, at the age of fifty-eight, Rousseau returned to Paris. He lived in relative seclusion at Ermenonville until he died, July 2, 1778.

Rousseau's Emile

Rousseau's *Emile* is a thought-provoking book. It is all the more so in the light of Rousseau's life and experiences. He possessed the ability to observe glaring faults in the French social and educational structure and to call attention to them in his writings in a dramatic way. He appeared at a time when man's social and educational institutions had become so solidified and stratified that they had lost touch with changing times and circumstances. Rousseau believed that the needs of educational reform included a return to nature, a development of the natural man, a simplification of the whole scholastic regime, a reassertion of the wholesomeness of childhood, and a removal of cramping restraints and

[14] Archer, *op. cit.*, p. 8.

clumsy educational machinery. *Emile* was published in 1762 when Rousseau was fifty years old. The fundamental idea on which all the proposed educational reforms were based was that the essential liberty of natural man should be safeguarded by education and really assured by the lawmakers.

The book is organized into five parts, or books. Book I deals with the years from infancy to age five; Book II, from age five to twelve; Book III, from age twelve to fifteen; Book IV, from age fifteen to twenty or twenty-two;[15] Book V discusses the education of women. The first four books represented what Rousseau believed to be the natural and important periods in the growth of the child. *Emile* is not merely a discussion of educational theory. It is an example of education in action, not in abstract statement but through the story of a child selected for experiment. The child is Emile. Rousseau's emphases in education would seem to be nature's own education, education by things and from men. There is no doubt at all that Rousseau's interest in education was deep and genuine; he believed that reform was urgently called for.

Rousseau approached the whole question of education from the point of view of social theory; he began, in *Emile*, to remold society by remolding the individual. His aim of education was to make the person a unit, a whole being, capable of finding himself in society. His theory of education was concerned with facilitating the direct and unconscious unfolding of the individual, with assuring the right of the natural man through thwarting outer hindrances and everything that might cause distortion. He felt that education must perform both negative and positive functions; it must clear away hindrances and must open a way for the natural development of the powers of the individual.

A main thesis of *Emile* seems to be that "everything is good . . . as it leaves the hand of the author of nature; everything deteriorates in the hand of man." Indeed, the first sentence of Book I is, "God makes all things good; man meddles with them and they become evil." Rousseau asserts that man develops in, rather than is molded by, society. The educational process he advocates is based on the assumption that the child's autonomous tendencies are sound, and that he need not, therefore, be subjected to authority. The order in which human abilities mature must be observed; this is the key to the education of natural man.

Emile is rather difficult to read because it is full of repetitions, digressions, and extraneous matter, and everywhere it is clogged with detail. Understanding of Rousseau's thought is further complicated by the fact that his philosophical system is unscientific, superficially rational, based

---

[15] This section includes an interpolated part, *Profession of Faith of a Savoyard Vicar*. This is the section of the book which caused the denunciation and banning by Catholics and Protestants and led to much of Rousseau's persecution.

on emotion, and more prophetic than philosophical.[16] This difficulty of reading is increased by the nature of Rousseau's brand of eloquence. He has been called a "coiner of happy phrases."[17] This has resulted in an emphasis on parts of his work rather than on the total message contained in it. Another reason for difficulty is that Rousseau lacked interest in empirical evidence, preferring instead his abstract propositions. His style and vocabulary put additional burdens upon the reader; he uses words in uncommon ways. A final impediment is provided by the difficulty of interpreting Rousseau's work in terms of his life. Rousseau himself anticipated something of this when he wrote: "My words are often contradictory, but I do not think there is any contradiction in my ideas."[18]

Book I of *Emile* deals with the period from infancy to age five. The main purpose to be achieved during this period is to make the child simple and rugged. This is the time for teaching the child how to preserve his own life when he becomes a man. To do this, self-knowledge and self-control become arts indispensable to life and happiness. Much of Book I is a preliminary presentation of the basic ideas of education in general, rather than a discussion of the particular age period. Rousseau explains at great length his ideas about the teacher. He states that one man only can educate one pupil. This teacher must be well educated himself, or he cannot lead others. Efficient teaching is a question of guidance more than of instruction. He also asserts that the teacher should not give precepts; he must let the student find them out for himself. Rousseau seems to emphasize self-education.

Further generalizations on the subject of education are delineated in Book I. Rousseau maintains that it is ordinary people who have to be educated; the others will find their way alone. He presumes that the poor man has no real need for formal schooling, for the education of his own station in life is forced upon him; he can rise to no other. Rousseau also expresses the view that education begins with life; experience precedes instruction. It is the recurrence of emotional experience which creates the force of habit. Education, therefore, should begin before the child can speak or understand. Logically, he presumes that "sense experiences are the raw material of thought."[19]

In Book II Rousseau deals with the years from five to twelve. It is in writing of this period that Rousseau's negativism seems most apparent. Education, he thinks, ought to be purely negative to shield the heart from vice and the mind from error. By negative education he means "to

[16] Rolland et al., *op. cit.*, p. xx.

[17] Cassirer, *op. cit.*, pp. 13–17.

[18] Jean Jacques Rousseau, *Emile,* translated by Barbara Foxley, E. P. Dutton & Co., Inc., New York, 1938, p. 72.

[19] Rousseau, *op. cit.*, p. 31.

do nothing and allow nothing to be done . . . not to gain time, but to lose it." He never tired of insisting upon the right of childhood to exist for its own sake. During this period, the main thing is to keep Emile in free and constant intercourse with nature. Rousseau suggests in Book II that education and educators should love children, indulge them in their sports, their pleasures, and their delightful instincts. For just as manhood has its place in the sequence of things, so childhood has its place in the sequence of human life. The man must be treated as a man and the child as a child. This is his reason for saying that the education of the early years should be negative. The child should be allowed to follow his own inclinations, for they are natural to him and therefore always right. Thus, for Rousseau, the most important, the most useful rule of education is: Do not save time, but lose it.

At age twelve, education really begins. This period, which is treated in Book III, covers the years from twelve to fifteen. Adolescence is the time for work, for instruction, and for inquiry. This period, then, marks the beginning of intellectual education. The motives for such education, according to Rousseau, should always be curiosity, interest, pleasure, and never constraint. For the spirit in Rousseau's system is to put Emile in the way of learning and to give him the power of grasping important things for himself. The choice of studies, then, will be based on the principle of utility within the range of the student's comprehension. First-hand knowledge is real knowledge. For example, Rousseau does not counsel students to learn science, but to discover it.

This point of view is, of course, consistent with Rousseau's opposition to authority and bookishness in education. As a matter of fact, he is quite systematic in his discouragement of the use of books or any other aids to education. He maintains that the misuse of books is the death of sound learning. Actually only one book appeared to have any value for this strange theorist: *Robinson Crusoe*. He granted this book some value because it afforded a complete treasury of natural education; it showed man how he could learn the means of self-preservation, and it emphasized the dignity of labor.

Three stages in this educational development are delineated by Rousseau; stages governed by necessity, usefulness, and finally, by what is fitting and right. He suggests that to limit our desires is the same thing as to increase our strength. For the only truths of value in life are those acquired by knowledge of man's relation to his fellowmen. In the educative process the pupil must learn that ignorance never did anyone any harm; error alone is fatal; and we do not lose our strength through ignorance, but through self-confidence. Curiously, barely five pages further, Rousseau says that if a student never makes mistakes he will never learn anything well. Evidently he distinguishes between error and mistake!

Basic to the education during these years is the question: What is the use of that? Rousseau says that "this is the sacred formula by which he and I [teacher and student] test every action of our lives."[20] Never tell the child what he cannot understand. It is not the teacher's business to teach the student the various sciences, but to give him a taste for them and to point out the methods of learning them when his taste is more mature. Rousseau asserts that "this is assuredly a fundamental principle of all good education."[21]

He proceeds then to point out that we badly need someone to teach us the art of learning with difficulty. For, as our apparatus becomes more ingenious, the coarser and more unskillful become our senses. He says, "We surround ourselves with tools and fail to use those which nature has provided everyone of us."[22] Thus, he reasserts, our real teachers should be experience and emotion. In organizing the educative process, Rousseau would encourage teaching by doing whenever possible; words should be used only when doing is impossible. The end of this process will be well-trained minds, which should be "the pillars on which human knowledge is most deeply engraved."[23]

Book III concludes with a few final and general comments. First, that we must fit a man's education to his real self, not to what is no part of him. It is disclosed here that the "great secret of education is to use exercise of mind and body as relaxation one to the other."[24]

Book IV covers the years from fifteen to twenty or twenty-two. Ethical and moral training are the prime concerns of this period. Rousseau thinks that the delay in beginning this phase of education is necessary because of the previous immature level of comprehension. "To announce a truth to those who are not intellectually mature enough to receive it, is equivalent to indoctrinating the mind with error."[25] Rousseau, in his "natural" religion, stresses two great truths: the existence of God and the existence of the soul of man. Beyond these, virtue is mainly a matter of the state of the heart. The institutions of religion become unimportant; the interactions of human beings are the important things. For Rousseau, morality is the end of religion. Ethical training is accomplished by turning self-love, which is potential alike for good or evil, to the interests of good. The foundations of morality are to be found in the sensibilities. The natural process in this formation will begin with self-love, develop into selfishness with its concurrent tendency to compare one's self with others,

[20] Rousseau, *op. cit.*, p. 142.
[21] *Ibid.*, p. 135.
[22] *Ibid.*, p. 139.
[23] *Ibid.*, p. 147.
[24] *Ibid.*, p. 165.
[25] *Ibid.*, p. 200.

and culminate in general well-being, which will generate a love of the human race and the realization that everyone is fundamentally like everyone else.

In Book IV Rousseau also decries a prevalent "rage for systems" in various subject areas, in proof of which he cites the way in which history was organized and taught during his time. During these years, he continues paradoxically, to guide a grown man, you must reverse all that you did to guide the child. Early education is a preparation of the child for education. Now, education should begin with the study of the essentials of humanity, of all that really constitutes mankind. Here, he asserts, the study of history is valuable for it reveals men as they are and provides a basis for judging them. In institutionalized education, history was being subjected to the wrong approach. As a remedy, Rousseau suggests the use of Thucydides, because he relates only those facts which can be of value in developing judgment. In fact, Rousseau claims that all ancient authors were better because they were nearer to nature.

Continuing this discussion, he asserts that the proper study of mankind involves three prerequisites: a great wish to know man, a great impartiality of judgment, and a sensitive heart, capable of understanding human passion and calm enough to be free from passion.[26] He suggests a parallelism that should be considered: Society must be studied in the individual and the individual in society.

Turning then to the restlessness of youth, which seemed to be quite evident during those times, Rousseau notes that teachers complain that the energy of this age makes their pupils unruly. However, he intimates that possibly the teachers themselves are to blame, for, far from being a hindrance to education, this "enthusiasm of education is its crown and coping stone."[27] If a pupil sees the value of a teacher's efforts, his appreciation will inculcate respect for authority and natural discipline.

Book V is concerned with Emile's search for a proper life companion and his eventual marriage. This part contains more narrative than the previous books, and it terminates with the expectation of Emile's first child. The task of education by the teacher is complete; the father now assumes that role for his child. Most of this part of the book is concerned with the education of girls, and much of it is today anachronistic because of the drastic changes in the status of women. The basic theme is the same—natural development in education. Rousseau begins by pointing out that woman differs from man only in degree. He suggests, again ironically, that in man and woman nature has contrived to make two beings alike and yet different. The man should be strong and active; the woman should be weak and passive; the one must have both the power and the will; it is enough that the other should offer little resistance.

[26] *Ibid.*, p. 206.
[27] *Ibid.*, p. 194.

He contends that "woman is specially made for man's delight."[28] The passions are restrained in men by reason, in women by modesty. Woman's inequality under the law is right because of the force of reason. Yet, curiously, stronger men are produced because of strong women, weaker— in the sense of softer—men from weak women.

The difference in the sexes necessitates a difference in education. A woman's education must be planned in relation to man, for she is the source of his early education. The ends of women's education are to be pleasing in men's sight, to win men's respect and love, to train men to manhood, to counsel and console them, and to make men's lives pleasant and happy. Of prime importance in achieving these goals is the teaching of self-control. In other words, utility governs man's education while "what will please man" governs woman's education. Since woman is not governed by reason, she needs more authority and guidance in education. She should be taught to love duties by considering the advantages to be derived from them. Since men reason and women observe, the latter's studies should be thoroughly practical and directed toward the study of man and the formation of taste. The ultimate objectives are taste without deep study, talent without art, and judgment without learning.

Epitomizing this approach is Sophy, Emile's perfect mate, whom he finds, naturally, while wandering through the countryside. Her practical accomplishments include needlework, lace-making, and housekeeping. Her religion is reasonable and simple, with few doctrines and fewer observances; her morality has been taught in the guise of pleasure and fun. Sophy comes from the lower level of society, for, Rousseau admits, in a class society, it is better to marry beneath one's station than above.

Another portion of Book V is concerned with the culmination of Emile's natural education, the final phase of becoming a social being. He begins by suggesting that we, as human beings, are bound to be what nature has made us at any given age. In developing his social theory of education, we must remember that all our natural inclinations are right. Rousseau advocates a theory based on this principle, the theory of the social contract: "Every one of us contributes his goods, his person, his life, to the common stock, under the direction of the general will; while as a body we receive each member as an indivisible part of the whole."[29] Rousseau maintains that the social contract is, or should be, the foundation of all civil society, and it is in the nature of this contract that we must seek the nature of the society formed by it. This is natural because there is not and cannot be any other fundamental law, properly so called, except the social contract. The two contracting parties are the individual and the public. This contract, in operation in society, will

[28] *Ibid.*, p. 322.
[29] *Ibid.*, p. 424.

admit the existence of free individuals, who do what is right voluntarily, because they desire it, and not through a sense of duty. Rousseau adds that "the further we get from equality, the greater the change in our natural feelings."[30] This socializing process is to be achieved in education by the processes already set forth: first, self-love; then, selfishness; and finally, love of humanity.

The book is concluded by Emile's acknowledgment that he owes much to his teacher, that he will always need him and his example, and that it is now his turn to do the same for his anticipated son. In *Emile* Rousseau has proposed, not a plan for education, but a doctrine to inspire it. He was fully aware of what he was doing, and never for a moment did he believe that he was providing anything more than literary inspiration and broad educational goals for those who follow in his footsteps. It is impossible to point to the direct results of Rousseau's views on education, yet it is easy to find educators who were influenced by him; perhaps it is impossible to find one who was not. Of all of the educators of the modern world who looked to Rousseau for inspiration and consciously tried to apply his theory in practice, none stands out more clearly than Johann Heinrich Pestalozzi.

THE NATURAL METHODOLOGY OF PESTALOZZI (1746–1827)

Johann Heinrich Pestalozzi was born at Zurich on January 12, 1746, of Italian Protestant refugees who had settled in that city toward the middle of the sixteenth century. His father died when he was five, and after this his mother had to practice a most rigid economy. "My mother," Pestalozzi was to write later, "sacrificed herself with the most utter self-devotion to the bringing up of her three children, depriving herself of everything which at her age and in her surroundings could have had attractions for her."[31] Pestalozzi attributes to this exclusively maternal influence his exaggerated sensitivity, and the lack of manly qualities which a paternal example would have helped to develop. Throughout his school life he was awkward and clumsy, and he always lacked the polish and social graces of the typical gentleman. While he was in school he made few friends and was often the brunt of his schoolmates' jokes. Equally disappointing to him was what he considered to be an extremely unrealistic education. "We imagined we could prepare ourselves thoroughly for the petty civic life in one of the Swiss cantons, by a superficial school knowledge of the great Greek and Roman civic life."[32]

[30] *Ibid.,* p. 369.
[31] Quoted in A. Pinloche, *Pestalozzi and the Foundation of the Modern Elementary School,* Charles Scribner's Sons, New York, 1912, pp. 3–4.
[32] *Ibid.,* p. 7.

Education became Pestalozzi's profession almost by accident. He had studied for the ministry and actually undertook the work of a pastor for a very brief period. He became so disturbed emotionally while giving his first sermon that he decided to give up any aspirations he had for an ecclesiastical career. He was familiar with Rousseau's works, especially *Emile,* and when the ministry no longer held any attraction for him, he turned to education. Almost as a matter of faith, he accepted the Rousseauistic doctrine of natural education, and to implement this doctrine in a practical way he bought a farm on which he hoped to operate a school according to Rousseauistic principles. Although no one could have had more sincere intentions, the man was simply not prepared to operate a school of any kind. He had ideals, but he had little else. In time the debts piled too high for any kind of management. Pestalozzi's first educational venture failed.

Pestalozzi knew in a very general way what he wanted to accomplish; the failure of his school-farm experiment led him to develop a more thorough plan. The first steps in this plan were made when Pestalozzi undertook to educate his own son according to the ideas contained in Rousseau's *Emile.* He even went so far as to name his son, Jacques, after Rousseau. Pestalozzi envisioned an educational environment which would offer opportunities for work experiences and elementary learning. At the same time, he never lost sight of Rousseau's proposals; he was consistent in seeking a method that would follow the order of nature, and he was resolute in organizing a curriculum of significant experiences that would lead to high goals.

Almost from the beginning of his ventures into education, Pestalozzi engaged in writing books and pamphlets on various social topics, including education. The first part of his most important work, *Leonard and Gertrude,* appeared in 1781. In it he described a village community, and called the attention of his readers to the conditions under which so many of the lower classes lived. Throughout *Leonard and Gertrude* Pestalozzi stressed two points which are fundamental to his theory of education: the necessity of extending sympathy or, at the very least, justice to the poor, and the importance of a mother's love, personified in Gertrude, the heroine of the story.

In 1785, he published the second and third parts of *Leonard and Gertrude.* In the second part, he drew up a list of the various kinds of injustice and tyranny that were prevalent. In the third part, he pointed to the remedies that should be put into force to alleviate the sad conditions. The first reform, he advised, should begin with the schoolmaster, the second with the school. "After all," he said, "we can do very little with the people, unless the next generation is to have a very different training from that which our schools furnish. The school ought really to stand in the closest connection with the life of the home, instead of, as now, in strong contradiction to it."[33] He went on to condemn the unprogressive, old-fashioned schoolteacher who could neither read nor write, and he criticized, in particular, the sanitary conditions in the village schools.

Leonard and Gertrude is a didactic novel. In Pestalozzi's story the old-fashioned schoolmaster is replaced by a young lieutenant, who is a disabled war veteran. Like the hero in an old-time melodrama, the lieutenant begins his crusade against filth, laziness, and disorder. Gertrude lends moral support by insisting that what she has done with ten children, the new teacher can do with forty. When the new type of education begins in the story, the children do a great deal of manual work and receive instruction in the three R's. Teaching methods are much emphasized: how to maintain good order without harshness, how to encourage good habits, and how to instruct from nature in those things that are most essential. The children are taught to pay particular attention to what they see and hear because accurate observation through the senses is the first step toward real knowledge. The author puts it this way: "Besides reading, all were to learn writing and arithmetic, which previously had only been taught to the more wealthy, in private lessons. . . . He [the lieutenant] cared for their heads as he did for their hearts, demanding whatever entered them should be plain and clear as the silent moon in the sky. To insure this, he taught them to see and hear with accuracy, and he sought to give them a thorough training in arithmetic; for he was convinced that arithmetic is the natural safeguard against error in the pursuit of truth."[34]

The third volume of this educational novel was intended to demonstrate how the same beauty and strength that characterized nature could likewise be found in men, and in the fourth part, Pestalozzi was concerned with the inadequacies of the legal system and drew up long lists of suggested reforms. The young, up-to-date schoolmaster was shown to be the only person who could bring about any great improvement in the laws that govern society, and his views and suggested reforms, inspired the ruler of a neighboring principality to put into effect laws that would protect his subjects against corruption, abuse, and the miscarriage of justice.

After completing the four parts of *Leonard and Gertrude*, Pestalozzi believed that he had communicated his message to the world. He was surprised and dismayed to discover that it was not understood. Thereafter, almost everything that he wrote, including *How Gertrude Teaches*

---

[33] Johann H. Pestalozzi, *Leonard and Gertrude*, translated and abridged by Eva Channing, D. C. Heath and Company, Boston, 1906, p. 118.

[34] *Ibid.*, pp. 153 and 157.

Her Children, was written to explain the deeper meaning in *Leonard and Gertrude.* Almost everything that he did was a practical implementation of the ideals that were clothed in the fiction of *Leonard and Gertrude.* Pestalozzi became a schoolmaster in the most practical sense.

At Stanz he assembled and instructed a number of children who had lost their homes because of the ravages of the French Revolution. He tried to do in the orphanage school at Stanz what the lieutenant had done in the novel. But there were factors in the real situation at Stanz that could not be found in the fictional community he had described. He met hostility from the predominantly Roman Catholic population, who considered him to be an intruder and a heretic. He tried hard, nevertheless, to create a family spirit in the community, with mutual feelings of love, gratitude, and unselfish regard for others. In spite of Pestalozzi's high ideals and his hopes for achieving good, the school was closed and the children were moved elsewhere. By this time, Pestalozzi's knowledge of teaching techniques and practical school problems and children's broad interests had been greatly enriched. When he started out to be an educator he was only a theorist; now, in addition to the theory, to which he remained true, he had all the knowledge that the practical schoolmaster must have. As far as teaching techniques were concerned, he was especially interested in those that would cultivate the powers of attention, observation, and memory. It is interesting to learn how his insights into methodology were formed; he has given us a glimpse of this formation. "As I had to teach the children single-handed, I learned the art of teaching many at once, and as I had no other means than that of repeating aloud to them and making them repeat what I had said after me, the idea occurred that they should draw, write and work while they learned."[35] Pestalozzi felt that this oral repetition by the children while they were actively engaged in another job, not only formed the vocal cords, exercised attention and memory, but at the same time prepared the children for doing work in a lifetime activity in which the attention had to be divided without being distracted.[36]

While he was at the Burgdorf school, Pestalozzi attempted to concentrate on the teaching of reading by one simple method of instruction. Since he believed sound to be the first elementary means of instruction,

[35] Quoted in Pinloche, *op. cit.,* pp. 33–34.

[36] Pestalozzi's first assistant at the school in Burgdorf leaves us his impression of this method: "He [Pestalozzi] had almost brazen lungs, and anyone who had not, would have to give up all idea of speaking or rather shouting continuously as he did. Even if I had had such lungs myself, I should often have desired that he and his class, might have used more moderation and lowered their voices. There were other points on which I could not entirely agree with him: He wanted to teach two subjects at the same time: he tried especially to combine exercises in speaking with freehand drawing and writing." (Quoted in Pinloche, *op. cit.,* p. 41.)

he collected combinations of syllables and had the children repeat them aloud. It appeared to him that it was only common sense that sounds should be stamped on the mind before the first letters are put before the child's eyes and any exercises in formal reading are begun. This type of approach, somewhat similar to phonetic analysis, made his students appear more advanced than students taught by the conventional methods, though whether their greater achievement was apparent or real remained an open question. Herbart, for one, had some doubts about the method, although he was in general agreement with Pestalozzi on many points about the educative process. In commenting on the method, he said: "The committing to memory of names, sentences, and the apparent lack of concern as to whether it was all understood cause me to doubt and put questions."[37]

In the Institute of Education which he opened and in the book, *How Gertrude Teaches Her Children*, Pestalozzi advanced both actual and written educational principles which he hoped to perpetuate. The book, published in 1801, was made up of a series of fourteen letters. The main idea expressed in *How Gertrude Teaches Her Children* was that first impressions of objects or sense perceptions are the basis for our knowledge, and that it is possible to establish a natural method of classification for them. Education would and should become a science, obeying definite laws. The knowledge gained from sense impressions could be clarified and developed by means of three concepts: number, form, and language. This is the way Pestalozzi put it: "When a confused conglomeration of objects is brought before our eyes, and we wish to dissect it and gradually make it clear to ourselves, we have to consider three things: (1) how many things and how many kinds of things there are before our eyes, i.e., their number; (2) what they are like, i.e., their form; (3) what they are called, i.e., their names."[38] According to this view, children should be taught to consider each object that is brought before them both as a separate unit in itself and as a member of a family of related objects; and they should consider in the same way the words which apply to or describe the object studied.

Through the use of objects which gave the child the sense perceptions so essential to learning, the child could see that the data assembled by his own observation were real and meaningful. The teacher, in turn, could present a problem mainly by questions phrased in terms of the child's observations, and the child's interest would stimulate his mind to work on a solution. This was the beginning of the "object lesson" as

[37] Quoted in Melvin C. Baker, *Foundations of John Dewey's Educational Theory*, King's Crown Press, New York, 1955, p. 62.

[38] Johann H. Pestalozzi, *How Gertrude Teaches Her Children*, translated by Lucy E. Holland and F. C. Turner, 5th ed., C. W. Bardeen, Syracuse, N.Y., 1915, p. 47.

a formal approach in teaching methods. Counting objects would provide for significant experiences in arithmetic; drawing them would give lessons in form and would be related to writing; instruction in their names could develop a knowledge of language. Good teachers would develop techniques that would engage the student (self-activity), and this activity would produce the best results when it followed the psychological order of learning, passing from the simple to the complex, from the known to the unknown. Pestalozzi was certain that by this time education would have provided the means of giving the right experiences, the right training and environment, to produce the right kind of citizen for the state. Both of Pestalozzi's chief goals—improving the condition of the individual man and improving society by the cumulative bettering of the state members of society—would be achieved by education.

It was largely through Pestalozzi's insistence upon the three main principles of his method that educators began to place more stress upon teacher preparation. The reduction of all subjects to unanalyzable elements, the teaching of these subjects by carefully graded steps, the use of the object lesson and the oral teaching of all subjects, the subordination of the textbook and the greater emphasis placed on perception, individual judgment, and generalization made the preparation of a better-educated and more skillful teacher an imperative.[39]

Pestalozzi's Influence and the Main Points of His Pedagogy

A quarter of a century before Pestalozzi's death, he achieved the kind of stature and fame that no one could have predicted for him when he was forty years old. He was made a citizen of the French Republic, was honored by kings and heads of state, and was accepted as a man worth listening to by philosophers, psychologists, and educators. His influence on the educational patterns of European states was impressive. Every country in Europe looked to him for some advice or inspiration. Prussia was especially marked by his influence. American education, too, was to come under his magic spell.[40]

---

[39] The object lesson, especially, became an important tool in methodology. It may have been that it was used excessively, as is suggested by the following: . . . just as the spirit of classical humanism degenerated into concentration on the form of the classics to the virtual neglect of their contents, so did such Pestalozzian ideas as the use of objects in teaching and the principle of proceeding from the simple to the complex degenerate into emphasis on the mastery of isolated steps in a given procedure, attention to minute detail . . . without much attention being given to the content of the sense experience." (Walter B. Kolesnik, *Mental Discipline in Modern Education,* University of Wisconsin Press, Madison, 1958, p. 17).

[40] See pp. 476–477.

The main achievements of Pestalozzian pedagogy may be summarized as follows:

1. The aim of education was nothing more nor less than the betterment of mankind. This ideal provided the kind of inspiration that modern states needed, along with the humanitarianism that it generated, to move in the direction of democratic education. Whatever steps were taken along the road to greater educational opportunity, national education was always set in the context of the practical, and this concern was, in every way, in keeping with the views of Pestalozzi.

2. Education was given its initial impulse toward becoming a scientific study. Up to this time, knowledge of education was largely unsystematic and indefinite and sometimes invalid. When Pestalozzi appeared on the educational scene, no one thought that teaching and learning were in any way scientific, or if they did think of education as a science, they said very little about it. Although Pestalozzi himself was not a scientist, when his work was finished the bases for a science of education had been laid.

3. The order of learning that Pestalozzi emphasized, without always knowing the technical points involved, brought out the importance and relationship of developmental psychology to teaching techniques and curriculum building. The whole movement toward child study may be traced to Pestalozzi.

4. The object-lesson technique brought the senses and sense training—realism of a kind, directed toward idealist ends—into sensitive positions in teaching and learning.

5. Pestalozzi's whole approach to education made a new kind of teacher absolutely necessary. Now the teacher needed to be well educated and skilled in the art of teaching. Since no magic could produce such an expert instructor, formal teacher training was begun. In other words, modern teacher education may look to Pestalozzi as its "father."

SUMMARY

In many important ways the circumstances surrounding education in the eighteenth century were no more conducive to quality or to opportunity than in previous centuries. Yet the eighteenth century was more sensitive to the needs for education and more fully aware of its values and of the possibilities for national good and national greatness that might flow from it than any other century had been. In every European country sentiments on the subject generated ferment; in some countries, notably in Prussia, this ferment was translated into practical educational reforms; in other countries, chiefly in France, the tendencies toward reform were channeled into theories. So Prussia was the place for action; France provided many of the ideals. The best illustration of this point is found in the history of national education in the eighteenth century: La Chalotais in his *Essay on National Education* laid the theoretical groundwork that Prussia put into operation. In Prussia we see the first concrete steps taken toward creating a national or state system of education, and there, too, we see the clearest example of compulsory attendance in schools.

The great historical figures of the century are Jean Jacques Rousseau and Johann Heinrich Pestalozzi. Though there is no evidence that the two ever met, they did share an intellectual comradeship. Rousseau, much dismayed at what he saw in schools and teaching, and prompted by his own undoubted genius, proposed a return to natural education. In his great work, *Emile*, he proposed principles for education that were almost completely negative. "Do the opposite of what is now being done," he advised, "and you will almost always be doing right." For all his interest in education, it must be admitted that Rousseau was no schoolmaster and showed no interest in becoming one. He expounded theories; their application was left to others.

Pestalozzi took up the work where Rousseau stopped. He tried to construct an educational process based on Rousseauistic ideals. Naturally, because he was operating on the level of a schoolmaster, he could not afford the literary flights of fancy that had engaged Rousseau. Pestalozzi's work was far more practical and could be applied. Two principal books set forth his main doctrines and educational practices: *Leonard and Gertrude* and *How Gertrude Teaches Her Children*. In the areas of methodology, child study, motivation, and teacher training, Pestalozzi made important contributions to the modern educational scene.

Questions and Exercises for Study and Discussion

1. Describe educational conditions in Europe in the eighteenth century. How did they differ from those of the seventeenth century? Did they preface any special developments in the nineteenth century?
2. How would you distinguish the modern university from the medieval university?
3. Give a brief report on the cultural and intellectual significance of the Enlightenment.
4. How did sensationalism affect education? Who were its champions?
5. What was the status of the Society of Jesus in eighteenth-century France?
6. Prepare a brief report on the life and career of Louis-René de la Chalotais.
7. What were the objections that La Chalotais raised against Jesuits and, generally speaking, against religious teachers?

8. Report on La Chalotais's plan for national education.
9. Explain the first steps toward national systems of education in France, Germany, and England.
10. Evaluate Basedow's role in German education.
11. Summarize the educational theory of Jean Jacques Rousseau.
12. Do you see Pestalozzi as a prophet of modern methodology in education? In what ways was Pestalozzi a follower of Rousseau?

13

Science, Nationalism,
and Education

The nineteenth century reaped the rewards of the educational philosophizing of the eighteenth century. Rousseau had awakened the educators of the world. Not all of them were followers of Rousseau, of course, but none, not even those who opposed him most violently, could afford to ignore what he had said. Even in what appeared to be his most flagrant rejections of common sense, there were some things to be learned. And if the influence of Rousseau began to wane, there was the work of Pestalozzi still going on for twenty-seven years of the nineteenth century to remind the schoolmasters and the educational theorists that Rousseau had spoken and that educational practitioners were still trying to apply his theories. Pestalozzi continued to be a force in education well into the nineteenth century. It is fair to say that his work had more effect on the educational patterns of this century than that of any other educator.

In addition to the theoretical and practical questions that educators met in their own research or in discussions with an aroused public, other movements added to the intellectual ferment of the nineteenth century. This was a century of many reforms and changes, and as it faced new conditions, it tried to keep intact its inheritance from the eighteenth century.

One of the inheritances was the economic realignment that had been undertaken sometime in the eighteenth century. What we have in mind was, of course, the onset of the industrial revolution. This change in the economic picture brought about almost immediately changes in the social structure; changes in the social structure while not necessarily

397

demanding changes in educational opportunity, did, in fact, impel men to argue heatedly for them. Then there was the political inheritance that the century had left, with its burden of political philosophy that both went into and grew out of the French Revolution. Liberty, equality, fraternity: these were words that had profound meaning and unusual appeal. And who could deny that both their meaning and their appeal affected the destinies of education?

But politics took education down many roads. It was not enough to argue for greater opportunity for the individual. There were many complexions of political thought to be considered, and education was asked to adjust to them. The most significant adjustments were expressed in the form of national education. This was the time when the great national school systems began to take their shape. Later in this discussion, we shall look at their evolution and their significance for the nineteenth century.

Finally, there was the question of faith in education. Sometimes faith meant a kind of humanitarian conception that could see nothing but good coming from an unequivocal commitment to national education. But this was only one side of the coin. Faith could mean also the commitment to the kind of education that would offer opportunity for students to develop their religious faith. Thus, in the movement for national systems of education directly under the control of the state, the desire for an education with some religious perspective was not obliterated. Of course, not every national school system made provisions for religious education; some did and some did not. It was at this point that the whole matter became involved in controversy.

We might say, with some justice, that the distinctive characteristics of the nineteenth century were nationalism, democracy, and anti-clericalism. With these preoccupations in mind, men could argue for a national system of education that was open to all and that provided opportunity of various types for the variety of individuals who would come to school, and also for a control vested in the people themselves rather than in religious communities or persons.

We shall see something more of these characteristics as they influenced educational thought and practice in this century. National systems of education involved both the first and the last characteristics. Outstanding educational leaders and thinkers—Herbart and Froebel are probably the best examples—translated into practical school programs the democratic principles that heretofore had been discussed only by philosophers and political theorists. Because the democratic tendencies were felt in the national school systems that came into clearer focus in this century, we shall begin with the men who were largely responsible for furthering democracy in education.

JOHANN FRIEDRICH HERBART AND THE SCIENCE
OF EDUCATION

Herbart (1776–1841) was both an educational philosopher and a teacher. He had all the abilities of a Rousseau, yet at the same time he had the pedagogical interests of a Pestalozzi. Perhaps the most interesting and significant thing that can be said about Herbart is that he tested his own theories. Had Herbart not been able to carry his theories down to the level of proof, we should probably not be studying about him today. He was a thorough and searching thinker, and an educational scientist.

Herbart was born in Oldenburg, Germany, in the year 1776. His early childhood was spent under the watchful eye of his mother. He received his elementary education from the local pastor, and his secondary education, which was completely classical, in the local Gymnasium. At the age of eighteen the young Herbart was ready for the university. Since his father had decided that he would follow the profession of law, young Herbart entered the University of Jena. The only unusual feature about Herbart's university studies, aside from the fact that he was especially successful, was that his mother accompanied him to college and looked out for him while he was there. Her indulgence extended to the point where she cultivated relationships for him; her solicitude was responsible for the special friendship that sprang up between Herbart and Schiller. Largely as a result of this friendship and also of Herbart's lukewarm feeling for the law, the young man's attention was turned to philosophy and education. About the time that Herbart came in contact with him, Schiller was writing his *Letters on the Aesthetic Education of Man*, and this book may have been the original spark that kindled Herbart's interest in education. From being interested in education in the early nineteenth century to becoming a disciple of Pestalozzi was only a short step, but, contrary to the general view, Herbart did not take this step very quickly. He left the University of Jena in 1797 and undertook a commission offered to him to tutor the three sons of a Swiss government official. It was not until after he had finished this assignment, in 1800, that Herbart met Pestalozzi, and even then Pestalozzi was hardly in a position to exert a great influence on him. Besides, Herbart had already laid some of the foundations for his educational theory by the time he first came in contact with Pestalozzi. That Herbart followed his own road does not detract from the fame of Pestalozzi, but it does give greater credit to Herbart's dedication to the work of education. Although it should be denied that Herbart was a disciple of Pestalozzi, it can be admitted that there was some cross-fertilization of their thoughts.[1]

[1] Robert Ulich, *History of Educational Thought*, American Book Company, New York, 1950, pp. 271–272.

Herbart's position gave him far more power to exert influence than Pestalozzi had ever been able to achieve; from his exceptional record at the University of Jena it was easy for him to move to the position of tutor for the children of a well-placed family. When this tour of duty came to an end, Herbart was ready to share his thoughts with others. He wanted to write. His writings, plus the general reputation that he had already achieved in the academic world, brought him a university appointment. He became professor of philosophy and pedagogy at the University of Königsberg in 1809. By this time, however, he had already formed quite definite views with regard to education, and had also worked out the philosophical positions which he defended throughout his career.

When we speak of Herbart, we often find it necessary to distinguish between Herbart the philosopher and Herbart the educator. Of course we should not assume from this that philosophy and education are so far apart that a man who is both a philosopher and an educator is a divided man. For Herbart the difference between philosophy and any other field of knowledge was certainly a matter of emphasis. In his philosophical writings (and generally speaking, it is possible to distinguish Herbart's writings into two categories, philosophical and pedagogical-psychological) he is critical of the separation that was more or less regularly being made between philosophy and other sciences. He was consistent in his belief that academic philosophy was not a kind of supernatural wisdom that could lead and direct other fields of knowledge. In an early work on philosophy, entitled *On the Study of Philosophy*, Herbart expressed simply and sincerely his view as to the role that philosophy should play:

Which relationship should Philosophy set up between herself and the other sciences, and between herself and life? Would she like to be considered as ruler, superior through her new and unknown weapons, menacing and formidable? Or would she rather prefer to be considered a native in her environment, as kin and friend, needy of ever-new acknowledgment and approval? . . . If the power of the human mind is strong enough simultaneously to expand itself into the width as well as the depth of life, then all the sciences, each separately and yet all united, ought to produce philosophy as their indispensable complement, and they ought never to cease in this endeavor. It is the limitations of the human mind which force us everywhere to divide labor, and which split knowing into portions of knowledge that philosophy has been severed from the totality of thought. . . . Thus philosophical thinking, unfortunately, has led to philosophy as a special and isolated branch of scholarship.[2]

Perhaps a word more should be added on Herbart's philosophy. Though it is not unusual to call Herbart a philosophical realist, this

[2] Quoted in *ibid.,* pp. 272–273.

designation is only partly true. Apparently he was a realist only in the sense that he believed there was a world of real things behind the appearances that we know. He believed, also, that the soul's nature, simple though it is, is totally beyond our knowledge and will always remain so. We do, however, have some knowledge of the experiences or the impressions that are made on the soul—what we call mental states—but we are not in a position to know anything of their origin or the nature of the real soul on which the impressions are made. At the same time Herbart accepted the view of the soul or the mind that had been offered somewhat earlier by John Locke.[3] For Herbart, as for Locke, the mind was originally a *tabula rasa*. All ideas are, without exception, the products of time and experience. Although this is only a brief and sketchy treatment of Herbart's philosophical views, it does provide us with some foundation for looking more closely at his educational doctrines. These were presented in the following works: *ABC of Sense Perception, The Application of Psychology to the Science of Education, Letters and Lectures on Education, Outlines of Educational Doctrine, The Science of Education: Its General Principles Deduced from Its Aim and the Aesthetic Revelation of the World,* and *A Textbook in Psychology.*

In Herbart's thinking about education he tried to integrate and accommodate theory to practice. He was convinced that the aims of education could not be arrived at or even discussed without reference to the meaning of human existence, and that the starting point for any theory of education, therefore, is the nature of man. Now his question is this: What is the best way for us to get at the fundamental meaning of man's nature? Here is where he turned to psychology, or more specifically, to the empirical approach, in the hope that it would throw additional light on the central issue. In other words, Herbart was by no means turning his back on the traditional answers that had been given concerning the nature of man; he was only seeking additional information that could supplement and perhaps confirm what was already known. But psychology was something more than this. It provided a basis upon which the technique of teaching could be more firmly and scientifically established. In the history of education, it would be hard to find a man who devoted more attention to laying a foundation for methodology than Herbart. And he was especially successful; his efforts produced results. He established an institute for the training of teachers, not the first such school, it is true, but the first so scientifically oriented, where men and women were instructed in techniques of teaching that could be established on an experimentally verifiable foundation and where they were imbued with some of the spirit that had inspired Herbart to begin such work in the first place.

[3] See pp. 360–361.

Herbart's Aim of Education

In the opening sentence of his *Science of Education* Herbart comes right to the point on the subject of the end of education. "The one and whole work of education may be summed up in the concept of morality." Herbart meant that the goal of education is the production of good men. This was not the first time in the history of education that the formation of men had been called the goal of education. As a matter of fact, education in its broadest meaning could have no other objective. Yet the educational traditions with which Herbart was most familiar and the point of view that he had met at the university looked upon education as principally an intellectual enterprise. So there was something new in Herbart's outlook, although it was only a newness of emphasis.

But when we say that Herbart regarded the proper and ultimate end of education to be moral, we must add that Herbart was thinking of education on the most basic level; he was not writing about what might be done in school or at home or elsewhere, but rather, about everything that is or can be done to form the individual under all possible auspices and at all possible times. It was Herbart's impression—and it has long been a common Christian view—that the worth of a man is measured by his will and not by his intellect. Herbart would have the educator, who is not necessarily the teacher or the instructor, concern himself with all those things that go to make up the good man.

This generalization would be sufficient for most educational thinkers; it had satisfied many in the past. But the various parts of morality had to be spelled out for Herbart, for generalization was not good enough for him. Morality was made up of what he called the "five moral ideas": freedom, completeness, good will, right, and equity. Education was thus aiming at making a man who would know what he ought to do on every occasion and how to do it. It would be concerned with giving him the bases of instruction so that he would be a broad man; and this was the teacher's task. It would be a matter of cultivating in him the right ideas with respect to what we today call brotherhood. Education would, in addition, have the job of establishing in the individual an attitude that regularly respected the rights of others, both their persons and their property. Finally, there was the moral idea of equity. The educational assignment here was to inculcate the idea of reward for good behavior and punishment for bad or evil behavior. The man who had assimilated these five moral ideas and had made them part of his system of values was, as far as Herbart was concerned, a good man. When education had produced such a good man, it had done its work well.

Producing the good man was, then, the great aim of Herbart's pedagogy. But, as we have suggested above, not all of this was the proper work of the teacher; only one part was especially his responsibility. This is what Herbart referred to as the idea of perfection or completeness, which needed instruction to fulfill its task. And this is where Herbart's celebrated doctrine of interest made its appearance.

Although Herbart's doctrine of interest has had its greatest effect in methodology, it played an important role in the objectives that he assigned to all of education. On this level Herbart thought of interest in terms of breadth. The interest that he advocated was to be many-sided, and he expected that the teacher, more than anyone else, would have the responsibility for developing broad interests in the children who came to him for instruction. To have many interests would give a person a number of obvious advantages, but for Herbart the most important was that an individual with wide interests would be in a better position to form character and persevere in good action. But the teacher could go farther. It was really his task to create in the mind of the learner an interest in the good life, the life of sound character. Of course, this was not a responsibility that rested solely on the teacher's shoulders, for other institutions that were engaged in the general work of education would share it with him to a certain extent. But since it was the school's role to deal with matters of instruction and since interest was related to instruction, the teacher had a responsibility for developing interest. But Herbart's work did not stop with setting goals. He tried to formulate scientific procedures whereby teachers could be more certain of the results of their work and reasonably sure that they were actually contributing to the formation of a child's character. In other words, Herbart was trying to find out, by scientific methods, how knowledge, the outcome of instruction, might be converted to virtue. His research carried him over into the science of education, and in this area he achieved his greatest reputation.

We should not leave this phase of Herbart's educational thought without making it clear that Herbart was always willing to distinguish between education and instruction. It has often been said that Herbart deplored attempts to make such a distinction, yet without it a great deal of his thought would not have made much sense. Education was the total cultivation of the individual, a lifelong and lifelike process. Herbart never doubted that it was more important than instruction, but on the other hand, he never denied that instruction was a necessary part of education. Its role was to emphasize the moral ideal and impress upon the student the wonder and value of the good life. Herbart never tired of repeating that the final aim of education was the formation of character. He recognized that the teacher would have to exercise extreme care, even in carrying out his commitment to character building, so as not to cripple the individuality of the child through an overzealous approach to his mission. Still, the foundation for the formation of character was, according to Herbart, to get the learner to accept transcendent values so that the criteria for morality would be his own.

Methods of Teaching

The foundation on which Herbart's methodology rests is psychological. By the time he was ready to present a method for teaching, he had pretty well abandoned speculative psychology and embarked upon experimentation. Herbart's methods of teaching are based on an experimental psychology. From the experimental approach he tried to develop a scientific and systematic theory of learning, and from learning it was only a short step to method. At the same time, he opened the gates of education to influences from other sciences, especially from medicine and psychology.

One of the foundations in psychology that Herbart laid for his method had to do again with the matter of interest. This was his explanation of the dominance of one idea or interest over others that might be contending for places in the mind. According to Herbart, the contest was simply a struggle on the part of these various interests or experiences to command the attention of the learner. The most recent experiences had some advantage in the contest and would tend to rise more quickly into consciousness and persevere more stubbornly than older experiences. While this theory may have been nothing more than an application of the so-called law of recency to learning experiences, it did have an influence on methods. If the teacher wants to utilize certain ideas that the child has or build on certain experiences that are part of his background, he must help these ideas and experiences to emerge on the level of consciousness. He must aid them in their struggle for supremacy over the other ideas of the child.

This is all part of a kind of conditioning process. The interests of the child are put into a certain frame of reference, and certain ideas or habits of action are derived from them. New experiences will be made to fit into the background of these past experiences and become part of a preformed frame of reference. Manipulating interest, then, was for Herbart an important part of the educative process. But this matter of interest could not be touched without certain dangers. Broad interests were eminently desirable, but broad interests that were held with a kind of passivity were really of no great value. It was necessary that a certain intensity should be coupled with the many-sidedness of which we have already spoken, provided it did not become exaggerated and lead the child away from vitally held interests. A mind that concentrates on one single interest to the exclusion of others is a one-sided mind. Method, then, becomes to a large extent a matter of controlling the voltage of interest. Neither too much nor too little, but always broad.

The question may well be asked: How broad should these interests be? Herbart thought the range of interest should be equivalent to the range of life itself. Yet he was quick to realize that such a wide approach to interest would not give much guidance to the teachers who were faced with the problems of dealing with schoolchildren's concerns. For pedagogical purposes, he classified interests into those that had to do with nature, on the one hand, and with society, on the other: interests that had to do with the physical world in which the child lived, and interests that arose regularly and appropriately from the social world in which he also lived. Neither source of interest, that is, neither world, could be neglected in the education of the child. This twofold classification of interest received further analysis and classification. Herbart divided the child's interests in the physical world and the social world into knowledge interests and ethical interests. The knowledge interests, which, of course, are subsumed under both the physical and the social world, would have to do with information about these worlds, interpretations of this information on a normative level, and finally, attempts to see the aesthetic values, the beauty, in them. Ethical interests, of no less importance than the knowledge interests, were directed at man, that is, at the individual man with whom students would come in contact; at men, that is, at societies or civic communities that men organize; and at God. Herbart was neither oblivious of, nor opposed to, the interest that men have in the Divine Being. He saw this as a social relationship.

Herbart's classification of interests had meaning right down to the level of the the teacher who is teaching and the student who is learning. The classification of the objects of interest was relevant first to the curriculum and then to the techniques of teaching. According to Herbart (and he is still operating well within the logical limits of his theory of education), the curriculum should consist of two main groups of studies, the historical and the scientific. Of the two, he considers the historical the more important, because the historical studies are obviously more humanistic. It is remarkable that this man, who has been called the father of the science of education, should have felt that human questions were always to be in the foreground of the educational process. It should be understood, however, that this was a matter of emphasis, and that Herbart by no means intended to relegate the scientific parts of the curriculum to second place. He could not have been true to his doctrine of many-sided interest nor would he have been optimistic about the attainment of the goals he set for education, if he had reduced part of the life of man to a definitely subordinate role. He wanted education to produce the moral man, but he did not believe that morality could be achieved by the presentation of moral ideas alone. "Do you believe," he asked, "that by moral ideas alone you can teach man how to act? Man stands in the midst of nature . . . he must know himself and his powers, and the forces around him who can help him." The work of the curriculum is not simply to present material from the various fields of knowledge. This must be done, of course, but there must also be some principle of integration, if the desired outcome of education—the truly moral man—is to emerge from the process. Herbart's argument brings us to the point where we should look more closely at the actual methods of teaching that he endorsed.

The Herbartian teacher would have to be concerned with three things primarily when he begins his presentation to the students. Before we touch on these three things, we should make clear that Herbart assumes that the teacher will be in a position of authority and that his purpose is to teach the child what he does not know. If there is any question about this, that is, about the fact that there is knowledge which can be taught or communicated, then Herbart's system and all of his thought become a meaningless jumble of words. The principal concerns for the teacher are: to relate the new lesson to what the child already knows; to help him to retain what has been taught; and to seek to maintain a high level of interest in the student, not only for what is currently being learned, but for learning in general. All of this means, of course, that teaching and learning are dynamic processes. Instruction depends on the dynamics of description, analysis, and synthesis. These are, or may be, discrete types of instruction, but Herbart emphasizes the teacher's obligation to employ them all in the effort to achieve good instruction.

Perhaps interest is central to all of this. As we have said before, the teacher's presentation must begin with ideas that are meaningful to the student. The teacher must find the student's level of maturity, it is true, but he must also find his level of experience. If either level is not found, then it is a foregone conclusion that the student's interest cannot be aroused to the point where it can lead to instructional goals. If the various levels are not reached, then the school is really standing in the way of the children's growth and development. Yet we know (and Herbart had no difficulty in seeing this) that individuals must do certain things in society, and that society will not always wait for them to become interested in learning how to do them. In practice, the student may have to accept some teaching for which he is neither psychologically nor experientially ready. The nature of things demands this, and it can hardly be opposed by the nature of learning. But on a broader and more significant level the question arises of how individual and social motives may be served by instruction in school. The social motives—better expressed as the needs of society—may open to the learner broad avenues of human knowledge and human experience, and may eventually disclose to him social values upon which the very foundation of civilized society rests. All of this means that the teacher should follow students' interests whenever such a procedure is to their advantage, but it means, too, that the teacher should lead students into those experiences that will be good for them and for the society in which they are to live. They will need the experiences if they are to share in protecting the stability and vitality of society. The students who are instructed on this broad level, where their own interests as well as the needs of society form the basis for their instruction, are exposed to what Herbart called a liberal education.

There is nothing in education for which Herbart is more famous than the "five formal steps of instruction." This fame is somewhat misplaced, for such a recipe for teaching was not of Herbart's making. He never supposed that teaching and learning could be put on a simple mechanical level. The steps of instruction, although they may find a basis in Herbart's pedagogical theory, should not be attributed to him; they belong rather to those of his disciples who were associated with the nineteenth-century normal schools and were looking for a clear-cut and precise method of teaching which could be communicated to the students. The five steps attributed to Herbart were: preparation, presentation, association, systemization, and application.

As we have said, Herbart never intended that the stages of instruction which he outlined should be followed mechanically, for he was acutely aware of the complexity of learning processes and of the instructional procedures necessary to meet them. He could not have advocated the employment of a simple, set, and mechanical method of teaching. Still, we must not divorce Herbart so completely from these steps that we fail to see the basis for them in his work. In his *Science of Education* Herbart used his theory of psychology and his theory of education and instruction to devise four steps or levels of approach to instruction, namely, clearness, association, system, and method. By the use of these steps Herbart hoped to indicate that a unified and coherent method of instruction ought to be followed if the child was to be helped to concentrate on the material that was presented to him, to learn it, and to retain it. By "clearness" Herbart meant that the child should not be confused by an inappropriate presentation of a subject, but that he should be able to understand what he is being made to learn. He would not understand it thoroughly, of course, for then there would be no need to present it to him, but he would understand it at least on the level of recognition. The presentation, then, would develop this level of recognition into a level of more complete knowledge, where the child would grasp the information that had been presented. The next step was "association." Herbart talked of apperceptive masses, by which he meant those bodies of experience already stored or held by the learner. Association was a matter of relating the new experience, the material which had just been learned, to old experiences, ideas, or convictions already in the mind of the student. The next step was "system." By this Herbart meant that once the new learning came into the mind ,and was associated with past learning, it should be organized into a more meaningful and systematic order. New learning would be put into the proper categories of past experience and would thus take on greater significance for the learner. Finally, there was the step of "method." Method meant that the student, as a kind of an end result of this order of learning, would be in such possession of his knowledge that he would be able to apply it. He would be able to make the transfer of the things that he had learned to the practical realities of the life that faced him. In other places Herbart referred to his steps in different language: He spoke of instruction that was illustrative, consistent, elevating, and applicable. When he used these terms in this context, he meant nothing really different from the terms clearness, association, system, and method. Herbart did not cast method into an unchangeable mold, although the same cannot be said of his followers. No part of Herbart's educational theory was ever admired more or followed more closely than that part which led to the formation of the five formal steps of teaching. As a partial evaluation, we may add that even though Herbart's method was misused by his followers, there were some good results from this misuse. No methodologist in the history of education ever took a more positive stand with respect to a systematic order of teaching than Herbart, and his followers paid regular allegiance to this order.

FROEBEL AND A NEW DIMENSION TO EDUCATION

Friedrich Wilhelm August Froebel (1782–1852), a German educational reformer, was born at Oberweissbach, Thuringia, in southern Germany. Because his father was fully occupied with his duties as a Lutheran pastor and his mother died before he was a year old, young Froebel was left to the rather negligent care of brothers and servants. His stepmother lost interest in him when her own son was born. An uncle later retrieved some of the neglect and chaos of the boy's life by taking him in and providing him with an opportunity for education. But Froebel's mind was not on his books, and the uncle, thinking that the boy did not have the capacity of mind necessary for learning, apprenticed him to a forester. At seventeen he left the forest. By this time his insights had matured sufficiently for him to see that somehow the schooling that he had received had missed the point. So we may say that Froebel's interest in educational reform dates from an early period in his life.

In 1799 Froebel went to the University of Jena, not apparently as a student but only to visit his brother, and while he was there he became intrigued with the possibilities of obtaining a higher education himself. The story is that, because of his own inadequate educational background, he enrolled in university studies of a somewhat preparatory sort. His stay at Jena was short. From the university he drifted from one position to another, was imprisoned for debt, and finally accepted a position as teacher of drawing in a Frankfort normal school. It was in this position that Froebel found the fulfillment of his overwhelming desire to serve mankind. In his *Autobiography* he reported that he had found something he had never before known but had always longed for in his life as a teacher. After two years with the Pestalozzian Institute of Frankfort, Froebel realized that his preparation for the profession of teaching was not all that it should have been and that he could not continue without a more substantial scholastic background. He decided to pursue his studies and obtain more experience with children. At the same time he seemed to realize that there was a dimension to teaching and learning that had not yet been fully exploited. He began to see that the method of instruction must be directed by the laws of development of the human mind as well as by those of the subjects to be taught. He had, at this early date in his career, the intuition that the essence of method is the art of adapting to the momentary stage of development in the student the corresponding aspect of the subject. This law of development became the central principle in his pedagogy, and it was the law that he was determined to understand more completely.[4]

To arrive at this end he studied more of Pestalozzi, at Yverdun, and experimented with a model group of boys whom he observed particularly at play. From the Pestalozzian surroundings Froebel emerged with mixed emotions. According to his own testimony, he was impressed by what he saw, but he was puzzled and disturbed too. In 1811 he went to the Universities of Göttingen and Berlin in pursuit of knowledge which would be helpful to him in the educational reform that he hoped to bring about. There is every indication that with his newly found zeal for educational reform, Froebel did remarkably well in his university studies despite the impediment of a faulty background. In 1814 he interrupted his university studies and enlisted in the Prussian army. His purpose in entering the military forces was wholly patriotic, for he was intent upon defending his fatherland in this renewal of the Napoleonic wars. But the military experience, besides satisfying his sense of patriotism, enriched his thinking on other subjects. He saw more clearly than ever before the values of discipline and united action, and he met two

[4] H. C. Bowen, *Froebel and Education by Self Activity*, Charles Scribner's Sons, New York, 1901, pp. 15–16.

men, Langethal and Middendorff, who later became his associates in promoting the new educational ideal.

In 1814 Froebel and his associates settled in Berlin, where Froebel obtained a situation in a museum. This gave him time to study in preparation for the opening of a new type of school, and it gave his followers time to catch up with him in their educational thinking. Within a year or so he was ready to apply his theory of education by development. He began on a trial basis for a short time with a few students in Berlin. After this he engaged in a two-year trial period at the village of Griesheim and then opened his first formal school at Keilhau, with twelve students. This was in 1817. Froebel remained with the Keilhau school until 1831, when he turned it over to his associates and went to Switzerland. During all this time the school with which Froebel was connected was an elementary school. It was still too early for Froebel's ideas on the kindergarten. In 1826 Froebel published his *The Education of Man.* This is an extremely complex book, but it is his one formal exposition of his educational views, and it sets forth his high hopes for the educational enterprise. In 1836 Froebel turned his attention to the education of young children. It was in education on this level that Froebel was to make his indelible mark on the history of education. In 1840 he opened the Universal German Kindergarten, and for the next twelve years he devoted all of his attention to the progress of these institutions throughout Germany.

Froebel's Philosophy

Froebel's philosophy, which is basic to all of his theories about education, places him squarely in the tradition of idealism. Some writers have seen enough similarity between him and Rousseau to call Froebel a German copy of the French philosopher. On the level of educational ideas, ideals, and practices there are many similarities between Froebel and Rousseau and Froebel and Pestalozzi. On the more basic level of philosophical principles there is little, if any, similarity.

Unity is Froebel's dominant principle. All things are related, connected, unified, whether or not this unity can be detected. The ultimate source of the unity, the principle of all unification, is God. The whole purpose of education is to enable men to fulfill themselves, to complete themselves, to attain unity with God.

Although Froebel was an idealist and a pantheist, he did not go so far in his idealism as to deny or ignore the facts of the world. It was by means of the facts of the world, by finding in them the clues to unity, that men would become educated and would be completed. Added to Froebel's principle of unity is his general conception of organic evolution. He believed that man grew much as plants and animals grow, with this difference: Plants and animals develop according to a definite inner law of their nature; man, being endowed with a mental nature, is able to shape many of the elements of his own development. Here again education, which may be simply the opportunity for development, becomes extremely important. Step by step, stage by stage, man moves forward, building on what he has constructed before. No stage of development is unimportant; possibly the first years of life, the foundational years, are most important. In the various stages of development men will be confronted by different problems and opportunities. The principle of unity that flows through all these various stages is self-activity. By being self-active, man comes closer to God, who is an ever-active spirit. The challenge that faces education, then, is to bring man closer to God and while doing so to enable man to become more completely himself.

Froebel and Education

Although Froebel's philosophy was basic to his educational theory, it is a complex, idealistic philosophy which is difficult to understand and more difficult to explain. For this reason we shall not dwell on the philosophical phases of Froebel's thought but shall go directly to his educational plans and practices.[5]

1. Most educational thinkers concerned themselves first with the aims of education. Froebel was no exception. He saw quite clearly the relationship between goals and means. Froebel envisaged a twofold aim for education. One part of the general aim was to produce in the individual a firm, pure, and strong will.[6] The other part, which is somewhat difficult to interpret, is to "lead and guide a man [through education] to clearness concerning himself and in himself, to peace with nature, and to unity with God."[7] In brief, Froebel was saying that education's chief purposes should be moral and, in a broad sense, social.

2. Froebel's theory of development had considerable relevance to the means of education, curriculum and methodology. He believed that there were definite, and for a time, discrete, periods of development through which children passed. These periods were knit together or unified in an educational experience by self-activity. Learning by doing, as a principle in education, knew no more ardent champion than Froebel. What should the child learn? According to Froebel, the fundamental object of instruction was not knowledge, but habits, skills, will, and character. The curriculum, then, would not need to have an orthodox or even a uniform content. It could be made up of those activities and experiences which

---

[5] Both are dealt with in a concise, lucid manner in Ulich, *op. cit.*, pp. 284–291.

[6] Friedrich Wilhelm August Froebel, *The Education of Man,* translated by W. N. Hailmann, D. Appleton & Company, Inc., New York, 1892, p. 96.

[7] *Ibid.*, pp. 4–5.

would seem to lead a child toward the strength of character or will that was prized so highly.[8] This attention to the steps of development in the learning processes made Froebel a forerunner of the whole developmental movement in psychology and in some ways an anticipator of the progressive movement in education.

3. One of the first steps in the maturation of the child is play. Before play begins, the child becomes aware of his surroundings, of the physical world in which he lives. Then he begins to play in and with that world. According to Froebel (and this was a principle that formed an important role in his building of the kindergarten), play is an outward expression of the child's inner action and life. It was, Froebel believed, the most spiritual activity in which a child could engage. Much of education, certainly most of the activities in the kindergarten, should be set in the context of play. This was, of course, just a step in the developmental process, for in Froebel's educational plan children did not always play. Play which combined attention with relaxation, purpose with independence, and discipline with freedom led the child up the ladder of maturity.

4. Besides coming in contact with the world in a playful way, the child should be given every opportunity and every encouragement to get in direct contact with nature. Froebel would not release the boy in the pasture or in the woods in quite the same way that Rousseau would have done. Yet he was every bit as convinced as Rousseau that the study of nature forms one of boyhood's deepest interests, and Froebel's own devotion to nature and nature study carried over into his school plans. In the programs of studies that he constructed for the schools with which he was associated, he always included weekly excursions out into the fields, so that children could come in contact with nature. This same interest led Froebel to endorse mathematical studies, by means of which man could measure or describe nature, and literary studies, especially those that had nature as their subject, and all forms of art and artistic skills that could come in contact with nature.

5. Froebel made two outstanding contributions to modern education. One was the kindergarten; the other was social education. Before the time of Froebel, social education was not unknown nor did it go completely uncultivated; still, educational theorists and practitioners did not devote much space or time to the development of the child's social nature. The school was a place for intellectual or moral formation, and social formation could and would take place outside the school, outside the ambit of formal education's responsibility. Much of this was changed by Froebel. First of all, his philosophical principle of unity envisioned the child as part of a whole, destined to a fuller and more complete life

[8] *Ibid.,* p. 16.

by sharing more fully in the life of the whole. Knowing and participating in the totality of mankind's hopes and aspirations was the supreme purpose of social education. No educator before Froebel and few after him perceived more clearly than he the importance of human relations and the role the schools could play in advancing them.

6. Froebel's most important single contribution to education and the thing for which he is most of all remembered is the kindergarten. This was a school—a preschool perhaps, in the strict sense—which did not have preparation for later schooling as its chief purpose. The kindergarten was a place in which children could grow, develop, and learn in an entirely natural way. Froebel's first kindergarten was established in Blankenburg in 1837. It met with some difficulties that first year and did not operate on a permanent basis until 1840. From Germany the kindergarten spread to many parts of the world. In America, the kindergarten was introduced by Mrs. Carl Schurz, a coworker of Froebel's in Germany, in 1855, at Watertown, Wisconsin. This was a German-speaking kindergarten. The first English-speaking kindergarten was opened in Boston, Massachusetts, in 1860, by Elizabeth Peabody. The kindergarten became a part of the public school system in the United States in 1873, in St. Louis, Missouri, under the direction of the superintendent of schools there, William T. Harris.

THE DEVELOPMENT OF NATIONAL SCHOOL SYSTEMS

While Herbart and Froebel were organizing and rearranging patterns for educational experience in the nineteenth century, the great states of the world were undertaking the work of reorganizing their school systems. Reorganization also went on in a number of smaller states, but it was from the great states that the impetus for educational control usually came. The great states had obviously more to gain or lose through an educational system. Germany, France, and England were deeply engaged with the question of national education. Because of her later importance in world affairs, we include Russia in this discussion.

Educational Reform in Germany

The motivation for educational reform in Prussia arose out of the bitter experiences of defeat that that nation had suffered at the hands of Napoleon. In 1806 the French under the great Napoleon had defeated the Prussians at Jena, and in 1807 the French imposed on Prussia the unpalatable terms of the Treaty of Tilsit. A nation with less fibre, made up of weaker people, might have succumbed; not Prussia. The defeat at the hands of the French was not accepted as an opportunity for retreating from the main currents of European political life, but was taken as a challenge to recoup the losses and once again become a nation of power and prestige. How was this to be done? Part of the answer was provided by Johann Gottlieb Fichte (1762–1814) in his *Addresses to the German People*. Fichte selected education as the instrument for reform and revitalization of the German nation. He gave two reasons for his choice. First, education was an area of activity that the French had left entirely in German hands. Apparently the French were unaware of the power of education, even though their theorists had for at least a century been writing and talking about the great national weapon that could be fashioned out of education. Second, it was an obvious instrument for use in re-creating the vitality of German nationalism. The picture is so often drawn of Fichte speaking his mind within the hearing of the French sentries on Unter den Linden that students of the history of education must be inclined to think of Fichte as a spy rather than a philosopher. Actually, Fitche's addresses can hardly be viewed as audacious acts. One need not detract from the patriotism or the courage of the man, to say that as far as the French were concerned, education was a neutral question, about which Fichte was free to say anything he wanted. In a way, then, not only Fichte, but Prussia too, had a free hand in shaping and reshaping educational affairs.

In Germany education was a spark of inspiration. From it the movement for unification of the German states got its initial impetus, and from unification the Germans turned to political reform and then to the creation of a new military system. Finally, they were back to education again, and now, with the newly constituted German nation, there was both the time and the opportunity to remold education along national lines. Education was to be used to generate patriotism and citizenship, and ultimately to advance the position of the German nation in Europe and in the world. The final objective of the education that was offered under the state's auspices was devotion to the fatherland. The German people seemed to want a guarantee that never again would they be subjected to the humiliation of a Jena or a Tilsit, and they asked education to give them this guarantee. Their view was entirely reasonable and honorable. Who can object because a nation and its people want to be cultural and scientific leaders of the world? It is out of such dreams that greatness comes. And who can charge Germany with excessive nationalism, when all of the states of Europe were engaged in the same enterprise? It is true that Germany rejected cosmopolitanism, even as Fichte rejected the view that he had once held that the future of Europe lay in the creation of a European state. But all the other states of Europe rejected cosmopolitanism too.

What was the main element of reform in the German system? Briefly, it was to reconstruct educational opportunity so that it would fit students for real life. Intellectual education had to take a secondary position in this new scheme of things, for it was moral education, more accurately patriotism, that Germany sought. Now, in intellectual education the main thing was to awaken the powers of the mind and to encourage independence of thought. This was the new pattern of education that was offered to the German nation; it was accepted with enthusiasm, and everyone became devoted to the ends that the educational leaders valued so highly.

The reform movement made drastic changes in the schools. Friedrich Wilhelm von Humboldt (1767–1835) was appointed minister of education, or director of public instruction, in 1808. It was his job to achieve the goals that were accepted as the end of educational reconstruction. He did his work well, and although he was in office for only about eighteen months, laid a foundation for German education that even today has not been disturbed materially.

One of Von Humboldt's first moves was to establish a new university, the University of Berlin. Its founding came at such an inopportune time, from a financial point of view, that one must conclude that the Germans were committed to a new university as an essential part of educational reconstruction. It is true that the University of Halle some years before had incorporated the idea of academic freedom as an internal guarantee of the professor's right to search for truth. But the University of Berlin, a state institution, went even further: At Berlin the university was granted full liberty to manage its own affairs, namely, all those things that had to do with study and the administration of university life. This was independence that no university had ever enjoyed before. In addition to exercising this independence, which, as time proved, was much more than a theoretical thing, the state institution created something of a new conception of a university's function. The main emphasis was laid on scientific research. Though this emphasis, it should be pointed out, was not an exclusive one, there is no doubt that teaching was of secondary importance. The example of the University of Berlin could not be ignored by other German universities, and so we begin to see the model of a university that was to have a great effect on all higher education everywhere in the world for at least the next 150 years. And this model was responsible to a large extent for the type of university education that developed in the United States.

At about the same time that the reforms in university studies and structure were being achieved, the secondary schools in Germany were undergoing some transformation. Certain secondary schools, *Gymnasien,* which were selected as preparatory schools for the university, were the only avenues that led to university study. In order to control the quality of instruction given in these institutions, the director of education instituted a teacher's examination. The attention that Von Humboldt gave to teachers' qualifications for teaching in these preparatory schools tended to raise the status of teachers who were associated with them. What had, years before, been thought of as a special preserve for the clergy was now restricted to those who were specially prepared for teaching on such a level. The curriculum, too, was revised. The old Gymnasium had been a classical school; this was the inheritance from Sturm. The new Gymnasium remained essentially though not exclusively a classical school, but instead of emphasizing the attainment of pure Latin, it handled the classics as repositories of the great ideas of mankind. From these great ideas students were expected to gain inspiration for great achievements. In addition to the classics, which, as we have said, were still central studies, the curriculum offered opportunities for more generalized individual preparation. Mathematics, science, and German found positions of considerable importance in the school program. In order to do everything that ought to be done with such a curriculum, the length of the course was set at nine years, at the end of which time a state examination was administered. Students who were successful on this examination were qualified to attend any German university.

Except for the establishment of what was called a *Progymnasium,* other reforms or revisions of secondary education had to wait until later in the century. The *Progymnasium* was a six-year school intended for the middle-class boys who, for one reason or another, could not look forward to university studies. These schools did not include Greek in their curricula; sometimes they excluded the classics altogether. The principal and most regularly found components of the curriculum were modern languages and science. There is some reason for believing that this school was established on an uncertain basis and, until 1832, was conducted in an uncertain, almost chaotic, way. After 1832 a state examination was administered to students who attended the middle school. Those who passed were able to fulfill their military obligation to the state with only one year's service, and after this, minor state offices were available to them. The other types of secondary schools that were established later in the century had two things in common: They broadened the curriculum to include those subjects that were relevant to modern scientific pursuits, and they opened their doors to boys and girls who under the old system could hardly have hoped to attend a secondary school. In addition, some of the new secondary schools or the new types of secondary education prepared students for the university. Thus, the exclusiveness of the old Gymnasium was partly broken down.

The changes in elementary education were somewhat less dramatic. They were, nevertheless, of equal significance. All elementary education became public and free. Attendance in school was compulsory from the ages of six to fourteen. Teachers were selected with greater care; almost all of them were men. Methods of teaching were set in a context that placed a special premium on the development of practical intelligence. Objectives were centered on the development of allegiance and devotion to national ideals. With such a system—and such a system did become a reality—illiteracy practically disappeared in Germany.

It should be added that the ideas and plans advanced by Pestalozzi had considerable influence on German education.[9] Fichte, of course had made many references to Pestalozzi in his discussion on education. He seemed to think of Pestalozzi as a kind of educational savior. In addition to this, the German government sent a number of teachers and educational supervisors and directors to study under or with Pestalozzi. Yet, with all this admiration for him, there was an element of distrust, for Pestalozzi had advocated popular and democratic education, and German elementary education, in spite of its excellent features, was not democratic. Not all German children attended the same type of elementary school. Those from the so-called better social classes attended special elementary schools, where they were given an academic preparation that would fit them for the type of secondary school they could reasonably expect to attend. Thus, for these students, the elementary school was really a preparatory school for the Gymnasium. For the other students in the German *Volksschulen,* the elementary schools, their experiences in reading, writing, arithmetic, and religion were intended, along with the vocational training in the "continuation schools," to train them or prepare them for life.

We should mention here one last outcome of German educational reconstruction: the further development of the theory and practice of education. Teachers' schools were organized to prepare teachers for the schools of the country, and in these schools there was a remarkable development of educational theory and methodology. The chief mover in this development, who voiced the principal doctrines on which such theories and practices were based, was Herbart.[10]

Educational Reconstruction in France

Nineteenth-century France did not escape from, or try to avoid, the current emphasis on national education. In France, however, the reform movements, which were often simply the steps taken toward establishing a national system of education, were never as thorough or as successful as those taken by Germany. And in France, the system that was established was far from permanent.

[9] See pp. 388–393.
[10] See pp. 404–408.

By the time Napoleon gained power in France, the educational doctrines of La Chalotais[11] were pretty well known and fairly generally accepted among that part of the French population that counted. Therefore, when Napoleon issued the decrees in 1806 and 1808 that made French education a tool of the state, there was little alarm and, generally speaking, only isolated pockets of opposition. This is somewhat surprising, because the Napoleonic policy of absolutism in education was quite opposed to the educational policy that might be abstracted from the ideology of the Revolution. The Revolution, if nothing else can be said for it, was carried on for freedom. Napoleon's policy and the decrees that put it into effect were diametrically opposed to the doctrine that the principal purpose of education is to build personal individuality and from individual strengths to move on to the formation of a strong and resilient society. In other words, the policy that Napoleon made effective in the first decade of the nineteenth century reversed the trend that had been going on for more than a quarter of a century in French educational practice. How powerless is tradition, how weak and ineffective are ideals, in the face of strength and authority!

With no more than a cynical nod in the direction of the educational traditions and ideals of the French, Napoleon took control of all education in France by creating what is called the University of France. We are aware of the place of France in the history of education, and we recognize that some of the solidest traditions in higher education had their foundation in France. The University of Paris, the mother of universities, had its birth on French soil; and in no other country were the purposes of the university or the freedom that higher teaching and study entailed more energetically defended than in France. But the Revolution changed much of this. Suffice it to say that when the Revolution had accomplished its work, the universities of France had disappeared. In the aftermath of the Revolution, central schools came into existence. These schools, in many ways part of education's higher level, tried to combine interests in literary and industrial studies. Their career was brief, and the record was not too precise, nor was it especially distinguished. It was at this point in history that Napoleon created the University of France.

All the educational institutions that were engaged in studies above the elementary level were made part of the University of France. It should be made clear at the outset that the University of France was an administrative unit, established to control education, and that it had no teaching function as such. Its control over education in France was complete. But the University showed no interest whatever in elementary education, which, for the most part, was left to wither and die. The

[11] See pp. 370–373.

university system inaugurated or reestablished practices in education that were almost always open to suspicion. It was a rigid system: The schools were run in the same way that a military unit was operated. Time was given for teaching and learning, it is true, but instruction was given in a very narrow and especially severe context. There was no time for thinking, for thought could be dangerous. Everyone, every student and every teacher, was under the most severe form of discipline. Nothing could be done that the regulations of the University of France did not authorize.

It may be noted that the French system had many admirers in other countries. There is little reason to doubt that it was an efficient system—a good way to control education, but a poor way to bring about the intellectual and moral autonomy of persons. Some of the states of the United States were anxious to follow the French model, although it may be said that they were never quite willing to accept the authoritarianism with which French education in this period was branded.

We have already said that the scheme of Napoleon for controlling education left elementary education pretty much out of the picture. It is true that Napoleon required the schools—especially the *collèges* and *lycées*—to offer some training classes for the teachers who were or would be in the elementary schools. Yet, even so, it could hardly be claimed that the French had anything remotely resembling a system of elementary education. Most of the opportunity for elementary education was provided by the schools of the Christian Brothers. The Brothers were permitted to continue their work because Napoleon happened to approve of what they were doing. Still, in a country as vast as France and with her growing population, it was simply impossible for any one teaching congregation to provide all the opportunity that was needed on education's most elementary level. We mean no special indictment of the Brothers, then, when we say that private means for elementary education were inadequate. In an absolute sense, private elementary education was a failure, although in a relative sense, one might well admire its many remarkable accomplishments. Neither the monitorial school idea, imported from England, nor any other plan devised during the first thirty years of the nineteenth century solved France's educational problem. If the Revolution had hurt education more than it helped it, the Restoration brought about no renaissance in education on any level. An inquiry into the state of French education in 1833 revealed conditions that were exceedingly bad.[12]

With education in the hands of the state, the vitality of French educational thinking began to evaporate. The minds that would have

[12] This was the inquiry that followed the 1832 report of Victor Cousin (1792–1867) on the structure and standards of Prussian education.

turned to educational questions saw the futility of doing so and turned their attention to other fields of intellectual endeavor where obstacles were not so awesome. Yet there were a few sparks of inspiration left. The activity in French educational thought took two main directions. One was toward domestic education, especially the education of girls. This, with the exception of Fénelon's *Treatise on the Education of Girls* written in 1687, had been a neglected subject for centuries. The other was the creation of new societies in which education could play a special role.

In connection with the first direction that was taken, the name of Mme Necker de Saussure (1765–1841) stands out especially. Despite this new theoretical emphasis, it should be mentioned that on the practical level the education of French girls was not completely neglected. Catholic teaching sisterhoods were conducting more than five thousand schools for girls about this time. Besides Mme de Saussure, Mme de Staël, Mme Campan, Mme de Remusat, and Mme de Guizot are some of the other names to be mentioned in this connection; but it was Mme de Saussure, in *Progressive Education*, written about 1838, who made the greatest impression. Without all of Rousseau's negativism, Mme de Saussure could be thought of as a kind of feminine Rousseau. In spite of some striking similarities, she differed with Rousseau very pointedly on the education of women. The third volume of her *Progressive Education* takes up the issue, and in this volume she rejects almost everything that Rousseau had written in his last book of *Emile*.[13] In her plan, education for girls would be much broader than anything Rousseau proposed. To put it briefly, according to Mme de Saussure, a girl was to be given the opportunity to develop her personality to the fullest. In doing so she was to become a qualified member both of the household and of society.

If Mme de Saussure's views were somewhat novel, they were not, it would seem, really revolutionary. This was an approach that was left to St. Simon (1760–1825), Fourier (1772–1837), Jacotot (1770–1840), and Edouard Seguin (1812–1880). The latter may not have been a true revolutionary but apparently he did share the ideals of one who was, St. Simon. Only a word can be said here about the role that these men played in French educational thought. St. Simon's aim was to break with most social traditions and create new communities that would not be controlled by the interests that were then controlling society. Since these new communities would be somewhat isolated and mainly self-sufficient, education would have to turn more and more in the direction of vocational preparation and training. St. Simon's social views would also have endorsed strong moral purposes for the schools. Fourier's plan was more drastic: Children would have been taken from the home when

[13] See pp. 386–387.

they were infants, and all of their upbringing would have been conducted in small communities under the care of special persons. Fourier's views on education, which were for the most part eminently practical, were contained in his *Natural Education.* Jean Jacques Jacotot's *Universal Education,* which appeared in 1822, made at least a temporary impression on teachers, when it set forth ideas that advocated the startling and truly revolutionary view that a teacher could teach things of which he himself was ignorant if he had the right method. Jacotot proposed to give teachers the right method. The implications of Jacotot's thought are surely evident when one considers that a great deal of attention was being given at this time, for political reasons, to broadening the base of educational opportunity. A universal method that required of teachers almost nothing in the way of competence caused education-minded politicians to look a second time. When they actually did look a second time, they found very little that was substantial, very little that was educationally attractive.

Finally, there was Edouard Seguin. The significance of his work should not be slighted. He was a pioneer in the educational work for retarded children. One author has called him the "apostle of the idiot" because of the principles that he laid down with regard to the education and training of such children. In his book on *Idiocy,* Seguin established important positions for the education of defectives. These were positions that Maria Montessori (1870–1952) demonstrated to be valid when she began her work many years later.

English Education

Steps taken for the establishment of a national system of education for England were somewhat retarded. While both Germany and France were making some progress in connection with popular education, England's attitude seemed to be one of indifference. The reluctance on the part of the state to take any action did not mean that no one in England was interested in educational reform or that it was not needed. The industrial revolution had ushered in many changes in English life. Most importantly, the factory system motivated certain changes in, or realignments of, living conditions; the factory system led to conditions in urban living that were so bad that they obviously had to be reformed first. Such things as education would have to await more basic social and economic reforms. The common man, when he or his leaders became articulate, demanded change, and in education he demanded greater opportunity. The middle class, on the other hand, was in a position to resist many of the demands of the common man because it, too, was strong and articulate. Mercantilism seemed to support the conditions that were so prevalent in England.

Yet it is not true that nothing at all was done. As early as 1802, the "Health and Morals of Apprentices Act" was passed. This act limited the working hours of apprentices to twelve a day and directed that every apprentice be given some instruction in reading, writing, and arithmetic during the first four years of his apprenticeship. This instruction was to be given according to the age and ability of the apprentice, and the costs of such instruction were to be borne by the master. The instruction that this act required was to be given in a place especially prepared either in the factory or in the workshop. In spite of the legislation, which was, no doubt, a step forward, little was done. It would appear that the law was not enforced with any vigor. Thus the English child, especially the child of the workingman, had to mark time until 1833, when another act that had relevance to education, The Factory Act, was passed.

The act of 1833 prohibited the employment of children under nine years of age, made two hours of instruction each day compulsory for children between the ages of nine and thirteen, and appropriated £20,000 for the purpose of building schoolhouses in which the children of the poorer classes might receive some instruction. By 1870 England had made enough progress in the direction of a national system of education to include all children in the elementary system. From that date on, English education was engaged in consolidating the gains that had been made in the previous seventy years. This consolidation took the form principally of broadening the requirements for compulsory attendance in elementary schools and, in time, of making more adequate provisions for secondary education so that it became more nearly on a popular level.

Two nineteenth-century figures stand out especially as English educational reformers and theorists, Robert Owen (1771–1858) and Herbert Spencer (1820–1903).

Owen was one of the nineteenth century's most ardent proponents of popular education. According to his views of education, expressed in *A New View of Society,* or *Essays on the Formation of Human Character,* education, more than anything else, was responsible for the making of men, and society was man's teacher as much as the school. Thus, Owen sought to bring about social reforms that would provide a more suitable frame of reference in which education or schooling could do its work. But this was not enough; he sought to reform education, too. Toward this end he suggested that a number of changes should be made all the way up the educational ladder. The infant school was unquestionably his best known effort at reform. The infant school was really an elementary school that offered opportunity for elementary studies to poor children between the ages of five and ten. Owen's educational experiment, a school called the New Institution, was conducted in the community of New Lanark, near Glasgow. It would be hard to believe that anything of any great consequence for educational practice could have made its way out of this institution. On the other hand, it is surely true that Owen generated a great deal of sympathy for the cause of education with his work, and he formulated the humanitarian outlook that was absolutely confident of the power of education to regenerate men and reform societies.

If Robert Owen was important to the future of education, Herbert Spencer was even more important. Naturalistic education of the twentieth century is almost entirely indebted to him for its foundations. Besides, Spencer was very much opposed to national education, since he was convinced that only harm could come from creating a system of education under political control. At any rate, Spencer was not powerful enough to stop national education, although he and other Englishmen of like mind did retard its development in England for a number of years. His place in the history of education, however, is reserved not because of any of the stands that he took in opposition to national education, but because of his views as to the purposes of education in general. In an essay written about 1861, "What Knowledge Is of Most Worth?", Spencer discussed the aims of education. It may be fair to claim that this essay, more than any other educational document of the nineteenth century, gave direction to the educational thought and practice of the twentieth century. What was Spencer's answer? What knowledge is of most worth? According to Spencer, it is scientific knowledge and especially that kind of scientific knowledge that leads to individual development. For him the individual's development is always first; social formation is always second. Literary education is nothing more than a "poor relative" in instruction. It is practically meaningless when compared with the kind of knowledge that can help individuals solve life's problems. This distrust of traditional knowledge is found not only in the essay "What Knowledge Is of Most Worth?" but also in Spencer's other essays, "Moral Education," "Intellectual Education," and "Physical Education."[14] In general, it can be said that Spencer completes the educational traditions that had their inception with Rousseau and Pestalozzi. His views, moreover, exemplify the individualism that was so characteristic of nineteenth-century English education.

Education in Russia

It is hardly possible to compare nineteenth-century developments of national systems of education in other European countries with those of

[14] These essays were published in reviews in England and were later united and republished in the United States in book form. See Herbert Spencer, *Education: Intellectual, Moral, and Physical,* Appleton-Century-Crofts, Inc., New York, 1927.

Russia. Russia's educational consciousness was slow in forming. Peter the Great and Catherine the Great, who belong to the seventeenth and eighteenth centuries, were responsible for the foundations of Russian education. In the nineteenth century we may mention Czar Alexander I (1801–1825) and Nicholas I (1825–1855) in connection with Russian education, but we cannot easily indicate the contributions that they made. More often than not, educational historians are content to say that they continued the work of their predecessors, although the educational work of their predecessors is not very obvious. Alexander II (1855–1881) was responsible for what one may call the beginnings of a national system of education in Russia, by establishing a state system of elementary schools that were open to all children. There was no such thing as compulsory attendance in these schools, however, and it is not possible to be precise about their effects. Apparently the ideal of popular education was accepted slowly, if not reluctantly, in Russia. About the time of the Bolshevist revolution (1917) no more than one-fourth of the children who were of school age were attending school, and less than one-quarter of the population of Russia was literate. The great educational advances in Russia belong to the next century.

SUMMARY

The nineteenth century was anxious to accept its educational inheritance. The ferment that characterized the two preceding centuries was still in evidence, and the outcomes from it were directed along practical lines toward the improvement of education. Two prominent educators attract our attention, Herbart and Froebel. As a result of Herbart's many accomplishments in education and psychology, it is possible to refer to him as the father of the science of education. His work made its greatest impression on the methods of teaching. Froebel was an idealist, who tried to reshape education along idealistic lines. In the main he failed. Yet in one area he was eminently successful. He founded the kindergarten—an institutional outgrowth of his educational philosophy—in 1837, and this institution has been his most important contribution to education.

The large educational movements of the nineteenth century had to do with national education. States began to see the relationship between education and national life and national goals. State systems came into existence. National education had its first and highest development in Prussia, then in Germany, then France, and finally England.

Questions and Exercises for Study and Discussion

1. What significance or meaning does the expression "science of education" have?
2. Trace the evolution of the science of education.
3. Explain Rousseau's and Pestalozzi's roles in building a science of education.
4. Report on the life of Herbart.
5. How did Herbart's work influence methodology? What are the "formal steps"?
6. Present Herbart's fundamental views on education. Are they accepted still?
7. Did Herbart influence the science of education in the United States?
8. Report on Froebel's life.
9. How did Froebel's philosophical views touch his theory of education by development?
10. Report on the early history of the kindergarten and discuss Froebel's relationship to the kindergarten.
11. Compare nineteenth-century educational reforms and innovations in Germany with those in France.
12. Report on nineteenth-century education in Russia.

14

Education in the United States

A PERIOD OF TRANSPLANTATION, 1635 TO 1750

The English colonists in America were not directly exposed to the educational movements of Europe in the seventeenth century. Many of the European practices were missing from the somewhat primitive educational opportunities that were offered to children in colonial America. Later, America was able to pick and choose and to profit to some degree from the experiments and mistakes that were made in Europe. But when the colonists were clearing the wilderness, the educational ferment that was being generated in Europe had very little effect upon their schools. Yet not all of the educational institutions, practices, and ideas of America are home-grown. If seventeenth-century European educational thought did not affect the American colonies much, the same cannot be said of eighteenth- and nineteenth-century European educational theory. It very definitely made its way across the Atlantic.

An essential characteristic of the social attitude of colonial New England was the contempt in which all democratic practices were held. The basis of modern American education—democracy—could not be found in the colonies. Another characteristic which profoundly influenced society and education was the colonists' absorption in religion. Religion was the dominant intellectual interest. In all the colonies of New England, with the exception of Rhode Island, the men responsible for the course of events were primarily concerned with the establishment of Bible commonwealths, and with the maintenance of an ecclesiastical social order sustained by a class-structured society.

Education had to come to the New England commonwealths in the context of an unequivocal repugnance for democracy, a definite limitation of the rights of suffrage and social status, and a conviction that the state should be subordinated to the church. Wherever schools were found in New England, these were the conditions and accepted convictions under which they operated.

In New England, where we find the earliest beginnings of education in America, there was a definite commitment to mental and moral training (although possibly not to schooling under formal auspices for all the children of the colony), which had its source in the religious ideals that the governing class espoused. To put it briefly, their religious beliefs led them to the conviction that a learned ministry was absolutely essential to the well-being of their creed. Since they knew that without educated leaders their sect would wither and die, they advocated the creation of educational opportunity that would produce and sustain a competent ministry. There are many different opinions as to why the colonists of New England, especially those in Massachusetts Bay, wanted schools and education. The reasons suggested range all the way from the desire on the part of the New England Puritans to cultivate liberal education to their conviction (and that of the leaders in some of the other American colonies) that education must and would serve the needs of institutionalized religion and the interests of a class-structured society.[1] Just where the truth lies on this question of educational purpose is hard to say. But we do not find much evidence to support the view that the educational intent of the Puritans was liberal or that the institutions that were founded or the ideals that surrounded instruction could lead very naturally to liberality of mind. The typical attitude of the New England colonist was that educational goals had to subserve superior interests; the most superior of all interests was religion. Education, then, was set in this context. It was religious in content and purpose. It was practical.

This attitude did not necessarily retard educational development. Institutionalized religion is not always tempted to stand in the way of educational opportunity or intellectual enlightenment. It was precisely because the ideals that they respected necessitated education that the colonists of New England set about making provisions for schooling. Almost from the beginning there was some sentiment in favor of offering educational opportunity rather generously. Not everyone concurred. The traditional attitude with which the colonists were familiar was that each man should be educated according to his means, and a vocal and effective portion of society did not want to assume any responsibility for education. Others seemed to support a kind of collectivism in education in New England, and believed that the community had some responsi-

---

[1] For further insight into the conflicting views of the early system of education in New England, see Samuel Eliot Morison, *The Puritan Pronaos,* New York University Press, New York, 1936, p. 30; Edgar W. Knight, *Education in the United States,* 3d ed., Ginn & Company, Boston, 1951, p. 85; and Merle Curti, *The Social Ideas of American Educators,* Charles Scribner's Sons, New York, 1935, pp. 4–5.

bility for the instruction of its members. Although this principle may not have been especially effective in providing widespread opportunity, we must not forget that it was responsible for town organization for education. The famous educational acts of the Massachusetts colony were logical expressions of this principle. The foundation of school organization was the town.

The town, of course, arose out of the peculiar circumstances and needs of the New England community and was not created for educational purposes. It was a compact type of settlement that was able to adapt itself to the needs of the people. The inhabitants of the town may have been farmers, fishermen, or businessmen. The town's area was not usually less than twenty square miles or more than forty, but in every case the size of a town depended upon the colony's legislative body. If a congregation or a group of people wanted to organize a town, they did so by petitioning the colonial government; and if the colonial government granted their petition, it marked out the boundaries of the town. The title to the land was assigned to proprietors, the affluent members of the community. The town, therefore, was a kind of corporate entity. With its legal creation, the town assumed an important place in colonial political life. Now it was able to send representatives to the colonial legislature, and it was given a good deal of freedom in the conduct of local affairs. There were broad areas for local action at this time; in some things—possibly education could be included—the local town unit was autonomous. But to return to town organization: When the town received its legal recognition from the colonial legislative unit, its officers began to assign plots of land in the village on which the proprietors and inhabitants could build their homes. Other plots were assigned for other purposes. A farmer would be allotted another plot of land on the outskirts of the village where he could till the soil; an artisan would be allotted a place in the village where he could build his shop. This land was assigned to the inhabitants of the town and was legally held by them. Yet not all the land of the town was assigned to private ownership. Pasture land and wooded areas, for instance, were reserved for common use, and there was no individual ownership of the commons.[2] After all the inhabitants of the newly formed town had had their property designated, the town may still have had some undistributed land. Such land was simply held by the town for future assignment. A newcomer to the town could apply for a portion of the land that remained unclaimed, and if the town board voted its approval, a plot of land would be assigned to the newcomer.

[2] For a broader appraisal of the town in New England life, see John Fairfield Sly, *Town Government in Massachusetts,* Harvard University Press, Cambridge, Mass., 1930.

It was in New England that the town meeting came into prominence. The town meeting was a forum in which the affairs of the community were conducted. In such a system, although there were many signs of democracy, there was no such thing as popular government even on the town level. Only qualified members of the town could participate in the discussions of the town meeting and vote the decisions, and usually the qualifications were stated in terms of an individual's status in the town: Was he a householder? What was his estate worth? Did he have a good reputation? All of these questions demanded a proper answer. In addition to these other requirements, an attained age of twenty-four was usually demanded.[3]

Thus, the town was governed by an oligarchy. But this was not a permanent arrangement, for the seeds of this system's destruction were in it from the very beginning. The original system of political control that was established in New England was indebted to institutionalized religion for its support. As religion became weaker, authoritarianism in government tended to become weaker too. New England was, after all, a frontier. Democracy has always thrived better on the frontier than anywhere else. Repression and regulation are the weapons of authoritarianism, and these weapons were becoming progressively less effective in the New England of the seventeenth century. Church leaders were aware of the diminution of their authority. But in spite of their desperate efforts to maintain control and power over the people, the ministers of the gospel saw this power gradually slip away from them. At one time their political, economic, social, and even religious authority went unquestioned. This condition of affairs changed. Magistrates and gentlemen as well as ministers were losing their power. The man who was coming into the picture, not yet a man to be given control in any democratic sense but a man to be reckoned with, nevertheless, was the common man. There were a number of reasons for these decided shifts in society which we cannot consider here.[4] We are concerned mainly to know that in this social ferment the first steps were taken in the interest of education.

The first advance, which was also the most famous and perhaps the most effective, was made by the Massachusetts Act of 1642. In this act we have the first example of compulsory education in the English American colonies. Between 1642, when the Massachusetts statute was passed, and 1671, all of the New England colonies except Rhode Island enacted laws which required that the children of the commonwealths be edu-

[3] *Ibid.*, pp. 75–76.
[4] On this point, see M. W. Jernegan, *The American Colonies, 1492–1750*, Longmans, Green & Co., Inc., New York, 1929, pp. 179 ff.; and Ralph Barton Perry, *Puritanism and Democracy*, Vanguard Press, Inc., New York, 1944.

cated. It must be emphasized, however, that compulsory education did not necessarily mean schooling. None of these early acts required the communities to establish schools or required anyone to attend a public institution. The legislation that made education compulsory put upon the home the burden of offering what were considered to be the minimum essentials for a Bible commonwealth. If the home would not or could not accomplish the goals that the law set up, then it was assumed that the child would be removed from the home or from the master to whom he had been apprenticed and put in a place where he could obtain the required education. This was a departure from the English laws on which these statutes were based—the Statute of Apprentices of 1562 and the English Poor Law of 1601—for the first English laws had not made anything more than the care of children a social obligation. If for any reason a child was removed from the home, from his parents or master, the responsibility of society was to see that he had food and shelter, nothing else. New England, slightly more humanitarian in its outlook, went a little beyond this and required that such a child receive not only some trade training but some academic education as well.

The Massachusetts Act of 1642 was, then, the first law in English America to make education compulsory for children. It was up to the selectmen of the town to determine whether or not the requirements of the law had been fulfilled. If they were not, if the children were not taught a calling or a trade and could not read well enough to understand the principles of religion or the capital laws of the colony, the parents could be fined, or the children could be removed from the home or from the care of the master. The Massachusetts law of 1642 was the model legislation for other colonies that enacted similar laws. Its main features remained even in the new law in 1648. In this new law the selectmen were to see that the children in their jurisdiction were able to read perfectly in English in order that they might be able to arrive at an understanding of the laws of the colony. The children were also to be taught the orthodox catechism so thoroughly that they would be able to answer questions on it. The provision for teaching a trade or calling remained much as before; parents or masters were "to bring up their children and apprentices in some honest lawful calling, labor, or imployment." The selectmen, with the help or advice of two magistrates, could remove children from situations wherein the law was not being fulfilled and apprentice them to some master who would abide by the law. Under such conditions boys were apprenticed until they were twenty-one and girls until they were eighteen.[5]

The motives for the enactment of this law in the colonies were evi-

[5] M. W. Jernegan, *Laboring and Dependent Classes in Colonial America, 1607–1783,* University of Chicago Press, Chicago, 1931, pp. 91–95.

dently economic, religious, and educational. The economic and religious motives are too obvious to require further comment. The educational motive, however, was not a pure one. It was put in the same context of educational goals that surrounded the school for the common man in the dual systems.[6] In other words, reading was stressed solely or mainly for the value that this skill would have in controlling a population that was completely regulated down to the finest details of an individual's life.

As we have said, all the New England colonies save Rhode Island passed such statutes. The next question is: How well or how exactly were these laws enforced? Though a serious effort was no doubt made to enforce them, a number of children in the colonies did not have the educational or vocational opportunity that the law assumed they would have. The cause of popular education, we must believe, was advanced a great deal by the example and effects of the Massachusetts law of 1642 and the laws modeled after it; but the laws themselves were not permanent, and the tradition that was begun for compulsory education met with at least temporary frustration. Late in the seventeenth century— from 1686 to 1689 to be exact—all of the New England colonies were united in a dominion under the governorship of Sir Edmund Andros. Colonial charters were revoked during this regime, and the laws that pertained to compulsory education were repealed or rendered ineffective. Thus, as the seventeenth century came to a close, much of the foundation that had been laid for popular education had been uprooted, and the tradition that was initiated with the Massachusetts Act of 1642 was sidetracked and stalled.

But before these unfortunate happenings interrupted educational progress, some of the colonies had taken another step forward. They legislated with regard to schools. Perhaps the progressive colonist realized that a law which required the accomplishments of education needed to be implemented. Again Massachusetts took the lead and passed the famous "Old Deluder Satan Act." Even before the Massachusetts colony took what is regarded by many as the most significant step in furthering the cause of public and free schools, some of the towns were already making provisions for the education of their children. Compulsory-education statutes placed an unequal and, in some cases, an impossible burden on the people of the towns, and many people opposed efforts to carry them out. But the laws were on the books, and the towns had to obey them. Some towns established schools and supported them. The school-establishment movement was by no means a popular one, however, and perhaps not more than a half-dozen towns brought such schools into existence before 1647. Those that did provided for the school's main-

[6] See pp. 416–417.

tenance in a number of ways: Some taxed the people of the town; others used land that belonged to the town for the support of the school; still others were fortunate in having wealthy citizens who donated whatever was necessary for the support of the school. Few, however, overlooked the source of income or school support that was the student himself, and tuitions or rates were almost always charged.[7] It is not possible to find any free school during this period. This generalization is meant to include the famous Boston Latin School, which, it is often said, was a free school. Although the Boston Latin School may have been planned as a free school, in actual practice it was not.

A good deal of activity on the part of the towns and of sentiment among the people was directed toward the establishment of town schools. This increasing interest provided a basis for the famous Massachusetts Act of 1647. We know from experience that much cultivation of the public mind is necessary before the enactment of social legislation and that few, if any, laws are very far in advance of the public desire for such legislation. The Act of 1647, although it encountered some opposition, probably expressed the people's will. And it should be observed that the act was well within the limits of the educational tradition that originated in Europe and was reinforced in this country first in the law of 1642. The legislation of 1647 required the towns of Massachusetts, if they had fifty or more householders, to appoint a teacher to teach any children who came to him the skills of reading and writing. The law provided for the support of the teacher in this way: "[his] wages shall be paid either by the parents or masters of such children, or by the inhabitants in general, by way of supply, as the major part of those that order the prudentials of the town shall appoint."[8] The warning was given that the charges should not be higher than the going rate. But the law went beyond providing for a mere reading-and-writing master. It demanded that every town whose population was greater than one hundred householders supply the children with "a grammar school, the master thereof being able to instruct youth so far as they may be fitted for the university."[9] The law provided that fines should be levied against those towns that did not comply with the statute. Perhaps it should be added here, and somewhat by way of anticipating what will be presented shortly, that the university for which these youths were to "be fitted" was Harvard College.

This law became the model for educational legislation in the other

[7] Jernegan, *Laboring and Dependent Classes in Colonial America, 1607–1783*, pp. 72–82.

[8] Quoted in Edward J. Power, *Education for American Democracy*, McGraw-Hill Book Company, Inc., New York, 1958, p. 37.

[9] *Ibid.*, p. 38.

colonies of New England. It was followed in every colony except Rhode Island. There are good reasons for thinking of this law, the "Old Deluder Satan Act," as the foundation for American public education. Yet the motives of those who were active in obtaining passage of the act were not at all attuned to ideals that today would be recognized as vital to the support of public education. The people of the colonies, we must admit, wanted the advantages of education, knew that the reading of good literature would bring them something of value, and were for, rather than against, literacy. But this was only part of the picture, and a rather inchoate part at that. The real motives behind the Massachusetts Act of 1647 and other laws like it had to do with religious and political authority. Education was to enable the masses to understand and obey the regulations of the church and the laws of the state. The act was religious, civic, and social in its outlook, and literary values were not foremost in the minds of those who supported the legislation. Perhaps the outstanding feature of the law of 1647 was that it recognized the state as an instrument for education. This was the beginning of a legal precedent that is still with us.

In general, the law of 1647 was apparently not too well observed for the first half century after its passage. There is a good deal of dispute among historians on this point; some claim that the law was not honored at all; others insist that it was followed faithfully. In any event, education became more popular, and the means of education were more generously distributed. Whether or not these were direct effects of the law of 1647 and its tradition may be disputed.

COLONIAL SCHOOLS

Four types of schools were found in the New England colonies: the dame school, the town school, the Latin grammar school, and the college. All were transplanted schools; that is, their chief characteristics were imported from Europe.

The Dame School

The dame school is more difficult to understand than any of the other colonial schools. The difficulty is not in understanding its nature, for it was a simple school in which the elements of reading, spelling, and religion were taught, but rather in understanding why it should have existed at all. The dame school was always outside the context of public education. It was an extension of the home's educational function rather than a downward extension of the school, and it disappeared when the functions of the elementary school became broader. One of the reasons why the dame school was able to maintain itself as long as it did was

that the town school—the type of school that came into existence following the legislation of 1647—often required that entering students be
able to read. This would seem to us an unusual requirement, but it was
made often enough to keep the dame school a rather necessary establishment. The teacher in the dame school was usually a woman of the community who had the time, the necessary skill, and the room to conduct a
school. The school was kept in her kitchen (thus the name "kitchen
school"), and fees were charged. Because these schools were outside the
ambit of public responsibility, there are few records of them and little
basis on which to write much of their history. Yet it may be true, as
some writers have suggested, that some dame schools, for one reason or
another, did receive some public support.[10]

If the dame school appears to us an oddity, we must remember that
it was a more logical outcome of current educational theory than the
town school. The most fundamental of all educational beliefs then was
that the individual, not society, was responsible for his own education.
We have already remarked that there were two points of view on this
matter,[11] but it should be clear that the dame school found its support
in the view that the child's education is first, and probably exclusively,
a responsibility of the home. If the home determined that some delegation of its educational function was necessary, the dame school was ready
to take over.

The Town School

When the town school first appeared as an import from England, its
curriculum consisted of writing and arithmetic. This was a continuation
of the scribal tradition in education;[12] the school's main purpose was to
educate clerks. But in New England it was almost impossible to keep
reading out of the elementary school's curriculum, for the most necessary
of the elementary skills was reading, not arithmetic or writing. Thus,
the town school in New England, following the prescript of the Act of
1647, became at first a reading school. Before long, however, the school
was devoting its attention to the three R's, not the three R's of the
twentieth century, but of the seventeenth: reading, writing, and religion.
Arithmetic was thought to be a mercantile skill and was not commonly
taught except in the towns that enjoyed a commercial status. In spite of
this tendency to isolate skills as they had been isolated before, the colonists soon came to include in their schools the content that is now universally accepted as proper to the elementary school.

[10] See Newton Edwards and Herman G. Richey, *The School in the American
Social Order*, Houghton Mifflin Company, Boston, 1947, p. 68.
[11] See pp. 427–428.
[12] See pp. 14 and 22.

The town school was not always an elementary school. When a town had more than one hundred householders, its obligation was to have a school which would "fit youth for the university." Clearly, the law of 1647 intended that the town school should go beyond elementary subjects in its offerings. In spite of this legal obligation, the towns apparently employed one master and charged him with the responsibility of teaching youth the first elements of education and with instructing more advanced students in the mysteries of the Latin language and the classics.

The town school, then, was, as the law required, a reading-and-writing school. There seems to be no need to distinguish between the reading school and the writing school after compulsory-school laws were adopted in the New England colonies.[13] For a few years before these laws were passed in Massachusetts in 1647, it may have been true that a reading school was maintained separately from a writing school, but we have little historical assurance for this statement. It should not be forgotten that the town system provided also for the more advanced education of youth. In many respects the town school was a secondary school and a Latin school, although it is surely true that most of the boys who came to the colonial colleges had attended, not a town school, but a private Latin grammar school.

The Latin Grammar School

The first permanent school established in English America was the Boston Latin Grammar School. This was a school that could trace its educational inheritance all the way back to the schools of the Hellenistic period. In a number of important respects it had changed but little from the schools common in that age.[14] Its more recent progenitor was, however, the classical school, the Gymnasium, of Sturm. The Latin grammar school came to New England recommended highly by the traditions of the Protestant Revolt and the Renaissance. It would be a mistake to think that the colonists of New England could create a Latin school modeled exactly after the Latin grammar schools of England, and it would be overgenerous to think that they could or would create an institution with the liberality of purpose that the English Latin grammar school came in time to have. The Latin grammar school of New England was first and foremost a religious institution. Its curriculum contained the usual classical subjects, although no attention was given to mathematics, science, modern language, or history. The school's content was narrowly and exclusively classical. The fathers of the colony and the founders of the school had little real interest in the classics, but they

[13] A compulsory-school law required the establishment of schools or the appointment of teachers. It is not to be confused with compulsory-attendance laws.

[14] See pp. 120–122.

were interested in the making of minds, and they followed the theory of the day which maintained that the best way to form the mind was to study the classics. They followed the theory of mental discipline and insisted that it be applied without exception to all secondary school subjects. What a boy learned was much less important than how his mind was formed. This must have been an unavoidable conclusion, for it would surely be hard to prove that the Latin tongue and the literature of the classics could have had a practical value for the people of New England. Even the boys who were thinking of the ministry as their life's work could not be sure that the knowledge of the classics that they obtained from their studies would have any real utility for them. Yet the Latin grammar school had only one commission: to prepare boys for college. Since the colleges were classical schools, the New England college was in a position to dictate objectives to the Latin grammar schools for many years to come.

The Latin grammar school was never a highly popular institution in New England or elsewhere in America. It was a school that catered to the so-called better classes; it pretended to be a school for the elite, and it maintained an exclusive policy of admissions. In addition to this, it was a school exclusively for boys.

The Latin grammar school was the best evidence that the New England attitude toward education was not democratic. A boy's education was primarily a matter for individual initiative and means. Although the Latin school did at times receive some public support in the form of money or land grants, this support was never regular, and it was never given in such a way that the private control of the institution was jeopardized. To a greater extent than the colonial colleges, the Latin grammar school repelled the threat of state or colonial intervention and control. Even the law of 1647 and its educational aftermath did little to disrupt the placid existence of the Latin school. The grammar master that the towns employed was really no threat to the established Latin school. The prestige of the Latin school was such that boys who wanted to go to college and maintain their position in the class-structured society could ill afford to ignore the opportunity that the school offered.

Although we may charge the Latin school with lack of democracy and with an inability to revise its curriculum according to the changes that were taking place in the world, we can hardly show that the Latin school did not achieve its own objectives. It did not pretend to be anything other than what it was. The records of these schools, their permanency and their success, as well as the successful careers of so many of their students, surely suggest that the schools were institutions that merit our respect, although we may want to withhold endorsement from the theory of secondary education that they espoused.

The College

About 1635 the fathers of the city of Boston were instrumental in creating the Boston Latin Grammar School; one year later the fathers of the Massachusetts Bay colony created the first college in English America. It is significant that the first colony-wide action in the interest of education was directed at higher education. By an action of the General Court, the colonial legislature, £400 were appropriated for the establishment of a college. This was the school that was to become Harvard.

Why was Harvard founded? Clearly, for the purpose of perpetuating the learned ministry. Now, preparing men for the ministry meant a good deal more than merely teaching boys some ritual for the performance of ceremonials. Congregationalism was not ritualistic; neither was it evangelistic. Puritanism in the wider sense was an intellectual creed or assent as well as a religious confession. It was to maintain the status of intellectualism in society as well as to sustain the religious doctrine embraced by the colony that the college was founded. In this primarily religious purpose standards of scholarship or literary quality were not forgotten, and the college established outside of Boston, now Harvard, was an entirely respectable academic institution. Yet, it was by no means a school that was committed to liberal objectives. Although all Harvard graduates did not become ministers, the first reason for the establishment of the college was to prepare men for that calling. In this objective the college founded in Massachusetts was not different from the vast majority of colleges that appeared later on the colonial scene.

If Harvard's chief purpose was to prepare ministers, how was this purpose accomplished? What experiences, academic and otherwise, did the students have at the college? How was it organized, and how was it governed, and what precedents did this college set for American higher education? To these questions we can give only a partial answer here.

The preparation of ministers for the Congregational church departed from what might be called orthodox seminary training. This departure was possible because, as we have said, the creed demanded little in the way of ritualistic compliance, and as a matter of fact, when the prospective preacher left the college he was not even ordained. Ordination was left to the congregation. More importantly, however, the minister was looked up to as a leader in society and a teacher. This latter role had been attached to the Christian ministry in the early days of the Church, and the attachment had been maintained. The Congregational minister, although there were certain points of doctrine on which he had to be orthodox, was expected to examine and analyze the truths of

Christianity and interpret them to his congregation. He was not expected to be a purveyor of church doctrine. He had to be an educated man to fulfill the role created for him, and education that fitted him best for the role was the traditional classical education that had been inherited by the modern period from the Renaissance. The prospective minister who passed through Harvard's halls followed an intellectual program that seemed to be the liberal arts. Grammar, logic, rhetoric, geometry, and astronomy were taught the young men, as were ethics, metaphysics, natural science, and possibly some Hebrew, Greek, and ancient history. Latin was the language of instruction. This was the single curriculum at Harvard; regardless of the vocational aspirations of a young man, this was the course of studies that he was required to pursue.

The chief, and sometimes the only, teacher in the college was the president. Now and then the finances of the college would permit that he be provided with the assistance he needed. Assistants would teach some of the lower classes; usually they were young men who had just graduated with their bachelor's degree and were waiting for a call from some congregation. They did not regard their teaching activity as anything more than what it was, a steppingstone to the ministry. The college president was himself a minister. He taught a full load at the college, ministered to a nearby congregation, and looked after all of the domestic needs of the boys at the school. In addition to this, the college president was expected to conduct a campaign to strengthen the institution. This campaign was, of course, a money-raising venture.

With all the responsibilities, the president at Harvard, like the presidents at other colonial colleges, had little real authority. College government was exercised from the outside. That is to say, the men who ruled the college, the trustees of the institution, were not part of the teaching staff or the administration. They were ministers, magistrates, and businessmen, who saw nothing unusual or incongruous about their taking the reins of control and making the basic decisions for an institution with which they had had only a very limited experience. Perhaps this was the major precedent that was initiated by Harvard, for with few exceptions the control of American colleges and universities continues to be from the outside.

In addition to Harvard, the colonial college that preceded all the rest in America, the following permanent colonial colleges were founded before 1769: William and Mary, 1693; Yale, 1701; Princeton, 1746; Columbia, 1754; the University of Pennsylvania, 1755; Brown, 1765; Rutgers, 1766; and Dartmouth, 1769. These were the colleges that set the tone for American higher education, and to some degree they are still exercising a function of leadership. And with the exception of the University of Pennsylvania, founded as the College, Academy, and Charitable School of Philadelphia, all were founded with a definite denominational affiliation. At least in the beginning, they shared the common objective of providing ministers for the churches.

COLONIAL EDUCATION OUTSIDE NEW ENGLAND

Early education in New England was so distinctive and so purposeful that it often overshadows colonial education elsewhere in the colonies. Of course our great interest in education in New England is justified in the light of history, but we should not on this account ignore the really fruitful developments and precedents for education that were generated elsewhere in colonial America. No one will find the beginnings of the American public school system in Pennsylvania, New York, or in the Southern colonies, but in spite of the lack of striking innovations in educational policy, this region made some contributions that should not be entirely obscured.

When we begin to examine the educational position of the Middle colonies and the South, we realize that the people, the motives for colonization, and the social and political environment were all drastically, almost dramatically, different from the North. We can hardly expect that educational opportunity in these regions would be the same as that offered by the Puritans in New England.

In New York and Pennsylvania the educational policy seemed to be to let things alone. Of course in these two colonies there was no real question of church domination. In the first place, the state was too strong to let the church exercise control; and in the second, far too many denominations were represented for any one to gain a dominant position and retain it. The policy was one of educational *laissez faire* so far as the state was concerned. Schooling became an individual matter or a matter for the separate congregations or sects to deal with. Here in the Middle colonies we find the precedent established for parochial systems of schools.

The South followed the educational policy that had been honored for so many decades in England. The economic and social arrangements of the South tended to sustain this policy so effectively that anything resembling public responsibility for education, except in the case of orphans and paupers, was difficult to find. Since the colony was most reluctant to provide any other kind of educational opportunity, the endowed, charity, and denominational school was the type that developed. Denominationalism in education in the South was so pronounced that the College of Georgia, now the University of Georgia, was actually, although not nominally, a denominational school in its first years.[15]

---

[15] On this point, see E. Merton Coulter, *College Life in the Old South*, University of Georgia Press, Athens, Ga., 1951, pp. 151 ff.

On the whole, the institutional provisions for education in the Middle and Southern colonies reflected the inherited traditions and customs of the colonists as well as the dominant economic, social, and political conditions of the colonies. The most characteristic thing about education on all levels in this block of colonies was its diversity, whereas in New England the outstanding feature was uniformity.

Catholic Education in New America

We can find no very clear record of American Catholic schools before the Revolutionary War. The reasons for this are clear. There were probably not more than 22,000 Catholics in English America in 1775. Such a small Catholic population, dispersed as it was and often with abstracted political privileges, could not have supported many Catholic schools. Even when Catholic schools were established, the Catholic colonist often found that it served his interests best to keep the existence of the schools in strict confidence. Nothing could be gained by keeping records of the progress of such schools in colonies where Catholicism was despised and often legally proscribed. There was no great disposition among the American Catholic pioneers to maintain historical archives, and besides, many of the colonial Catholic schools were part of missionary activities of which few accounts could be kept.

The first opportunities for Catholic education within the present boundaries of the United States were provided by Franciscan friars in Florida and New Mexico. In New Orleans, where an Ursuline Academy was founded in 1727, in St. Louis, Detroit, Vincennes, and upper Maine, Catholic educational ventures were undertaken and met with relatively good success. The first Catholic schools in the English colonies were organized in Maryland under the direction of the Jesuits. A school founded at St. Mary's City about 1640 was probably the first Catholic school in that section; it may not have been more than an elementary school. A secondary school was opened by the Jesuits in Newton, Maryland, as early as 1673. A Catholic school was started in New York City about 1685. We can be fairly definite about these early school foundations, but about a number of other Catholic schools in Maryland, Pennsylvania, and other colonies it is not possible to be precise.

Wherever Catholic schools were found, they reflected the traditional practices of Catholic schools in Europe. Thus, in every sense, Catholic schools were transplanted schools.

THE TRANSITION, 1750 TO 1820

The second period in the development of American education opened with the founding of the Academy and closed with the creation of the American high school. These are events, however, that should be taken as landmarks; in actual fact they are more the effects than the causes of educational ferment.

Reshaping the American Mind

When education was first brought to America, it reflected in institutions and ideals its indebtedness to the country from which it had been transported. The colonial period proper, that is, the years from 1635 to 1750, was in educational matters an old and conservative period, however venturesome it may have been in settlement and colonization. The ideals by which men lived were the tested and true ideals of the past, and no one questioned their validity. It never entered the minds of the thinking men that the world was passing them by, but this, in fact, was what was happening. The question was not whether the ideals were valid for all time (for who could test them in any ultimate fashion?) but whether they were relevant to the present time. As far as education was concerned, it became clearer and clearer that the theories that dominated it were not entirely relevant, but even this realization did not bring about any educational revolution. The period which we have under consideration now was a period of marked evolution, which affected the schools and all education in a very significant way. On the other hand, this evolution was never so forceful that it upset all of the old schools. There were many pockets of resistance to change and many outposts of inertia, and some of the outworn ideals of the early period were never discarded. By way of summary, we may say that the fundamental characteristics of the old society were that (1) the colonies had a close political tie with the mother country; (2) the culture was inherited from the mother country, and the conservative wisdom of the age determined that this culture be preserved; (3) society was organized into a fairly rigid class structure; and (4) the religious tradition, especially that of Puritan New England, dominated almost all of life. These are characteristics that may be listed by way of summary, as we have said, but they may be placed also in juxtaposition with the characteristics of the new period. It is the new period that concerns us most now, and in its changed character we find the American mind taking on a new, broader, and more democratic dimension.

The fundamental question was: Who is man and what sort of society is best for him? This is an unavoidable and constant social and human inquiry. What the world is like in any period influences the kind of answers that men give. We must indicate at the outset that the answers to fundamental questions were not what they had been before. This change in philosophy led to a distinctive intellectual climate, one in which new and sometimes radical ideas concerning man, society, and education might be generated.

As much as anything else, the Enlightenment was a factor in causing men to reevaluate their thinking.[16] The Enlightenment was not a very positive force in the history of thought, but if it did nothing else it did motivate men to examine the assumptions upon which they had operated. The general code of the Enlightenment was to denounce authority, whatever its source, and to depend only on those assumptions that could be tested in the clear light of pure reason. Whatever the evils of such a system may have been, the new life that invigorated science came, in part, from the Enlightenment. We need mention only the names of men of the stature of Rutherford (1749–1819), Cavendish (1731–1810), Bergman (1735–1784), Lavoisier (1743–1794), and Volta (1745–1827) to make the point a little clearer. Yet, in spite of the unmistakable influence generated by the Enlightenment, we must not think that scientific thought rushed through an unguarded door and was welcomed with open arms by those who waited inside. Actually the higher schools and the American colleges had little time for the thought that came from the Enlightenment. Most of the schools of higher learning were actively opposed to anything that scientific education might represent. And the lower schools, of course, are never in a position to introduce new ideas. By their very nature they must reflect what society has already accepted as tested values to be transmitted. This constitutes a marked difference between higher and lower schools: Colleges, but more especially universities, should be in the vanguard of culture and thought; secondary and elementary schools must bring up the rear. Neither the Enlightenment nor science actually invaded the schools of America, yet both came in time to influence them. Slowly but surely the movement contributed to changes in the purposes and curricula of the colleges, in the hopes and aspirations of lower schools, and brought about a democratic system of education in the United States.

Faith in the power of knowledge, coupled with the unwillingness to accept the conservative wisdom of the previous age, a wisdom that made human progress unlikely if not impossible, brought about still further changes. The root of this new way of thinking may be called humanitarianism. Its most important constituent was the idea of human progress. Man was able, according to this view, to control the world and other men in such a way that progress would be inevitable and possibly even infinite. The key to the whole program of human progress was knowledge. And who could speak of knowledge without thinking at once of schools and the means for education? With such a deep and sincere faith, a faith not to be despised or scorned, education came to be a kind of religion. Men could become excited about it, and they could defend its virtues with infectious arguments and seductive devices. Of course it would be unreasonable to suppose that this new humanitarianism

[16] See p. 368.

was not challenged by the old order, for it contained in it the seeds that could destroy the old order. If society's stamina is to be found in knowledge, and if knowledge is available and waiting to be found and is not an exclusive prerogative of an aristocracy, the aristocracy loses its position of influence. No one gives up easily those things that he values highly. Who could expect the so-called better classes to capitulate without a struggle?

One thing leads to another. When the Enlightenment called upon reason to testify, it did not merely suggest that revelation and authority based thereon were undependable; it stated so explicitly. As the effects of the Enlightenment moved across the land and as men became more and more enamored of humanitarianism, there was greater and greater secularization of thought and feeling in America. The first step in this direction was recorded when religion began to lose its hold on the intellectual life of the eighteenth century. The clearest example of the ground that was being lost by denominationalism was that whereas before the Revolution nine colonies had established churches, within a few years after it, the established church was almost totally a thing of the past.

The philosophical idea was expressed, and more often than not in clear and precise language, that men are equal before the law and that they should have greater opportunity for political and social equality. The testing ground for this theory of social equality and social mobility as well as for freedom and self-reliance was the vast frontier that the new world afforded to men and their families. The frontier was the incubator for democracy.

Democracy as an ideal is one thing; democracy as a reality, both political and social, is another. The idea came first; the reality was a long time in being achieved. Yet the first steps in translating ideas into reality were taken in this context when a new political order was established in which social democracy and democratic institutions could be born and where they could grow. This was the framework that education needed for its rebirth. It was possible within such a framework to construct new ideals and generate new patterns of instruction. Finally, we come to the question of means—not means on the level of the internal functioning of a school, but means of a broad social type. Where was the support for education to come from? Although this was a question that may not have been articulated before 1820, it was a problem that was understood. It belonged to the question of the economic levels of society, and it involved a variety of considerations that had to do with production, distribution, and consumption. Although we look in vain for what can be called a definite economic theory, that is, a theory in a formal and completely authentic sense, we can see that a number of economic interests did come into conflict. The most noticeable were those of the capitalists, on the one hand, and the agrarians on the other. There were the interests of the businessmen, the bankers, and the professional men, and there were the interests of the farmers, the artisans, and the common men. More often than not these interests were at odds. Each side formulated a set of doctrines and expressed them as coherently as possible in the hope of defending vested interests. The period that contained all this ferment, from say 1750 to 1820, was the period of transition. During these years intellectual battles were being waged whose outcomes made a foundation upon which democratic education could rest. The greatest strides in the direction of democratic education were taken by the two most important men of the period, Benjamin Franklin and Thomas Jefferson. Each contributed a great deal to American educational theory and practice.

Benjamin Franklin (1706–1790)

Benjamin Franklin had an engaging personality, an inventive mind, and a character that appreciated practical achievements. These traits were of considerable importance to him and to the country he served. Franklin, more than anyone else in this country or in Europe, understood the desire of the common man for independence, success, and intellectual illumination. This insight into men's desires and motives may have come to Franklin because he himself was once one of these common men, who, by reason of his own great ability and the learning he had obtained through his own efforts, had become an uncommon man. Besides this understanding of man's drive to lift himself out of his mediocrity, Franklin had a vision of America: He knew that the new world had a potential that up to his day had not even been tapped. He knew that the standards of the past could not be applied to the world that was just unfolding. Franklin was anything but an educational conservative, although there is no evidence that he ever advocated a truly revolutionary program for any of the schools that he founded.

If we compare his *Proposals Relating to the Education of Youth in Pensilvania* with what was being done in the better schools of the day (1749), we conclude that he was committed to important changes in education. There is a vast difference between what was being done at eighteenth-century Harvard, for example, and what Franklin thought should have been done. He was never willing to stop with theory. He wanted theories applied. When he set down the proposals for the academy, he followed through to see that the academy was founded.

The academy was a secondary school that embodied in its program of studies and its creed for education everything that Franklin had included in his famous *Proposals*. The theme, or basic philosophy of the academy was this: "As to their studies, it would be well if they could be taught every thing that is useful, and every thing that is ornamental: But art is long, and their time is short. It is therefore proposed that they learn those things that are likely to be most useful and most ornamental. Regard being had to the several professions for which they are intended."[17]

Franklin's views on education were not entirely original. He was restating the positions of many educational thinkers who had preceded him. Yet Franklin did make two proposals that, while not original, had far-reaching and lasting effects upon the American system. One had to do with the nonsectarian context in which American public education came to be set, and the other involved the emphasis upon utility in education. The first is easy to detect; American public education has a long history of nonsectarianism. The second may be found in the attention that has, in the past century, been given to the study of English. This concentration of attention has led to a shift of emphasis from the study of other languages which amounts to a virtual exclusion of them from the curricula of American schools. Perhaps Franklin may not be held responsible for the monolingual type of education that has become so common in America, but it is clear that he supported the inclusion of utility-centered subjects such as mathematics, the mechanic arts, and the methods of scientific experimentation, in the secondary school program. Following the model that Franklin provided in the Academy of Philadelphia, the secondary school in this country tended to become an English school rather than a classical school. We do not mean to imply that all of the classical schools were closed with the advent of Franklin's school, nor should we think that this tendency toward English education in the secondary school was never challenged. Yet, if Franklin had had his way, they would have been closed and English education would not have been challenged. Franklin had little time for the dead languages. As it was, the academies became exceedingly popular. They were generously supported by states, towns, and counties, and their founding was encouraged in every section of the country. The academy movement probably reached its height about 1850, when there were more than 6,000 academies, with more than 12,000 teachers, and about 260,000 pupils. It should be remembered, however, despite the generous public support they received, that academies were tuition schools and therefore closed to many children. They were never genuine public institutions.

The conviction that Franklin expressed everywhere in his writings is that man's general welfare ought to be and must be improved. Man's welfare is dependent on internal as well as external factors. Perhaps it depends most of all upon the intellectual illumination of each man. And

[17] Thomas Woody (ed.), *The Educational Views of Benjamin Franklin*, McGraw-Hill Book Company, Inc., New York, 1931, p. 178.

this illumination, Franklin would say, was not gained merely by coming in contact with disparate kinds of knowledge, but by pursuing all knowledge that would lead to the improvement of the general state of man. Franklin was utility-minded, there is no doubt of that, but he was not a narrow utilitarian. He understood the meaning of utility in the very same way that his age understood it, namely, anything that would lead to the betterment of mankind. Of course intellectual cultivation could not always be developed independently. A social agency was implied, and this social agency, the school, was charged with the mission of "making men" who in turn could make better worlds in which men could live. There was nothing ignoble or small about Franklin's educational vision. He stimulated America to move toward a commitment to universal public education. The realization of this ideal did not come in Franklin's day, but without Franklin it might not have come at all.

Thomas Jefferson (1743–1826)

Thomas Jefferson's major interest was the preservation of the democratic experiment. He was proud of the system of political organization that he had helped to bring into existence, and he wanted it perpetuated for the generations of Americans who would follow. This could best be done, Jefferson was convinced, by a system of public education. Education was the chief guardian and the principal lifeline of democracy; without education, democracy would perish. We cannot doubt the validity of Jefferson's view.

In order that education in the new world might provide the kind of foundation that Jefferson thought necessary for democracy, it would first of all have to be secular. It was not enough to distinguish education from religion; it was essential, Jefferson thought, to free the people from the coercion of religion. This meant creating a social environment wherein men would be entirely free to do as they pleased on matters involving religion. There were good reasons for the views that Jefferson held. History holds all kinds of examples of religious tyranny, and he wanted none of it in this country. Jefferson was not merely a theorist on this question of religious freedom. He was a member of the committee for the revision of the Virginia constitution (1776–1779), and as a result of his work on this committee an Act for Establishing Religious Freedom was passed by the Virginia Assembly in 1779. Another result of the committee's efforts, equally important to the future of America, was the Bill for the More General Diffusion of Knowledge. This bill contained the essentials of Jefferson's educational policy. Although it never became law in the commonwealth of Virginia, this bill did create an ideal of universal education without which American democracy surely could not have prospered. This bill is worth looking at a little more closely.

According to the proposal, Virginia would be divided into sections, called "hundreds," and each of these sections would have a school wherein reading, writing, and arithmetic were to be taught at public expense to all free children in the section. This opportunity would be given to each student for a period of three years, after which, although the public would no longer bear the expense of instruction, the child could remain in school if he wanted to. For every ten sections an educational supervisor would be appointed; he would presumably be a man fully qualified in learning and in the business of keeping schools.

In addition to the elementary system, Jefferson's plan provided for the establishment of secondary schools on a statewide basis. Twenty secondary school districts were to be organized in the colony. Each was to have a grammar school, which would be built and maintained by the public. It was to be located on a hundred-acre plot of land, and it was to have all the equipment necessary for keeping the boys in residence while they attended the school. Many of the boys would pay tuition, but provisions were to be made for giving scholarships to boys who could not pay tuition fees. The scholarship system was worked out with considerable mathematical intricacy. It is doubtful that it would have worked had it been put to a test, yet it did embody the practical realization that all of the boys chosen for the scholarship program would not succeed in school: The scholarships would be diminished each year until by the end of six years of instruction there would be only one-half as many scholarship students as in the beginning. The school was to have been a combination of the Latin grammar school and the academy. Although not a high school in the twentieth-century sense, it was a prophetic anticipation of the high school.

This secondary school system was intended to prepare qualified students for the College of William and Mary. Although this purpose was noted because William and Mary was already operating, the private college was not to be a permanent part of the system. Jefferson asked that a state university, the University of Virginia, be established. This would give the state a publicly supported college in which religion would not intrude. A system of state scholarships was planned for the state university: Twenty students from the grammar schools would receive such scholarships. In addition to the scholarship students, anyone who was qualified and could afford the costs could attend the state university.

The plan that Jefferson proposed was not accepted in 1779, and when he offered it again in 1817, it was again rejected by the legislature. This is evidence, surely, that most of the people were not ready for universal elementary education. It is evidence, too, that Jefferson was far in advance of the people and that he was giving them a goal toward which the educational enterprise might strive. Although the bills which he proposed did not become law in Virginia, his efforts were not totally without success. One of the areas in which his influence was felt was in state provisions for education: Many of the states, now sensitive to the Jeffersonian arguments and able to see that education and schooling were closely related to state objectives, began to put into their constitutions and statutes provisions that indicated that the state was now ready to assume some responsibility for education. Jefferson undoubtedly led the states in their movement toward the support and supervision of public education.

It would be hard to overestimate the influence that Thomas Jefferson had on American education. There is little real doubt that the ideal of universal education is to be attributed to him. But Jefferson had a strong interest in higher education too. It was important for him that the common man should be prepared to govern himself and that the progress of mankind should not be inhibited by institutions of higher learning that were nearly, if not actually, anti-intellectual. More than anything else, when Jefferson called for reforms in higher education, he was asking the colleges of the day to turn from their preoccupation with religion and make a real intellectual commitment to science and social responsibility. It was his view that the colleges should be concerned with real life. He was convinced that they should prepare leaders for the world that actually existed. All of these proposals were important to the evolution of higher education in America; but it should not be forgotten that Jefferson was also the first educational theorist in America to advance the theory of curricular electivism. In other words, he would have replaced the rigid curriculum of the earlier centuries, one in which students had no choice as to what they would study, with a curriculum that would give them a chance to select their courses according to their interests and abilities.

Catholic Education in Transition

The period from 1750 to 1820 was a transitional period in America, a time for many important social and political innovations. We have showed that education on all levels was called upon to serve American ideas more fully. This was the period in which Catholic education responded to the same call and began to show definite signs of increasing vitality.

Basic to any achievements in Catholic education was the more effective organization of the Church in America. Rev. John Carroll was appointed Prefect Apostolic of what is now the Eastern United States in 1784. At this time there was nothing that could be called a system of Catholic education: There were no Catholic colleges and only a few elementary and secondary schools. As a matter of fact, it was not yet clear that a separate system of Catholic schools was necessary. Father Carroll seemed to believe that the existing schools of the day were suitable and that it would be necessary only to establish a seminary for the education of priests.[18] Very shortly, however, Carroll modified his view; he found that the regular schools of the country were quite anti-Catholic and that they could not be used by Catholic children without danger to their faith. He turned his attention at once to the establishment of schools that would provide the necessary kind of educational opportunity. Yet he was able to establish only a few schools through his own efforts. The best known of these were Georgetown Academy (1786) and St. Mary's College and Seminary of Baltimore (1799). After 1790, when Carroll was consecrated Bishop of Baltimore, he provided exceptional leadership in broadening the base for Catholic education.

Perhaps the major problem that faced Bishop Carroll when he tried to keep the growth of Catholic education parallel to the growth of the Church in America was the shortage of qualified teachers. To help solve this problem, five American religious communities for women were founded, and many others were brought to the United States from Europe. Yet progress was slow. New teaching communities could not spring into action overnight—they needed time to grow and mature— and the religious teachers who came from Europe needed time in which to learn English and become accustomed to America and her ways before they could be most effective. Despite these obstacles and many others, Catholic education responded to the clearer vision of America, and as the Catholic Church grew in this great new country so also did Catholic education. No very adequate set of statistics is available for this period to reflect the growth of Catholic elementary and secondary schools. We must be satisfied to say that both diocesan and parish-sponsored, as well as independent Catholic elementary and secondary schools, increased in stature and numbers. It is possible to be somewhat more precise about Catholic college developments: Eight Catholic colleges were founded before 1820. They were Georgetown (1786), St. Mary's College, Baltimore (1799), St. Thomas Aquinas College, Kentucky (1807), Mt. St. Mary's College, Emmitsburg, Maryland (1808), New York Literary Institute, New York City (1809), St. Louis University (1818), Louisiana College, New Orleans (1819), and St. Joseph's College, Bardstown, Kentucky (1819). Three of these colleges are still in existence as colleges or universities: Georgetown, Mt. St. Mary's, and St. Louis.[19]

[18] John Gilmary Shea, *History of the Catholic Church in the United States,* J. G. Shea, New York, 1886–1892, vol. II, p. 260.
[19] See Edward J. Power, *A History of Catholic Higher Education in the United States,* The Bruce Publishing Company, Milwaukee, 1958, p. 333.

THE AMERICAN EDUCATIONAL AWAKENING, 1820 TO 1900

The third general period of American educational history spanned most of the nineteenth century. At the beginning of the period it would have been impossible to speak in any strict sense of an American educational system. When the period came to an end, the system was complete, and the structure was present for democratic opportunity in education. We cannot easily determine which of the three periods—transplantation, transition, or awakening—was the most important, but neither can we overestimate the importance of the years of educational awakening.

Education for Citizenship

About 1820, although there were tendencies in the direction of non-sectarianism in education, the American school was set in a religious atmosphere; the purpose of education was religious, and the content of education, although it was not mere catechism, was also mainly religious. It would be fair to say, then, that although early American education was not medieval education all over again, its ultimate objective was other-worldly. The directors of education were churchmen; for the most part they decided not only what would be taught but who the teachers would be. The teachers, although not much can be said for their qualifications, generally measured up to the expectations that were held out for education. The period after 1820, sometimes called the period of educational awakening, was heir to much of the secular thought of earlier years. Both Franklin and Jefferson were listened to. Although religious perspectives were not immediately altered in the schoolroom or religious content expurgated from the school syllabus, the educational interests of the people were no longer set in a narrow religious framework. Education was beginning to have a new mission. Education for citizenship was the new goal, and soon it was accepted in all publicly supported schools.

The extent of public education in the early years of the period is a matter sometimes disputed. By 1820 or 1830 many of the states had enacted statutes that promised the establishment of public school systems. Yet the meaning of *public* was not always precise, and the provisions for education made by the various states did not go much beyond an endorsement of the general expectation that all the children of the state should learn to read and write. Not even in New England did all the children of school age always attend public schools at public expense. And, of course, 1820 or 1830 is still too early for compulsory-attendance legislation, although such legislation did become a reality during the early part of the period of awakening. The most progressive legislation up to 1820 was the Northwest Ordinance of 1785. According to this legislation—an excellent example, incidentally, of national interest in education—section 16 of every township in the Northwest Territory was to be reserved for school purposes, and the income from such land was to be used for the schools. But the land that was set aside produced little revenue, and no state could have afforded to conduct a system of universal elementary schooling on the income from the national land grant. Not all of the states, moreover, participated in this grant from the national government.

Though the ideal of public education may have been acceptable, the idea of free education was somewhat repugnant to the American temperament. A long history of charity schools and pauper schools had made the American public understandably suspicious of the practice of free education. A great deal of evidence indicates how reluctant parents were to send their children to free schools. James Carter, in his *Essays on Popular Education*, referred to the unwillingness of the people of as progressive a state as Massachusetts to send their children to the schools that were supported out of public funds. Such schools were considered inferior. And not only the public free schools were affected by such an attitude. In the second decade of the nineteenth century, the Jesuit college in St. Louis found that if it adhered to the rule of the Society and offered instruction to its students gratuitously, the students of the quality that the Jesuits wanted would not come to the school. In the interest of preserving the ideals of education which their school was founded to serve, and in order to make the school appear academically respectable to the people of St. Louis, the Jesuits had to charge tuition. The tuition that was levied, while very moderate, was nevertheless enough to induce students to come, for now the school could not be regarded as a pauper school.[20] How curious it was that the free school idea had to fight two very different kinds of opposition. On the one hand, some people opposed the free schools because they did not want to pay for them or did not believe them to be consistent with democratic principles. On the other hand, other people were unwilling to send their children to schools that did not charge fees for instruction.

Opportunities for free public education were extremely limited at the outset of this period. One of the major accomplishments of the years after 1820 was the establishment of the principle that elementary schools, open to all, should be provided for the children of the country and that they should be able to attend such schools without either paying rates or being exposed to the ridicule of attending a pauper school. Some historians think that the foundations of free public education are to be found in the Eastern United States, and their view is supported by a

[20] On this point, see *ibid.* pp. 161–165.

great deal of evidence. Others think that in the Eastern United States the traditions of private education and of pauper and charity education were so strong that the free school idea could not readily take root, and that the West may have been the section of the country in which the free public school was accepted and developed. The free schools about which we are talking, it should be understood, were, with few exceptions, simple elementary schools which offered the rudiments. Despite opposition, the free school became an accepted and tested institution. By 1840, the free school, open to all the children of all the people, was the foundational institution in the American educational system. It may be called the common school.

The Common School

The common school grew out of the idea that the needs of a democratic government and of a democratic society require the majority of the people to be literate. The first objective of the common school was literacy. In time, of course, the common school was confronted with the problem of broadening and deepening its educational program, but in the beginning these schools were reading-and-writing schools and nothing more. Educational ideals are one thing; educational practice is another. It was a long step from the ideals expressed in the writings of Jefferson to the erection of publicly supported schools in which universal elementary education was possible. This long step was retarded at many points. The first and probably the most effective opposition came from the people who did not want to pay for public schools. The argument that they used is one that from that time to this has been used to block every forward movement or broadening of opportunity in public education, namely, that the economic resources of the country could not afford a system of schools that educated all the children of the land.

The second point of opposition was to be found on the level of educational control. In order to have an effective system of public elementary education, it was felt necessary to curtail the power of the districts.[21] These pockets of educational control had operated with near autonomy since the early years of the nineteenth century, and they were reluctant to give up any of the precious control that tradition and the disuse of state educational authority had won for them.[22] In the light of history it would seem obvious that the demand for more effective state supervision was unavoidable if the system of schools promising universal ele-

[21] For the origin and growth of the district in New England, see Walter Herbert Small, *Early New England Schools,* Ginn & Company, Boston, 1914, pp. 33 ff.

[22] The finest recent study of the history of the common school is by Lawrence A. Cremin, *The American Common School,* Teachers College, Columbia University, New York, 1951.

mentary education was to become an effective reality. Yet the light of history casts a clearer backward shadow, and the general opinion of the day seemed to be that although the state could and probably should aid in financing education on the local level, it should not set any of the standards according to which the schools were to operate. Eventually state supervision became a fact, but its realization was slow, and it was achieved only by overcoming concentrated and diligent opposition.

Finally, the hold that organized religion had on education was not relinquished without a fight. The churches, so long effective instruments in providing opportunity for education and exercising control over it, were no more willing to give up their schools than they would have been to give up their churches; the ministers were as reluctant to give up their dominant positions on school committees as they would have been to cede their pulpits to the deists. In time they had to relinquish the control they had exercised over education, and in time it was necessary to take denominational religion out of the common school. Had it not been for the decision to make public education nonsectarian, the experiment with universal elementary education might not have succeeded. The continued existence of the common school hung in the balance. Here were the alternatives: either to keep sectarianism in the common schools and sacrifice them, or to remove sectarianism and save the schools. In 1827 Massachusetts took the lead in requiring that all of its common schools exclude denominational teaching from the school syllabus. Neither God nor religion, in the general sense, was expelled from the school, but the distinctive teachings of the sects were no longer welcome, and according to law, they were not permitted. Thus, we see that before the common school could prosper, before it could be the instrument for extending democratic opportunity, it was necessary that three important battles be waged and won: the battles of support, supervision, and sectarianism.[23]

Public men of vision, educational organizations (the Western Literary Institute, the American Lyceum, and various conventions called to support educational causes), educational journalism, foreign example, and a generation of educational statesmen led the fight for the free common school. Space does not permit anything more than a word about these sources of support, except for the last, the educational statesmen. It is impossible to overlook the work of Horace Mann in the history of education in the United States, and to Mann's name may be added those of James Carter and Henry Barnard. There were many others, it is true, but these men were the great figures. The greatest and most influential of all was Horace Mann.

[23] I have dealt with these battles at greater length in my *Education for American Democracy*, pp. 136–148.

Horace Mann (1796–1859)

The most adequate characterization of Horace Mann is to say that he was a humanitarian. First of all, he believed in man. After having had an intimate connection with it in his early childhood and young manhood, he had rejected the Calvinistic doctrine of depravity. He never doubted that through education man could become perfect. This was a revolutionary doctrine, which ran counter to the accepted and central tradition that education was to be offered to those who could profit from it. Although a person's capacity for education depended upon many things, unacceptable social status and background were usually sufficient reasons to exclude otherwise capable children from the opportunities good schools afforded. From Mann's point of view, or from any point of view, the doctrine of perfectibility, coupled with education as its chief instrument, had broad social implications. This doctrine, reinforced by practical proposals for education, urged upon the American public the idea that if education were more generously distributed, not only would individuals be better and more humane, but society, too, would be freed from vice, crime, poverty, and other social ills. In a way this doctrine might appear to have a socialistic flavor. Yet, if it had implications for the status of the individual in society, it had, also, the advantage of promoting the industrial welfare; and thus, though perhaps indirectly, it was a doctrine that came in time to claim capitalism as an ally.

Mann appeared on the educational scene when a reformer of his type was most needed. Irrespective of the quality of his ideas, he was a resolute, even a stubborn reformer. After having once made up his mind, he never turned aside, never doubted for a moment that the decision he had made was the right one.[24]

About the time Mann began to take an active role in the affairs of the state of Massachusetts, industrialization, urbanization, and many other social problems were facing the country. All of these issues were related to the question of elementary education. And of course it should not be assumed that Mann was operating in a vacuum; the way had been prepared for him by others, most notably by James Carter (1795–1849), who had for years been working, writing, and speaking for the cause of popular education. These were days of ferment, and education did not escape the attention of those who were most directly involved in the social upheaval.

Mann's first official connection with education came when he was

[24] For more detailed discussions of Mann's life and work, see Raymond B. Culver, *Horace Mann and Religion in the Massachusetts Public Schools,* Yale University Press, New Haven, 1929; and Burke A. Hinsdale, *Horace Mann and the Common School Revival in the United States,* Charles Scribner's Sons, New York, 1898.

appointed secretary to the State Board of Education in Massachusetts. This appointment was made in 1837. From this time until he died, Horace Mann was the firmest friend public education in America had.

Within a few months after assuming the office of secretary, Mann reported on the conditions of education in the state. The report was based on the findings of an investigation he had conducted. He had found, first of all, that the school committees—the boards responsible for the district schools—were rarely doing their duty. They were practically ignoring the schools and permitting teachers of uncertain quality to teach in them. In addition, he found that the children who needed the common school most of all did not attend it regularly; more than one-third of the children did not go to school in the winter, and an even greater proportion remained away from school in the spring. All of these shortcomings were magnified by the fact that the school term was short; the school sessions were kept in buildings that were unfit; there were no libraries in the schools; there were few common adoptions of textbooks for children in a single class; and there was hardly any grading of instruction. But these features, bad as they were, were made even worse by the fact that the public was apathetic about the common schools. The public seemed almost to expect that the common schools would be schools of low quality; certainly they did not seek any improvement in them. Private and sectarian schools were supposed to be the places where one could get a good education. This was a state of affairs and an attitude toward public education that Mann could not tolerate. Most of all, he would not accept the assumption that the common school could not offer an educational experience of high quality. His whole purpose as secretary —and this is a point that is too often misunderstood—was a simple one: to make the common school experience worthwhile and significant for the students who attended. He was completely unwilling to accept the often repeated claim that a sectarian school could prepare young people for their duties as citizens more adequately than the public school could. He set out to prove that this was not true, and to a great extent he succeeded.

Mann's task was never an easy one. First of all he had to educate most of the adult population to his way of thinking. To do this he inaugurated a public relations campaign for the common schools that more than anything else called their existence to the attention of the public. Public acceptance of public education was his first goal.

Throughout his long and illustrious career Mann played an important role in laying the foundation for public education. This foundation included such things as public support, public control, nonsectarianism, and the broadening of the curriculum and the recruitment of qualified teachers in order to give the child in a public school a first-rate educational experience. In a large and important way, Horace Mann succeeded. Perhaps we should add, in the interest of presenting a balanced view, that Mann was somewhat arbitrary in his actions and very determined in his beliefs. He made many enemies, but he thrived on controversy. Of course controversy was useful to Mann. What better way was there to attract attention to education than by engaging in a fully reported controversy? So Mann had quarrels with churchmen, with newspapermen, with publishers, with schoolmasters.

We should touch on one last point before we leave the great educational reformer. Among people who are convinced that education must have a clear denominational orientation, the name of Horace Mann is often anathema. Their wrath is misdirected. Nothing in Mann's record or in the writings for which he is most famous, the twelve *Annual Reports*, would substantiate the claim that he was an opponent of religion. On the contrary, Mann was a friend of religion as he was a friend of the Bible. In his *Common School Journal* and elsewhere he wrote in the interest of the common schools, and he believed sincerely that the common schools could not become quality schools unless they were freed from the crippling sectarianism that had plagued the earlier schools of the country. The aftereffects of nonsectarianism are not the question here. If we ask whether Horace Mann was opposed to religion and tried to drive God out of the American schoolroom, the answer must be an unequivocal no.

What Mann did in Massachusetts was done in Rhode Island and Connecticut by Henry Barnard (1811–1900). In addition, Barnard was the first United States Commissioner of Education. He took that office in 1867. It may be said that Barnard was more of a scholar and writer than Mann. He was responsible for a great body of educational literature; and besides this, he was an inveterate traveler and investigator, who brought to American education the best of foreign examples.

The Content of the Common School

Before we leave the common school of the nineteenth century we should discuss briefly its content, its organization, and the experiences a student in such a school might have. Irrespective of the changes that were constantly taking place in the society that the school was expected to serve, the school itself, its character and its curriculum, changed but little. It took a minor educational revolution to make the common school a graded school; it took a good deal more than that to broaden its program in such a way that young men and women could get from it an adequate social, civic, and economic education.

Gradually overcoming a definite resistance, changes came slowly but surely to the common school. At the beginning of the period of awakening it was a considerably different institution from what it was at the end of the nineteenth century. The early common school had been a reading-and-writing school. Spelling was added and became part of the reading-and-writing syllabus, and geography had a fairly early introduction to American elementary education. What was taught in any of the subjects offered was, for the most part, what the textbook had between its covers, for the teachers in those schools were seldom able to go beyond the printed text. So the expansion of the common school curriculum, because it did lean so heavily on the texts that were used, had to await the appearance of new textbooks.

Reading and writing, studying the Bible, and spelling made up the usual common school program. The materials used for reading and writing were often religiously oriented; this may have been one of the reasons for the proscription of such materials from the schools of Massachusetts in the Act of 1827. Spelling was taught first from the text prepared by Noah Webster, *The First Part of the Grammatical Institute of the English Language.* Although the whole work extended to three volumes, the latter two were devoted to grammar and reading. From 1783 to 1836, when Parsons' *Analytical Spelling Book* appeared, Webster's book had the market pretty much to itself and to a great extent controlled the curriculum of the common school. Parsons' book was probably a little better fitted to the needs of the time and of the school that was opening its doors to more and more people. There was a challenging and intriguing statement in the preface to Parsons' speller: "Parents who have little skill in teaching can learn their children to read, where there are no schools, and adults with little assistance can learn by themselves."[25] The study of arithmetic, heretofore reserved for schools in commercial districts, was stimulated by the introduction of Colburn's *First Lessons in Arithmetic on the Plan of Pestalozzi.* This book appeared in 1821. The book itself marked the beginning of a pedagogical revolution, for the lessons that Pestalozzi had taught brought the teaching of arithmetic down to the level of the object lesson. It is reasonable to expect that the students who had to use Colburn's text were, to say the least, more satisfied with their mathematical experience than the students who had studied the subject in the earlier schools.

There were signs that the curriculum would be broadened when geography was added to the elementary school syllabus. Up to about 1821, when Woodbridge prepared his *Rudiments of Geography,* the subject had been reserved pretty much for the classical schools and colleges. After 1821, geography was a fairly common subject in the lower schools. Of course, to take a subject from the secondary school and put it in the

[25] Quoted in Clifton Johnson, *Old-time Schools and Schoolbooks,* The Macmillan Company, New York, 1904, p. 226.

elementary school's program was not an extraordinary procedure; this shift is a regular occurrence in the history of curricula. But in the years when the elementary school was experiencing its greatest growth in the United States, such happenings were even more understandable, for the common school student had no real hope of going further up the educational ladder. The common school was to be his only formal educational experience. He was to be exposed to the things that were best for him individually and that would best prepare him to be a good citizen. Goodrich's *Method of Telling about Geography* was published in 1830, and for some time these two texts held a position of considerable authority in elementary education. History, too, was added, for it, more than any other subject, could contribute to the formation of good citizens. With the strong emphasis on citizenship, it is not surprising that the teaching of history was set in a definite nationalistic context. But of all these new materials of instruction, none could command the attention of the student and the educational historian as do the *McGuffey Readers* that were published first in 1836.

As the school program became broader and the number of years to be devoted to elementary education increased, the educators of the day found it imperative that the instruction be graded more formally than first, second, and third readers, etc. Grading, though unavoidable, was a long time in coming. It was to become one of the achievements of the common school of the nineteenth century. But before grading was instituted, children just went to school and sometimes repeated what they had previously mastered. Although it may be argued that grading of instruction and the establishment of an age-grade complex has weakened twentieth-century education, it can hardly be maintained that grading of instruction was not a step forward in the nineteenth century.

Finally we should say a word about the teachers in the common schools. Not much need be said, if one is looking only for good things to say. There was always the exceptional teacher, of course, but for the most part the teachers in these schools were really not qualified to be there. The nineteenth century saw the greatest improvement in the quality of teaching. When the century began almost anyone could teach in a common school; when the century came to an end teacher education and teachers' requirements were observed carefully in every state system of education. The normal schools and the teachers colleges offered programs for teacher training and education,[26] but, more than that, these

[26] For the history of teacher education in the United States, see Vernon L. Mangum, *The American Normal School: Its Rise and Development in Massachusetts*, Warwick and York, Incorporated, Baltimore, 1928; and Jessie M. Pangburn, *The Evolution of the American Teachers College*, Teachers College, Columbia University, New York, 1932.

institutions were subject to state supervision, and after 1852 prospective teachers were usually required to attend them. For all its shortcomings, no century may claim greater developments in the teaching art, or greater improvements in the opportunities offered youth for education.

Secondary Education

Up to nearly the end of the first quarter of the nineteenth century, the only secondary schools in evidence in the United States were Latin grammar schools and academies. Neither fully met the country's needs for secondary education. By the time the high school was founded in 1821, the academy had lost most of its distinctive features and to all intents and purposes was little different from the Latin grammar school which had preceded it in America. Since we have already described these two older types of secondary education in the United States, we do not need to repeat their features here.[27] It is enough to say that neither of these schools seemed to satisfy the ever-increasing demands made on secondary education. The demand for secondary education during the first seventy-five years of the nineteenth century was not universal or popular, but there was an obvious need for a kind of secondary education that the established schools did not offer. It was to meet this demand that the high school came into existence.[28]

The high school was founded with the intention of offering educational opportunity to boys who wanted to become merchants and mechanics. The Boston English Classical School, renamed the Boston English High School in 1824, was established for this reason. Its chief difference from other secondary schools of the day was that it was under public control and support and it offered a "good English education." There was still no thought that secondary education could be without classical curricula. A classical curriculum had meant, of course, that the Latin and probably the Greek classics would be taught. Offering the classics in English was an innovation of the first order of importance. When the school was established on a more solid foundation, the classics in Latin were able to find their way back into the curriculum, although they could no longer dominate it. But apart from the curricular innovation, the distinctive character of the American high school, as it was established in 1821, was that it was to prepare students, boys at first and then both boys and girls, for life. It did not prepare for the colleges to which the students might go, for most of the boys and girls were not going to college

---

[27] See pp. 435–436 and 444–445.

[28] For the early history of the high school and the high school movement, see Elmer E. Brown, *The Making of Our Middle Schools*, Longmans, Green & Co, Inc., New York, 1902; and Emit D. Grizzel, *Origin and Development of the High School in New England before 1865*, The Macmillan Company, New York, 1923.

but to the life they would lead as adults when they left high school. The first high schools were terminal schools. It may be said that the redefinition of the high school's purpose after 1890 was really nothing more than a return to the institution's original objective and an admonition that it be true to its original purpose.[29]

Another important feature associated with the high school must not be neglected: The high school was publicly supported and controlled and was open and free to any qualified student.

The high school in Boston was a successful experiment. Yet though it germinated the high school idea, the multiplication of high schools was due not so much to the model that existed in Boston as to the Massachusetts law of 1827—the High School Act, sometimes called the James Carter High School Act—which required the establishment of high schools or the employment of teachers who could teach high school subjects in every Massachusetts town that had a population of five hundred or more. This was the beginning of a movement that within two decades had spread throughout New England and to most of the Western states. Still, the high school was not a popular institution. It was recognized as a desirable addition to the educational system, but it was not entirely acceptable as a part of publicly supported and publicly controlled education. Many people were convinced that the high school could never become part of the public school system because it would be impossible for the public to support such an addition. Others, not so much impressed with the financial argument, insisted that the high school was really part of higher education, that it had nothing to do with the preparation of citizens, and therefore that it could not be a legal part of the public school system.

Even though the latter argument would have little standing in the mid-twentieth century, it did influence many minds in the nineteenth century. State constitutions had generally accepted the commission to provide public education to the people of the state by the constitutional invocation that "the state legislature shall establish and maintain a system of public education." The question was: What is public education? Where does it start and where does it end? Those who claimed that the high school was part of higher education were saying, in effect, that the high school could not be supported by public money, that it would not be constitutional to do so, for the state's constitution had not provided for the support of higher education. This impasse blocked the high schools in many of the states, and retarded high school expansion and development.

[29] The *Report* of the Committee of Ten was mainly responsible for the redefinition of the high school's purpose. For a discussion of this point, see Power, *Education for American Democracy,* pp. 180–185.

In 1859 the Michigan legislature passed a law permitting certain types of school districts to establish high schools and support them out of public money. This law may be regarded as the beginning of the high school movement in Michigan, but compared to the precedents that arose out of the interpretation of the law, the law itself is of little historical importance. In keeping with the Michigan High School Act, a number of school districts founded high schools. One such school district was School District Number One of the village of Kalamazoo. But the high school in Kalamazoo met with opposition, which arose, not out of the fact that Charles Stuart and others who joined with him were opposed to high school education, but that they did not believe the High School Act of 1859 was constitutional. They brought their complaint to the courts. It was this litigation that led to the famous Kalamazoo decision that established the legal status of the high school in Michigan. In the decision the court upheld the constitutionality of the Act of 1859 and in effect defined the high school as part of public education. The decision of the Michigan court served as a precedent for similar decisions in other states. For the first time, then, the supporters of the high school movement knew where they stood; they knew now that no legal obstacles would stand in the way of the high school's natural evolution. The Kalamazoo decision was a great victory for the high school and brought it to the brink of popularity. Achievement of true popularity was due to another important event in the history of the American high school, the *Report* of the Committee of Ten.

In 1890 a committee of the National Education Association was appointed to study the relationship between high schools and secondary schools and colleges on the question of college entrance requirements. For the past several decades the colleges had controlled the secondary schools with their college entrance requirements. In 1890 relatively few students attended high schools who did not anticipate college entrance, and high schools and secondary schools in general could not afford to ignore the curricular demands that the colleges imposed. In a very real sense the high school's curriculum was in the colleges' grip, and this domination curtailed the growth of the high school. The committee was appointed to find some way to resolve the touchy issues that arose between secondary schools and colleges.

The Committee of Ten did not conform exactly to its original commission. Rather, it decided to take a long and careful look at the high school. As a result of this examination, the Committee redefined the high school's purpose: It said that its essential purpose was to prepare students for life. While the college-preparatory function of secondary education was duly recognized by the Committee of Ten, the important purpose of the high school was set in a terminal context. In other words, the high school was to find its objectives in what young people would do when they left school. This terminal context was accepted because it was believed that only a relatively small percentage of the high school population would ever go to college. The high school experience would conclude the formal schooling for most of the students.[30]

It was the *Report* of the Committee of Ten, along with the Kalamazoo decision, that made the high schools popular institutions in the United States. Within a few years after the Committee's *Report* appeared in 1893—the Kalamazoo decision had been rendered in 1874—the high school was attracting about as many students in one year as it had in its entire history up to that time. While the high school did not eliminate other kinds of secondary education, no other kind of secondary education after 1895 could rival the high school in popularity. With the creation and popularization of the high school, the American educational ladder was complete; a student could climb all the way from elementary school through the public university. And now we turn from this brief survey of the high school to the last rung of the American educational ladder, higher education.

American Higher Education

Naturally we cannot determine a precise point in history when the colleges of America were freed from the religious control to which they had been subjected since the founding of Harvard in 1636. At best this freedom was only a relative thing, for in a number of colleges, especially those under Catholic auspices, the religious direction of instruction became even more important. The Catholic colleges of the United States began to make their appearance just as the general college movement in America took a turn in the other direction. By the time we get to the last half of the nineteenth century, the day of the denominational college is really in the past, while the day of the state university and the state college is just dawning. We do not mean to say that none of the denominational colleges made significant contributions to the life of America. Even though the period of its greatest influence was over, the denominational college of the late nineteenth century and of the twentieth century, for that matter, was still in a position to exercise a tremendous force for good in American higher education.[31]

[30] For more details on the position taken by the committee, see the *Report of the Committee of Ten on Secondary School Studies,* U.S. Bureau of Education, 1893.

[31] For a discussion of the motives which led to the founding of Catholic colleges in what is now the United States, see Power, *A History of Catholic Higher Education in the United States,* pp. 25–48; for a discussion of the rise and development of the state university, see John S. Brubacher and Willis Rudy, *Higher Education in Transition,* Harper & Brothers, New York, 1958, pp. 139–171.

There were two main objections to the denominational college: One was that it was not democratic enough either in its control or in its choice of students. The other was that it did not respond to the needs of the times as quickly as the public thought it should. In a way, because the college of the past continued to live in the past and neglected to update its curriculum, the public lost confidence in the denominational college as an educational institution and lost confidence, too, in the minister-president who directed the school.[32]

When the public lost confidence in these older colleges, it began immediately to demand changes. Effective changes could be made in only two ways. One was to develop a state college system. There was some precedent for this action, because from as early as 1785 state colleges had existed in America. The other was to assume control over these denominational colleges and to conduct them in such a way that the public's confidence would be restored. The states were successful in assuming control of a number of the nonpublic colleges and in requiring them to operate their programs in accordance with the dictates of public officers. But in one dramatic instance the state failed in its effort to control nonpublic higher education. This was at Dartmouth College.[33] According to the United States Supreme Court, the college, which had a colonial charter, could not be interfered with by the state. Thus not only Dartmouth College but other private colleges as well could find legal security in their charters. But the security that chartered colleges could find did not extend to the newly founded institutions of the nineteenth century that did not have state charters. As a matter of fact, the decision in the Dartmouth College case led the states to tighten up their practices of issuing charters and led them, too, to pass laws which made it illegal for a college to carry on its work without a state charter.[34]

Although we could hardly argue that the Dartmouth College decision deprived the state of authority in higher education, the decision definitely limited its control. Possibly the decision prompted the states to establish higher educational systems of their own. At any rate, the state college movement began and flourished in the last half of the nineteenth century.[35]

[32] These points are dealt with in detail and with remarkable historical perspective by George P. Schmidt, *The Liberal Arts College*, Rutgers University Press, New Brunswick, N. J., 1957; and Richard Hofstadter and C. DeWitt Hardy, *The Development and Scope of Higher Education in the United States*, Columbia University Press, New York, 1952.

[33] See Brubacher and Rudy, *op. cit.*, pp. 33–36.

[34] The aftereffects of the Dartmouth College decision are dealt with by Donald G. Tewksbury, *The Founding of American Colleges and Universities before the Civil War*, Teachers College, Columbia University, New York, 1932, pp. 142–154.

[35] This, again, is a matter of emphasis, for it is clear that there were state colleges long before this time. See Brubacher and Rudy, *op. cit.*, pp. 139 ff.

The state universities were especially conscious of the new dimension added to university purposes: research. Although many of the newly founded or newly expanded state schools were unable at once to undertake research programs or highly advanced graduate programs, no state university was oblivious of the attractiveness of such activities. In time these state institutions answered the call for technological development and social science research, and also for medical schools, legal departments, and schools of engineering, all of which departments had a vital social significance. Research was soon being organized, and graduate work was introduced especially after 1876, when the Johns Hopkins University in Baltimore provided a model which other American universities could copy. And there was another expansion: Higher education accepted new students in its hallowed halls. These new students were women. The first beginnings of the coeducation movement in higher education were made at Oberlin College in 1833 and were followed by Antioch College in 1853, Syracuse University in 1850, and the University of Iowa in 1856. At about the same time, or possibly a few years earlier, the separate woman's college grew out of the academies or seminaries that for some years had been operated for girls. We find such well-known colleges as Mount Holyoke, Rockford, and Vassar, to name only three. In all, more than sixty colleges for women were founded before 1860, although we may justifiably inquire whether all of these so-called colleges were really of collegiate rank.

One of the chief reasons for the development of coeducational programs in the colleges that heretofore had been for men, and for the founding of colleges for women was that women now, in the greater and broader development of popular education, had ways of applying the knowledge that they might gain in college studies. In other words, now that the lower schools needed women teachers, the girls could go to college in order to develop salable skills. With this incentive the college programs for women increased spectacularly. But the colleges were not the first institutions to respond to the need for properly educated teachers. The general willingness of the colleges to enter the field of teacher education was not much in evidence before the normal schools and teachers colleges cultivated this area of professional training.

As a public institution the normal school dates from 1839, and as a private school from about 1822. Its purpose was, without pretense or fanfare, to teach people who wanted to be elementary school (common school) teachers something about the art of teaching. The normal school was usually not interested in content and therefore did not offer a college course. Its commitment was to communicate techniques of teaching. The normal school lasted for about fifty years in the United States, and during these years some very famous normal schools came into existence.

The most famous of all was the Oswego Normal School at Oswego, New York.[36] Between 1830 and 1880 public and private normal schools could be found in every state in the union. When the elementary school program was broadened and when the high school became a permanent and popular part of the educational system, the normal school no longer seemed adequate to the task of preparing teachers for America's schools. A new kind of teacher was needed, and a new kind of institution for teacher education came into existence. This was the teachers college.

Public and private teachers colleges were founded, and both types undertook to prepare men and women to teach in elementary and secondary schools. As teachers colleges grew, normal schools declined. At present, in the mid-twentieth century, the normal school has completely disappeared, and teachers colleges in the United States educate about one-half of the country's teachers. In addition, many teachers colleges, although they may no longer be called by this name, have complete university programs wherein qualified students may earn all the advanced degrees that are usually granted in the graduate schools of the country.

Developments in Catholic Education

By 1820 there were approximately 195,000 Catholics in the United States. They, too, were ready for the educational awakening, for like their fellow citizens, they were eager for a better social climate in which to live and work. Catholics could and did support universal education because they could understand that a more generous distribution of educational opportunity would benefit the whole nation. The consequences of universal education were as great a boon to Catholics as they were to anyone else. Thus, while Catholics generally approved and supported the development of the common schools, they sought also to expand and improve their own schools. The Church in America had grown, and its needs as well as the nation's prompted a renewal of interest in education. With the extension of the nonsectarian common school, a system of Church schools seemed even more important to Catholics. They were also in a better position to support such schools than they had been, and the supply of teachers to direct these educational activities was considerably better too. Communities of brothers, sisters, and priests were able to accept schools in the parishes and to establish independent Catholic schools of their own.

As early as 1829, in the First Provincial Council of Baltimore, the Church in America made a general pronouncement on education. In its decree, the Fathers of the Council recommended the establishment of

[36] See J. P. Gordy, *Rise and Growth of the Normal School Idea in the United States,* U.S. Bureau of Education Circular of Information, no. 8, 1891.

schools in which children could be taught the principles of faith and morality as well as the elements of a literary education. It may be remarked that this decree was enacted just two years after Massachusetts had prohibited sectarian teaching in the common schools. The Massachusetts law was not aimed especially at Catholics, but because of it Catholics were alerted to the greater need for their own schools, now that the nonsectarian trend in the common schools had become so definite.

The next important Church legislation on the subject of Catholic education came in the First Plenary Council in 1852. In the decree on education the Fathers of the Council admonished the bishops to establish schools in connection with all the churches and to support these schools out of church funds if necessary. The Second Plenary Council, held in 1866, did not advance much beyond the position already taken in previous councils. It did, however, call attention to the need for more teaching communities, and it advised pastors to select lay teachers with great care when they were unable to procure religious teachers. In addition, the people were urged to support Catholic parish schools.

In 1884 the Third Plenary Council enacted what have ever since been regarded as definitive decrees on education. In general, the position taken was that parents are obliged to provide their children with an education that does not exclude religion. Normally this education is to be obtained in Catholic parish schools. The Fathers of the Council realized that many parishes did not have schools and that some parish schools were of inferior caliber. The decrees stated, therefore, that every church was to have a parochial school within two years of the promulgation of the decrees. It was the definite understanding of the prelates that parochial schools were to be at least the equivalent of the public schools of the country. Despite the positive language of the educational decrees of the Third Plenary Council, the standard established by that Council for parochial schools in connection with the churches has not yet been achieved.

During the years of awakening, Catholic education was faced with issues other than those pertaining to internal growth. Compulsory-attendance legislation, enacted first in 1852, seemed to many Catholics to be an invasion of parental rights in education. There was the danger, too, that as the state gained greater control over education, attendance in state schools might be required. The Oregon law of 1922, declared unconstitutional in 1925 in *Pierce v. Society of Sisters*, 268 U.S. 510, and the proposed amendments to Michigan's constitution in 1920 and 1924, threatened such compulsion. The creation of the Federal Department of Education in 1867 alerted Catholics and others to the dangers of central control of education. With these and other apparent threats to their intellectual and educational security, Catholic educators could seldom rest easily. Yet their greatest problem was financing their own schools. In New York City in the 1840s, Archbishop John Hughes had made an unsuccessful appeal to the city council for an allotment of public money for the support of Catholic schools in the city. Thereafter church-related schools were almost never assigned any public funds, although such assignments had been fairly common before 1840. The second dimension of nonsectarianism—that public funds may not be used for religious purposes—came into full force.

This was the period, too, when Catholic secondary schools and colleges became more numerous. Separate secondary schools for boys and girls were opened by the teaching communities; diocesan high schools (central high schools) were founded; and parish high schools began to become more common. In curricular and cocurricular programs these schools kept pace with the educational progress of the time. The Catholic college movement was accelerated too. From 1786 to 1850, forty-two Catholic colleges were founded, of which ten survived. From 1850 to 1900, one hundred and fifty-two colleges for men were founded, of which forty-five survived. The movement to establish Catholic colleges for women began somewhat later in the period; by 1905, eighteen Catholic colleges for women had been founded. Catholic higher education was not content to grow only in numbers of institutions. To better achieve the best ideals in Catholic higher education, the Catholic University of America was established in the Third Plenary Council of 1884. It was intended to be a graduate school, and during its first years it offered no formal undergraduate programs. Catholic higher education developed in still another direction when coeducation was introduced. Some colleges that had enrolled men only now began to offer educational opportunities to women. DePaul University in Chicago, in 1914, was the first Catholic college for men to become completely co-educational.

Finally, it should be mentioned that in its quest for ever higher quality and in view of its nationwide status, Catholic education sponsored a national organization to further its objectives and represent it to the public: the National Catholic Education Association, founded in 1904.

SUMMARY

The first schools in English America were transplanted schools; that is, they were really European schools brought to the new world in the hope that they would help the colonists achieve their ideals and their dreams. Although colonization differed from one section of the new country to another, education tended to follow the established old-world patterns. The first major break with tradition came in Massachusetts in the famous laws of that colony. These laws were passed in 1642 (the compulsory-education law) and 1647 (the compulsory-school law). The typical schools of the transplantation were colleges, town schools, Latin grammar schools, and dame schools (elementary schools).

Eventually it became clear that the old institutions would not do in the new setting, and efforts were made to found new schools or reform old ones. These enterprises were undertaken, generally speaking, during the period of transition, from 1750 to 1820. During this period the new schools that attract our attention are the academies and the state universities. Benjamin Franklin and Thomas Jefferson were active in inculcating new ideals for the educational enterprise of the new country.

With a theoretical foundation inherited from the transition, the period of educational awakening, from 1820 to 1900, translated these theories into practice. In these years elementary education was made nearly universal and became almost entirely free. Elementary schools (common schools) were supported and controlled by the public. High schools came into existence and in time became the American contribution to secondary education. The Kalamazoo decision and the *Report* of the Committee of Ten must be noted in the development of the high school.

Higher education, too, was subject to tremendous change. The most notable changes were in the development of state universities, which brought an entirely new tone to higher education, and in the establishment of graduate and professional schools and programs related to society's needs.

Questions and Exercises for Study and Discussion

1. In what principal ways was education in colonial America transplanted education?
2. What were the objectives of education in colonial New England? Explain the purpose and effect of the Massachusetts Acts of 1642 and 1647.
3. Explain the role of the New England town in education in the colonial years.
4. Describe colonial schools.
5. Was the educational pattern in colonial America uniform, or did it differ from region to region? Discuss.
6. Report on Catholic education in colonial America.
7. Compare and contrast the educational theories of Benjamin Franklin and Thomas Jefferson. On the level of educational practice, what do you associate with each man?
8. Report on the life, times, and career of Horace Mann.
9. What prompted the rise of the common school? What were the school's main features and what did it become?

10. Discuss the American educational objective of citizenship. What place does this objective have in the history of education?
11. Show how the Kalamazoo decision strengthened the position of the American high school.
12. Prepare a special report on the proposals and effects of the *Report* of the Committee of Ten.
13. Describe the developments in American Catholic education in the United States since the Civil War.
14. Prepare a report on the evolution of teacher education in the United States.

15

American Education in the Twentieth Century

The nineteenth century was a century of educational change. A great deal that was done in that century has had lasting effect, yet the century of ferment was so busy with its new ideas and the sources that generated them that it had little time to consolidate its gains or to look forward to the containment of new educational horizons. For the most part, this has been the work of the first sixty years of the twentieth century.

POPULARIZATION OF EDUCATION

The important forces of the nineteenth century made themselves felt by the last decade of the century, and education in all levels became more popular. By popularity of education we mean the place that schools, both public and private, occupy in the public mind. From 1890 to the outbreak of the Second World War, the record of educational history is mainly one of growth. During this period a steadily increasing percentage of the school-age youth of America was attending school. The increase in high school and college enrollments was at a phenomenal rate. The school term was lengthened, and by 1918 all the states had compulsory attendance laws which made universal education a virtual reality. The schools, from the lowest to the highest, were given more adequate financial support, and the salaries of teachers more than doubled during these years. In 1890, 44 per cent of the population from five to seventeen years of age was in school. By 1930 this proportion has changed to 67 per cent; in 1960 it was 79 per cent. From 1890 to 1930 the school year was increased from 135 to 172 days; and by 1960 the school year in most of the states was at least 180 days.

Throughout this period of growth there were obvious rays of sunshine. The educational establishment was better off than it had ever been before, and the quality of educational opportunity was higher. But there were clouds too. Some sections of the country lagged behind others. The figures of growth given above are averages; some states and some regions were far behind these averages.

When we enter the twentieth century, we find a complete American school system. The educational ladder extends from the primary school through the university. It is possible now for Americans to speak of a nearly authentic democratic system of education. We see, too, that this ideal of democracy in education involved another consideration, namely, how far it was possible and right to control private education. American society was a pluralistic society; it needs were many and varied, and, in addition, America had a strong tradition of private control and support of education, as she had a strong tradition of religiously oriented education. Both private and religiously integrated education had lost ground in the late years of the nineteenth century. There was so much devotion to democratic education as the twentieth century began that private, church-related education was in real danger of becoming extinct. Many people argued that private and church-related education could not be democratic and that it could not serve the best interests of a growing America. Their arguments were heeded, and the call went out for the suppression of all but the state schools. Another prerogative of the schools was in danger. In the interest of achieving curricular uniformity, the demand was voiced and again heeded and in some states converted into law, that only certain subjects be taught and that they be taught in a certain way. Some states, Nebraska for instance, proscribed the teaching of foreign languages to children who had not yet finished the eighth grade. About the time of the First World War, the prevailing tendencies threatened to leave little room in education for agencies other than the state, if the state had its way. This was one of the prices that education had to pay for popularity. But it was too high and also too unrealistic a price. In time, both of the extravagant claims of the state, that it alone could be the educator of youth and that it alone could decide what was best for youth to study, were struck down by the United States Supreme Court. In the famous Oregon decision (1925), the Court issued a decree that protected not only the rights of the private schools involved in the litigation, but also the rights of all non-public education in the United States.[1] In 1923 the United States Supreme Court ruled on the Nebraska law that had prohibited the

[1] For a fuller discussion of the relevance of the Oregon decision to private education in the United States, see Edward J. Power, *Education for American Democracy*, McGraw-Hill Book Company, Inc., New York, 1958, pp. 47–49 and 89–92.

teaching of languages other than English to elementary school students. The Court held that the Nebraska statute was unconstitutional. The Court's ruling thus protected the right of parents to determine what their children should study.[2]

The relationship of these points to the popularization of education may seem, at first, to be somewhat remote. On closer examination, however, we see that the legal foundation that was given to private education in the Oregon decision had the effect of making education more popular and more generously distributed. In the language question, the Court gave the parents some control over the schools, and in this way enabled the schools to gain parental confidence. Gaining the confidence of those who are first of all responsible for the education of children is more than half the battle for popularizing education.

EDUCATIONAL OPPORTUNITY

The question of educational opportunity, as it was asked in the first sixty years of the twentieth century, had two dimensions: first, the extension of opportunity, both horizontally and vertically; second, the opening of schools to all the children of all the people without regard to race, color, or creed. Both dimensions were immensely important to the future of education in the United States and also to the position of the United States on the scale of world opinion.

Many kinds of inequality may exist in an educational system. There is inequality when a student of superior capacity is placed in a classroom with children of far less ability and also when a student of inferior ability is put in a classroom with superior youngsters. Yet when we speak of inequality of educational opportunity in the twentieth-century American school, we really have only one thing in mind: the Negro in American education.

In many of the states of the union the practice was followed for years of maintaining "separate but equal" facilities for Negro children; there was a separate system of schools for Negro children and a separate system for white children. This practice had had the support of the United States Supreme Court in *Plessy v. Ferguson*.[3] In 1954 the United States Supreme Court in *Brown v. Kansas*,[4] on the authority of the Fourteenth Amendment, overturned the separate but equal doctrine, maintaining that there could be no such thing as a separate but equal public facility, and notified the states in which the doctrine was applied that public schools would have to be integrated with "all deliberate speed." The

---

[2] *Ibid.*, pp. 86–89.

[3] *Plessy v. Ferguson*, 163 U.S. 537. The decision in this case was rendered in 1890.

[4] *Brown v. Kansas*, 347 U.S. 483.

directions of the Court were accepted somewhat reluctantly in certain sections of the country, notably in Little Rock, Arkansas, and it was what happened in these sections that made the news. Such headlines tended to obscure the fact that thousands of other communities in the North and South were quietly bringing their schools into line with the fundamental law of the land.

The other dimension of opportunity tried to find its solution in the realignment of the school system. During the late nineteenth century, when the high school became a regular and legally recognized public institution, the American school system took a definite shape. By 1890 or so it was possible, as we have said, to speak of the American educational ladder, an integrated system of schools that began with the primary school and ended with the university. It was, for the most part, open to all American children; at any rate, there was no dual system such as could have been found in Europe during the same period.[5] In the establishment of such a system, American educational theory committed itself to popular education on all levels. This inclusiveness gave rise to the charge that American schools had no standards, that they were not real intellectual agencies, and that they were definitely inferior to their European counterparts. It must be understood, of course, that in any discussion of the relative merits of European and American education we must consider what the two systems are driving at. We should do the same thing when we debate about education in the United States and in the Soviet Union. Many of the complaints directed at American education are based on a faulty understanding of its purposes. In the next section we shall review the evolution of American educational theory.

To return to the development of the American ladder, we may say that the twentieth century witnessed the following extensions: Elementary schools were extended downward; secondary education was extended downward, and so was higher education. These downward extensions fashioned four new steps for the American educational ladder: nursery school, the kindergarten, the junior high school, and the junior college. The latter is now more generally referred to as the community college. Each of these new educational units was brought into existence primarily to provide greater opportunity for education.

THE AMERICAN TEACHING TRADITION

Indebted though it was to the educational theory and practice of Europe, American education came in time to have a teaching tradition of its own. Before 1900 it could have been described as European edu-

[5] See pp. 416–417.

cation all over again. But education and the schools outgrew their parent institutions of the nineteenth century, whether these institutions were found in America or in Europe. Education in America became a big business, and the doors of the schools were opened to all. Public education had a rapid growth, but it was to gain even greater stature in the twentieth century. It was in this growth and in the delving into the ground of theory from which it sprang that the American teaching tradition came into being.

It would hardly have been possible to speak of a native pedagogy in nineteenth-century America. The names of Pestalozzi, Herbart, and Froebel were far too prominent for American educators to think that they themselves could be independent. But the important point to be observed here is that the Americans who had studied under the influence of the best pedagogical minds of Europe were now in a position to prepare a generation of American educators. One of the leaders in building the American teaching tradition was Francis W. Parker (1837–1902). As superintendent of schools in Quincy, Massachusetts, Parker introduced a method which has since been called the Quincy method. Although there is nothing unusual about it when viewed from the perspective of the third quarter of the twentieth century, it was extremely novel when it was introduced by Parker in the waning years of the nineteenth century. The general idea was that the formalism of the old-time schoolroom should be eliminated in favor of a classroom in which learning and living would be made to complement each other. In other words, Parker introduced the practice that was later to be labeled progressive education. It should be noted that Parker's new method and his liberalism in teaching did not go unchallenged; the people of Quincy were determined to see whether or not the methods that had been used in teaching their children were valid. A long and somewhat wearying investigation was undertaken. The people wanted to know whether their youngsters could spell, read, write, and compute. It was found that the pupils who learned these skills by the new method were able to perform as well if not better than those who had learned them by the old method. Parker left Quincy for Chicago, to become director of the University of Chicago's School of Education. His connection with the school was brief, however, for he died in 1902.

In a way, then, Parker was the founder of the American educational tradition; but it was John Dewey (1859–1952) who cultivated what Parker had invented and gave it the stature of a real teaching tradition.

John Dewey was born in Burlington, Vermont, in 1859. He attended the public schools in Burlington and the University of Vermont. Following his graduation from college, Dewey became a schoolteacher and for two years or so was the schoolmaster of a country school. During this brief interlude his interest in the world of ideas was stimulated to such an extent that he returned to the University of Vermont to take an informal postgraduate course in philosophy. After a year or so at the University of Vermont, he enrolled at the Johns Hopkins University of Baltimore—a school that had achieved a reputation for excellence in a few short years and one which attracted most of the outstanding students of the United States of that day—where he pursued graduate study in philosophy. At Johns Hopkins he came in contact with the famous G. Stanley Hall (1844–1924) and the leading idealist philosopher in America of the day, George S. Morris (1840–1889). When Dewey completed his studies at Johns Hopkins, he took his Ph.D. degree and accepted a teaching appointment at the University of Michigan. His teaching field was philosophy, although for those who like to think of Dewey as a psychologist, it might be mentioned that his doctoral dissertation was on the "Psychology of Immanuel Kant." From the University of Michigan Dewey went to the University of Minnesota, where he stayed for two years, and then he returned to the University of Michigan. From Michigan he went to the University of Chicago.

Although Dewey's academic area was philosophy, he began to show unusual interest in education, and within two years after his appointment to the faculty of the University of Chicago he had organized a school, the Laboratory School of the University of Chicago. Dewey's interest in education was not as unusual as it may appear, for he always regarded the school as the best testing place for philosophical doctrines. The laboratory school was, therefore, an entirely natural outlet for his philosophical interests. This school was an experimental school, and the idea caused almost as much excitement as the new methods of teaching and learning that it practiced. Experimenting with children was then thought to be a radical departure from orthodox procedure.

From the Laboratory School at the University of Chicago John Dewey led an educational revolution.

The essential elements of this revolution have been described, praised, and criticized in various ways. Basically, Dewey wanted to turn the schools back to a closer relationship with life. In the early chapters of this book we examined educational practices that tended to separate learning from living or ignored the essential relationship that ought to exist between teaching and reality, between instruction and the world of people and things.[6] Again, and especially in the hands of Dewey and his followers, the school was turned in the direction of affinity with real life situations, and the shibboleths most characteristic of this new direction described education as a matter of "teaching students, not subjects," or of "educating the whole child." Another pregnant statement was,

[6] See pp. 121–125.

"Education is not a preparation for life; it is life." There was just enough truth in the new catch phrases to make them attractive, and just enough unreal pedantry in the old-school situation to warrant a kind of grand rejection. The motives of men are not easy to assess. Yet whatever the educators' motives were in this case, they led men to accept the new kind of education at least on a trial basis, assuming, no doubt, that it could not be any worse than the kind of instruction, arid and incomplete and unreal, with which the age was most familiar.

Aside from a new methodology that was based primarily on the animal nature of man, a method incidentally that educators have discovered should never be overlooked, this new view in education first set out to free the curriculum from the grip of formalism. As the elementary school of the nineteenth century developed, it became a graded school with a fairly rigid curriculum. The age-grade relationship became an unwieldy thing. Regardless of a child's ability, he was put in the grade to which his age assigned him, and he was kept in that grade until he was one year older. Another kind of formalism resulted from the idea that there was a definite and prescribed subject matter waiting to be mastered, a subject matter that could not be altered by anyone. The idea was deeply ingrained in educational practices. Textbooks were prepared for the various subjects in each of the several grades, and it became the teacher's duty to see that the material in the book was covered. Most of the pupil's time was spent in mastering the textbook, a task which meant memorizing the details that were touched on in the book. Too often these exercises had little or no meaning for the children. If these features led to educational unpleasantness in the early years of the nineteenth century when educational popularity was yet to come, think of the wrath they incurred in the early years of the twentieth century, when the school population had already attained some of the proportions that phenomenal growth had promised!

The unreality and irrelevance of the elementary curriculum had not been ignored all these hundred or more years. Reform movements were undertaken before Dewey, but they did not enjoy any special success. There was, for example, the Oswego movement. This was an attempt to apply the principles of Pestalozzian methodology, to substitute concrete experiences with common objects for the memorization of textbook content.[7] The movement advocated a diminishing emphasis on the "book" in the elementary school. The kindergarten movement that was introduced to America in 1855 and was grafted to the American public school system in St. Louis, Missouri, under the sponsorship of William T. Harris (1835–1909), in 1873, lent new inspiration to the belief that children should be active if they are to learn: that self-activity is the basis of all

[7] See pp. 393–394.

learning. Even the Herbartian movement was ready to lend a hand by assailing the prevalent organization of content and by criticizing the outworn methods of teaching that were in use. Perhaps the criticism was not so much that the methods were outworn as that they were without solid psychological foundations. Then there was the work of Parker. In addition to the many other reforms that he advocated, Parker wanted elementary education to be built around a core of common experiences, and he wanted the elementary schools to follow the general educational plan of Froebel. In the end none of these reforms was accepted. Rather, it was John Dewey and the Progressive Education Association that made the greatest gains in attacking formalism and wresting education from its clutches. It is true, of course, that many of the ideas of these progressives, Dewey included, were not original with them. They borrowed from Rousseau, Pestalozzi, Herbart, Froebel, as well as from others. That they did so does not lead us to criticize them. Regardless of the indebtedness that these progressives may have had to educational thinkers of the past, the main source of their inspiration and the major architect of what may be called progressive education was John Dewey.[8] He challenged the education of the past as well as the education of the present in a number of important books: *School and Society* (1899), *How We Think* (1909), *Democracy and Education* (1916), *Human Nature and Conduct* (1922), and *Experience and Education* (1938). These, of course, are only a few of the books that Dewey wrote, and hundreds of articles could be added to them. The central purpose of all his writing and teaching was to create the new educational tradition of which we have spoken. The first step in creating such a tradition and one which would have a definite commitment to democracy would be to formulate a new theory of education. And so we find the reason for Dewey's preoccupation with educational philosophy, a philosophy that challenged both the ends and the means of the traditional levels of education.

The Progressive Education Association, organized in 1918, was an especially active agency in promoting and spreading the ideas of John Dewey, although in later years Dewey was often critical of the PEA.[9] It could boast such names as William Heard Kilpatrick and Harold Rugg, but there were hundreds of other, lesser figures who took their places in this movement. Whatever our final evaluation of progressive education may be, we cannot believe that it will be susceptible to the charge

[8] See Martin S. Dworkin, *Dewey on Education, Selections,* Classics in Education no. 3, Bureau of Publications, Teachers College, Columbia University, New York, 1959.

[9] See L. A. Cremin, *The Transformation of the School,* Alfred A. Knopf, Inc., New York, 1961.

of insincerity that is sometimes leveled at progressive educators. Their devotion to the cause of education is one thing that stands out greatly in their favor. In spite of the dedication which the progressive educators felt to the reform they had undertaken, they met with a good deal of opposition, although the record of history will show that the opposition was not very effective. This opposition came generally from essentialists or traditionalists. The labels are not especially helpful in identifying the people who were opposed to progressive education, but in a general way such opposition arose out of the belief that the educational practices of progressives were really antieducational. The practices most commonly advocated by progressives, often following Dewey but sometimes misinterpreting him, were these: to create a school situation in which learners have a great deal of freedom, to stress child initiative and self-activity, to abandon logically arranged and formally taught subjects in favor of projects, to have children themselves formulate meaningful and proximate educational objectives, and to emphasize personality building and social adjustment. In a word, the schools were to be turned back to the children, and, in the best progressive terminology, they were to be places that stressed living rather than learning.

This is probably the place to indicate that a number of educators and teachers who were close to the controversy that was being waged refused to join either side. They thought neither of winning nor of losing a theoretical point; their one object was to organize and conduct the best schools possible for the youth of America. Many educators were actually eclectic in their educational position, taking what they thought was good from the several theoretical positions and trying to fashion the best educational program possible. This is not to say that arguments did not continue from entrenched positions. The progressives challenged the traditionalists and vice versa; the challenge was accepted; and the educational duel was fought and refought. No one was the winner in any of these battles of educational ideology. The question may be asked: Were there not many losers? When the Progressive Education Association disbanded in 1944, its dissolution was not by any means a surrender, for the association did not really disappear; it only changed. It was known as the American Education Fellowship until 1955, when it finally disbanded.

Dewey's kind of progressive education made itself felt most on the level of elementary education. But the revolution that touched the elementary schools and led to such ferment for forty years or more did not ignore secondary education. Progressivism touched the high school of the twentieth century in the following ways: (1) It reinforced the definition of the high school made by the Committee of Ten; (2) it supported a standardizing of the goals of the high schools' curriculum—the goals set forth in the report of the Committee on Reorganization of Secondary Education, which met in 1918 and produced the famous Seven Cardinal

Principles of Secondary Education;[10] and (3) it promoted an increase in the number of subjects in the high school so that the differences in ability of students might be served by a variety of curricular offerings. The changes seem laudable, and we can hardly maintain that the high school could or should have taken some other direction. And with the greater perspective of time, we must admit that none of the three points listed above was characteristic of progressivism in any special way. It was the spirit and practice of electivism that committed the high school to the progressive views of the Progressive Education Association. In other words, when the high schools accepted the doctrine of electivism and the theory of equivalence of studies that supports it,[11] the opponents of progressivism claimed that the high schools had been captured by progressive practices in education. The same thing occurred when the "Carnegie unit," a quantitative measure of a student's progress, was applied to the evaluation of high school work. Eventually, in the Eight-year Study, we find the Progressive Education Association conducting a study to test the merits of the traditional preparatory secondary school program.[12]

In spite of the progressive tendencies that seemed to become attached to it, the American high school was neither regressive nor anti-intellectual. The high schools of the United States tried to adapt their programs to the ever-increasing high school population; but at the same time, with the addition of new subjects, with the organization of the curriculum to meet individual needs, and with the introduction of vocational curricula and guidance programs, they achieved an excellence that had never before been dreamed of.

While public education was growing, private education was not standing still. The most remarkable developments in private education in the United States were to be found in the Catholic school system. This system had come into existence with the Third Plenary Council of 1884.[13]

BUILDING A SCIENCE OF EDUCATION

When schools were first brought to America, education was primarily an art; that is, whatever the teacher did in his schoolroom was best described as artistic, although we can easily understand why some

[10] The Seven Cardinal Principles of Secondary Education are: health, command of the fundamental processes, worthy use of leisure, worthy home membership, citizenship, vocational efficiency, and ethical character.

[11] In its simplest terms, the theory of equivalence of studies means that one study is as good as any other so long as it is taught well and studied hard.

[12] The general report of the Eight-year Study was published under the title *Adventures in American Education*, Harper & Brothers, New York, 1942.

[13] See J. A. Burns and Bernard J. Kohlbrenner, *A History of Catholic Education in the United States*, Benziger Bros., New York, 1937.

historians would avoid using the term. In any event, a fairly well-organized content could be communicated to pupils. There was not, however, any great body of communicable knowledge about the art or the process of teaching. Something was known in a very general way about the child's nature, but it was not set in a psychological or pedagogical frame of reference. Something was known, again in a general way, about the school's relation to society, and Rousseau's work was well enough known to stimulate thought. There were some general discussions of teaching methods, following the ideas of Pestalozzi, but these, of course, were not highly developed or well known when the first schools were founded in America. In other words, education had to wait a long time before it became a science, before knowledge about it was organized in a meaningful way.

Perhaps we can say that Herbart was the father of the science of education.[14] At any rate, by the middle of the nineteenth century in the United States, something was known about Herbart's work in the psychology and methodology of teaching. Students who were interested in education—and there were many by this time—went to Europe to study under the men who were pioneering in the science of education, men who were trying to discover and understand the essential nature of the teaching and learning process. Foremost among these European professors was Herbart. His impact on American education had already been mentioned.[15] Slightly less important than Herbart was Wilhelm Wundt (1832–1920). Wundt published his *Principles of Psychology* in 1874, and from that time on the relationship of experimental psychology to the teaching-learning processes became more and more important. In America the great William James (1842–1910), following the psychological pattern of the day, published his *Principles of Psychology* in 1890. More than any other book on psychology, James's book sensitized educators to the place that psychology must play in teaching and learning. The movement started by James was accelerated by James McKeen Cattell (1860–1944) and G. Stanley Hall (1844–1924). The great figure, however, after American psychology and American psychologists had been impressed by functionalism and behaviorism and various other psychological "isms," was Edward L. Thorndike (1874–1949). No American psychologist has had greater effect on the American school than this man. The system that he developed, although he is not credited with inventing it, is called *connectionism*. Thorndike's work was started at Harvard University, under the celebrated William James, but he transferred to Columbia University, where he continued and completed his work and where he stayed to influence the entire educational world. Thorndike

[14] See pp. 399–402.
[15] See p. 474.

pioneered in the field of educational measurement. He was deeply involved in the question of transfer of training. He was concerned with individual differences and with the isolation of certain mental capacities. He studied questions of skill learning and was interested in the issues of growth and development. He concerned himself with adult learning, and he formulated the famous system of connectionistic, S-R bond, psychology.

Thorndike's influence on American education was profound. The system that he developed—the S-R theory and its explanation of learning following mainly the laws of effect, exercise, and readiness—was widely acclaimed. This acclaim was due, in part, at least, to the fact that Thorndike's explanation, to say nothing at all about its validity, was one that could be followed with relative ease. It explained clearly how learning takes place, in terms that teachers could understand. It is true that the explanation was mechanistic, that is, learning was described as a purely mechanical process; but it is also true that the physical bases of learning cannot be questioned or denied. Thus, because of its merit and its intelligibility, Thorndike's theory achieved unusual popularity. Most teachers of the early twentieth century were followers of Thorndike, whether or not they knew or would acknowledge their discipleship. Teachers' manuals were organized according to the doctrines that Thorndike had defined. Thorndike's great work, three imposing volumes in which the bulk of his connectionistic theory is to be found, is *Educational Psychology*, published in 1913. It now enjoys the distinction of an educational classic.

The scientific tradition that was reinforced by the work of Thorndike and his followers led to the mental-testing movement. One of the chief forces advocating the more general employment of mental tests was the newly formed American Psychological Association. Yet relatively little headway was made until the success of the mental test was unequivocally demonstrated by Alfred Binet (1857–1911). Binet, a Frenchman, began his work in 1895, and ten years later America was ready for the mental test. In spite of the recognition that must be given to Binet and to Theodore Simon (1873–   ), the real credit for the testing movement must go to Lewis B. Terman (1877–1956). In 1916 Terman revised and published the Binet test, and from that time on, Terman's scale and subsequent revisions of it have been deservedly popular in the educational world. With this movement, the IQ, the intelligence quotient, was introduced to American education. The testing movement received further acceleration from the United States Army, which devised Alpha and Beta scales for the testing of intelligence. The idea was, of course, that the results of such tests would be used to place the First World War inductees in positions for which their capacity most fitted them. In spite of psychologists' inexperience with such instruments on such a large scale and some extraordinary and unexpected outcomes from such use, the army program did serve to dramatize the value of tests and the variety of uses to which they could be put. The practical character of testing was demonstrated.

Building on the mental test, education inaugurated the measurement movement, with its tests of aptitude and achievement. Such tests were accompanied by statements about their validity and reliability. Most important of all, these tests were standardized, so that their results could be compared with norms that had been established by previous administrations of the tests. The test, through the device of standardization, was made to tell a great deal by means of comparative techniques. Testing had an important effect on teaching. Teachers and students became test-conscious. They became interested in the quantitative evaluation that these tests made of learning activities.

Another step in building a science of education was the survey movement. The school survey was far from being a novelty in the nineteenth century: Horace Mann's *Annual Reports* had been surveys or reports of surveys.[16] Wilhelm von Humboldt's work in Germany and Victor Cousin's in France were related to the survey. They had examined schools and teaching and had reported on what they found. This is the essence of the survey. In the late nineteenth century and in the early twentieth, school districts began to employ qualified people to conduct surveys. Some of these survey reports were of considerable importance in the field of educational literature. One of the first formal surveys was the one conducted in Boise, Idaho, under the supervision of Calvin Kendall. This began a movement that was followed in most of the nation's larger cities. The school survey became so important that the 1914 Yearbook of the National Society for the Study of Education was devoted to it.

The first surveys were simple affairs. As time went on and as school systems became larger and more complex, the survey had to be more extensive and more carefully conducted. Perhaps the best, or best-known survey in the United States was the 1935 cost-and-character survey conducted by the New York State Regents.

In addition to surveys and testing, the educational scientists turned their attention to the curriculum. Without going into the details of this aspect of the science of education, we can say that those who advocated the application of science to curriculum believed that the academic program needed the invigorating effects that such a scientific approach could give it. One of the favorite means for approaching curriculum in the early years of this movement was to analyze the job of living—"job analysis"—and then put into the school's curriculum those things that

[16] See p. 456.

such an analysis indicated ought to be there. Job analysis was only one of the many scientific approaches to curriculum construction. The general purpose was, of course, to make the curriculum of the school a more useful instrument for forming the minds and characters of youth. Whatever one may think of the outcomes of some of the scientific studies, their general purposes are not subject to criticism. The greatest problem facing the scientific curriculum builder was that no agreement could be arrived at, with science or without it, as to whether the curriculum should consist of subject matter or whether it should provide a frame of reference in which young people could have worthwhile experiences. These problems are still real; they have not been resolved in educational history.

Curriculum, testing, etc., were points that needed attention, but to them must be added the study of the child himself. This was the study in which the science of education made its greatest progress. Modern education has many instruments for coming to know the child better, and it is using these instruments in clinics and study centers the country over. So far as the history of the child-study movement is concerned, one may mention that it received its original impetus from Rousseau, an added impetus from Pestalozzi and Froebel and, in America, from G. Stanley Hall.

Finally, the science of education turned its attention to the problem of exceptional children. From as early as 1817, when Thomas Gallaudet (1787–1851) established a school for the deaf, concern has been shown for the education of exceptional children. There are many categories of the exceptional, and progress of surprisingly high quality has been made in all of them; the curriculum of the schools for such children, the qualifications and the special education of teachers who are to teach them, and the medical and psychological care that they need, are all matters for study and continuing interest.

EDUCATIONAL THEORY

In the eighteenth and nineteenth centuries America was too busy laying the foundations for education, too busy building schools, finding money to support them, and preparing teachers to instruct the ever-increasing numbers of students, to think about formulating a theory of education. American educators were probably not insensible to the place that theory has in education but were too occupied with practical matters to do more than accept, largely without question, the basic elements of theory that had come to them from Europe. In Europe, in the eighteenth and nineteenth centuries, educational theory had made large and impressive gains. From another point of view, we may say that American educators were actually molding a new educational theory. The commitment they made to universal education almost implies an antecedent theory; and democratic education and the principle of equality of opportunity that it embraced are in themselves the beginning of a new theory. Yet, with all of this ferment and the solid practice that arose out of it, in a formal sense not much was done to articulate a new or a distinctive educational theory. That contribution to American education was made in the twentieth century.

We have mentioned the attempts to formulate an American teaching tradition,[17] and we know, of course, that tradition was part of the theoretical problem. Despite the acceptance of this new tradition (and we have seen how it progressed), it was still a fact that a formal educational theory was lacking.

America's educational theorist was John Dewey. Dewey, who led the American educational revolution on the level of practice, was the philosopher who formulated a new theory of education. But Dewey did not do this work without some help from others. The two men who broke ground for him were Charles Sanders Peirce (1839–1914) and William James (1842–1910).

Peirce's role in the history of American pragmatism is less well known than that of James or Dewey. It was a role that had to do mainly with the early formulation of the basic idea of pragmatism, an idea that was accepted by the men who followed him and expanded it into a philosophical system. The idea was this: "To determine the meaning of an idea, put it into practice in the objective world of actualities, and whatever its consequences prove to be, these constitute the meaning of the idea."[18] Peirce was not concerned especially with devising any test for truth. He may not even have been concerned with truth; he wanted to find out what an idea meant. His method for discovering the meaning was to try the idea out, for he believed that through testing its meaning would be disclosed. At the same time, Peirce was not especially interested in education. He was not a teacher, not at least in the usual sense, and he had no university chair from which to promulgate his philosophical ideas. The result was that his influence was felt only among a few. Significantly, this influence did not miss James, and through James it came to rest on Dewey.

The popularization of the pragmatic idea or criterion was left to others, among whom the most effective was William James. Few teachers and writers of greater popularity than James have appeared on the American scene. He took the criterion that Peirce had proposed and gave it general currency in philosophical circles. In the hands of James the criterion

---

[17] See pp. 473–479.

[18] J. Donald Butler, *Four Philosophies and Their Practice in Education and Religion*, rev. ed., Harper & Brothers, New York, 1957, p. 434.

was used much as Peirce had wanted it used. Both men believed that once the idea was tested in the world of affairs, its meaning could be depended upon; in other words, that a certain permanency attached to the outcomes of the pragmatic test. The pragmatism that was developed by Peirce and popularized by James was changed by John Dewey.

We have already seen something of the background and academic career of John Dewey.[19] He took the pragmatic inheritance that Peirce and James offered and converted it into a philosophical system that was to bear his distinctive mark. With Dewey, though not with those who preceded him, pragmatism adopted a naturalistic outlook, or, we might say that to the extent that this brand of pragmatism had a metaphysic, that metaphysic was naturalistic. Where both Peirce and James had been willing to believe that ideas once tested had a degree of permanency, Dewey regarded truth as relativistic. This line of thought was all worked out on a philosophical level, although it was not without meaning for education. Applying it, Dewey established the school as a social institution with social objectives. The school had always had some social objectives, but with this new educational theory the social purposes came to dominate all others. It was not the school's main function to communicate the inheritance of the past, although this might be done, but rather to put the student in direct relation with the society in which he lived. He was to learn what he needed to know not by reading about it but by living it. The school environment was to be informal, and the educational process was to be set in a context in which the student could be given an opportunity to learn what he needed to know. The objectives of education were not to be determined in advance; they were not outlined in long and impressive lists of goals; they were to be worked out as the children lived and learned in the schools.

It is hard to know where the theories of Dewey stopped and those of his followers began. A long list of names belong to the general pragmatic tradition, but all these men may not have been close and careful followers of Dewey. Besides, there were changes in Dewey's pedagogical creed. True to his pragmatism, Dewey did not formulate one position on educational doctrine and refuse to budge from it. Thus, it is difficult for the historian of American education to trace the evolution of Dewey's thought and pragmatic practices in education. Such close studies will have to be left for other books. We must be content here with the broad, although at times somewhat dissatisfying, outlines of that evolution.

In the development of educational theory in America, Dewey and those who followed him more or less closely form a group which, for

[19] See pp. 474–475.

want of a better name, we call progressives. Those who opposed the ideas and practices of Dewey and his followers we may call essentialists.

Essentialists

There were, it should be said at the outset, two kinds of essentialism: One was represented by William C. Bagley (1874–1946), a professor of education at Columbia University's Teachers College. Bagley was the leader of a group of educators who called themselves essentialists and who had organized in an effort to give effective opposition to the progressive education movement. The other kind of essentialism, which was not a product of the essentialistic society, advocated a return to the fundamentals in education. Among those who associated themselves with the generalized movement, one could find all kinds of educational opinion and educational philosophy. They did agree on one point, however— that a common core to basic culture consists of the essentials of civilized life, and that this common core ought to be communicated steadfastly in all the schools of the land. Eventually this latter essentialistic group broke up into many splinter groups. It was in these groups that the beginnings of certain present-day educational theories are to be found, namely, realism, idealism, rational humanism, and Christian humanism.

Whatever form these various schools of thought took, they maintained in common some opposition to the means that were used by the progressives, although they may not have scorned all the outcomes that the progressives obtained with their new methods. At the same time, the progressives were not immune to the criticisms heaped on them. In 1930 they attempted to prove that the new education was superior to anything that the traditional or essentialist educators had to offer. They organized the Eight-year Study. This was an attempt to find scientific verification for the claims that the progressives had been making about the superiority of the kind of education they advocated. It involved a comparison of the performance of high school students who were subjected to the older methodology and the older objectives, on the one hand, and the students who were exposed to the new pedagogy, on the other. Two groups were formed, and they were to be followed from the first year of high school all the way through college. The study, beginning in 1930, lasted until 1938. In general, the report favored the new pedagogy. According to the conclusions drawn from the study, it seemed to be a fact that the new pedagogy was superior in most areas of study. Although many essentialists took issue with these conclusions as well as with the design of the study, the report of the Eight-year Study was supported by the Progressive Education Association, the Carnegie Corporation, and the General Education Board and was quite generally accepted. The outcome was that the high school's course, and to some extent its standards of achievement, were open to even greater liberalization.[20]

During the first half of the twentieth century, the character of the high school changed a great deal. Many more students entered the school and stayed for a greater length of time. More importantly, they came with a variety of motives and capacities. The high school had become a popular institution. It was no longer a school for the elite and it was no longer thought of as a college-preparatory institution. The high school had no alternative but to change. It could not have remained the kind of school it had been at the beginning of the century and claimed any kind of popular support. These changes in the high school led to criticisms that the high school, in becoming more democratic, was losing its academic soul.[21]

HIGHER EDUCATION IN THE TWENTIETH CENTURY

With the advent of the twentieth century, most educators felt fairly sure that they understood higher education. It was clear to them that the college or the university was a place where academically minded young men, and some young women, could go to pursue their studies and where they could prepare themselves as leaders in the professions and in society. The colleges did not assume any general obligation for the education of teachers, for they felt too committed to their ideas of liberal learning to admit curricula for the professional teacher-education student. The college was the last great haven for the education of the elite. The elementary school was the first to open its doors to all the children of all the people. Then the high school did the same thing. But the college kept its doors closed to all but the few, who had to be especially prepared to meet the admission tests that were erected. The college of 1890 or even of 1905 was a secure place. The college had assumed its form, and those who were its administrators assumed that it would never really change. The college was a finished institution.

Yet, as the century wore on and as the country came to the Great Depression, it was beginning to appear uncertain whether or not the college was going to be able to escape the changes that social progress had required from the lower institutions. Because it was not easy for people to find productive work during the years of the economic depression, more and more students who otherwise might not have

[20] On this point, see W. M. Aikin, *The Story of the Eight-year Study*, Harper & Brothers, New York, 1942.

[21] For some of the works that contain these criticisms of the high school, see Adolphe E. Meyer, *Educational History of the American People*, McGraw-Hill Book Company, Inc., New York, 1957, p. 324.

thought of continuing their education came to the colleges. The colleges admitted them. This was the first break in the wall of resistance. Then, as the colleges became somewhat more liberal in admitting students, they began to discover that not all of the students they admitted were willing to go through the anachronistic programs prepared for them. For one reason or another, mainly lack of interest or inability to succeed, the students resisted the college course of the studies.

Some years before the twentieth century began, as early as 1872, Charles W. Eliot (1834–1926), the dynamic president of Harvard College from 1869 to 1909, introduced the elective program. This program made it possible for students in the college to select the studies in which they were interested. Following the theory of equivalence of studies that was implied in the *Report* of the Committee of Ten, colleges could graduate students who had accumulated a certain number of credit hours. The important point was not the consistency and integrity of the student's development, but the number of credits he had. If he had accumulated 120 hours of college credit, he had enough to take the bachelor's degree.

This liberalization of degree requirements led to the expansion of college study programs and to a multiplication of college degrees. At one time the only degree granted by the American college was the B.A. (bachelor of arts). With this development, dozens of bachelor's degrees were invented.

This liberalization had other effects also. Some college officers became concerned about the new direction that colleges were taking. They feared that the intellectual talents of the few might be wasted by being exposed to such democratizing programs as the colleges were then experimenting with. They decided to establish separate colleges, or a separate branch of the college, which would serve as an additional screening device. This device was to operate on the first two years of the college course. It was called the junior college. During the first years, while the student was in the junior college, he was expected to prove himself. If he did not do so, he left the college. This was the first step in the junior college movement.

The next step was to create junior colleges that were separate from four-year institutions. Some of these junior colleges, which were both public and private, thought of themselves as feeder institutions for four-year colleges and universities; others were simply going through a growth period and were looking forward with hope and optimism to the time when they would become four-year institutions. The junior college movement was successful in that it made college opportunity available to many students who otherwise would not have had it. Following the *Report of the President's Commission on Higher Education* in 1947, the junior college received even greater attention, for this report advocated the establishment of junior colleges in many places where they did not at that time exist. The report referred to them as community colleges, saw them as new additions to the local public high school, and suggested that their objectives be set both in a preparatory and a terminal context. In other words, the new community colleges that were envisioned in the report were to offer academic programs for those who wanted them and could profit from them, and to offer nonacademic programs to students who wanted such programs. The community college touched on such areas as adult education, continuing education, vocational education, and the reeducation of workers for industry.[22]

In addition to these movements that were responsible for broadening higher education considerably, the colleges and the universities to a certain extent liberalized their programs. Most noticeably, they added summer school programs, accelerated programs (these were added mostly during the Second World War), and night school programs. Besides, many new professional schools were founded, and colleges expanded their foundations to make room for professional schools. New units in higher education, usually called institutes, appeared, to offer specialized training or education in a variety of skills and subjects.

The meaning of higher education, by the time we reach the sixth decade of the twentieth century, is evidently considerably different from what it was at the beginning of the century. Contemporary American higher education is schooling or training beyond the high school, no matter what its content or its purposes may be. It may be scientific, professional, academic, nonacademic, technical, or vocational. And, although it is usually commenced after the high school years, it is not necessary for all who participate in higher education programs to have a high school diploma.

While the frontiers of higher education were extended considerably during the first half of the twentieth century, and while more and more students came to attend some kind of institution for higher education, there were many signs that some of the conventional values of higher education were in danger of being lost. The loss was not so much in the direction of lower standards for the ordinary college or university, but rather in the direction of overspecialization. There was a time, early in the century, of course, when it was assumed that the high school was the place for general or liberal education. Liberal education, according to the conventional educational wisdom, was intended to give the student a foundation upon which he could build and from which he could go in almost any direction. As long as the high schools remained

[22] "Higher Education for American Democracy," *Report of the President's Commission on Higher Education*, Washington, D.C., 1947.

true to their older purpose, the college could go rather safely down the road to specialization. But with the change in the high school course, many students came to the colleges without the foundational preparation that the colleges felt they should have. This posed something of a dilemma: Should the colleges go on with specialization and ignore the inadequate backgrounds of the students, or should they accept responsibility for giving students foundational experiences? Two important studies of the 1940s addressed themselves to this issue. One was the report of a committee of the faculty of Harvard University, *General Education in a Free Society* (1945), and the other was the *Report of the President's Commission on Higher Education* (1947). Both reports deplored the lack of attention given to general or liberal education, and both subscribed to the view that the real danger in American higher education was overspecialization, by which they meant specialization without the proper grounding in basic studies of English, literature, science, mathematics, and social science. Both advocated a reorganization of the college curriculum which would make more room for such liberalizing subjects.

Passing from criticism to action, the University of Chicago, beginning with the administration of Robert M. Hutchins in 1929, instituted a program whereby students were to spend their first two years of college pursuing studies in the broad fields of human knowledge covering the humanities and the sciences. At the end of this two-year curriculum, students could present themselves for examinations and, if successful, would be granted the bachelor's degree. Then they would begin their university studies in those areas in which they wished to specialize. The Chicago Plan was by no means widely acclaimed, for by this time American colleges and universities, as well as accrediting associations that they had organized, were committed to a four-year course leading to the bachelor's degree. While the Chicago Plan made a brave beginning and showed some promise of creating a renaissance in higher education, it ran into too much resistance and was much less influential than was at first anticipated. No other American college followed the lead of the University of Chicago. When President Hutchins left Chicago, the plan was abandoned.

A brief survey of the movements in twentieth-century American higher education should not leave unnoticed the effects that the GI Bill of Rights, in its educational provisions, had on American higher education after the Second World War. According to the Federal legislation, men and women who had served in the Armed Forces of the United States were eligible for subvention through college based on the number of months they had served. It is estimated that about six million men and women took advantage of the GI Bill of Rights and attended colleges of their choice. More than any other instrumentality that was brought into play in the century, the GI bill served to popularize higher education. This bill was a force almost without equal in the history of American higher education.

After the Second World War, although to some extent the movement had set in before the war, colleges and universities became especially aware of their duty to conduct scientific investigation. Research programs of various kinds, almost all of them devoted to pure and applied research related to science, were undertaken by higher schools. Government, industry, private foundations, and the schools themselves supported these programs. Many of them, of course, were and are related to those areas of scientific knowledge that can be of value to America in national defense. Yet in spite of the practical and critical nature of the work in which the colleges are involved, the college community tends to benefit, and the college and the university tend to achieve a more significant role in the nation's life. At the same time, however, it has been argued that the college, in becoming a research institution for the Federal government, is again putting itself in jeopardy; it is in danger of losing those humanistic values that the college and the university, as teaching agencies principally, must continue to cherish and communicate. Regardless of the motives for research, it would certainly seem to be true that the college and the university of the mid-twentieth century are more research-conscious and more science-conscious than they ever were in the past.

Perhaps a word ought to be added here concerning the students themselves: their interests, their values, and the goals that they seek through the college course. In the nineteenth century students attended college for the same reasons that students are attending college in this century, for self-improvement and professional advancement. The nostalgic appeal is sometimes made for a return to the college-student type of the good old days. The facts are, however, that the college student of the good old days was much the same as his present-day counterpart. Both attended the college to develop skills and achieve knowledge and understandings that would enable them to advance in the world of affairs. This is not to say, of course, that students never studied for the simple joy of learning, but the purely liberal approach to learning in higher education has never had a very warm welcome in reality, whatever theoretical appeal it may have had.

The college student of the twentieth century, especially in the years from 1930 to 1960, came to the college with much better preparation than his predecessors. He was motivated to achieve the values that society considered important. Since we have already said something about the college course, what we have to say now will be directed at the fringes of college life, at the college student's amusements, his entertainment, and his recreation. At one time these things were reserved for the free time of the student. In the modern college, cocurricular or extracurricular activities are pointed in the direction of caring for the students' leisure time. Thus it is possible for us to see the activities in which students engage becoming a regular, almost an official, part of college life, whereas before they were thought to be outside the ambit of college influence. The most noticeable among many emphases in this part of college life is upon athletics. The major appeal that colleges made to the public from 1920 to 1960 was in athletics, especially in football. During certain seasons of the year the public eye is focused on the colleges, not looking for scholars or scientists but for athletes with prowess on the gridiron. Yet in spite of the considerable attention such fringe activities receive, we can still claim that the colleges of the 1960s offer the best and most well-rounded opportunities for learning and intellectual development that higher education has ever presented.

Among the many crucial issues that face American colleges in the last half of the twentieth century, one stands out especially; it involves the recruitment of an entirely competent faculty. With the ever-increasing enrollments in the colleges, college faculties must continue to grow. But the problem has been and continues to be to find these fully qualified men and women. Faculties of the colleges may easily be downgraded by bringing in teachers from the lower schools, many of whom are fitted neither by temperament, training, nor scholarly instincts to be fully adequate college teachers. But this is a problem for the future to solve. It is not one that the historian can settle or even illuminate.

There are, of course, many features of the academic community that attract people to it, as there are features that drive them away or dissuade them from joining. The most important of the deterrent forces in the years from 1920 to 1955 involved academic freedom. After the First World War and again after the Second World War, many members of the college teaching community were suspected of being, if not actually disloyal to their country, at least of doubtful dependability. Government committees, citizens groups, and the public press began to question the qualifications of many of the members of the academic community. Teachers were dismissed from their teaching positions under supposedly suspicious circumstances and with less than conclusive evidence, when the searching eye of public inquiry was directed at them. History will record that few colleges were willing to stand behind the faculties they had organized when questions were raised concerning an individual teacher's loyalties. It has been said of the colleges that they preferred popular approval to honor.

Unlike workers and some other professional people, college teachers have been reluctant to organize for their own protection. Although college teachers have a professional organization, the American Association of University Professors, fewer than 20 per cent of the college teachers in America have joined this professional organization. Yet this Association, with what strength it has, has been in the vanguard whenever the rights and responsibilities of college faculties have been threatened. Without any question at all, one of the major issues touching the teachers of twentieth-century American colleges has been the question of academic freedom.

INTERNATIONAL EDUCATION

Today's world, a decade beyond the mid-twentieth century, is unavoidably conscious of the various nations that make it up. Perhaps we have all been tardy in realizing the importance of understanding the world and all the people in it. From an American point of view, not enough attention was paid to education in other countries, or even to the hopes and aspirations of the people of other countries before about 1925. It is obvious, of course, that in the early years of America's educational activity a great deal of content and method was borrowed from the older European states. Yet the borrowing was usually done without a very thorough understanding of how the schools that America adopted and adapted were to serve the communities that had given them birth. In 1926 the Commission on Intellectual Cooperation was organized. This was the first step in seeking international cooperation and understanding through education. About the same time, the International Bureau of Education was created. Although its objectives were about the same as those of the CIC, it had the backing of the nations that took part in the enterprise and it was in part supported by them. It sought to achieve the objective of international understanding and greater good will among nations by serving as a clearinghouse for information about the different member nations. The Bureau also organized international conferences to which scholars and articulate citizens were invited. It did not achieve any very notable success. The United States did not join the International Bureau of Education until 1958. In spite of this discouragement, the Bureau did make important progress, if only in calling attention to the need for greater international understanding.

In addition to these attempts to promote understanding, the great powers of the 1930s—Great Britain, France, and Germany, and the United States after 1939—created departments or divisions of cultural relations in their foreign ministries. In spite of the promise of such a movement, in actual operation these departments did little more than represent the culture or the cultural point of view of the country involved. In a way, these departments served the cause of national propaganda, and in some instances, we are led to believe, their programs were little better than the vacuum in cultural communications that generally had existed before.

In the Americas of the 1930s and thereafter there was regional cooperation which looked forward to better understanding among the states of North and South America. Programs of regional cooperation were directed at facilitating all kinds of informational and cultural exchanges among the various countries involved. Teachers, students, publications, art, radio programs, etc., were exchanged.

Besides the activities mentioned above, we might speak of the Institute of International Education as well as of the various programs sponsored by the United States government for the exchange of students and professors: the Fulbright grants. In American higher education, also, the study of comparative education—comparative systems of education as well as ideals and national motives—has received greater attention.

Finally, there is the United Nations Educational, Scientific, and Cultural Organization (UNESCO), founded in London in 1945 on the premise that since it is in the minds of men that wars are begun, it is in the minds of men that the defenses of peace must be constructed. Under this motto the purposes of UNESCO are to spread information in order that there may be greater international understanding, and to create a climate in the various countries of the world in which it will be possible for all people to pursue truth freely and objectively. Both purposes should lead, if they are achieved, to a better world and to a better life for the people who inhabit it. On the practical level, UNESCO sought to attain these high ideals by sponsoring an international student exchange (an exchange of ideas by an exchange of all the instruments that convey ideas), by promoting programs that would reduce illiteracy in all the countries of the world, especially the newly organized national states, and finally, by assisting all the countries of the world in raising their educational and cultural standards.

It is still too early to assess the value of UNESCO. There is no doubt that many of its programs have met with considerable success and have been widely accepted. On the other hand, it is also true that in those areas of the world where a free flow of information would do the most good in the cause of world understanding and world peace, access to such information has been limited. In Asia and Africa, where the need is the greatest, either force or lack of skill seems to stand in the way of gaining or disseminating objective information. Force is used when some other country or some powerful figure does not want informed people. Suppression of truth has always been the chief weapon of the tyrant. Lack of skill, inability to communicate or to understand, also stands in the way of progress, not only for the underdeveloped regions of the world but for the developed regions as well.

The objections to UNESCO and its programs have been voiced in a number of ways. Actually, however, they stem from one essential attitude —nationalism. The purposes of UNESCO lead ultimately to a one-world philosophy and a one-world level of action. The one-world idea is surely opposed by all who defend nationalistic ideals. Yet if a sober look is taken into the future, the choice is not between one world and several national states, but rather between one world and no world.

A LOOK TO THE FUTURE

It is not within the province of the historian to look to the future. Historians have rarely made good prophets. And who could dare to be a prophet when space is man's next frontier to conquer? Nevertheless, we should try to say a word about education's relation to the future. It is clear that exchange programs of various kinds, involving students, teachers, leading citizens, technological and scientific missions, are not only here to stay but are to be expanded dramatically in the years ahead. There are many new frontiers to conquer, and the chief weapon will be education.

In the United States itself the future should bring about three principal advances. First, the part that the Federal government will play in financing education will be increased greatly. This will be done without encroachment on the traditional legal relationship that has existed between the states and the Federal government in the matter of responsibility and authority for education. If we are to broaden the base for financial support of education, if we are to bring about that kind of equality of educational opportunity that can come only through greater and more generous and more equitable financial support of America's schools, then we must establish some kind of Federal program of educational support. Such support should not disturb any of the prized features of localism in American school organization. Whether or not the Federal government contributes to the support of schools, the schools will still belong to the people. Second, equality of educational opportunity as it touches on the questions of who may attend schools, what schools they may attend, and how they are treated when they get there is a problem for the future to resolve. The time must come, and it will come within the next two decades, when all children of America, regardless of the color of their skin, the race of their ancestors, or the religion of their choice, will be given the opportunity everywhere in American schools to fulfill the promise of their God-given talents. The opportunity will be offered, for it is inevitable. The only limit that will be placed on educational progress will be established by the individual himself. Such limits will be found in motivation and capacity. Finally, as we look into the future, we are convinced that the education of adults is going to become far more important than it has been in the recent past. Adult education, not on the level of vocational or entertainment education, but on the level of good, solid liberal education, has a promising outlook. The time may soon come when young people will attend schools first to achieve competence in those skills and knowledges and practical techniques with which they earn a living. After they are earning their living and have achieved a higher level of maturity, they will return to school in search of that intellectual formation that makes man more fully human.

SUMMARY

Many of the hopes for education in the United States were realized in the twentieth century. Free public schools were made universally available, and opportunity for all children was expanded greatly. The teaching tradition of the past was reformed and reinvigorated in order that teaching and learning might accommodate the expanding needs of a democratic society. Knowledge about the art of teaching and the science of education was organized, and consistent efforts were made to increase the body of knowledge about teaching and learning. The educational consciousness of the twentieth century was capped in a new theory of education called pragmatism. The leading educational philosopher of the century was John Dewey. The last rung of the educational ladder, higher education, was subject to important changes. In a word, higher education was brought more closely in line with democratic educational ideals.

While all these important educational developments have been taking place in the United States, education throughout the world has been reawakening to the needs and hopes of mankind. The greatest need is for understanding among men and nations; the greatest hope is still for peace and human equality.

Questions and Exercises for Study and Discussion

1. Discuss the major steps in the popularization of American education.
2. What is the meaning of "the American teaching tradition"? Is there such a thing?
3. How did the progressive education movement start? What were its successes? Its failures?
4. Report on the academic career of John Dewey.

5. In what principal ways has John Dewey influenced education in the United States?
6. What were the major developments in American elementary education in the first half of the twentieth century?
7. What were the major developments in American secondary education in the first half of the twentieth century?
8. What were the major developments in American higher education in the first half of the twentieth century?
9. Prepare a paper containing your predictions of things to come in international education.
10. Prepare a report containing your views of the future of American education.

References for Further Reading

Ancient Education (Chapters 1 to 5)

Adamson, J. E.: *The Theory of Education in Plato's Republic*, Swan Sonnenschein, London, 1903.

Aristotle: *Nicomachean Ethics*, with an English translation by H. Rackham, Loeb Classical Library, Harvard University Press, Cambridge, Mass., 1926.

———: *Politics*, with an English translation by H. Rackham, Loeb Classical Library, Harvard University Press, Cambridge, Mass., 1932.

Barclay, William: *Educational Ideals of the Ancient World*, Collins, London, 1959.

Bosanquet, Bernard: *The Education of the Young in the Republic of Plato*, Harvard University Press, Cambridge, Mass., 1901.

Breasted, J. H.: *The Dawn of Conscience*, Charles Scribner's Sons, New York, 1947.

Burnet, John: *Aristotle on Education*, Harvard University Press, Cambridge, Mass., 1928.

Capes, W. W.: *University Life in Ancient Athens*, Stechert-Hafner, Inc., New York, 1922.

Cole, P. R.: *Later Roman Education*, Teachers College, Columbia University, New York, 1909.

Davidson, Thomas: *Aristotle and Ancient Educational Ideals*, Charles Scribner's Sons, New York, 1901.

———: *Education of the Greek People*, Appleton-Century-Crofts, Inc., New York, 1904.

Dobson, John F.: *Ancient Education and Its Meaning to Us*, Longmans, Green & Co., Inc., New York, 1932.

Drever, James: *Greek Education: Its Practice and Principles*, G. P. Putnam's Sons, New York, 1912.

Forbes, Clarence A.: *Greek Physical Education*, Appleton-Century-Crofts, Inc., New York, 1929.

Freeman, Kenneth J.: *Schools of Hellas*, 3d ed., The Macmillan Company, New York, 1922.

Galt, Howard S.: *A History of Chinese Educational Institutions*, Arthur Probsthain, London, 1951.

Gardiner, E. Norman: *Athletics of the Ancient World,* Oxford University Press, New York, 1930.

Goldenweiser, Alex A.: *Anthropology: An Introduction to Primitive Culture,* Appleton-Century-Crofts, Inc., New York, 1937.

Gwynn, Aubery: *Roman Education from Cicero to Quintilian,* Oxford University Press, New York, 1926.

Haarhoff, Theodore J.: *Schools of Ancient Gaul: A Study of Pagan and Christian Schools in the Last Century of the Western Empire,* Oxford University Press, New York, 1920.

Hambly, W. D., and Charles Hose: *Origins of Education among Primitive Peoples,* St. Martin's Press, Inc., New York, 1926.

Hobhouse, W.: *The Theory and Practice of Ancient Education,* Stechert-Hafner, Inc., New York, 1910.

Hoebel, E. Adamson: *Man in the Primitive World,* McGraw-Hill Book Company, Inc., New York, 1958.

Jaeger, Werner W.: *Paideia: The Ideals of Greek Culture,* translated by Gilbert Highet, Oxford University Press, New York, 1945.

Kenyon, Frederic G.: *Books and Readers in Ancient Greece and Rome,* Oxford University Press, New York, 1932.

Lane, Fred: *Elementary Greek Education,* C. W. Bardeen Company, Syracuse, New York, 1895.

Laurie, S. S.: *Historical Survey of Pre-Christian Education,* Longmans, Green & Co., Inc., New York, 1895.

Lodge, Rupert C.: *Plato's Theory of Education,* Harcourt, Brace & World, Inc., New York, 1948.

Mahaffy, J. P.: *Greek Life and Thought,* The Macmillan Company, New York, 1896.

——: *Old Greek Education,* Harper & Brothers, New York, 1881.

——: *Social Life in Greece,* St. Martin's Press, Inc., New York, 1913.

Marrou, H. I.: *A History of Education in Antiquity,* translated by George Lamb, Sheed & Ward, Inc., New York, 1956.

Maspero, G. C. C.: *Life in Ancient Egypt and Assyria,* Grolier Society, Inc., New York, 1906.

——: *The Dawn of Civilization: Egypt and Chaldaea,* SPCK, London, 1901.

Monroe, Paul: *Source Book in the History of Education for the Greek and Roman Period,* The Macmillan Company, New York, 1921.

Nettleship, Richard L.: *The Theory of Education in the Republic of Plato,* University of Chicago Press, Chicago, 1906.

Plato: *The Republic,* Loeb Classical Library, Harvard University Press, Cambridge, Mass., 1930–1935, vols. I and II.

——: *The Laws,* Loeb Classical Library, G. P. Putnam's Sons, New York, 1926, vols. I and II.

Quintilian: *Institutes of Oratory,* translated by H. E. Butler, Loeb Classical Library, Harvard University Press, Cambridge, Mass., 1921, vols. I–IV.

Smail, W. M.: *Quintilian on Education,* Oxford University Press, New York, 1938.

Swift, Fletcher H.: *Education in Ancient Israel,* The Open Court Publishing Company, La Salle, Ill., 1919.

Thorndike, Lynn: *A Short History of Civilization,* Appleton-Century-Crofts, Inc., New York, 1926.

Todd, A. J.: *The Primitive Family as an Educational Agency,* G. P. Putnam's Sons, New York, 1913.

Van Hook, Larue: *Greek Life and Thought,* Columbia University Press, New York, 1937.

Walden, John W. H.: *The Universities of Ancient Greece,* Charles Scribner's Sons, New York, 1909.

Westaway, Katherine M.: *The Educational Theory of Plutarch,* University of London Press, Ltd., London, 1922.

Wie, Francis C. M.: *The Spirit of Chinese Cultures,* Charles Scribner's Sons, New York, 1947.

Wilkins, A. S.: *National Education in Greece in the Fourth Century B.C.,* Stechert-Hafner, Inc., New York, 1911.

————: *Roman Education,* The Macmillan Company, New York, 1914.

Wilson, J. A.: *The Culture of Ancient Egypt,* University of Chicago Press, Chicago, 1951.

Woody, Thomas. *Life and Education in Early Societies,* The Macmillan Company, New York, 1949.

Early Christian and Medieval Education (Chapters 6 to 8)

Abelson, Paul: *The Seven Liberal Arts,* Teachers College, Columbia University, New York, 1906.

Artz, Frederick B.: *The Mind of the Middle Ages,* Alfred A. Knopf, Inc., New York, 1953.

Auchmuty, James J.: *Irish Education,* Hodges, Figgs and Co., Dublin, 1937, and George G. Harrap & Co., Ltd., London, 1937.

Bigg, Charles: *The Christian Platonists of Alexandria,* Macmillan & Company, Ltd., London, 1886.

Cassidy, Francis P.: *Molders of the Medieval Mind,* B. Herder Book Company, St. Louis, 1944.

Cassiodorus Senator, Flavius Magnus Aurelius: *An Introduction to Divine and Human Readings,* translated, with an introduction and notes, by Leslie Webber Jones, Columbia University Press, New York, 1946.

Compayré, J. G.: *Abelard and the Origin and Early History of the Universities,* Charles Scribner's Sons, New York, 1893.

Daly, Lowrie J.: *The Medieval University,* Sheed & Ward, Inc., New York, 1961.

DeWulf, Maurice: *Scholasticism Old and New,* translated by P. Coffey, Benziger Bros., New York, 1907.

Drane, A. T.: *Christian Schools and Scholars,* new ed., Benziger Bros., New York, 1924.

Duckett, Eleanor S.: *Alcuin, Friend of Charlemagne; His World and His Work,* The Macmillan Company, New York, 1951.

Ellspermann, Gerald L.: *The Attitude of the Early Christian Latin Writers toward Pagan Literature and Learning*, The Catholic University of America Press, Washington, D.C., 1949.

Gábriel, Asztrik: *Student Life in Ave Maria College, Medieval Paris*, Publications in Medieval Studies, Notre Dame, Ind., 1955.

———: *The Educational Ideals of Vincent of Beauvais*, The Mediaeval Institute, University of Notre Dame, Notre Dame, Ind., 1956.

Graham, Hugh: *The Early Irish Monastic Schools*, Talbot Press, Ltd., Dublin, 1923.

Graves, Frank P.: *What Did Jesus Teach? An Examination of the Educational Material and Method of the Master*, The Macmillan Company, New York, 1925.

Haskins, Charles H.: *Studies in the History of Medieval Science*, Harvard University Press, Cambridge, Mass., 1929.

———: *The Renaissance of the Twelfth Century*, Harvard University Press, Cambridge, Mass., 1927.

———: *The Rise of Universities*, Holt, Rinehart and Winston, Inc., New York, 1923.

Healy, John: *Ireland's Ancient Schools and Scholars*, Sealy, Bryers, and Walker, Dublin, 1893.

Hodgson, Geraldine: *Primitive Christian Education*, T. & T. Clark, Edinburgh, 1906.

Hugo of St. Victor: *Didascalicon; a medieval guide to the arts*, translated, with an introduction and notes, by Jerome Taylor, Columbia University Press, New York, 1961.

Kibre, Pearl: *The Nations in the Mediaeval Universities*, Medieval Academy of America, Boston, 1948.

Kleinz, John Paul: *The Theory of Knowledge of Hugh of St. Victor*, The Catholic University of America Press, Washington, D.C., 1944.

Laistner, M. L. W.: *Christianity and Pagan Literature in the Early Roman Empire*, Cornell University Press, Ithaca, N.Y., 1951.

Laurie, S. S.: *Rise and Early Constitutions of Universities*, Appleton-Century-Crofts, Inc., New York, 1903.

Leach, A. F.: *Educational Charters and Documents*, Cambridge University Press, New York, 1911.

———: *Schools of Medieval England*, Methuen & Co., Ltd., London, 1915.

Magevney, E.: *Christian Education in the Dark Ages*, Catholic Library Association, New York, 1900.

———: *Christian Education in the First Centuries*, The Cathedral Library Association, New York, 1907.

Mayer, Mary Helen: *The Philosophy of Teaching of St. Thomas Aquinas*, The Bruce Publishing Company, Milwaukee, 1929.

McCann, Justin: *The Rule of St. Benedict*, Burns, Oates & Washbourne, Ltd., London, 1952.

McCormick, John E.: *St. Thomas and the Life of Learning*, Marquette University Press, Milwaukee, 1937.

McGarry, Daniel D.: *The Metalogicon of John of Salisbury*, University of California Press, Berkeley, Calif., 1955.

Morgan, James: *The Psychological Teaching of St. Augustine*, Robert Scott, London, 1932.

Mullinger, J. Bass: *The Schools of Charles the Great*, Stechert-Hafner, Inc., New York, 1911.

Norton, A. O.: *Readings in the History of Education: Medieval Universities*, Harvard University Press, Cambridge, Mass., 1909.

Patch, Howard Rollin: *The Tradition of Boethius*, Oxford University Press, New York, 1935.

Paetow, L. J.: *Battle of the Seven Liberal Arts*, University of California Press, Berkeley, Calif., 1914.

——: *The Arts Course at Medieval Universities*, University of Illinois Press, Urbana, Ill., 1910.

Parry, Albert W.: *Education in England in the Middle Ages*, University of London Press, London, 1920.

Poole, R. L.: *Illustrations of the History of Medieval Thought and Learning*, 2d ed., The Macmillan Company, New York, 1940.

Rait, Robert S.: *Life in the Medieval University*, The Macmillan Company, New York, 1912.

Rand, Edward K.: *The Founders of the Middle Ages*, Harvard University Press, Cambridge, Mass., 1928.

Rashdall, Hastings: *Universities of Europe in the Middle Ages*, new ed., Oxford University Press, New York, 1936.

St. Augustine: *Concerning the Teacher* and *On the Immortality of the Soul*, translated by G. G. Leckie, Appleton-Century-Crofts, Inc., New York, 1938.

St. Jerome: *On Female Education*, in Henry Barnard's *American Journal of Education*, vol. 5, pp. 593–598.

St. John Chrysostom: *Concerning the Education of Children*, translated by John Evelyn, in William Upcott (ed.), *Miscellaneous Writings of John Evelyn*, Henry Colburn, London, 1825.

Schachner, Nathan: *The Medieval Universities*, J. B. Lippincott Company, Philadelphia, 1938.

Seybolt, Robert F.: *The Manuale Scholarium*, Harvard University Press, Cambridge, Mass., 1921.

Sherrill, L. J.: *The Rise of Christian Education*, The Macmillan Company, New York, 1944.

Taylor, H. O.: *The Medieval Mind*, The Macmillan Company, London, 1930,

Taylor, Jerome: *The Origin and Early Life of Hugh of St. Victor: An Evaluation of the Tradition*, The Mediaeval Institute, University of Notre Dame, Notre Dame, Ind., 1957.

Thorndike, Lynn: *University Records and Life in the Middle Ages*, Columbia University Press, New York, 1944.

Townsend, W. J.: *The Great Schoolmen of the Middle Ages*, Hodder & Stoughton, Ltd., London, 1881.

Waddell, Helen: *The Wandering Scholars*, Constable & Co., Ltd., London, 1927.

Walsh, J. J.: *The Thirteenth, Greatest of Centuries*, 5th ed., Catholic Summer School Press, New York, 1924.

Watson, Foster: *The English Grammar Schools to 1660,* Cambridge University Press, New York, 1908.

West, Andrew F.: *Alcuin and the Rise of Christian Schools,* Charles Scribner's Sons, New York, 1909.

Modern European Education (Chapters 9 to 13)

Adams, John: *The Herbartian Psychology Applied to Education,* D. C. Heath and Company, Boston, 1897.

————: *The Evolution of Educational Theory,* The Macmillan Company, New York, 1912.

Adamson, J. W.: *English Education, 1789–1902,* Cambridge University Press, New York, 1930.

————: *Pioneers of Modern Education,* Cambridge University Press, New York, 1905.

Ascham, Roger: *The Scholemaster,* edited by D. C. Whimster, Methuen & Co., Ltd., London, 1934.

Bacon, Francis, *The Advancement of Learning,* and *Novum Organum,* rev. ed., John Wiley & Sons, Inc., New York, 1944.

Barker, Ernest: *British Universities,* Longmans, Green & Co., Inc., New York, 1946.

Barnard, Henry C.: *Pestalozzi and His Educational System,* C. W. Bardeen, Syracuse, N.Y., 1906.

————: *The French Tradition in Education,* Cambridge University Press, New York, 1922.

Battersby, W. J.: *De La Salle: A Pioneer of Modern Education,* Longmans, Green & Co., Inc., New York, 1949.

Becker, Carl H.: *Secondary Education and Teacher Training in Germany,* Teachers College, Columbia University, New York, 1931.

Bowen, H. C.: *Froebel and Education by Self Activity,* Charles Scribner's Sons, New York, 1901.

Boyd, William: *The Educational Theory of Jean Jacques Rousseau,* Longmans, Green & Co., Inc., New York, 1911..

Cannon, M. A.: *The Education of Women during the Renaissance,* The Catholic University of America Press, Washington, D.C., 1916.

Castiglione, Baldassare: *The Book of the Courtier,* translated by L. E. Opdycke, Charles Scribner's Sons, 1903.

Cavenagh, F. A.: *James and John Stuart Mill on Education,* Cambridge University Press, New York, 1931.

Champagnac, E. T.: *Mulcaster's Elementarie,* Oxford University Press, New York, 1925.

Comenius, Johann Amos: *The Great Didactic,* translated and edited by M. W. Keatinge, Adam & Charles Black, Ltd., London, 1921–1923.

Compayré, Gabriel: *Jean Jacques Rousseau and Education from Nature,* translated by R. P. Jago, Thomas Y. Crowell Company, New York, 1907.

Connell, W. F.: *The Educational Thought and Influence of Matthew Arnold,* Routledge & Kegan Paul, Ltd., London, 1950.

Darroch, Alexander: *Herbart and the Herbartian Theory of Education,* Longmans, Green & Co., Inc., New York, 1903.

Davidson, Thomas: *Rousseau and Education According to Nature,* Charles Scribner's Sons, New York, 1898.

Dawson, Christopher: *The Crisis of Western Education,* Sheed & Ward, Inc., New York, 1961.

De Garmo, Charles: *Herbart and the Herbartians,* Charles Scribner's Sons, New York, 1904.

Eby, Frederick (ed.): *Early Protestant Educators,* McGraw-Hill Book Company, Inc., New York, 1931.

Elyot, Thomas: *The Boke Named the Governour,* Kegan Paul, Trench, Trubner & Co., London, 1883.

Erasmus, Desiderius: *The Education of a Christian Prince,* edited by Lester K. Born, Columbia University Press, New York, 1936.

Farrell, Allan P.: *The Jesuit Code of Liberal Education,* The Bruce Publishing Company, Milwaukee, 1938.

Farrington, F. E.: *French Secondary Schools,* Longmans, Green & Co., Inc., New York, 1910.

Fitzpatrick, Edward A.: *La Salle, Patron of All Teachers,* The Bruce Publishing Company, Milwaukee, 1951.

Froebel, Friedrich Wilhelm August: *The Education of Man,* translated by W. N. Hailmann, D. Appleton & Company, Inc., New York, 1892.

————: *Pedagogics of the Kindergarten,* translated by Josephine Jarvis, Appleton-Century-Crofts, Inc., New York, 1905.

Hamlyn, V. W. C.: *The Universities of Europe at the Period of the Reformation,* G. Shrimpton, Oxford, 1876.

Hans, Nicholas: *History of Russian Educational Policy,* P. S. King & Staples, Ltd., London, 1931.

Herbart, Johann F.: *Outlines of Educational Doctrine,* translated by A. F. Lange, The Macmillan Company, New York, 1901.

Herbart, Johann F.: *Science of Education: Its General Principles Deduced from Its Aim and the Aesthetic Revelation of the World,* translated by H. M. and E. Felkin, D. C. Heath and Company, Boston, 1908.

Hughes, James L.: *Froebel's Educational Laws for All Teachers,* Appleton-Century-Crofts, Inc., New York, 1904.

Hyma, Albert: *The Brethren of the Common Life,* Eerdmans, Grand Rapids, Mich., 1950.

Johnson, William H. E.: *Russia's Educational Heritage,* Rutgers University Press, New Brunswick, N.J., 1950.

Kant, Immanuel: *Educational Theory,* translated by E. F. Bucher, J. B. Lippincott Company, Philadelphia, 1904.

Keatinge, M. W.: *Comenius,* McGraw-Hill Book Company, Inc., New York, 1931.

Kilpatrick, William H.: *Froebel's Kindergarten Principles Critically Examined,* The Macmillan Company, New York, 1916.

La Fontainerie, Francois de: *French Liberalism and Education in the Eighteenth Century,* McGraw-Hill Book Company, Inc., New York, 1932.

————: *The Conduct of the Schools of Jean Baptiste de la Salle*, McGraw-Hill Book Company, Inc., New York, 1935.

Leach, A. F.: *English Schools at the Reformation*, Constable & Co., Ltd., Westminster, England, 1896.

Learned, W. S.: *The Quality of the Educational Process in the United States and Europe*, Carnegie Foundation Bulletin 20, New York, 1927.

Lilge, Frederic: *The Abuse of Learning: The Failure of the German University*, The Macmillan Company, New York, 1948.

Locke, John: *Educational Writings*, edited by John William Adamson, The Macmillan Company, New York, 1913.

Mallet, Charles E.: *A History of the University of Oxford*, Methuen & Co., Ltd., London, 1924–1927.

Maritain, Jacques: *Three Reformers: Luther, Descartes, Rousseau*, Charles Scribner's Sons, New York, 1929.

McGrath, Fergal: *Newman's University: Idea and Reality*, Longmans, Green & Co., Inc., New York, 1951.

McMahon, Clara P.: *Education in Fifteenth-century England*, Johns Hopkins Press, Baltimore, 1947.

McMurray, Charles A.: *The Elements of General Method Based on the Principles of Herbart*, The Macmillan Company, New York, 1903.

Moehlman, A. H., and J. S. Roucek: *Comparative Education*, The Dryden Press, Inc., New York, 1952.

Milton, John: *Milton on Education*, edited by Oliver M. Ainsworth, Cornell University Press, Ithaca, N.Y., 1928.

Monroe, Will S.: *A History of the Pestalozzian Movement in the United States*, C. W. Bardeen, Syracuse, N.Y., 1907.

————: *Comenius and the Beginnings of Educational Reform*, Charles Scribner's Sons, New York, 1900.

Montaigne, Michel de: *The Education of Children*, translated by L. E. Rector, D. Appleton & Company, Inc., New York, 1899.

Mullinger, J. Bass: *The University of Cambridge*, Cambridge University Press, New York, 1873–1911.

Newman, John Henry Cardinal: *The Idea of a University*, Longmans, Green & Co., Inc., New York, 1919.

Painter, F. V. N.: *Great Pedagogical Essays*, American Book Company, New York, 1905.

————: *Luther on Education*, Lutheran Publication Society, Philadelphia, 1889.

Paulsen, Friedrich: *German Education, Past and Present*, translated by T. Lorenz, Charles Scribner's Sons, New York, 1912.

————: *German Universities and University Study*, Charles Scribner's Sons, New York, 1906.

Pestalozzi, Johann H.: *How Gertrude Teaches Her Children*, 5th ed., translated by Lucy E. Holland and F. C. Turner, C. W. Bardeen, Syracuse, N.Y., 1915.

————: *Leonard and Gertrude*, translated and abridged by Eva Channing, D. C. Heath and Company, Boston, 1906.

Pius II: *De Liberorum Educatione,* translated with an introduction by Brother J. S. Nelson, The Catholic University of America Press, Washington, D.C., 1940.

Rousseau, Jean Jacques: *Emile,* translated by Barbara Foxley, E. P. Dutton & Co., Inc., New York, 1938.

St. Ignatius of Loyola: *Ratio Studiorum,* in Edward A. Fitzpatrick (ed.), *St. Ignatius and the Ratio Studiorum,* McGraw-Hill Book Company, Inc., New York, 1933.

Schwickerath, Robert, S. J.: *Jesuit Education: Its History and Principles,* B. Herder Book Company, St. Louis, 1904.

Smith, Frank: *A History of English Elementary Education, 1760–1902,* University of London Press, Ltd., London, 1931.

Spencer, Herbert: *Education: Intellectual, Moral, and Physical,* Appleton-Century-Crofts, Inc., 1927.

Turnbull, G. T.: *The Educational Theory of J. G. Fichte,* Liverpool University Press, Liverpool, 1926.

Vives, Juan Luis: *On Education,* a translation of *De Tradendis Disciplinis,* with an introduction by Foster Watson, G. P. Putnam's Sons, New York, 1913.

Walch, Sister M. Romana: *Pestalozzi and the Pestalozzian Theory of Education,* The Catholic University of America Press, Washington, D.C., 1952.

Watson, Foster: *Vives and the Renascence Education of Women,* Longmans, Green & Co., Inc., New York, 1912.

Woodward, William H.: *Desiderius Erasmus, concerning the Aim and Method of Education,* Cambridge University Press, New York, 1904.

———: *Vittorino da Feltre and Other Humanist Educators,* Cambridge University Press, New York, 1905.

———: *Studies in Education during the Age of the Renaissance, 1400–1600,* Cambridge University Press, New York, 1924.

American Education (Chapters 14 and 15)

Adams, Henry: *The Education of Henry Adams,* Houghton Mifflin Company, Boston, 1922.

Adams, Herbert B.: *Thomas Jefferson and the University of Virginia,* Contributions to American Educational History, no. 2, Washington, D.C., 1888.

Adler, Mortimer J., and Milton Mayer: *The Revolution in Education,* University of Chicago Press, Chicago, 1958.

Arrowood, Charles F.: *Thomas Jefferson and Education in a Republic,* McGraw-Hill Book Company, Inc., New York, 1930.

Baker, Melvin C.: *Foundations of John Dewey's Educational Theory,* King's Crown Press, New York, 1955.

Beck, Hubert P.: *Men Who Control Our Universities,* King's Crown Press, New York, 1947.

Bestor, Arthur: *Educational Wastelands,* University of Illinois Press, Urbana, Ill., 1953.

———: *The Restoration of Learning,* Alfred A. Knopf, Inc., New York, 1955.

Boas, Louise: *Women's Education Begins*, Wheaton College Press, Newton, Mass., 1935.

Bode, Boyd: *Progressive Education at the Crossroads*, Newsom and Company, New York, 1938.

Bode, Boyd: *Modern Educational Theories*, The Macmillan Company, New York, 1927.

Blum, Virgil C., S.J.: *Freedom of Choice in Education*, The Macmillan Company, New York, 1958.

Boone, R. G.: *Education in the United States*, D. Appleton & Company, Inc., 1890.

Borrowman, Merle L.: *The Liberal and Technical in Teacher Education*, Teachers College, Columbia University, New York, 1955.

Bowler, Sister M. Mariella: *A History of Catholic Colleges for Women in the United States of America*, The Catholic University of America Press, Washington, D.C., 1933.

Breed, Frederick S.: *Education and the New Realism*, The Macmillan Company, New York, 1939.

Brubacher, John S.: *The Public Schools and Spiritual Values*, Harper & Brothers, New York, 1944.

———, and Willis Rudy: *Higher Education in Transition*, Harper & Brothers, New York, 1958.

Burns, J. A., and Bernard J. Kohlbrenner: *A History of Catholic Education in the United States*, Benziger Bros., New York, 1937.

Butler, J. Donald: *Four Philosophies and Their Practice in Education and Religion*, rev. ed., Harper & Brothers, New York, 1957.

Butts, R. Freeman: *The American Tradition in Religion and Education*, The Beacon Press, Boston, 1950.

———: *The College Charts Its Course*, McGraw-Hill Book Company, Inc., New York, 1939.

———, and Lawrence Cremin: *A History of Education in American Culture*, Holt, Rinehart and Winston, Inc., New York, 1953.

Cassidy, Francis P.: *Catholic College Foundations and Development in the United States, 1677 to 1850*, The Catholic University of America Press, Washington, D.C., 1924.

Chalmers, Gordon, K.: *The Republic and the Person: A Discussion of Necessities in Modern American Education*, Henry Regnery Company, Chicago, 1952.

Childs, John L.: *American Pragmatism and Education*, Holt, Rinehart and Winston, Inc., New York, 1956.

Conant, James B.: *The American High School Today*, McGraw-Hill Book Company, Inc., New York, 1959.

Confrey, Burton: *Secularism in American Education*, The Catholic Education Press, Washington, D.C., 1931.

Cremin, Lawrence A.: *The American Common School*, Teachers College, Columbia University, New York, 1951.

———: *The Transformation of the School*, Alfred A. Knopf, Inc., New York, 1961.

Cubberley, E. P.: *Public Education in the United States,* Houghton Mifflin Company, Boston, 1934.

Culver, Raymond B.: *Horace Mann and Religion in the Massachusetts Public Schools,* Yale University Press, New Haven, Conn., 1929.

Curti, Merle: *The Social Ideas of American Educators,* Charles Scribner's Sons, New York, 1935.

Dearborn, Ned H.: *The Oswego Movement in American Education,* Teachers College, Columbia University, New York, 1925.

Dewey, John: *Democracy and Education,* The Macmillan Company, New York, 1916.

————: *My Pedagogic Creed,* E. L. Keelogg, New York, 1897.

———— : *School and Society,* rev. ed., University of Chicago Press, Chicago, 1915.

Eckleberry, R. H: *The History of the Municipal University in the United States,* U.S. Office of Education Bulletin no. 2, 1932.

Edwards, Newton, and Herman G. Richey: *The School in the American Social Order,* Houghton Mifflin Company, Boston, 1947.

Elsbree, Willard S.: *The American Teacher,* American Book Company, New York, 1939.

Flexner, Abraham: *Daniel Coit Gilman: Creator of the American Type University,* Harcourt, Brace & World, Inc., New York, 1946.

Franklin, Benjamin: *Proposals Relating to the Education of Youth in Pennsylvania,* University of Pennsylvania Press, Philadelphia, 1931.

Foerster, Norman: *The Future of the Liberal College,* Appleton-Century-Crofts, Inc., New York, 1938.

Foudy, John: *The Education Principles of American Humanism,* The Catholic University of America Press, Washington, D.C., 1945.

Goebel, Edmund, J.: *A Study of Catholic Secondary Education during the Colonial Period up to the First Plenary Council of Baltimore, 1852,* Benziger Bros., New York, 1937.

Goodsell, Willystine: *Pioneers of Women's Education,* McGraw-Hill Book Company, Inc., New York, 1931.

Grizzell, Emit D.: *Origin and Development of the High School in New England before 1865,* The Macmillan Company, New York, 1923.

Hansen, Allen O.: *Liberalism and American Education in the Eighteenth Century,* The Macmillan Company, New York, 1926.

Harper, Charles A.: *A Century of Public Teacher Education,* American Association of Teachers Colleges, New York, 1939.

Harvard Committee: *General Education in a Free Society,* Harvard University Press, Cambridge, Mass., 1945.

Hinsdale, Burke A.: *Horace Mann and the Common School Revival in the United States,* Charles Scribner's Sons, New York, 1898.

Hofstadter, Richard, and Walter P. Metzger: *The Development of Academic Freedom in the United States,* Columbia University Press, New York, 1955.

————, and C. De Witt Hardy: *The Development and Scope of Higher*

Education in the United States, Columbia University Press, New York, 1952.

Honeywell, Roy J.: *The Educational Work of Thomas Jefferson,* Harvard University Press, Cambridge, Mass., 1931.

Hutchins, Robert M.: *The Higher Learning in America,* University of Chicago Press, Chicago, 1936.

Hutchins, Robert M.: *The Conflict in Education in a Democratic Society,* Harper & Brothers, New York, 1953.

Jackson, Sidney L.: *America's Struggle for Free Schools,* American Council on Public Affairs, Washington, D.C., 1942.

James, William: *Talks to Teachers on Psychology,* new ed., Holt, Rinehart and Winston, Inc., New York, 1939.

Johnson, Clifton: *Old-time Schools and Schoolbooks,* The Macmillan Company, New York, 1904.

Kandel, I. L.: *American Education in the Twentieth Century,* Harvard University Press, Cambridge, Mass., 1957.

Knight, Edgar W.: *Education in the United States,* 3d ed., Ginn & Company, Boston, 1951.

Mann, Horace: *Report, Together with the Report of the Secretary of the Board, 1st–12th,* Dutton and Wentworth, Boston, 1838–1849, reprinted, Washington, D.C., 1947–1952.

McGucken, W. J.: *The Jesuits and Education,* The Bruce Publishing Company, Milwaukee, 1932.

Meriweather, Cloyer: *Our Colonial Curriculum, 1607–1776,* Capital Publishing Company, Washington, D.C., 1907.

Meyer, Adolphe E.: *Educational History of the American People,* McGraw-Hill Book Company, Inc., New York, 1957.

Miller, Perry: *The New England Mind,* The Macmillan Company, New York, 1939.

Monroe, Paul: *Founding of the American Public School System,* The Macmillan Company, New York, 1940.

Morison, Samuel E.: *The Founding of Harvard College,* Harvard University Press, Cambridge, Mass., 1935.

Nock, Albert J.: *The Theory of Education in the United States,* Harcourt, Brace & World, Inc., New York, 1932.

O'Connell, Geoffrey: *Naturalism in American Education,* Benziger Bros., New York, 1938.

O'Neill, James M.: *Religion and Education under the Constitution,* Harper & Brothers, New York, 1949.

Pangburn, Jessie M.: *The Evolution of the American Teachers College,* Teachers College, Columbia University, New York, 1932.

Power, Edward J.: *A History of Catholic Higher Education in the United States,* The Bruce Publishing Company, Milwaukee, 1958.

———: *Education for American Democracy,* McGraw-Hill Book Company, Inc., New York, 1958.

The Relation of Religion to Public Education: The Basic Principles, American Council on Education, Washington, D.C., 1947.

Ross, Earle D.: *Democracy's College,* Iowa State College Press, Ames, Iowa, 1942.

Small, Walter Herbert: *Early New England Schools,* Ginn & Company, Boston, 1914.

Tewksbury, Donald G.: *The Founding of American Colleges and Universities before the Civil War,* Teachers College, Columbia University, New York, 1932.

Thorpe, Francis N.: *Franklin's Influence in American Education,* U.S. Bureau of Education, 1903.

Walsh, James J.: *Education of the Founding Fathers,* Fordham University Press, New York, 1935.

Williams, E. I. F.: *Horace Mann: Educational Statesman,* The Macmillan Company, New York, 1937.

Wish, Harvey: *Society and Thought in Early America,* Longmans, Green & Co., Inc., New York, 1950.

Woefel, Norman: *Molders of the American Mind,* Columbia University Press, New York, 1933.

Woody, Thomas: *Educational Views of Benjamin Franklin,* McGraw-Hill Book Company, Inc., New York, 1931.

General Histories of Education

Boyd, William: *History of Western Education,* 6th ed. Adam & Charles Black, Ltd., London, 1952.

Brubacher, John S.: *A History of the Problems of Education,* McGraw-Hill Book Company, Inc., New York, 1947.

Butts, R. Freeman: *A Cultural History of Education,* McGraw-Hill Book Company, Inc., New York, 1946.

Cole, Percival R.: *History of Educational Thought,* Oxford University Press, New York, 1931.

Cubberley, Ellwood P.: *The History of Education,* Houghton Mifflin Company, Boston, 1920.

Eby, Frederick: *The Development of Modern Education,* 2d ed., Prentice-Hall, Inc., Englewood Cliffs, N.J., 1952.

———, and Charles F. Arrowood: *The History and Philosophy of Education: Ancient and Medieval,* Prentice-Hall, Inc., Englewood Cliffs, N.J., 1940.

Good, H. G.: *A History of Western Education,* The Macmillan Company, New York, 1947.

Graves, Frank P.: *A History of Education before the Middle Ages,* The Macmillan Company, New York, 1909.

———: *A History of Education during the Middle Ages,* The Macmillan Company, New York, 1910.

———: *A History of Education in Modern Times,* The Macmillan Company, New York, 1913.

Kandel, Isaac L.: *History of Secondary Education: A Study of the Development of Liberal Education,* Houghton Mifflin Company, Boston, 1930.

Kane, William T., S.J.: *An Essay toward a History of Education,* rev. ed., Loyola University Press, Chicago, 1954.

Knight, Edgar W.: *Twenty Centuries of Education,* Ginn & Company, Boston, 1940.

Marique, Pierre J.: *History of Christian Education,* Fordham University Press, New York, 1924–1932.

McCormick, Patrick J., and Francis P. Cassidy: *History of Education,* The Catholic Education Press, Washington, D.C., 1953.

Messenger, J. F.: *Interpretative History of Education,* Thomas Y. Crowell Company, New York, 1931.

Monroe, Paul: *Textbook in the History of Education,* The Macmillan Company, New York, 1905.

Moore, E. C.: *The Story of Instruction,* The Macmillan Company, New York, 1936–1938.

Mulhern, James: *A History of Education,* 2d ed., The Ronald Press Company, New York, 1959.

Ulich, Robert: *History of Educational Thought,* American Book Company, New York, 1950.

Index

513